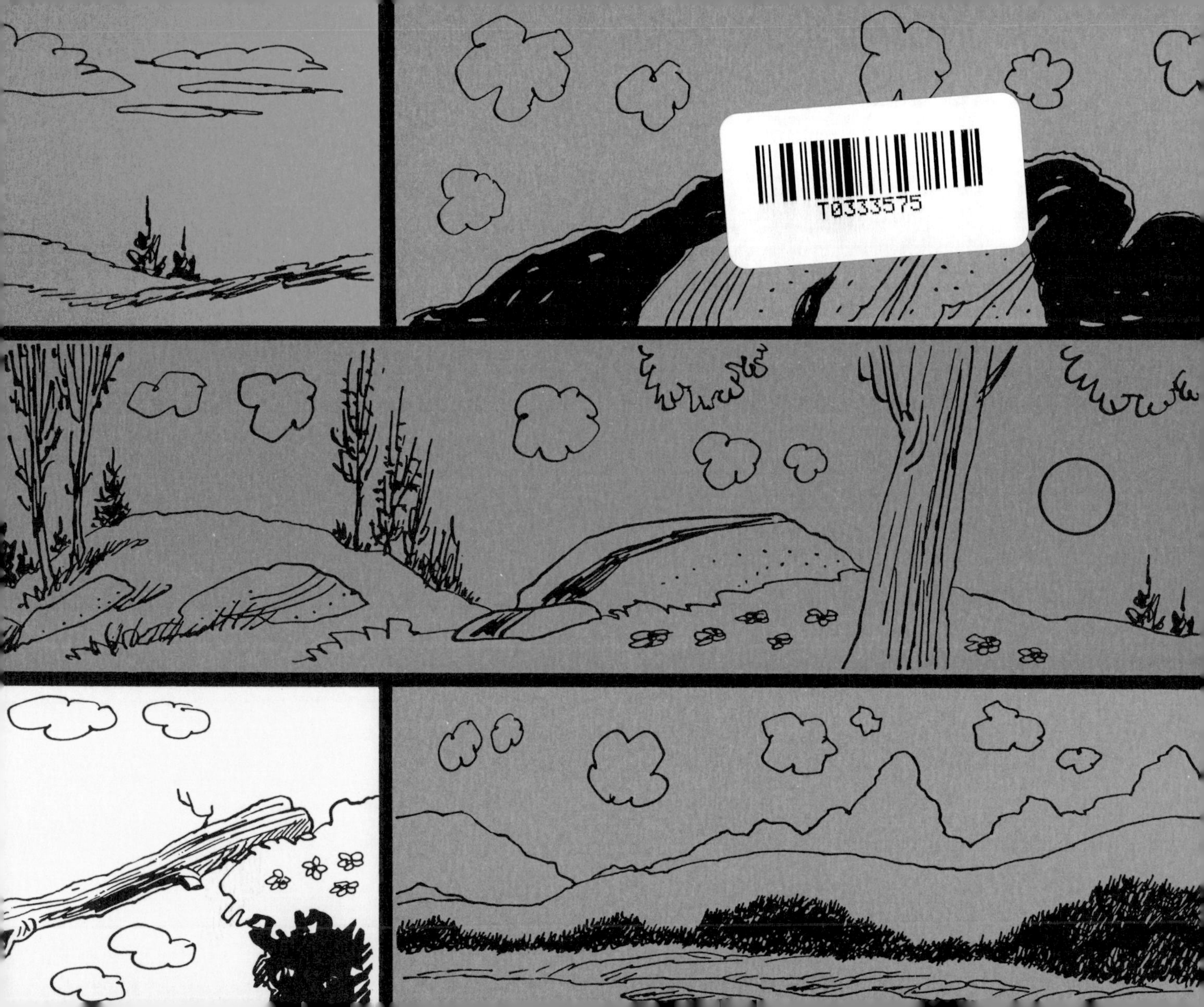

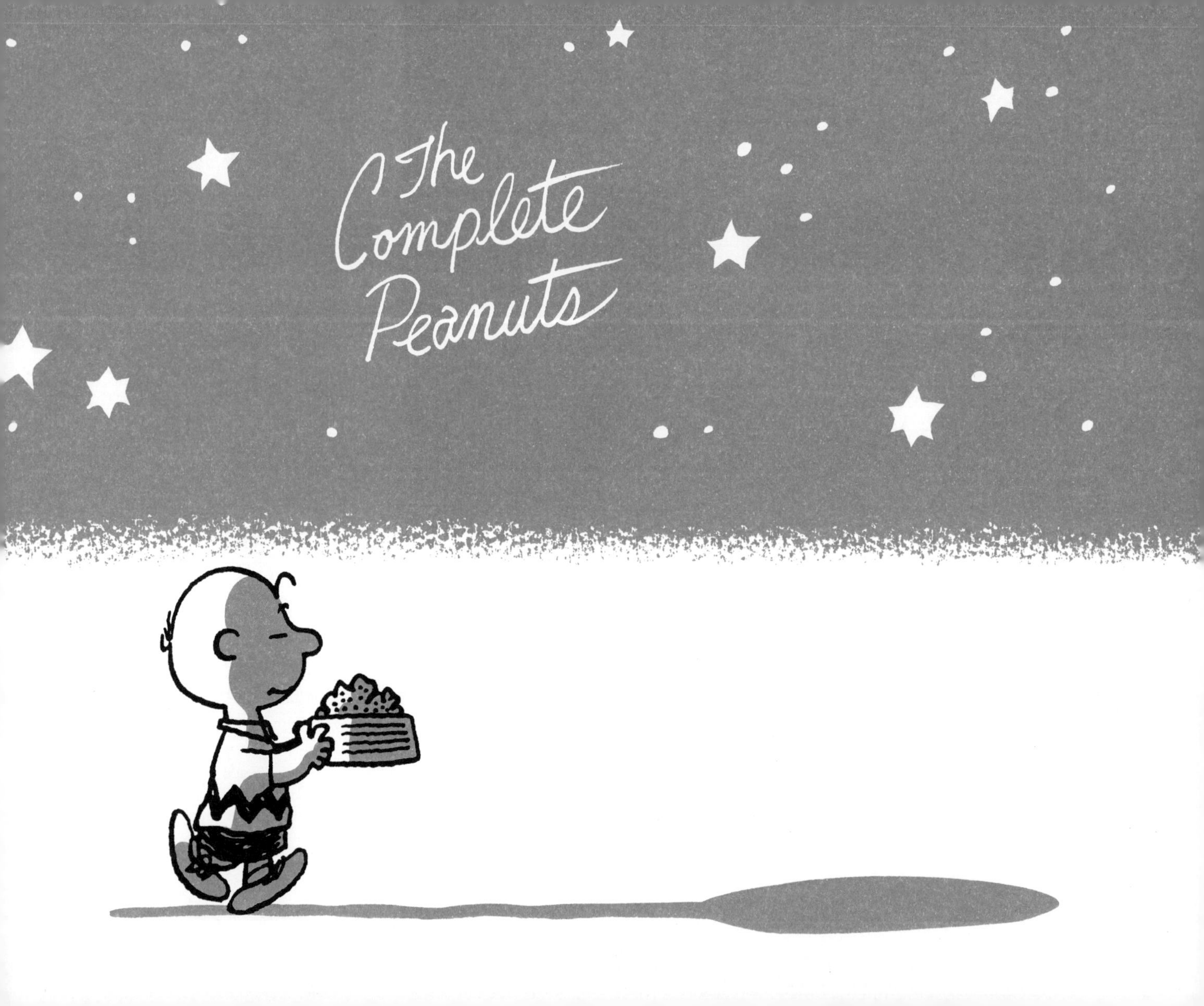
The Complete Peanuts

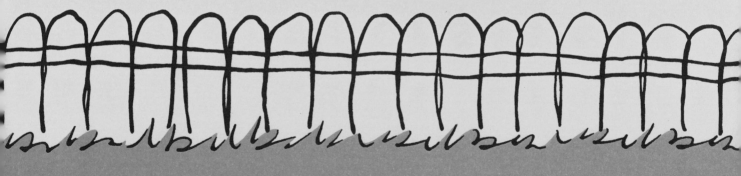

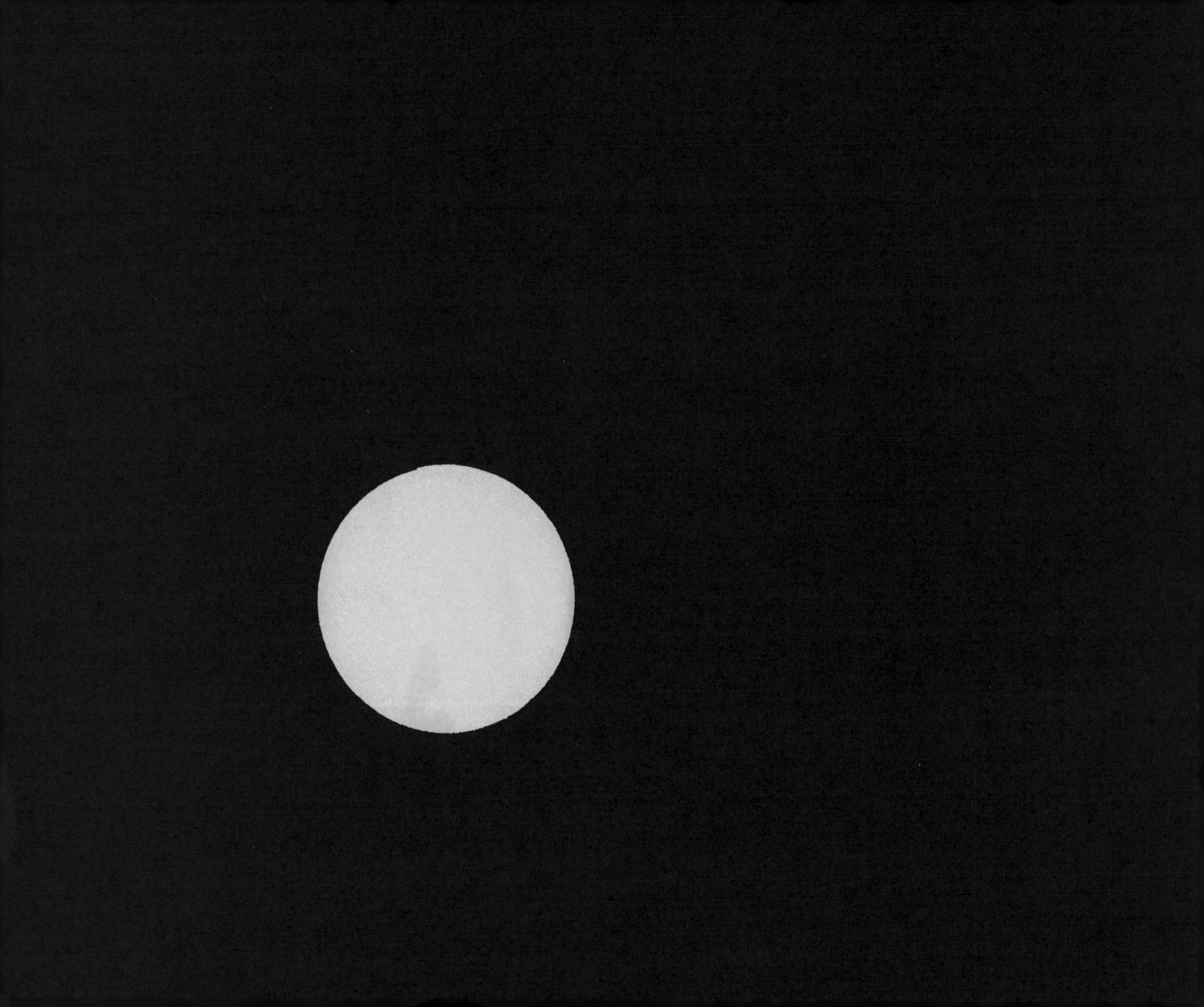

THE COMPLETE PEANUTS
by Charles M. Schulz

Editor: Gary Groth
Designer: Seth
Production Manager: Kim Thompson
Production, assembly and restoration: Paul Baresh
Archival assistance: Marcie Lee
Index compiled by Priscilla Miller
Associate Publisher: Eric Reynolds
Publishers: Gary Groth & Kim Thompson

Special thanks to Jeannie Schulz, without whom
this project would not have come to fruition.
Thanks also to John R. Troy and the
Charles M. Schulz Creative Associates,
especially Paige Braddock and Kim Towner.
Thanks for special support from Peanuts International, LLC.

First published in America in 2011 by Fantagraphics Books,
7563 Lake City Way, Seattle, WA 98115, USA

First published in Great Britain in 2014 by Canongate Books Ltd,
14 High Street, Edinburgh, EH1 1TE

2

British Library Cataloguing-in-Publication Data
A catalogue record for this book is available on request from the British Library.

ISBN 978 1 78211 102 3
Printed and bound in China
www.canongate.co.uk

CHARLES M. SCHULZ

THE COMPLETE PEANUTS

1981 TO 1982

"YEARS ARE LIKE
CANDY BARS..."

CANONGATE BOOKS

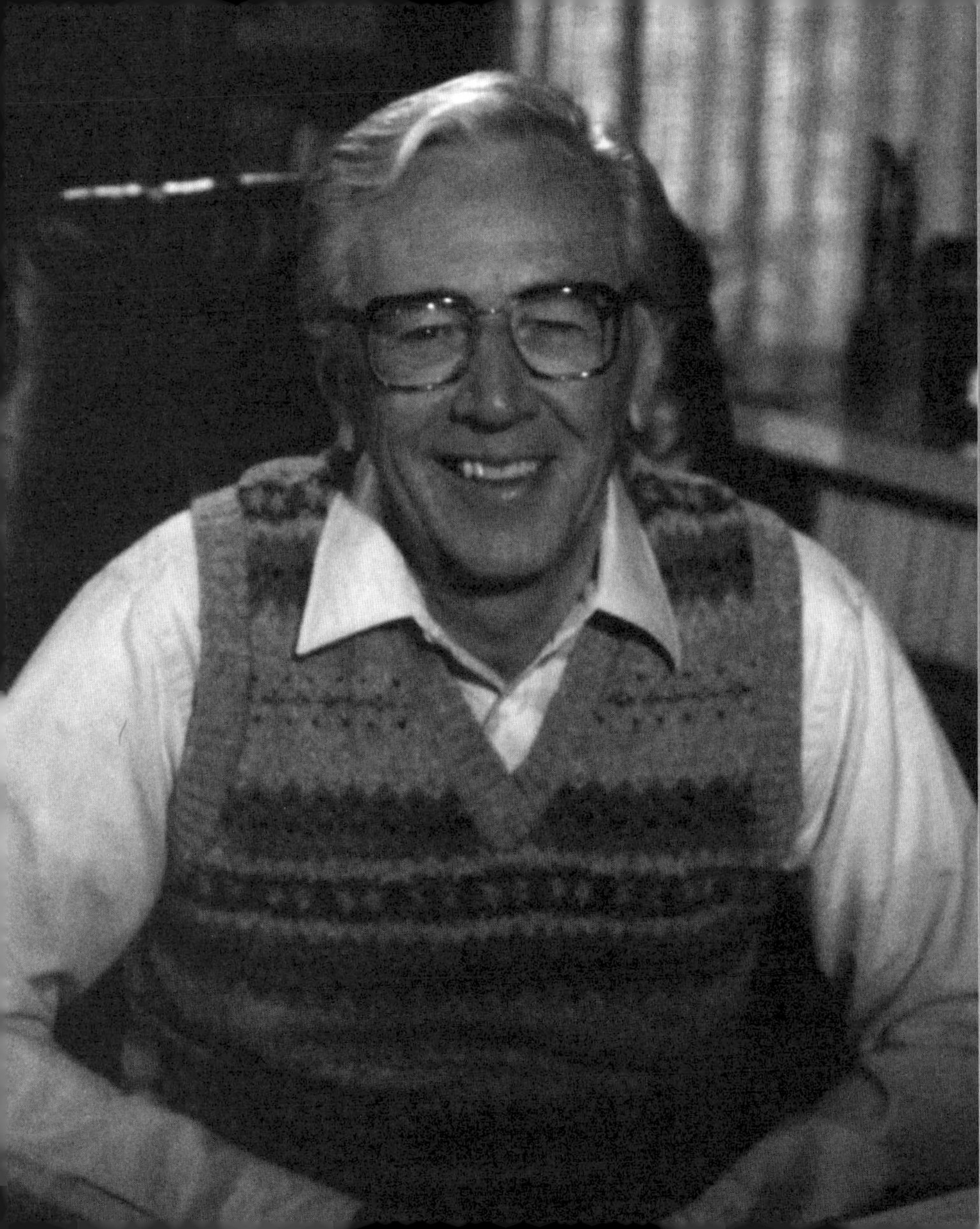

Charles M. Schulz in 1985 during the filming of *It's Your 20th Television Anniversary, Charlie Brown*. Courtesy of The Charles M. Schulz Museum and Research Center, Santa Rosa, California.

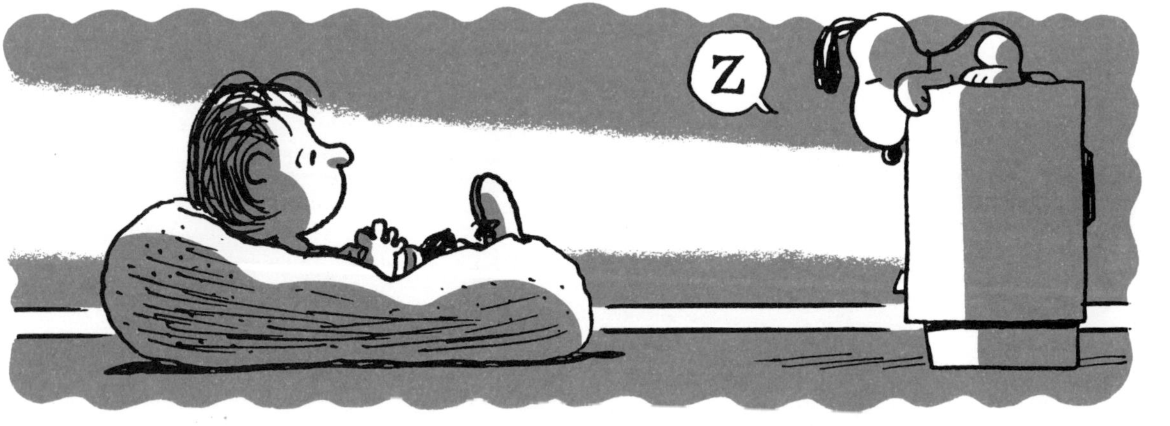
Z

FOREWORD by LYNN JOHNSTON

Right now, I am the same age as Sparky was when I first met him. I remember walking down a street with him in Washington DC after the Reuben Awards. His wife Jeannie and Cathy Guisewite (of the comic strip *Cathy*) were with us. Cathy and I were singing "Will you still need me, will you still feed me when I'm sixty-four?" and Sparky was not amused. He didn't want to be sixty-four. He wanted to stay young forever—like Charlie Brown and Linus and Lucy. He wanted time to stand still. He was a dreamer—which is what made him exceptionally talented, endlessly creative, competitive, funny, and sometimes sad. "If you want to know me, read my work," is what he told interviewers and fans who queried him. He was right. Charles Schulz explored his private thoughts, his philosophy, and his life in *Peanuts*.

The interesting thing about doing a comic strip is—you have control of an entire world. It's a world of your own invention, but it's a world, just the same. You know what's going to happen to people and when... and, you know what they will say about it. You know who the bullies are and whose heroism will save the day. You control the conversations, the situations, and even the weather. You can be any one of the characters you invent at any given time—allowing your inner selves to come forth. You slip into the body of the malicious meanie as easily as you become a sweet, gentle, and introspective friend. You are, in essence, the "creator," which is what the folks at the syndicates call us! We are the creators of a small, black-and-white window through which everyone is invited to look. Some folks want to open the door and come inside.

Inside that door: That's where a cartoonist goes. It's where the magic begins. I'll call it magic, because even those of us who do comic strips for a living wonder where the ideas come from and how they flow from mind to hand to paper. How do we generate ideas? Cartoonists, writers, actors, dancers, and musicians—performers of all kinds— are on "record" all the time. In order to bring an audience into an imaginary world, the real world has to be examined in minute detail. A simple bus ride, for example, is a library of resources.

Put yourself on an old green-and-white city bus. It's early in the evening and… let it be raining outside. Smell the exhaust, the dust, and the clothing of other passengers getting on. Look at them. Listen to their speech; watch their expressions, movements, and mannerisms. Now, press your hand against the seat in front of you. Feel the texture of the fabric it's made of. Hear the sound of the motor. Feel the movement of the bus. Watch the passing city streets through the fog on the window. Feel the dampness in the air, how it chills you to the bone. Be there. Can you do this? Yes you can, because you've done it before—and you were on "record."

Cartoonists use experience, intuition, impressions, and visual recordings to create an imaginary world. We explore, examine, and mirror what's around us. We might distort or exaggerate, but enough reality is maintained so that we can draw ourselves, and therefore others into something familiar, believable, and clear. A clear, sustainable fantasy is what a good comic strip is and the people who create them must live in both worlds.

Creative people are always accused of daydreaming! Daydreaming is just rewinding a mental video and watching it again. Sometimes we rewrite what happened. We embellish or extend it. Daydreaming is exactly what the word implies: dreaming, with the lights on and your eyes wide open. The difference is control! Being able to control and direct fantasy requires a unique talent. It's a wonderful gift—and it's often a curse. Daydreaming can take you away from things you should be dealing with; people you should be listening to—here and now. People who live with daydreamers have to know when the dream is happening and when it's OK to "step in." Because they are the editors, the partners, and often the targets of the "artist," they have to be objective, confident, responsible, and loyal. It isn't easy to live with a cartoonist. Along with the dreaming comes a theme-park ride of hilarity, silliness, laughter, and passion; confusion, anxiety, depression, and doubt. What if I never come up with another idea? What if my talents fail? What if... what if?

One day Sparky called me to say he was feeling miserable. He said his moods were all over the place: up and down. "I'm on the bungee cord of life," he said. "Sparky, that's a great punch line!" I told him. "You have a daily there!" He grumbled some more and I don't remember how the conversation ended, but he was not about to use my suggestion. He hated the idea of using someone else's ideas!

Every few weeks, we would talk on the phone, and some time later, he called to say he had run out of ideas. He couldn't think of a single thing. "What about 'bungee cord of life'?" I asked. "That was a great punch line!" "It was your idea," he said. "It was not!" I argued—and I repeated the conversation we'd had. "Well, if you're sure it was my idea and not yours, I'll use it." Six weeks later, the bungee strip appeared and he sent me the original—with the comment "For Lynn, who gives me all my best ideas."

We all have the same panic. The deadline is a cruel master, but without it, would we be so inventive and productive? Without the fear of failure, of letting our syndicate and our audience down, would we still put out 365 comic strips a year? Absolutely not! We need the anxiety as much as we need the applause. It's all part of the process.

My process was to sit in a comfortable place and write as if I were writing a script. Sparky's process was to doodle on a yellow legal pad. He would scribble faces with different expressions, bodies with different poses. "I'm trying to draw a funny picture," he'd say. "I'm waiting for something to happen." If you looked at the doodles, you'd see nothing, really to connect to the strip he would draw, but this was the catalyst that started the chemistry. It was the key to his personal imaginary door.

After the work is done, examined, judged worthy, and sent, there is a feeling of intense pleasure until the next week of work is due. I guess you could call it a "high." There is perhaps a mild connection between this work and an addiction. As much as cartoonists resent the process, the response is glorious. Whether it's laughter, commiseration, dissent, or applause, we need the audience reaction as much as we need the paycheck. Both reward you for hard work, for putting your heart and soul on the line. Both are the gauge by which you judge your own ability, and you go for "excellence" in order to maintain the flow. The letters, the interviews, the visitors can all be an intrusion, but you need them. There is tremendous competition for this audience. We compete with others in the business, but the heart of the competition is within ourselves. Perfection is never possible, but if you aim for perfection, you will undoubtedly achieve "very good." There is constant, self-inflicted pressure to improve your mind, your drawing prowess, and your ability to produce. You have to be your own worst critic, your own strict supervisor, and as such, you are never separated from your work. Being complacent, being satisfied, means you lose the game. If you stop trying to make the next strip better than the last, you are looking at the down side of your career. Sparky was this driven. It's what made him so successful. It's also what made him so complex, so compelling, and so interesting to us all.

Did he know he'd be so successful? "I don't do things that I think will fail," he would say, but there were times when I know he surprised himself. We were sitting together at one of the Christmas Ice shows he hosted at the Redwood Arena in Santa Rosa. Judy Sladky, who has been the character "Snoopy" for many years, had just completed a wonderful set and was skating off the ice. The show had been brilliant and the audience enthralled. Sparky leaned over and said to me, "Just think... there was a time when there *was* no Snoopy!" I looked at him to see if he was kidding, but he wasn't. Judy had once again brought Snoopy to life and Snoopy had thrilled us all.

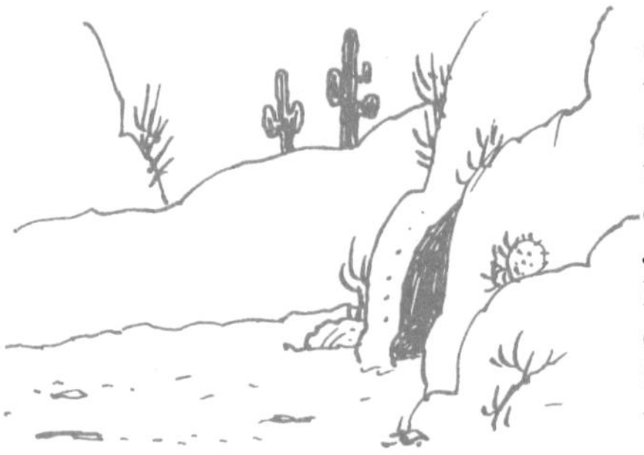

Judy has been Snoopy for so long that she wags her seat when she's happy—even when she's not in character! In order to make Snoopy real, Sparky carefully instilled his spirit in Judy. His spirit—meaning both his and Snoopy's. Sparky was, of course all of his characters, but Snoopy was the one through which he soared. Snoopy allowed him to be spontaneous, slapstick, silly, and wild. Snoopy was rhythm, comedy, glamour, and style. As Snoopy, Judy brought to the stage the best of Charles Schulz. As Snoopy, he had no failures, no losses, no flaws. Everyone loved Snoopy and as someone who often doubted if anyone really liked him, his own Snoopy had friends and admirers all over the globe. The cast of *Peanuts* characters had evolved as characters do, with their own quirks and personalities, but Snoopy had been a surprise. I was a good friend, had been a guest every year at the ice show for about seven years, and this was the first time I'd seen Charles Schulz genuinely awed by his own work.

That year, for his birthday, I gave Sparky a paper tube onto which I had rolled a long string of cartoon trombonists. He opened the package and then called me at home. "I suppose there are seventy-six trombones here," he said. I thought it was funny, but he wasn't laughing. "I don't want to be seventy-six," he said. "What if I die before I can finish my work?" I suggested he do a two-week storyline in which he wrapped up *Peanuts*. "Do an ending... have Linus give up his blanket, have Lucy apologize for something, have Charlie Brown kick the football! Then you can put it in a vault somewhere and bring it out when you're ready to." "I couldn't do that," he said. "It's like tempting fate! If I did that, something awful might happen. Besides... it's your idea."

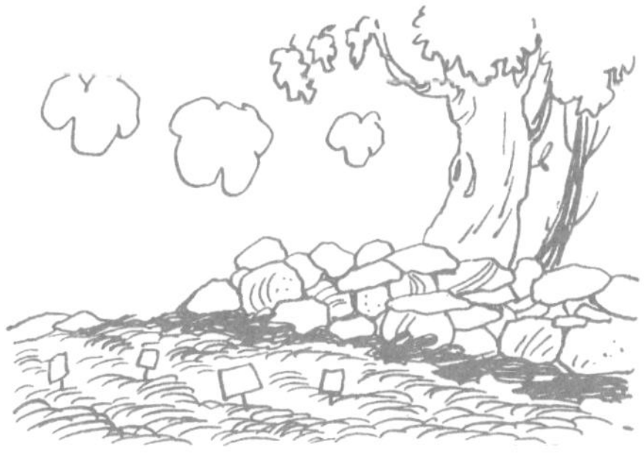

I last saw Charles Schulz in his hospital room. He was lying back on the bed, propped up on a pillow and I was sitting beside him. "It's not fair," he said to me honestly. "I'm not ready to go. I haven't finished yet. I still have so much to do!" He was angry with the powers that be for bringing things to an end this way. We talked about our work; being able to control a world of our own making, having the power to decide what happens to whom, and how and when... and, here he was—a creator, trapped in a reality he couldn't comprehend. Sparky died at the age of seventy-seven—and I had told him it would be a lucky year.

The most memorable friends are the ones you learn from. Sparky taught me to expect the best of myself and to push myself hard. He taught me to give my audience something uplifting. There are too many negatives in the world, and we get far too much of it. He complimented, reinforced, and encouraged me when I lacked confidence, but his friendship said it all. It was what kept me going. If Sparky liked what I was doing, then I'd be OK.

At the age of sixty-four and now retired, I want to do for others what he did for me. I want to encourage the next generation of cartoonists and comic artists to do what they are driven to do—and to do it to the best of their ability. I want to set a good example, because he set the bar for me. If you look at the legacy *Peanuts* has become, you know it can be done—it's just a matter of time.

Somewhere, there are other men or women with a gift that will drive them to greatness... and how fortunate they are to have Charles Schulz as a guide.

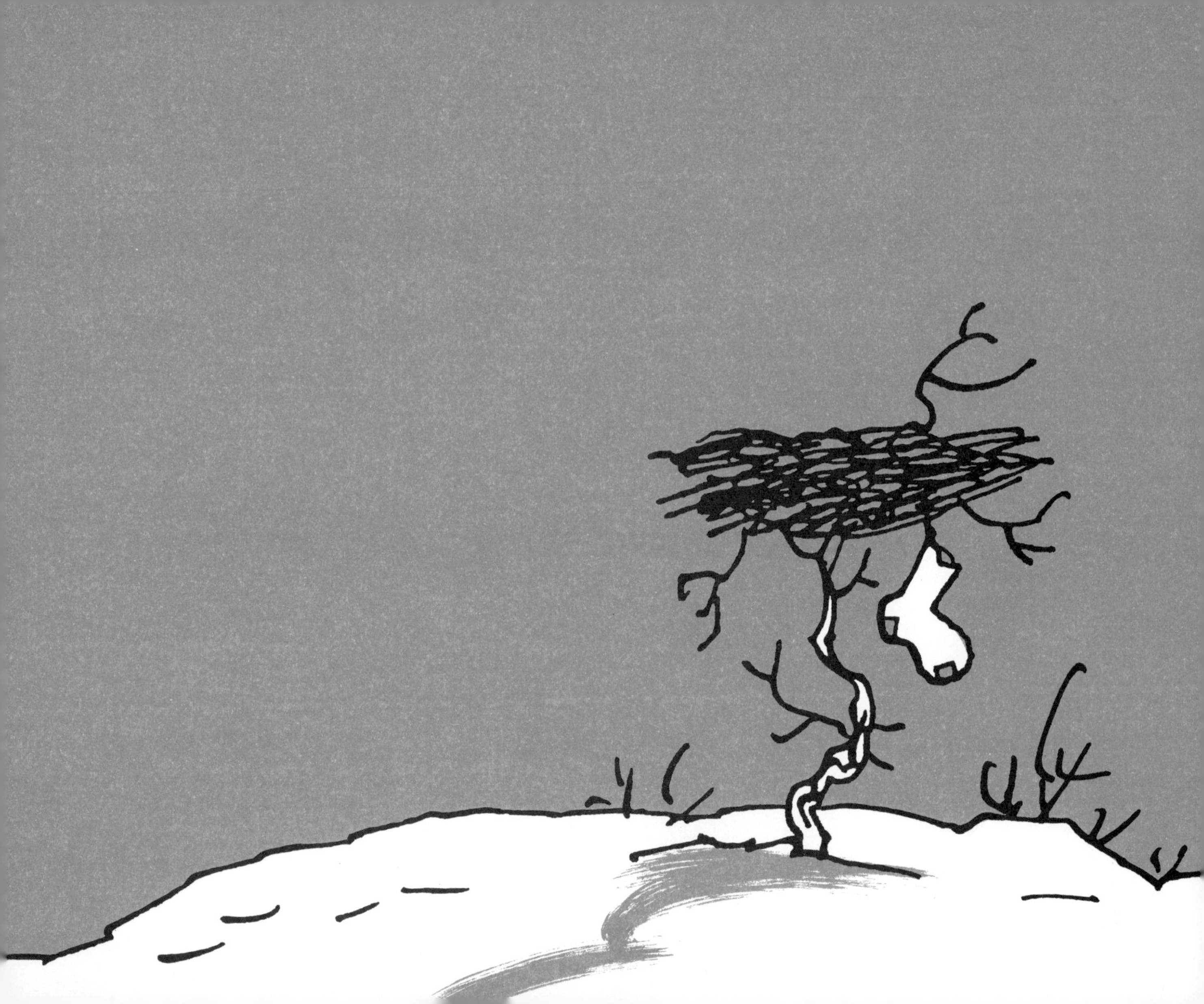

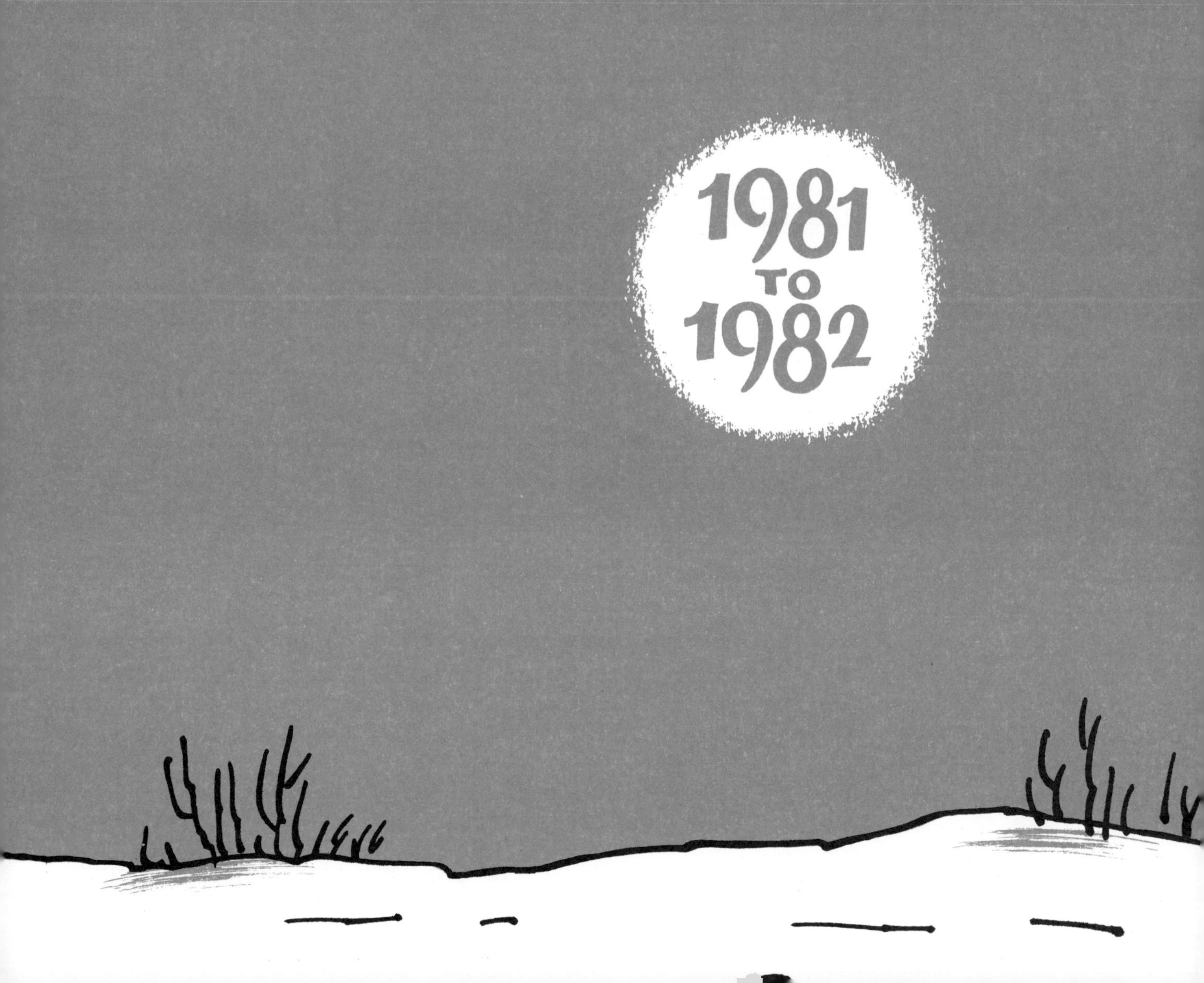
1981
TO
1982

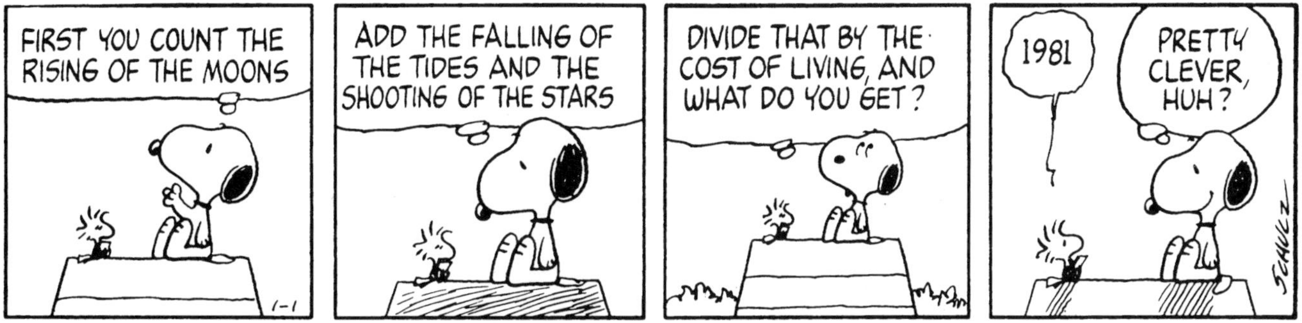
FIRST YOU COUNT THE RISING OF THE MOONS
ADD THE FALLING OF THE TIDES AND THE SHOOTING OF THE STARS
DIVIDE THAT BY THE COST OF LIVING, AND WHAT DO YOU GET?
1981
PRETTY CLEVER, HUH?

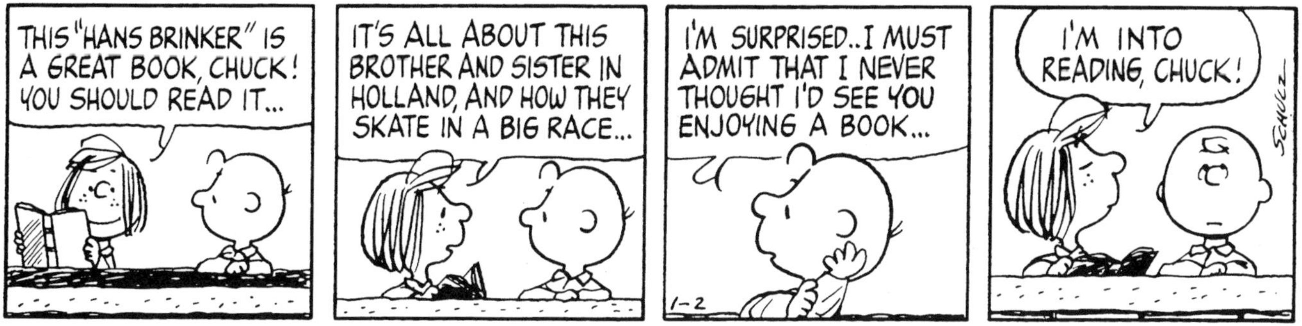
THIS "HANS BRINKER" IS A GREAT BOOK, CHUCK! YOU SHOULD READ IT...
IT'S ALL ABOUT THIS BROTHER AND SISTER IN HOLLAND, AND HOW THEY SKATE IN A BIG RACE...
I'M SURPRISED..I MUST ADMIT THAT I NEVER THOUGHT I'D SEE YOU ENJOYING A BOOK...
I'M INTO READING, CHUCK!

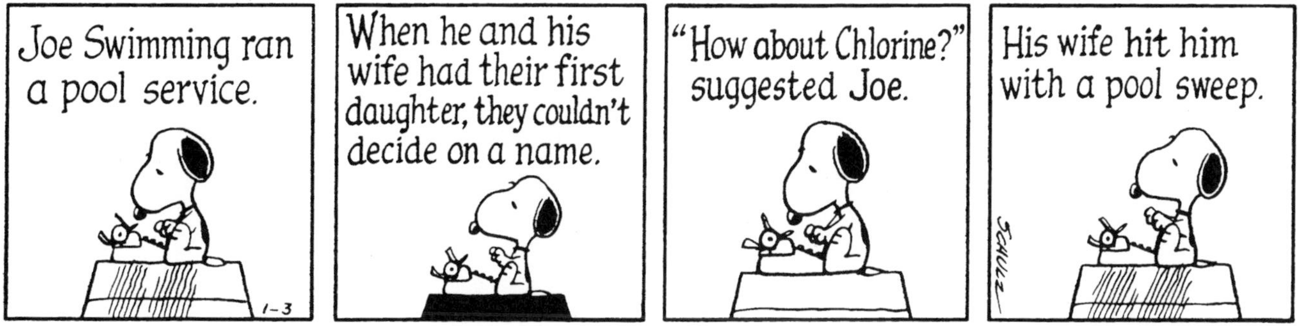
Joe Swimming ran a pool service.
When he and his wife had their first daughter, they couldn't decide on a name.
"How about Chlorine?" suggested Joe.
His wife hit him with a pool sweep.

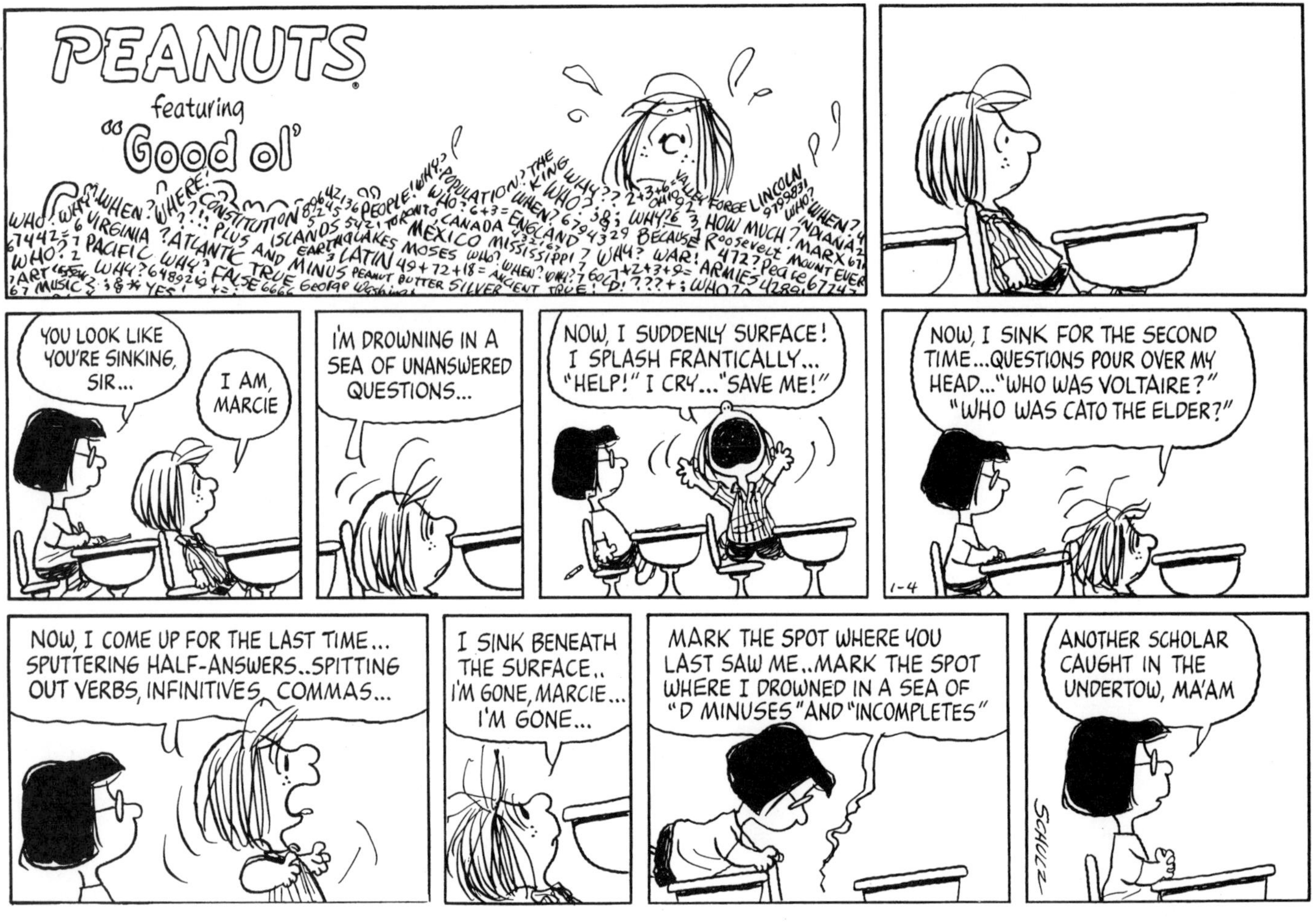
PEANUTS
featuring
"Good ol'"
YOU LOOK LIKE YOU'RE SINKING, SIR...
I AM, MARCIE
I'M DROWNING IN A SEA OF UNANSWERED QUESTIONS...
NOW, I SUDDENLY SURFACE! I SPLASH FRANTICALLY... "HELP!" I CRY..."SAVE ME!"
NOW, I SINK FOR THE SECOND TIME...QUESTIONS POUR OVER MY HEAD..."WHO WAS VOLTAIRE?" "WHO WAS CATO THE ELDER?"
1-4
NOW, I COME UP FOR THE LAST TIME... SPUTTERING HALF-ANSWERS..SPITTING OUT VERBS, INFINITIVES, COMMAS...
I SINK BENEATH THE SURFACE.. I'M GONE, MARCIE... I'M GONE...
MARK THE SPOT WHERE YOU LAST SAW ME..MARK THE SPOT WHERE I DROWNED IN A SEA OF "D MINUSES" AND "INCOMPLETES"
SCHULZ
ANOTHER SCHOLAR CAUGHT IN THE UNDERTOW, MA'AM

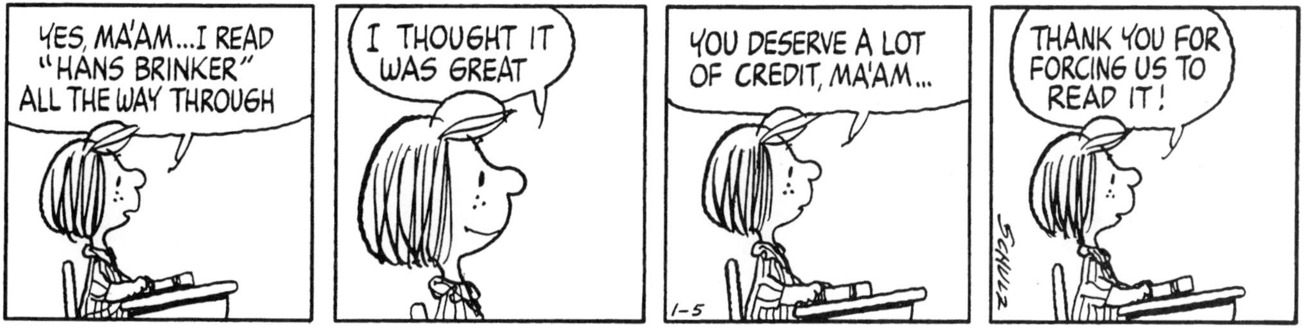
YES, MA'AM...I READ "HANS BRINKER" ALL THE WAY THROUGH
I THOUGHT IT WAS GREAT
YOU DESERVE A LOT OF CREDIT, MA'AM...
THANK YOU FOR FORCING US TO READ IT!
1-5
SCHULZ

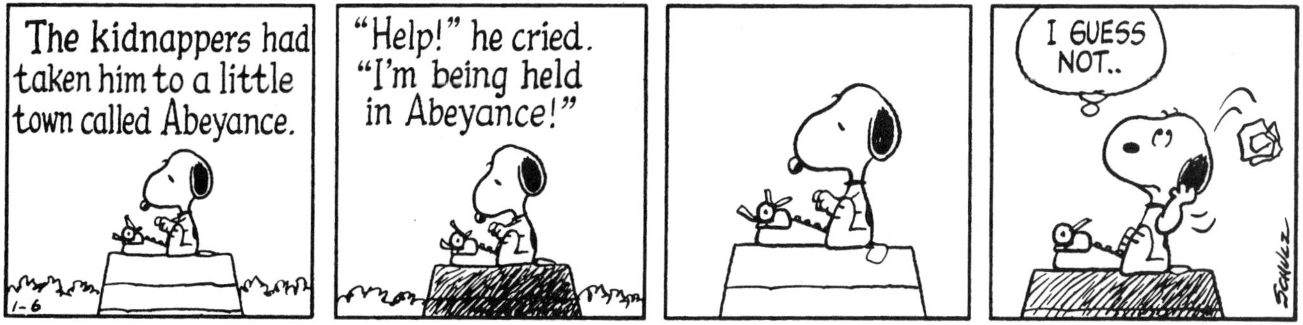
The kidnappers had taken him to a little town called Abeyance.
"Help!" he cried. "I'm being held in Abeyance!"
I GUESS NOT..
1-6
SCHULZ

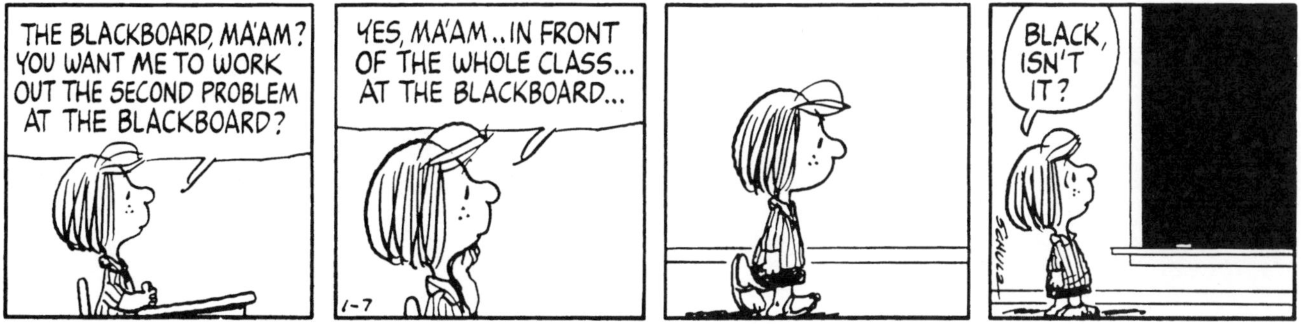
THE BLACKBOARD, MA'AM? YOU WANT ME TO WORK OUT THE SECOND PROBLEM AT THE BLACKBOARD?
YES, MA'AM..IN FRONT OF THE WHOLE CLASS... AT THE BLACKBOARD...
BLACK, ISN'T IT?
1-7
SCHULZ

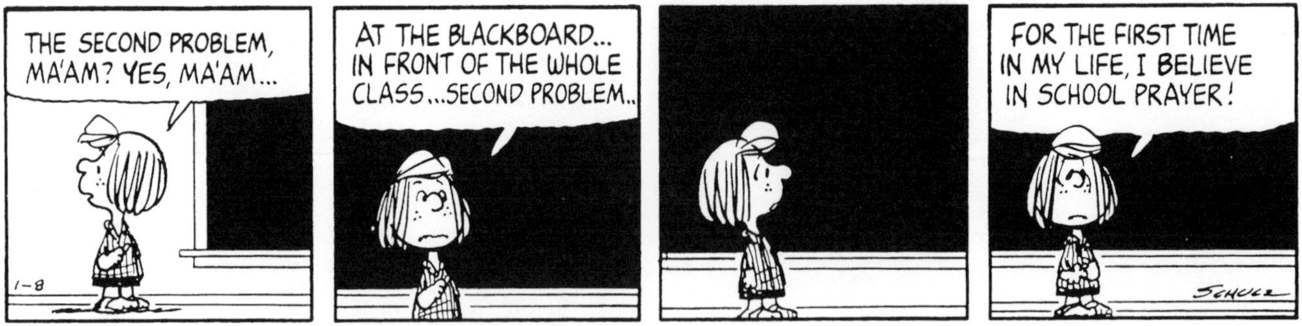
THE SECOND PROBLEM, MA'AM? YES, MA'AM...
1-8
AT THE BLACKBOARD... IN FRONT OF THE WHOLE CLASS...SECOND PROBLEM..
FOR THE FIRST TIME IN MY LIFE, I BELIEVE IN SCHOOL PRAYER!
SCHULZ

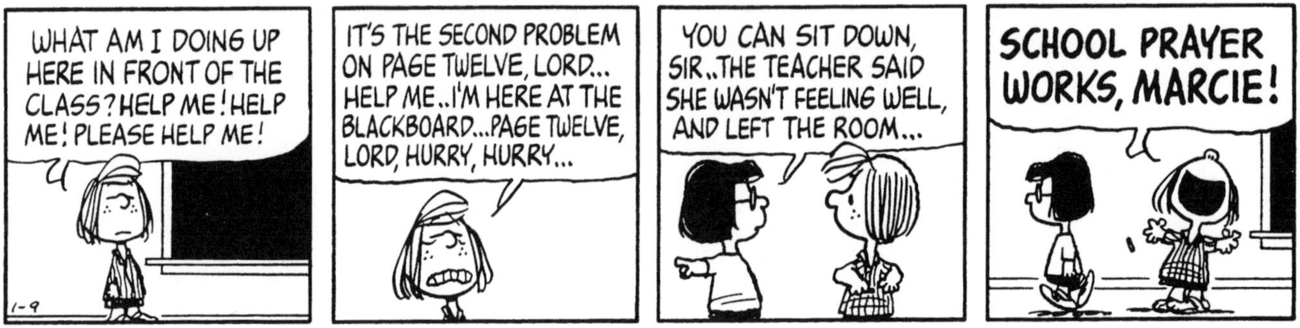
WHAT AM I DOING UP HERE IN FRONT OF THE CLASS? HELP ME! HELP ME! PLEASE HELP ME!
1-9
IT'S THE SECOND PROBLEM ON PAGE TWELVE, LORD... HELP ME..I'M HERE AT THE BLACKBOARD...PAGE TWELVE, LORD, HURRY, HURRY...
YOU CAN SIT DOWN, SIR..THE TEACHER SAID SHE WASN'T FEELING WELL, AND LEFT THE ROOM...
SCHOOL PRAYER WORKS, MARCIE!

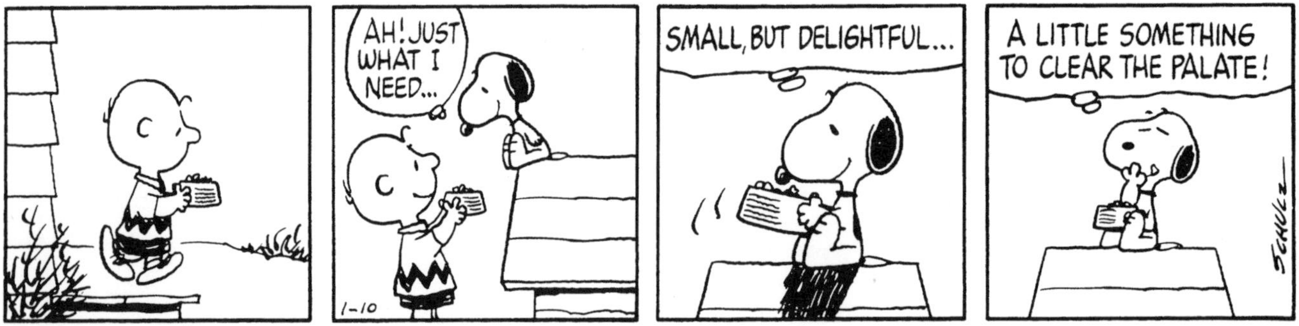
AH! JUST WHAT I NEED...
1-10
SMALL, BUT DELIGHTFUL...
A LITTLE SOMETHING TO CLEAR THE PALATE!
SCHULZ

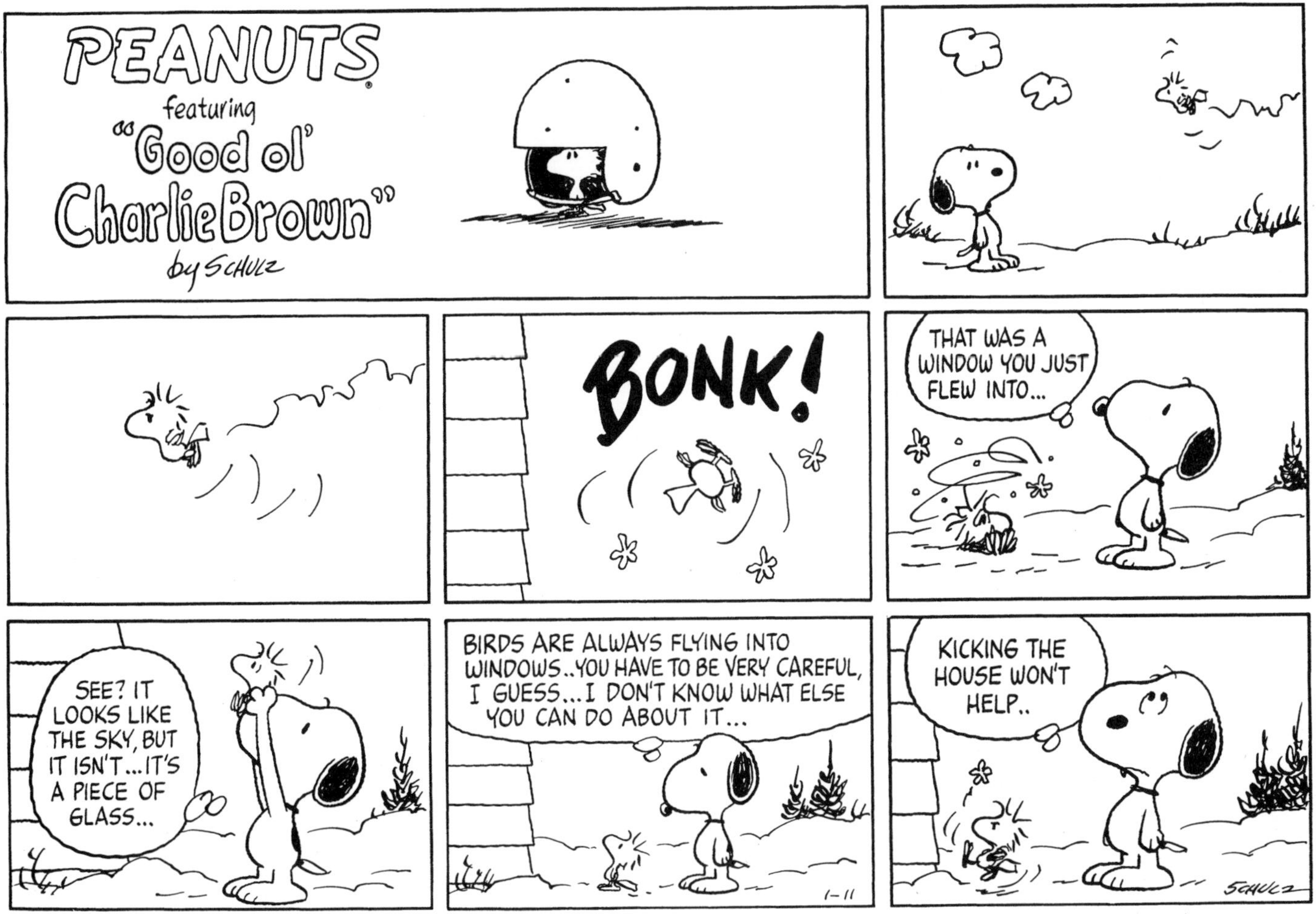
PEANUTS
featuring
"Good ol' Charlie Brown"
by SCHULZ
BONK!
THAT WAS A WINDOW YOU JUST FLEW INTO...
SEE? IT LOOKS LIKE THE SKY, BUT IT ISN'T...IT'S A PIECE OF GLASS...
BIRDS ARE ALWAYS FLYING INTO WINDOWS..YOU HAVE TO BE VERY CAREFUL, I GUESS...I DON'T KNOW WHAT ELSE YOU CAN DO ABOUT IT...
1-11
KICKING THE HOUSE WON'T HELP..
SCHULZ

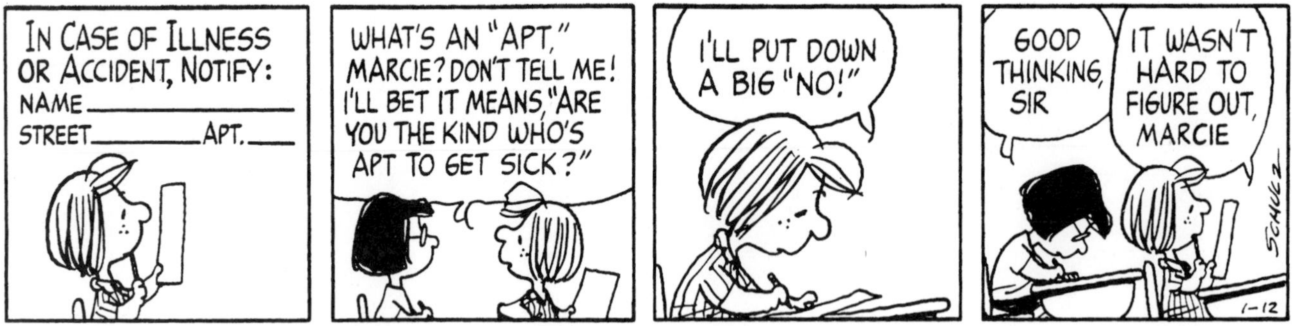
IN CASE OF ILLNESS OR ACCIDENT, NOTIFY:
NAME ______
STREET ______ APT. ____
WHAT'S AN "APT," MARCIE? DON'T TELL ME! I'LL BET IT MEANS, "ARE YOU THE KIND WHO'S APT TO GET SICK?"
I'LL PUT DOWN A BIG "NO!"
GOOD THINKING, SIR
IT WASN'T HARD TO FIGURE OUT, MARCIE
SCHULZ
1-12

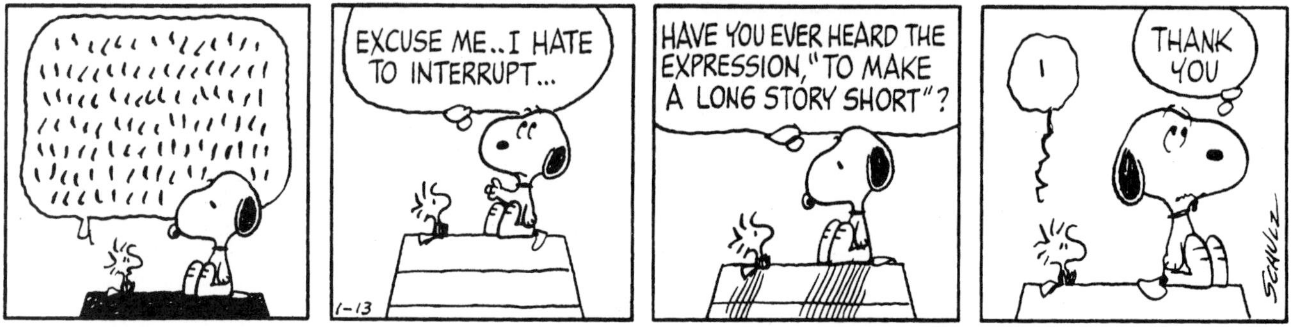
EXCUSE ME..I HATE TO INTERRUPT...
1-13
HAVE YOU EVER HEARD THE EXPRESSION, "TO MAKE A LONG STORY SHORT"?
I
THANK YOU
SCHULZ

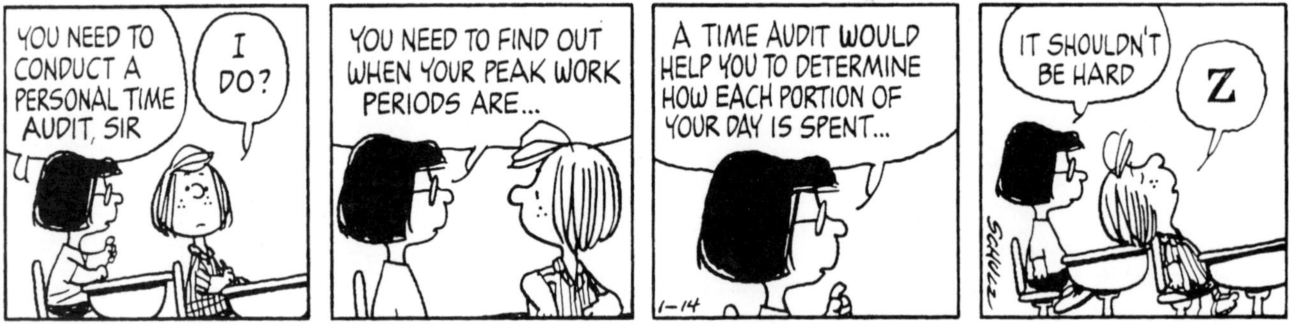
YOU NEED TO CONDUCT A PERSONAL TIME AUDIT, SIR
I DO?
YOU NEED TO FIND OUT WHEN YOUR PEAK WORK PERIODS ARE...
A TIME AUDIT WOULD HELP YOU TO DETERMINE HOW EACH PORTION OF YOUR DAY IS SPENT...
1-14
IT SHOULDN'T BE HARD
Z
SCHULZ

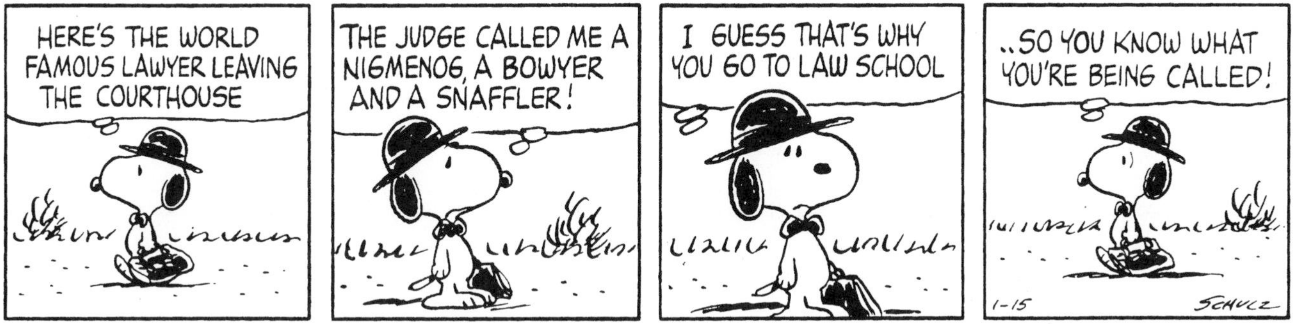
HERE'S THE WORLD FAMOUS LAWYER LEAVING THE COURTHOUSE
THE JUDGE CALLED ME A NIGMENOG, A BOWYER AND A SNAFFLER!
I GUESS THAT'S WHY YOU GO TO LAW SCHOOL
..SO YOU KNOW WHAT YOU'RE BEING CALLED!
1-15
SCHULZ

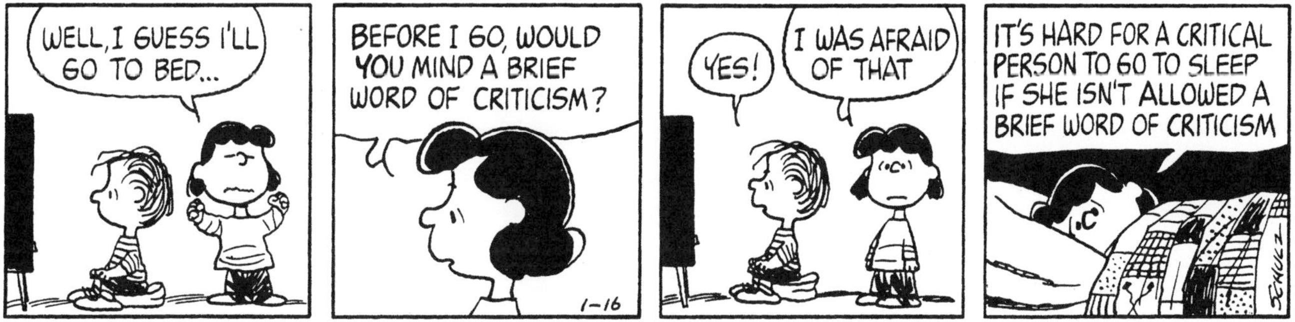
WELL, I GUESS I'LL GO TO BED...
BEFORE I GO, WOULD YOU MIND A BRIEF WORD OF CRITICISM?
1-16
YES!
I WAS AFRAID OF THAT
IT'S HARD FOR A CRITICAL PERSON TO GO TO SLEEP IF SHE ISN'T ALLOWED A BRIEF WORD OF CRITICISM
SCHULZ

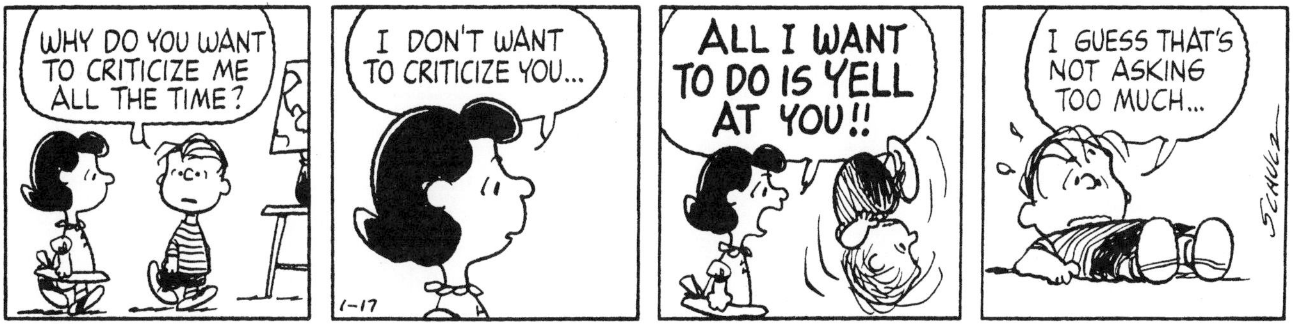
WHY DO YOU WANT TO CRITICIZE ME ALL THE TIME?
I DON'T WANT TO CRITICIZE YOU...
1-17
ALL I WANT TO DO IS YELL AT YOU!!
I GUESS THAT'S NOT ASKING TOO MUCH...
SCHULZ

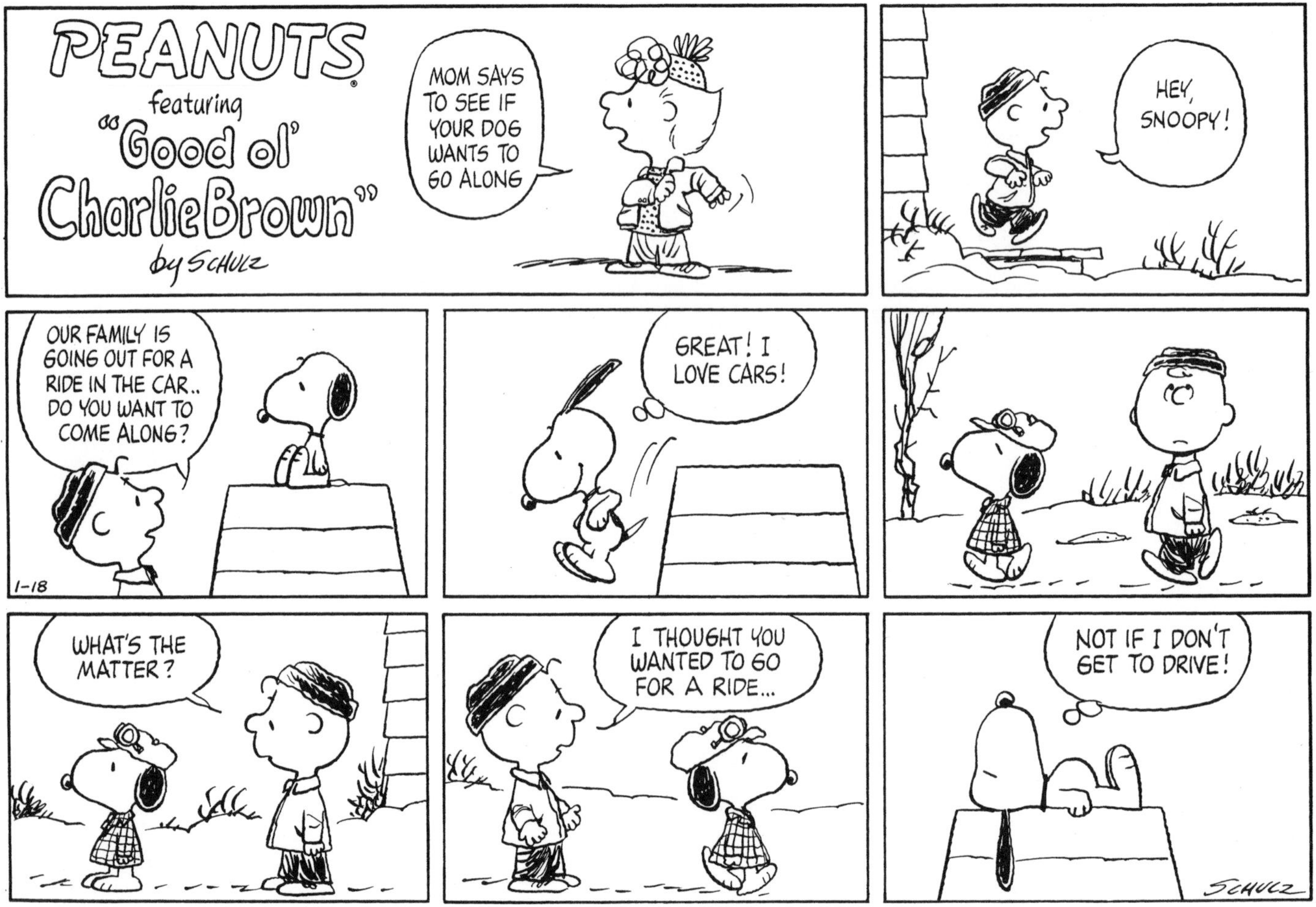
PEANUTS
featuring "Good ol' Charlie Brown"
by SCHULZ
MOM SAYS TO SEE IF YOUR DOG WANTS TO GO ALONG
HEY, SNOOPY!
OUR FAMILY IS GOING OUT FOR A RIDE IN THE CAR.. DO YOU WANT TO COME ALONG?
1-18
GREAT! I LOVE CARS!
WHAT'S THE MATTER?
I THOUGHT YOU WANTED TO GO FOR A RIDE...
NOT IF I DON'T GET TO DRIVE!
SCHULZ

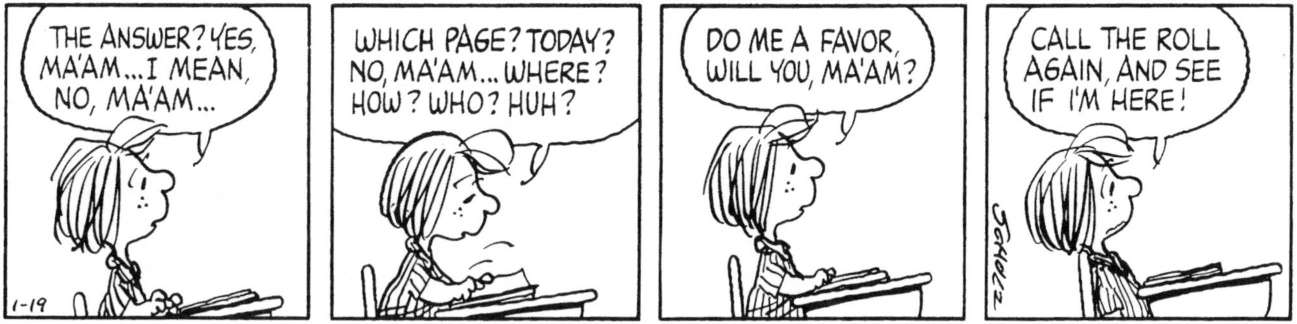
THE ANSWER? YES, MA'AM... I MEAN, NO, MA'AM...
WHICH PAGE? TODAY? NO, MA'AM... WHERE? HOW? WHO? HUH?
DO ME A FAVOR, WILL YOU, MA'AM?
CALL THE ROLL AGAIN, AND SEE IF I'M HERE!
1-19
SCHULZ

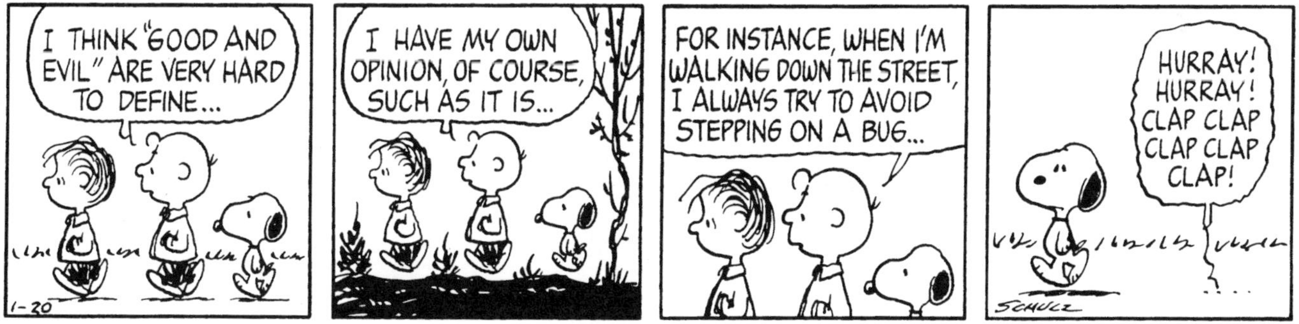
I THINK "GOOD AND EVIL" ARE VERY HARD TO DEFINE...
I HAVE MY OWN OPINION, OF COURSE, SUCH AS IT IS...
FOR INSTANCE, WHEN I'M WALKING DOWN THE STREET, I ALWAYS TRY TO AVOID STEPPING ON A BUG...
HURRAY! HURRAY! CLAP CLAP CLAP CLAP CLAP!
1-20
SCHULZ

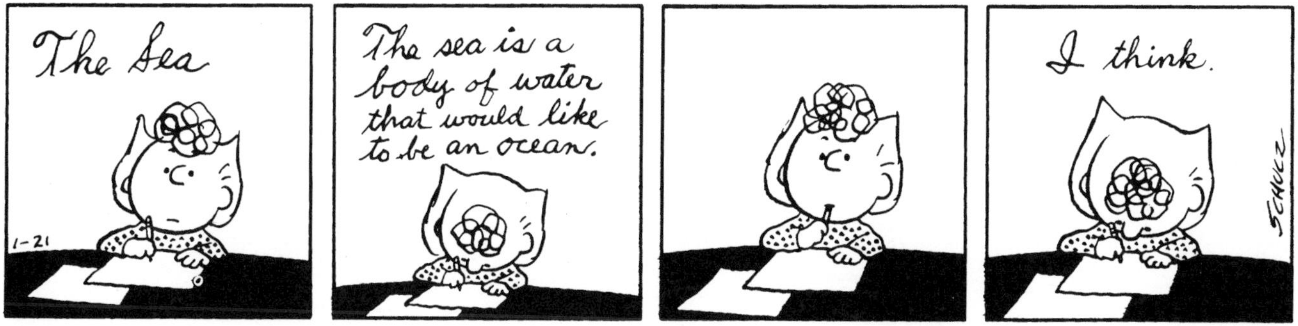
The Sea
The sea is a body of water that would like to be an ocean.
I think.
1-21
SCHULZ

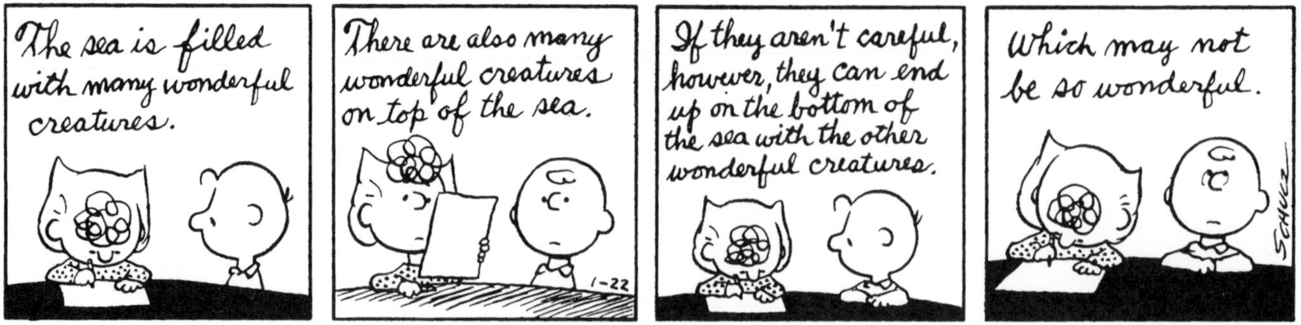
The sea is filled with many wonderful creatures.
There are also many wonderful creatures on top of the sea.
1-22
If they aren't careful, however, they can end up on the bottom of the sea with the other wonderful creatures.
Which may not be so wonderful.
SCHULZ

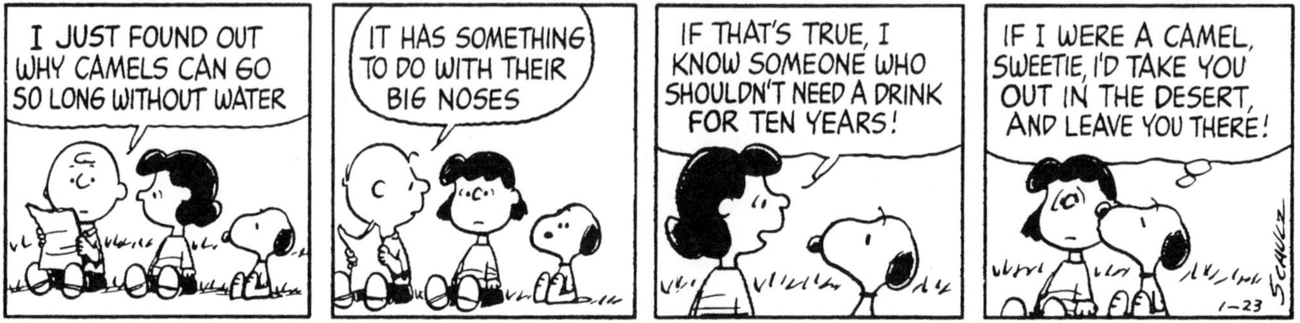
I JUST FOUND OUT WHY CAMELS CAN GO SO LONG WITHOUT WATER
IT HAS SOMETHING TO DO WITH THEIR BIG NOSES
IF THAT'S TRUE, I KNOW SOMEONE WHO SHOULDN'T NEED A DRINK FOR TEN YEARS!
IF I WERE A CAMEL, SWEETIE, I'D TAKE YOU OUT IN THE DESERT, AND LEAVE YOU THERE!
SCHULZ
1-23

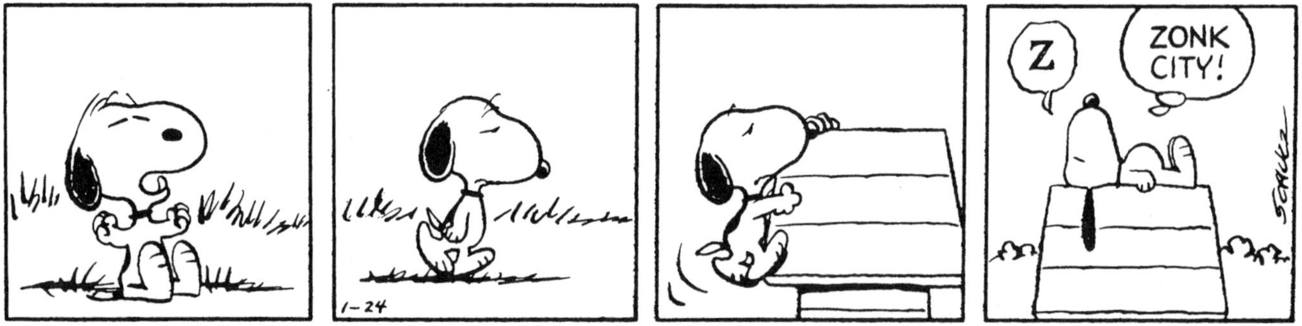
1-24
Z
ZONK CITY!
SCHULZ

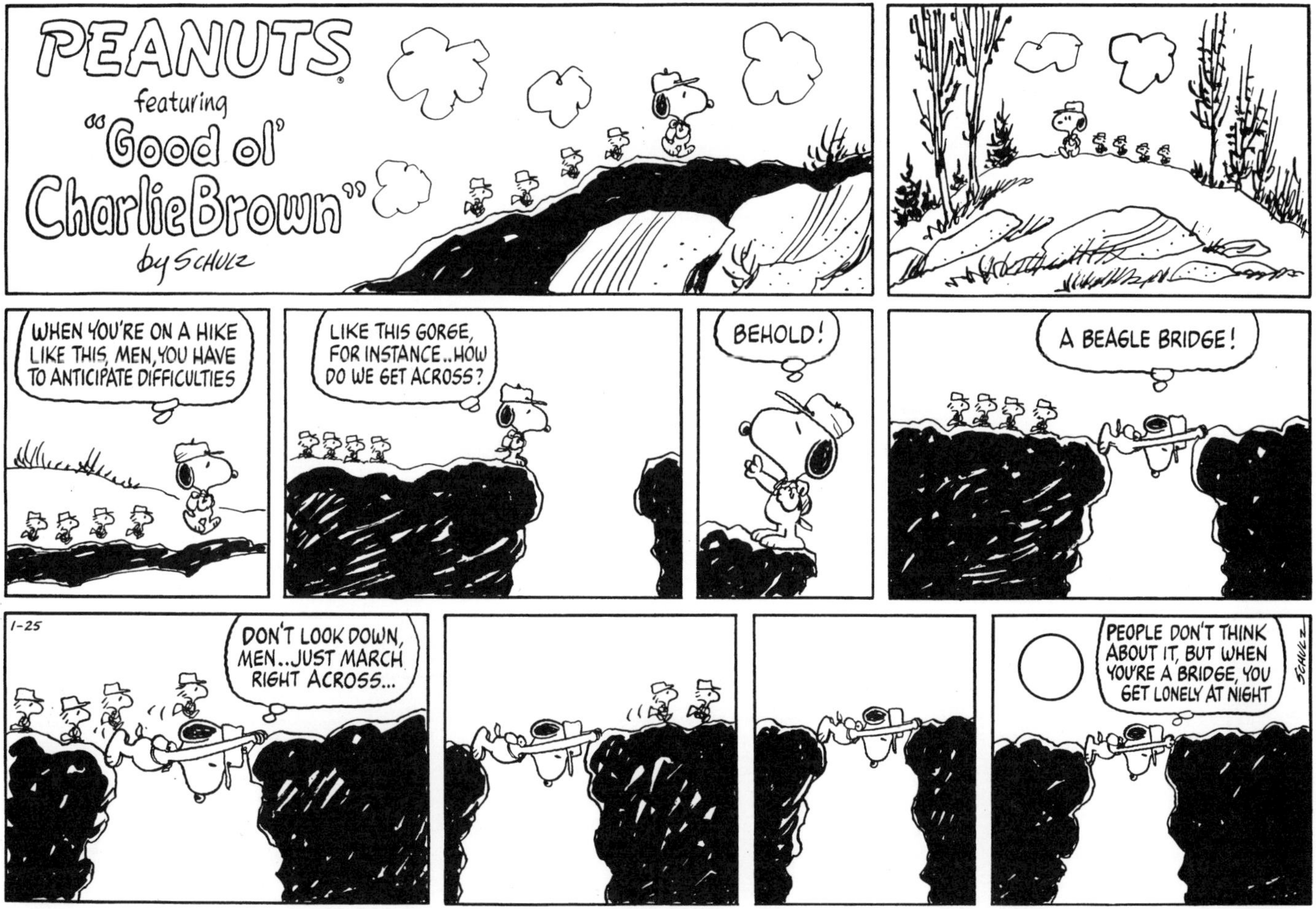
PEANUTS
featuring
"Good ol' CharlieBrown"
by SCHULZ
WHEN YOU'RE ON A HIKE LIKE THIS, MEN, YOU HAVE TO ANTICIPATE DIFFICULTIES
LIKE THIS GORGE, FOR INSTANCE..HOW DO WE GET ACROSS?
BEHOLD!
A BEAGLE BRIDGE!
1-25
DON'T LOOK DOWN, MEN..JUST MARCH RIGHT ACROSS...
PEOPLE DON'T THINK ABOUT IT, BUT WHEN YOU'RE A BRIDGE, YOU GET LONELY AT NIGHT
SCHULZ

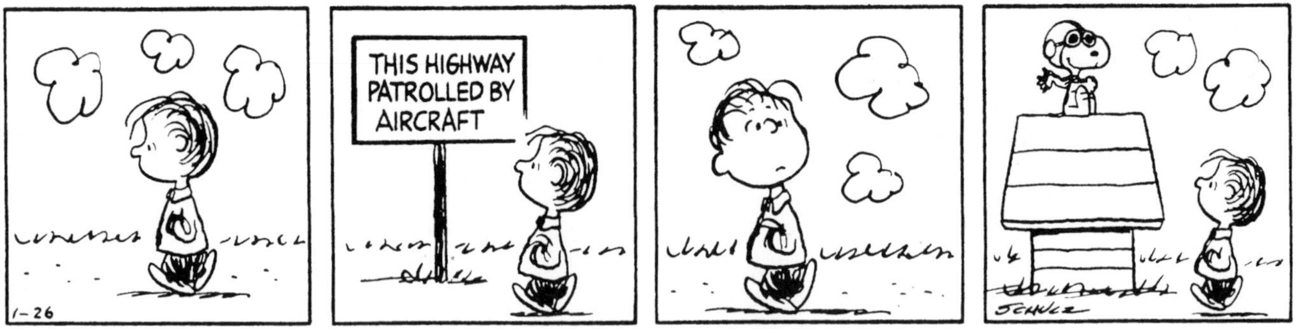
THIS HIGHWAY PATROLLED BY AIRCRAFT
1-26

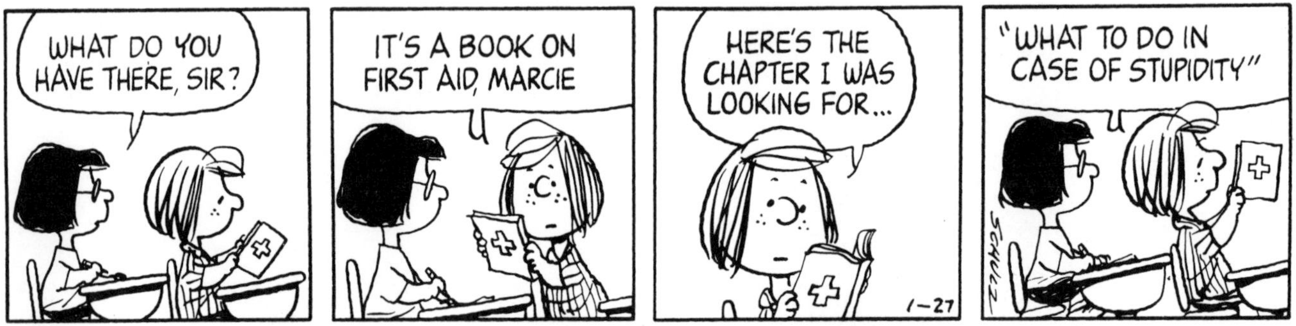
WHAT DO YOU HAVE THERE, SIR?
IT'S A BOOK ON FIRST AID, MARCIE
HERE'S THE CHAPTER I WAS LOOKING FOR...
"WHAT TO DO IN CASE OF STUPIDITY"
1-27

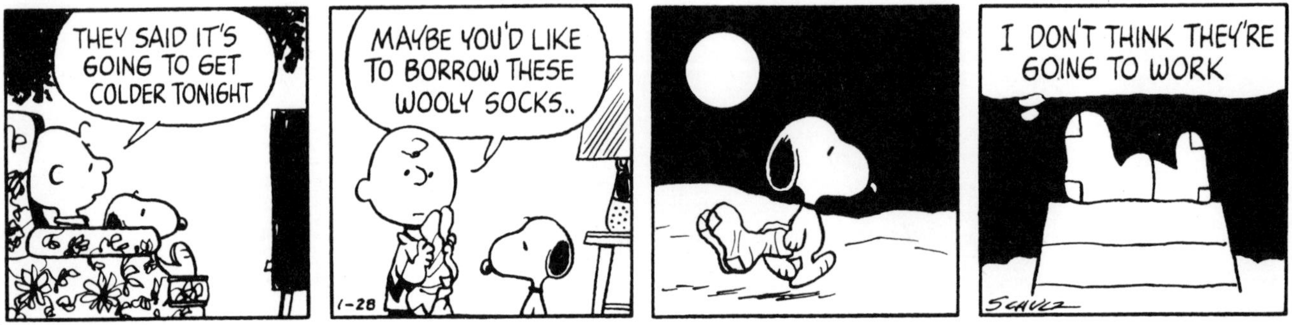
THEY SAID IT'S GOING TO GET COLDER TONIGHT
MAYBE YOU'D LIKE TO BORROW THESE WOOLY SOCKS..
I DON'T THINK THEY'RE GOING TO WORK
1-28

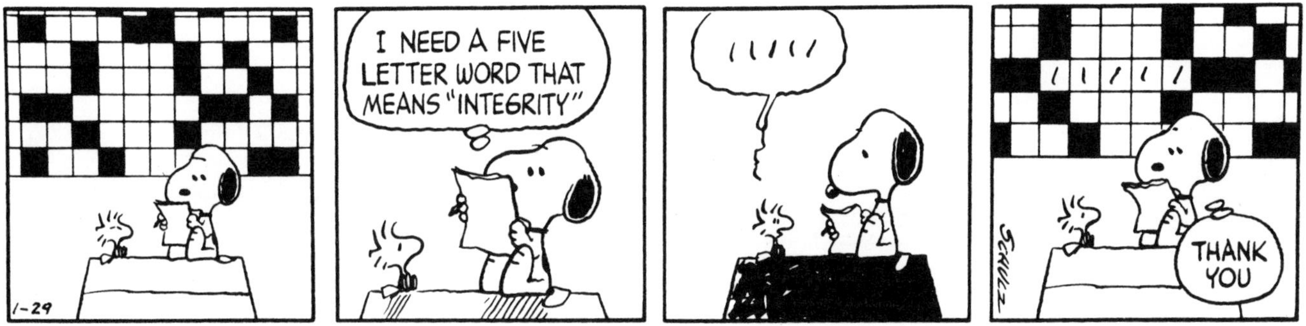
1-29
I NEED A FIVE LETTER WORD THAT MEANS "INTEGRITY"
SCHULZ
THANK YOU

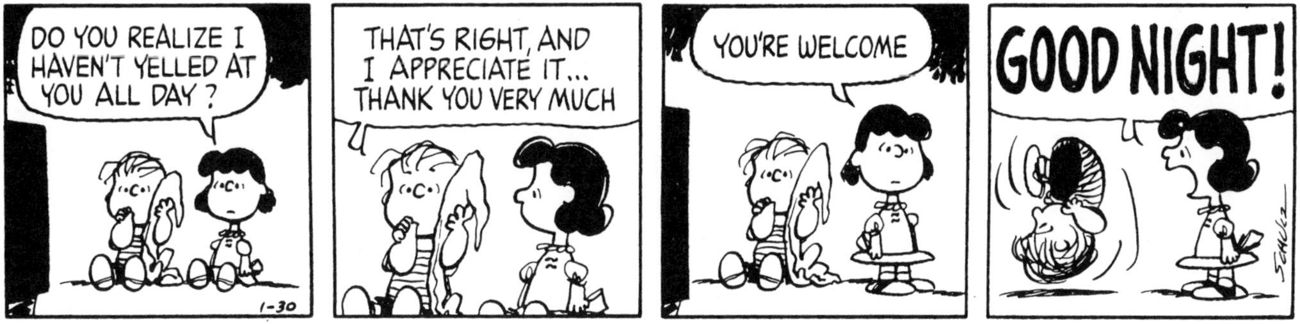
DO YOU REALIZE I HAVEN'T YELLED AT YOU ALL DAY ?
1-30
THAT'S RIGHT, AND I APPRECIATE IT... THANK YOU VERY MUCH
YOU'RE WELCOME
GOOD NIGHT!
SCHULZ

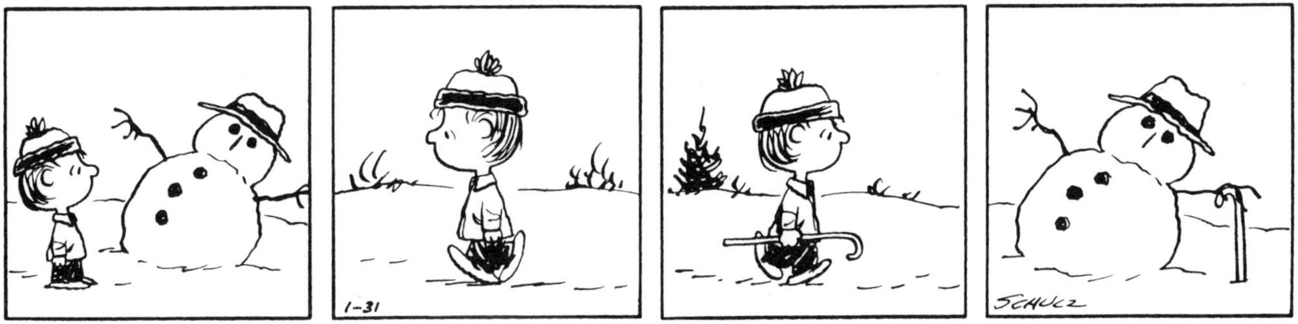
1-31
SCHULZ

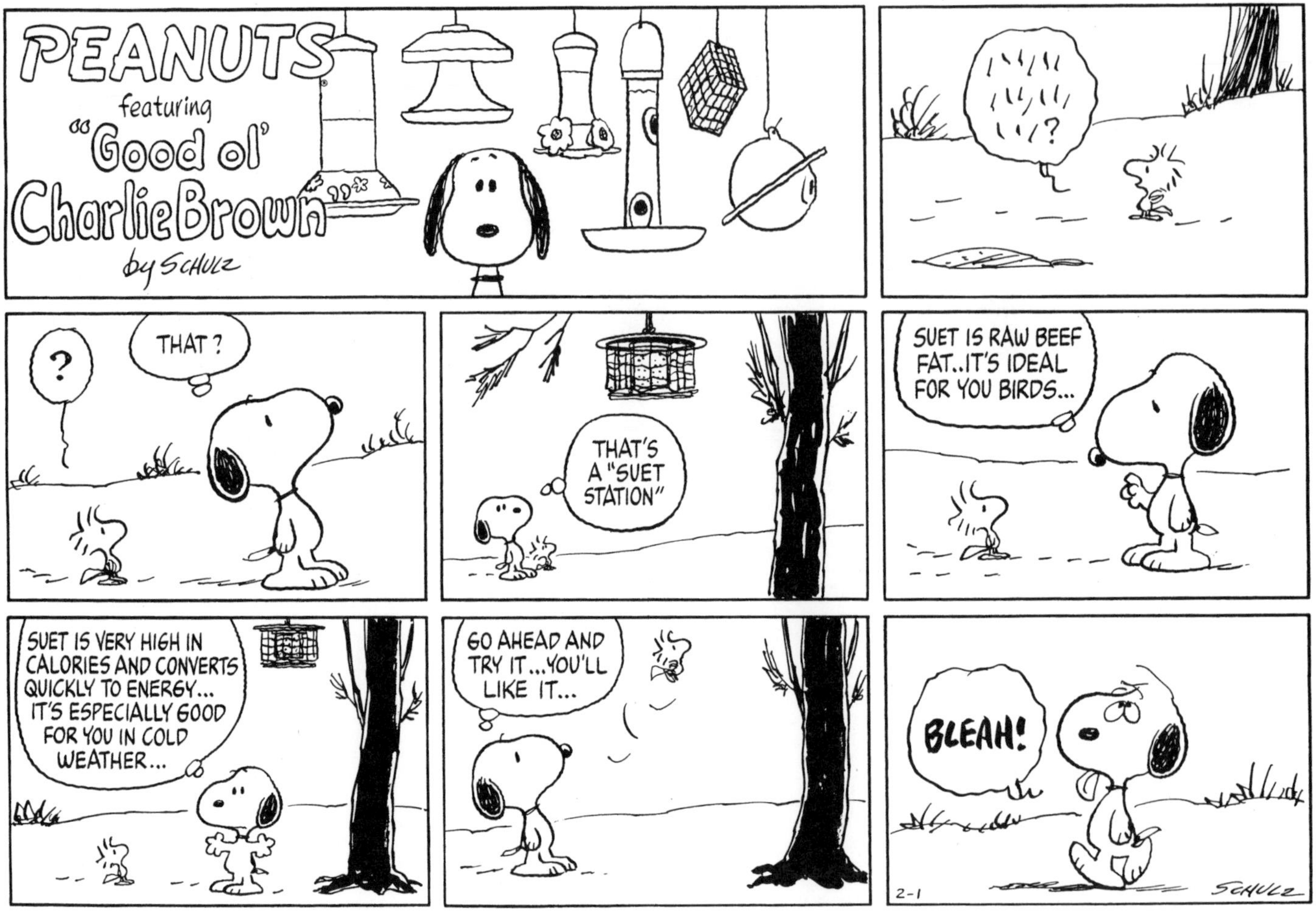
PEANUTS
featuring "Good ol' CharlieBrown"
by SCHULZ
?
?
THAT ?
THAT'S A "SUET STATION"
SUET IS RAW BEEF FAT..IT'S IDEAL FOR YOU BIRDS...
SUET IS VERY HIGH IN CALORIES AND CONVERTS QUICKLY TO ENERGY... IT'S ESPECIALLY GOOD FOR YOU IN COLD WEATHER...
GO AHEAD AND TRY IT...YOU'LL LIKE IT...
BLEAH!
2-1
SCHULZ

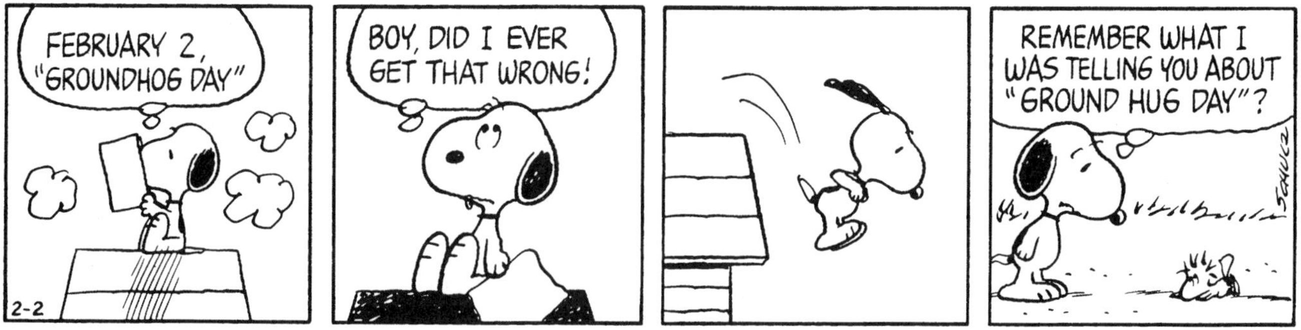
FEBRUARY 2, "GROUNDHOG DAY"
BOY, DID I EVER GET THAT WRONG!
REMEMBER WHAT I WAS TELLING YOU ABOUT "GROUND HUG DAY"?
SCHULZ

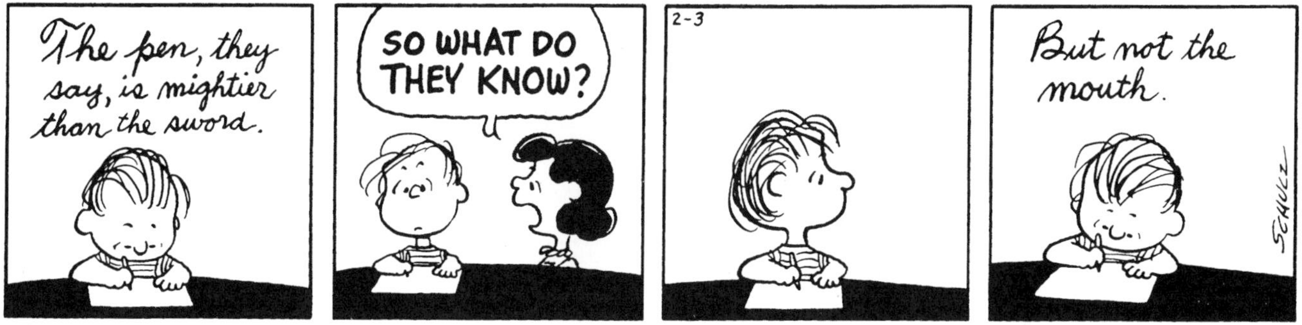
The pen, they say, is mightier than the sword.
SO WHAT DO THEY KNOW?
But not the mouth.
SCHULZ

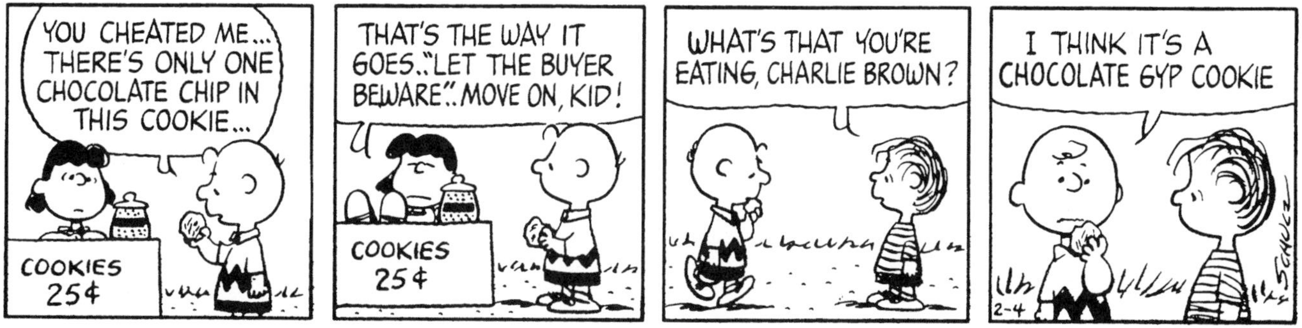
YOU CHEATED ME... THERE'S ONLY ONE CHOCOLATE CHIP IN THIS COOKIE...
COOKIES 25¢
THAT'S THE WAY IT GOES.."LET THE BUYER BEWARE".. MOVE ON, KID!
COOKIES 25¢
WHAT'S THAT YOU'RE EATING, CHARLIE BROWN?
I THINK IT'S A CHOCOLATE GYP COOKIE
SCHULZ

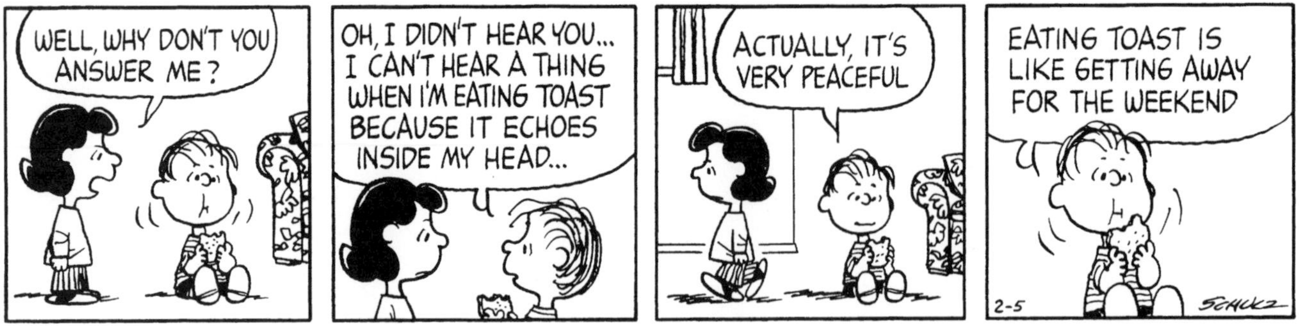
WELL, WHY DON'T YOU ANSWER ME?
OH, I DIDN'T HEAR YOU... I CAN'T HEAR A THING WHEN I'M EATING TOAST BECAUSE IT ECHOES INSIDE MY HEAD...
ACTUALLY, IT'S VERY PEACEFUL
EATING TOAST IS LIKE GETTING AWAY FOR THE WEEKEND
2-5
SCHULZ

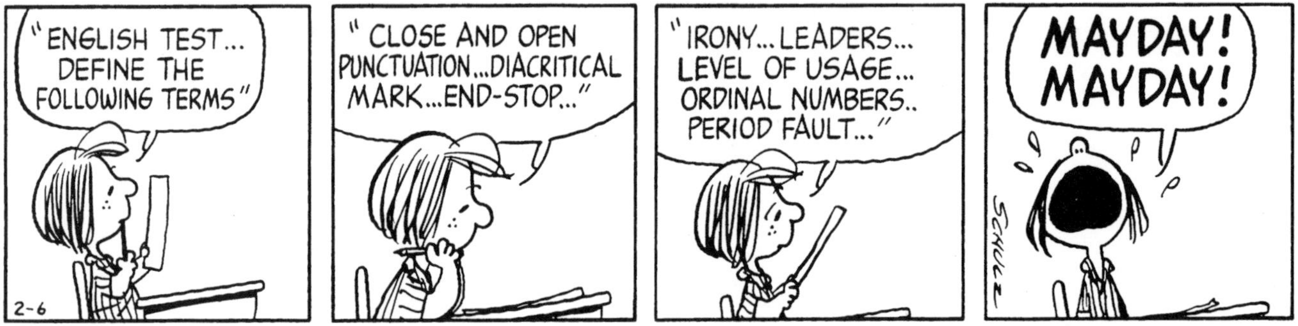
"ENGLISH TEST... DEFINE THE FOLLOWING TERMS"
2-6
" CLOSE AND OPEN PUNCTUATION...DIACRITICAL MARK...END-STOP..."
"IRONY... LEADERS... LEVEL OF USAGE... ORDINAL NUMBERS.. PERIOD FAULT..."
MAYDAY! MAYDAY!
SCHULZ

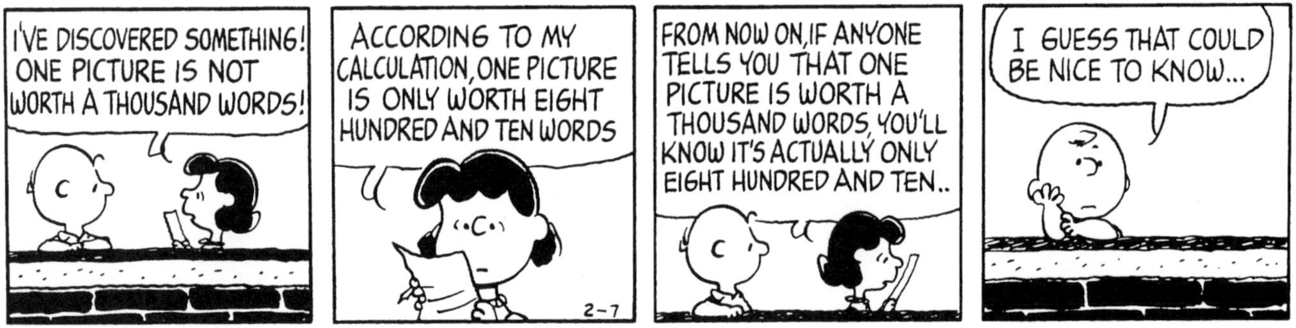
I'VE DISCOVERED SOMETHING! ONE PICTURE IS NOT WORTH A THOUSAND WORDS!
ACCORDING TO MY CALCULATION, ONE PICTURE IS ONLY WORTH EIGHT HUNDRED AND TEN WORDS
2-7
FROM NOW ON, IF ANYONE TELLS YOU THAT ONE PICTURE IS WORTH A THOUSAND WORDS, YOU'LL KNOW IT'S ACTUALLY ONLY EIGHT HUNDRED AND TEN..
I GUESS THAT COULD BE NICE TO KNOW...

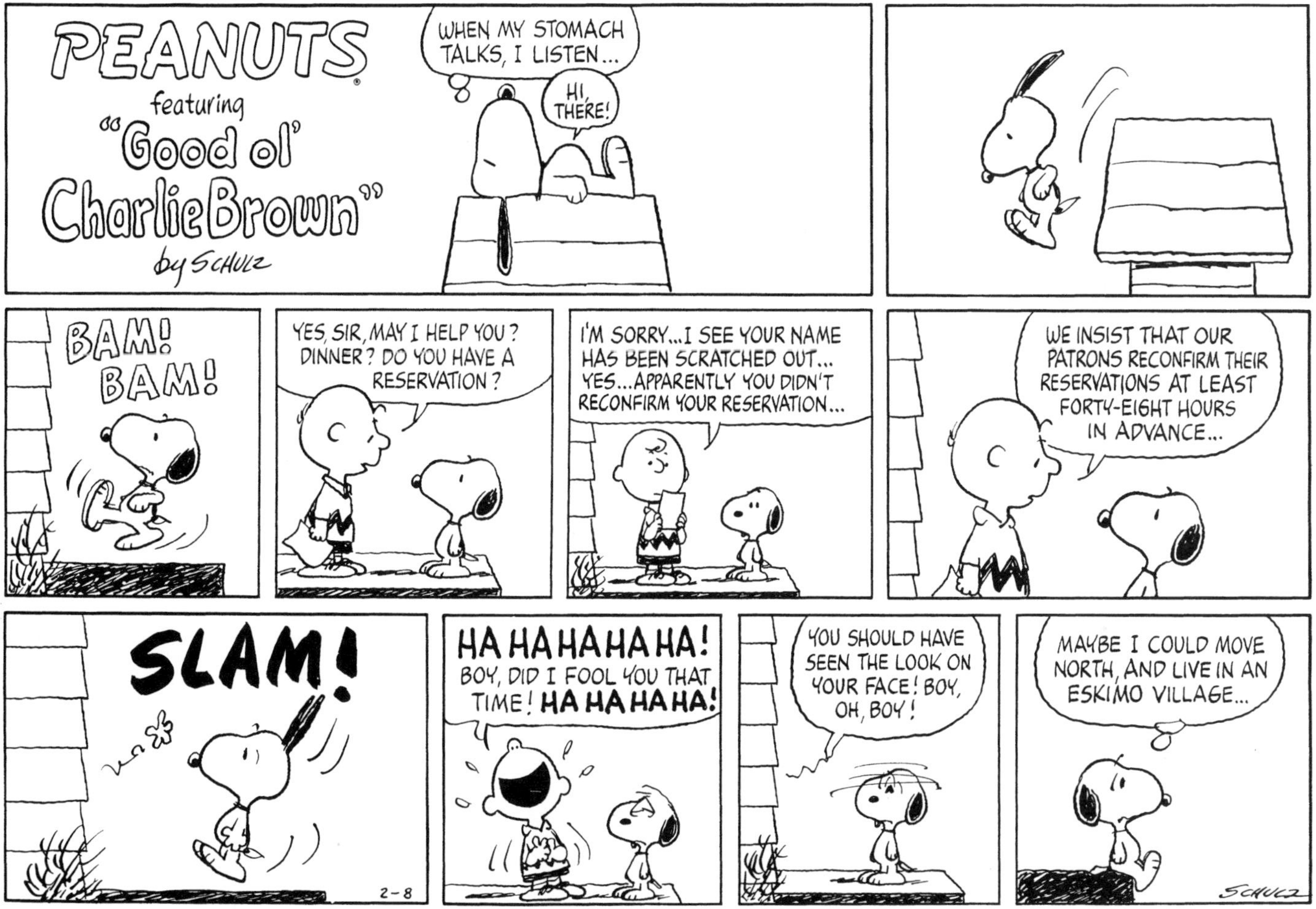
PEANUTS
featuring "Good ol' Charlie Brown"
by SCHULZ
WHEN MY STOMACH TALKS, I LISTEN...
HI, THERE!
BAM! BAM!
YES, SIR, MAY I HELP YOU? DINNER? DO YOU HAVE A RESERVATION?
I'M SORRY...I SEE YOUR NAME HAS BEEN SCRATCHED OUT... YES...APPARENTLY YOU DIDN'T RECONFIRM YOUR RESERVATION...
WE INSIST THAT OUR PATRONS RECONFIRM THEIR RESERVATIONS AT LEAST FORTY-EIGHT HOURS IN ADVANCE...
SLAM!
2-8
HA HA HA HA HA HA! BOY, DID I FOOL YOU THAT TIME! HA HA HA HA HA!
YOU SHOULD HAVE SEEN THE LOOK ON YOUR FACE! BOY, OH, BOY!
MAYBE I COULD MOVE NORTH, AND LIVE IN AN ESKIMO VILLAGE...
SCHULZ

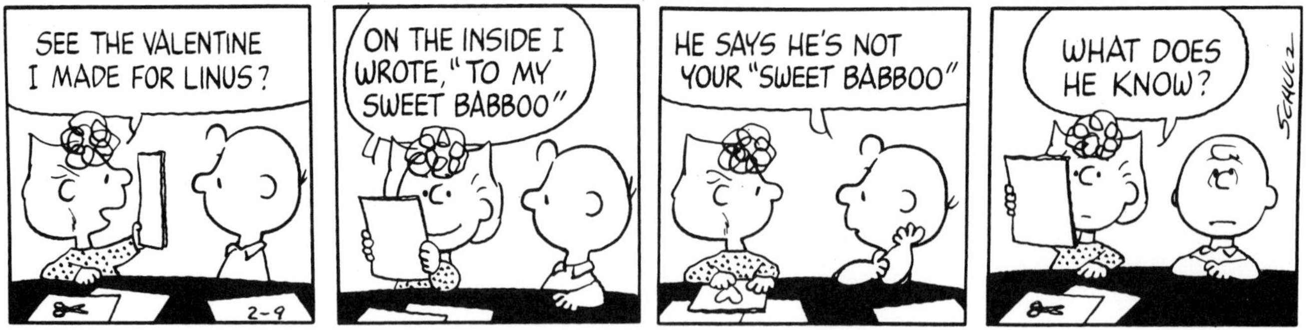
SEE THE VALENTINE I MADE FOR LINUS?
2-9
ON THE INSIDE I WROTE, "TO MY SWEET BABBOO"
HE SAYS HE'S NOT YOUR "SWEET BABBOO"
WHAT DOES HE KNOW?
SCHULZ

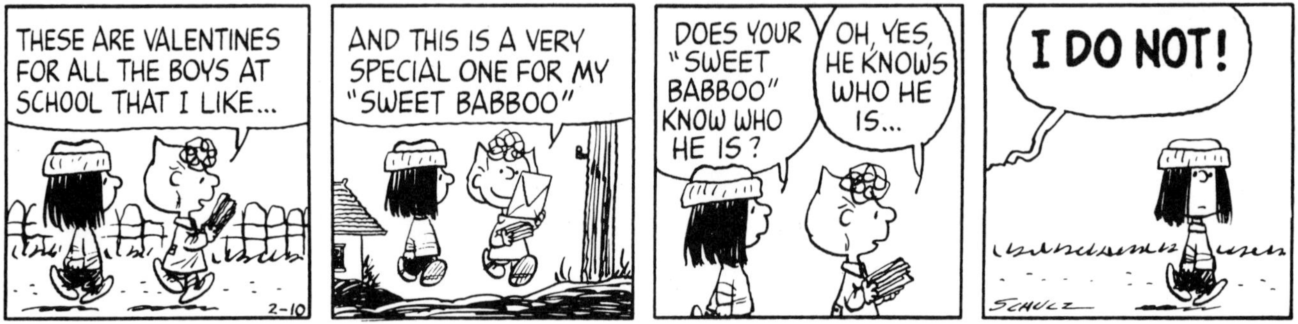
THESE ARE VALENTINES FOR ALL THE BOYS AT SCHOOL THAT I LIKE...
2-10
AND THIS IS A VERY SPECIAL ONE FOR MY "SWEET BABBOO"
DOES YOUR "SWEET BABBOO" KNOW WHO HE IS?
OH, YES, HE KNOWS WHO HE IS...
I DO NOT!
SCHULZ

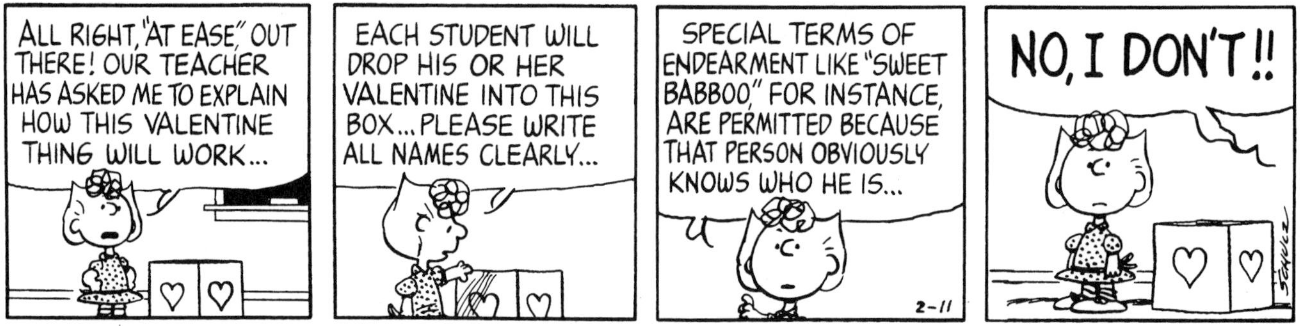
ALL RIGHT, "AT EASE," OUT THERE! OUR TEACHER HAS ASKED ME TO EXPLAIN HOW THIS VALENTINE THING WILL WORK...
EACH STUDENT WILL DROP HIS OR HER VALENTINE INTO THIS BOX... PLEASE WRITE ALL NAMES CLEARLY...
SPECIAL TERMS OF ENDEARMENT LIKE "SWEET BABBOO," FOR INSTANCE, ARE PERMITTED BECAUSE THAT PERSON OBVIOUSLY KNOWS WHO HE IS...
2-11
NO, I DON'T!!
SCHULZ

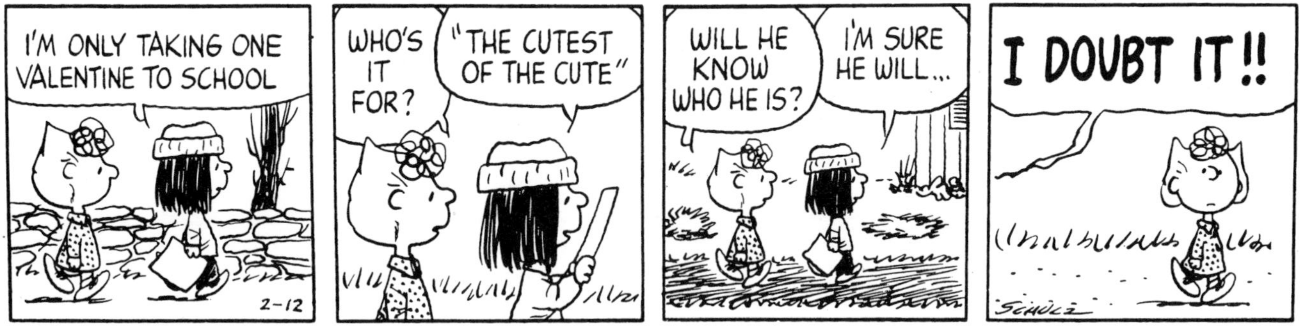
I'M ONLY TAKING ONE VALENTINE TO SCHOOL
2-12
WHO'S IT FOR?
"THE CUTEST OF THE CUTE"
WILL HE KNOW WHO HE IS?
I'M SURE HE WILL...
I DOUBT IT!!
SCHULZ

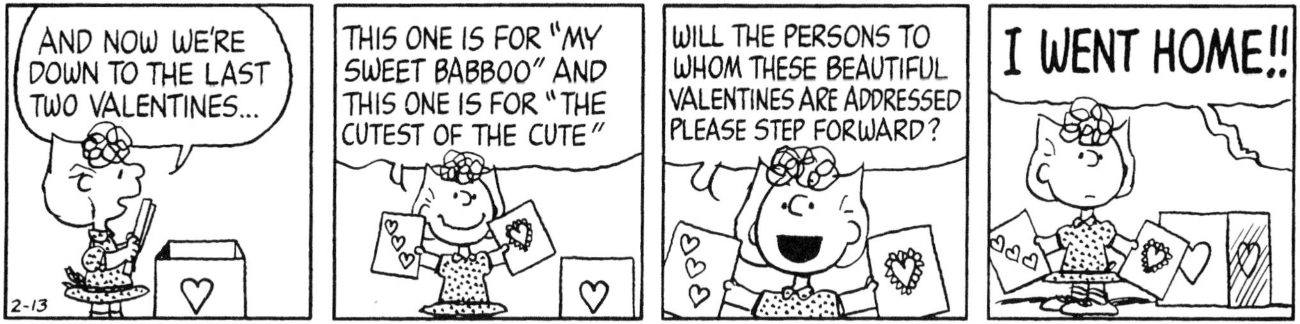
AND NOW WE'RE DOWN TO THE LAST TWO VALENTINES...
2-13
THIS ONE IS FOR "MY SWEET BABBOO" AND THIS ONE IS FOR "THE CUTEST OF THE CUTE"
WILL THE PERSONS TO WHOM THESE BEAUTIFUL VALENTINES ARE ADDRESSED PLEASE STEP FORWARD?
I WENT HOME!!

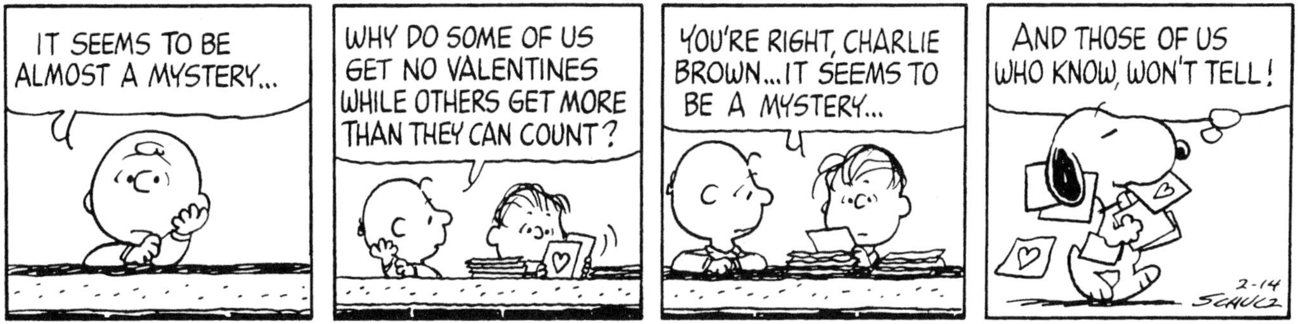
IT SEEMS TO BE ALMOST A MYSTERY...
WHY DO SOME OF US GET NO VALENTINES WHILE OTHERS GET MORE THAN THEY CAN COUNT?
YOU'RE RIGHT, CHARLIE BROWN...IT SEEMS TO BE A MYSTERY...
AND THOSE OF US WHO KNOW, WON'T TELL!
2-14
SCHULZ

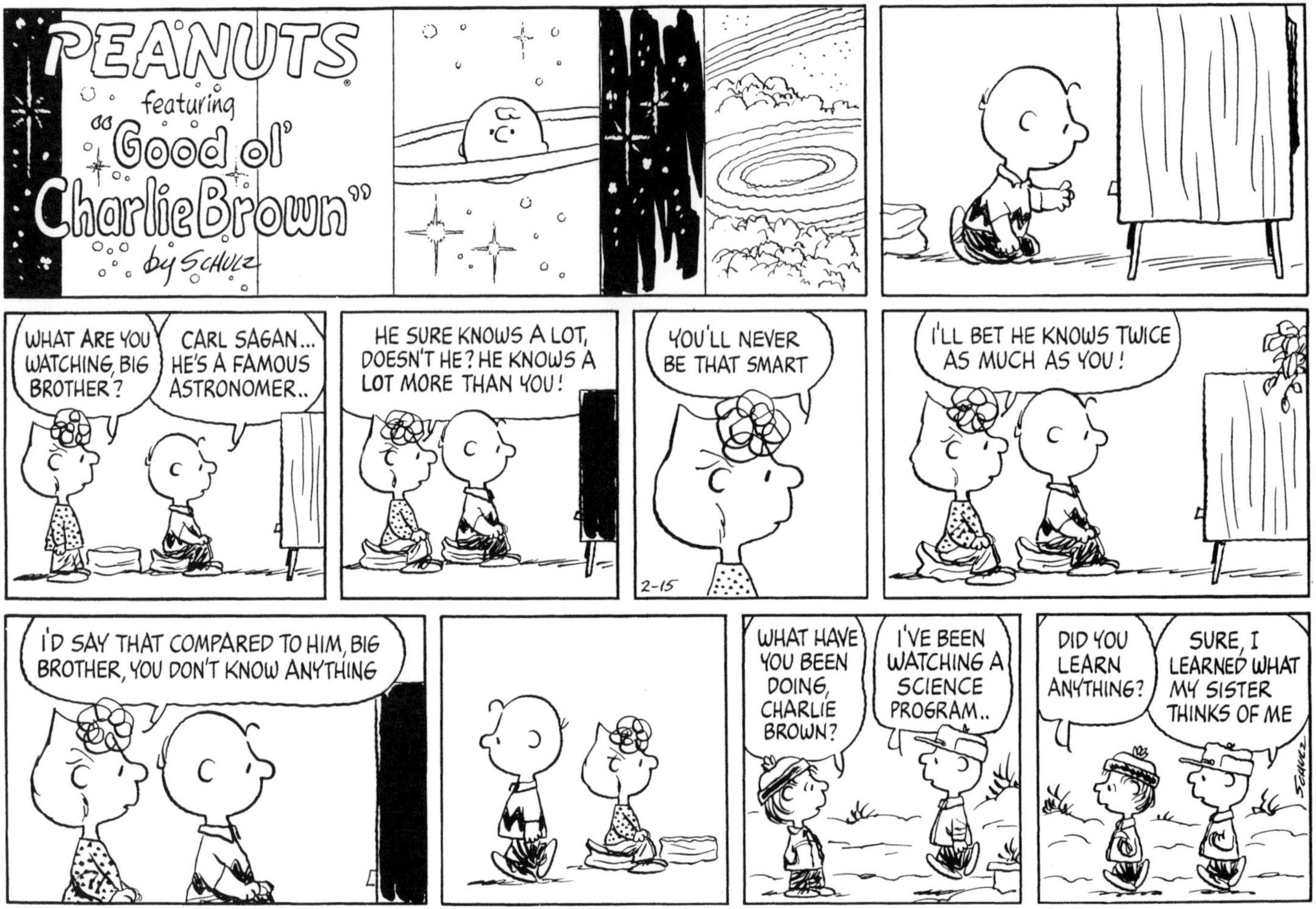
PEANUTS
featuring
"Good ol' Charlie Brown"
by SCHULZ
WHAT ARE YOU WATCHING, BIG BROTHER?
CARL SAGAN... HE'S A FAMOUS ASTRONOMER..
HE SURE KNOWS A LOT, DOESN'T HE? HE KNOWS A LOT MORE THAN YOU!
YOU'LL NEVER BE THAT SMART
2-15
I'LL BET HE KNOWS TWICE AS MUCH AS YOU!
I'D SAY THAT COMPARED TO HIM, BIG BROTHER, YOU DON'T KNOW ANYTHING
WHAT HAVE YOU BEEN DOING, CHARLIE BROWN?
I'VE BEEN WATCHING A SCIENCE PROGRAM..
DID YOU LEARN ANYTHING?
SURE, I LEARNED WHAT MY SISTER THINKS OF ME
SCHULZ

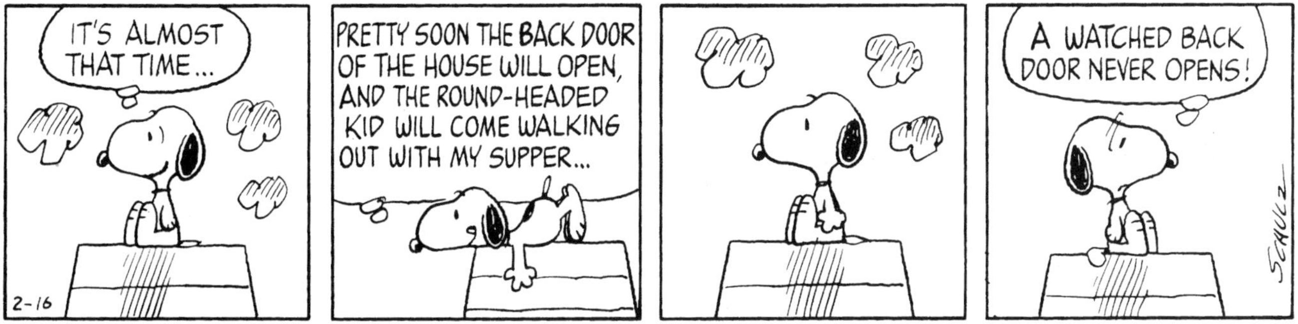
2-16
IT'S ALMOST THAT TIME...
PRETTY SOON THE BACK DOOR OF THE HOUSE WILL OPEN, AND THE ROUND-HEADED KID WILL COME WALKING OUT WITH MY SUPPER...
A WATCHED BACK DOOR NEVER OPENS!
SCHULZ

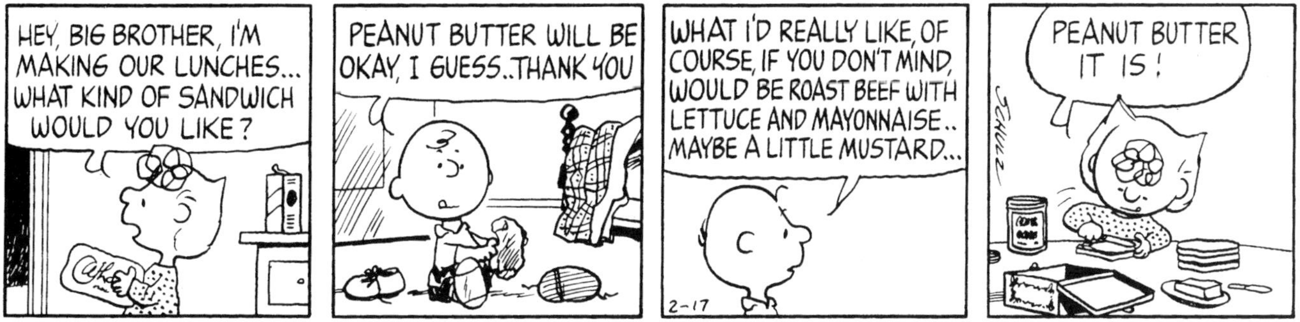
HEY, BIG BROTHER, I'M MAKING OUR LUNCHES... WHAT KIND OF SANDWICH WOULD YOU LIKE?
PEANUT BUTTER WILL BE OKAY, I GUESS..THANK YOU
WHAT I'D REALLY LIKE, OF COURSE, IF YOU DON'T MIND, WOULD BE ROAST BEEF WITH LETTUCE AND MAYONNAISE.. MAYBE A LITTLE MUSTARD...
2-17
SCHULZ
PEANUT BUTTER IT IS!

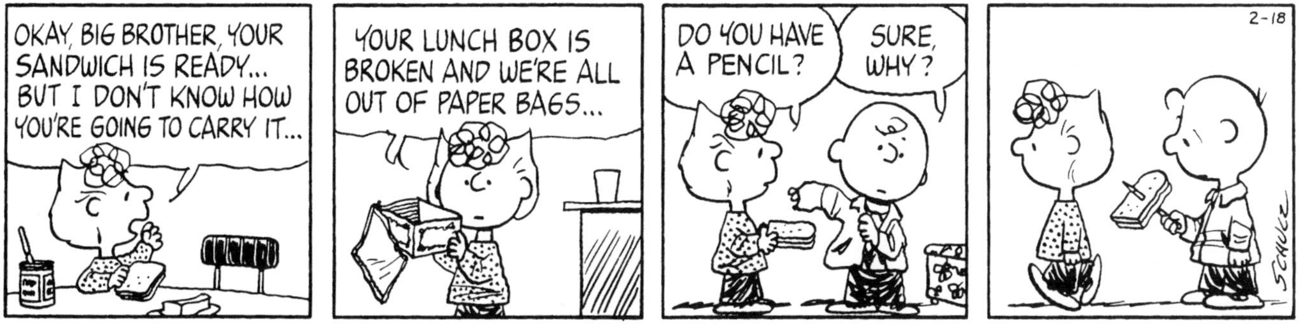
OKAY, BIG BROTHER, YOUR SANDWICH IS READY... BUT I DON'T KNOW HOW YOU'RE GOING TO CARRY IT...
YOUR LUNCH BOX IS BROKEN AND WE'RE ALL OUT OF PAPER BAGS...
DO YOU HAVE A PENCIL?
SURE, WHY?
2-18
SCHULZ

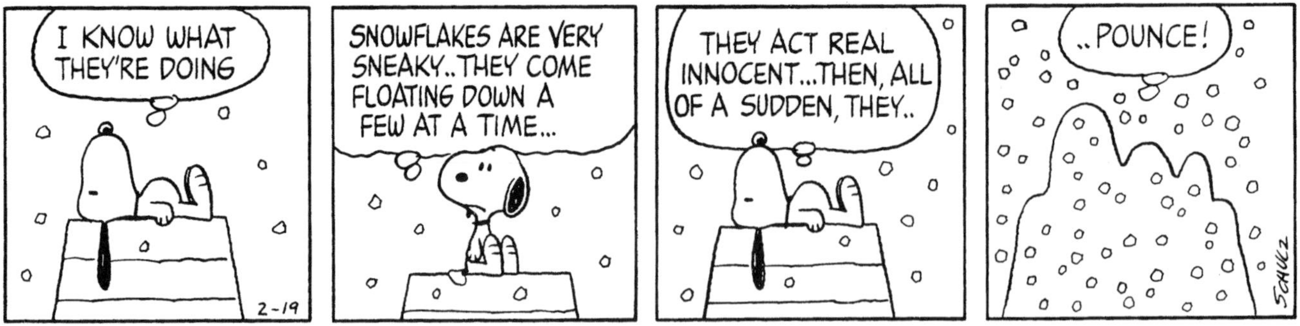
I KNOW WHAT THEY'RE DOING
2-19
SNOWFLAKES ARE VERY SNEAKY.. THEY COME FLOATING DOWN A FEW AT A TIME...
THEY ACT REAL INNOCENT...THEN, ALL OF A SUDDEN, THEY..
..POUNCE!
SCHULZ

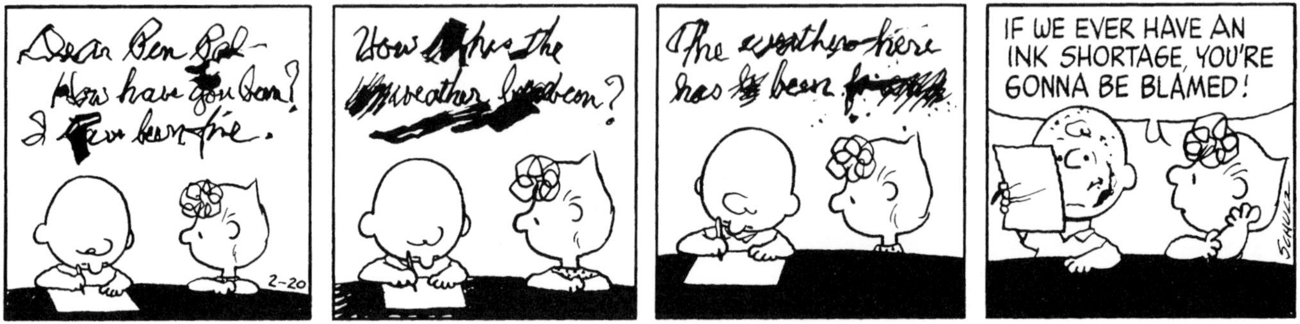
Dear Ben Bob-
How have you been?
I have been fine.
2-20
How has the weather been?
The weather here has been
IF WE EVER HAVE AN INK SHORTAGE, YOU'RE GONNA BE BLAMED!
SCHULZ

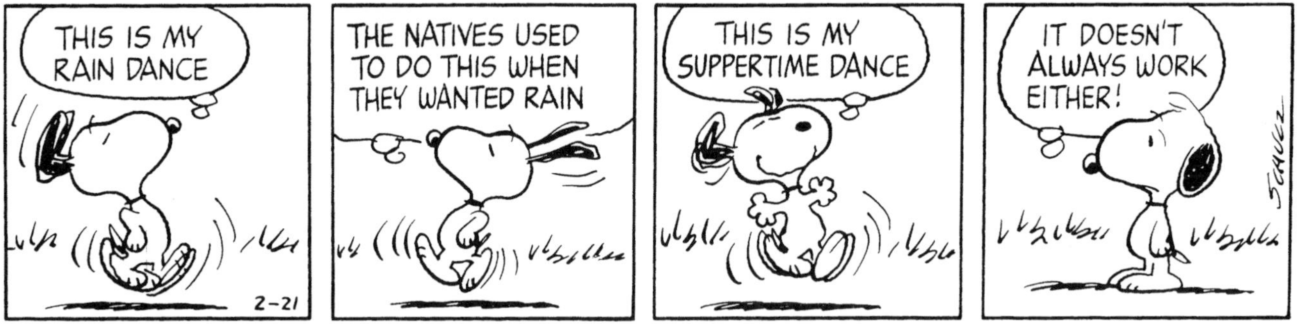
THIS IS MY RAIN DANCE
2-21
THE NATIVES USED TO DO THIS WHEN THEY WANTED RAIN
THIS IS MY SUPPERTIME DANCE
IT DOESN'T ALWAYS WORK EITHER!
SCHULZ

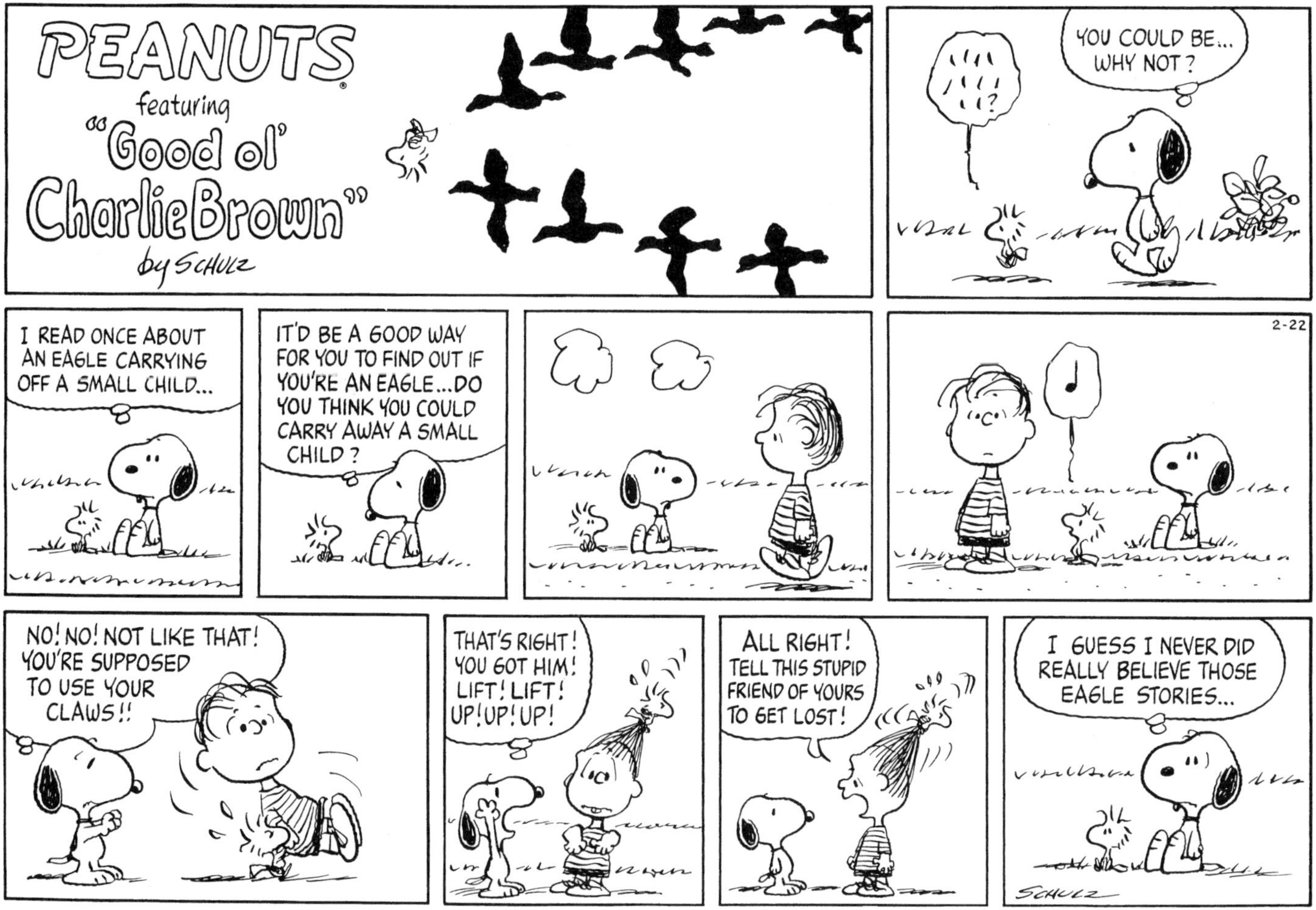
PEANUTS
featuring "Good ol' CharlieBrown"
by SCHULZ
YOU COULD BE... WHY NOT?
I READ ONCE ABOUT AN EAGLE CARRYING OFF A SMALL CHILD...
IT'D BE A GOOD WAY FOR YOU TO FIND OUT IF YOU'RE AN EAGLE...DO YOU THINK YOU COULD CARRY AWAY A SMALL CHILD?
2-22
NO! NO! NOT LIKE THAT! YOU'RE SUPPOSED TO USE YOUR CLAWS!!
THAT'S RIGHT! YOU GOT HIM! LIFT! LIFT! UP! UP! UP!
ALL RIGHT! TELL THIS STUPID FRIEND OF YOURS TO GET LOST!
I GUESS I NEVER DID REALLY BELIEVE THOSE EAGLE STORIES...
SCHULZ

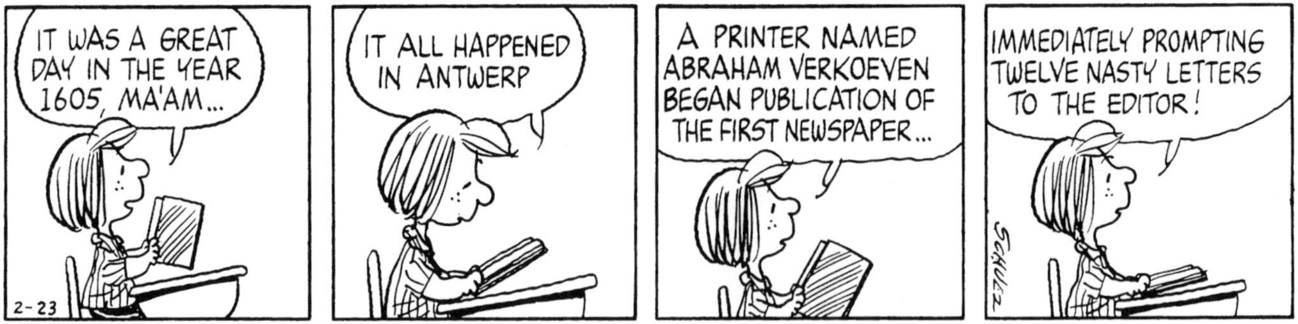
IT WAS A GREAT DAY IN THE YEAR 1605, MA'AM...
2-23
IT ALL HAPPENED IN ANTWERP
A PRINTER NAMED ABRAHAM VERKOEVEN BEGAN PUBLICATION OF THE FIRST NEWSPAPER...
IMMEDIATELY PROMPTING TWELVE NASTY LETTERS TO THE EDITOR!
SCHULZ

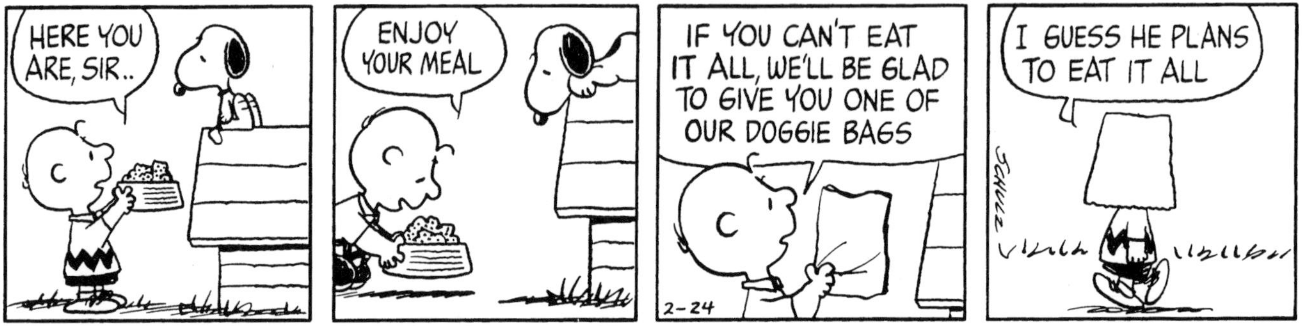
HERE YOU ARE, SIR..
ENJOY YOUR MEAL
IF YOU CAN'T EAT IT ALL, WE'LL BE GLAD TO GIVE YOU ONE OF OUR DOGGIE BAGS
2-24
I GUESS HE PLANS TO EAT IT ALL
SCHULZ

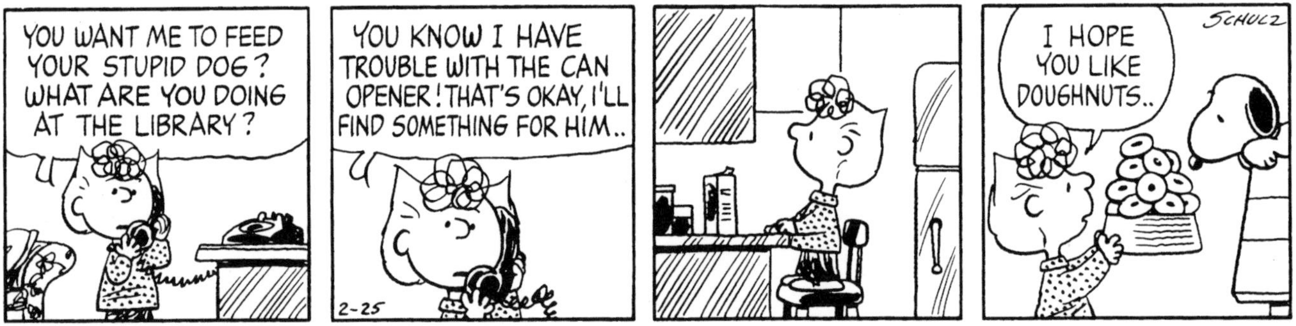
YOU WANT ME TO FEED YOUR STUPID DOG? WHAT ARE YOU DOING AT THE LIBRARY?
YOU KNOW I HAVE TROUBLE WITH THE CAN OPENER! THAT'S OKAY, I'LL FIND SOMETHING FOR HIM..
2-25
SCHULZ
I HOPE YOU LIKE DOUGHNUTS..

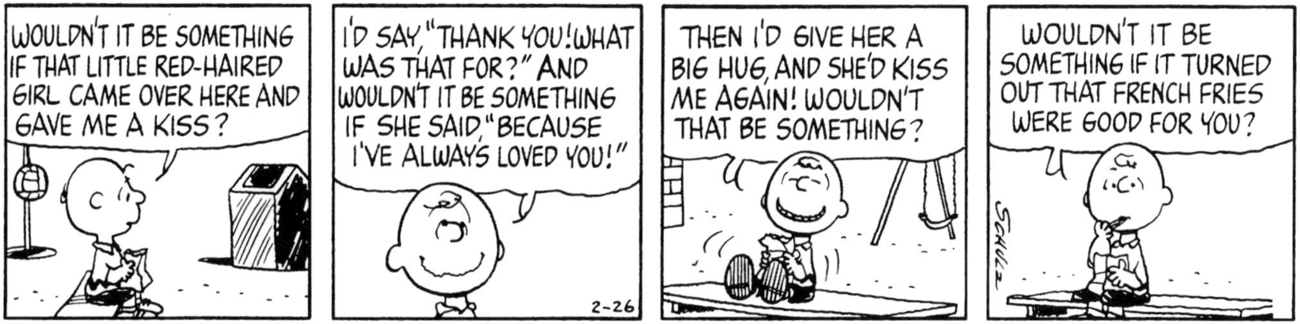
WOULDN'T IT BE SOMETHING IF THAT LITTLE RED-HAIRED GIRL CAME OVER HERE AND GAVE ME A KISS?
I'D SAY, "THANK YOU! WHAT WAS THAT FOR?" AND WOULDN'T IT BE SOMETHING IF SHE SAID, "BECAUSE I'VE ALWAYS LOVED YOU!"
2-26
THEN I'D GIVE HER A BIG HUG, AND SHE'D KISS ME AGAIN! WOULDN'T THAT BE SOMETHING?
WOULDN'T IT BE SOMETHING IF IT TURNED OUT THAT FRENCH FRIES WERE GOOD FOR YOU?
SCHULZ

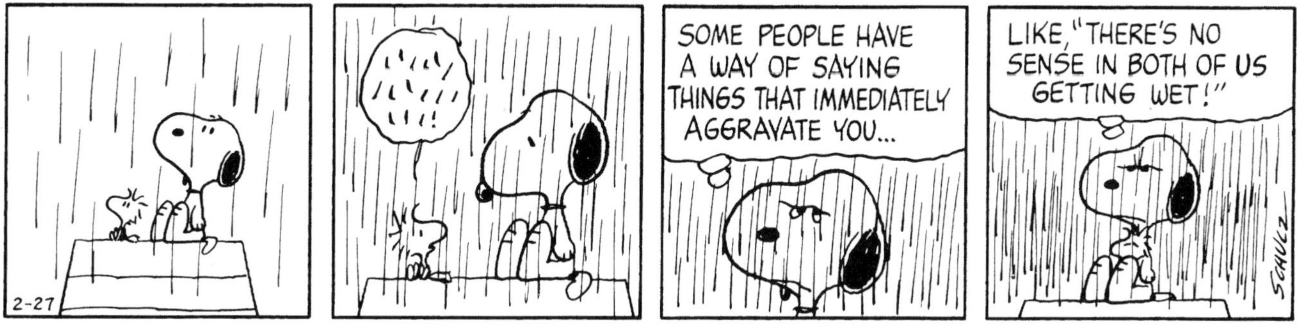
2-27
SOME PEOPLE HAVE A WAY OF SAYING THINGS THAT IMMEDIATELY AGGRAVATE YOU...
LIKE, "THERE'S NO SENSE IN BOTH OF US GETTING WET!"
SCHULZ

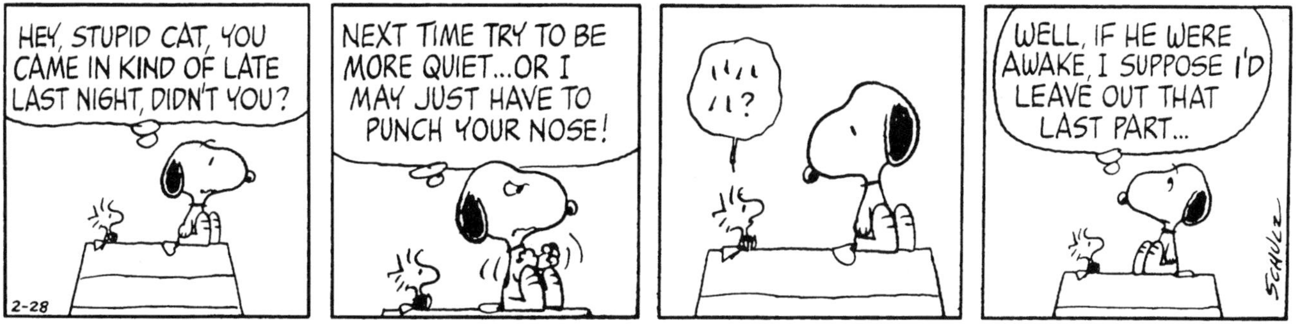
HEY, STUPID CAT, YOU CAME IN KIND OF LATE LAST NIGHT, DIDN'T YOU?
2-28
NEXT TIME TRY TO BE MORE QUIET...OR I MAY JUST HAVE TO PUNCH YOUR NOSE!
?
WELL, IF HE WERE AWAKE, I SUPPOSE I'D LEAVE OUT THAT LAST PART...
SCHULZ

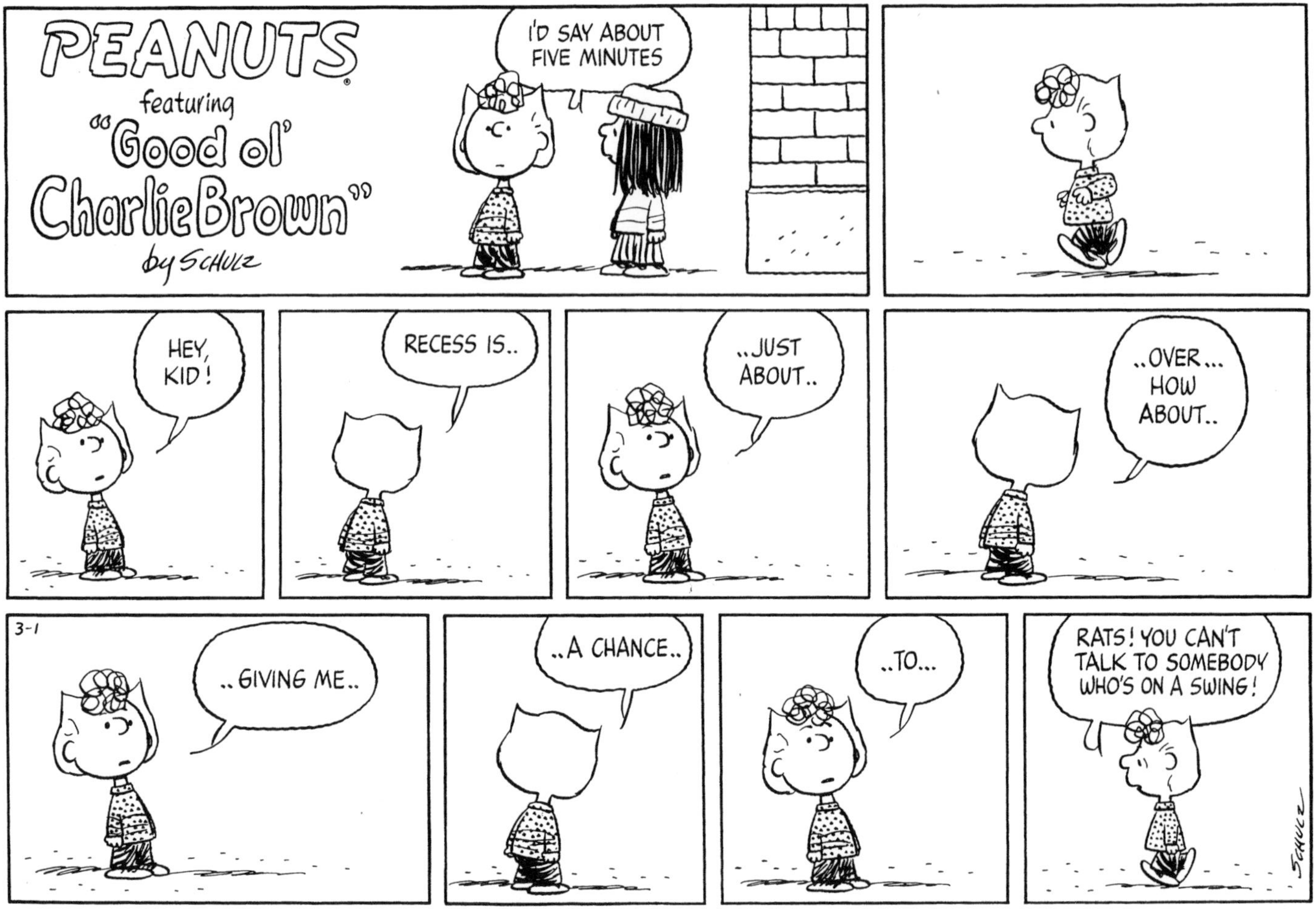

PEANUTS
featuring "Good ol' Charlie Brown"
by SCHULZ
I'D SAY ABOUT FIVE MINUTES
HEY, KID!
RECESS IS..
..JUST ABOUT..
..OVER... HOW ABOUT..
3-1
..GIVING ME..
..A CHANCE..
..TO...
RATS! YOU CAN'T TALK TO SOMEBODY WHO'S ON A SWING!
SCHULZ

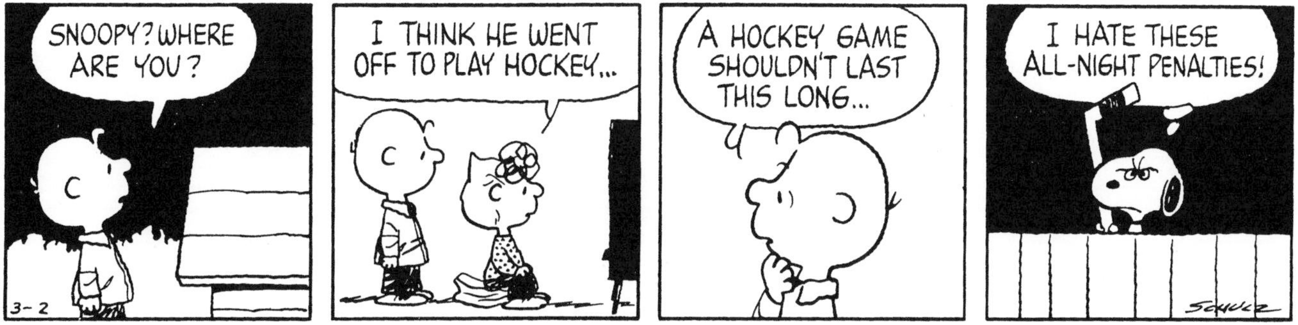
SNOOPY? WHERE ARE YOU?
I THINK HE WENT OFF TO PLAY HOCKEY...
A HOCKEY GAME SHOULDN'T LAST THIS LONG...
I HATE THESE ALL-NIGHT PENALTIES!

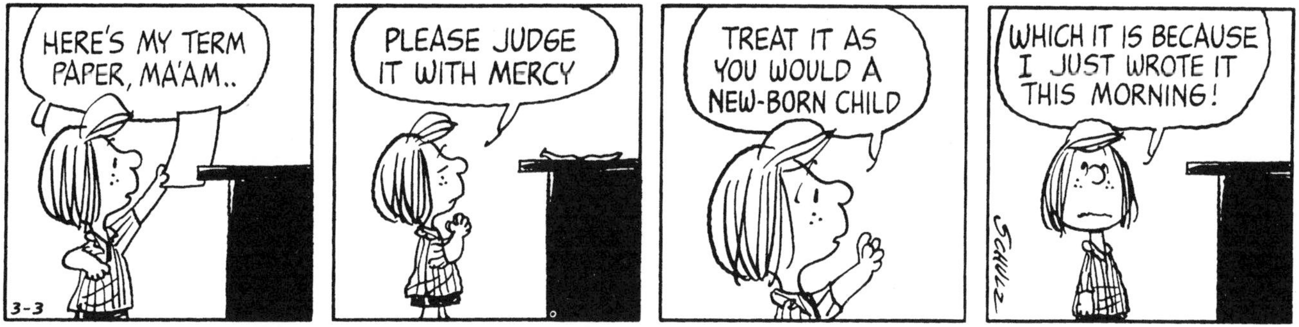
HERE'S MY TERM PAPER, MA'AM..
PLEASE JUDGE IT WITH MERCY
TREAT IT AS YOU WOULD A NEW-BORN CHILD
WHICH IT IS BECAUSE I JUST WROTE IT THIS MORNING!

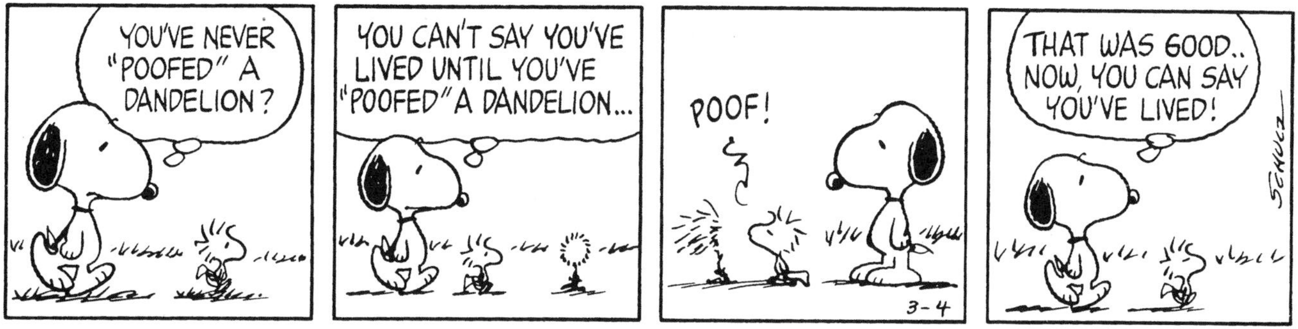
YOU'VE NEVER "POOFED" A DANDELION?
YOU CAN'T SAY YOU'VE LIVED UNTIL YOU'VE "POOFED" A DANDELION...
POOF!
THAT WAS GOOD.. NOW, YOU CAN SAY YOU'VE LIVED!

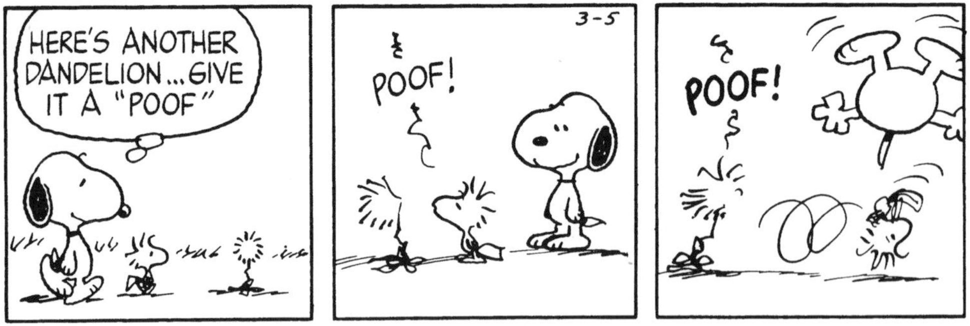
HERE'S ANOTHER DANDELION...GIVE IT A "POOF"
3-5
POOF!
POOF!
SORRY..I DIDN'T KNOW THEY EVER "POOFED" BACK
SCHULZ

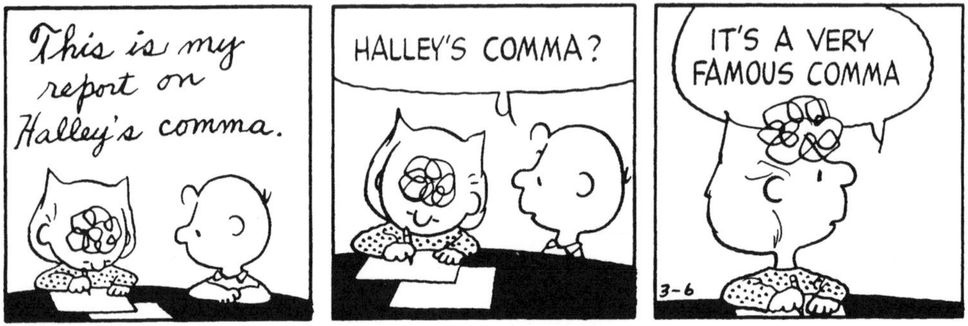
This is my report on Halley's comma.
HALLEY'S COMMA?
IT'S A VERY FAMOUS COMMA
3-6
HE PROBABLY WROTE HOME A LOT
SCHULZ

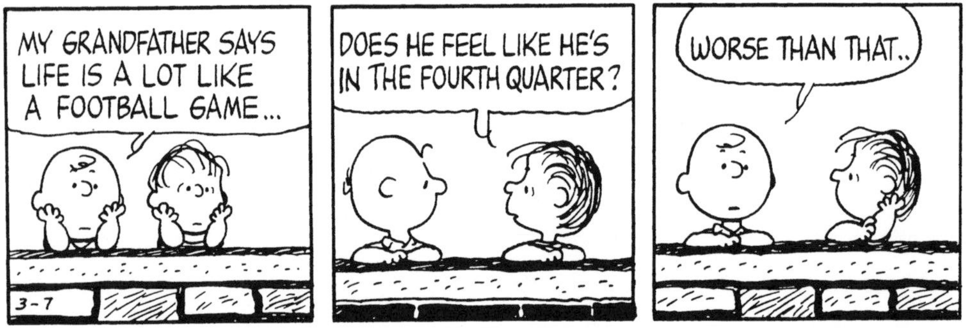
MY GRANDFATHER SAYS LIFE IS A LOT LIKE A FOOTBALL GAME...
3-7
DOES HE FEEL LIKE HE'S IN THE FOURTH QUARTER?
WORSE THAN THAT..
HE'S AFRAID HE DOESN'T HAVE ANY MORE "TIME OUTS"
SCHULZ

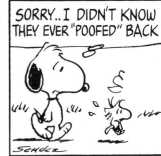

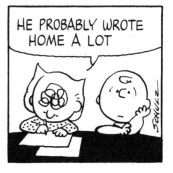

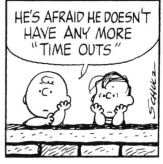

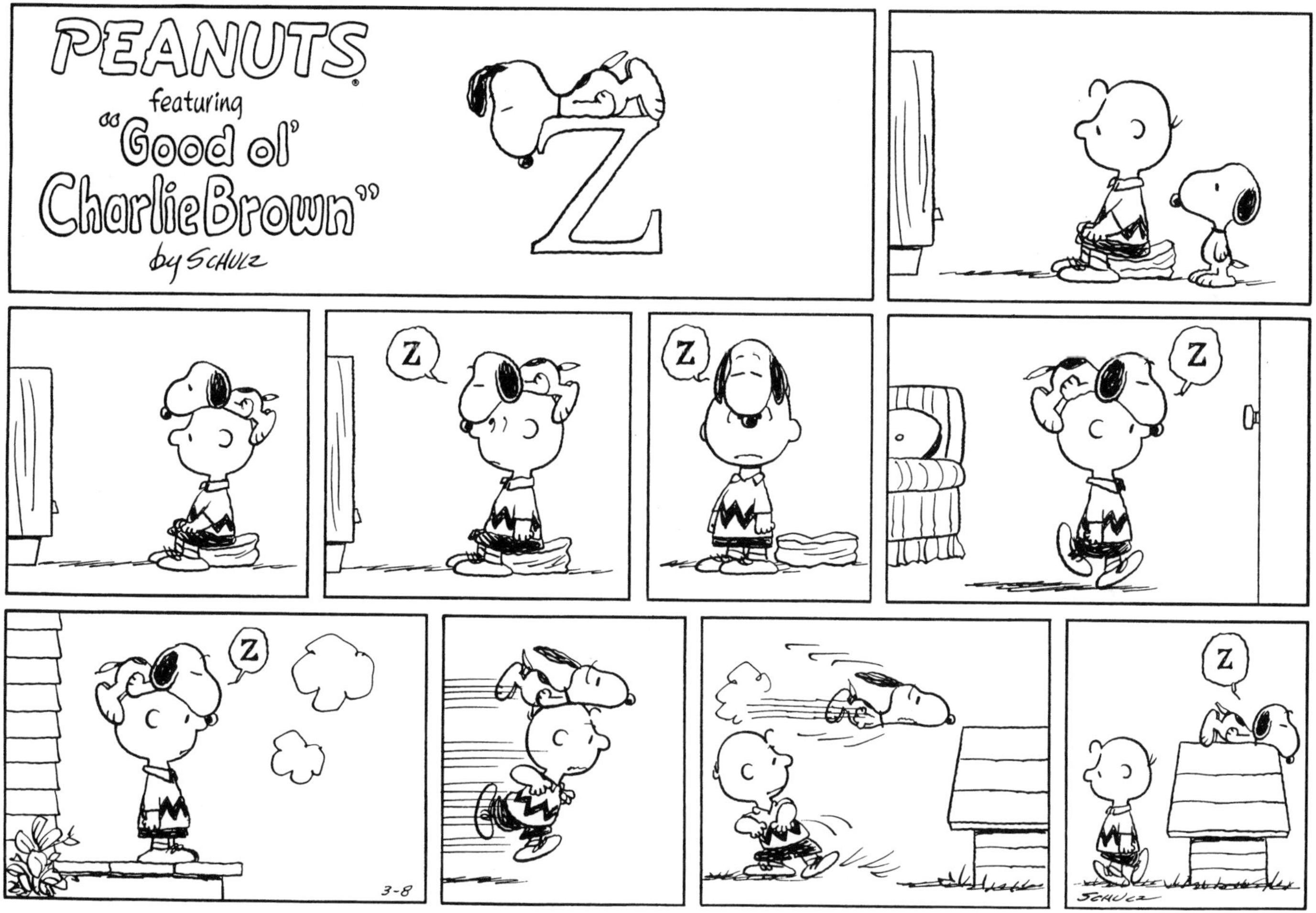
PEANUTS
featuring
"Good ol' CharlieBrown"
by SCHULZ
Z
Z
Z
Z
Z
Z
3-8
SCHULZ

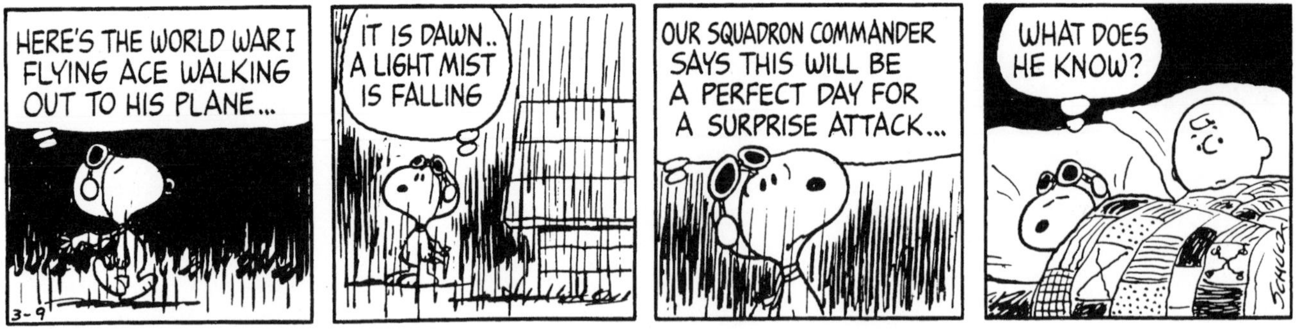
HERE'S THE WORLD WAR I FLYING ACE WALKING OUT TO HIS PLANE...
IT IS DAWN.. A LIGHT MIST IS FALLING
OUR SQUADRON COMMANDER SAYS THIS WILL BE A PERFECT DAY FOR A SURPRISE ATTACK...
WHAT DOES HE KNOW?
3-9

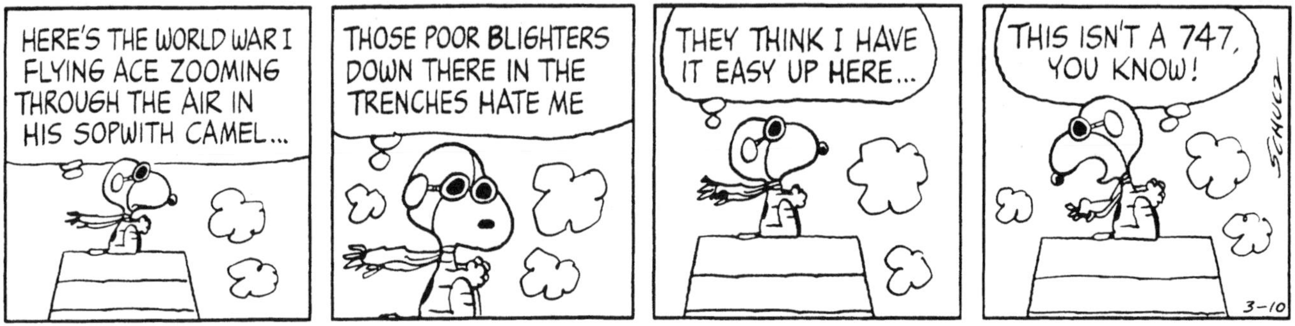
HERE'S THE WORLD WAR I FLYING ACE ZOOMING THROUGH THE AIR IN HIS SOPWITH CAMEL...
THOSE POOR BLIGHTERS DOWN THERE IN THE TRENCHES HATE ME
THEY THINK I HAVE IT EASY UP HERE...
THIS ISN'T A 747, YOU KNOW!
3-10

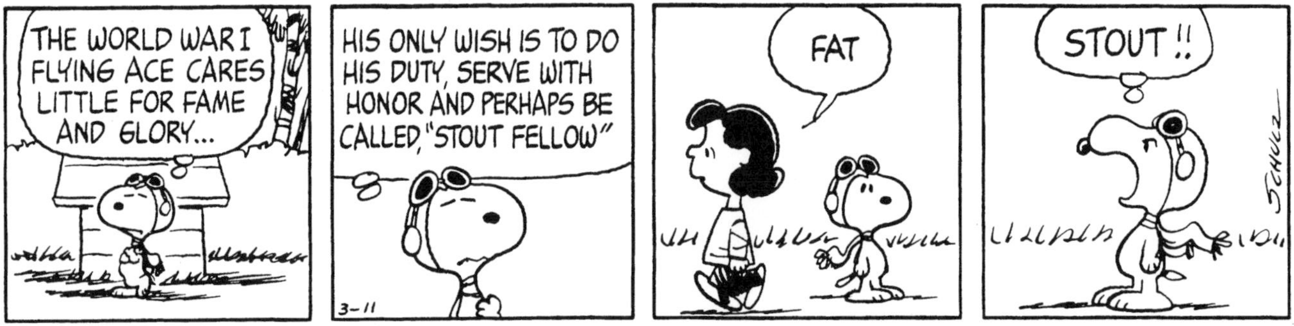
THE WORLD WAR I FLYING ACE CARES LITTLE FOR FAME AND GLORY...
HIS ONLY WISH IS TO DO HIS DUTY, SERVE WITH HONOR AND PERHAPS BE CALLED, "STOUT FELLOW"
FAT
STOUT!!
3-11

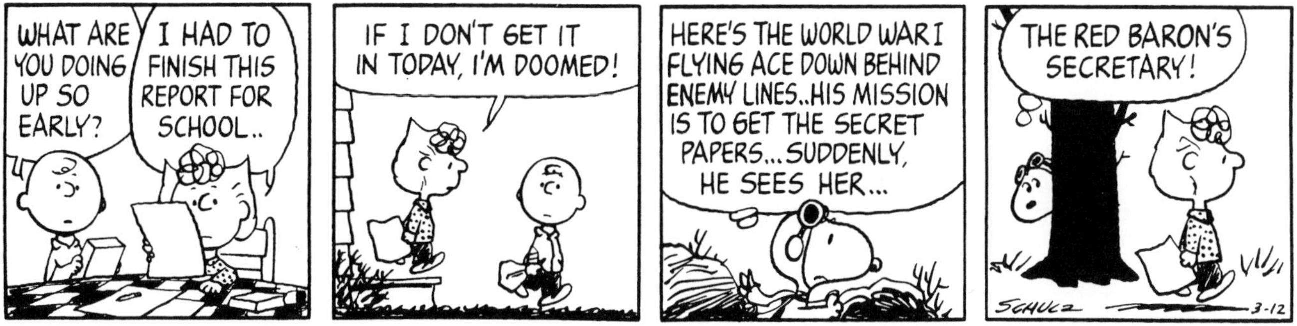
WHAT ARE YOU DOING UP SO EARLY?
I HAD TO FINISH THIS REPORT FOR SCHOOL..
IF I DON'T GET IT IN TODAY, I'M DOOMED!
HERE'S THE WORLD WAR I FLYING ACE DOWN BEHIND ENEMY LINES..HIS MISSION IS TO GET THE SECRET PAPERS...SUDDENLY, HE SEES HER...
THE RED BARON'S SECRETARY!
SCHULZ
3-12

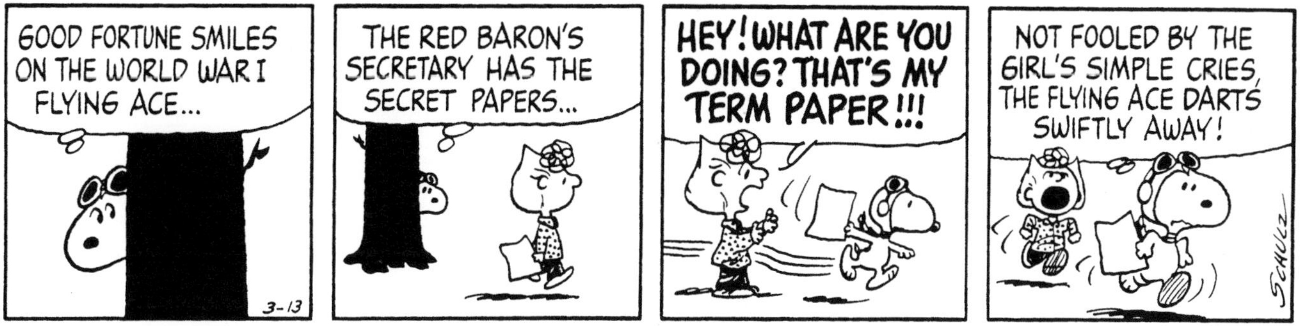
GOOD FORTUNE SMILES ON THE WORLD WAR I FLYING ACE...
3-13
THE RED BARON'S SECRETARY HAS THE SECRET PAPERS...
HEY! WHAT ARE YOU DOING? THAT'S MY TERM PAPER!!!
NOT FOOLED BY THE GIRL'S SIMPLE CRIES, THE FLYING ACE DARTS SWIFTLY AWAY!
SCHULZ

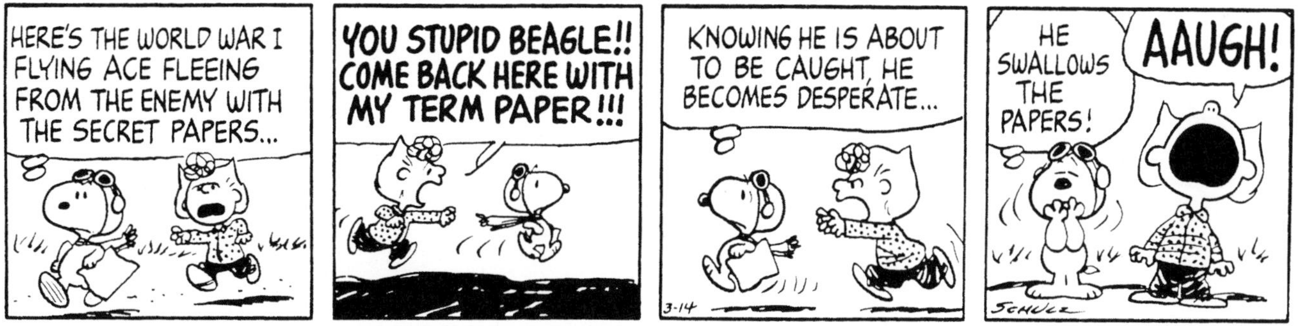
HERE'S THE WORLD WAR I FLYING ACE FLEEING FROM THE ENEMY WITH THE SECRET PAPERS...
YOU STUPID BEAGLE!! COME BACK HERE WITH MY TERM PAPER!!!
KNOWING HE IS ABOUT TO BE CAUGHT, HE BECOMES DESPERATE...
3-14
HE SWALLOWS THE PAPERS!
AAUGH!
SCHULZ

PEANUTS featuring "Good ol' Charlie Brown" by Schulz

HELP 10¢

THE DOCTOR IS [IN]

MAYBE I CAN PUT IT ANOTHER WAY...

PSYCHIATRIC HELP 10¢

THE DOCTOR IS [IN]

LIFE, CHARLIE BROWN, IS LIKE A DECK CHAIR...

LIKE A WHAT?

HAVE YOU EVER BEEN ON A CRUISE SHIP? PASSENGERS OPEN UP THESE CANVAS DECK CHAIRS SO THEY CAN SIT IN THE SUN...

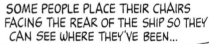

SOME PEOPLE PLACE THEIR CHAIRS FACING THE REAR OF THE SHIP SO THEY CAN SEE WHERE THEY'VE BEEN...

THE DOCTOR IS [IN]

OTHER PEOPLE FACE THEIR CHAIRS FORWARD...THEY WANT TO SEE WHERE THEY'RE GOING!

THE DOCTOR IS [IN]

PSYCHIAT HELP 10

ON THE CRUISE SHIP OF LIFE, CHARLIE BROWN, WHICH WAY IS YOUR DECK CHAIR FACING?

THE DOCTOR IS [IN]

3-15

PSYCHY HEL

I'VE NEVER BEEN ABLE TO GET ONE UNFOLDED...

THE DOCTOR IS [IN]

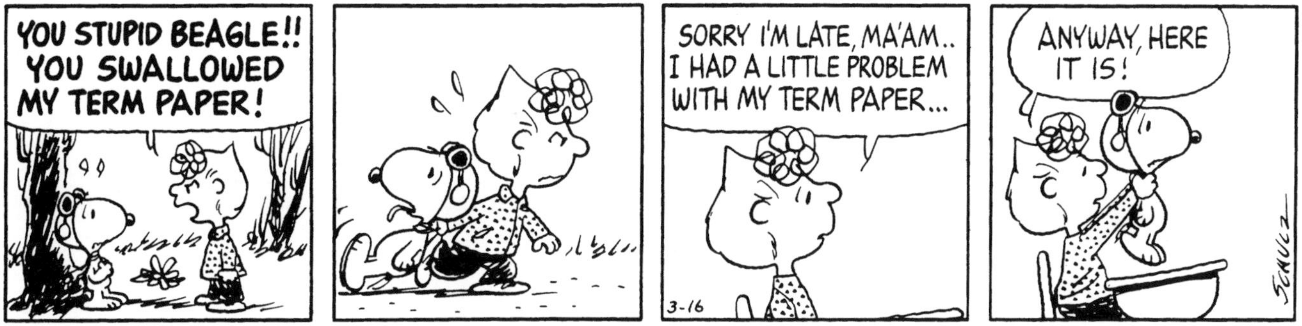
YOU STUPID BEAGLE!! YOU SWALLOWED MY TERM PAPER!
SORRY I'M LATE, MA'AM.. I HAD A LITTLE PROBLEM WITH MY TERM PAPER...
3-16
ANYWAY, HERE IT IS!
SCHULZ

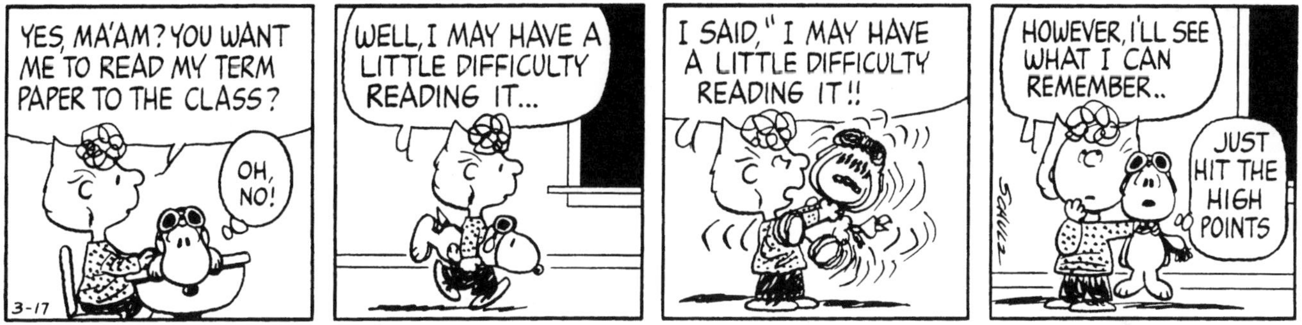
YES, MA'AM? YOU WANT ME TO READ MY TERM PAPER TO THE CLASS?
OH, NO!
3-17
WELL, I MAY HAVE A LITTLE DIFFICULTY READING IT...
I SAID, "I MAY HAVE A LITTLE DIFFICULTY READING IT!!
HOWEVER, I'LL SEE WHAT I CAN REMEMBER..
JUST HIT THE HIGH POINTS
SCHULZ

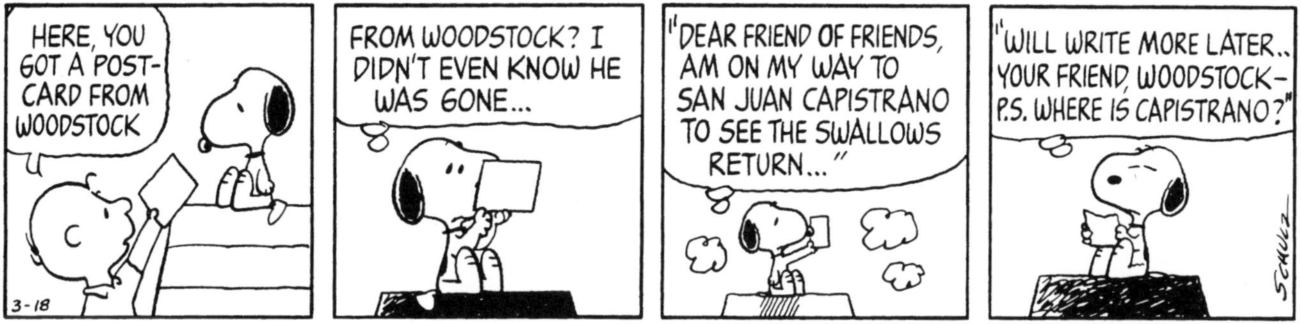
HERE, YOU GOT A POST-CARD FROM WOODSTOCK
3-18
FROM WOODSTOCK? I DIDN'T EVEN KNOW HE WAS GONE...
"DEAR FRIEND OF FRIENDS, AM ON MY WAY TO SAN JUAN CAPISTRANO TO SEE THE SWALLOWS RETURN..."
"WILL WRITE MORE LATER.. YOUR FRIEND, WOODSTOCK– P.S. WHERE IS CAPISTRANO?"
SCHULZ

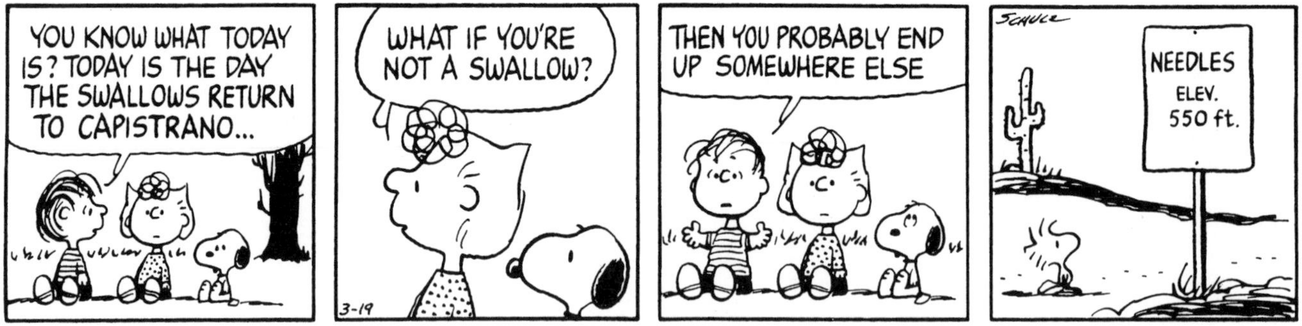
YOU KNOW WHAT TODAY IS? TODAY IS THE DAY THE SWALLOWS RETURN TO CAPISTRANO...
WHAT IF YOU'RE NOT A SWALLOW?
3-19
THEN YOU PROBABLY END UP SOMEWHERE ELSE
SCHULZ
NEEDLES
ELEV.
550 ft.

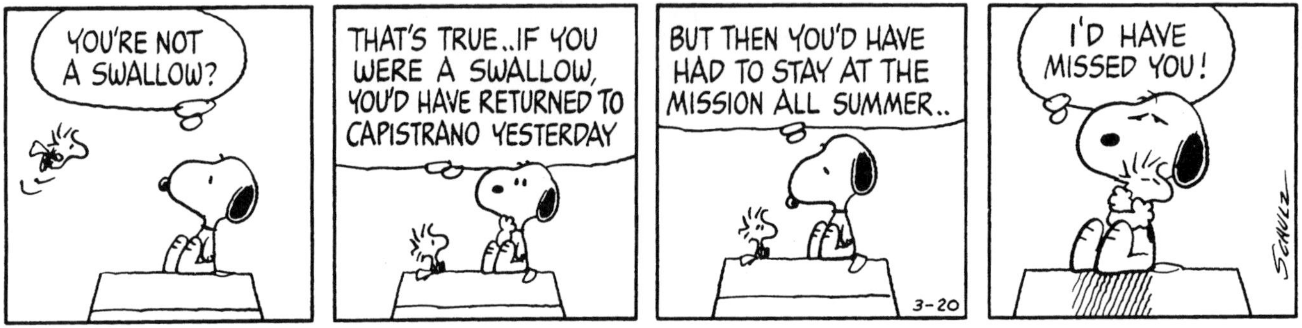
YOU'RE NOT A SWALLOW?
THAT'S TRUE..IF YOU WERE A SWALLOW, YOU'D HAVE RETURNED TO CAPISTRANO YESTERDAY
BUT THEN YOU'D HAVE HAD TO STAY AT THE MISSION ALL SUMMER..
3-20
I'D HAVE MISSED YOU!
SCHULZ

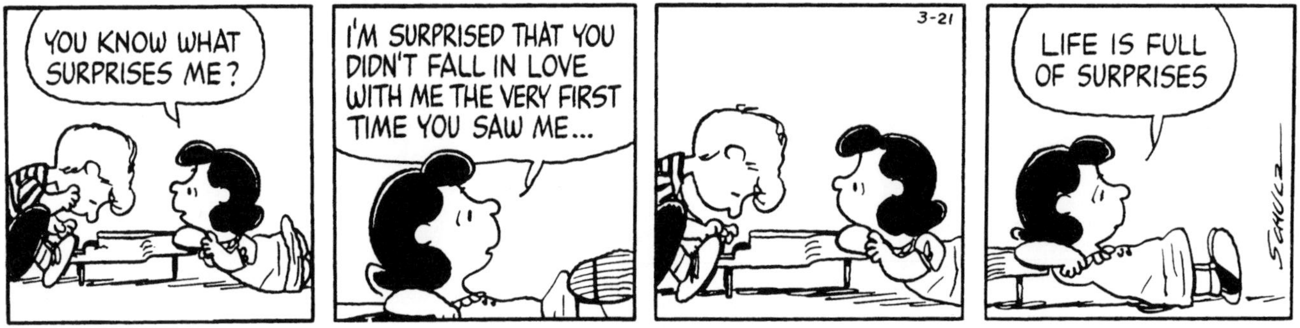
YOU KNOW WHAT SURPRISES ME?
I'M SURPRISED THAT YOU DIDN'T FALL IN LOVE WITH ME THE VERY FIRST TIME YOU SAW ME...
3-21
LIFE IS FULL OF SURPRISES
SCHULZ

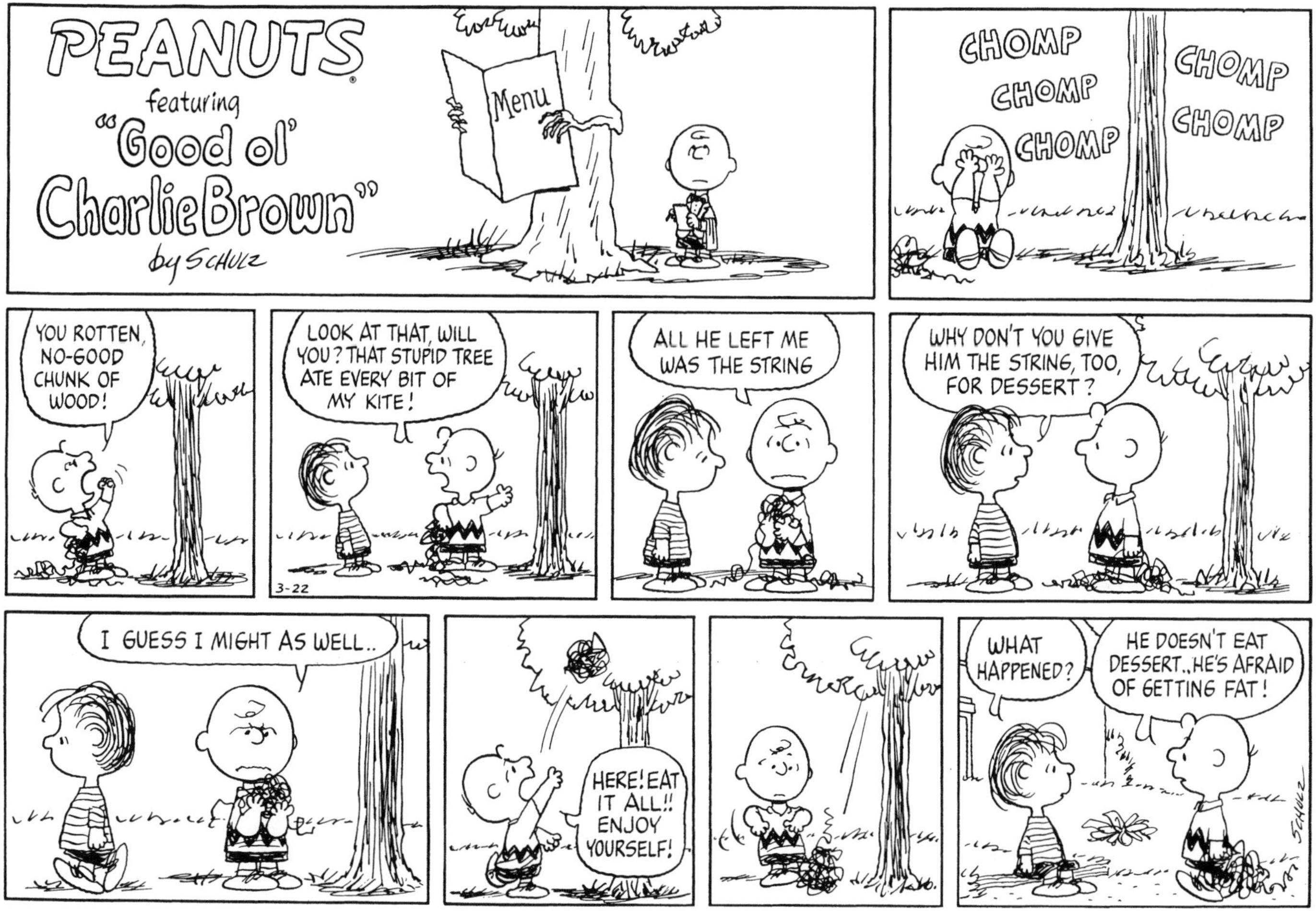
PEANUTS
featuring
"Good ol' Charlie Brown"
by SCHULZ
Menu
CHOMP CHOMP CHOMP
CHOMP CHOMP
YOU ROTTEN, NO-GOOD CHUNK OF WOOD!
LOOK AT THAT, WILL YOU? THAT STUPID TREE ATE EVERY BIT OF MY KITE!
3-22
ALL HE LEFT ME WAS THE STRING
WHY DON'T YOU GIVE HIM THE STRING, TOO, FOR DESSERT?
I GUESS I MIGHT AS WELL..
HERE! EAT IT ALL!! ENJOY YOURSELF!
WHAT HAPPENED?
HE DOESN'T EAT DESSERT.. HE'S AFRAID OF GETTING FAT!
SCHULZ

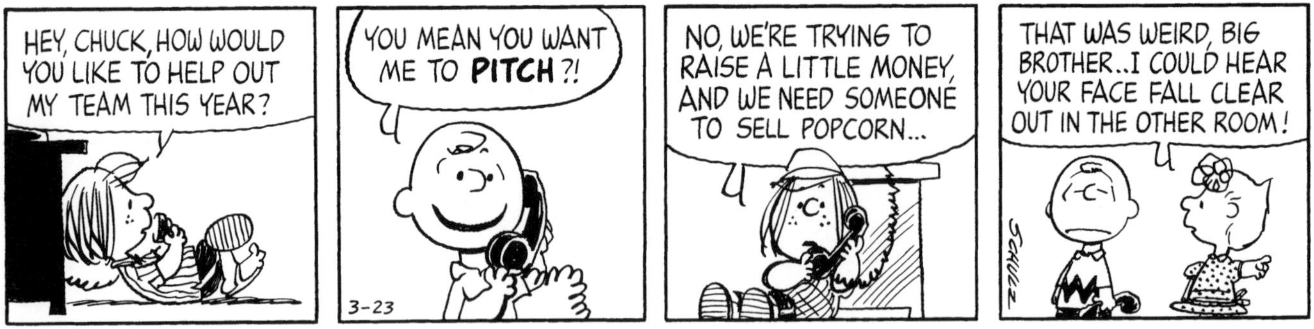
HEY, CHUCK, HOW WOULD YOU LIKE TO HELP OUT MY TEAM THIS YEAR?
YOU MEAN YOU WANT ME TO **PITCH**?!
3-23
NO, WE'RE TRYING TO RAISE A LITTLE MONEY, AND WE NEED SOMEONE TO SELL POPCORN...
THAT WAS WEIRD, BIG BROTHER..I COULD HEAR YOUR FACE FALL CLEAR OUT IN THE OTHER ROOM!
SCHULZ

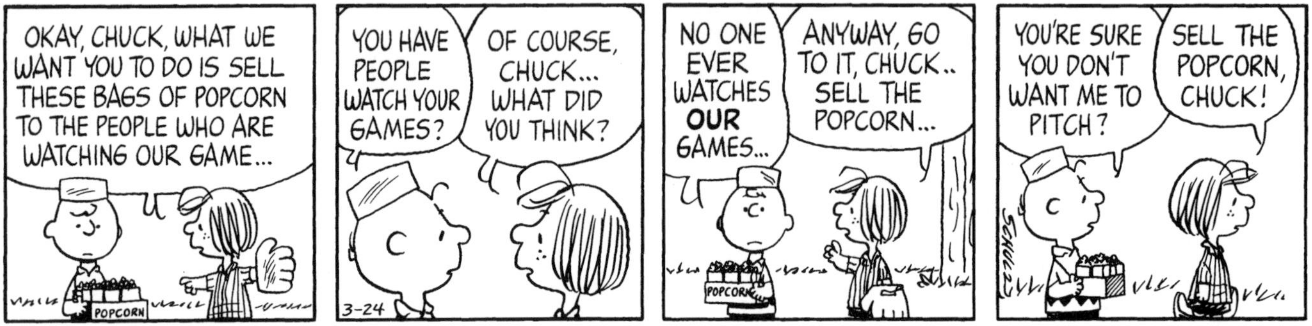
OKAY, CHUCK, WHAT WE WANT YOU TO DO IS SELL THESE BAGS OF POPCORN TO THE PEOPLE WHO ARE WATCHING OUR GAME...
POPCORN
YOU HAVE PEOPLE WATCH YOUR GAMES?
OF COURSE, CHUCK... WHAT DID YOU THINK?
3-24
NO ONE EVER WATCHES **OUR** GAMES...
ANYWAY, GO TO IT, CHUCK.. SELL THE POPCORN...
POPCORN
YOU'RE SURE YOU DON'T WANT ME TO PITCH?
SELL THE POPCORN, CHUCK!
SCHULZ

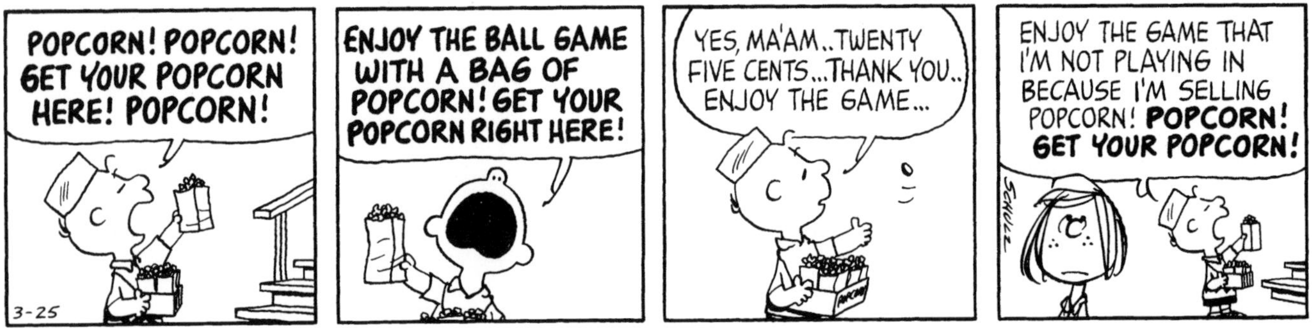
POPCORN! POPCORN! GET YOUR POPCORN HERE! POPCORN!
3-25
ENJOY THE BALL GAME WITH A BAG OF POPCORN! GET YOUR POPCORN RIGHT HERE!
YES, MA'AM..TWENTY FIVE CENTS...THANK YOU.. ENJOY THE GAME...
ENJOY THE GAME THAT I'M NOT PLAYING IN BECAUSE I'M SELLING POPCORN! **POPCORN! GET YOUR POPCORN!**
SCHULZ

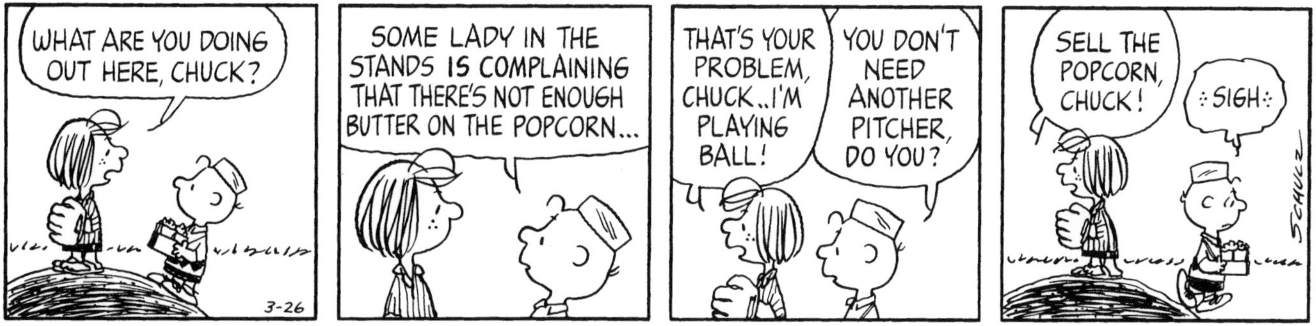
WHAT ARE YOU DOING OUT HERE, CHUCK?
3-26
SOME LADY IN THE STANDS IS COMPLAINING THAT THERE'S NOT ENOUGH BUTTER ON THE POPCORN...
THAT'S YOUR PROBLEM, CHUCK..I'M PLAYING BALL!
YOU DON'T NEED ANOTHER PITCHER, DO YOU?
SELL THE POPCORN, CHUCK!
SIGH
SCHULZ

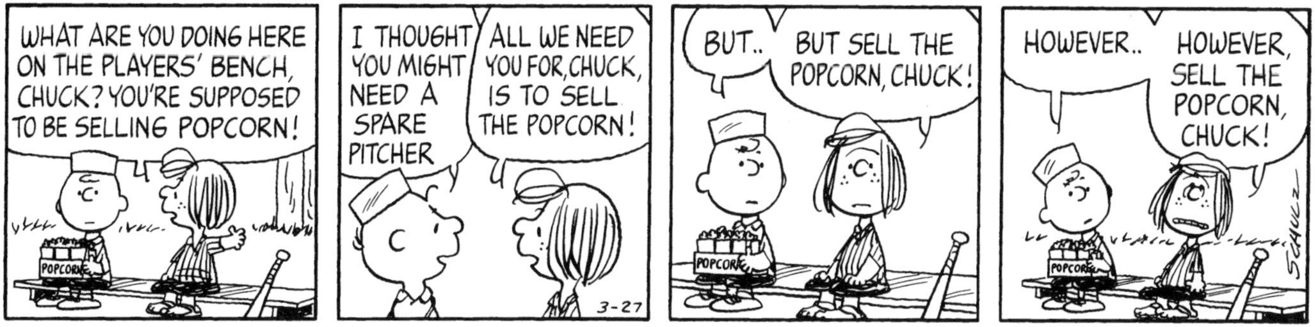
WHAT ARE YOU DOING HERE ON THE PLAYERS' BENCH, CHUCK? YOU'RE SUPPOSED TO BE SELLING POPCORN!
POPCORN
I THOUGHT YOU MIGHT NEED A SPARE PITCHER
ALL WE NEED YOU FOR, CHUCK, IS TO SELL THE POPCORN!
3-27
BUT..
BUT SELL THE POPCORN, CHUCK!
POPCORN
HOWEVER..
HOWEVER, SELL THE POPCORN, CHUCK!
POPCORN
SCHULZ

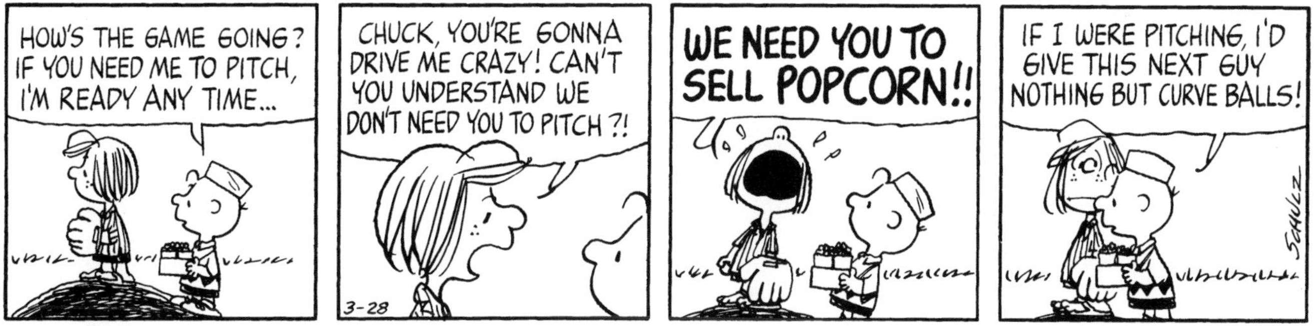
HOW'S THE GAME GOING? IF YOU NEED ME TO PITCH, I'M READY ANY TIME...
CHUCK, YOU'RE GONNA DRIVE ME CRAZY! CAN'T YOU UNDERSTAND WE DON'T NEED YOU TO PITCH?!
3-28
WE NEED YOU TO SELL POPCORN!!
IF I WERE PITCHING, I'D GIVE THIS NEXT GUY NOTHING BUT CURVE BALLS!
SCHULZ

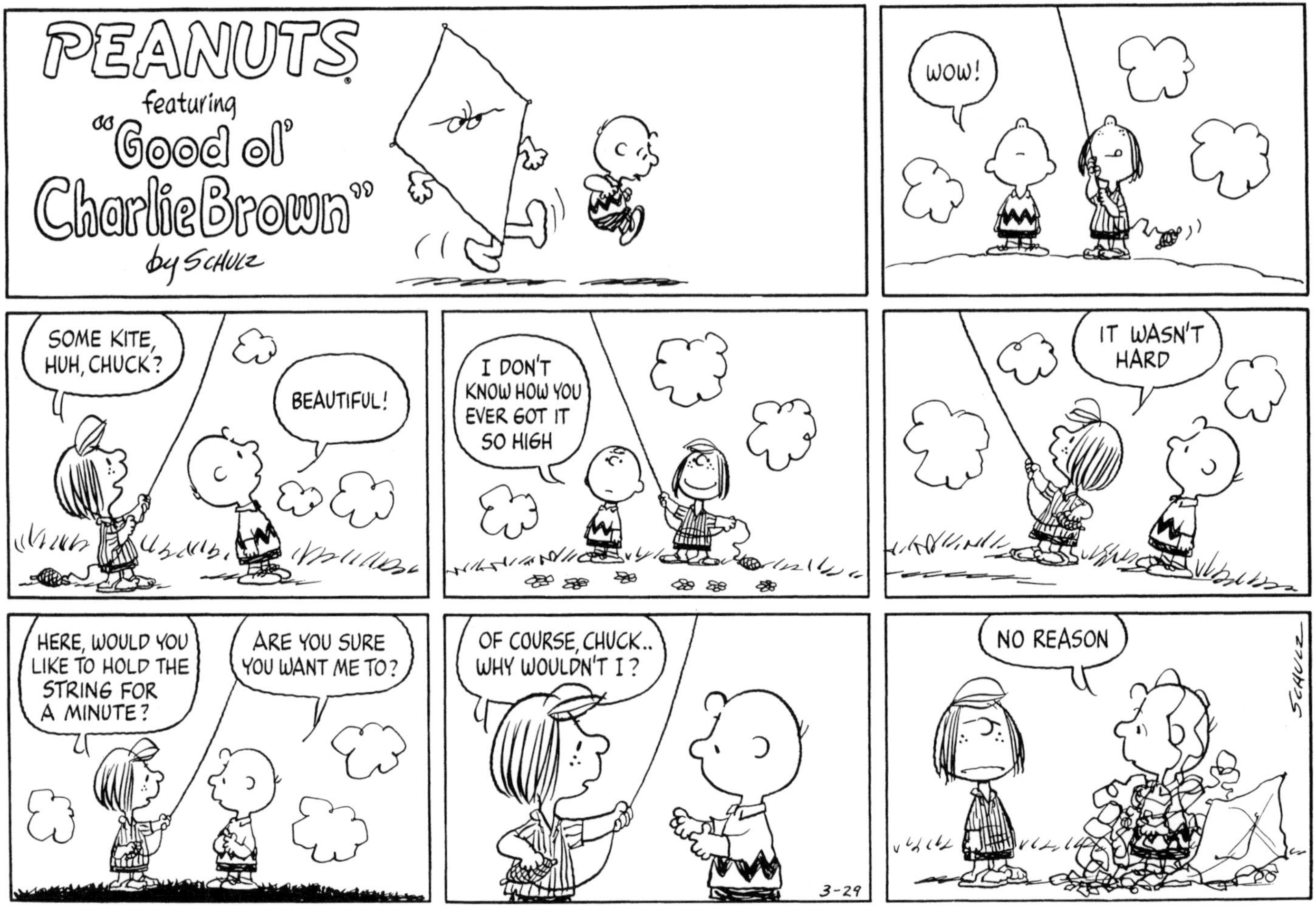
PEANUTS
featuring "Good ol' Charlie Brown"
by SCHULZ
WOW!
SOME KITE, HUH, CHUCK?
BEAUTIFUL!
I DON'T KNOW HOW YOU EVER GOT IT SO HIGH
IT WASN'T HARD
HERE, WOULD YOU LIKE TO HOLD THE STRING FOR A MINUTE?
ARE YOU SURE YOU WANT ME TO?
OF COURSE, CHUCK.. WHY WOULDN'T I?
3-29
NO REASON
SCHULZ

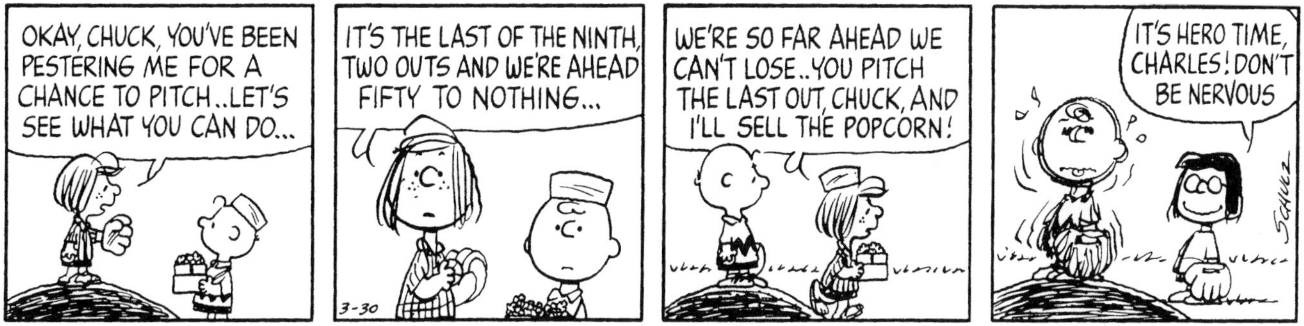
OKAY, CHUCK, YOU'VE BEEN PESTERING ME FOR A CHANCE TO PITCH..LET'S SEE WHAT YOU CAN DO...
IT'S THE LAST OF THE NINTH, TWO OUTS AND WE'RE AHEAD FIFTY TO NOTHING...
3-30
WE'RE SO FAR AHEAD WE CAN'T LOSE..YOU PITCH THE LAST OUT, CHUCK, AND I'LL SELL THE POPCORN!
IT'S HERO TIME, CHARLES! DON'T BE NERVOUS
SCHULZ

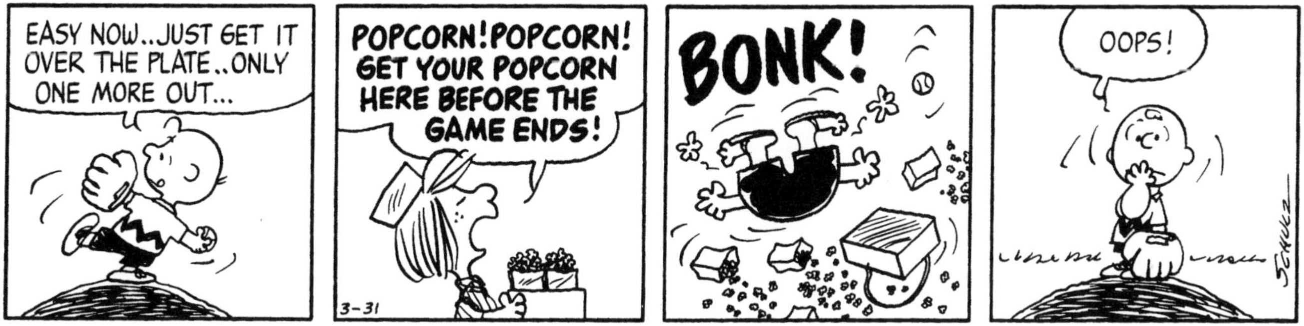
EASY NOW..JUST GET IT OVER THE PLATE..ONLY ONE MORE OUT...
POPCORN! POPCORN! GET YOUR POPCORN HERE BEFORE THE GAME ENDS!
3-31
BONK!
OOPS!
SCHULZ

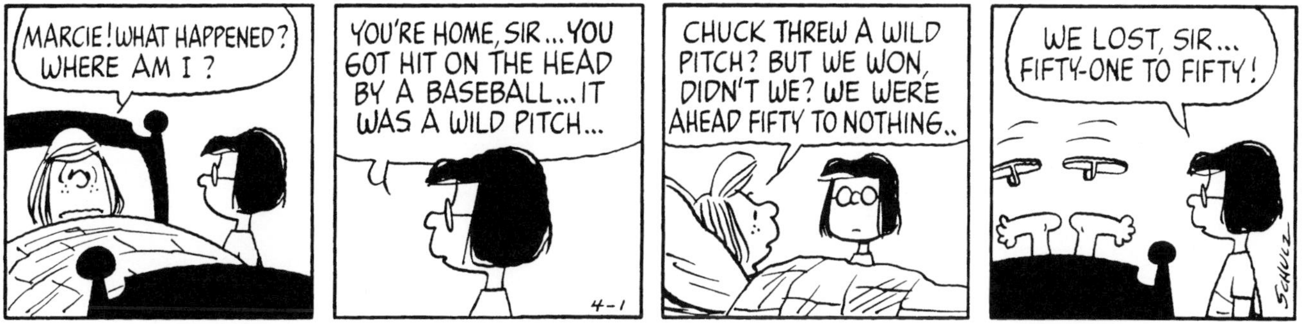
MARCIE! WHAT HAPPENED? WHERE AM I?
YOU'RE HOME, SIR...YOU GOT HIT ON THE HEAD BY A BASEBALL...IT WAS A WILD PITCH...
4-1
CHUCK THREW A WILD PITCH? BUT WE WON, DIDN'T WE? WE WERE AHEAD FIFTY TO NOTHING..
WE LOST, SIR... FIFTY-ONE TO FIFTY!
SCHULZ

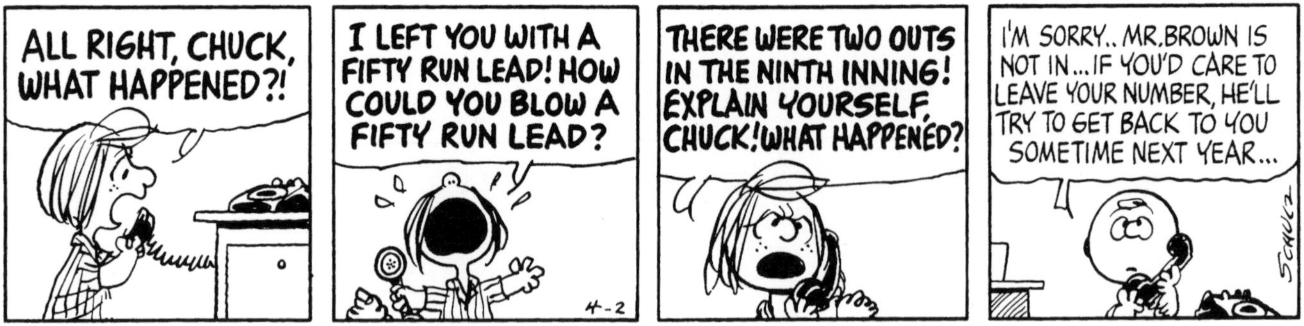
ALL RIGHT, CHUCK, WHAT HAPPENED?!
I LEFT YOU WITH A FIFTY RUN LEAD! HOW COULD YOU BLOW A FIFTY RUN LEAD?
4-2
THERE WERE TWO OUTS IN THE NINTH INNING! EXPLAIN YOURSELF, CHUCK! WHAT HAPPENED?
I'M SORRY.. MR. BROWN IS NOT IN... IF YOU'D CARE TO LEAVE YOUR NUMBER, HE'LL TRY TO GET BACK TO YOU SOMETIME NEXT YEAR...

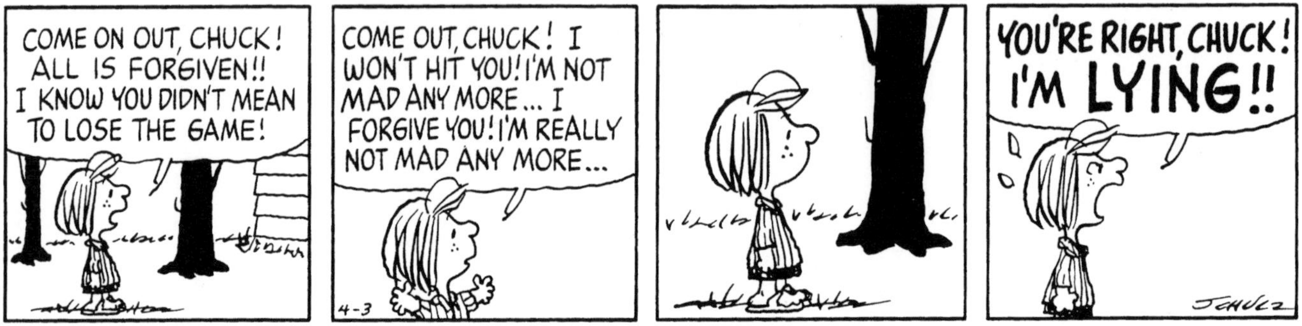
COME ON OUT, CHUCK! ALL IS FORGIVEN!! I KNOW YOU DIDN'T MEAN TO LOSE THE GAME!
COME OUT, CHUCK! I WON'T HIT YOU! I'M NOT MAD ANY MORE... I FORGIVE YOU! I'M REALLY NOT MAD ANY MORE...
4-3
YOU'RE RIGHT, CHUCK! I'M LYING!!

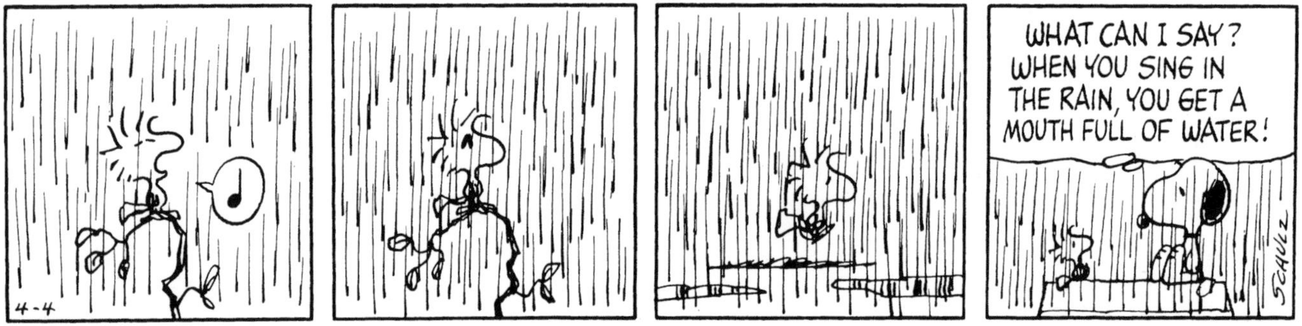
4-4
WHAT CAN I SAY? WHEN YOU SING IN THE RAIN, YOU GET A MOUTH FULL OF WATER!

PEANUTS
featuring "Good ol' Charlie Brown"
by SCHULZ
AHEM!
THIS IS MY REPORT ON "HANS BRINKER OR THE SILVER SKATES"
THE MAIN EMPHASIS OF MY REPORT WILL DEAL WITH THE STRANGE SECTION THAT BEGINS ON PAGE SEVENTY-TWO..
HERE WE HAVE THE STORY OF THE BOY WHO SAVED THE CITY BY PLACING HIS FINGER IN THE HOLE OF THE DIKE...
4-5
THUS, HE STOPPED THE LEAK THAT WOULD HAVE FLOODED THE CITY...HE WAS A HERO!
HOWEVER, WHAT IF THE BOY LOST THE USE OF HIS FINGER? COULD THE DOCTOR HAVE BEEN SUED FOR IMPROPER DIAGNOSIS?
AND WHAT IF THE BOY'S FAMILY BROUGHT A PERSONAL INJURY ACTION AGAINST THE CITY FOR FAILING TO PROPERLY MAINTAIN THE DIKE?
HAS ANYONE EVER THOUGHT OF THIS? ALL RIGHT, THEN, SUPPOSE WE..
MA'AM?
SIGH ANOTHER D MINUS..
SCHULZ

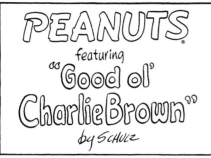

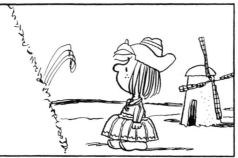

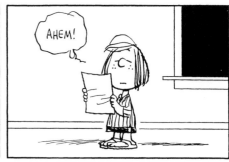

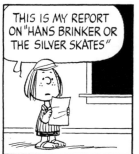

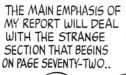

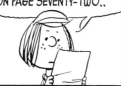

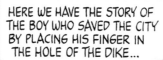

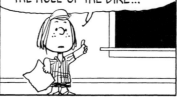

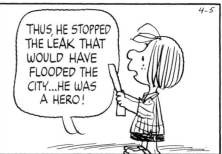

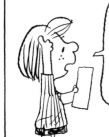

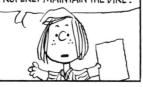

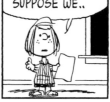

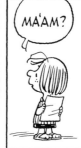

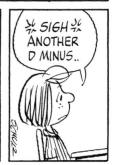

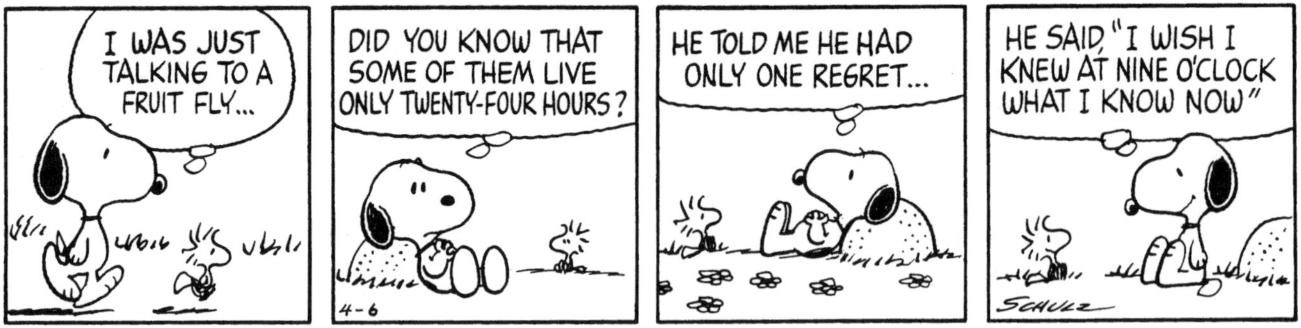
I WAS JUST TALKING TO A FRUIT FLY...
DID YOU KNOW THAT SOME OF THEM LIVE ONLY TWENTY-FOUR HOURS?
HE TOLD ME HE HAD ONLY ONE REGRET...
HE SAID, "I WISH I KNEW AT NINE O'CLOCK WHAT I KNOW NOW"

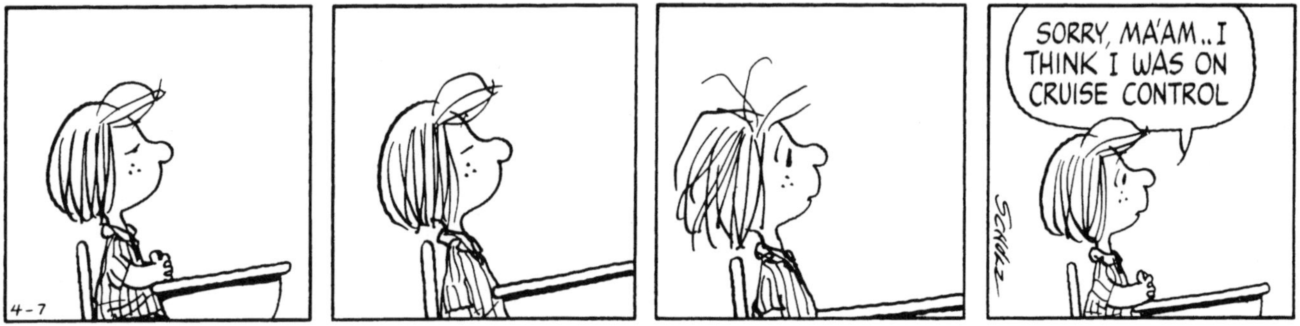
SORRY, MA'AM..I THINK I WAS ON CRUISE CONTROL

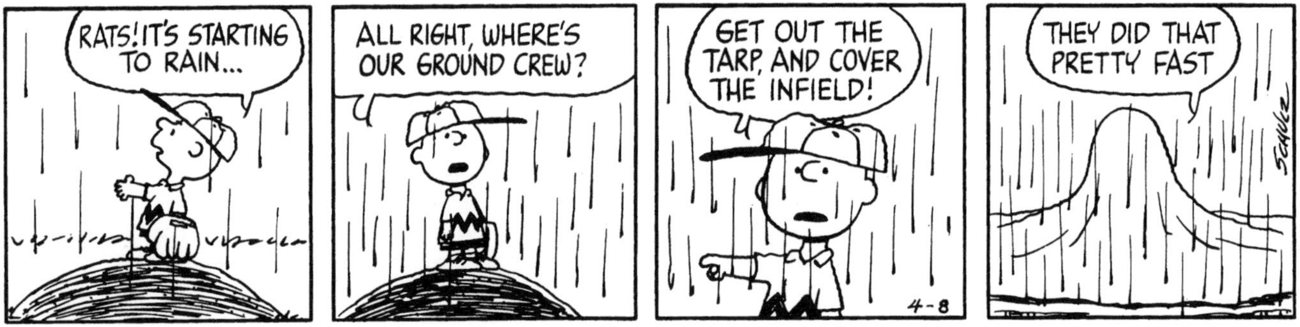
RATS! IT'S STARTING TO RAIN...
ALL RIGHT, WHERE'S OUR GROUND CREW?
GET OUT THE TARP, AND COVER THE INFIELD!
THEY DID THAT PRETTY FAST

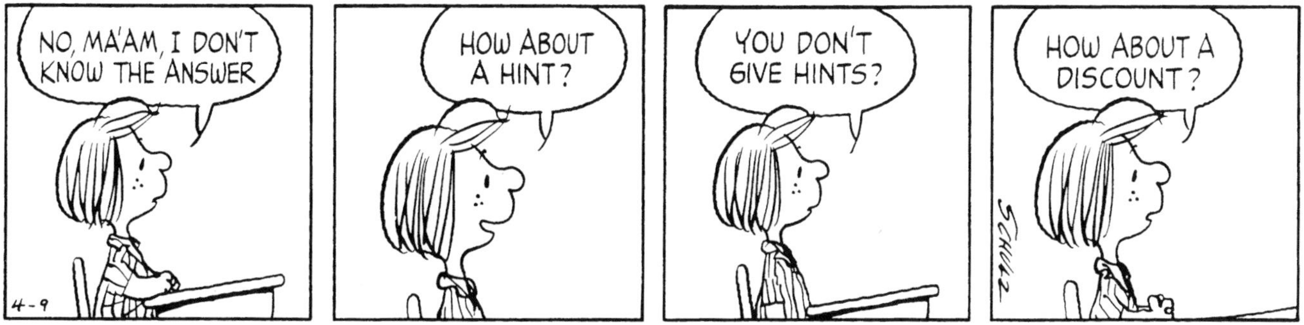
NO, MA'AM, I DON'T KNOW THE ANSWER
HOW ABOUT A HINT?
YOU DON'T GIVE HINTS?
HOW ABOUT A DISCOUNT?

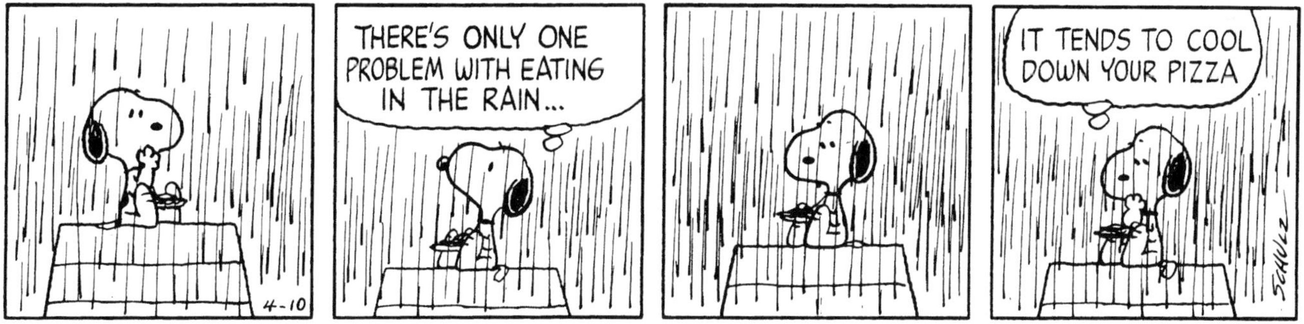
THERE'S ONLY ONE PROBLEM WITH EATING IN THE RAIN...
IT TENDS TO COOL DOWN YOUR PIZZA

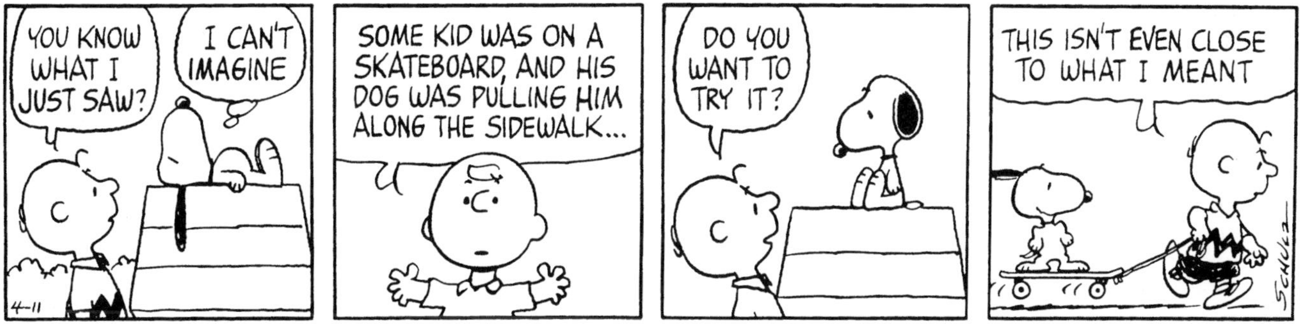
YOU KNOW WHAT I JUST SAW?
I CAN'T IMAGINE
SOME KID WAS ON A SKATEBOARD, AND HIS DOG WAS PULLING HIM ALONG THE SIDEWALK...
DO YOU WANT TO TRY IT?
THIS ISN'T EVEN CLOSE TO WHAT I MEANT

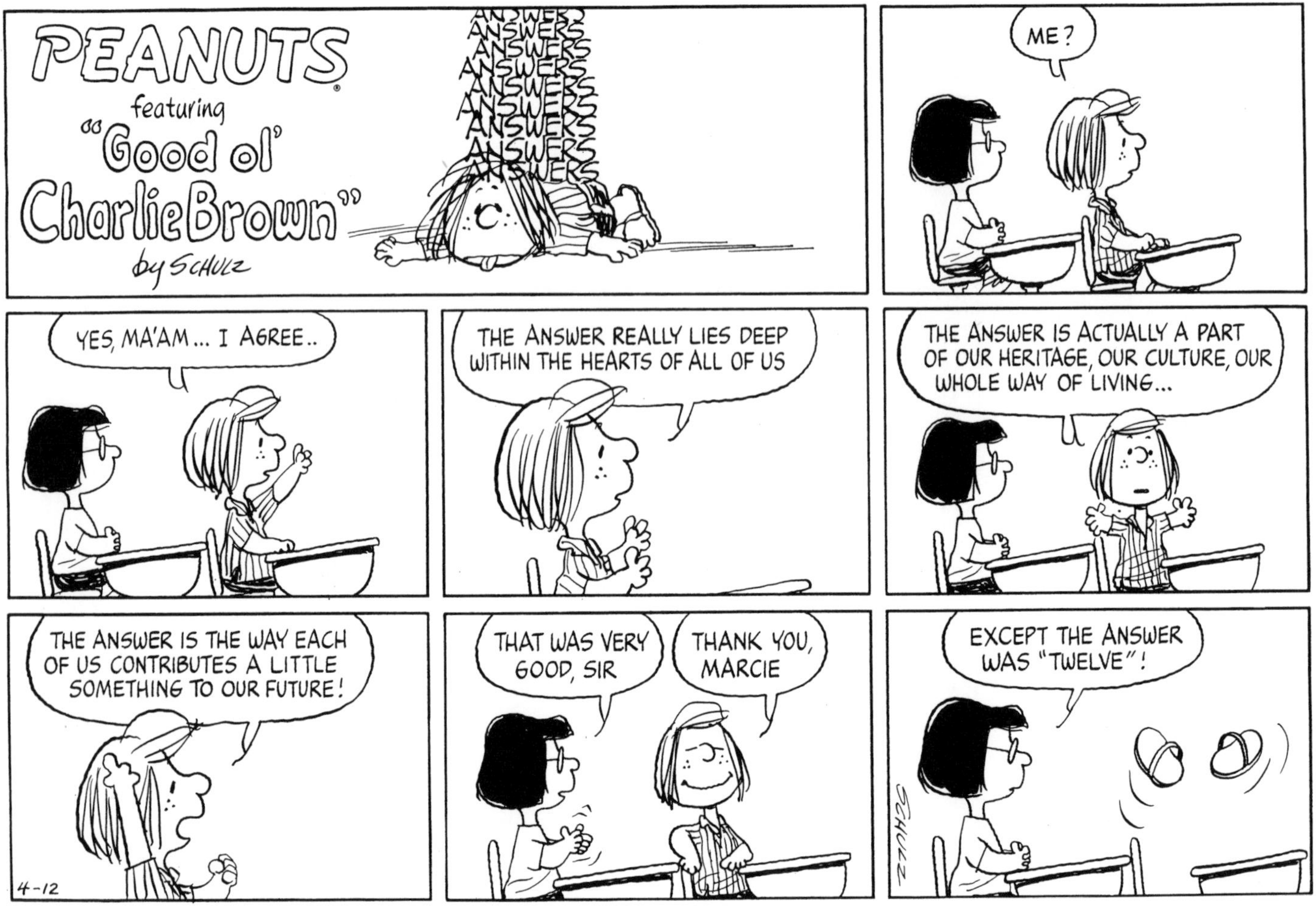
PEANUTS
featuring "Good ol' Charlie Brown"
by SCHULZ
ANSWERS ANSWERS ANSWERS ANSWERS ANSWERS ANSWERS ANSWERS ANSWERS ANSWERS
ME?
YES, MA'AM... I AGREE..
THE ANSWER REALLY LIES DEEP WITHIN THE HEARTS OF ALL OF US
THE ANSWER IS ACTUALLY A PART OF OUR HERITAGE, OUR CULTURE, OUR WHOLE WAY OF LIVING...
THE ANSWER IS THE WAY EACH OF US CONTRIBUTES A LITTLE SOMETHING TO OUR FUTURE!
4-12
THAT WAS VERY GOOD, SIR
THANK YOU, MARCIE
EXCEPT THE ANSWER WAS "TWELVE"!
SCHULZ

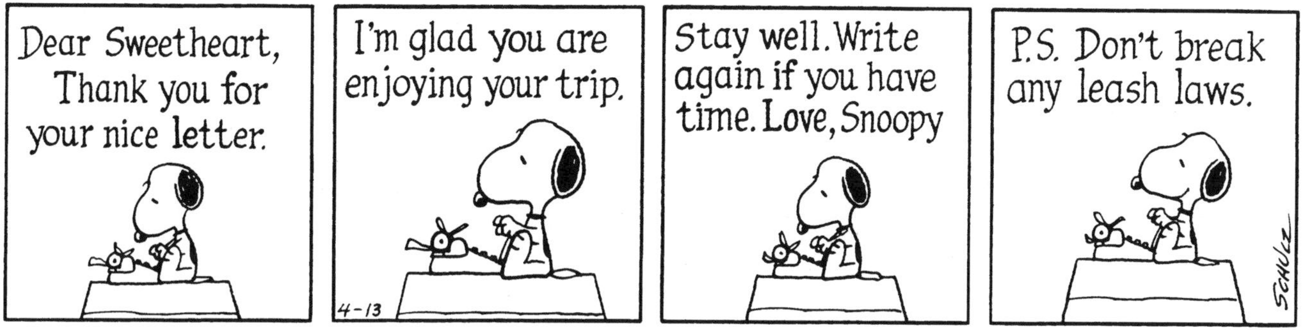
Dear Sweetheart,
Thank you for your nice letter.
4-13
I'm glad you are enjoying your trip.
Stay well. Write again if you have time. Love, Snoopy
P.S. Don't break any leash laws.
SCHULZ

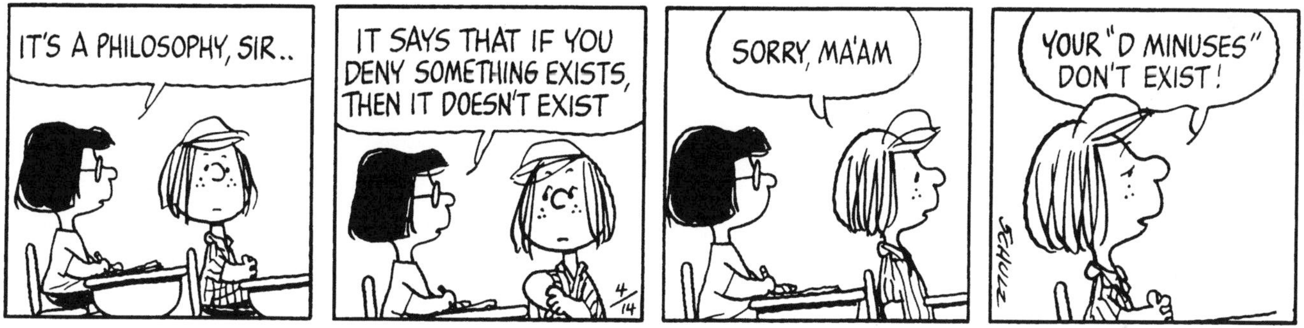
IT'S A PHILOSOPHY, SIR..
IT SAYS THAT IF YOU DENY SOMETHING EXISTS, THEN IT DOESN'T EXIST
4/14
SORRY, MA'AM
SCHULZ
YOUR "D MINUSES" DON'T EXIST!

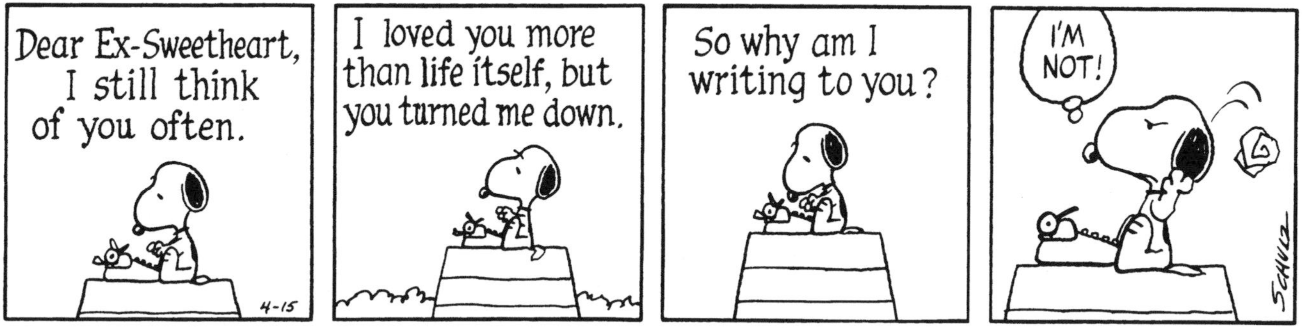
Dear Ex-Sweetheart,
I still think of you often.
4-15
I loved you more than life itself, but you turned me down.
So why am I writing to you?
I'M NOT!
SCHULZ

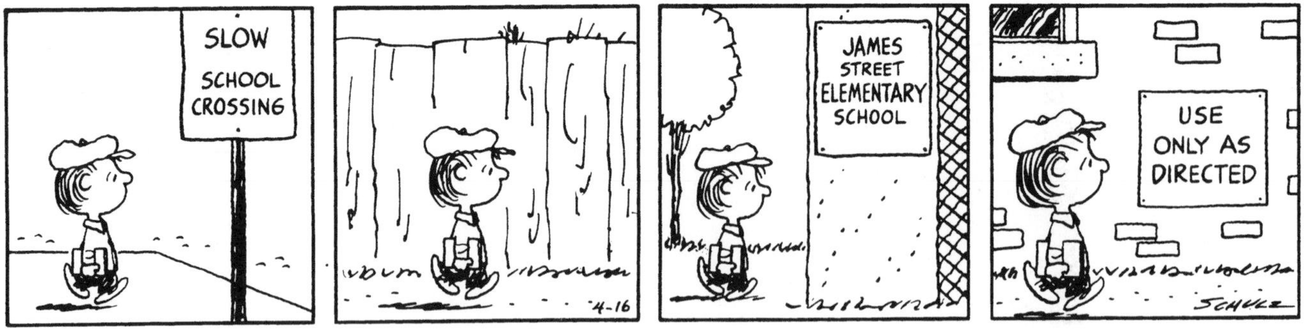
SLOW
SCHOOL CROSSING
4-16
JAMES STREET ELEMENTARY SCHOOL
USE ONLY AS DIRECTED
SCHULZ

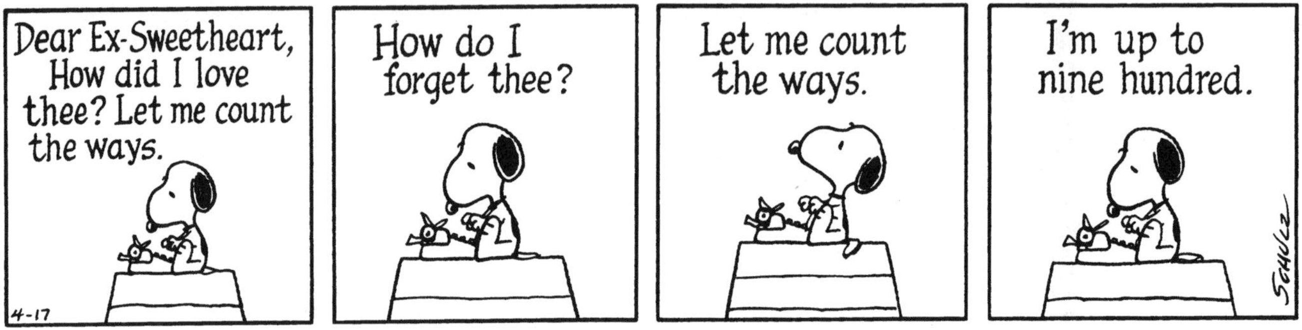
Dear Ex-Sweetheart,
How did I love thee? Let me count the ways.
4-17
How do I forget thee?
Let me count the ways.
I'm up to nine hundred.
SCHULZ

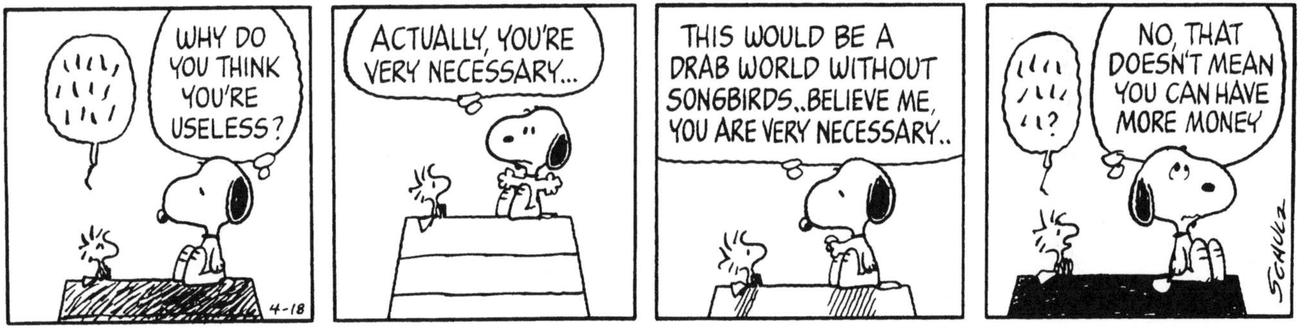
WHY DO YOU THINK YOU'RE USELESS?
4-18
ACTUALLY, YOU'RE VERY NECESSARY...
THIS WOULD BE A DRAB WORLD WITHOUT SONGBIRDS..BELIEVE ME, YOU ARE VERY NECESSARY..
NO, THAT DOESN'T MEAN YOU CAN HAVE MORE MONEY
SCHULZ

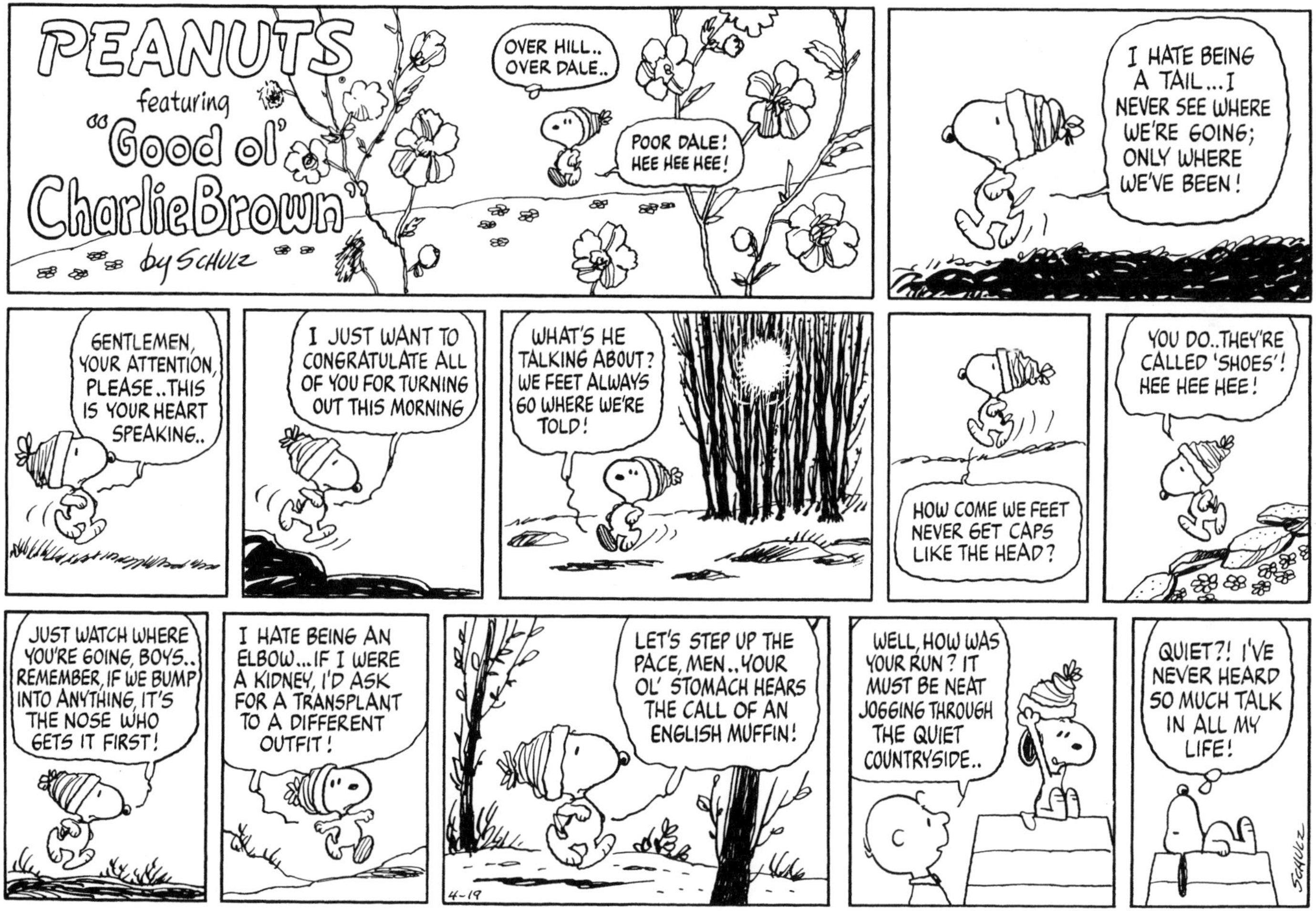
PEANUTS
featuring "Good ol' CharlieBrown"
by SCHULZ
OVER HILL.. OVER DALE..
POOR DALE! HEE HEE HEE!
I HATE BEING A TAIL...I NEVER SEE WHERE WE'RE GOING; ONLY WHERE WE'VE BEEN!
GENTLEMEN, YOUR ATTENTION, PLEASE..THIS IS YOUR HEART SPEAKING..
I JUST WANT TO CONGRATULATE ALL OF YOU FOR TURNING OUT THIS MORNING
WHAT'S HE TALKING ABOUT? WE FEET ALWAYS GO WHERE WE'RE TOLD!
HOW COME WE FEET NEVER GET CAPS LIKE THE HEAD?
YOU DO..THEY'RE CALLED 'SHOES'! HEE HEE HEE!
JUST WATCH WHERE YOU'RE GOING, BOYS.. REMEMBER, IF WE BUMP INTO ANYTHING, IT'S THE NOSE WHO GETS IT FIRST!
I HATE BEING AN ELBOW...IF I WERE A KIDNEY, I'D ASK FOR A TRANSPLANT TO A DIFFERENT OUTFIT!
LET'S STEP UP THE PACE, MEN..YOUR OL' STOMACH HEARS THE CALL OF AN ENGLISH MUFFIN!
4-19
WELL, HOW WAS YOUR RUN? IT MUST BE NEAT JOGGING THROUGH THE QUIET COUNTRYSIDE..
QUIET?! I'VE NEVER HEARD SO MUCH TALK IN ALL MY LIFE!
SCHULZ

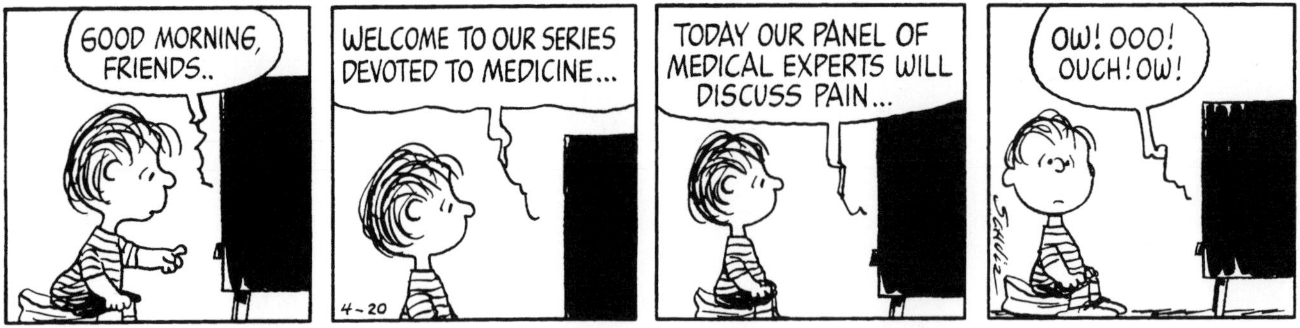
GOOD MORNING, FRIENDS..
WELCOME TO OUR SERIES DEVOTED TO MEDICINE...
TODAY OUR PANEL OF MEDICAL EXPERTS WILL DISCUSS PAIN...
OW! OOO! OUCH! OW!

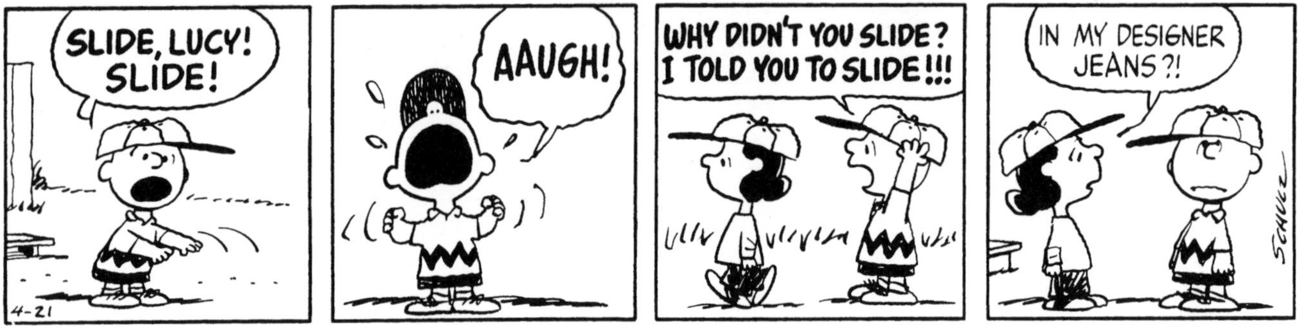
SLIDE, LUCY! SLIDE!
AAUGH!
WHY DIDN'T YOU SLIDE? I TOLD YOU TO SLIDE!!!
IN MY DESIGNER JEANS?!

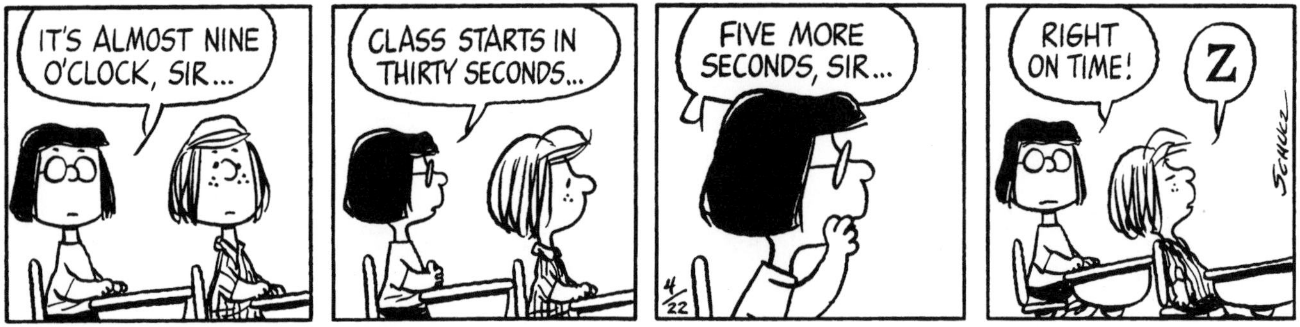
IT'S ALMOST NINE O'CLOCK, SIR...
CLASS STARTS IN THIRTY SECONDS...
FIVE MORE SECONDS, SIR...
RIGHT ON TIME!
Z

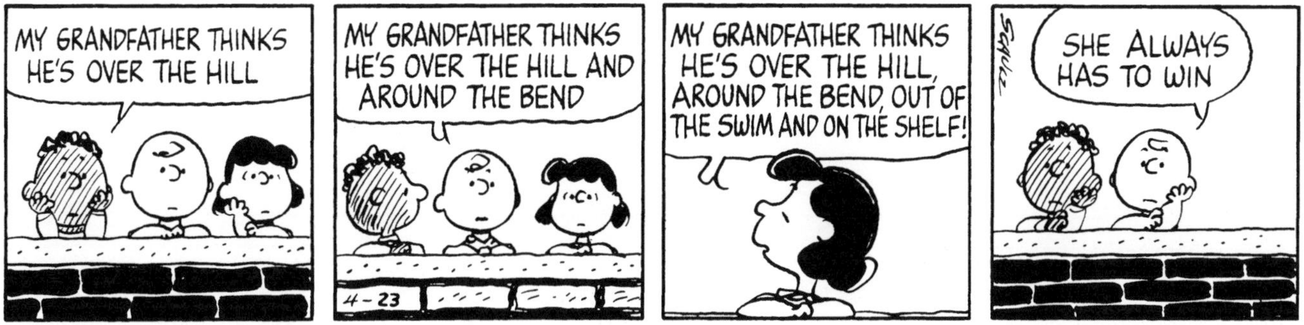
MY GRANDFATHER THINKS HE'S OVER THE HILL
MY GRANDFATHER THINKS HE'S OVER THE HILL AND AROUND THE BEND
4-23
MY GRANDFATHER THINKS HE'S OVER THE HILL, AROUND THE BEND, OUT OF THE SWIM AND ON THE SHELF!
SCHULZ
SHE ALWAYS HAS TO WIN

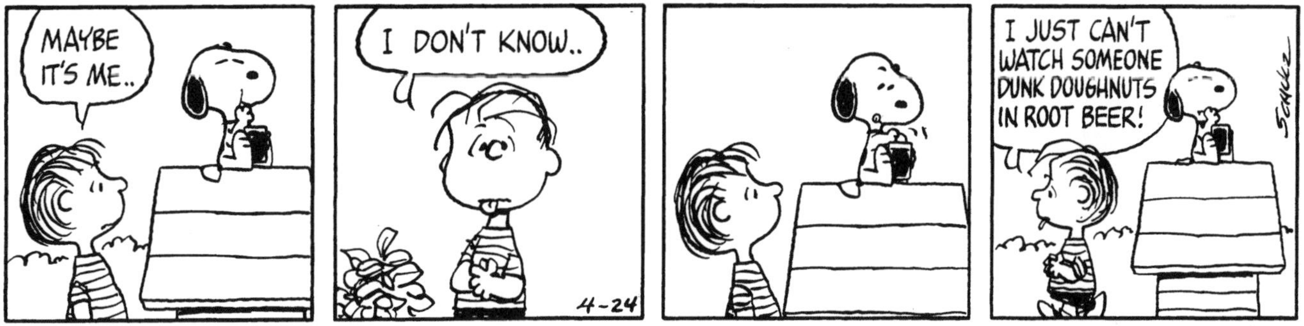
MAYBE IT'S ME..
I DON'T KNOW..
4-24
I JUST CAN'T WATCH SOMEONE DUNK DOUGHNUTS IN ROOT BEER!
SCHULZ

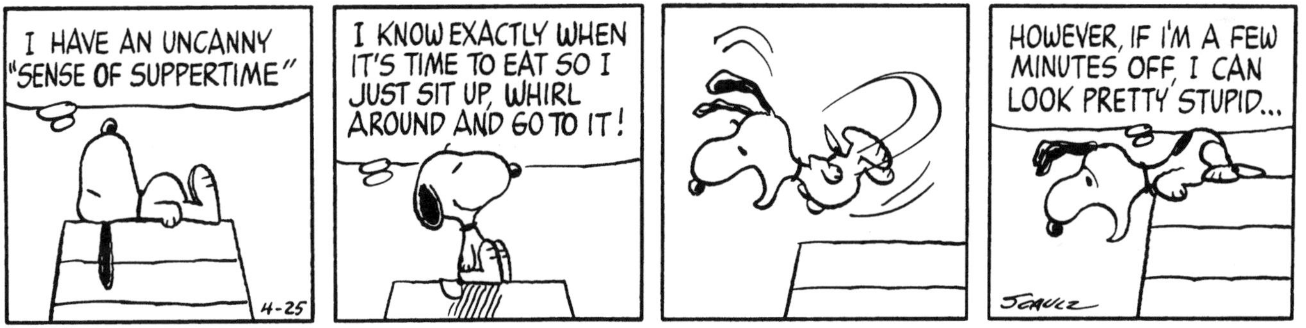
I HAVE AN UNCANNY "SENSE OF SUPPERTIME"
4-25
I KNOW EXACTLY WHEN IT'S TIME TO EAT SO I JUST SIT UP, WHIRL AROUND AND GO TO IT!
HOWEVER, IF I'M A FEW MINUTES OFF, I CAN LOOK PRETTY STUPID...
SCHULZ

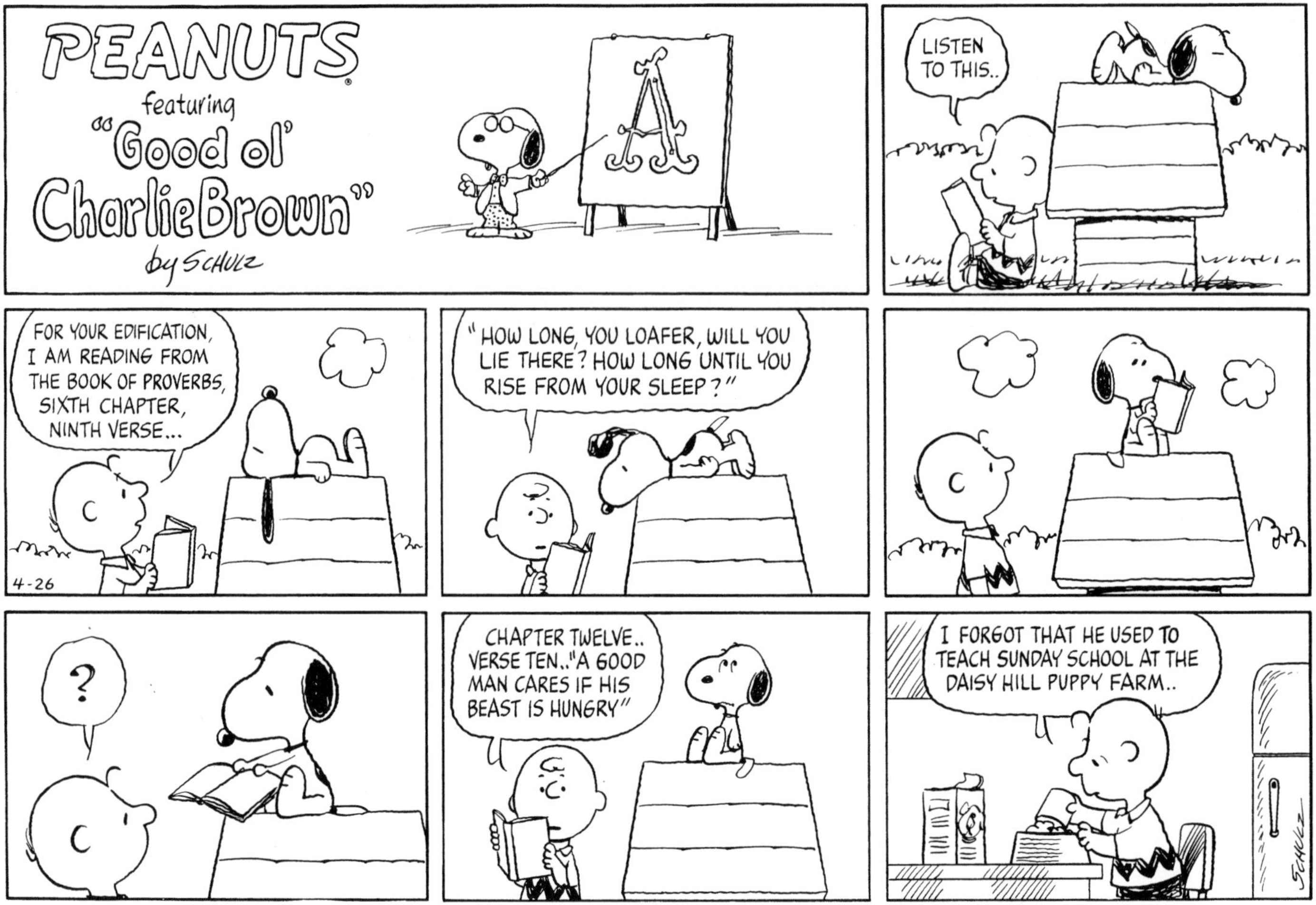
PEANUTS
featuring
"Good ol' Charlie Brown"
by SCHULZ
LISTEN TO THIS..
FOR YOUR EDIFICATION, I AM READING FROM THE BOOK OF PROVERBS, SIXTH CHAPTER, NINTH VERSE...
4-26
"HOW LONG, YOU LOAFER, WILL YOU LIE THERE? HOW LONG UNTIL YOU RISE FROM YOUR SLEEP?"
?
CHAPTER TWELVE.. VERSE TEN.."A GOOD MAN CARES IF HIS BEAST IS HUNGRY"
I FORGOT THAT HE USED TO TEACH SUNDAY SCHOOL AT THE DAISY HILL PUPPY FARM..
SCHULZ

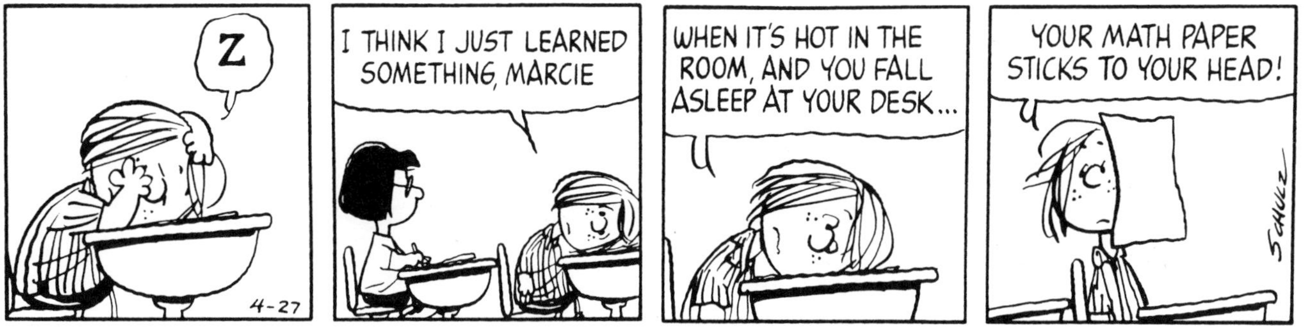
Z
I THINK I JUST LEARNED SOMETHING, MARCIE
4-27
WHEN IT'S HOT IN THE ROOM, AND YOU FALL ASLEEP AT YOUR DESK...
YOUR MATH PAPER STICKS TO YOUR HEAD!
SCHULZ

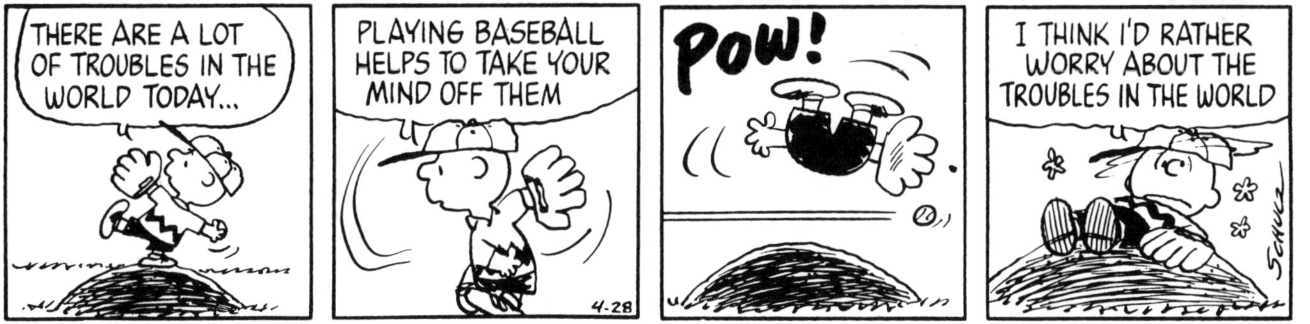
THERE ARE A LOT OF TROUBLES IN THE WORLD TODAY...
PLAYING BASEBALL HELPS TO TAKE YOUR MIND OFF THEM
4-28
POW!
I THINK I'D RATHER WORRY ABOUT THE TROUBLES IN THE WORLD
SCHULZ

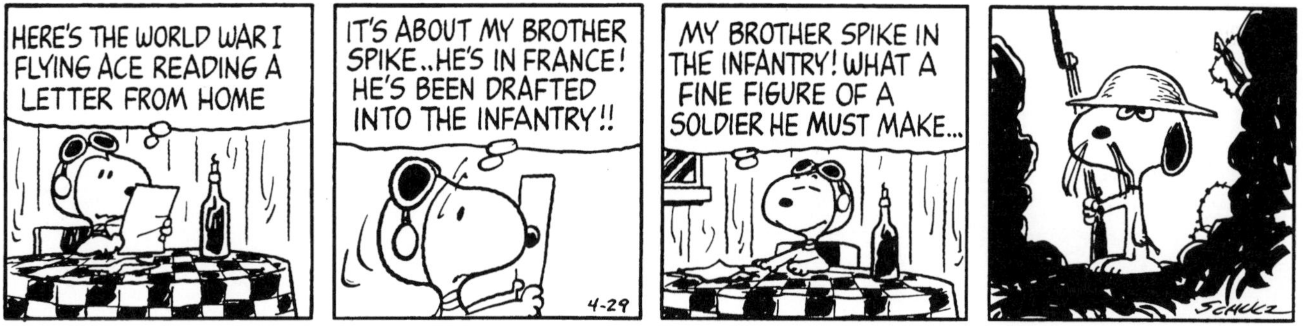
HERE'S THE WORLD WAR I FLYING ACE READING A LETTER FROM HOME
IT'S ABOUT MY BROTHER SPIKE..HE'S IN FRANCE! HE'S BEEN DRAFTED INTO THE INFANTRY!!
4-29
MY BROTHER SPIKE IN THE INFANTRY! WHAT A FINE FIGURE OF A SOLDIER HE MUST MAKE...
SCHULZ

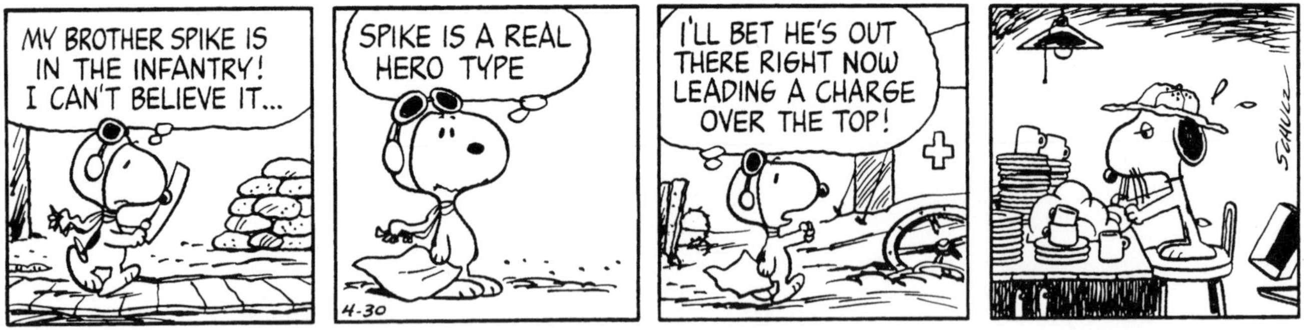
MY BROTHER SPIKE IS IN THE INFANTRY! I CAN'T BELIEVE IT...
SPIKE IS A REAL HERO TYPE
4-30
I'LL BET HE'S OUT THERE RIGHT NOW LEADING A CHARGE OVER THE TOP!
SCHULZ

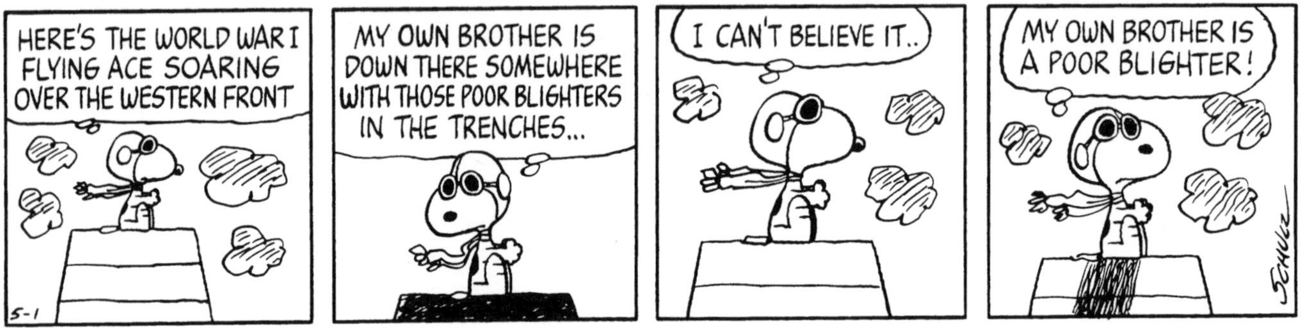
HERE'S THE WORLD WAR I FLYING ACE SOARING OVER THE WESTERN FRONT
5-1
MY OWN BROTHER IS DOWN THERE SOMEWHERE WITH THOSE POOR BLIGHTERS IN THE TRENCHES...
I CAN'T BELIEVE IT..
MY OWN BROTHER IS A POOR BLIGHTER!
SCHULZ

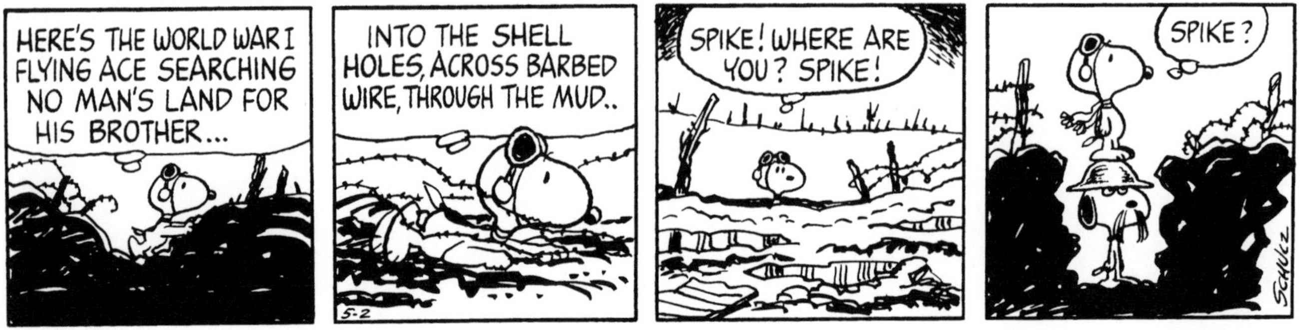
HERE'S THE WORLD WAR I FLYING ACE SEARCHING NO MAN'S LAND FOR HIS BROTHER...
INTO THE SHELL HOLES, ACROSS BARBED WIRE, THROUGH THE MUD..
5-2
SPIKE! WHERE ARE YOU? SPIKE!
SPIKE?
SCHULZ

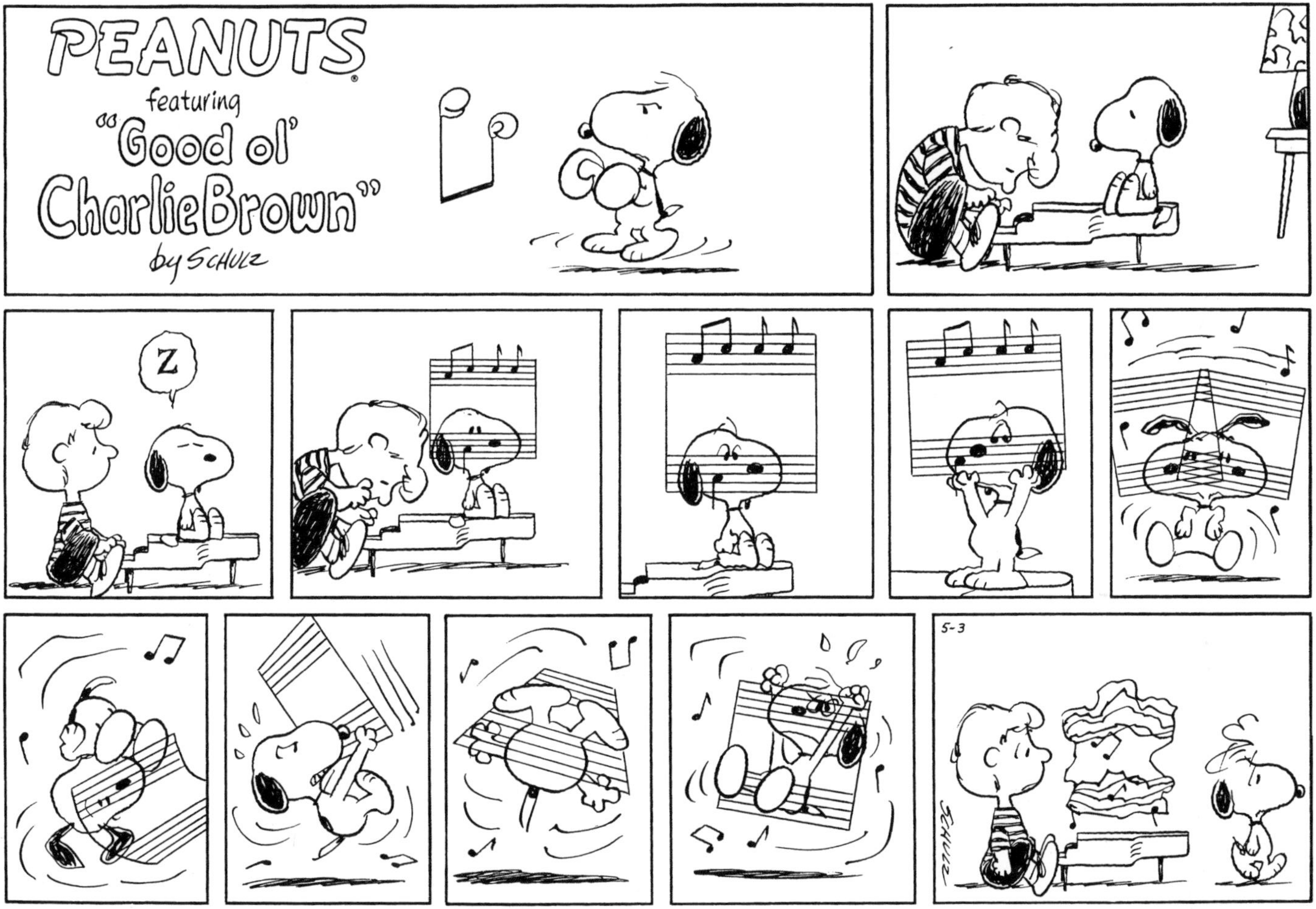
PEANUTS
featuring
"Good ol' CharlieBrown"
by SCHULZ
Z
5-3
SCHULZ

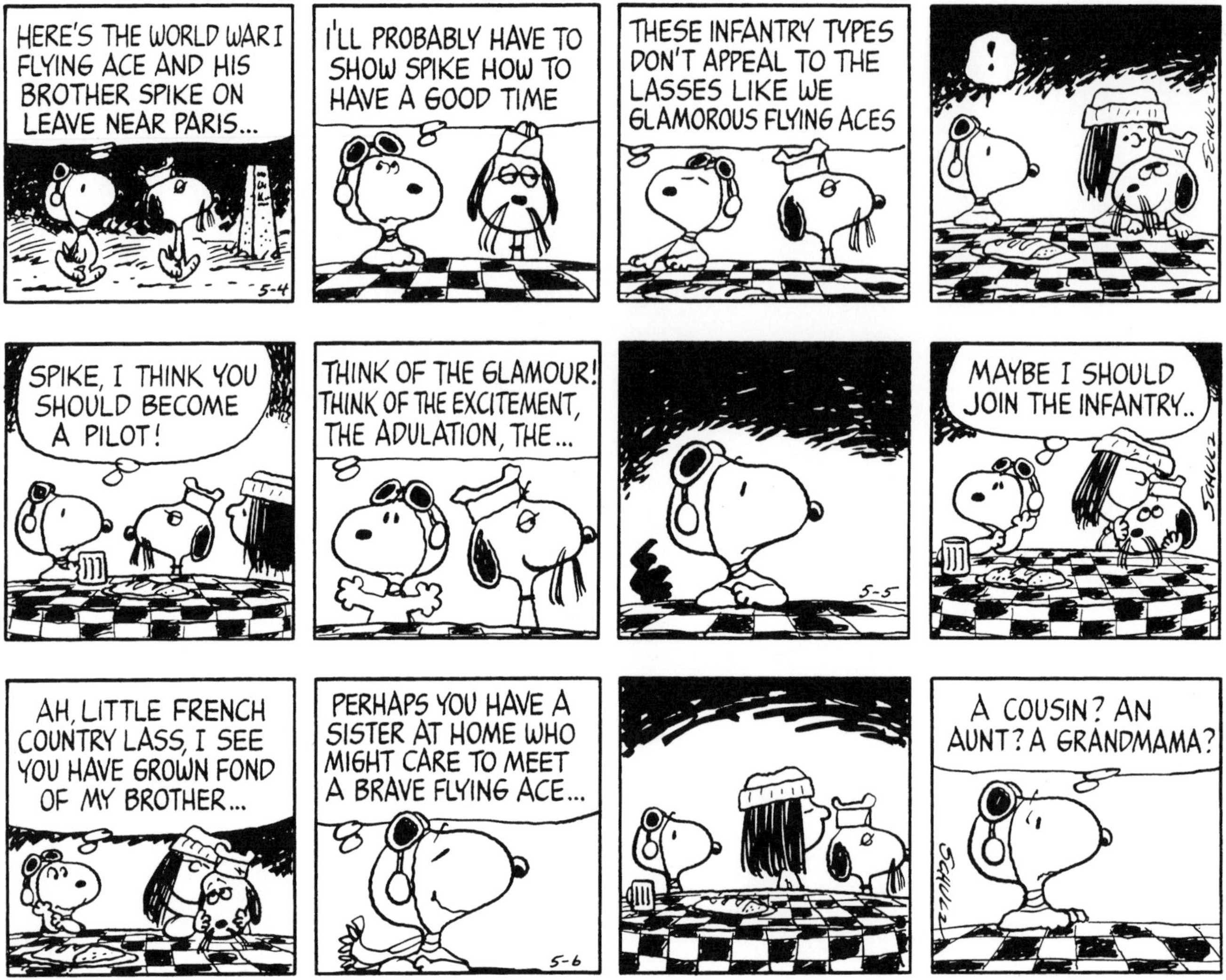
HERE'S THE WORLD WAR I FLYING ACE AND HIS BROTHER SPIKE ON LEAVE NEAR PARIS...
5-4
I'LL PROBABLY HAVE TO SHOW SPIKE HOW TO HAVE A GOOD TIME
THESE INFANTRY TYPES DON'T APPEAL TO THE LASSES LIKE WE GLAMOROUS FLYING ACES
!
SCHULZ
SPIKE, I THINK YOU SHOULD BECOME A PILOT!
THINK OF THE GLAMOUR! THINK OF THE EXCITEMENT, THE ADULATION, THE...
5-5
MAYBE I SHOULD JOIN THE INFANTRY..
SCHULZ
AH, LITTLE FRENCH COUNTRY LASS, I SEE YOU HAVE GROWN FOND OF MY BROTHER...
PERHAPS YOU HAVE A SISTER AT HOME WHO MIGHT CARE TO MEET A BRAVE FLYING ACE...
5-6
SCHULZ
A COUSIN? AN AUNT? A GRANDMAMA?

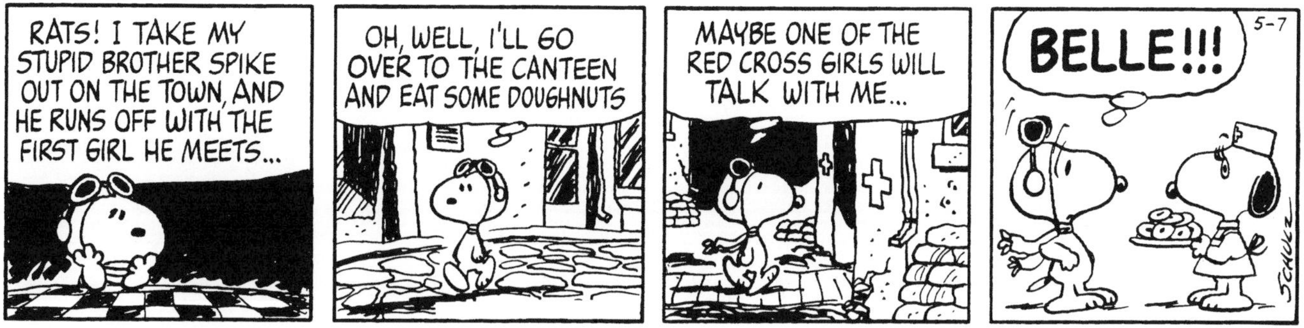
RATS! I TAKE MY STUPID BROTHER SPIKE OUT ON THE TOWN, AND HE RUNS OFF WITH THE FIRST GIRL HE MEETS...
OH, WELL, I'LL GO OVER TO THE CANTEEN AND EAT SOME DOUGHNUTS
MAYBE ONE OF THE RED CROSS GIRLS WILL TALK WITH ME...
BELLE!!!
5-7
SCHULZ

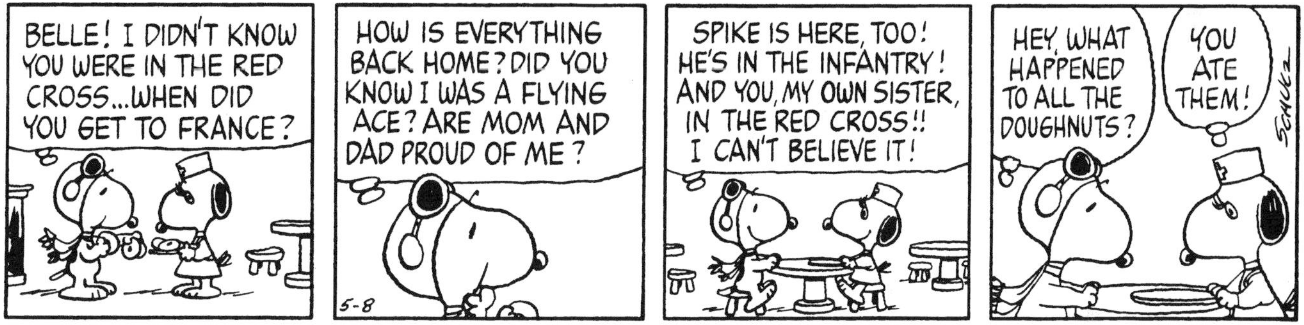
BELLE! I DIDN'T KNOW YOU WERE IN THE RED CROSS...WHEN DID YOU GET TO FRANCE?
HOW IS EVERYTHING BACK HOME? DID YOU KNOW I WAS A FLYING ACE? ARE MOM AND DAD PROUD OF ME?
5-8
SPIKE IS HERE, TOO! HE'S IN THE INFANTRY! AND YOU, MY OWN SISTER, IN THE RED CROSS!! I CAN'T BELIEVE IT!
HEY, WHAT HAPPENED TO ALL THE DOUGHNUTS?
YOU ATE THEM!
SCHULZ

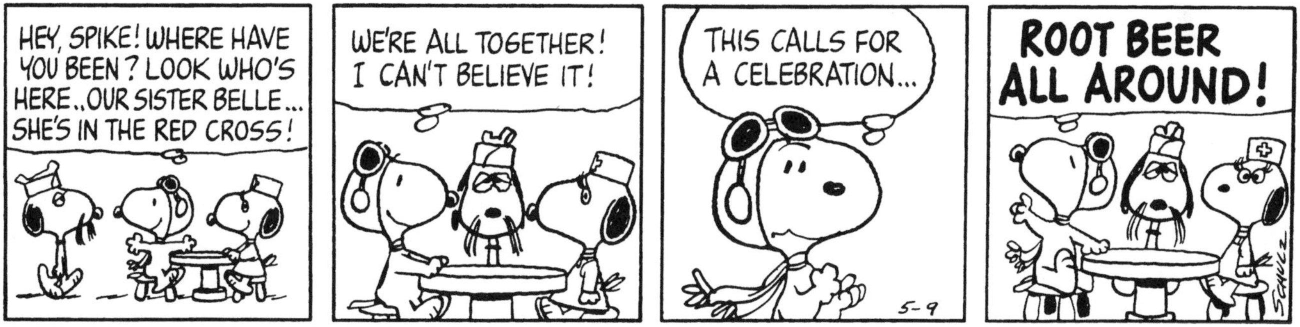
HEY, SPIKE! WHERE HAVE YOU BEEN? LOOK WHO'S HERE..OUR SISTER BELLE... SHE'S IN THE RED CROSS!
WE'RE ALL TOGETHER! I CAN'T BELIEVE IT!
THIS CALLS FOR A CELEBRATION...
5-9
ROOT BEER ALL AROUND!
SCHULZ

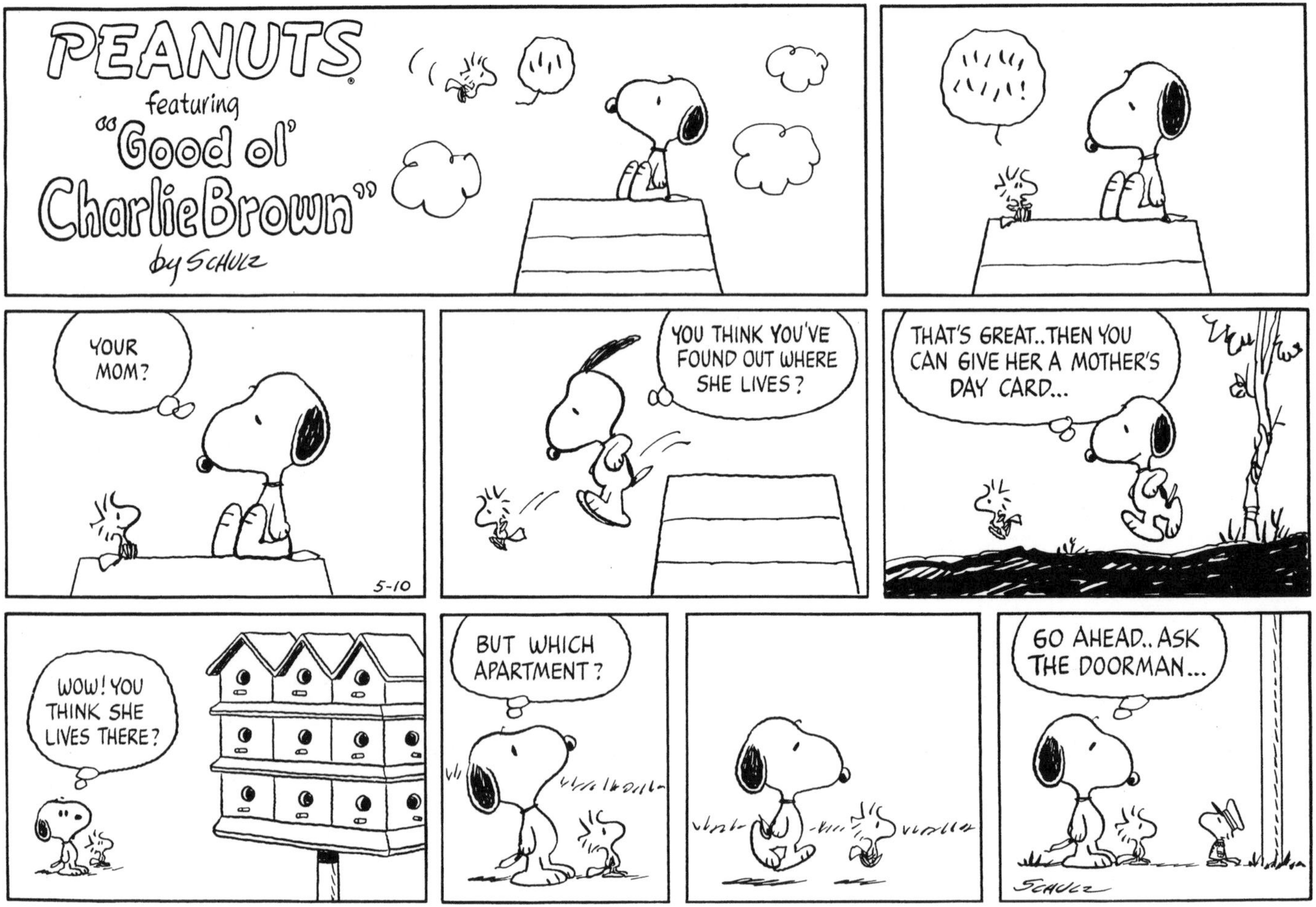
PEANUTS
featuring
"Good ol' CharlieBrown"
by SCHULZ
YOUR MOM?
5-10
YOU THINK YOU'VE FOUND OUT WHERE SHE LIVES?
THAT'S GREAT..THEN YOU CAN GIVE HER A MOTHER'S DAY CARD...
WOW! YOU THINK SHE LIVES THERE?
BUT WHICH APARTMENT?
GO AHEAD.. ASK THE DOORMAN...
SCHULZ

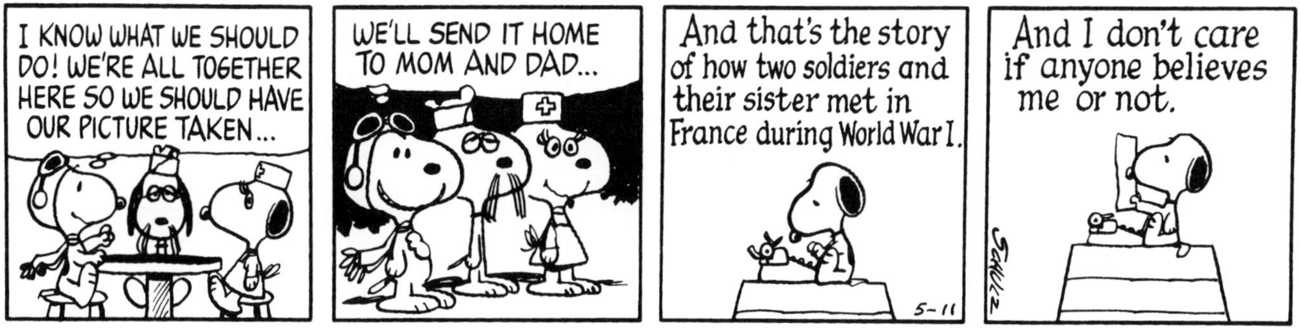
I KNOW WHAT WE SHOULD DO! WE'RE ALL TOGETHER HERE SO WE SHOULD HAVE OUR PICTURE TAKEN...
WE'LL SEND IT HOME TO MOM AND DAD...
And that's the story of how two soldiers and their sister met in France during World War I.
And I don't care if anyone believes me or not.
5-11
SCHULZ

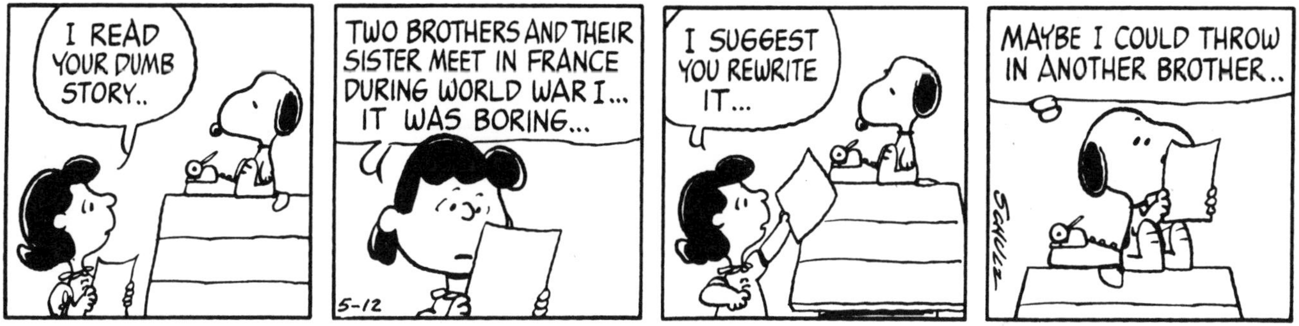
I READ YOUR DUMB STORY..
TWO BROTHERS AND THEIR SISTER MEET IN FRANCE DURING WORLD WAR I... IT WAS BORING...
5-12
I SUGGEST YOU REWRITE IT...
MAYBE I COULD THROW IN ANOTHER BROTHER..
SCHULZ

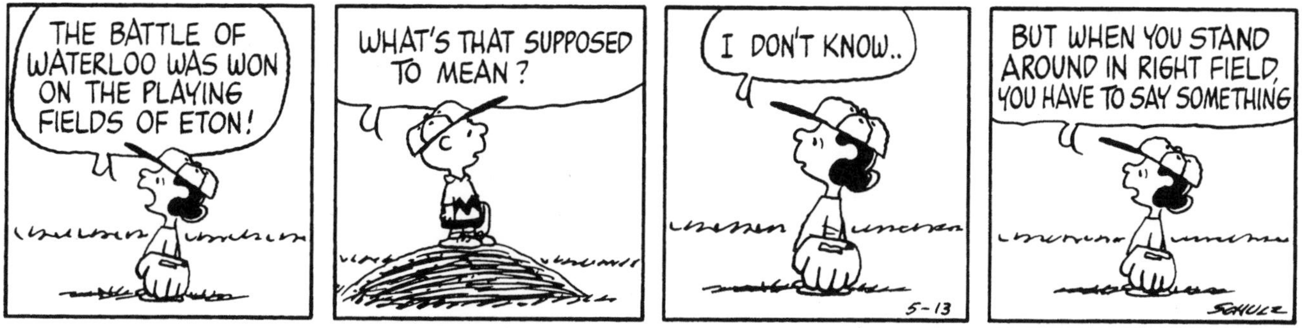
THE BATTLE OF WATERLOO WAS WON ON THE PLAYING FIELDS OF ETON!
WHAT'S THAT SUPPOSED TO MEAN?
I DON'T KNOW..
5-13
BUT WHEN YOU STAND AROUND IN RIGHT FIELD, YOU HAVE TO SAY SOMETHING
SCHULZ

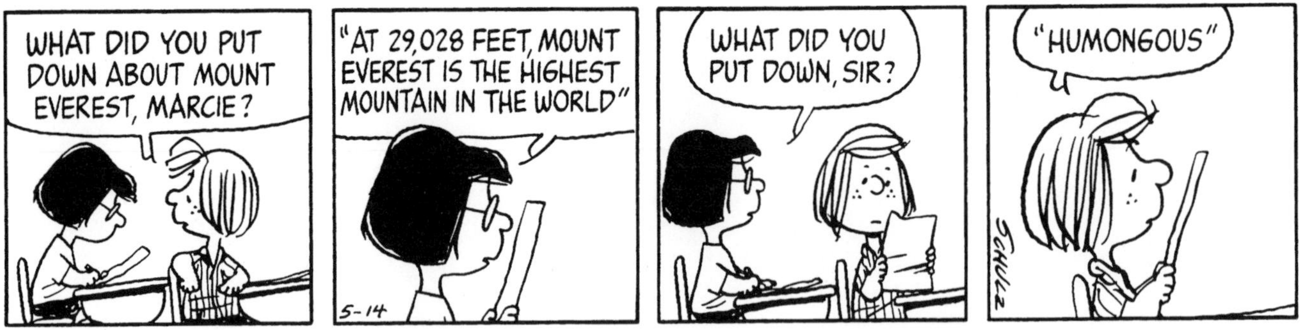
WHAT DID YOU PUT DOWN ABOUT MOUNT EVEREST, MARCIE?
"AT 29,028 FEET, MOUNT EVEREST IS THE HIGHEST MOUNTAIN IN THE WORLD"
5-14
WHAT DID YOU PUT DOWN, SIR?
"HUMONGOUS"
SCHULZ

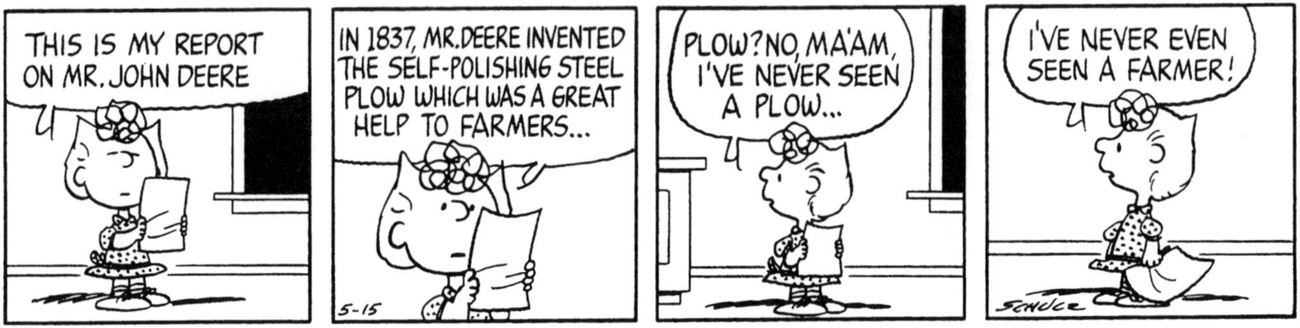
THIS IS MY REPORT ON MR. JOHN DEERE
IN 1837, MR. DEERE INVENTED THE SELF-POLISHING STEEL PLOW WHICH WAS A GREAT HELP TO FARMERS...
5-15
PLOW? NO, MA'AM, I'VE NEVER SEEN A PLOW...
I'VE NEVER EVEN SEEN A FARMER!
SCHULZ

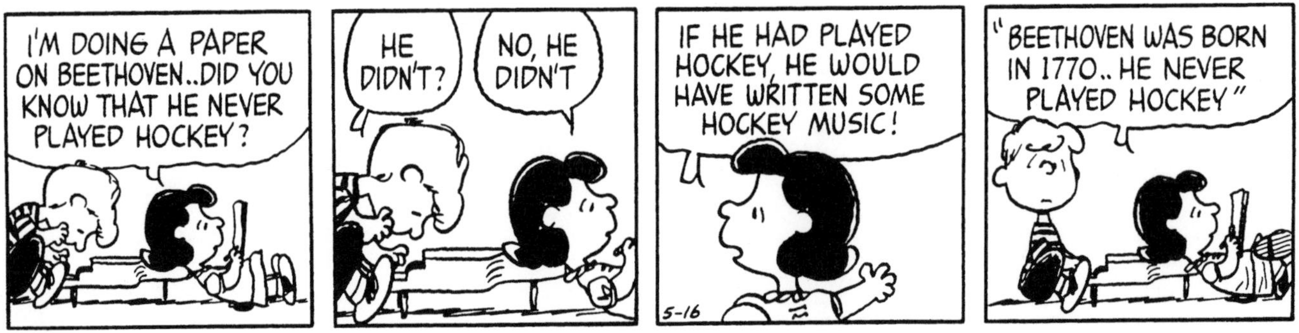
I'M DOING A PAPER ON BEETHOVEN..DID YOU KNOW THAT HE NEVER PLAYED HOCKEY?
HE DIDN'T?
NO, HE DIDN'T
IF HE HAD PLAYED HOCKEY, HE WOULD HAVE WRITTEN SOME HOCKEY MUSIC!
5-16
"BEETHOVEN WAS BORN IN 1770.. HE NEVER PLAYED HOCKEY"

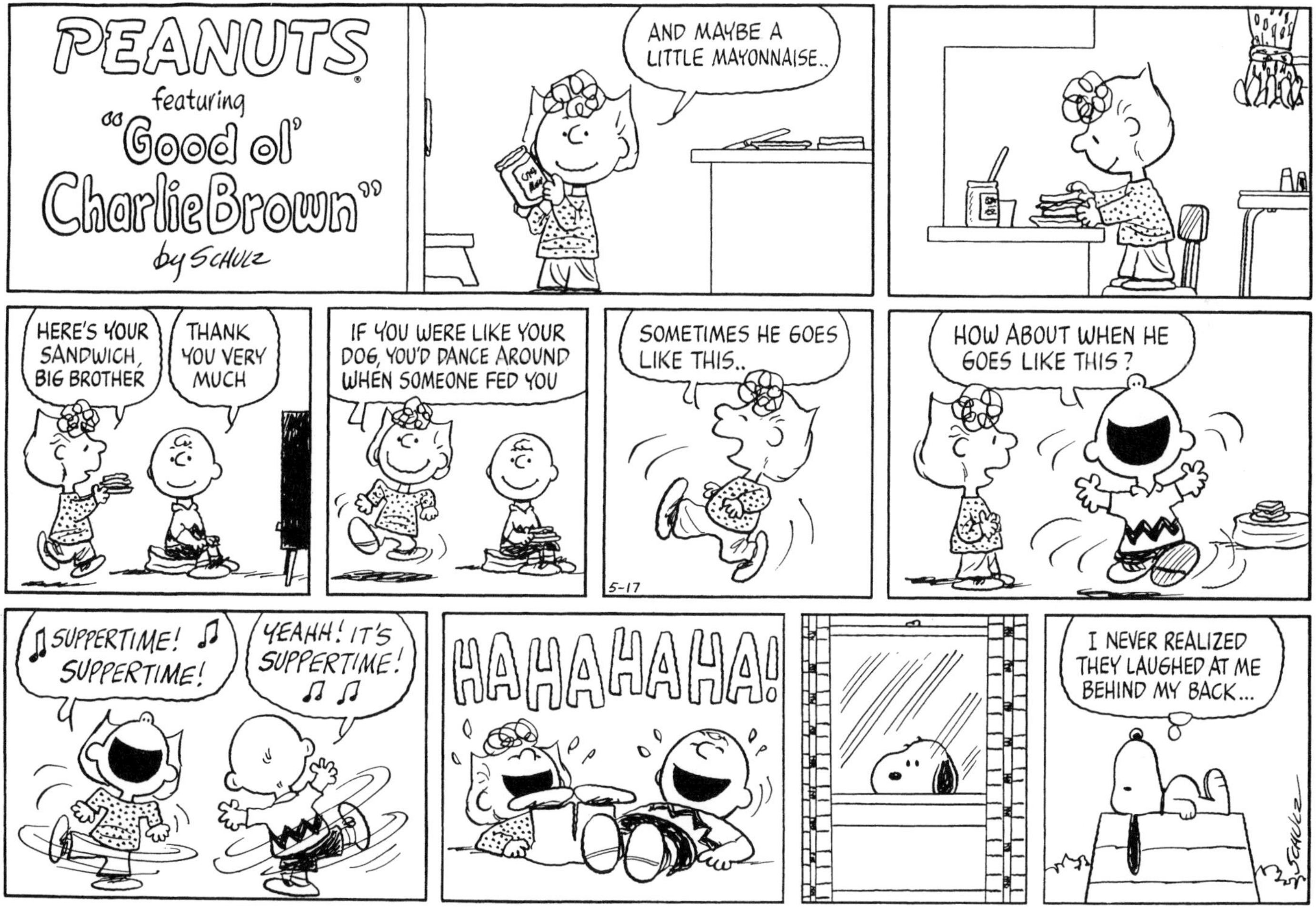
PEANUTS®
featuring "Good ol' CharlieBrown"
by SCHULZ
AND MAYBE A LITTLE MAYONNAISE..
HERE'S YOUR SANDWICH, BIG BROTHER
THANK YOU VERY MUCH
IF YOU WERE LIKE YOUR DOG, YOU'D DANCE AROUND WHEN SOMEONE FED YOU
SOMETIMES HE GOES LIKE THIS..
5-17
HOW ABOUT WHEN HE GOES LIKE THIS?
SUPPERTIME! SUPPERTIME!
YEAHH! IT'S SUPPERTIME!
HAHAHAHA!
I NEVER REALIZED THEY LAUGHED AT ME BEHIND MY BACK...
SCHULZ

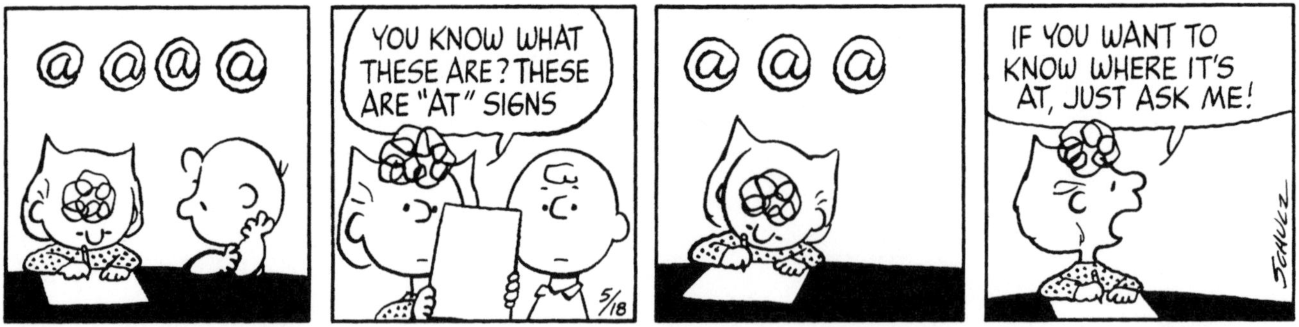
@ @ @ @
YOU KNOW WHAT THESE ARE? THESE ARE "AT" SIGNS
5/18
@ @ @
IF YOU WANT TO KNOW WHERE IT'S AT, JUST ASK ME!
SCHULZ

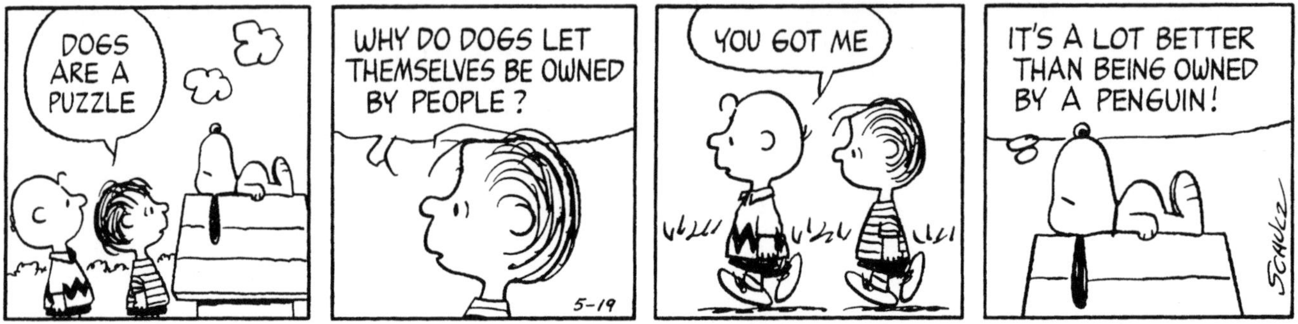
DOGS ARE A PUZZLE
WHY DO DOGS LET THEMSELVES BE OWNED BY PEOPLE?
5-19
YOU GOT ME
IT'S A LOT BETTER THAN BEING OWNED BY A PENGUIN!
SCHULZ

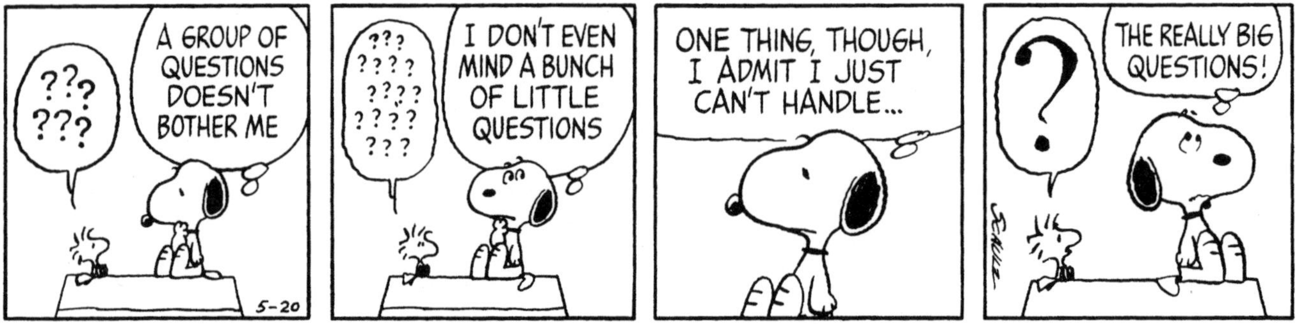
???
???
A GROUP OF QUESTIONS DOESN'T BOTHER ME
5-20
???
????
????
????
???
I DON'T EVEN MIND A BUNCH OF LITTLE QUESTIONS
ONE THING, THOUGH, I ADMIT I JUST CAN'T HANDLE...
?
THE REALLY BIG QUESTIONS!
SCHULZ

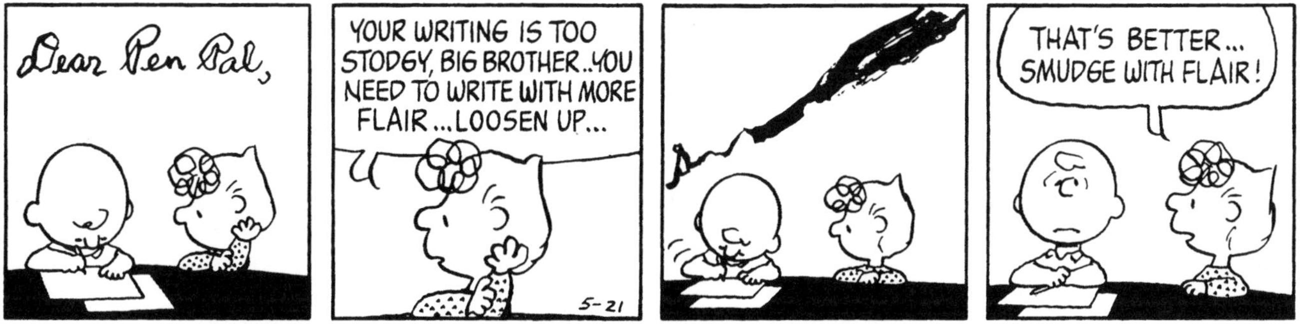
Dear Pen Pal,
YOUR WRITING IS TOO STODGY, BIG BROTHER..YOU NEED TO WRITE WITH MORE FLAIR...LOOSEN UP...
5-21
THAT'S BETTER... SMUDGE WITH FLAIR!

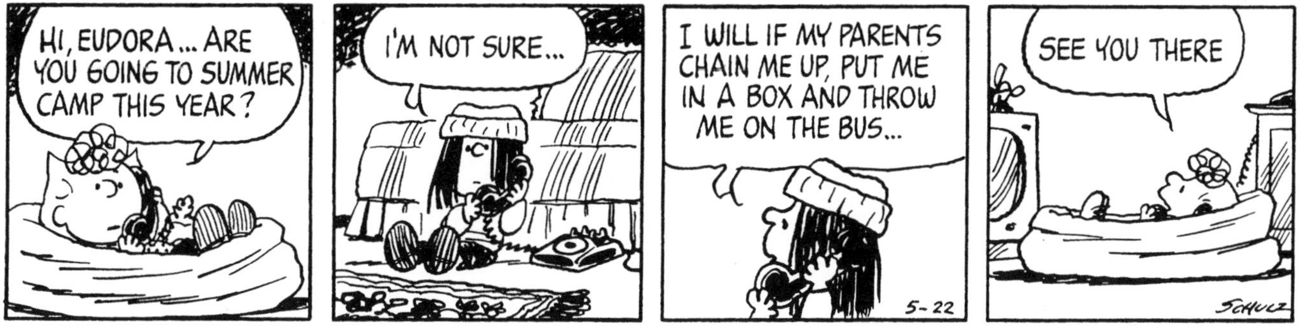
HI, EUDORA... ARE YOU GOING TO SUMMER CAMP THIS YEAR?
I'M NOT SURE...
I WILL IF MY PARENTS CHAIN ME UP, PUT ME IN A BOX AND THROW ME ON THE BUS...
5-22
SEE YOU THERE
SCHULZ

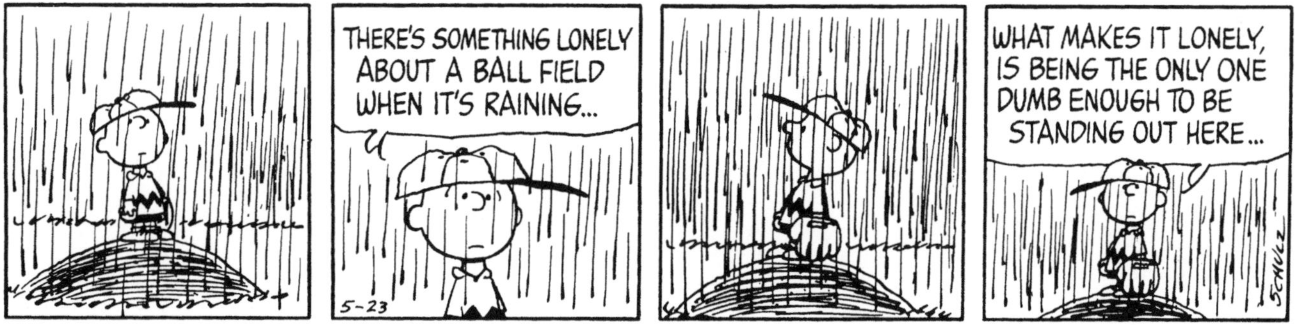
THERE'S SOMETHING LONELY ABOUT A BALL FIELD WHEN IT'S RAINING...
5-23
WHAT MAKES IT LONELY, IS BEING THE ONLY ONE DUMB ENOUGH TO BE STANDING OUT HERE...
SCHULZ

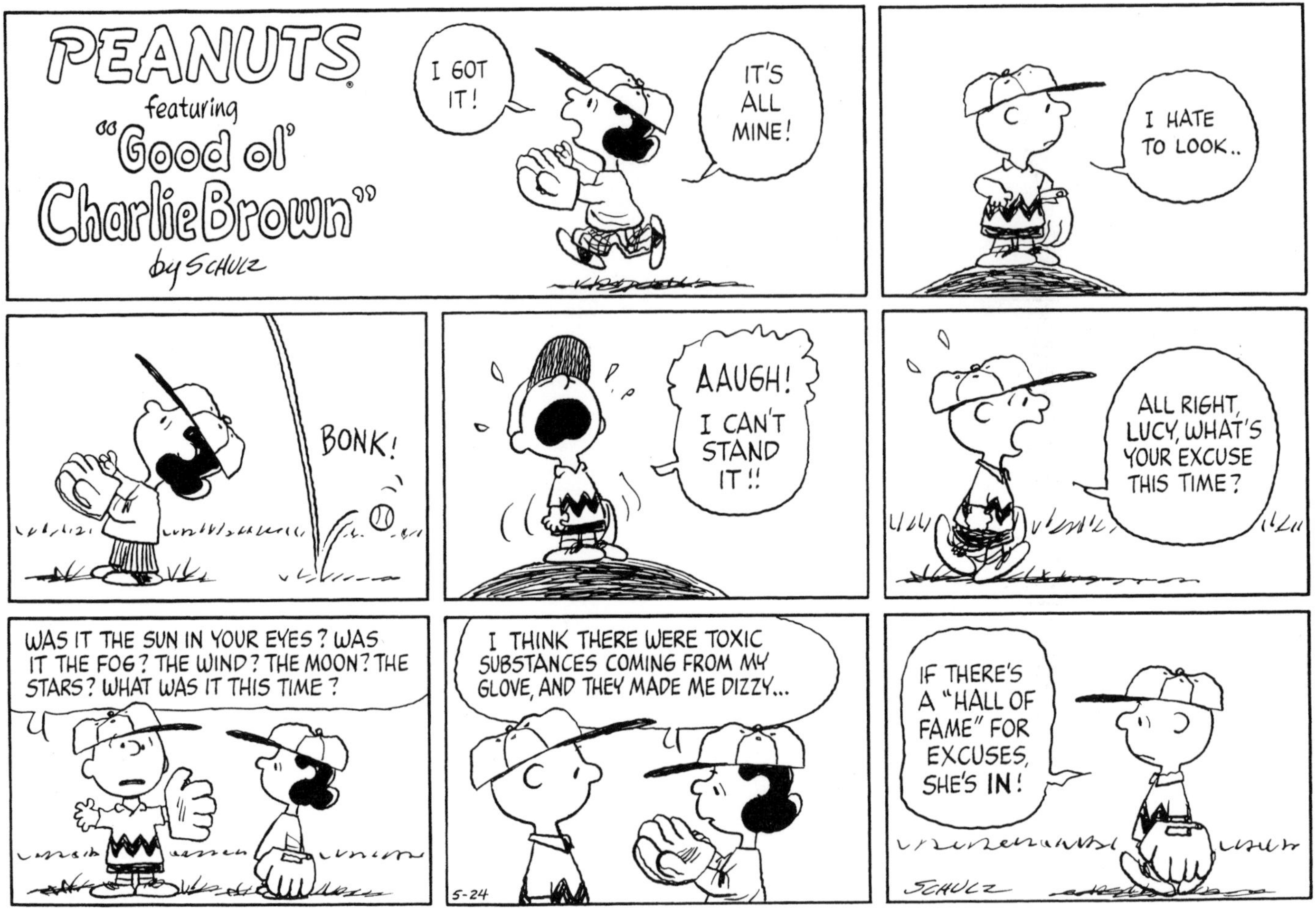
PEANUTS
featuring "Good ol' Charlie Brown"
by SCHULZ
I GOT IT!
IT'S ALL MINE!
I HATE TO LOOK..
BONK!
AAUGH! I CAN'T STAND IT!!
ALL RIGHT, LUCY, WHAT'S YOUR EXCUSE THIS TIME?
WAS IT THE SUN IN YOUR EYES? WAS IT THE FOG? THE WIND? THE MOON? THE STARS? WHAT WAS IT THIS TIME?
I THINK THERE WERE TOXIC SUBSTANCES COMING FROM MY GLOVE, AND THEY MADE ME DIZZY...
5-24
IF THERE'S A "HALL OF FAME" FOR EXCUSES, SHE'S IN!
SCHULZ

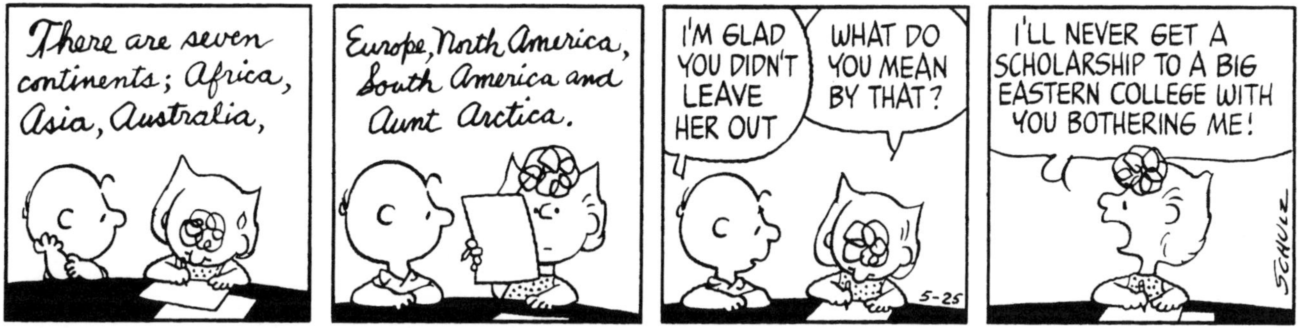
There are seven continents; Africa, Asia, Australia,
Europe, North America, South America and Aunt Arctica.
I'M GLAD YOU DIDN'T LEAVE HER OUT
WHAT DO YOU MEAN BY THAT?
5-25
I'LL NEVER GET A SCHOLARSHIP TO A BIG EASTERN COLLEGE WITH YOU BOTHERING ME!
SCHULZ

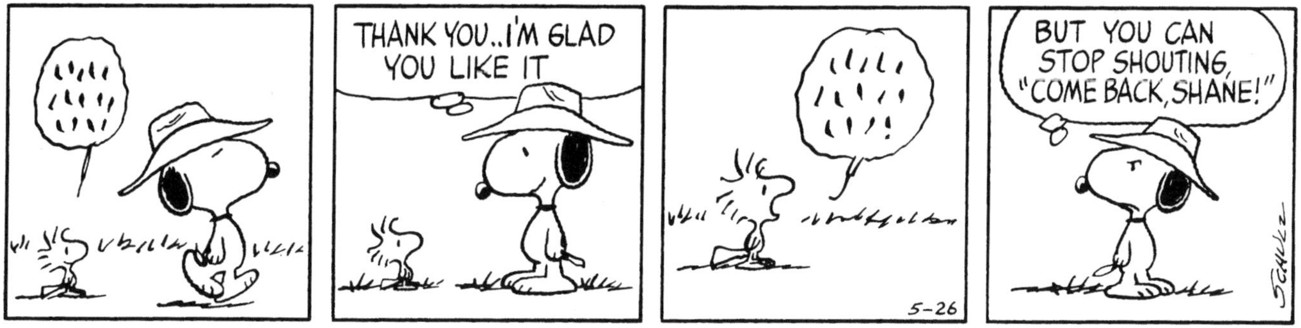
THANK YOU..I'M GLAD YOU LIKE IT
5-26
BUT YOU CAN STOP SHOUTING, "COME BACK, SHANE!"
SCHULZ

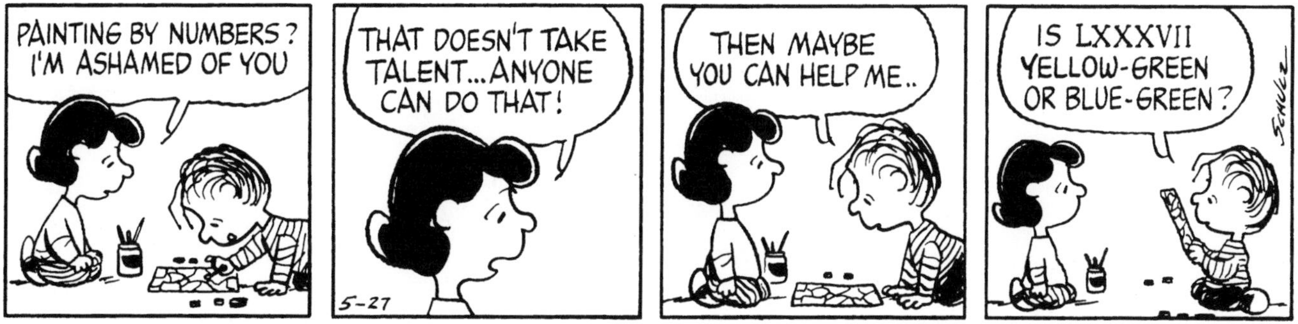
PAINTING BY NUMBERS? I'M ASHAMED OF YOU
THAT DOESN'T TAKE TALENT...ANYONE CAN DO THAT!
5-27
THEN MAYBE YOU CAN HELP ME..
IS LXXXVII YELLOW-GREEN OR BLUE-GREEN?
SCHULZ

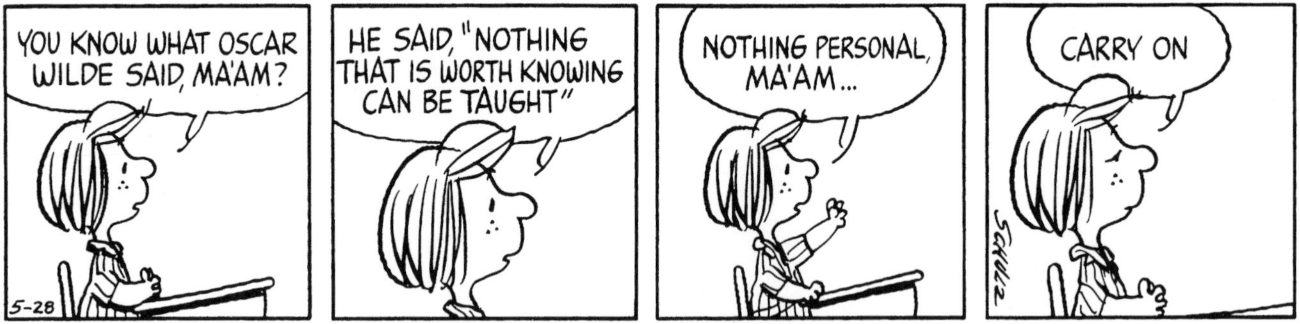
YOU KNOW WHAT OSCAR WILDE SAID, MA'AM?
HE SAID, "NOTHING THAT IS WORTH KNOWING CAN BE TAUGHT"
NOTHING PERSONAL, MA'AM...
CARRY ON
5-28
SCHULZ

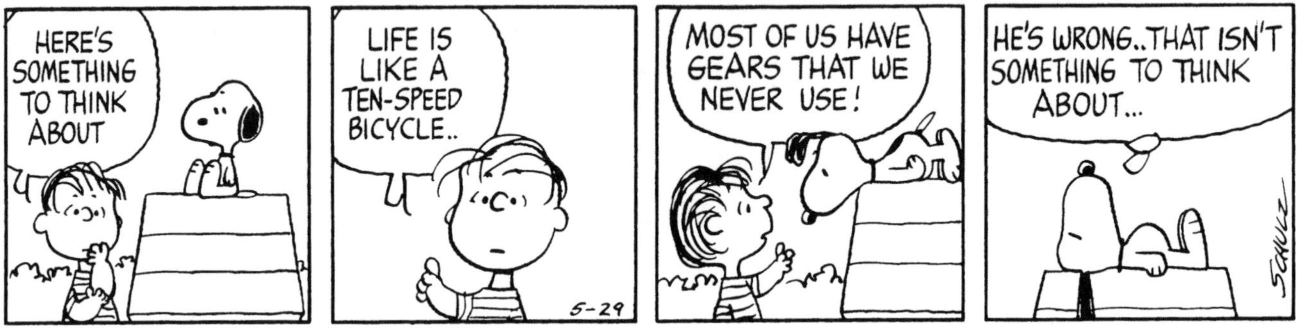
HERE'S SOMETHING TO THINK ABOUT
LIFE IS LIKE A TEN-SPEED BICYCLE..
MOST OF US HAVE GEARS THAT WE NEVER USE!
HE'S WRONG..THAT ISN'T SOMETHING TO THINK ABOUT...
5-29
SCHULZ

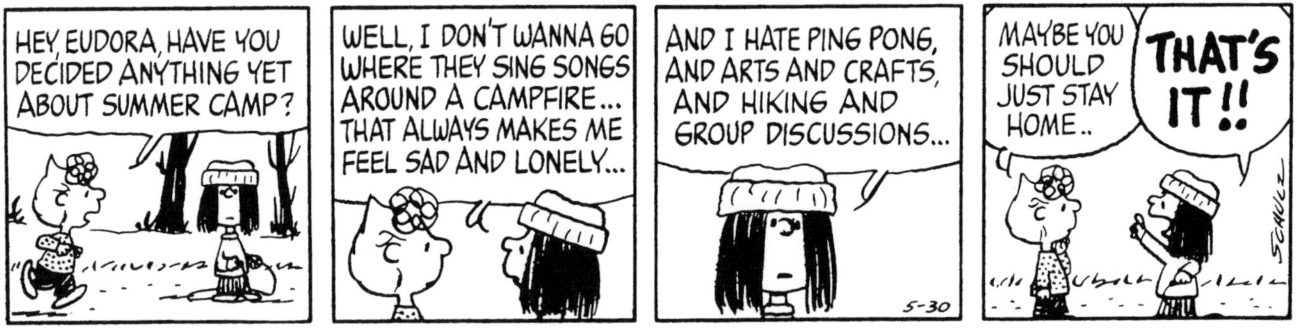
HEY, EUDORA, HAVE YOU DECIDED ANYTHING YET ABOUT SUMMER CAMP?
WELL, I DON'T WANNA GO WHERE THEY SING SONGS AROUND A CAMPFIRE... THAT ALWAYS MAKES ME FEEL SAD AND LONELY...
AND I HATE PING PONG, AND ARTS AND CRAFTS, AND HIKING AND GROUP DISCUSSIONS...
MAYBE YOU SHOULD JUST STAY HOME..
THAT'S IT!!
5-30
SCHULZ

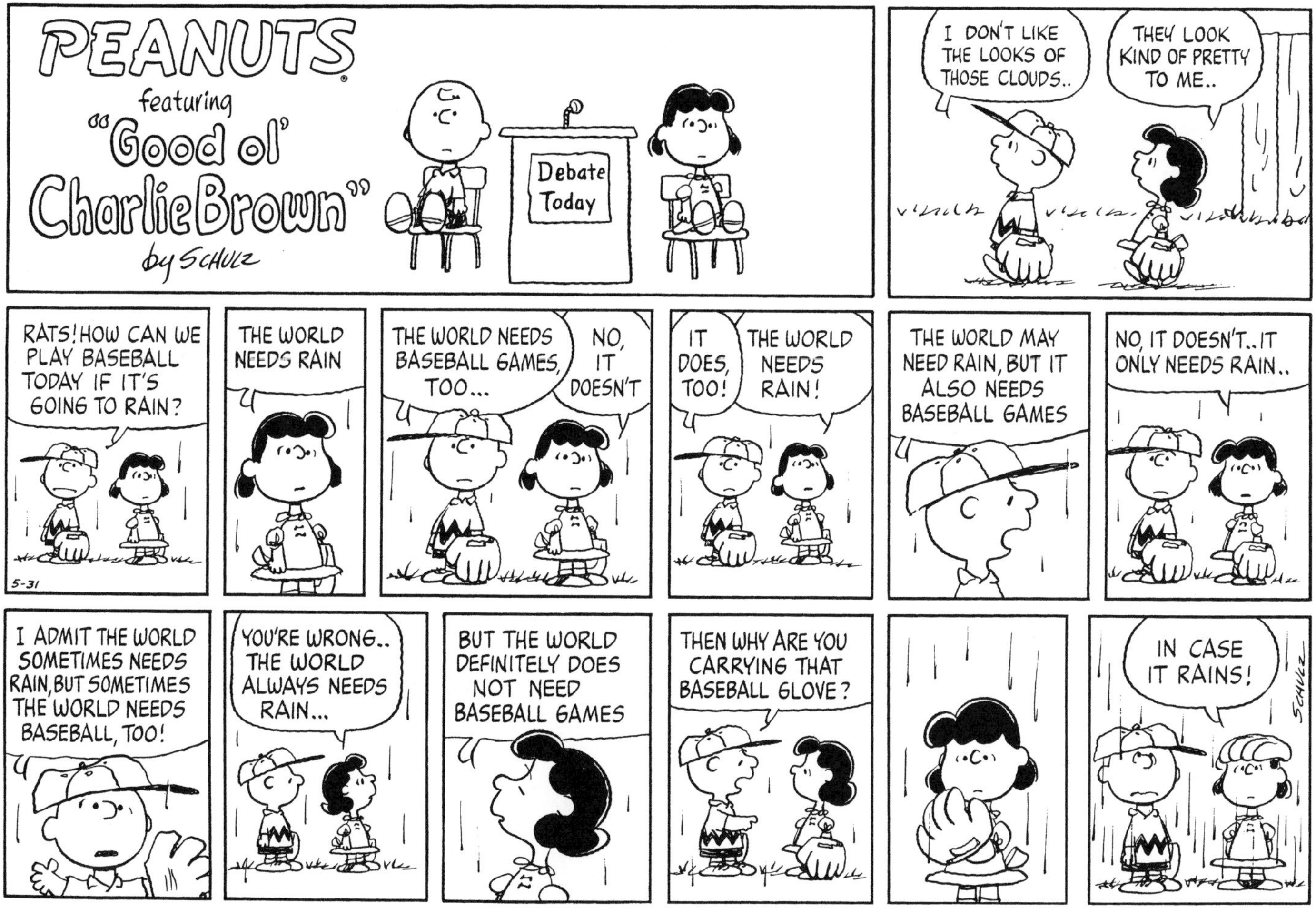
PEANUTS
featuring "Good ol' Charlie Brown"
by SCHULZ
Debate Today
I DON'T LIKE THE LOOKS OF THOSE CLOUDS..
THEY LOOK KIND OF PRETTY TO ME..
RATS! HOW CAN WE PLAY BASEBALL TODAY IF IT'S GOING TO RAIN?
5-31
THE WORLD NEEDS RAIN
THE WORLD NEEDS BASEBALL GAMES, TOO...
NO, IT DOESN'T
IT DOES, TOO!
THE WORLD NEEDS RAIN!
THE WORLD MAY NEED RAIN, BUT IT ALSO NEEDS BASEBALL GAMES
NO, IT DOESN'T.. IT ONLY NEEDS RAIN..
I ADMIT THE WORLD SOMETIMES NEEDS RAIN, BUT SOMETIMES THE WORLD NEEDS BASEBALL, TOO!
YOU'RE WRONG.. THE WORLD ALWAYS NEEDS RAIN...
BUT THE WORLD DEFINITELY DOES NOT NEED BASEBALL GAMES
THEN WHY ARE YOU CARRYING THAT BASEBALL GLOVE?
IN CASE IT RAINS!
SCHULZ

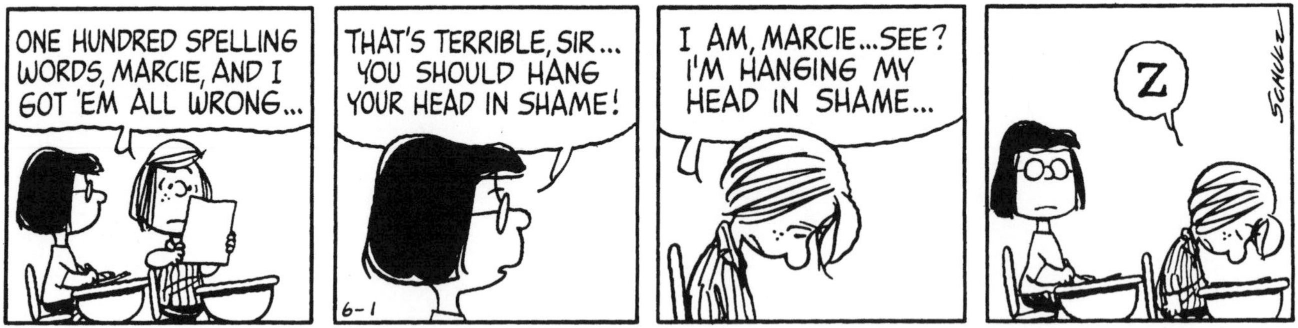
ONE HUNDRED SPELLING WORDS, MARCIE, AND I GOT 'EM ALL WRONG...
THAT'S TERRIBLE, SIR... YOU SHOULD HANG YOUR HEAD IN SHAME!
6-1
I AM, MARCIE...SEE? I'M HANGING MY HEAD IN SHAME...
Z
SCHULZ

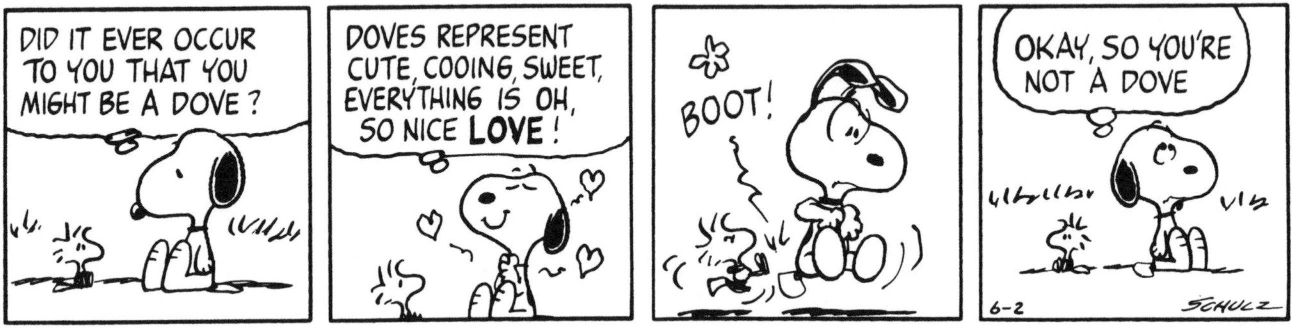
DID IT EVER OCCUR TO YOU THAT YOU MIGHT BE A DOVE?
DOVES REPRESENT CUTE, COOING, SWEET, EVERYTHING IS OH, SO NICE LOVE!
BOOT!
OKAY, SO YOU'RE NOT A DOVE
6-2
SCHULZ

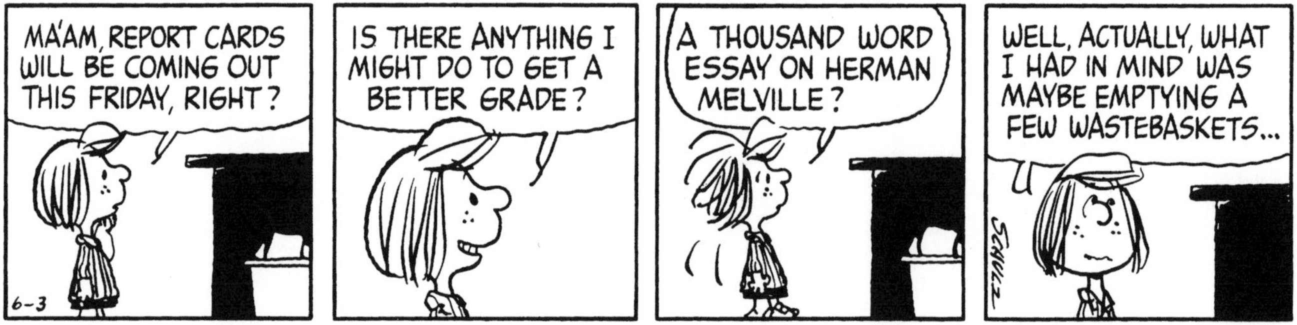
MA'AM, REPORT CARDS WILL BE COMING OUT THIS FRIDAY, RIGHT?
6-3
IS THERE ANYTHING I MIGHT DO TO GET A BETTER GRADE?
A THOUSAND WORD ESSAY ON HERMAN MELVILLE?
SCHULZ
WELL, ACTUALLY, WHAT I HAD IN MIND WAS MAYBE EMPTYING A FEW WASTEBASKETS...

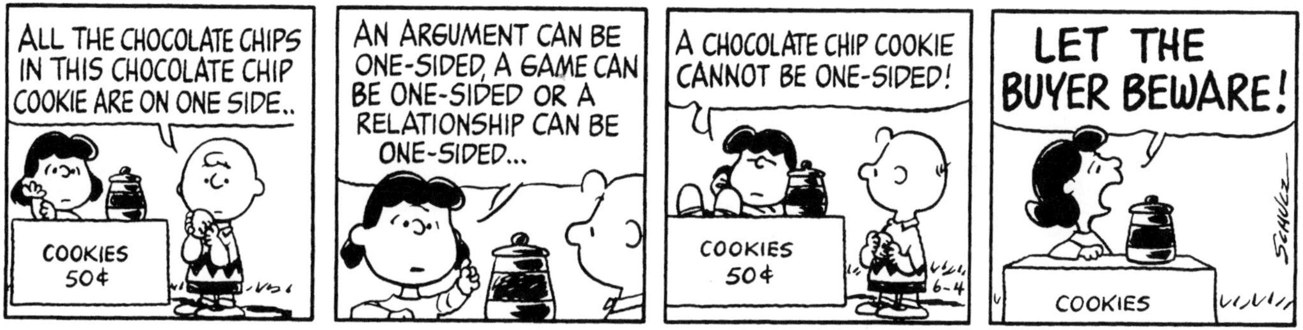
ALL THE CHOCOLATE CHIPS IN THIS CHOCOLATE CHIP COOKIE ARE ON ONE SIDE..
COOKIES 50¢
AN ARGUMENT CAN BE ONE-SIDED, A GAME CAN BE ONE-SIDED OR A RELATIONSHIP CAN BE ONE-SIDED...
A CHOCOLATE CHIP COOKIE CANNOT BE ONE-SIDED!
COOKIES 50¢
6-4
LET THE BUYER BEWARE!
COOKIES
SCHULZ

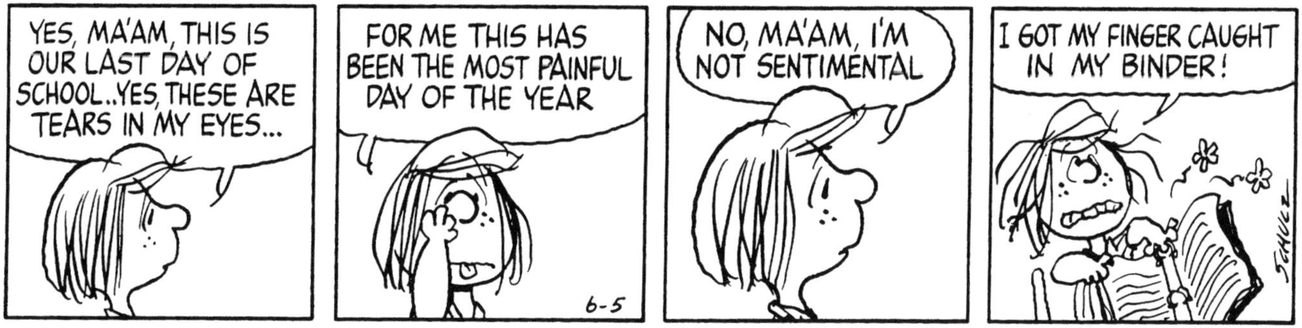
YES, MA'AM, THIS IS OUR LAST DAY OF SCHOOL..YES, THESE ARE TEARS IN MY EYES...
FOR ME THIS HAS BEEN THE MOST PAINFUL DAY OF THE YEAR
6-5
NO, MA'AM, I'M NOT SENTIMENTAL
I GOT MY FINGER CAUGHT IN MY BINDER!
SCHULZ

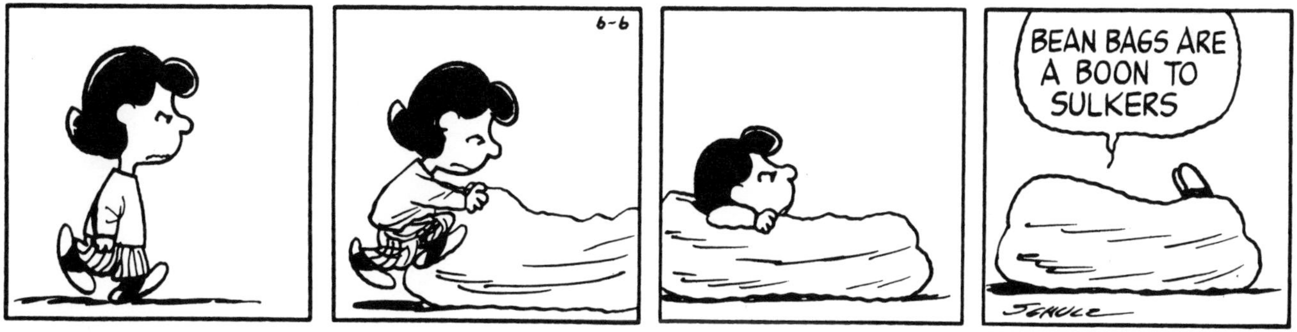
6-6
BEAN BAGS ARE A BOON TO SULKERS
SCHULZ

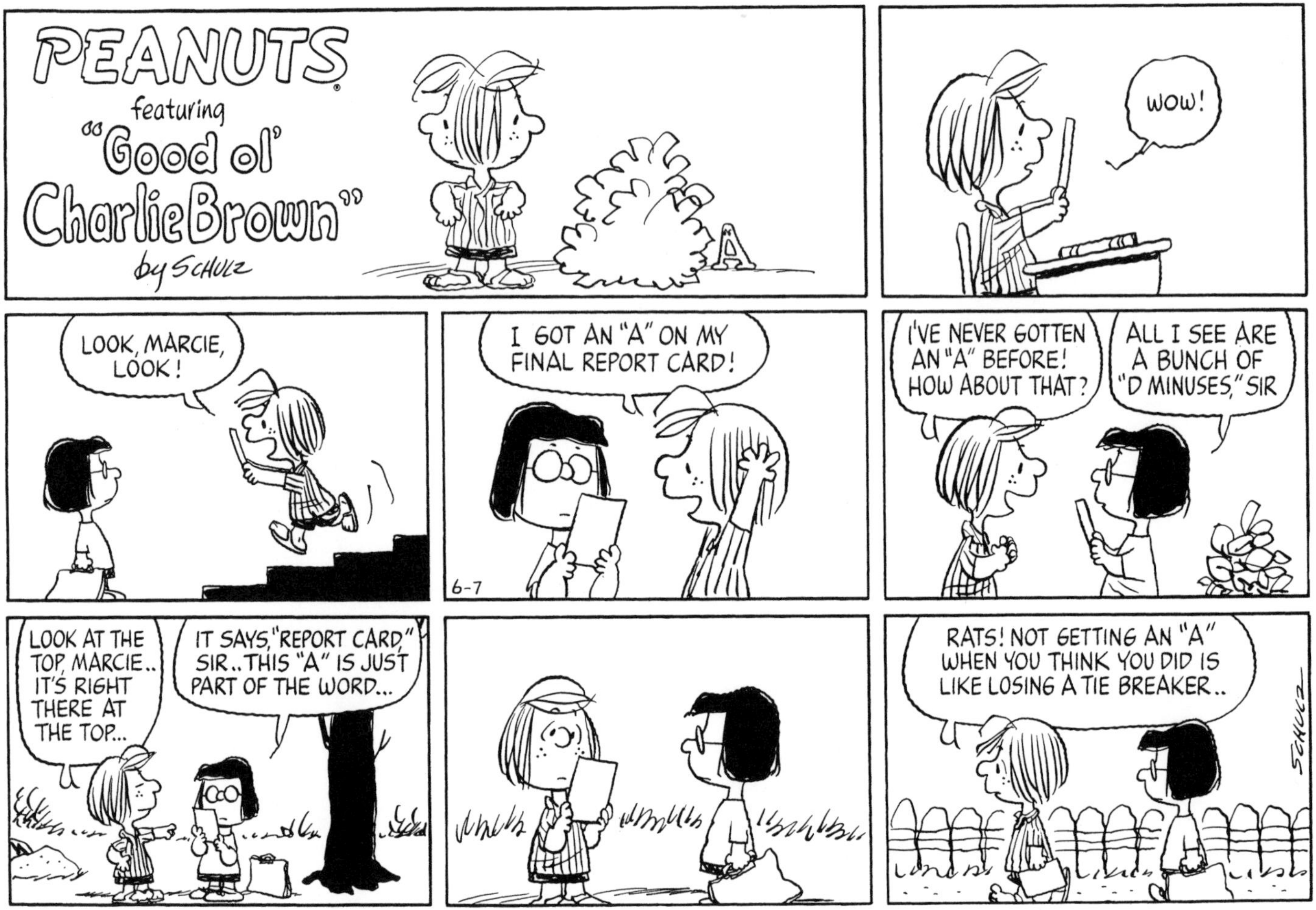
PEANUTS
featuring
"Good ol' Charlie Brown"
by SCHULZ
WOW!
LOOK, MARCIE, LOOK!
I GOT AN "A" ON MY FINAL REPORT CARD!
6-7
I'VE NEVER GOTTEN AN "A" BEFORE! HOW ABOUT THAT?
ALL I SEE ARE A BUNCH OF "D MINUSES," SIR
LOOK AT THE TOP, MARCIE.. IT'S RIGHT THERE AT THE TOP...
IT SAYS, "REPORT CARD," SIR.. THIS "A" IS JUST PART OF THE WORD...
RATS! NOT GETTING AN "A" WHEN YOU THINK YOU DID IS LIKE LOSING A TIE BREAKER..
SCHULZ

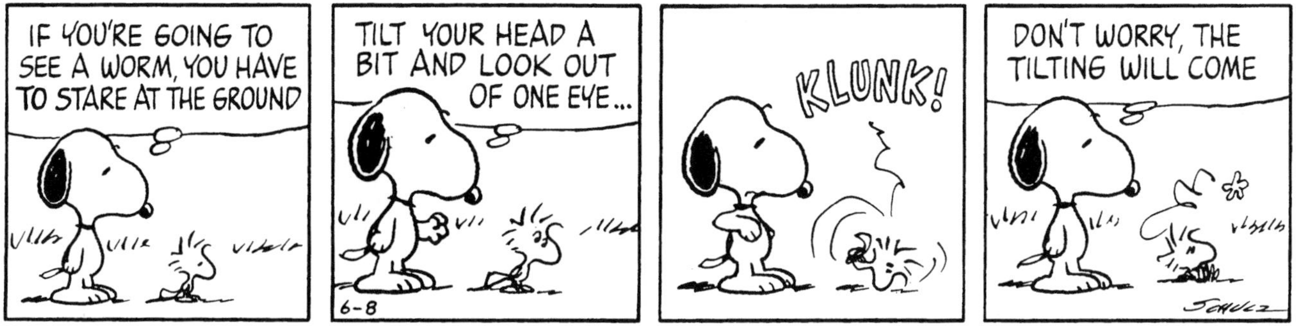
IF YOU'RE GOING TO SEE A WORM, YOU HAVE TO STARE AT THE GROUND
TILT YOUR HEAD A BIT AND LOOK OUT OF ONE EYE...
6-8
KLUNK!
DON'T WORRY, THE TILTING WILL COME

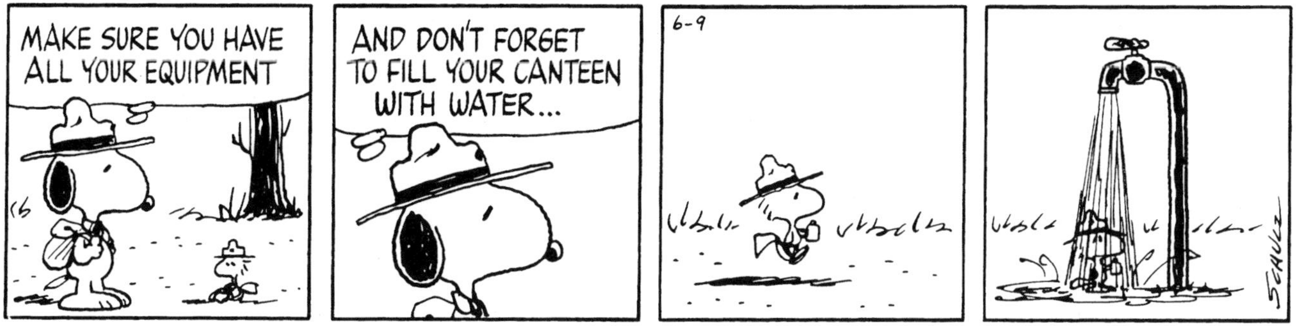
MAKE SURE YOU HAVE ALL YOUR EQUIPMENT
AND DON'T FORGET TO FILL YOUR CANTEEN WITH WATER...
6-9

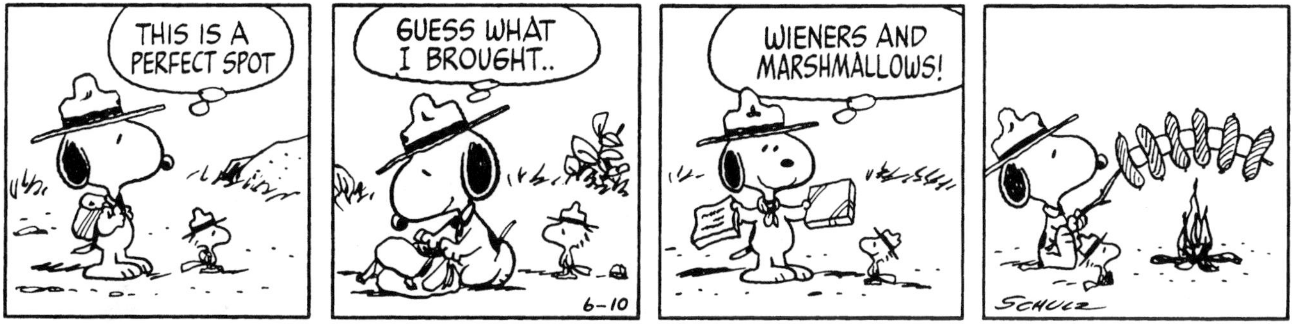
THIS IS A PERFECT SPOT
GUESS WHAT I BROUGHT..
6-10
WIENERS AND MARSHMALLOWS!

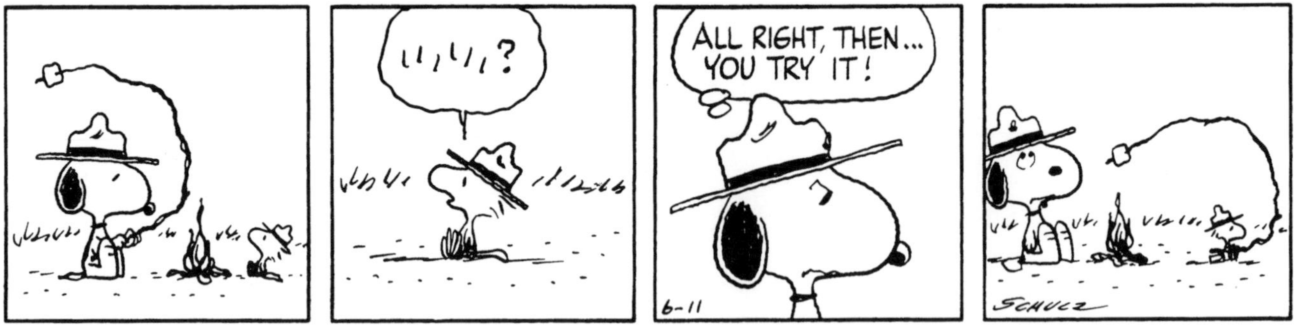
ALL RIGHT, THEN...
YOU TRY IT!
6-11
SCHULZ

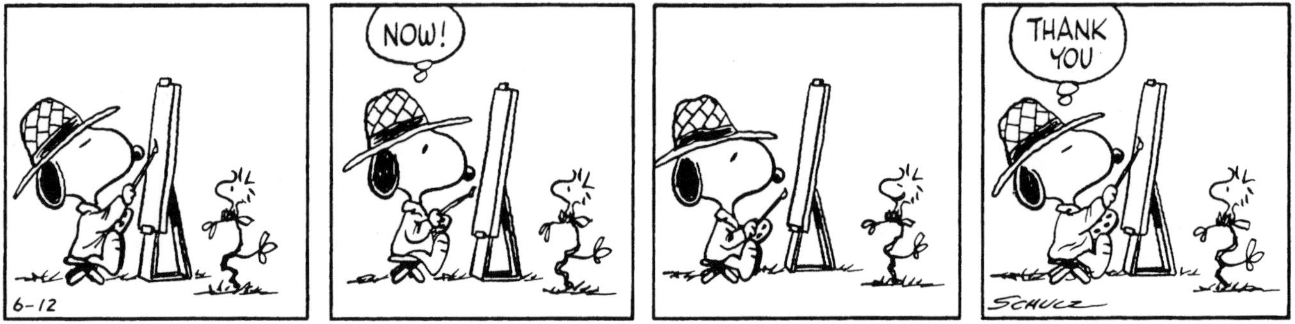
6-12
NOW!
THANK YOU
SCHULZ

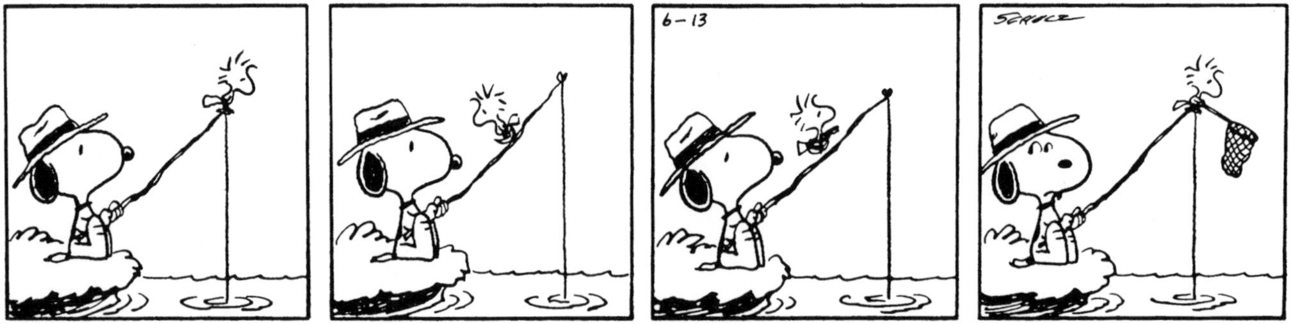
6-13
SCHULZ

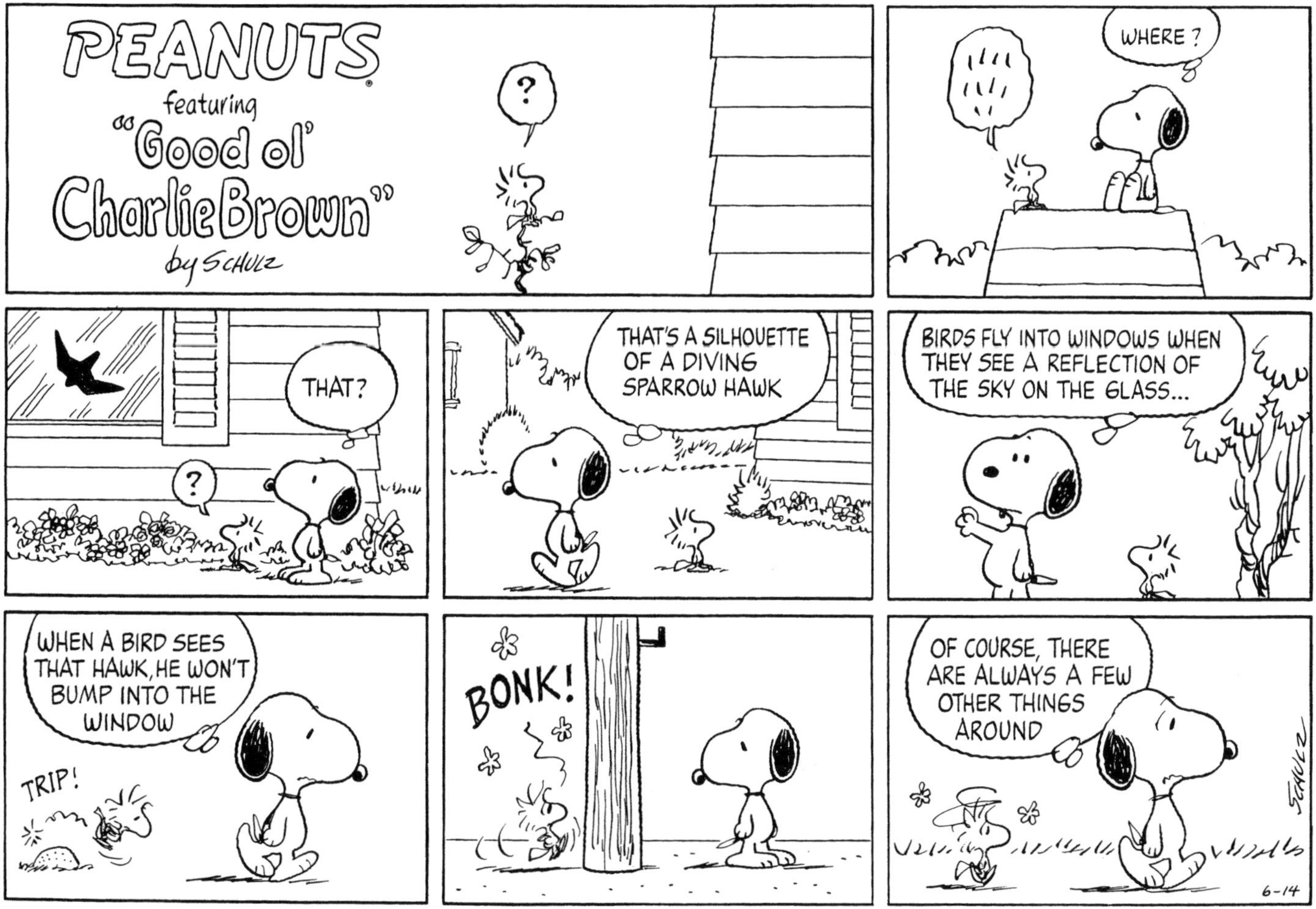
PEANUTS
featuring
"Good ol' CharlieBrown"
by SCHULZ
?
WHERE ?
THAT?
?
THAT'S A SILHOUETTE OF A DIVING SPARROW HAWK
BIRDS FLY INTO WINDOWS WHEN THEY SEE A REFLECTION OF THE SKY ON THE GLASS...
WHEN A BIRD SEES THAT HAWK, HE WON'T BUMP INTO THE WINDOW
TRIP!
BONK!
OF COURSE, THERE ARE ALWAYS A FEW OTHER THINGS AROUND
SCHULZ
6-14

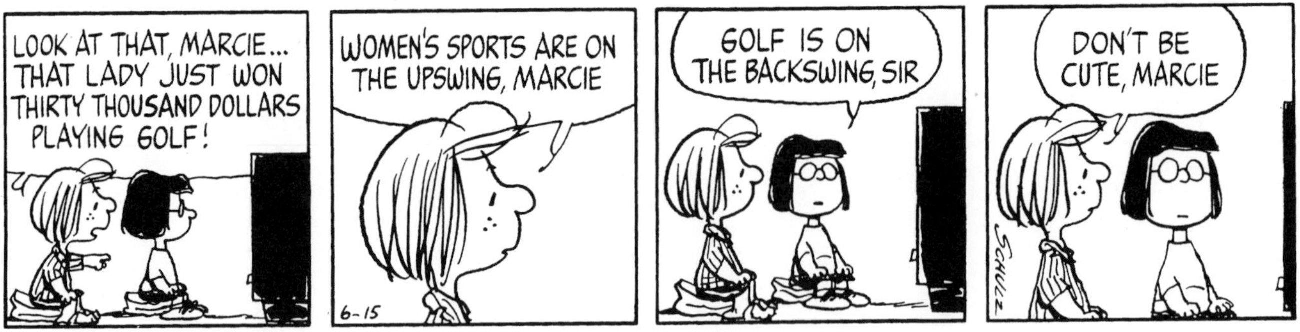
LOOK AT THAT, MARCIE... THAT LADY JUST WON THIRTY THOUSAND DOLLARS PLAYING GOLF!
WOMEN'S SPORTS ARE ON THE UPSWING, MARCIE
6-15
GOLF IS ON THE BACKSWING, SIR
DON'T BE CUTE, MARCIE
SCHULZ

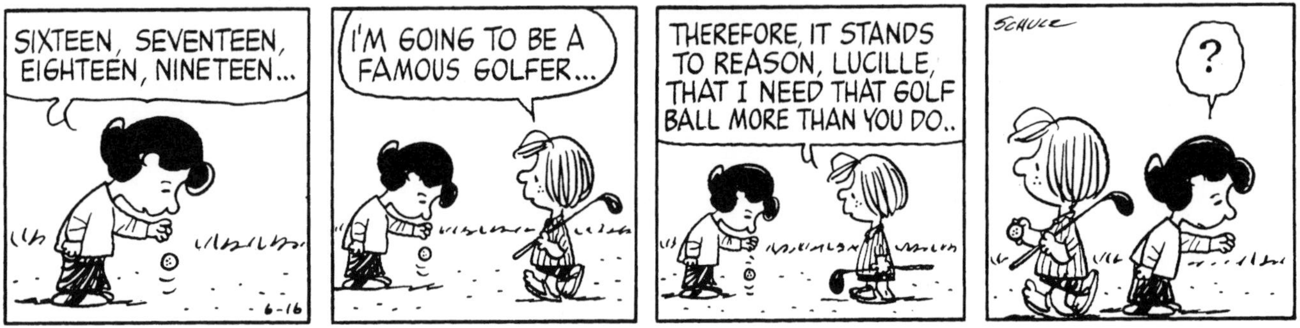
SIXTEEN, SEVENTEEN, EIGHTEEN, NINETEEN...
6-16
I'M GOING TO BE A FAMOUS GOLFER...
THEREFORE, IT STANDS TO REASON, LUCILLE, THAT I NEED THAT GOLF BALL MORE THAN YOU DO..
SCHULZ
?

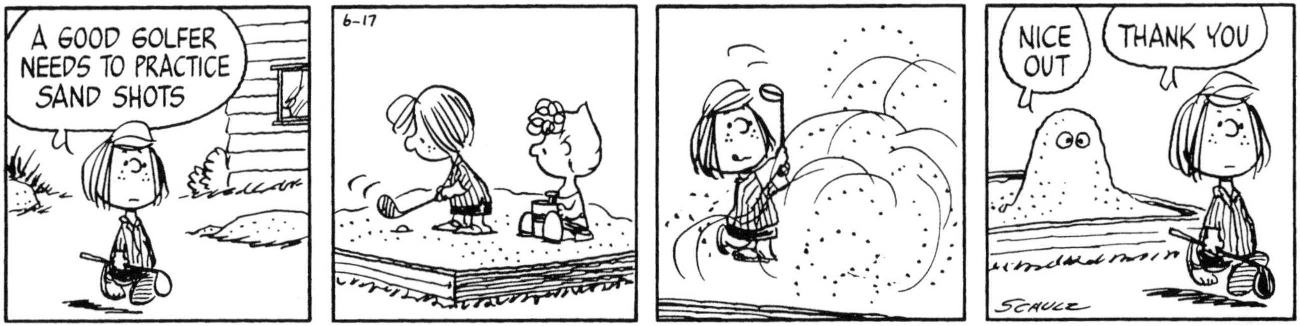
A GOOD GOLFER NEEDS TO PRACTICE SAND SHOTS
6-17
NICE OUT
THANK YOU
SCHULZ

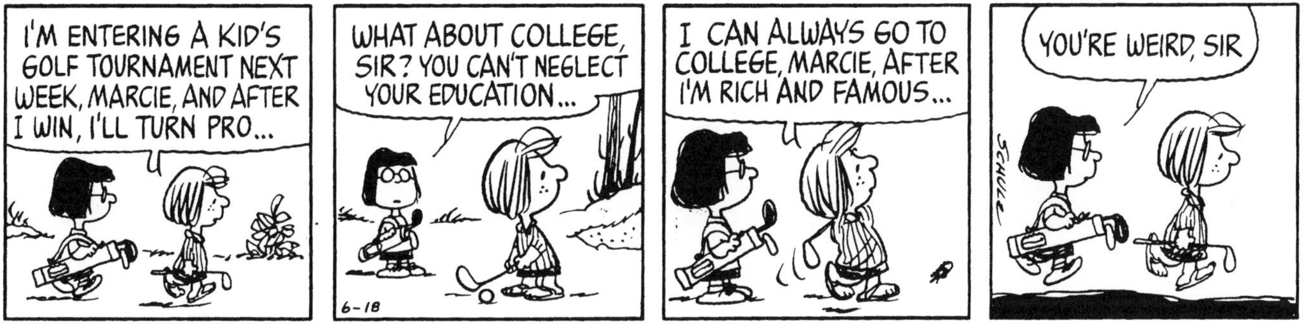
I'M ENTERING A KID'S GOLF TOURNAMENT NEXT WEEK, MARCIE, AND AFTER I WIN, I'LL TURN PRO...
WHAT ABOUT COLLEGE, SIR? YOU CAN'T NEGLECT YOUR EDUCATION...
6-18
I CAN ALWAYS GO TO COLLEGE, MARCIE, AFTER I'M RICH AND FAMOUS...
YOU'RE WEIRD, SIR
SCHULZ

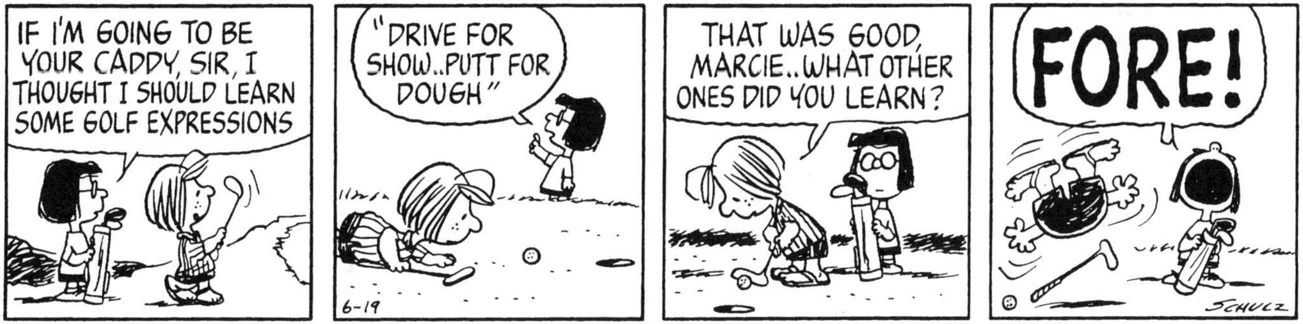
IF I'M GOING TO BE YOUR CADDY, SIR, I THOUGHT I SHOULD LEARN SOME GOLF EXPRESSIONS
"DRIVE FOR SHOW..PUTT FOR DOUGH"
6-19
THAT WAS GOOD, MARCIE..WHAT OTHER ONES DID YOU LEARN?
FORE!
SCHULZ

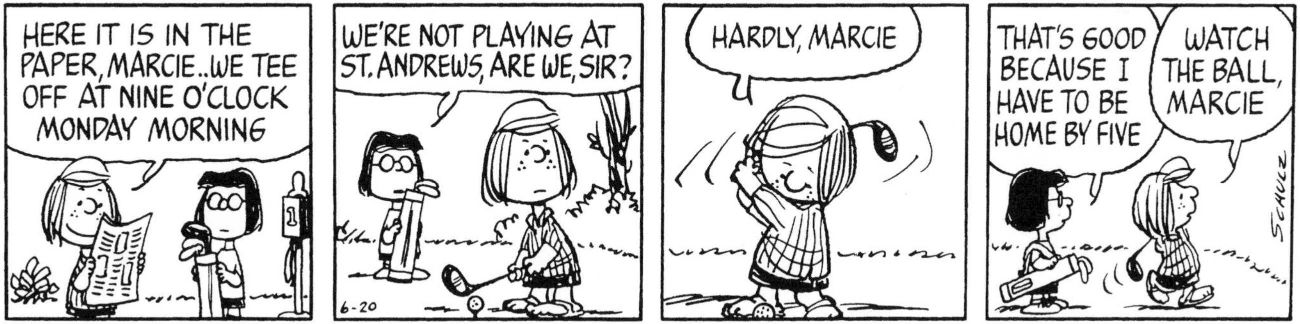
HERE IT IS IN THE PAPER, MARCIE..WE TEE OFF AT NINE O'CLOCK MONDAY MORNING
WE'RE NOT PLAYING AT ST. ANDREWS, ARE WE, SIR?
6-20
HARDLY, MARCIE
THAT'S GOOD BECAUSE I HAVE TO BE HOME BY FIVE
WATCH THE BALL, MARCIE
SCHULZ

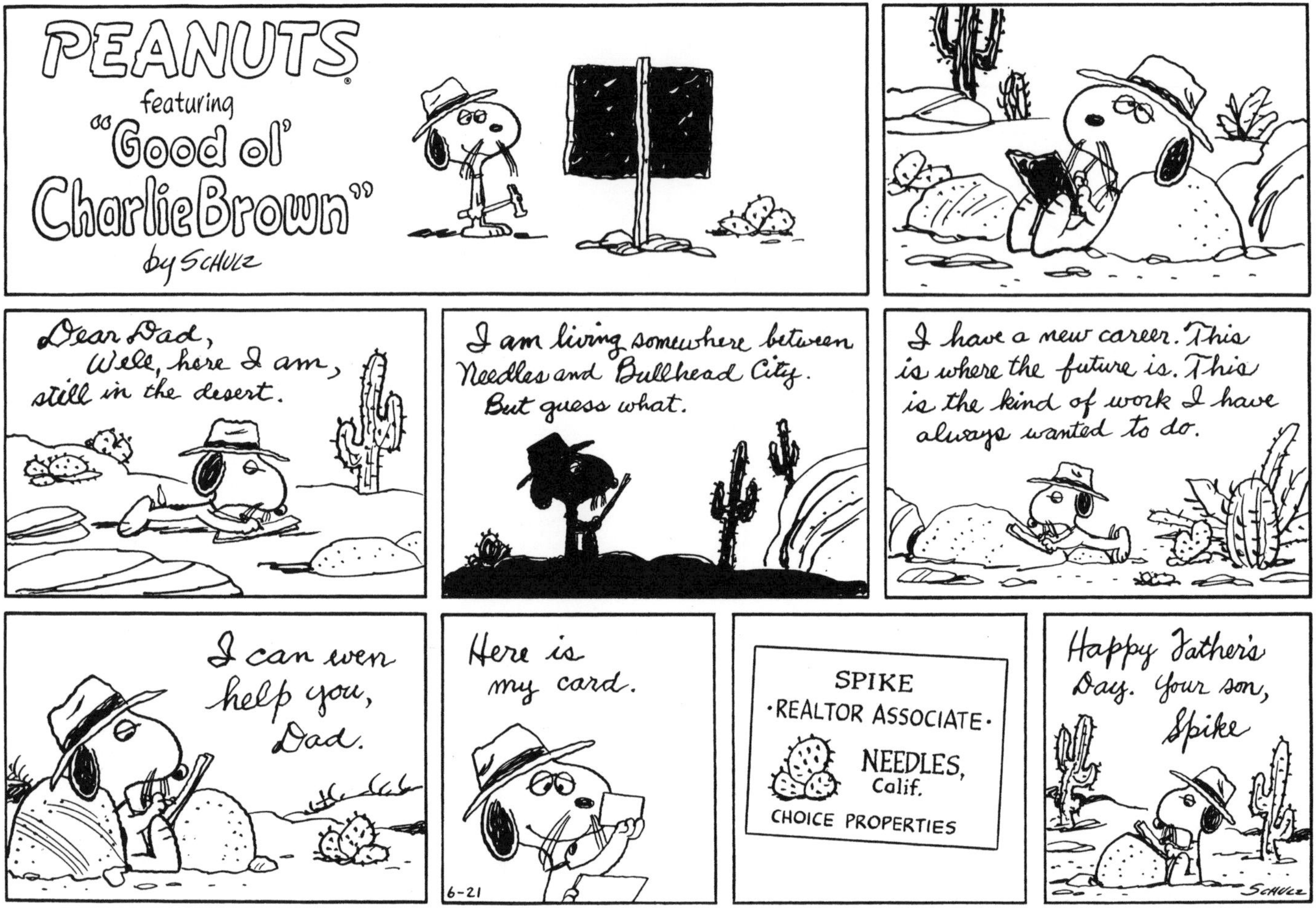
PEANUTS
featuring
"Good ol' Charlie Brown"
by SCHULZ
Dear Dad, Well, here I am, still in the desert.
I am living somewhere between Needles and Bullhead City. But guess what.
I have a new career. This is where the future is. This is the kind of work I have always wanted to do.
I can even help you, Dad.
Here is my card.
6-21
SPIKE
·REALTOR ASSOCIATE·
NEEDLES, Calif.
CHOICE PROPERTIES
Happy Father's Day. Your son, Spike
SCHULZ

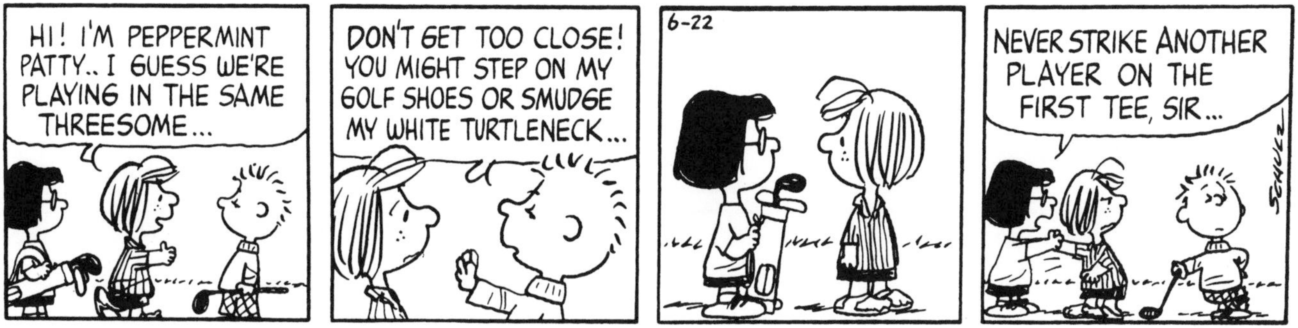
HI! I'M PEPPERMINT PATTY.. I GUESS WE'RE PLAYING IN THE SAME THREESOME...
DON'T GET TOO CLOSE! YOU MIGHT STEP ON MY GOLF SHOES OR SMUDGE MY WHITE TURTLENECK...
6-22
NEVER STRIKE ANOTHER PLAYER ON THE FIRST TEE, SIR...
SCHULZ

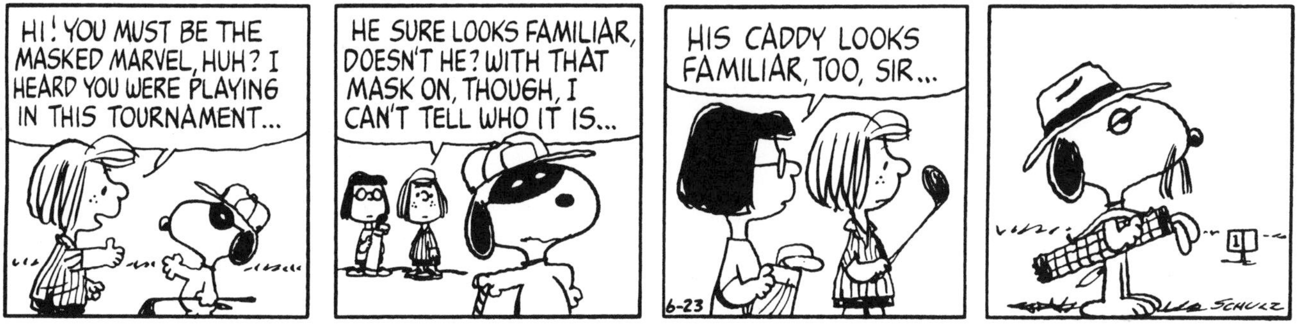
HI! YOU MUST BE THE MASKED MARVEL, HUH? I HEARD YOU WERE PLAYING IN THIS TOURNAMENT...
HE SURE LOOKS FAMILIAR, DOESN'T HE? WITH THAT MASK ON, THOUGH, I CAN'T TELL WHO IT IS...
HIS CADDY LOOKS FAMILIAR, TOO, SIR...
6-23
1
SCHULZ

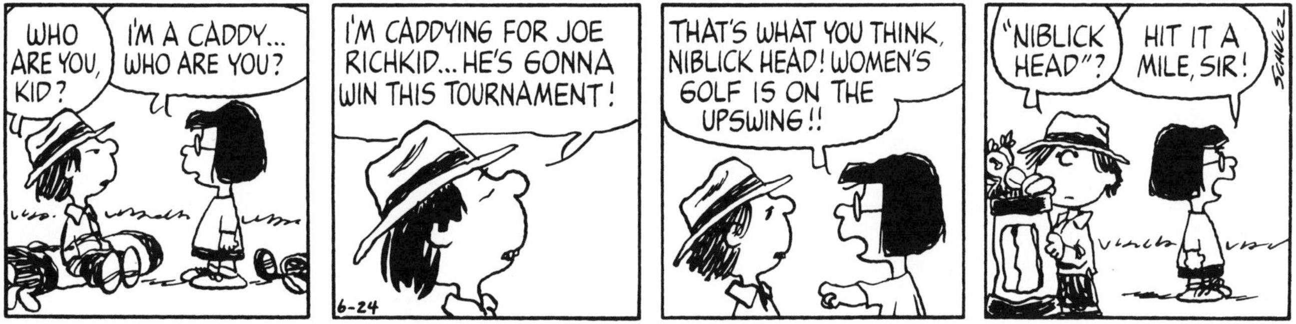
WHO ARE YOU, KID?
I'M A CADDY... WHO ARE YOU?
I'M CADDYING FOR JOE RICHKID... HE'S GONNA WIN THIS TOURNAMENT!
6-24
THAT'S WHAT YOU THINK, NIBLICK HEAD! WOMEN'S GOLF IS ON THE UPSWING!!
"NIBLICK HEAD"?
HIT IT A MILE, SIR!
SCHULZ

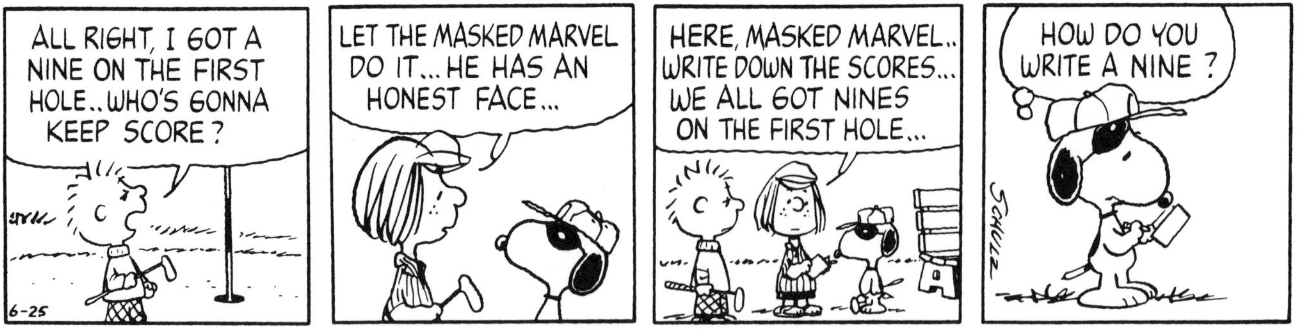
ALL RIGHT, I GOT A NINE ON THE FIRST HOLE..WHO'S GONNA KEEP SCORE?
6-25
LET THE MASKED MARVEL DO IT... HE HAS AN HONEST FACE...
HERE, MASKED MARVEL.. WRITE DOWN THE SCORES... WE ALL GOT NINES ON THE FIRST HOLE...
HOW DO YOU WRITE A NINE?
SCHULZ

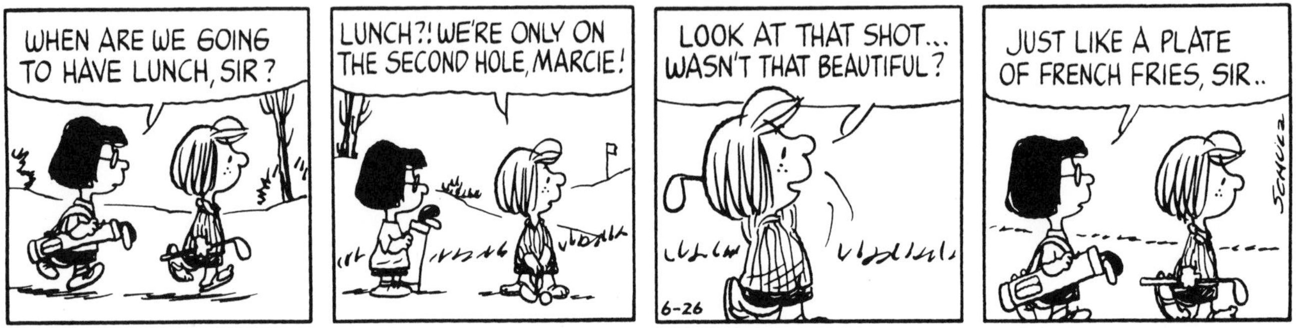
WHEN ARE WE GOING TO HAVE LUNCH, SIR?
LUNCH?! WE'RE ONLY ON THE SECOND HOLE, MARCIE!
LOOK AT THAT SHOT... WASN'T THAT BEAUTIFUL?
6-26
JUST LIKE A PLATE OF FRENCH FRIES, SIR..
SCHULZ

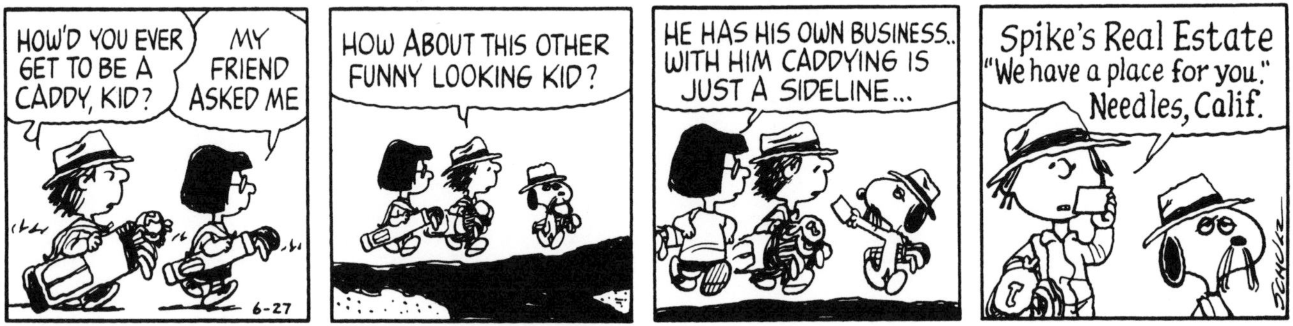
HOW'D YOU EVER GET TO BE A CADDY, KID?
MY FRIEND ASKED ME
6-27
HOW ABOUT THIS OTHER FUNNY LOOKING KID?
HE HAS HIS OWN BUSINESS.. WITH HIM CADDYING IS JUST A SIDELINE...
Spike's Real Estate
"We have a place for you."
Needles, Calif.
SCHULZ

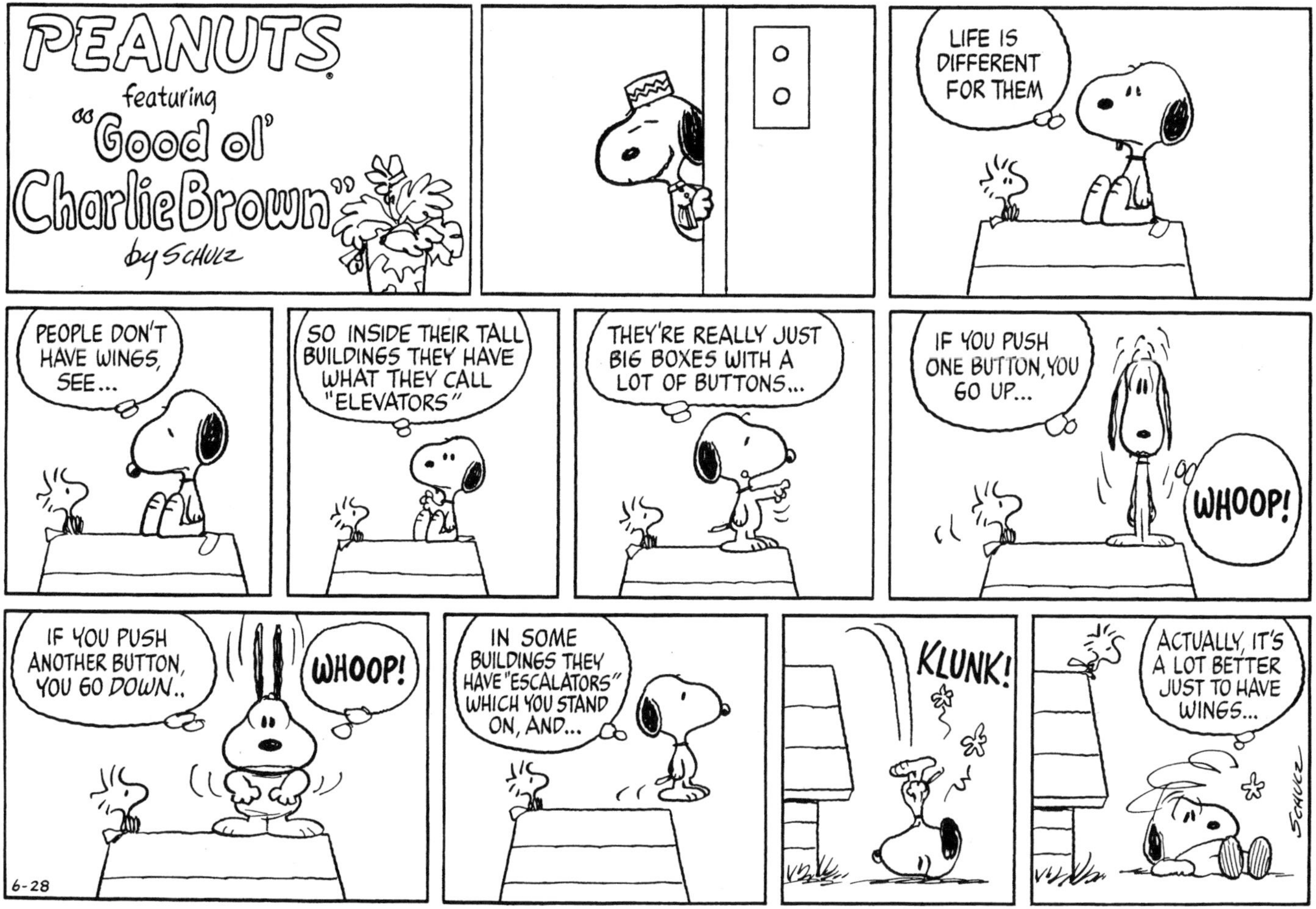
PEANUTS
featuring
"Good ol' CharlieBrown"
by SCHULZ
LIFE IS DIFFERENT FOR THEM
PEOPLE DON'T HAVE WINGS, SEE...
SO INSIDE THEIR TALL BUILDINGS THEY HAVE WHAT THEY CALL "ELEVATORS"
THEY'RE REALLY JUST BIG BOXES WITH A LOT OF BUTTONS...
IF YOU PUSH ONE BUTTON, YOU GO UP...
WHOOP!
IF YOU PUSH ANOTHER BUTTON, YOU GO DOWN..
WHOOP!
6-28
IN SOME BUILDINGS THEY HAVE "ESCALATORS" WHICH YOU STAND ON, AND...
KLUNK!
ACTUALLY, IT'S A LOT BETTER JUST TO HAVE WINGS...
SCHULZ

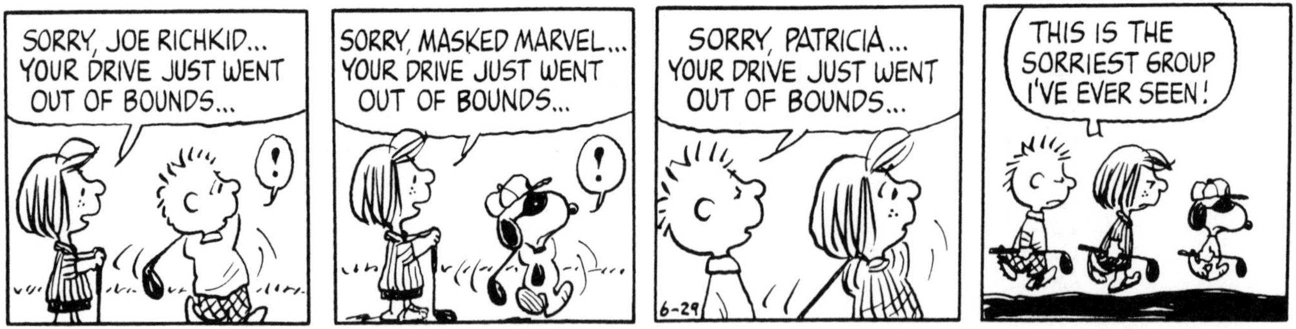
SORRY, JOE RICHKID... YOUR DRIVE JUST WENT OUT OF BOUNDS...
!
SORRY, MASKED MARVEL... YOUR DRIVE JUST WENT OUT OF BOUNDS...
!
SORRY, PATRICIA... YOUR DRIVE JUST WENT OUT OF BOUNDS...
THIS IS THE SORRIEST GROUP I'VE EVER SEEN!

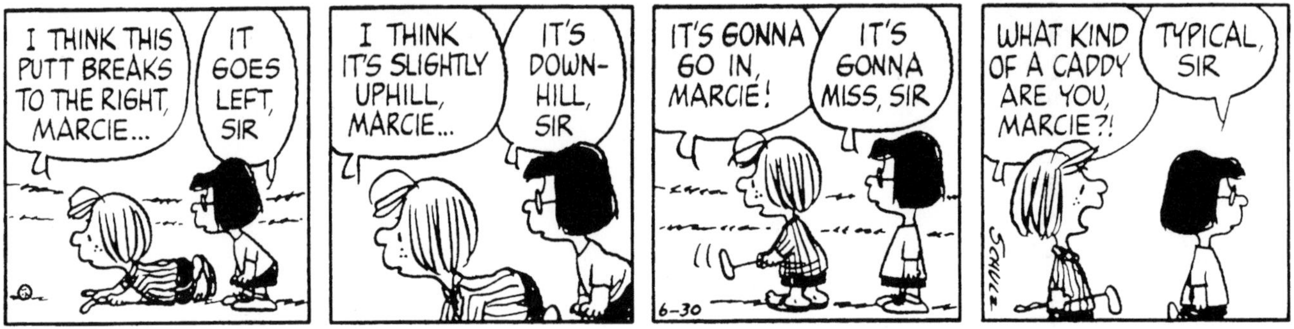
I THINK THIS PUTT BREAKS TO THE RIGHT, MARCIE...
IT GOES LEFT, SIR
I THINK IT'S SLIGHTLY UPHILL, MARCIE...
IT'S DOWNHILL, SIR
IT'S GONNA GO IN, MARCIE!
IT'S GONNA MISS, SIR
WHAT KIND OF A CADDY ARE YOU, MARCIE?!
TYPICAL, SIR

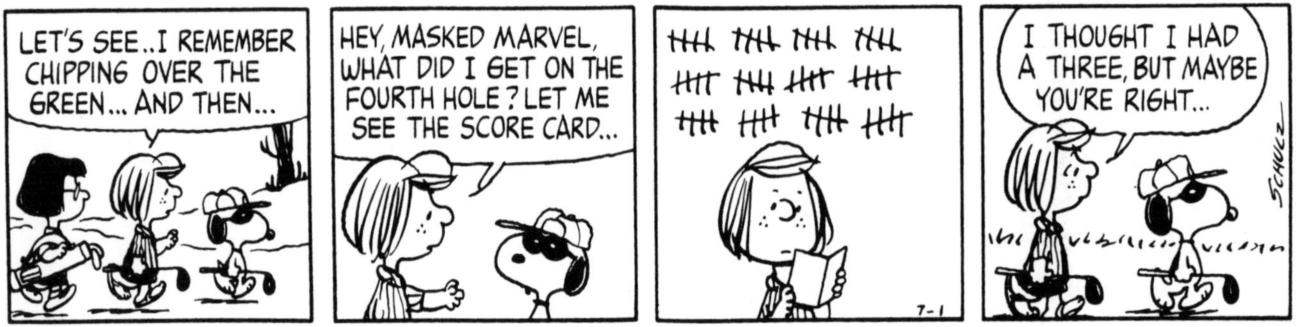
LET'S SEE..I REMEMBER CHIPPING OVER THE GREEN... AND THEN...
HEY, MASKED MARVEL, WHAT DID I GET ON THE FOURTH HOLE? LET ME SEE THE SCORE CARD...
I THOUGHT I HAD A THREE, BUT MAYBE YOU'RE RIGHT...

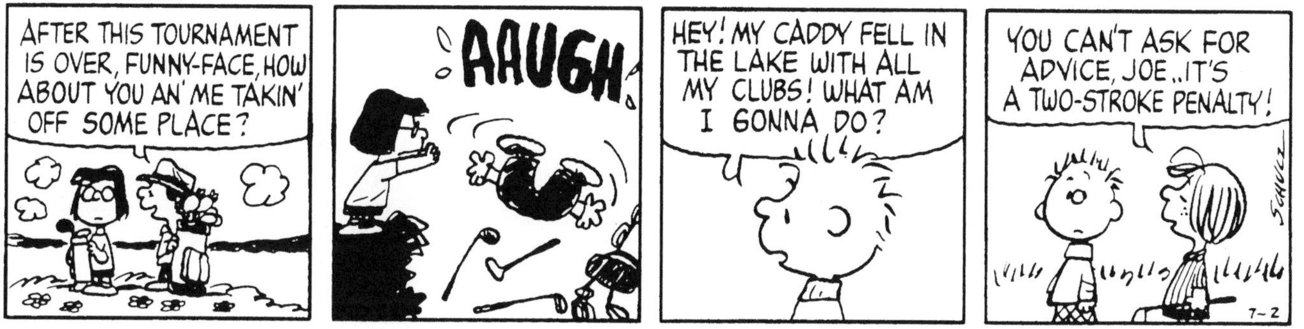
AFTER THIS TOURNAMENT IS OVER, FUNNY-FACE, HOW ABOUT YOU AN' ME TAKIN' OFF SOME PLACE?
AAUGH
HEY! MY CADDY FELL IN THE LAKE WITH ALL MY CLUBS! WHAT AM I GONNA DO?
YOU CAN'T ASK FOR ADVICE, JOE.. IT'S A TWO-STROKE PENALTY!
SCHULZ
7-2

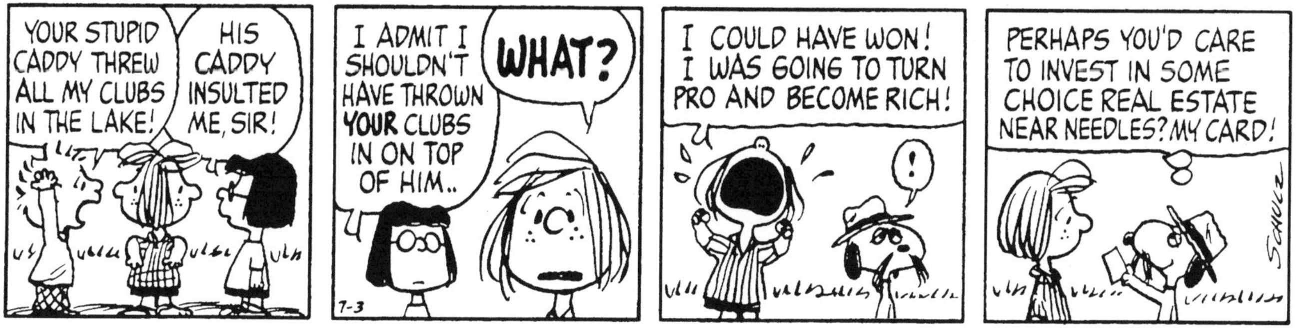
YOUR STUPID CADDY THREW ALL MY CLUBS IN THE LAKE!
HIS CADDY INSULTED ME, SIR!
I ADMIT I SHOULDN'T HAVE THROWN YOUR CLUBS IN ON TOP OF HIM..
WHAT?
7-3
I COULD HAVE WON! I WAS GOING TO TURN PRO AND BECOME RICH!
!
PERHAPS YOU'D CARE TO INVEST IN SOME CHOICE REAL ESTATE NEAR NEEDLES? MY CARD!
SCHULZ

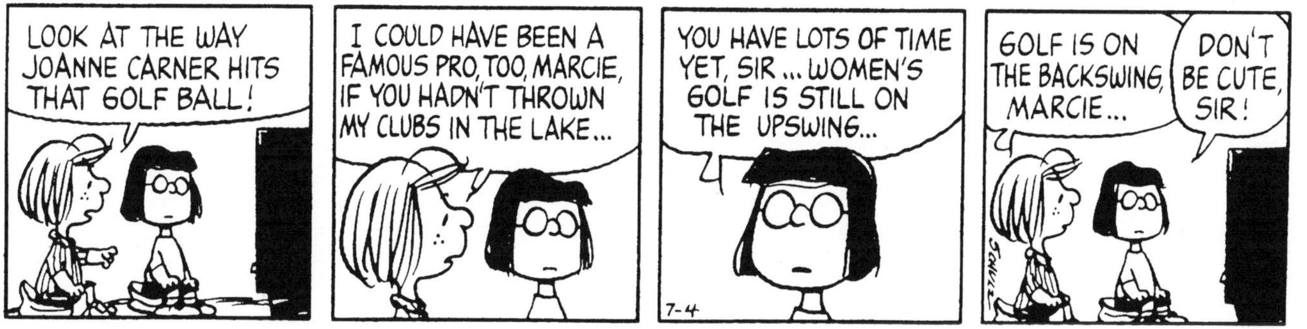
LOOK AT THE WAY JOANNE CARNER HITS THAT GOLF BALL!
I COULD HAVE BEEN A FAMOUS PRO, TOO, MARCIE, IF YOU HADN'T THROWN MY CLUBS IN THE LAKE...
YOU HAVE LOTS OF TIME YET, SIR ... WOMEN'S GOLF IS STILL ON THE UPSWING...
7-4
GOLF IS ON THE BACKSWING, MARCIE...
DON'T BE CUTE, SIR!
SCHULZ

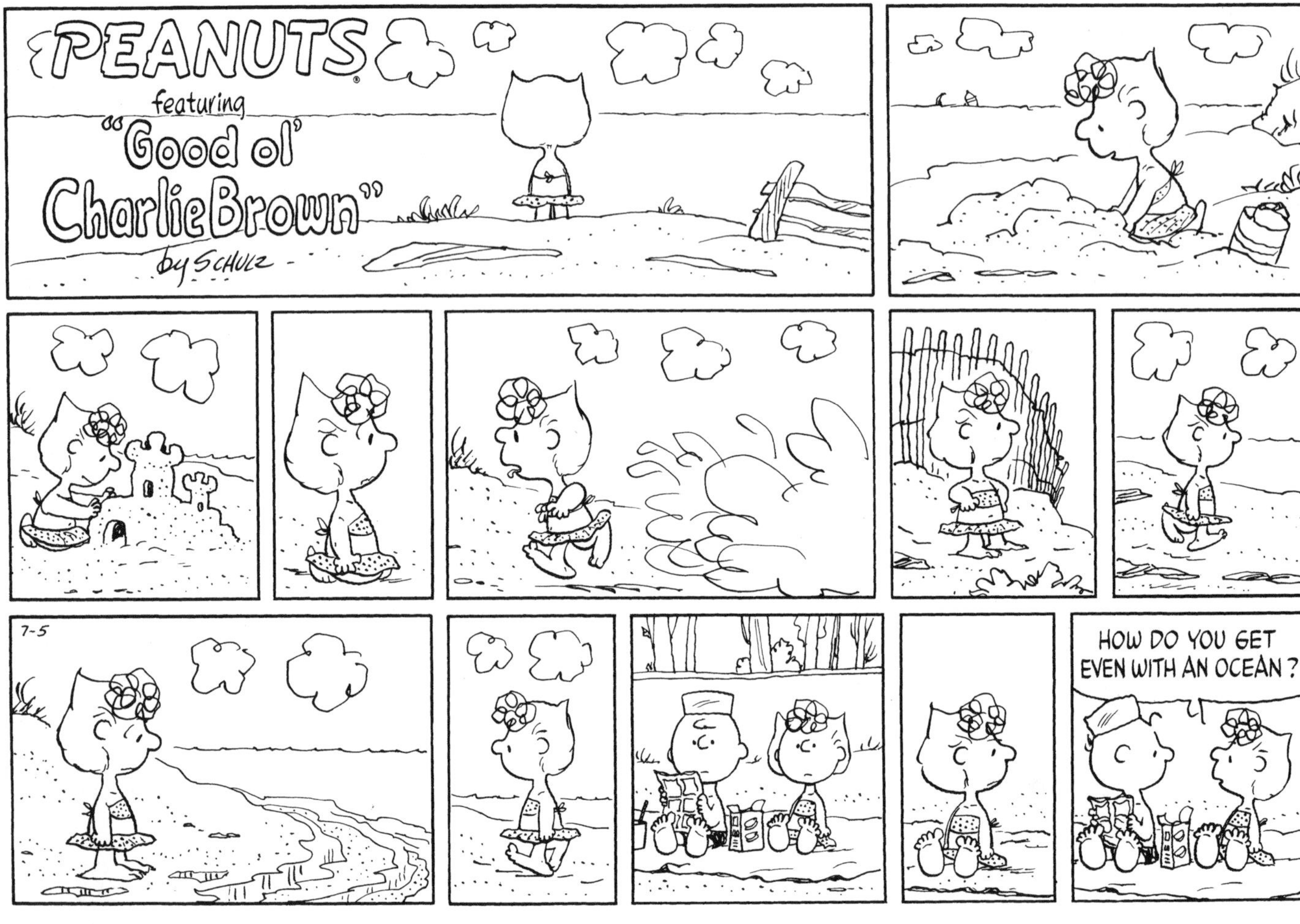
PEANUTS
featuring
"Good ol' Charlie Brown"
by SCHULZ
7-5
HOW DO YOU GET EVEN WITH AN OCEAN ?
SCHULZ

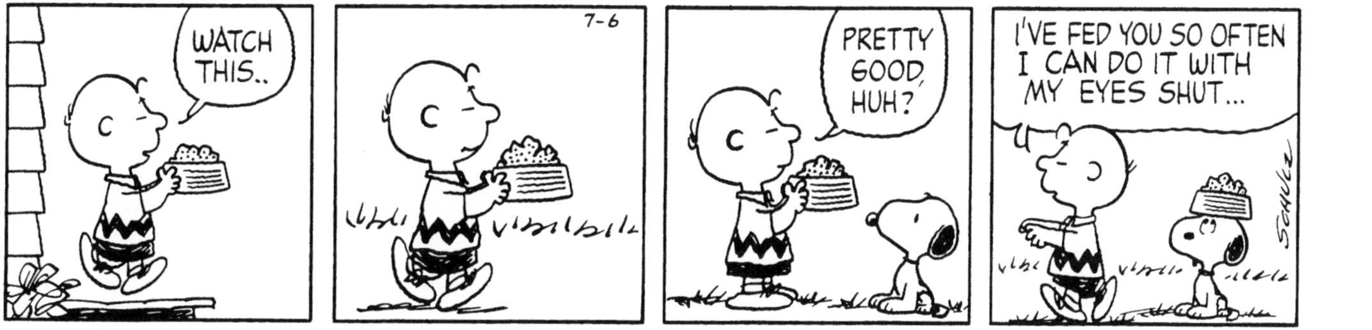
WATCH THIS..
7-6
PRETTY GOOD, HUH?
I'VE FED YOU SO OFTEN I CAN DO IT WITH MY EYES SHUT...
SCHULZ

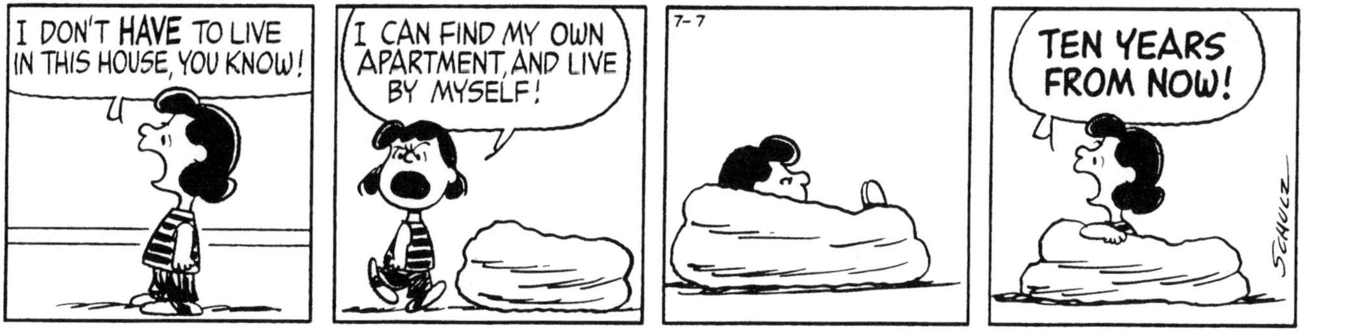
I DON'T HAVE TO LIVE IN THIS HOUSE, YOU KNOW!
I CAN FIND MY OWN APARTMENT, AND LIVE BY MYSELF!
7-7
TEN YEARS FROM NOW!
SCHULZ

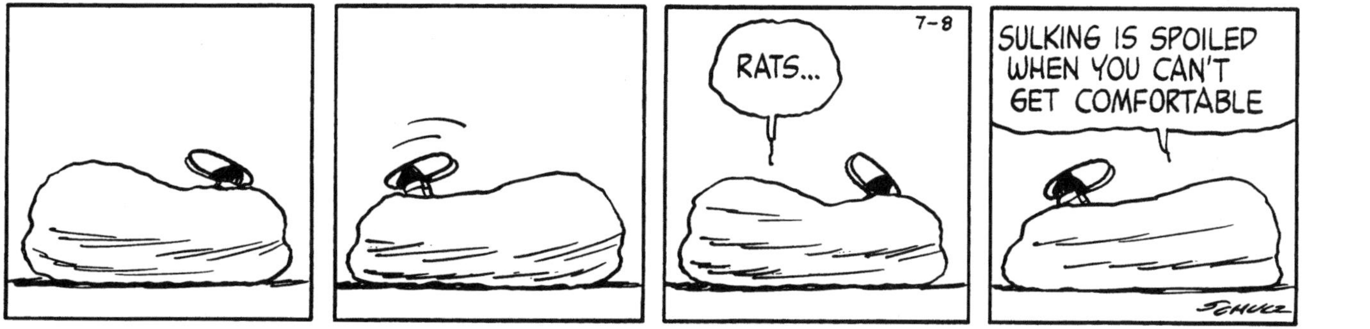
7-8
RATS...
SULKING IS SPOILED WHEN YOU CAN'T GET COMFORTABLE
SCHULZ

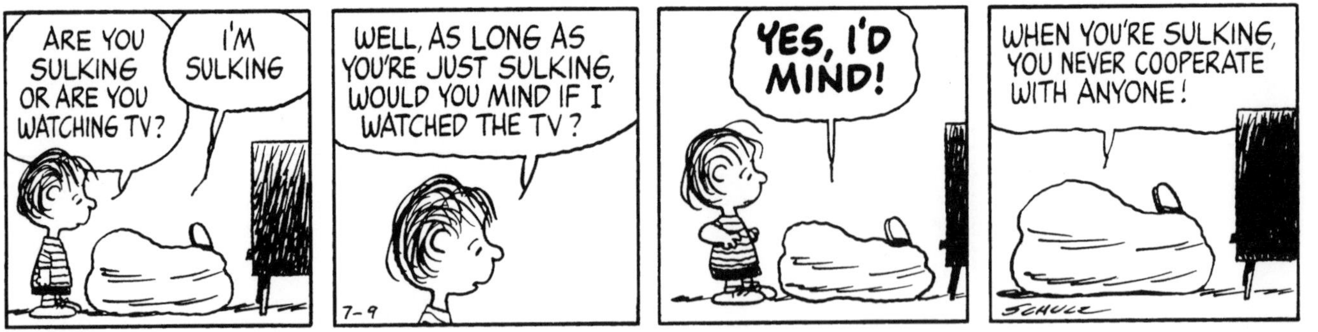
ARE YOU SULKING OR ARE YOU WATCHING TV?
I'M SULKING
WELL, AS LONG AS YOU'RE JUST SULKING, WOULD YOU MIND IF I WATCHED THE TV?
7-9
YES, I'D MIND!
WHEN YOU'RE SULKING, YOU NEVER COOPERATE WITH ANYONE!
SCHULZ

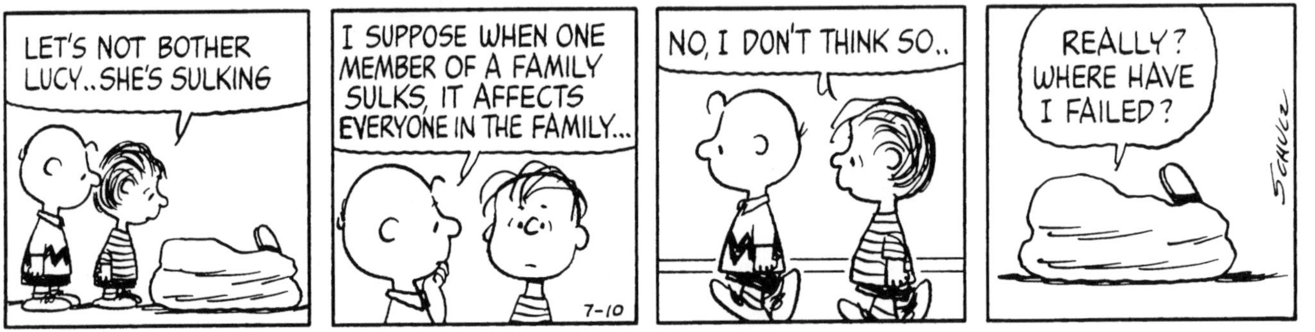
LET'S NOT BOTHER LUCY..SHE'S SULKING
I SUPPOSE WHEN ONE MEMBER OF A FAMILY SULKS, IT AFFECTS EVERYONE IN THE FAMILY...
7-10
NO, I DON'T THINK SO..
REALLY? WHERE HAVE I FAILED?
SCHULZ

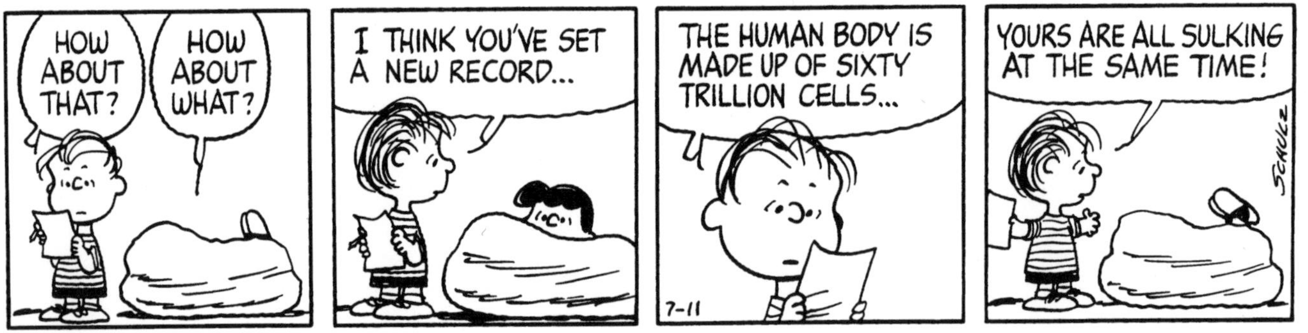
HOW ABOUT THAT?
HOW ABOUT WHAT?
I THINK YOU'VE SET A NEW RECORD...
THE HUMAN BODY IS MADE UP OF SIXTY TRILLION CELLS...
7-11
YOURS ARE ALL SULKING AT THE SAME TIME!
SCHULZ

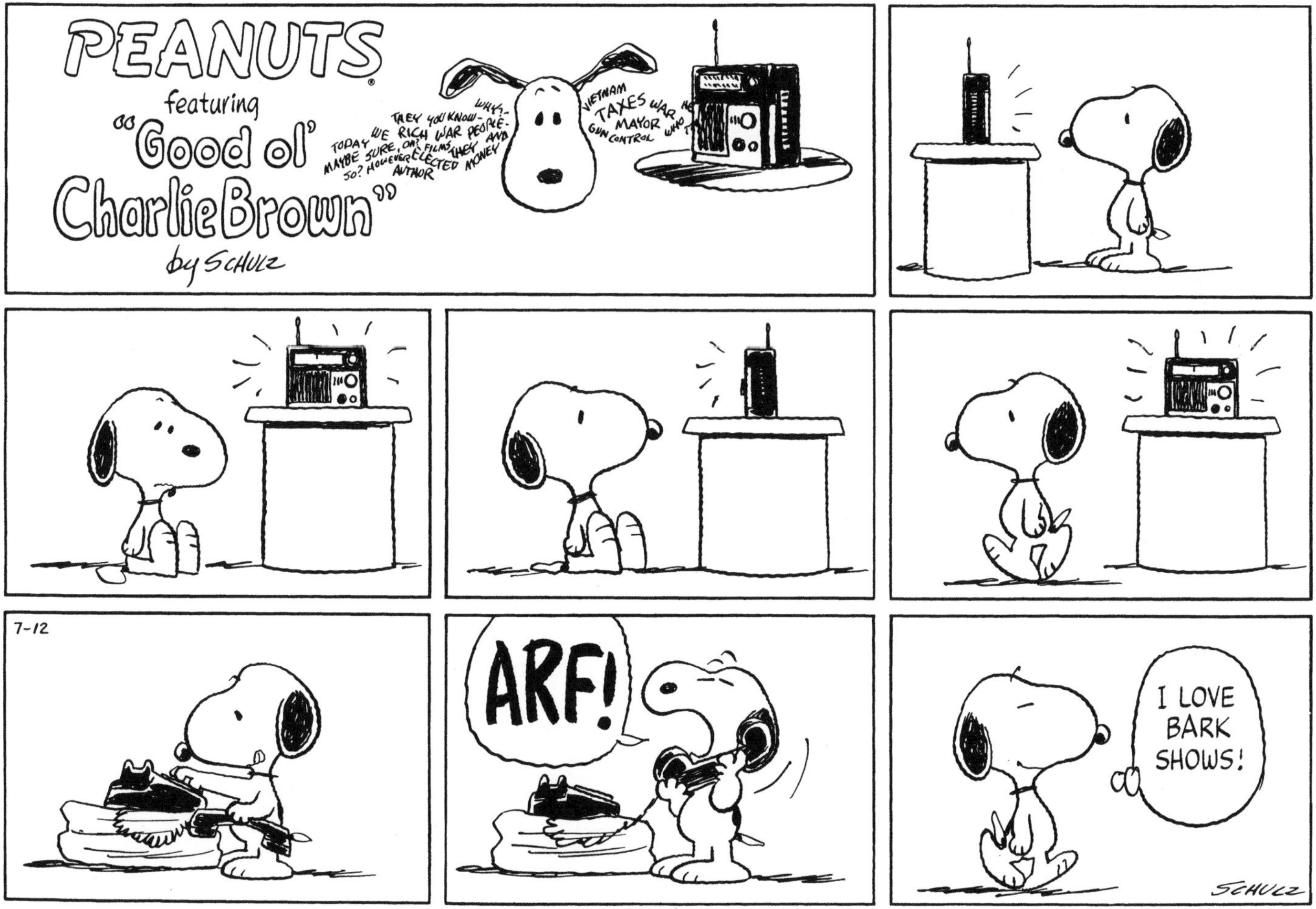
PEANUTS
featuring
"Good ol' Charlie Brown"
by SCHULZ
7-12
ARF!
I LOVE BARK SHOWS!
SCHULZ

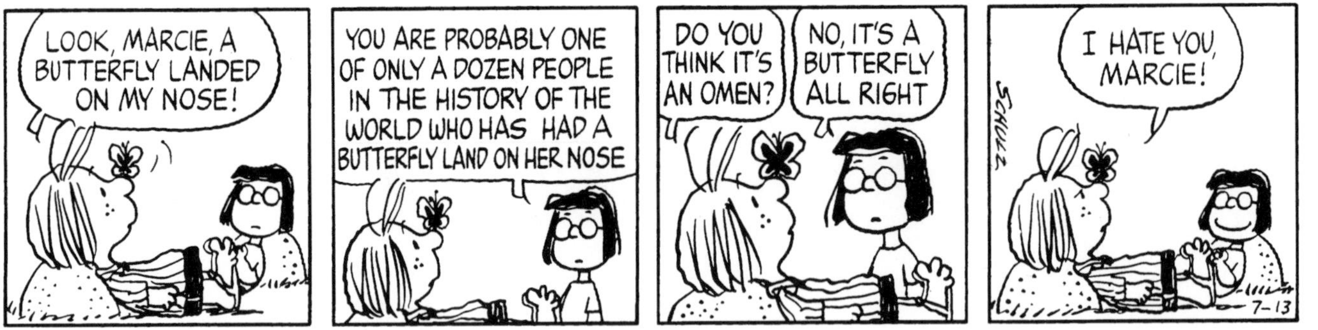
LOOK, MARCIE, A BUTTERFLY LANDED ON MY NOSE!
YOU ARE PROBABLY ONE OF ONLY A DOZEN PEOPLE IN THE HISTORY OF THE WORLD WHO HAS HAD A BUTTERFLY LAND ON HER NOSE
DO YOU THINK IT'S AN OMEN?
NO, IT'S A BUTTERFLY ALL RIGHT
SCHULZ
I HATE YOU, MARCIE!
7-13

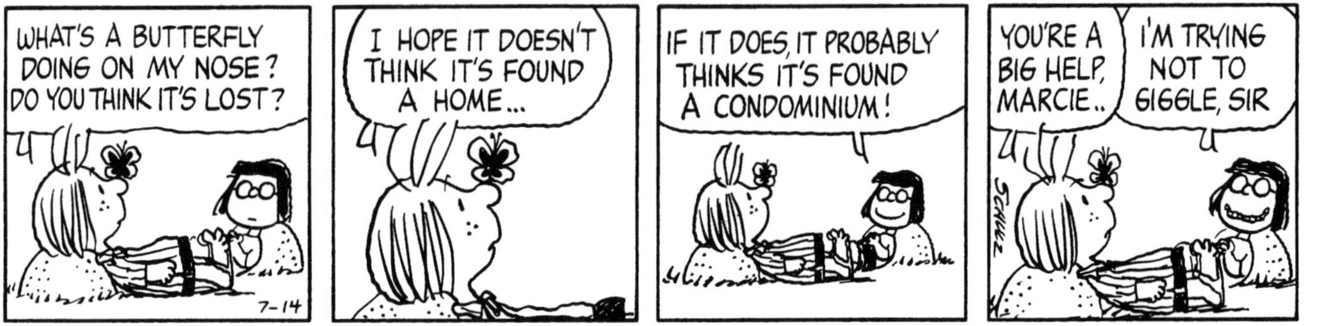
WHAT'S A BUTTERFLY DOING ON MY NOSE? DO YOU THINK IT'S LOST?
7-14
I HOPE IT DOESN'T THINK IT'S FOUND A HOME...
IF IT DOES, IT PROBABLY THINKS IT'S FOUND A CONDOMINIUM!
YOU'RE A BIG HELP, MARCIE..
I'M TRYING NOT TO GIGGLE, SIR
SCHULZ

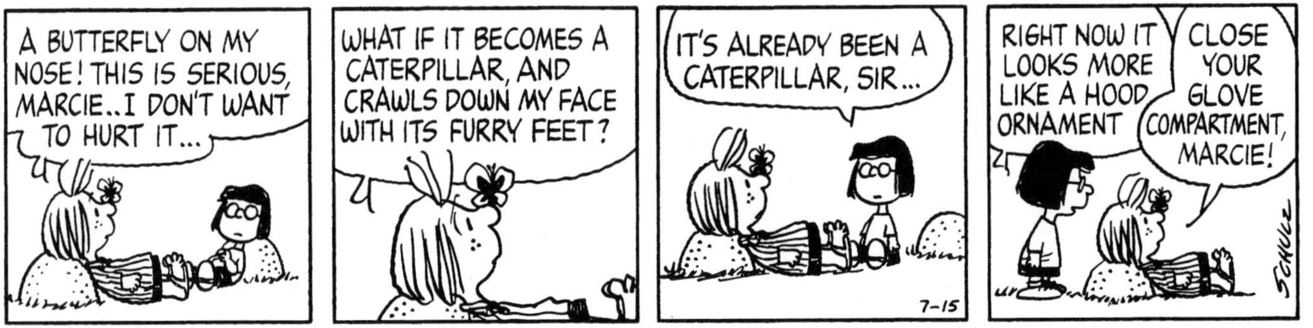
A BUTTERFLY ON MY NOSE! THIS IS SERIOUS, MARCIE..I DON'T WANT TO HURT IT...
WHAT IF IT BECOMES A CATERPILLAR, AND CRAWLS DOWN MY FACE WITH ITS FURRY FEET?
IT'S ALREADY BEEN A CATERPILLAR, SIR...
7-15
RIGHT NOW IT LOOKS MORE LIKE A HOOD ORNAMENT
CLOSE YOUR GLOVE COMPARTMENT, MARCIE!
SCHULZ

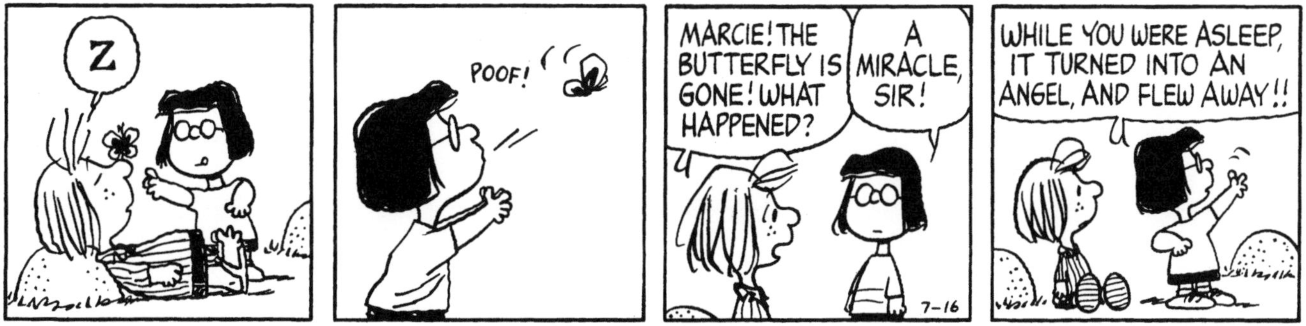
Z
POOF!
MARCIE! THE BUTTERFLY IS GONE! WHAT HAPPENED?
A MIRACLE, SIR!
7-16
WHILE YOU WERE ASLEEP, IT TURNED INTO AN ANGEL, AND FLEW AWAY!!

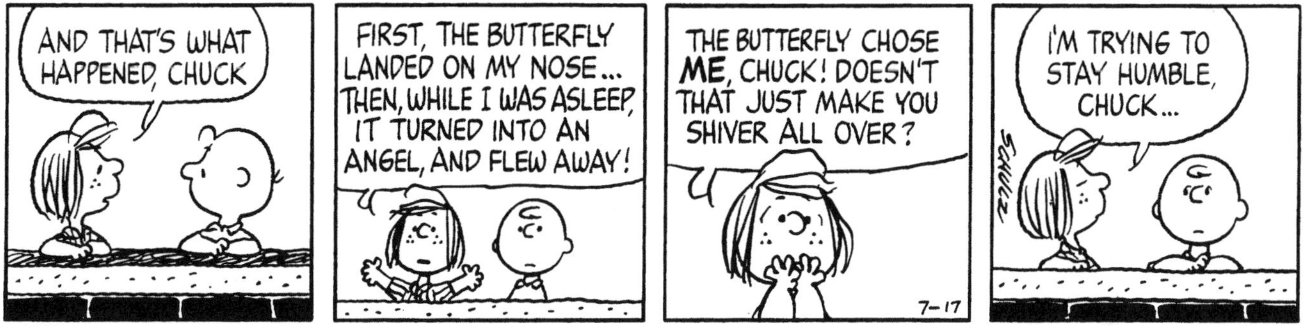
AND THAT'S WHAT HAPPENED, CHUCK
FIRST, THE BUTTERFLY LANDED ON MY NOSE... THEN, WHILE I WAS ASLEEP, IT TURNED INTO AN ANGEL, AND FLEW AWAY!
THE BUTTERFLY CHOSE ME, CHUCK! DOESN'T THAT JUST MAKE YOU SHIVER ALL OVER?
7-17
SCHULZ
I'M TRYING TO STAY HUMBLE, CHUCK...

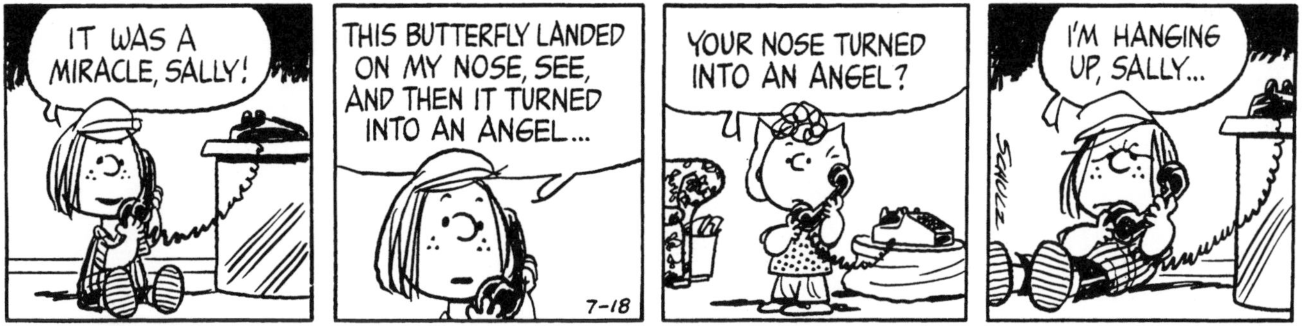
IT WAS A MIRACLE, SALLY!
THIS BUTTERFLY LANDED ON MY NOSE, SEE, AND THEN IT TURNED INTO AN ANGEL...
7-18
YOUR NOSE TURNED INTO AN ANGEL?
SCHULZ
I'M HANGING UP, SALLY...

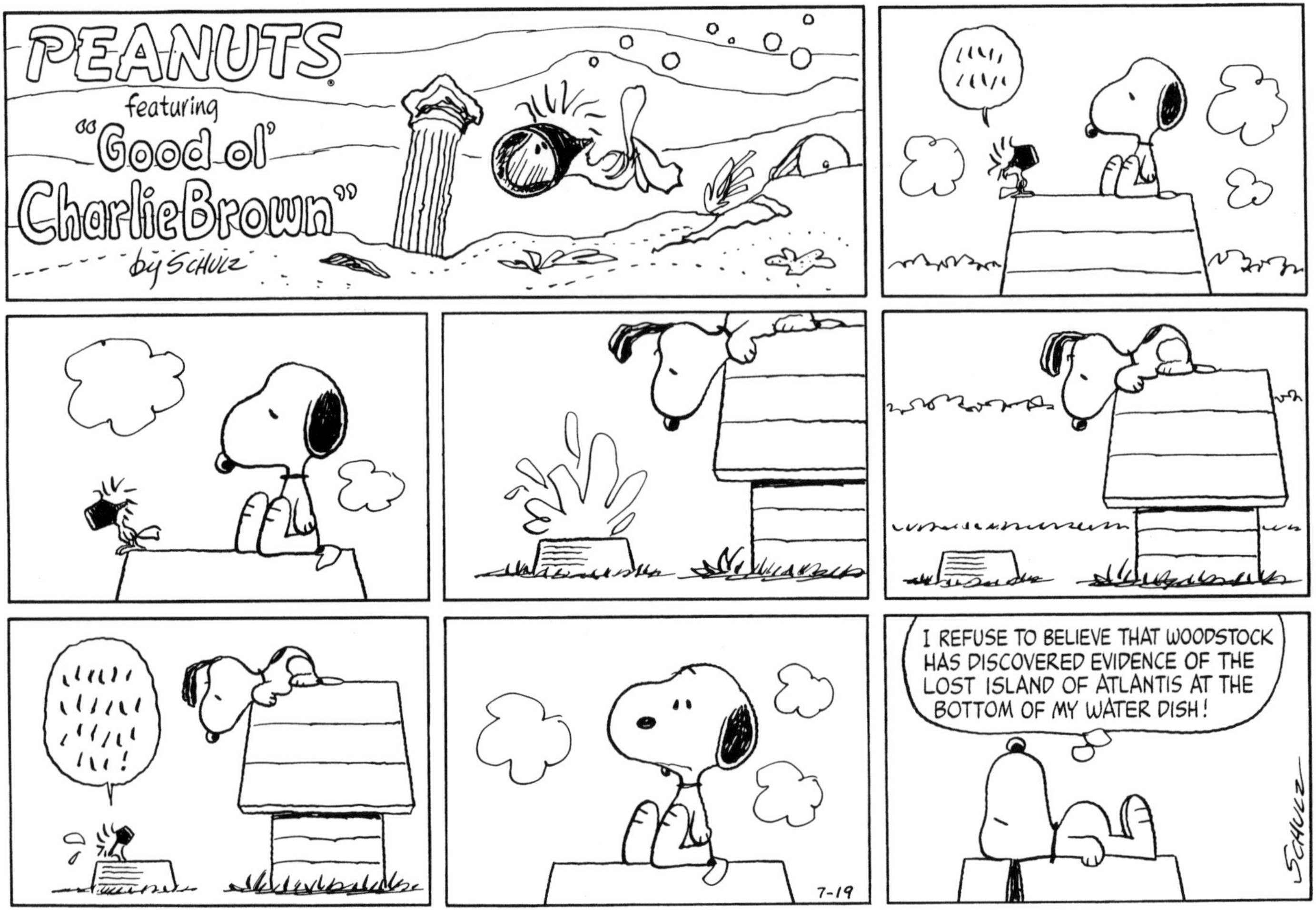
PEANUTS
featuring
"Good ol' CharlieBrown"
by SCHULZ
I REFUSE TO BELIEVE THAT WOODSTOCK HAS DISCOVERED EVIDENCE OF THE LOST ISLAND OF ATLANTIS AT THE BOTTOM OF MY WATER DISH!
7-19
SCHULZ

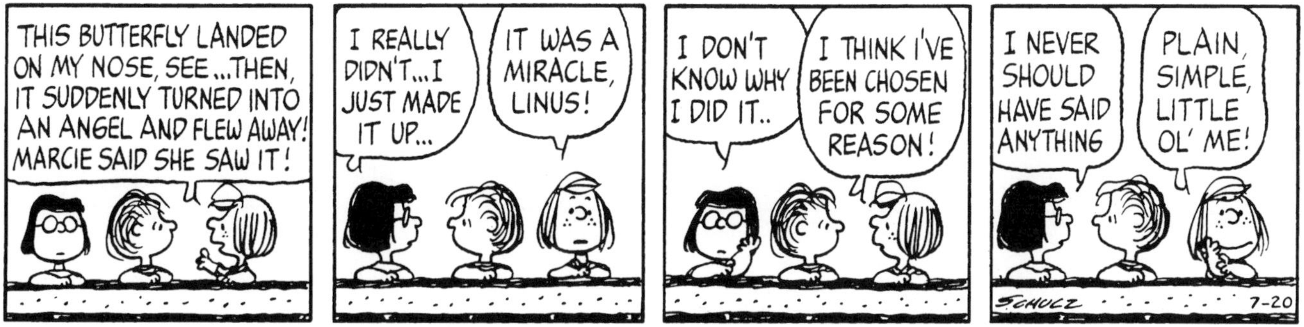
THIS BUTTERFLY LANDED ON MY NOSE, SEE...THEN, IT SUDDENLY TURNED INTO AN ANGEL AND FLEW AWAY! MARCIE SAID SHE SAW IT!
I REALLY DIDN'T...I JUST MADE IT UP...
IT WAS A MIRACLE, LINUS!
I DON'T KNOW WHY I DID IT..
I THINK I'VE BEEN CHOSEN FOR SOME REASON!
I NEVER SHOULD HAVE SAID ANYTHING
PLAIN, SIMPLE, LITTLE OL' ME!
SCHULZ
7-20

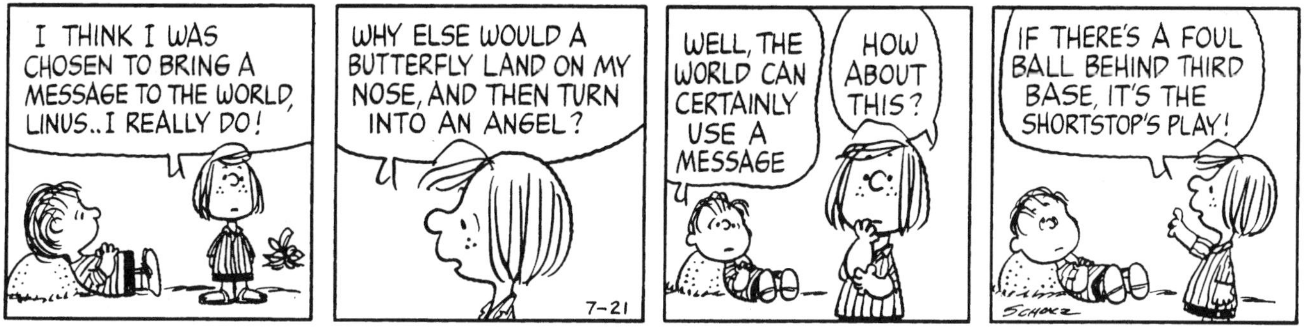
I THINK I WAS CHOSEN TO BRING A MESSAGE TO THE WORLD, LINUS..I REALLY DO!
WHY ELSE WOULD A BUTTERFLY LAND ON MY NOSE, AND THEN TURN INTO AN ANGEL?
7-21
WELL, THE WORLD CAN CERTAINLY USE A MESSAGE
HOW ABOUT THIS?
IF THERE'S A FOUL BALL BEHIND THIRD BASE, IT'S THE SHORTSTOP'S PLAY!
SCHULZ

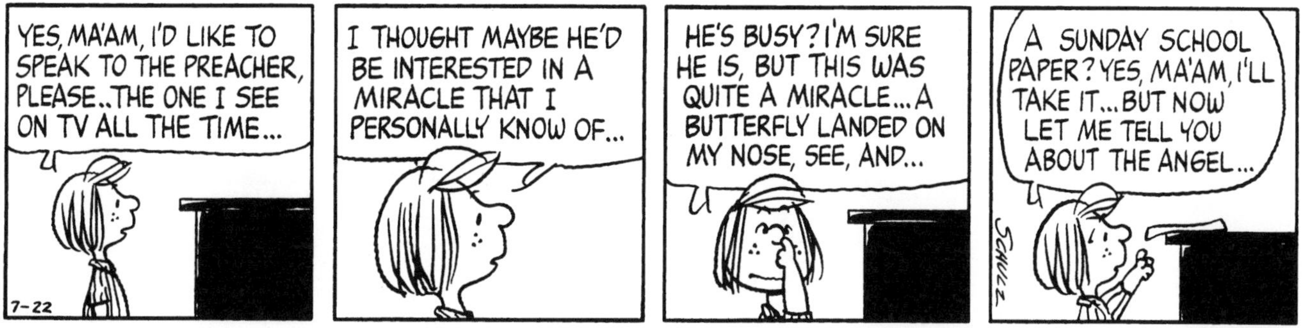
YES, MA'AM, I'D LIKE TO SPEAK TO THE PREACHER, PLEASE..THE ONE I SEE ON TV ALL THE TIME...
7-22
I THOUGHT MAYBE HE'D BE INTERESTED IN A MIRACLE THAT I PERSONALLY KNOW OF...
HE'S BUSY? I'M SURE HE IS, BUT THIS WAS QUITE A MIRACLE...A BUTTERFLY LANDED ON MY NOSE, SEE, AND...
A SUNDAY SCHOOL PAPER? YES, MA'AM, I'LL TAKE IT...BUT NOW LET ME TELL YOU ABOUT THE ANGEL...
SCHULZ

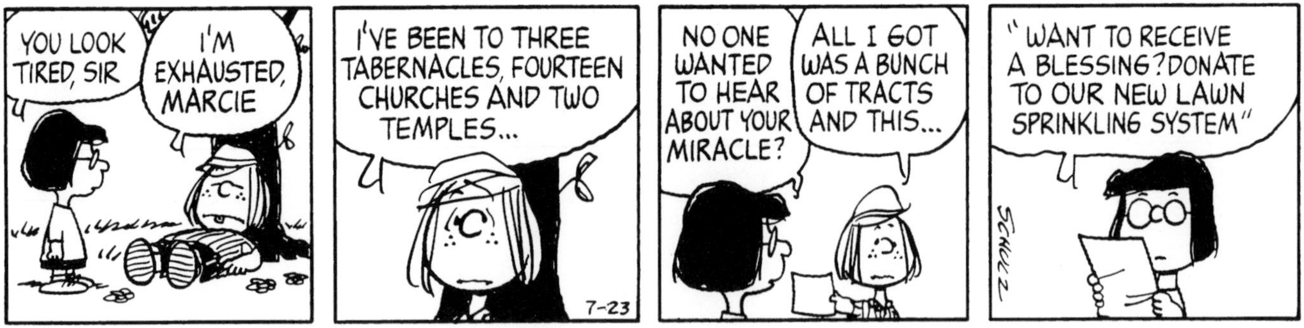

YOU LOOK TIRED, SIR
I'M EXHAUSTED, MARCIE
I'VE BEEN TO THREE TABERNACLES, FOURTEEN CHURCHES AND TWO TEMPLES...
7-23
NO ONE WANTED TO HEAR ABOUT YOUR MIRACLE?
ALL I GOT WAS A BUNCH OF TRACTS AND THIS...
"WANT TO RECEIVE A BLESSING? DONATE TO OUR NEW LAWN SPRINKLING SYSTEM"
SCHULZ

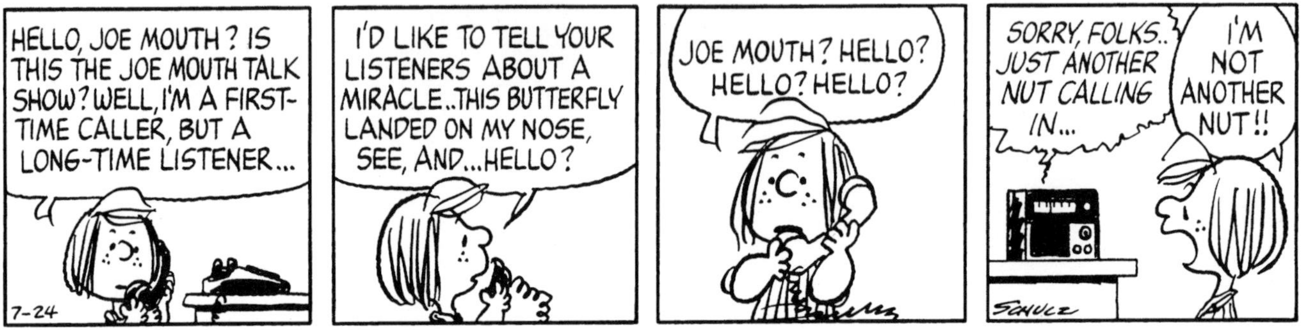

HELLO, JOE MOUTH? IS THIS THE JOE MOUTH TALK SHOW? WELL, I'M A FIRST-TIME CALLER, BUT A LONG-TIME LISTENER...
7-24
I'D LIKE TO TELL YOUR LISTENERS ABOUT A MIRACLE..THIS BUTTERFLY LANDED ON MY NOSE, SEE, AND...HELLO?
JOE MOUTH? HELLO? HELLO? HELLO?
SORRY, FOLKS.. JUST ANOTHER NUT CALLING IN...
I'M NOT ANOTHER NUT!!
SCHULZ

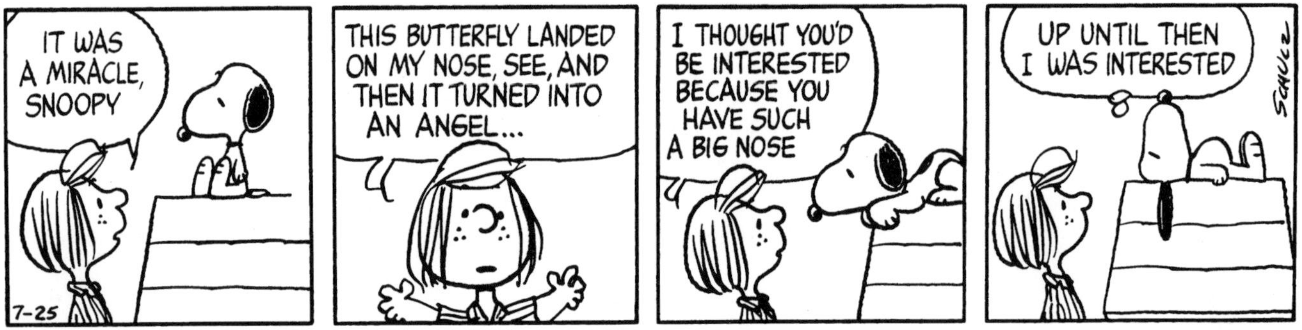

IT WAS A MIRACLE, SNOOPY
7-25
THIS BUTTERFLY LANDED ON MY NOSE, SEE, AND THEN IT TURNED INTO AN ANGEL...
I THOUGHT YOU'D BE INTERESTED BECAUSE YOU HAVE SUCH A BIG NOSE
UP UNTIL THEN I WAS INTERESTED
SCHULZ

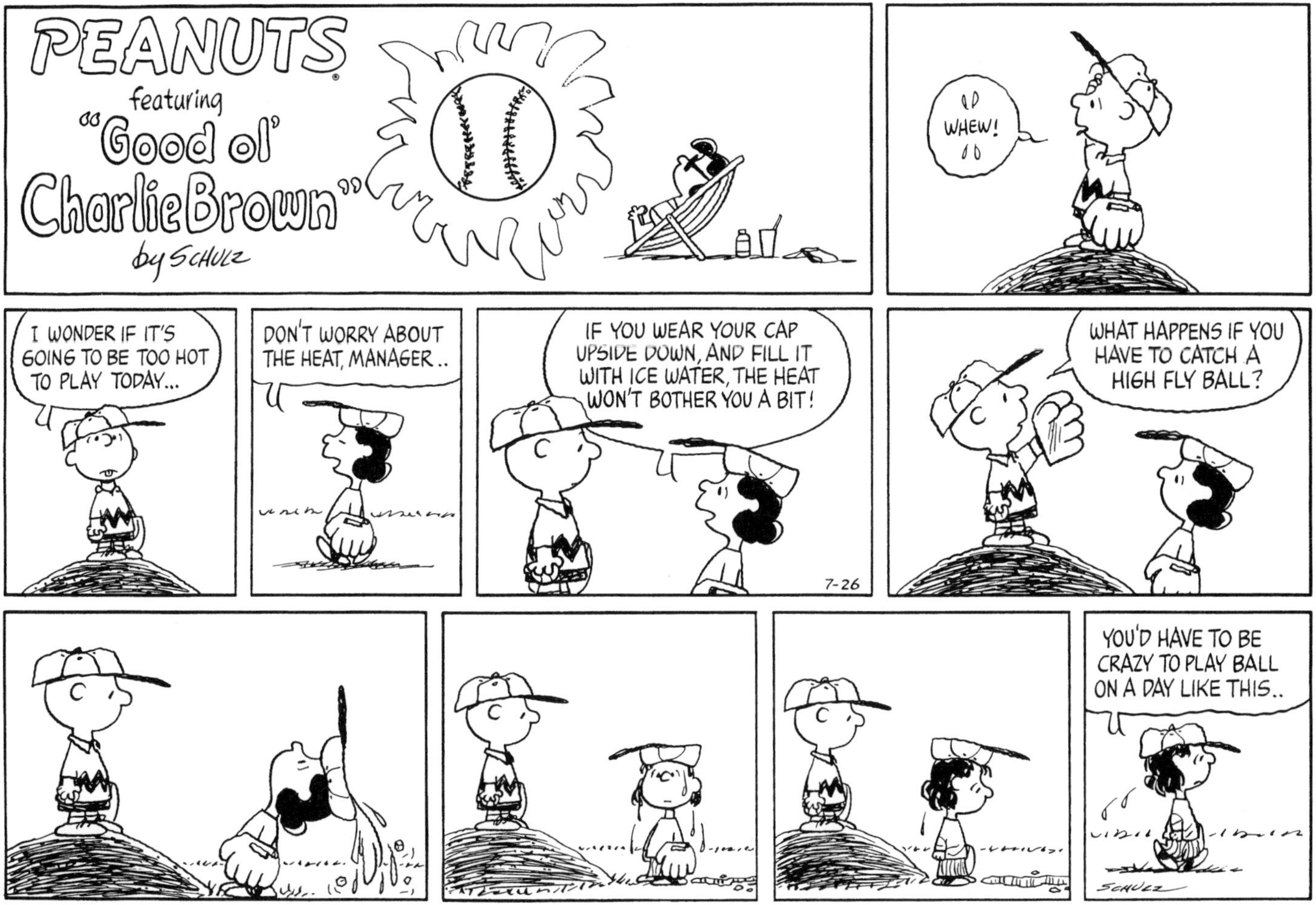
PEANUTS
featuring
"Good ol' Charlie Brown"
by SCHULZ
WHEW!
I WONDER IF IT'S GOING TO BE TOO HOT TO PLAY TODAY...
DON'T WORRY ABOUT THE HEAT, MANAGER..
IF YOU WEAR YOUR CAP UPSIDE DOWN, AND FILL IT WITH ICE WATER, THE HEAT WON'T BOTHER YOU A BIT!
7-26
WHAT HAPPENS IF YOU HAVE TO CATCH A HIGH FLY BALL?
YOU'D HAVE TO BE CRAZY TO PLAY BALL ON A DAY LIKE THIS..
SCHULZ

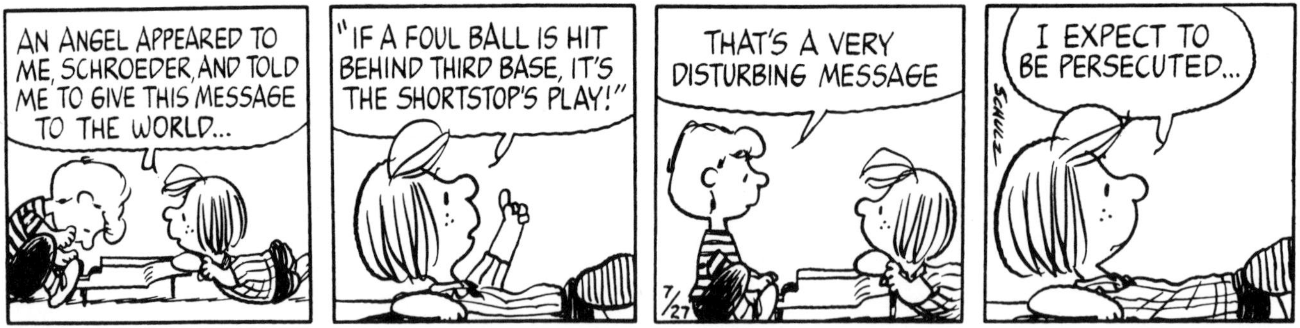
AN ANGEL APPEARED TO ME, SCHROEDER, AND TOLD ME TO GIVE THIS MESSAGE TO THE WORLD...
"IF A FOUL BALL IS HIT BEHIND THIRD BASE, IT'S THE SHORTSTOP'S PLAY!"
THAT'S A VERY DISTURBING MESSAGE
7/27
I EXPECT TO BE PERSECUTED...
SCHULZ

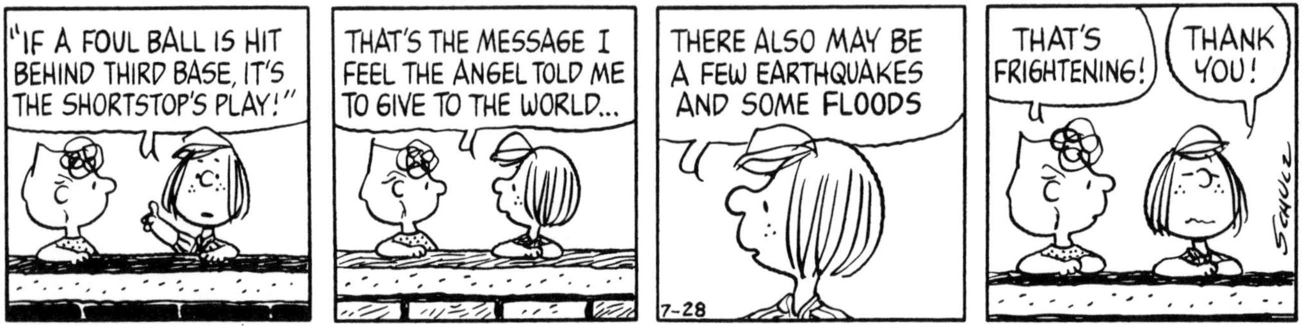
"IF A FOUL BALL IS HIT BEHIND THIRD BASE, IT'S THE SHORTSTOP'S PLAY!"
THAT'S THE MESSAGE I FEEL THE ANGEL TOLD ME TO GIVE TO THE WORLD...
THERE ALSO MAY BE A FEW EARTHQUAKES AND SOME FLOODS
7-28
THAT'S FRIGHTENING!
THANK YOU!
SCHULZ

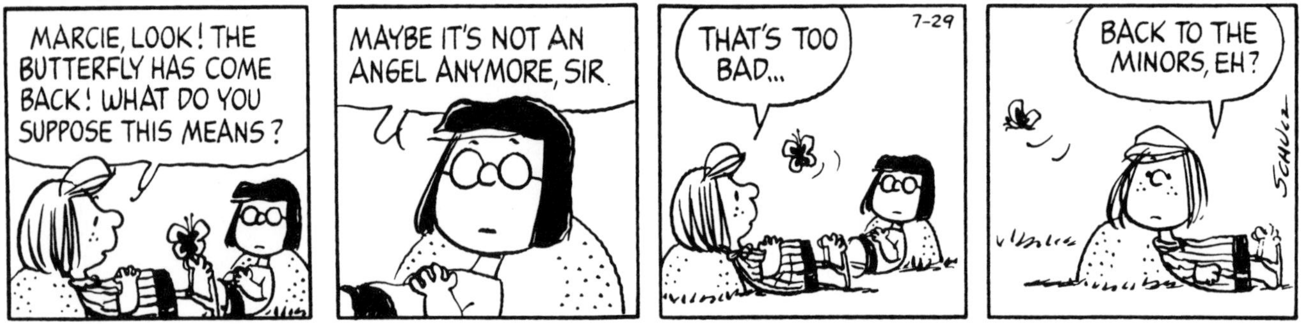
MARCIE, LOOK! THE BUTTERFLY HAS COME BACK! WHAT DO YOU SUPPOSE THIS MEANS?
MAYBE IT'S NOT AN ANGEL ANYMORE, SIR
7-29
THAT'S TOO BAD...
BACK TO THE MINORS, EH?
SCHULZ

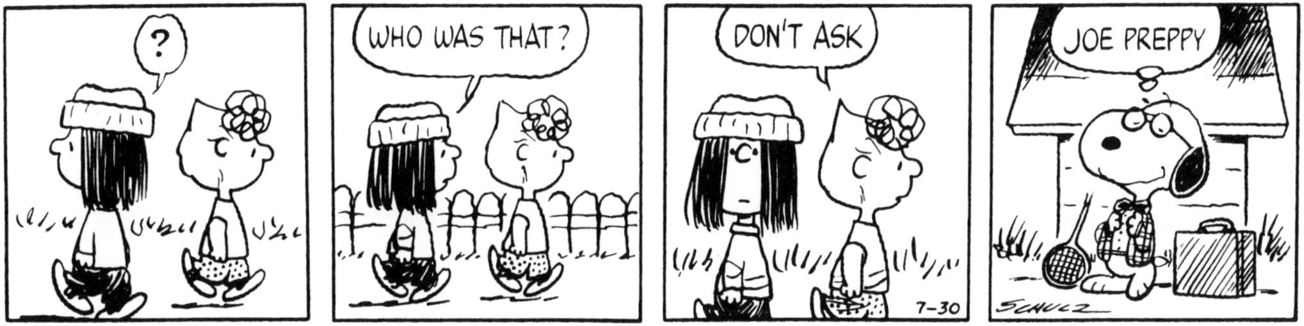
?
WHO WAS THAT?
DON'T ASK
JOE PREPPY

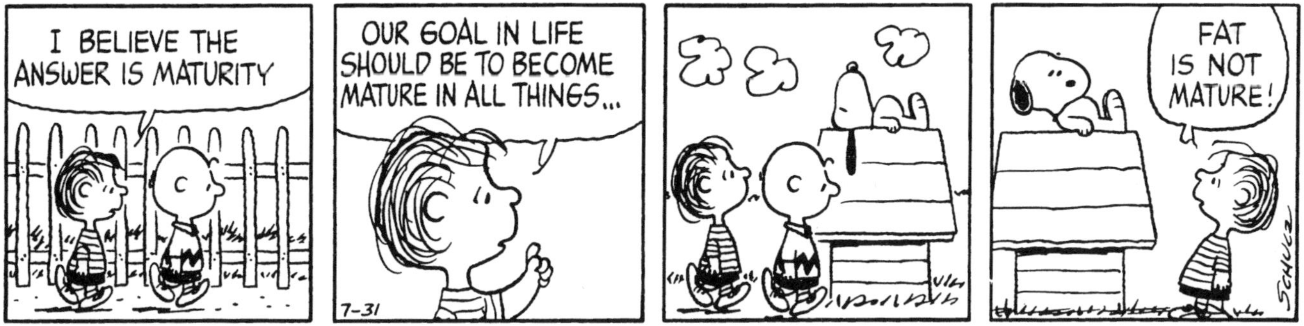
I BELIEVE THE ANSWER IS MATURITY
OUR GOAL IN LIFE SHOULD BE TO BECOME MATURE IN ALL THINGS...
FAT IS NOT MATURE!

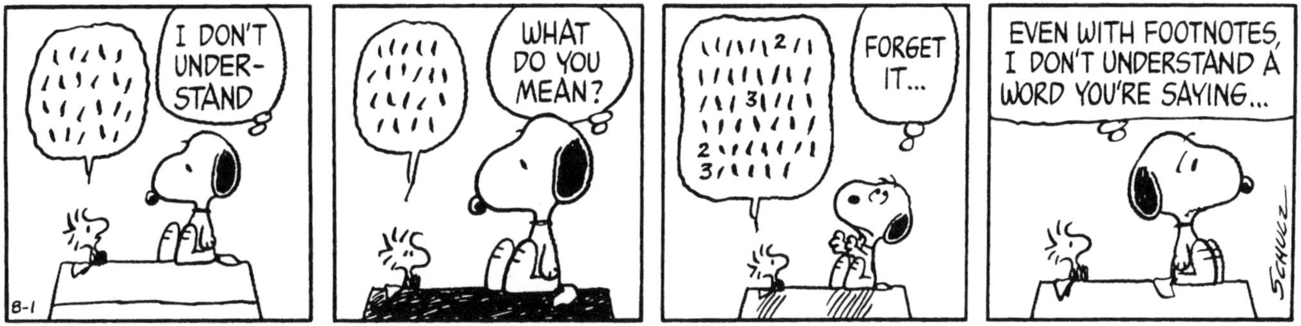
I DON'T UNDER-STAND
WHAT DO YOU MEAN?
FORGET IT...
EVEN WITH FOOTNOTES, I DON'T UNDERSTAND A WORD YOU'RE SAYING...

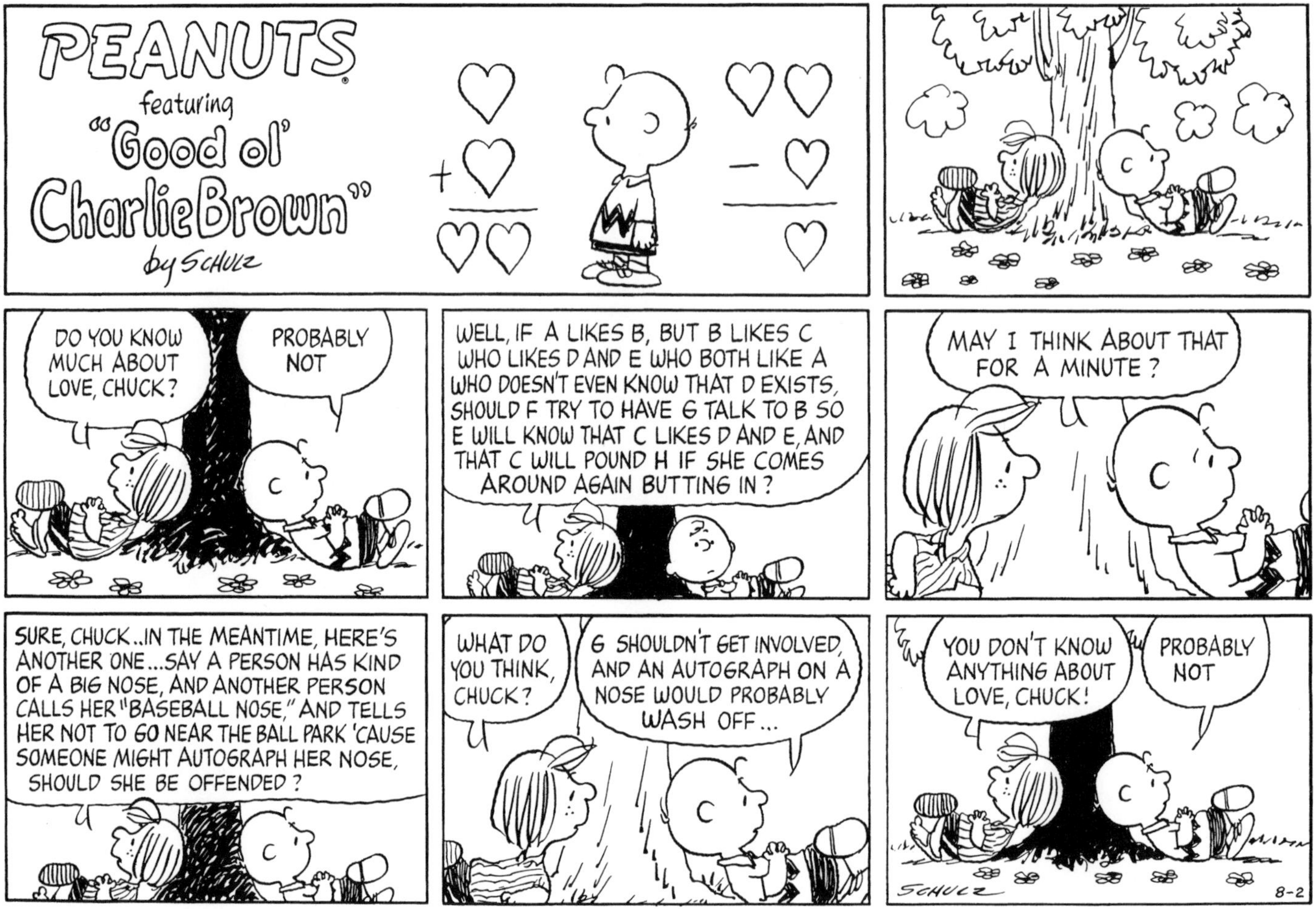
PEANUTS
featuring
"Good ol' CharlieBrown"
by SCHULZ
DO YOU KNOW MUCH ABOUT LOVE, CHUCK?
PROBABLY NOT
WELL, IF A LIKES B, BUT B LIKES C WHO LIKES D AND E WHO BOTH LIKE A WHO DOESN'T EVEN KNOW THAT D EXISTS, SHOULD F TRY TO HAVE G TALK TO B SO E WILL KNOW THAT C LIKES D AND E, AND THAT C WILL POUND H IF SHE COMES AROUND AGAIN BUTTING IN?
MAY I THINK ABOUT THAT FOR A MINUTE?
SURE, CHUCK..IN THE MEANTIME, HERE'S ANOTHER ONE...SAY A PERSON HAS KIND OF A BIG NOSE, AND ANOTHER PERSON CALLS HER "BASEBALL NOSE," AND TELLS HER NOT TO GO NEAR THE BALL PARK 'CAUSE SOMEONE MIGHT AUTOGRAPH HER NOSE, SHOULD SHE BE OFFENDED?
WHAT DO YOU THINK, CHUCK?
G SHOULDN'T GET INVOLVED, AND AN AUTOGRAPH ON A NOSE WOULD PROBABLY WASH OFF...
YOU DON'T KNOW ANYTHING ABOUT LOVE, CHUCK!
PROBABLY NOT
SCHULZ
8-2

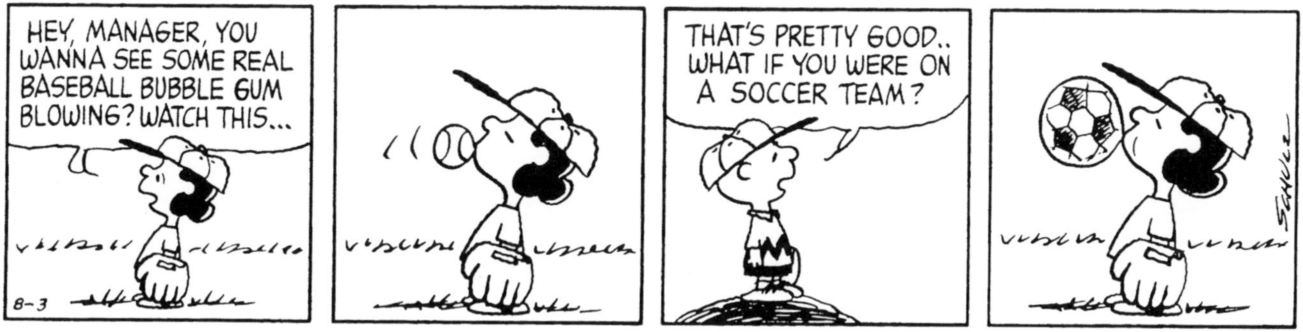
HEY, MANAGER, YOU WANNA SEE SOME REAL BASEBALL BUBBLE GUM BLOWING? WATCH THIS...
8-3
THAT'S PRETTY GOOD.. WHAT IF YOU WERE ON A SOCCER TEAM?
SCHULZ

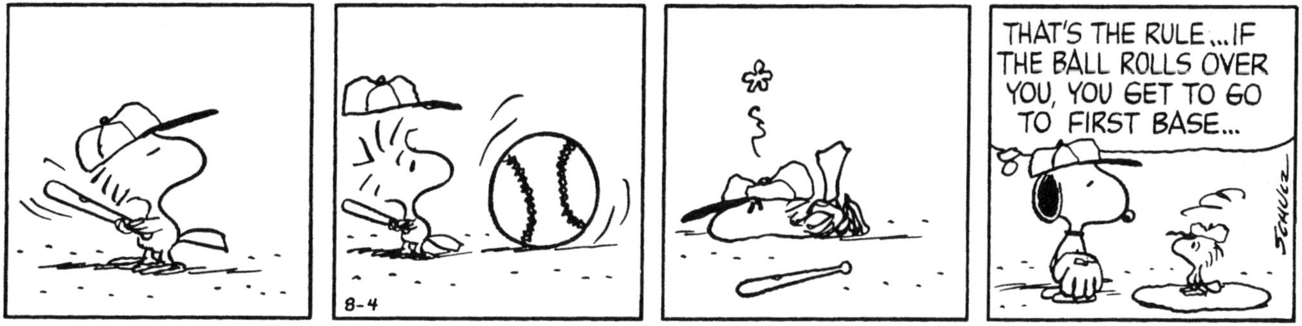
8-4
THAT'S THE RULE...IF THE BALL ROLLS OVER YOU, YOU GET TO GO TO FIRST BASE...
SCHULZ

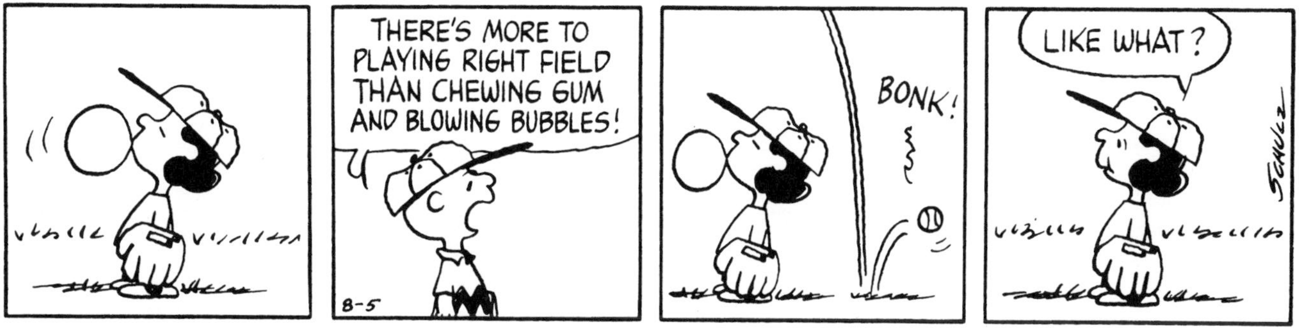
THERE'S MORE TO PLAYING RIGHT FIELD THAN CHEWING GUM AND BLOWING BUBBLES!
8-5
BONK!
LIKE WHAT?
SCHULZ

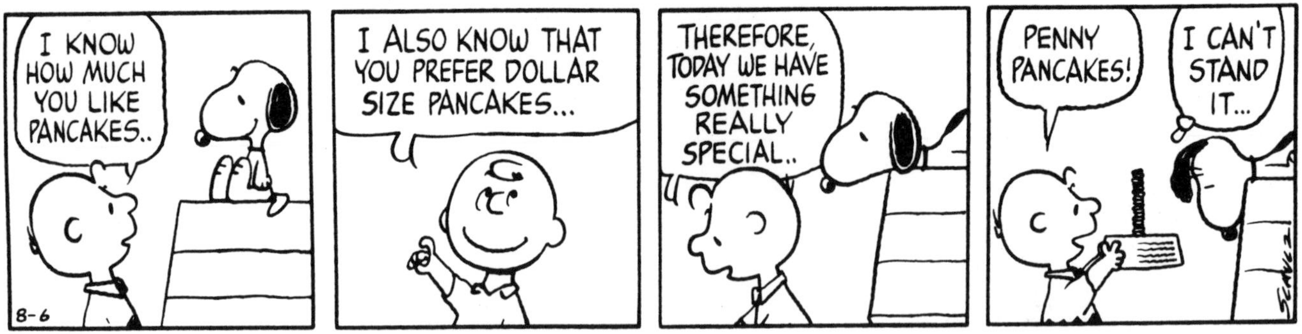
8-6
I KNOW HOW MUCH YOU LIKE PANCAKES..
I ALSO KNOW THAT YOU PREFER DOLLAR SIZE PANCAKES...
THEREFORE, TODAY WE HAVE SOMETHING REALLY SPECIAL..
PENNY PANCAKES!
I CAN'T STAND IT...

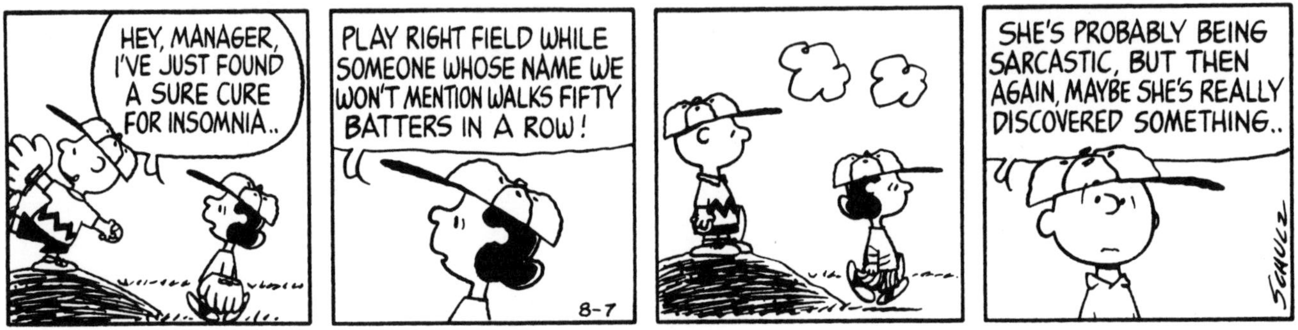
HEY, MANAGER, I'VE JUST FOUND A SURE CURE FOR INSOMNIA..
PLAY RIGHT FIELD WHILE SOMEONE WHOSE NAME WE WON'T MENTION WALKS FIFTY BATTERS IN A ROW!
8-7
SHE'S PROBABLY BEING SARCASTIC, BUT THEN AGAIN, MAYBE SHE'S REALLY DISCOVERED SOMETHING..

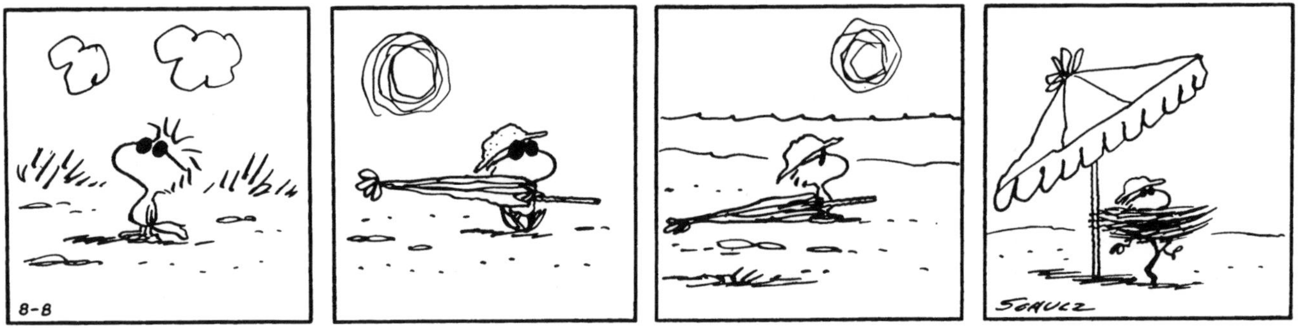
8-8

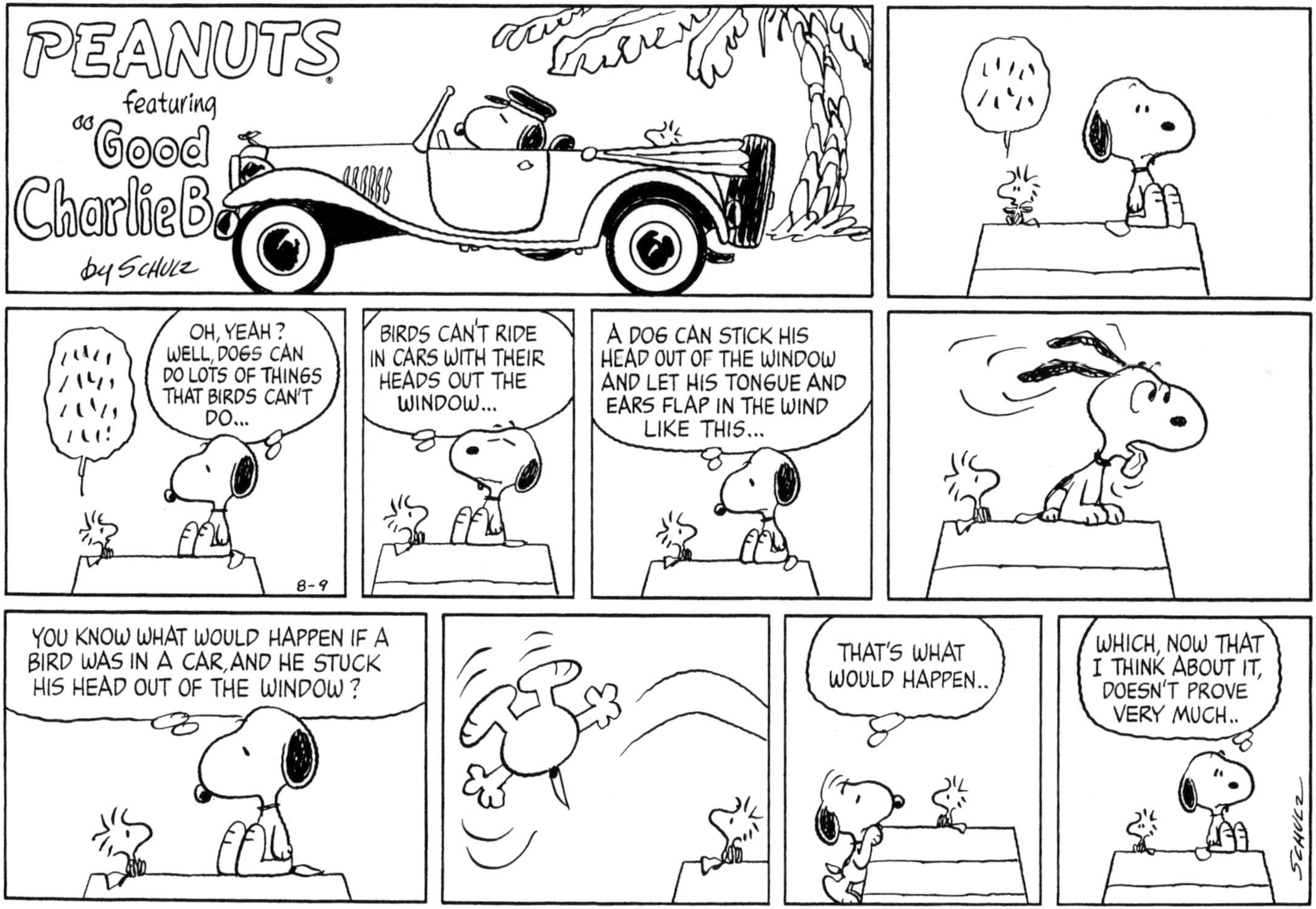
PEANUTS
featuring "Good ol' Charlie Brown"
by SCHULZ
OH, YEAH? WELL, DOGS CAN DO LOTS OF THINGS THAT BIRDS CAN'T DO...
8-9
BIRDS CAN'T RIDE IN CARS WITH THEIR HEADS OUT THE WINDOW...
A DOG CAN STICK HIS HEAD OUT OF THE WINDOW AND LET HIS TONGUE AND EARS FLAP IN THE WIND LIKE THIS...
YOU KNOW WHAT WOULD HAPPEN IF A BIRD WAS IN A CAR, AND HE STUCK HIS HEAD OUT OF THE WINDOW?
THAT'S WHAT WOULD HAPPEN..
WHICH, NOW THAT I THINK ABOUT IT, DOESN'T PROVE VERY MUCH..
SCHULZ

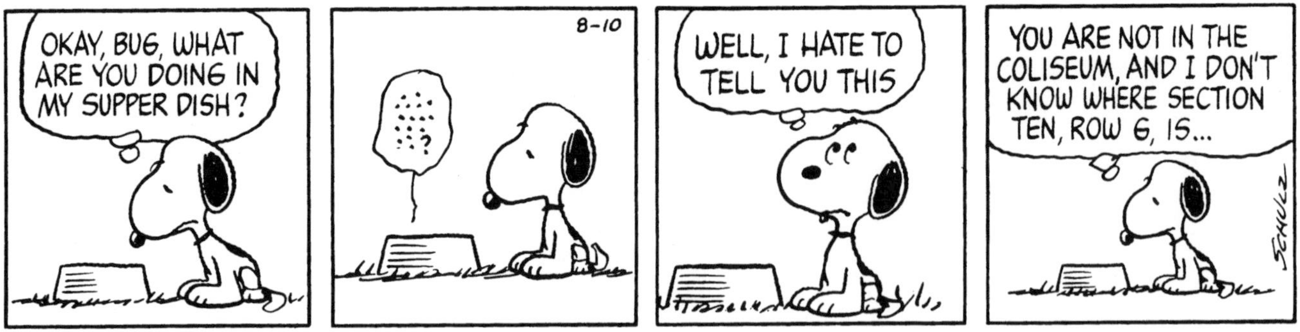
OKAY, BUG, WHAT ARE YOU DOING IN MY SUPPER DISH?
8-10
?
WELL, I HATE TO TELL YOU THIS
YOU ARE NOT IN THE COLISEUM, AND I DON'T KNOW WHERE SECTION TEN, ROW 6, IS...
SCHULZ

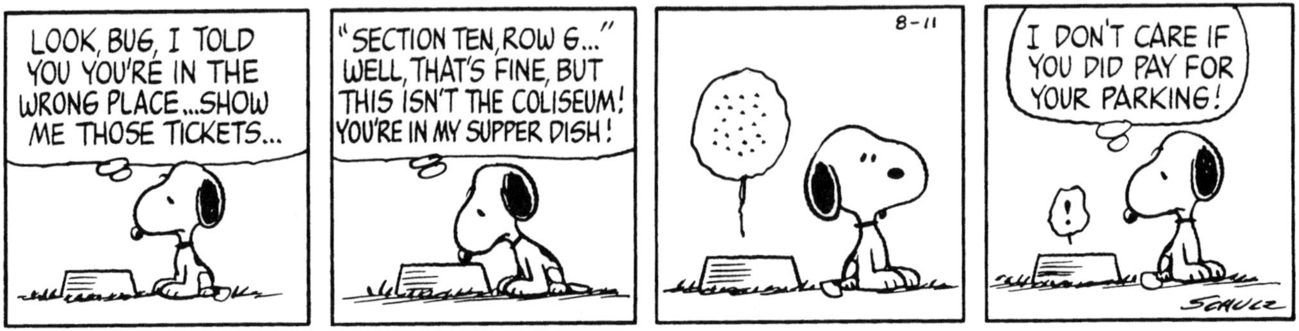
LOOK, BUG, I TOLD YOU YOU'RE IN THE WRONG PLACE...SHOW ME THOSE TICKETS...
"SECTION TEN, ROW 6..." WELL, THAT'S FINE, BUT THIS ISN'T THE COLISEUM! YOU'RE IN MY SUPPER DISH!
8-11
!
I DON'T CARE IF YOU DID PAY FOR YOUR PARKING!
SCHULZ

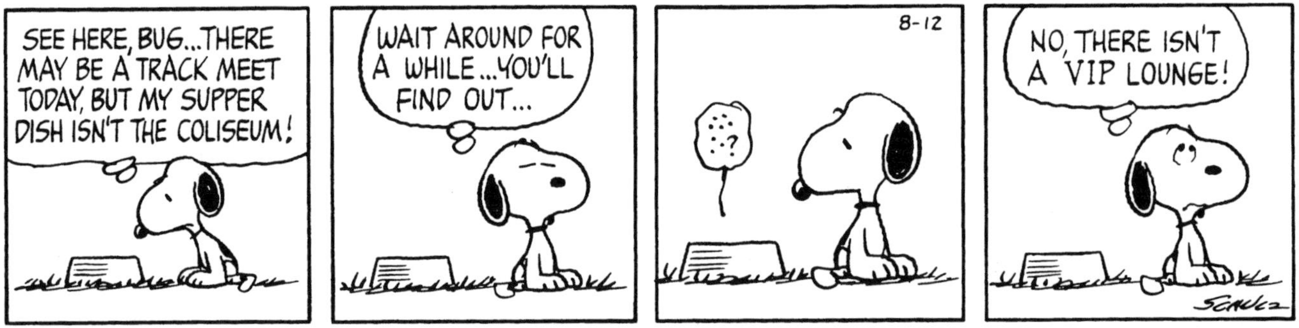
SEE HERE, BUG...THERE MAY BE A TRACK MEET TODAY, BUT MY SUPPER DISH ISN'T THE COLISEUM!
WAIT AROUND FOR A WHILE...YOU'LL FIND OUT...
8-12
?
NO, THERE ISN'T A VIP LOUNGE!
SCHULZ

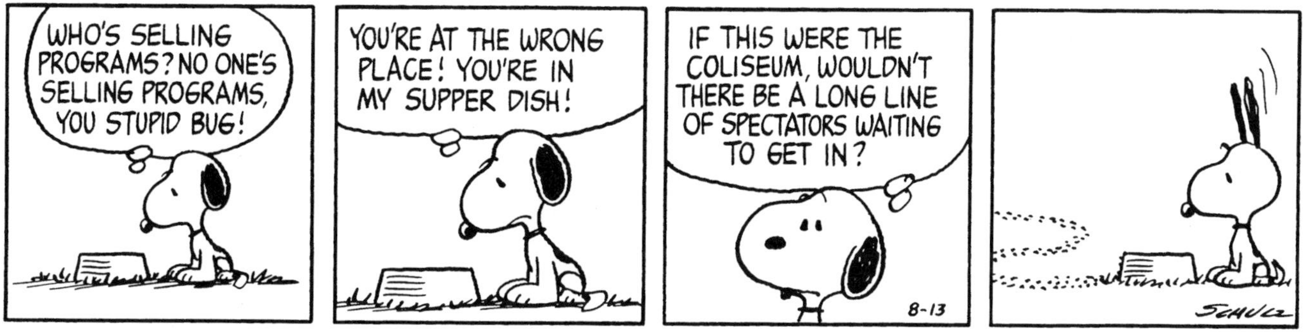
WHO'S SELLING PROGRAMS? NO ONE'S SELLING PROGRAMS, YOU STUPID BUG!
YOU'RE AT THE WRONG PLACE! YOU'RE IN MY SUPPER DISH!
IF THIS WERE THE COLISEUM, WOULDN'T THERE BE A LONG LINE OF SPECTATORS WAITING TO GET IN?
8-13
SCHULZ

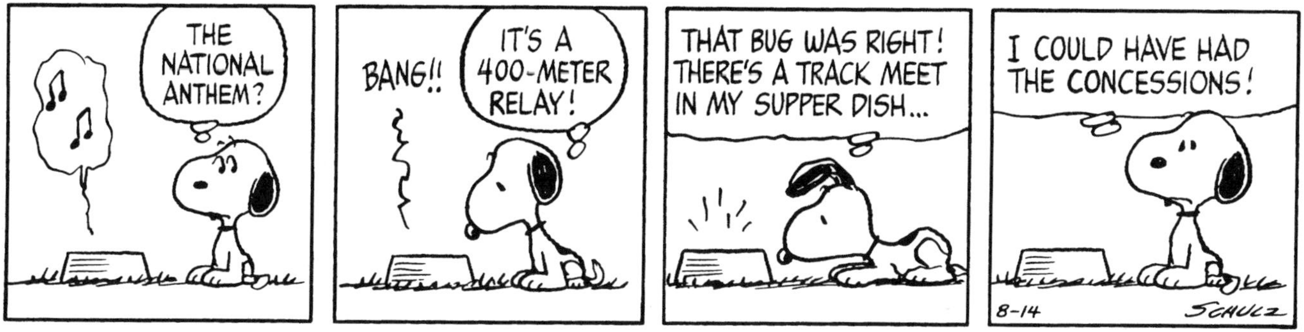
THE NATIONAL ANTHEM?
BANG!!
IT'S A 400-METER RELAY!
THAT BUG WAS RIGHT! THERE'S A TRACK MEET IN MY SUPPER DISH...
I COULD HAVE HAD THE CONCESSIONS!
8-14
SCHULZ

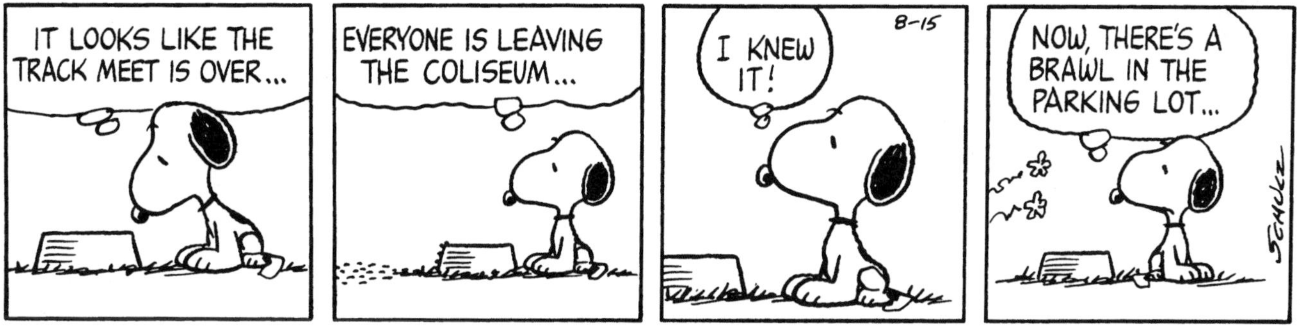
IT LOOKS LIKE THE TRACK MEET IS OVER...
EVERYONE IS LEAVING THE COLISEUM...
8-15
I KNEW IT!
NOW, THERE'S A BRAWL IN THE PARKING LOT...
SCHULZ

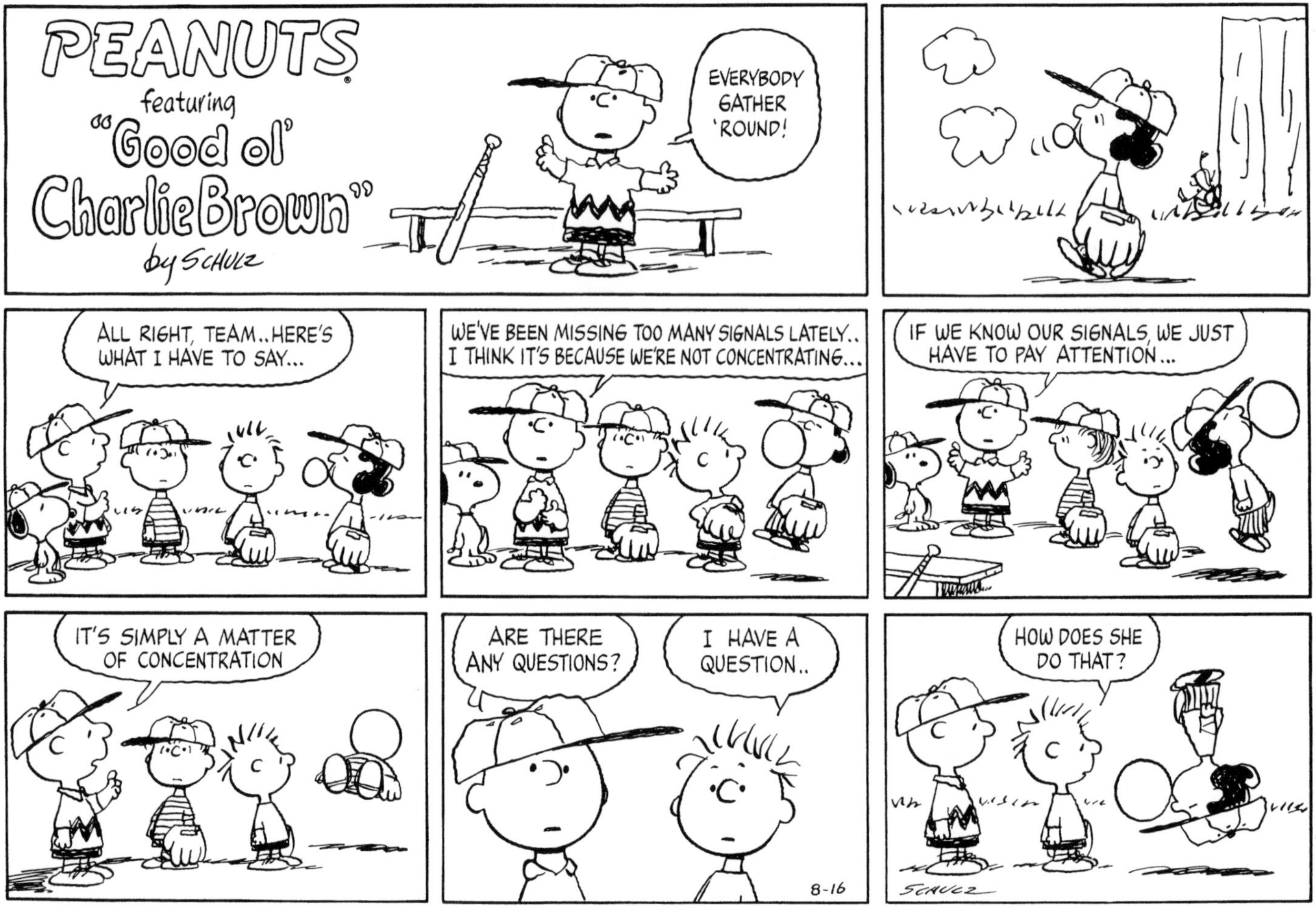
PEANUTS
featuring "Good ol' Charlie Brown" by SCHULZ
EVERYBODY GATHER 'ROUND!
ALL RIGHT, TEAM..HERE'S WHAT I HAVE TO SAY...
WE'VE BEEN MISSING TOO MANY SIGNALS LATELY.. I THINK IT'S BECAUSE WE'RE NOT CONCENTRATING...
IF WE KNOW OUR SIGNALS, WE JUST HAVE TO PAY ATTENTION...
IT'S SIMPLY A MATTER OF CONCENTRATION
ARE THERE ANY QUESTIONS?
I HAVE A QUESTION..
8-16
HOW DOES SHE DO THAT?
SCHULZ

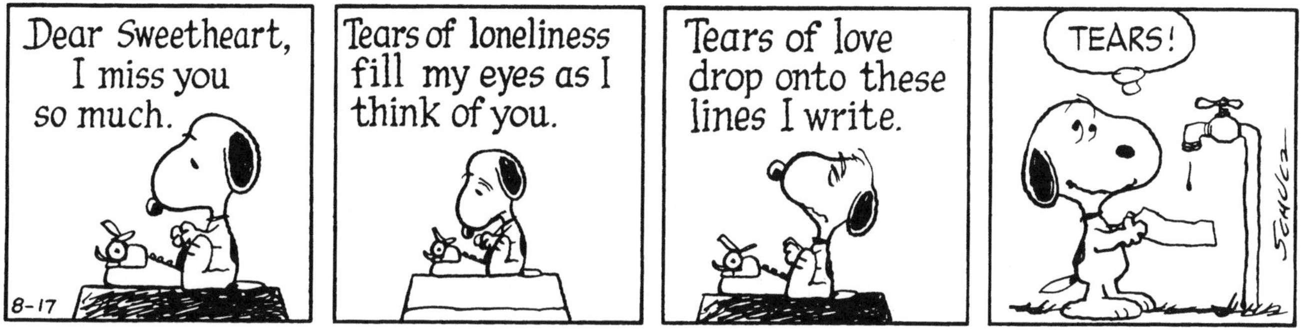
Dear Sweetheart, I miss you so much.
8-17
Tears of loneliness fill my eyes as I think of you.
Tears of love drop onto these lines I write.
TEARS!
SCHULZ

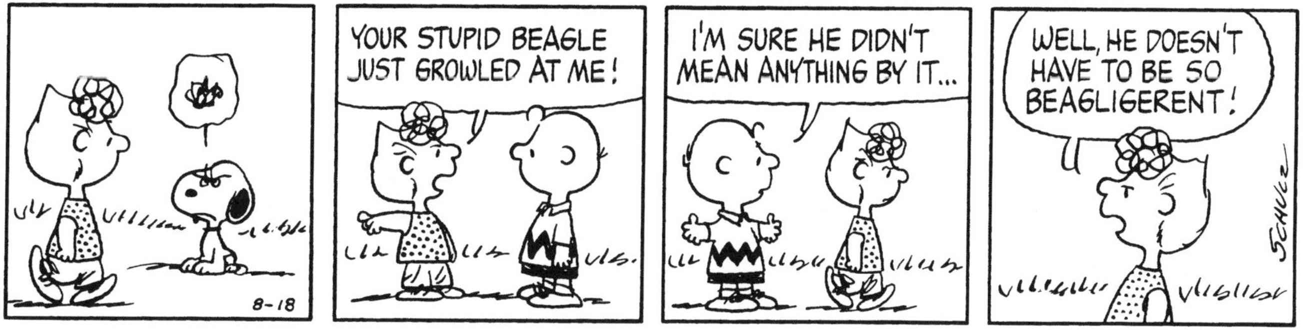
8-18
YOUR STUPID BEAGLE JUST GROWLED AT ME!
I'M SURE HE DIDN'T MEAN ANYTHING BY IT...
WELL, HE DOESN'T HAVE TO BE SO BEAGLIGERENT!
SCHULZ

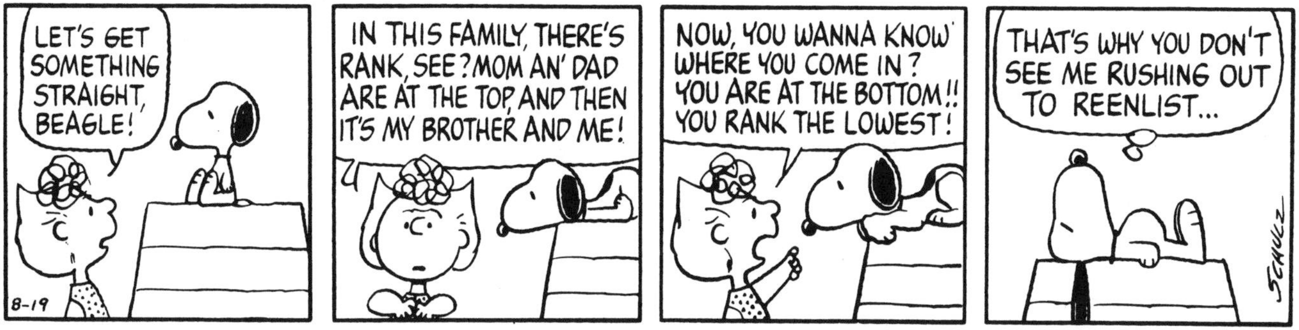
LET'S GET SOMETHING STRAIGHT, BEAGLE!
8-19
IN THIS FAMILY, THERE'S RANK, SEE? MOM AN' DAD ARE AT THE TOP, AND THEN IT'S MY BROTHER AND ME!
NOW, YOU WANNA KNOW WHERE YOU COME IN? YOU ARE AT THE BOTTOM!! YOU RANK THE LOWEST!
THAT'S WHY YOU DON'T SEE ME RUSHING OUT TO REENLIST...
SCHULZ

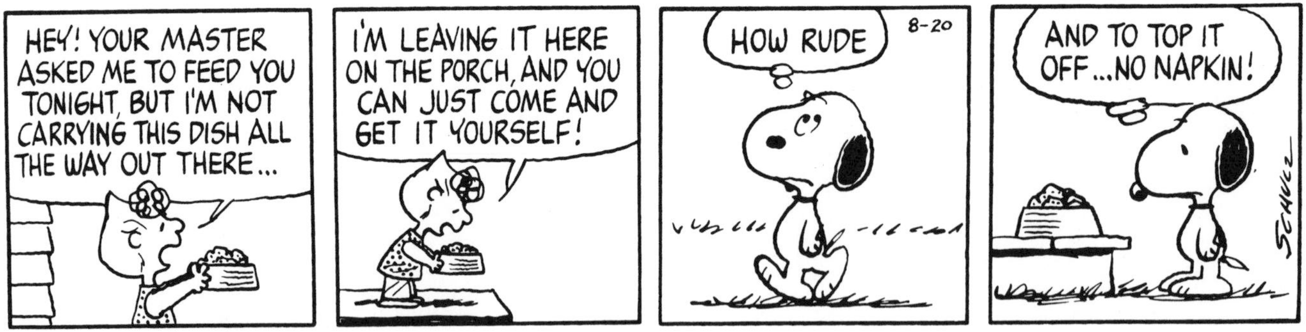
HEY! YOUR MASTER ASKED ME TO FEED YOU TONIGHT, BUT I'M NOT CARRYING THIS DISH ALL THE WAY OUT THERE...
I'M LEAVING IT HERE ON THE PORCH, AND YOU CAN JUST COME AND GET IT YOURSELF!
HOW RUDE
8-20
AND TO TOP IT OFF...NO NAPKIN!
SCHULZ

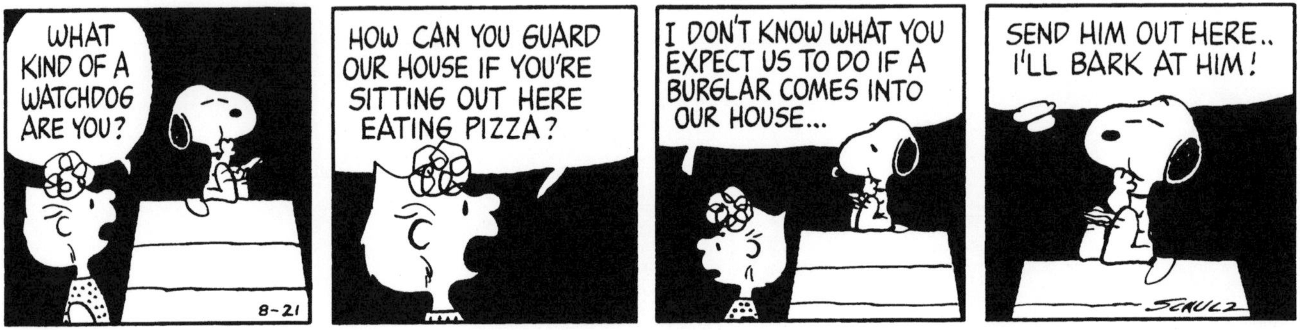
WHAT KIND OF A WATCHDOG ARE YOU?
8-21
HOW CAN YOU GUARD OUR HOUSE IF YOU'RE SITTING OUT HERE EATING PIZZA?
I DON'T KNOW WHAT YOU EXPECT US TO DO IF A BURGLAR COMES INTO OUR HOUSE...
SEND HIM OUT HERE.. I'LL BARK AT HIM!
SCHULZ

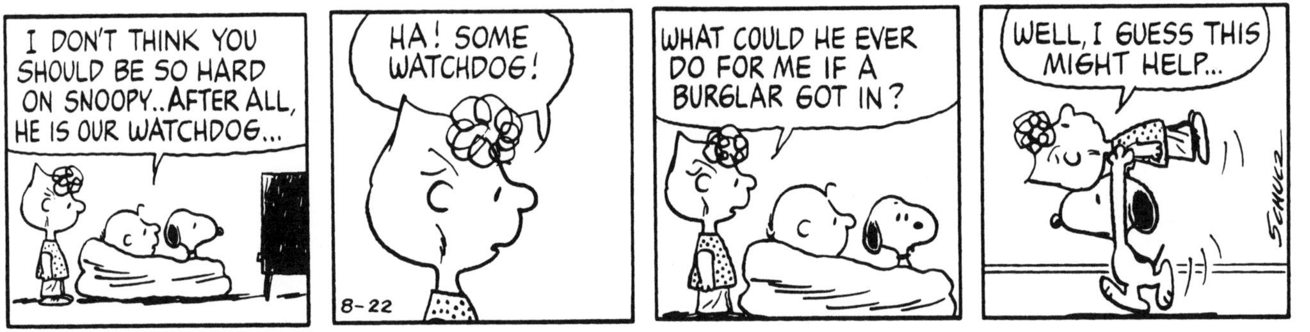
I DON'T THINK YOU SHOULD BE SO HARD ON SNOOPY..AFTER ALL, HE IS OUR WATCHDOG...
HA! SOME WATCHDOG!
8-22
WHAT COULD HE EVER DO FOR ME IF A BURGLAR GOT IN?
WELL, I GUESS THIS MIGHT HELP...
SCHULZ

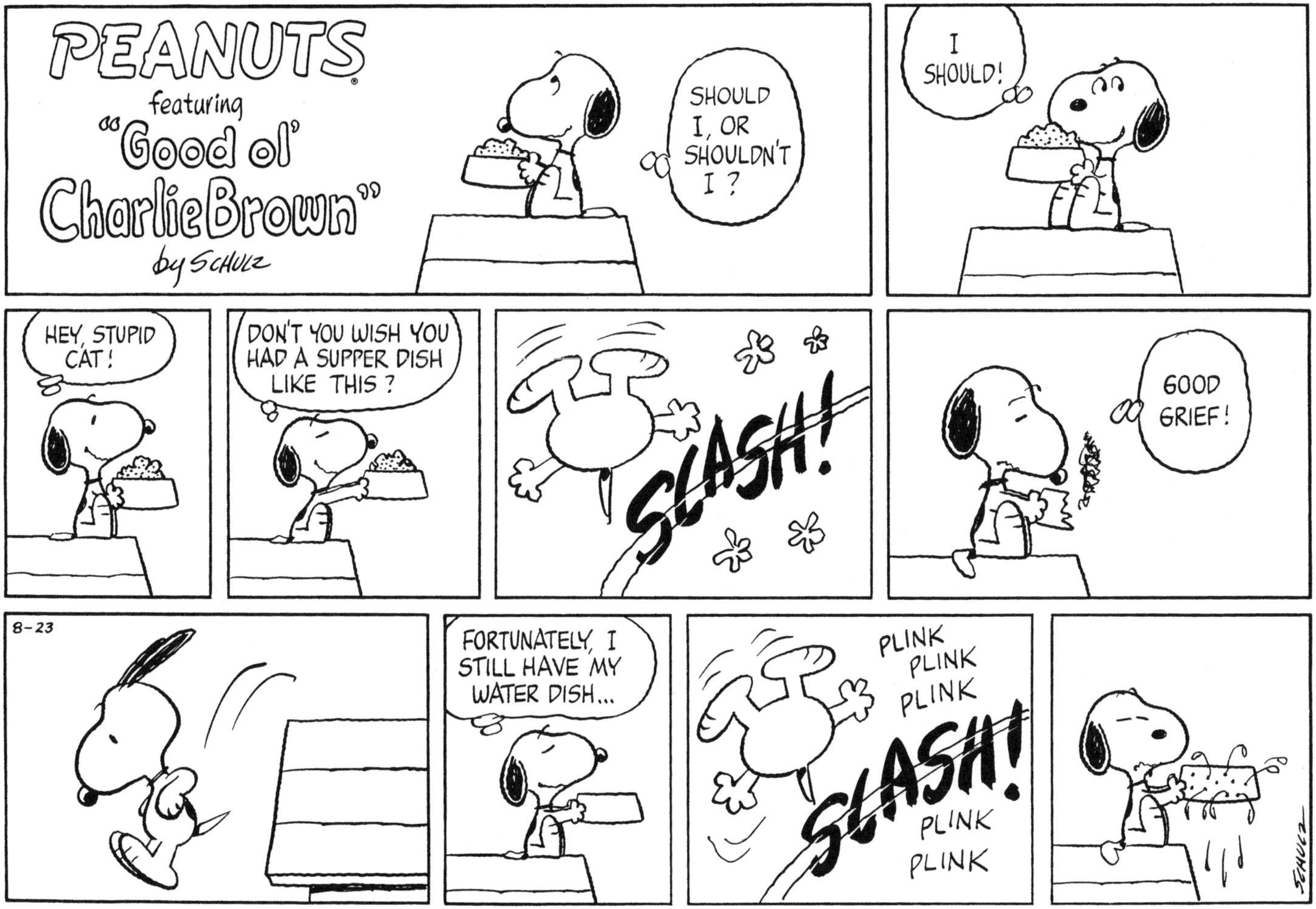
PEANUTS
featuring "Good ol' Charlie Brown"
by SCHULZ
SHOULD I, OR SHOULDN'T I ?
I SHOULD!
HEY, STUPID CAT!
DON'T YOU WISH YOU HAD A SUPPER DISH LIKE THIS ?
SLASH!
GOOD GRIEF!
8-23
FORTUNATELY, I STILL HAVE MY WATER DISH...
PLINK PLINK PLINK
SLASH!
PLINK PLINK
SCHULZ

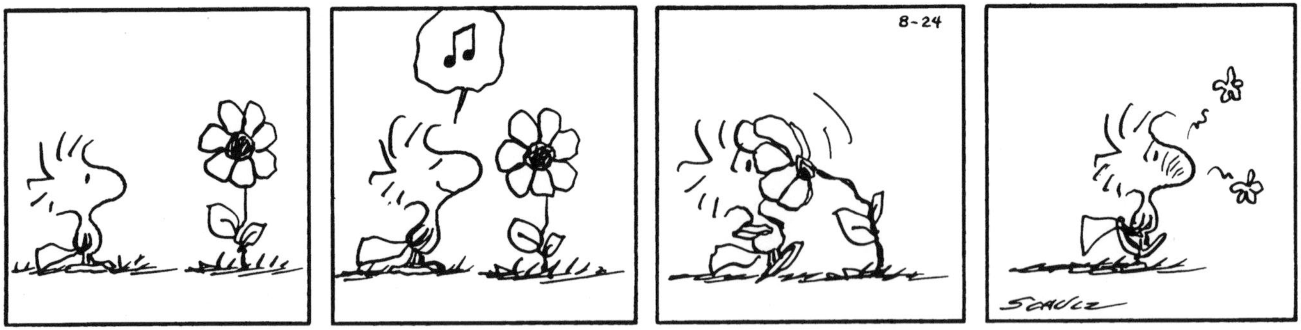
8-24
SCHULZ

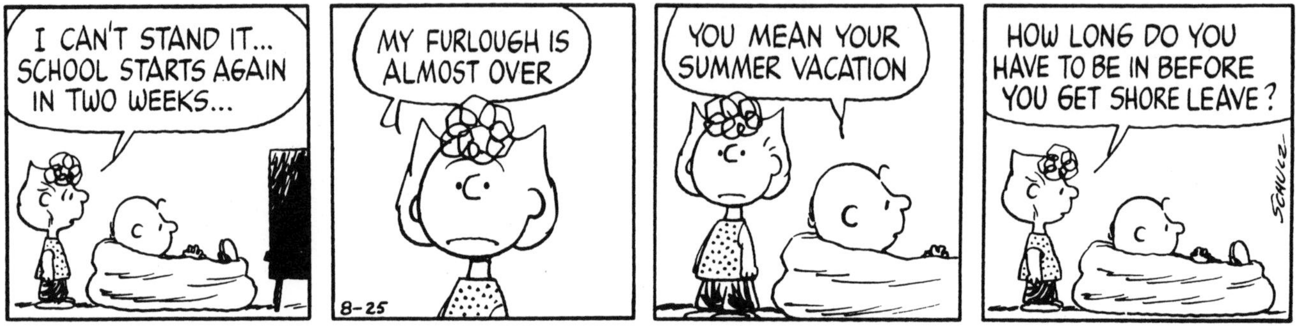
I CAN'T STAND IT... SCHOOL STARTS AGAIN IN TWO WEEKS...
MY FURLOUGH IS ALMOST OVER
8-25
YOU MEAN YOUR SUMMER VACATION
HOW LONG DO YOU HAVE TO BE IN BEFORE YOU GET SHORE LEAVE?
SCHULZ

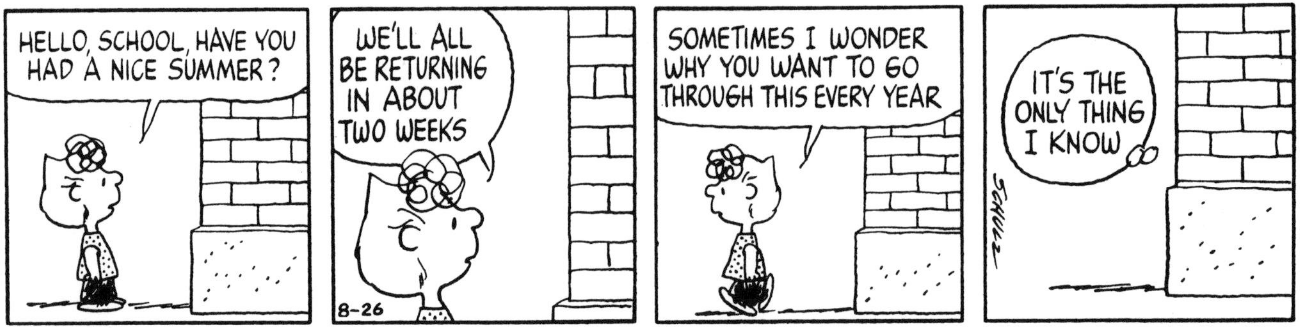
HELLO, SCHOOL, HAVE YOU HAD A NICE SUMMER?
WE'LL ALL BE RETURNING IN ABOUT TWO WEEKS
8-26
SOMETIMES I WONDER WHY YOU WANT TO GO THROUGH THIS EVERY YEAR
IT'S THE ONLY THING I KNOW
SCHULZ

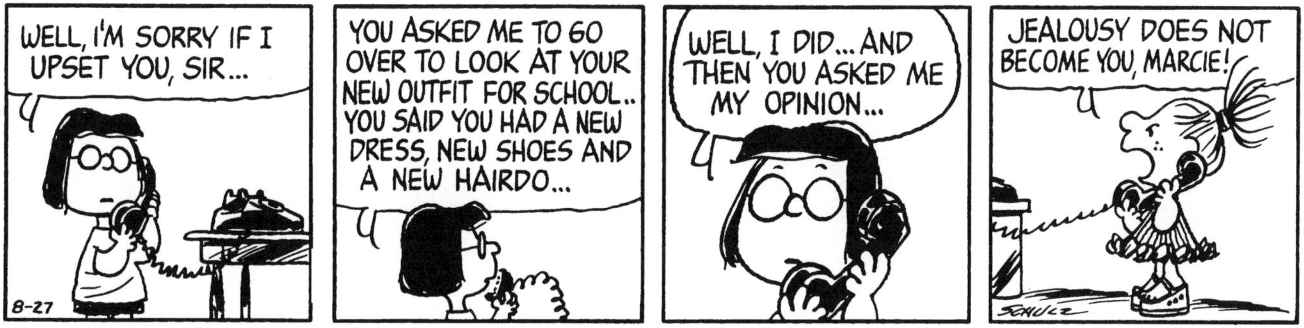
WELL, I'M SORRY IF I UPSET YOU, SIR...
8-27
YOU ASKED ME TO GO OVER TO LOOK AT YOUR NEW OUTFIT FOR SCHOOL.. YOU SAID YOU HAD A NEW DRESS, NEW SHOES AND A NEW HAIRDO...
WELL, I DID... AND THEN YOU ASKED ME MY OPINION...
JEALOUSY DOES NOT BECOME YOU, MARCIE!
SCHULZ

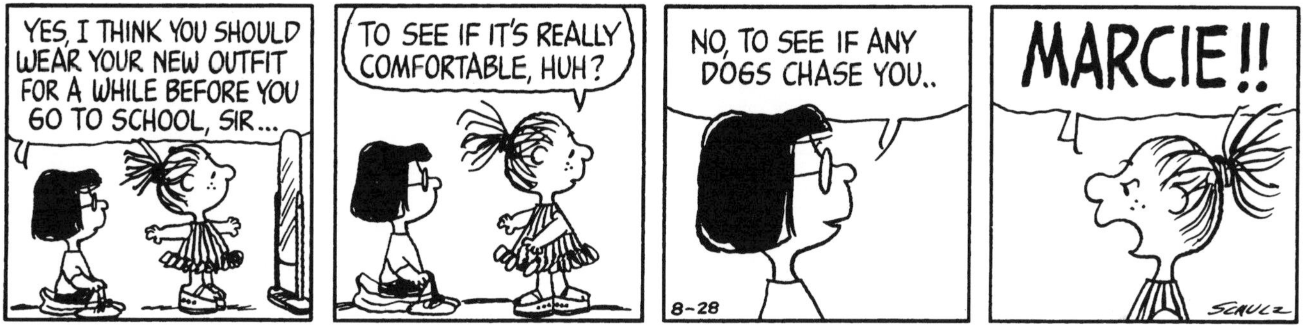
YES, I THINK YOU SHOULD WEAR YOUR NEW OUTFIT FOR A WHILE BEFORE YOU GO TO SCHOOL, SIR...
TO SEE IF IT'S REALLY COMFORTABLE, HUH?
NO, TO SEE IF ANY DOGS CHASE YOU..
8-28
MARCIE!!
SCHULZ

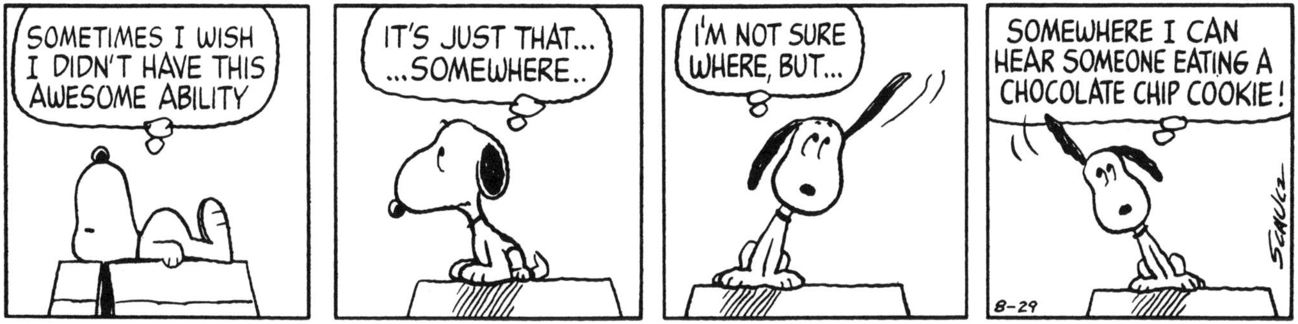
SOMETIMES I WISH I DIDN'T HAVE THIS AWESOME ABILITY
IT'S JUST THAT... ...SOMEWHERE..
I'M NOT SURE WHERE, BUT...
SOMEWHERE I CAN HEAR SOMEONE EATING A CHOCOLATE CHIP COOKIE!
SCHULZ
8-29

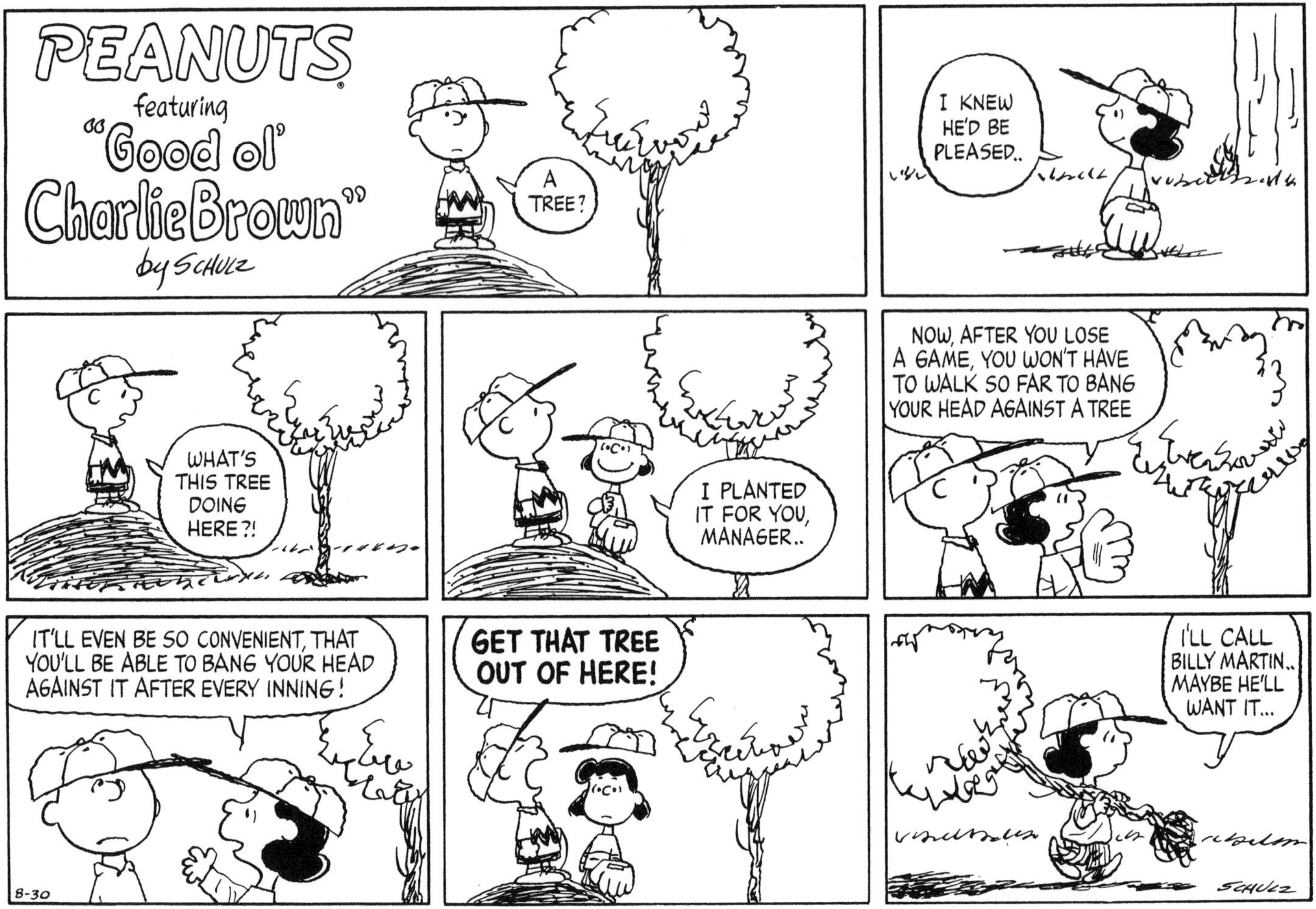
PEANUTS
featuring "Good ol' Charlie Brown"
by SCHULZ
A TREE?
I KNEW HE'D BE PLEASED..
WHAT'S THIS TREE DOING HERE?!
I PLANTED IT FOR YOU, MANAGER..
NOW, AFTER YOU LOSE A GAME, YOU WON'T HAVE TO WALK SO FAR TO BANG YOUR HEAD AGAINST A TREE
IT'LL EVEN BE SO CONVENIENT, THAT YOU'LL BE ABLE TO BANG YOUR HEAD AGAINST IT AFTER EVERY INNING!
8-30
GET THAT TREE OUT OF HERE!
I'LL CALL BILLY MARTIN.. MAYBE HE'LL WANT IT...
SCHULZ

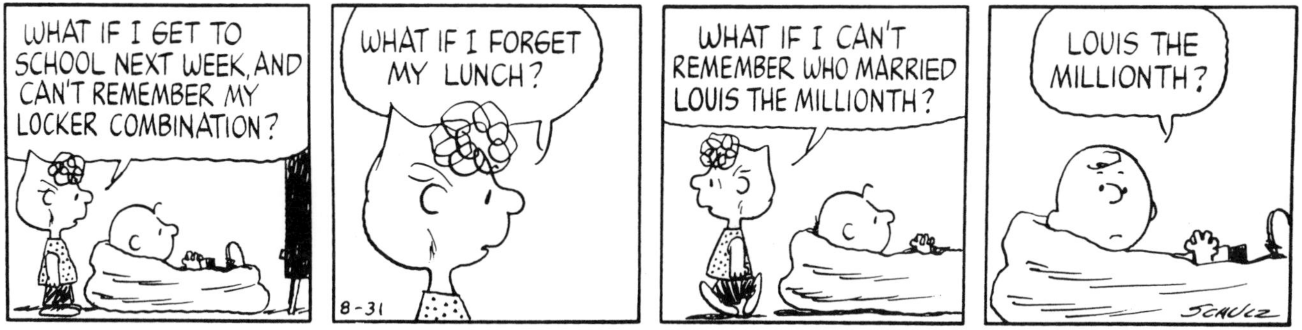
WHAT IF I GET TO SCHOOL NEXT WEEK, AND CAN'T REMEMBER MY LOCKER COMBINATION?
WHAT IF I FORGET MY LUNCH?
8-31
WHAT IF I CAN'T REMEMBER WHO MARRIED LOUIS THE MILLIONTH?
LOUIS THE MILLIONTH?
SCHULZ

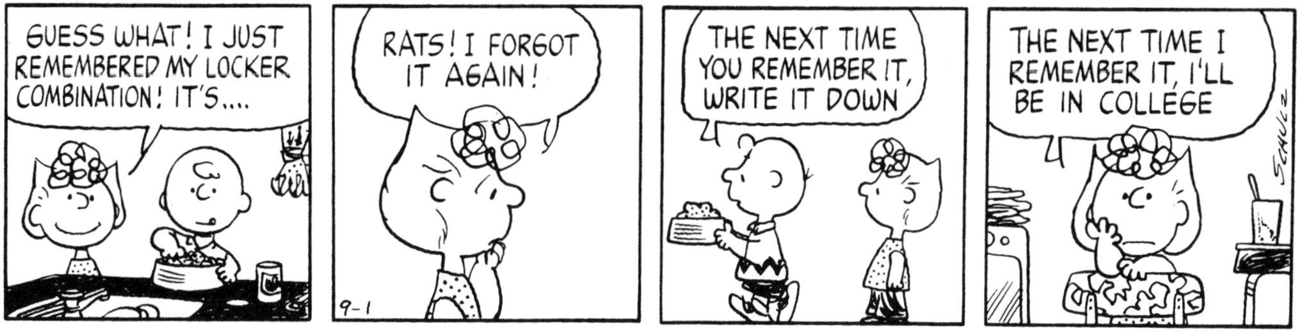
GUESS WHAT! I JUST REMEMBERED MY LOCKER COMBINATION! IT'S....
RATS! I FORGOT IT AGAIN!
9-1
THE NEXT TIME YOU REMEMBER IT, WRITE IT DOWN
THE NEXT TIME I REMEMBER IT, I'LL BE IN COLLEGE
SCHULZ

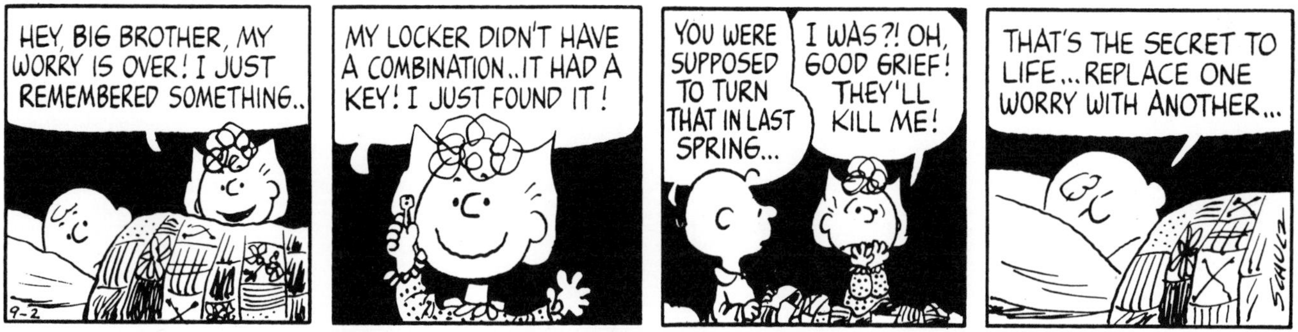
HEY, BIG BROTHER, MY WORRY IS OVER! I JUST REMEMBERED SOMETHING..
9-2
MY LOCKER DIDN'T HAVE A COMBINATION..IT HAD A KEY! I JUST FOUND IT!
YOU WERE SUPPOSED TO TURN THAT IN LAST SPRING...
I WAS?! OH, GOOD GRIEF! THEY'LL KILL ME!
THAT'S THE SECRET TO LIFE...REPLACE ONE WORRY WITH ANOTHER...
SCHULZ

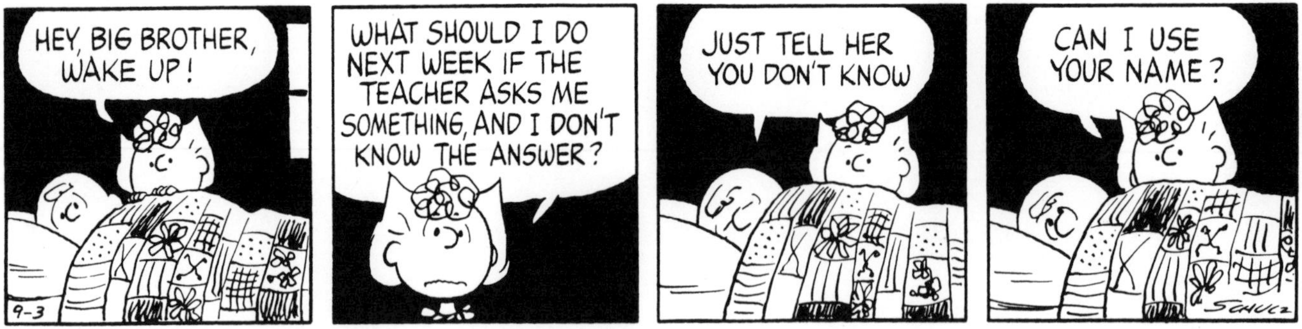
HEY, BIG BROTHER, WAKE UP!
9-3
WHAT SHOULD I DO NEXT WEEK IF THE TEACHER ASKS ME SOMETHING, AND I DON'T KNOW THE ANSWER?
JUST TELL HER YOU DON'T KNOW
CAN I USE YOUR NAME?
SCHULZ

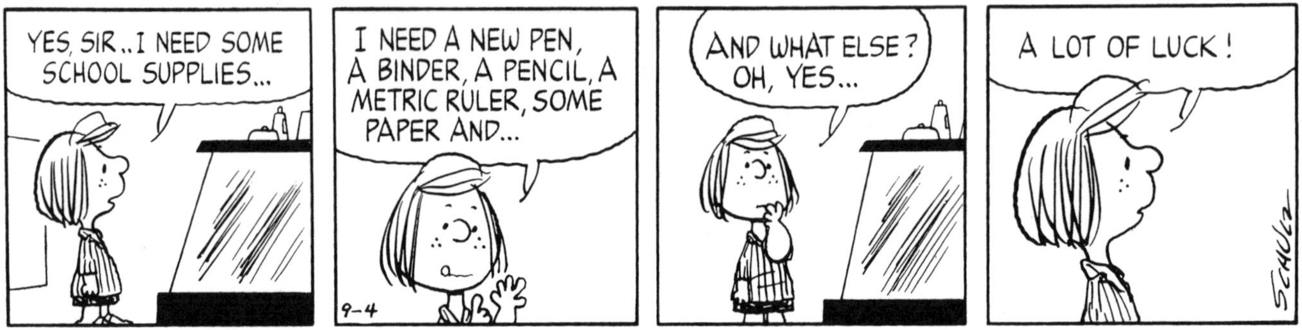
YES, SIR..I NEED SOME SCHOOL SUPPLIES...
I NEED A NEW PEN, A BINDER, A PENCIL, A METRIC RULER, SOME PAPER AND...
9-4
AND WHAT ELSE? OH, YES...
A LOT OF LUCK!
SCHULZ

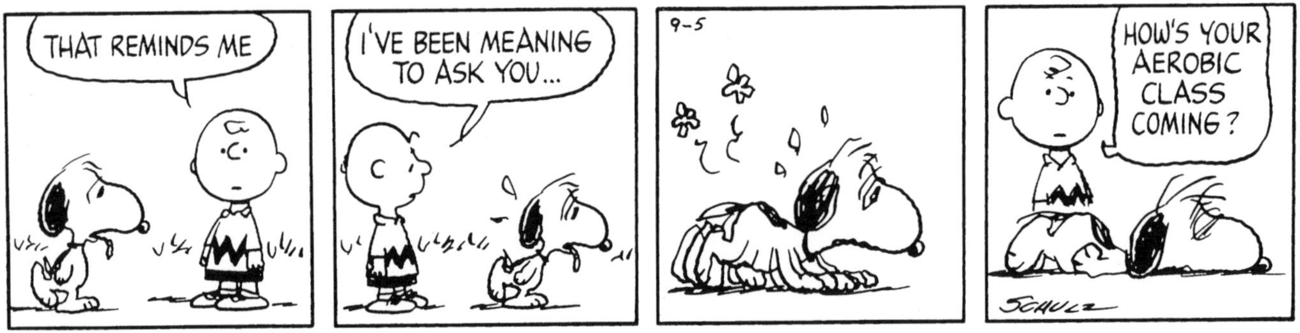
THAT REMINDS ME
I'VE BEEN MEANING TO ASK YOU...
9-5
HOW'S YOUR AEROBIC CLASS COMING?
SCHULZ

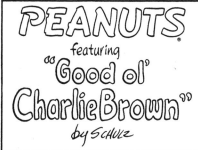

PEANUTS featuring "Good ol' Charlie Brown" by SCHULZ

THE OL' DESK.. CHALK DUST IN THE AIR...

IT'S ALL HERE!

THIS IS IT, MARCIE...

A NEW SCHOOL YEAR, AND WHAT I LIKE TO CALL,"THE EXCITEMENT OF LEARNING"

IT'S AN ADVENTURE THAT EVERYONE CAN ENJOY...

I MEAN, AFTER ALL, ISN'T THAT WHAT LIFE IS ALL ABOUT?

YES, MARCIE, THIS IS IT!

THAT WASN'T TOO BAD.."THE EXCITEMENT OF LEARNING" LASTED FOURTEEN SECONDS!

Z

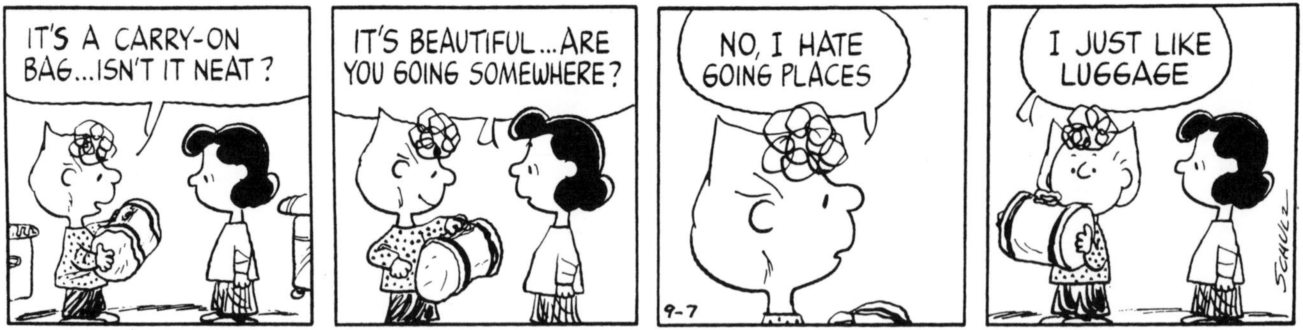
IT'S A CARRY-ON BAG...ISN'T IT NEAT ?
IT'S BEAUTIFUL...ARE YOU GOING SOMEWHERE ?
NO, I HATE GOING PLACES
I JUST LIKE LUGGAGE

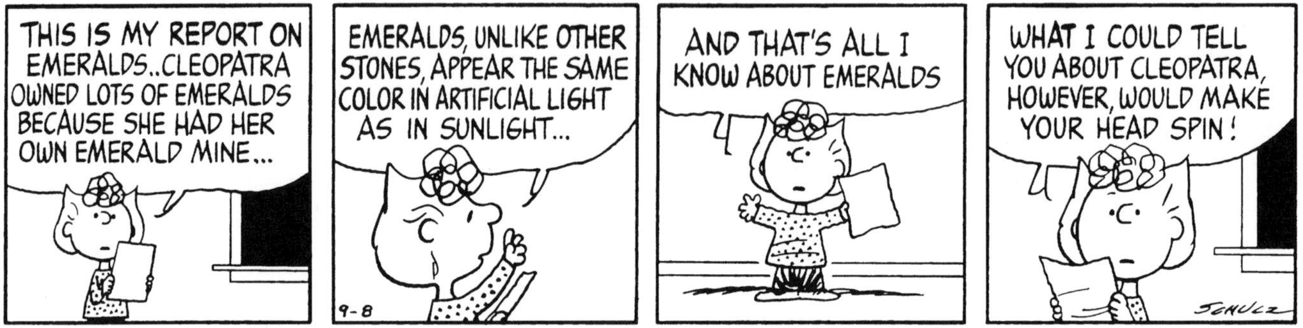
THIS IS MY REPORT ON EMERALDS..CLEOPATRA OWNED LOTS OF EMERALDS BECAUSE SHE HAD HER OWN EMERALD MINE...
EMERALDS, UNLIKE OTHER STONES, APPEAR THE SAME COLOR IN ARTIFICIAL LIGHT AS IN SUNLIGHT...
AND THAT'S ALL I KNOW ABOUT EMERALDS
WHAT I COULD TELL YOU ABOUT CLEOPATRA, HOWEVER, WOULD MAKE YOUR HEAD SPIN !

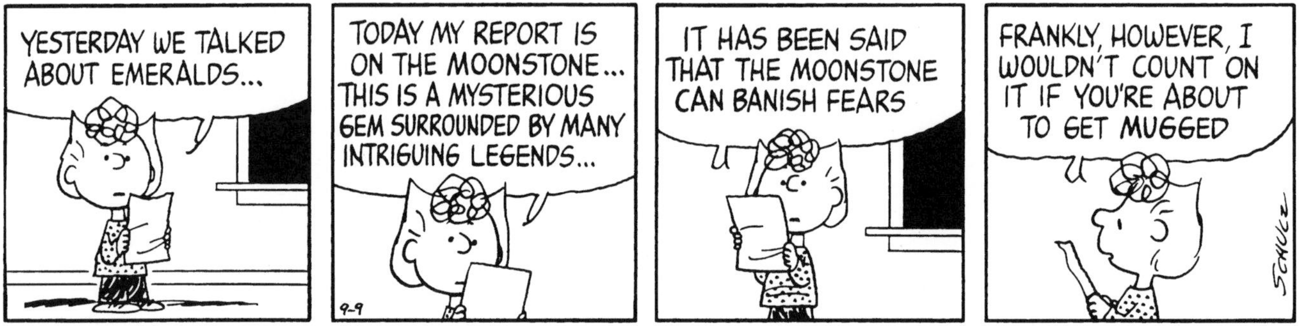
YESTERDAY WE TALKED ABOUT EMERALDS...
TODAY MY REPORT IS ON THE MOONSTONE... THIS IS A MYSTERIOUS GEM SURROUNDED BY MANY INTRIGUING LEGENDS...
IT HAS BEEN SAID THAT THE MOONSTONE CAN BANISH FEARS
FRANKLY, HOWEVER, I WOULDN'T COUNT ON IT IF YOU'RE ABOUT TO GET MUGGED

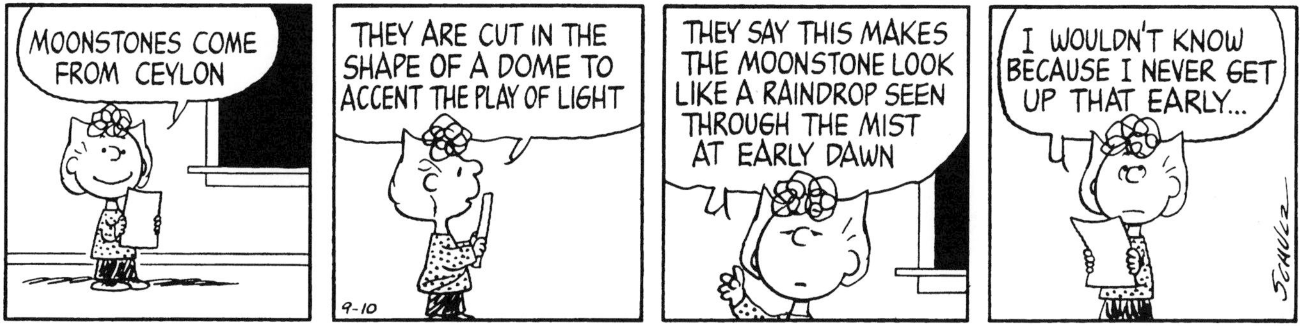
MOONSTONES COME FROM CEYLON
THEY ARE CUT IN THE SHAPE OF A DOME TO ACCENT THE PLAY OF LIGHT
9-10
THEY SAY THIS MAKES THE MOONSTONE LOOK LIKE A RAINDROP SEEN THROUGH THE MIST AT EARLY DAWN
I WOULDN'T KNOW BECAUSE I NEVER GET UP THAT EARLY...
SCHULZ

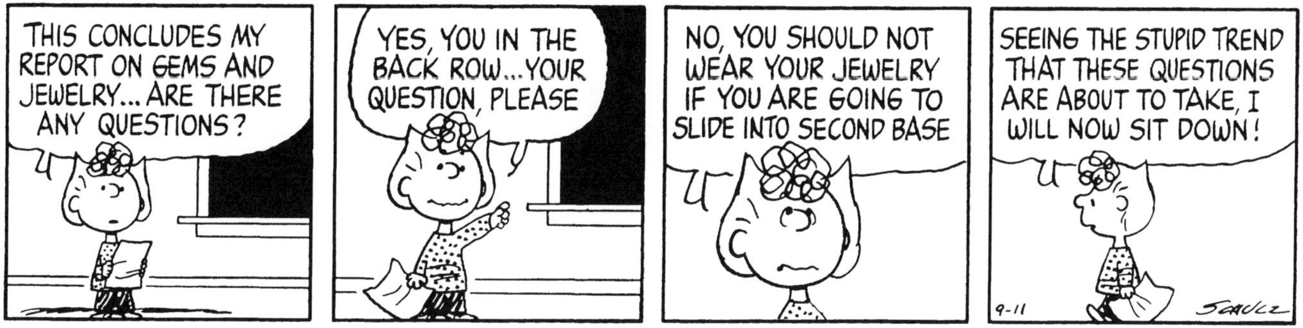
THIS CONCLUDES MY REPORT ON GEMS AND JEWELRY... ARE THERE ANY QUESTIONS?
YES, YOU IN THE BACK ROW...YOUR QUESTION, PLEASE
NO, YOU SHOULD NOT WEAR YOUR JEWELRY IF YOU ARE GOING TO SLIDE INTO SECOND BASE
SEEING THE STUPID TREND THAT THESE QUESTIONS ARE ABOUT TO TAKE, I WILL NOW SIT DOWN!
9-11
SCHULZ

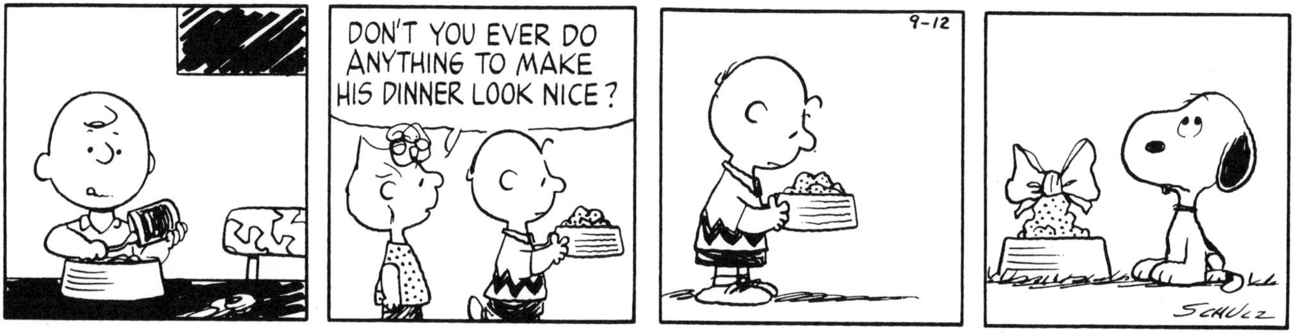
DON'T YOU EVER DO ANYTHING TO MAKE HIS DINNER LOOK NICE?
9-12
SCHULZ

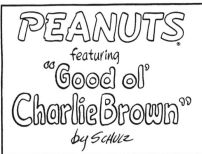
Peanuts featuring "Good ol' Charlie Brown" by Schulz

YES, MA'AM.. MORE THAN READY...

THEY'RE GONNA LOVE THIS, MARCIE!

THIS IS MY REPORT ON "WHAT I DID THIS SUMMER".. AT THE CONCLUSION, I WILL ANSWER QUESTIONS..

ONE DAY LATE IN THE SUMMER, I WAS LYING IN A MEADOW, WHEN SUDDENLY, A BUTTERFLY LANDED ON MY NOSE!

9-13

HA HA HA HA HA HA HA HA HA HA

WELL, I DIDN'T WANT TO BRUSH IT AWAY BECAUSE I MIGHT HURT IT...

AFTER A WHILE I MUST HAVE DOZED OFF.. WHEN I OPENED MY EYES, THE BUTTERFLY WAS GONE!

YOU'LL NEVER GUESS WHAT HAPPENED... IT HAD TURNED INTO AN ANGEL, AND FLOWN AWAY!

HA HA HA HA HA HA HA HA HA HA

WELL, THIS WAS OBVIOUSLY A MIRACLE! I HAD BEEN CHOSEN TO BRING A MESSAGE TO THE WORLD!

WHAT WAS THIS MESSAGE I WAS TO BRING TO THE WORLD? AFTER MUCH THOUGHT, I DECIDED IT WAS THIS, "A FOUL BALL HIT BEHIND THIRD BASE IS THE SHORTSTOP'S PLAY!"

HA HA HA HA HA HA HA HA HA HA

MA'AM, IF IT'S OKAY WITH YOU, I'LL TAKE THE QUESTIONS AFTER SCHOOL OUT IN THE ALLEY BEHIND THE GYM!

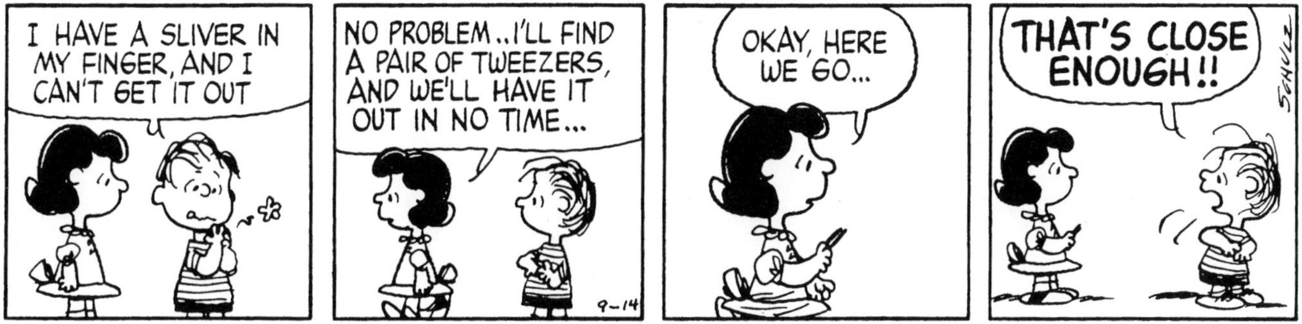
I HAVE A SLIVER IN MY FINGER, AND I CAN'T GET IT OUT
NO PROBLEM..I'LL FIND A PAIR OF TWEEZERS, AND WE'LL HAVE IT OUT IN NO TIME...
OKAY, HERE WE GO...
THAT'S CLOSE ENOUGH!!
SCHULZ
9-14

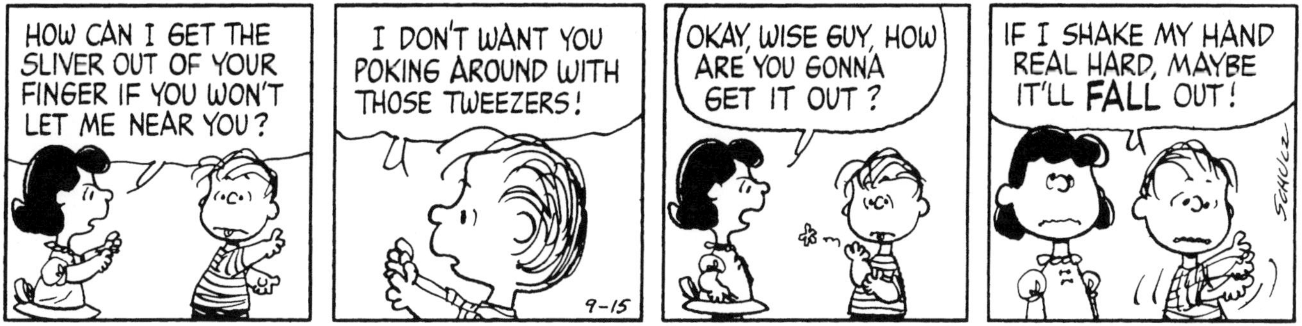
HOW CAN I GET THE SLIVER OUT OF YOUR FINGER IF YOU WON'T LET ME NEAR YOU?
I DON'T WANT YOU POKING AROUND WITH THOSE TWEEZERS!
OKAY, WISE GUY, HOW ARE YOU GONNA GET IT OUT?
IF I SHAKE MY HAND REAL HARD, MAYBE IT'LL FALL OUT!
SCHULZ
9-15

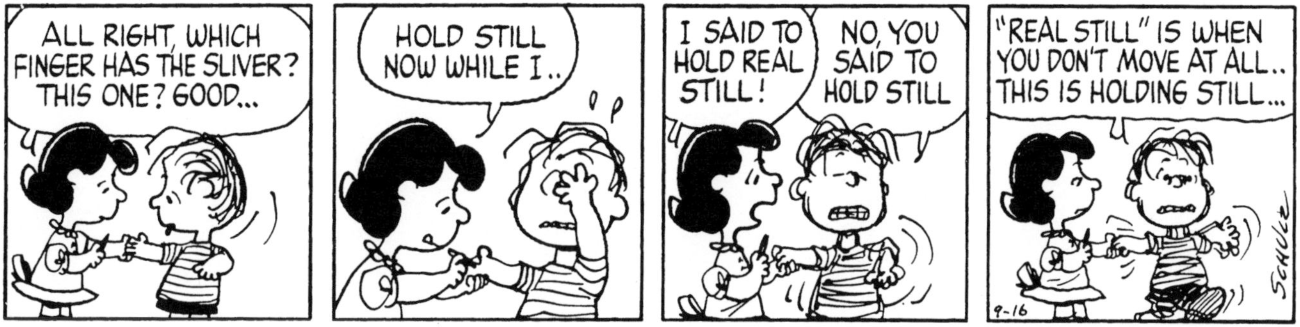
ALL RIGHT, WHICH FINGER HAS THE SLIVER? THIS ONE? GOOD...
HOLD STILL NOW WHILE I..
I SAID TO HOLD REAL STILL!
NO, YOU SAID TO HOLD STILL
"REAL STILL" IS WHEN YOU DON'T MOVE AT ALL.. THIS IS HOLDING STILL...
SCHULZ
9-16

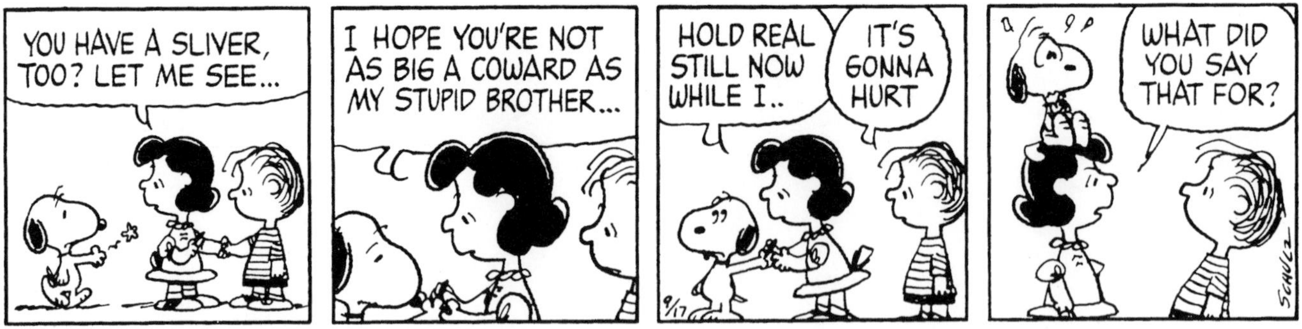
YOU HAVE A SLIVER, TOO? LET ME SEE...
I HOPE YOU'RE NOT AS BIG A COWARD AS MY STUPID BROTHER...
HOLD REAL STILL NOW WHILE I..
IT'S GONNA HURT
WHAT DID YOU SAY THAT FOR?

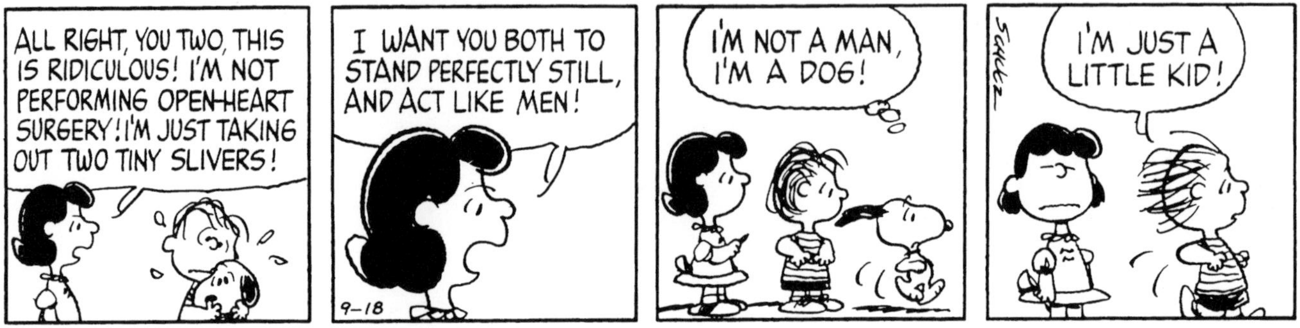
ALL RIGHT, YOU TWO, THIS IS RIDICULOUS! I'M NOT PERFORMING OPEN-HEART SURGERY! I'M JUST TAKING OUT TWO TINY SLIVERS!
I WANT YOU BOTH TO STAND PERFECTLY STILL, AND ACT LIKE MEN!
I'M NOT A MAN, I'M A DOG!
I'M JUST A LITTLE KID!

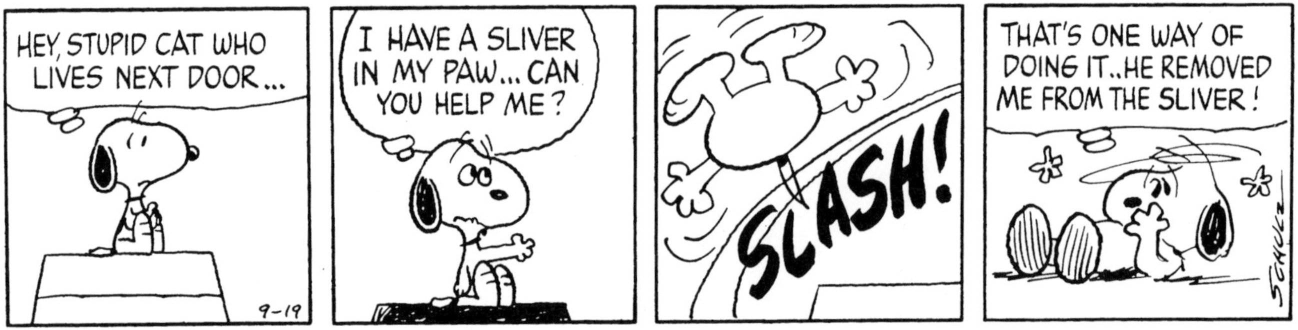
HEY, STUPID CAT WHO LIVES NEXT DOOR...
I HAVE A SLIVER IN MY PAW... CAN YOU HELP ME?
SLASH!
THAT'S ONE WAY OF DOING IT..HE REMOVED ME FROM THE SLIVER!

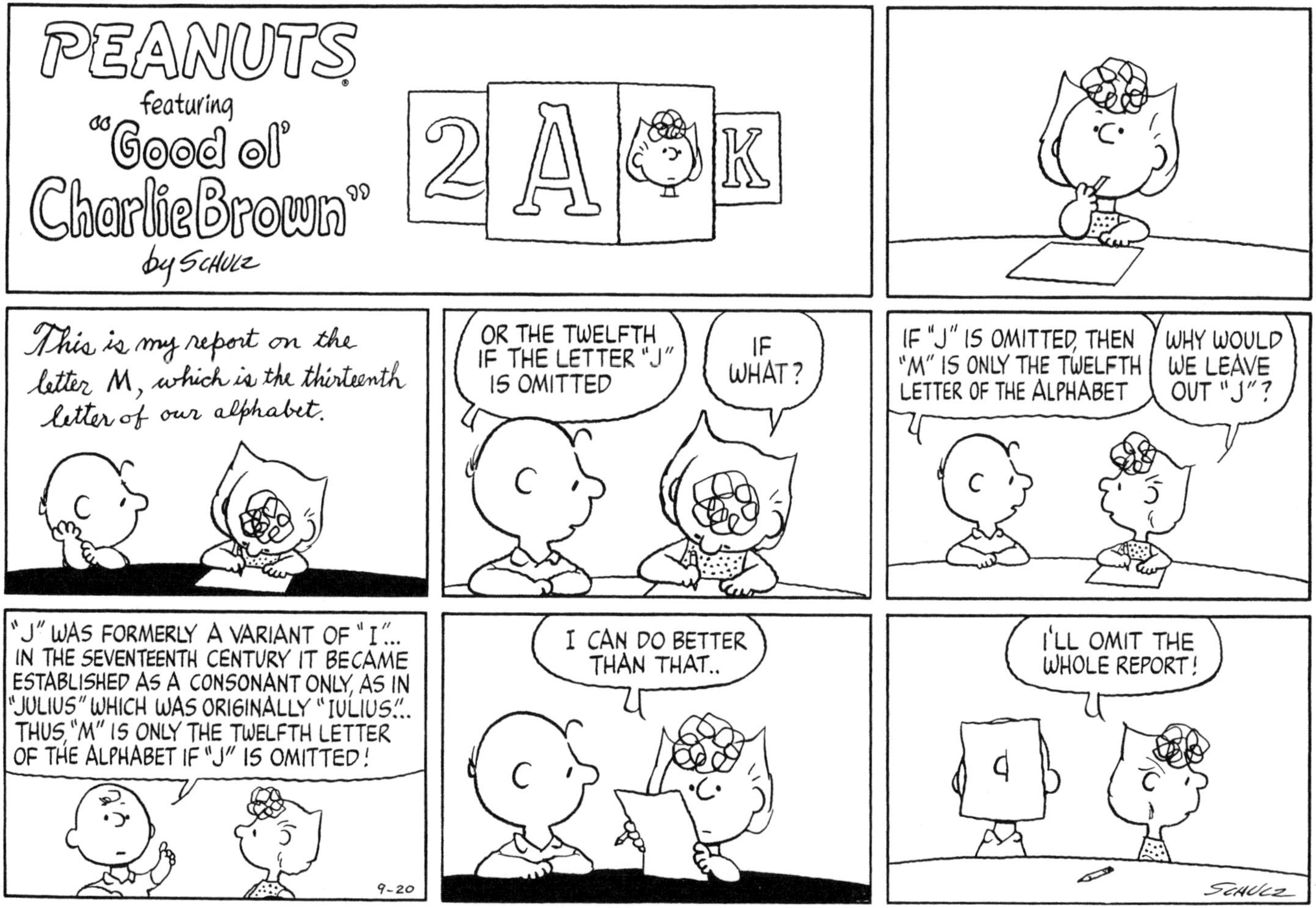
PEANUTS
featuring "Good ol' Charlie Brown"
by SCHULZ
2
A
K
This is my report on the letter M, which is the thirteenth letter of our alphabet.
OR THE TWELFTH IF THE LETTER "J" IS OMITTED
IF WHAT?
IF "J" IS OMITTED, THEN "M" IS ONLY THE TWELFTH LETTER OF THE ALPHABET
WHY WOULD WE LEAVE OUT "J"?
"J" WAS FORMERLY A VARIANT OF "I"... IN THE SEVENTEENTH CENTURY IT BECAME ESTABLISHED AS A CONSONANT ONLY, AS IN "JULIUS" WHICH WAS ORIGINALLY "IULIUS"... THUS, "M" IS ONLY THE TWELFTH LETTER OF THE ALPHABET IF "J" IS OMITTED!
9-20
I CAN DO BETTER THAN THAT..
I'LL OMIT THE WHOLE REPORT!
SCHULZ

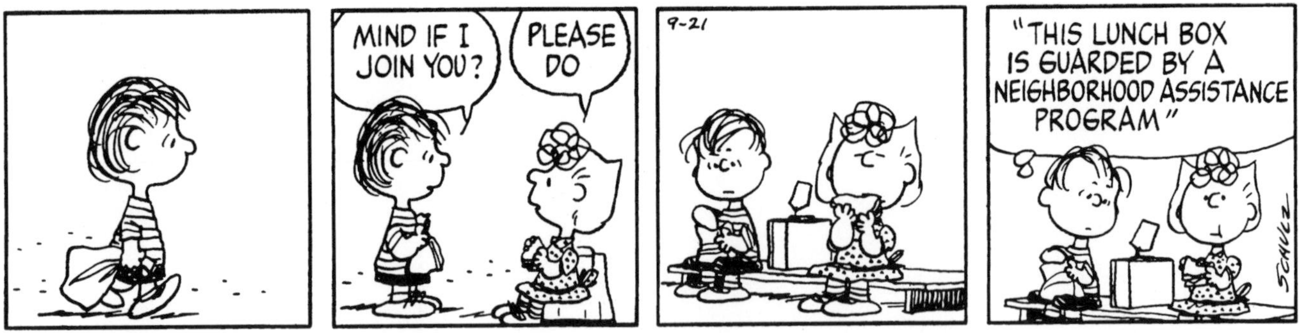
MIND IF I JOIN YOU?
PLEASE DO
9-21
"THIS LUNCH BOX IS GUARDED BY A NEIGHBORHOOD ASSISTANCE PROGRAM"
SCHULZ

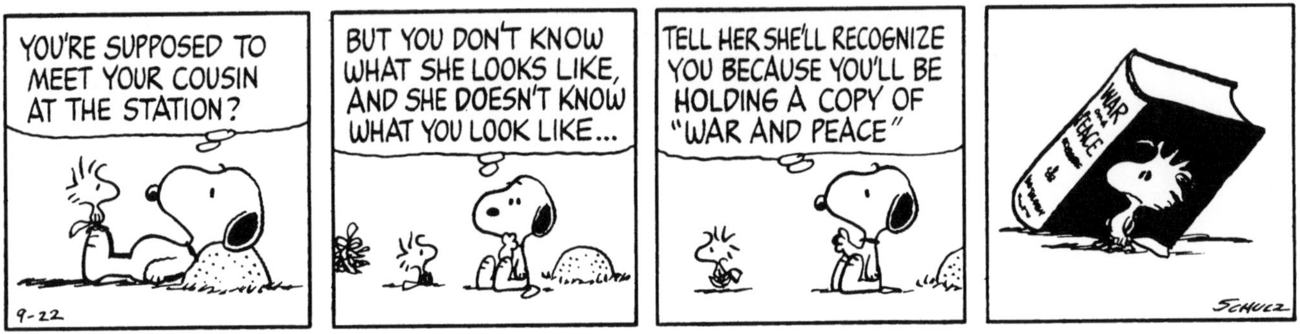
YOU'RE SUPPOSED TO MEET YOUR COUSIN AT THE STATION?
9-22
BUT YOU DON'T KNOW WHAT SHE LOOKS LIKE, AND SHE DOESN'T KNOW WHAT YOU LOOK LIKE...
TELL HER SHE'LL RECOGNIZE YOU BECAUSE YOU'LL BE HOLDING A COPY OF "WAR AND PEACE"
WAR AND PEACE
SCHULZ

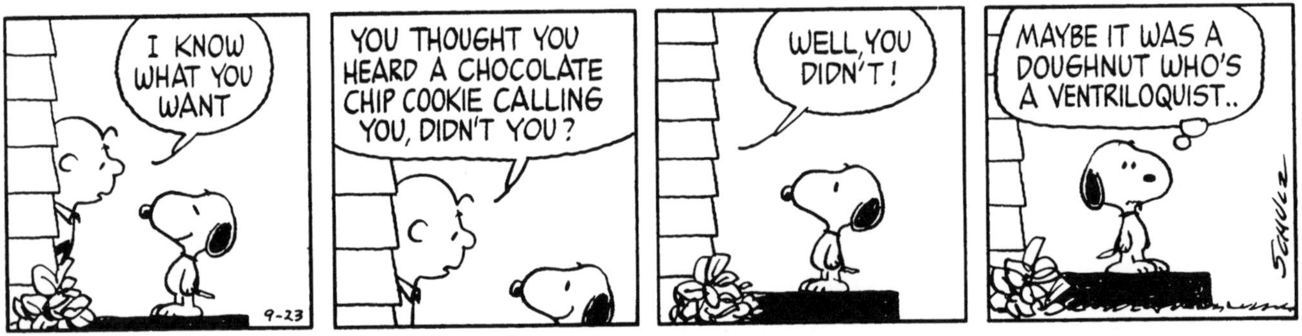
I KNOW WHAT YOU WANT
9-23
YOU THOUGHT YOU HEARD A CHOCOLATE CHIP COOKIE CALLING YOU, DIDN'T YOU?
WELL, YOU DIDN'T!
MAYBE IT WAS A DOUGHNUT WHO'S A VENTRILOQUIST..
SCHULZ

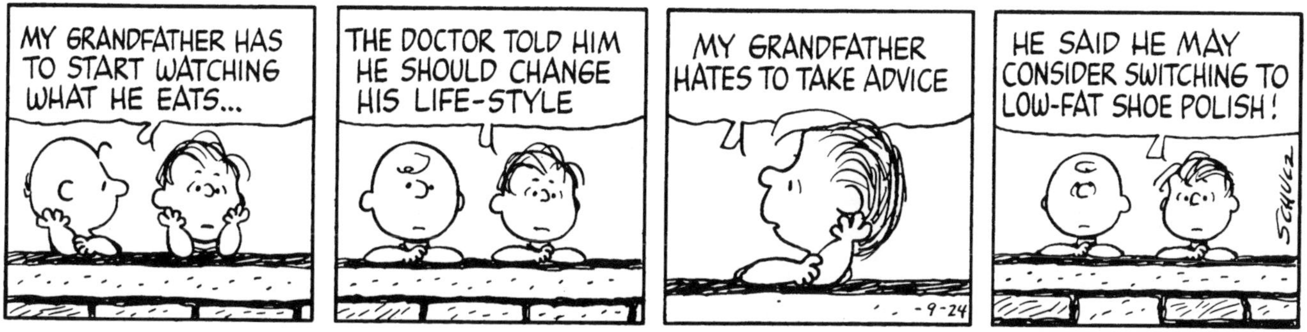
MY GRANDFATHER HAS TO START WATCHING WHAT HE EATS...
THE DOCTOR TOLD HIM HE SHOULD CHANGE HIS LIFE-STYLE
MY GRANDFATHER HATES TO TAKE ADVICE
HE SAID HE MAY CONSIDER SWITCHING TO LOW-FAT SHOE POLISH!
9-24
SCHULZ

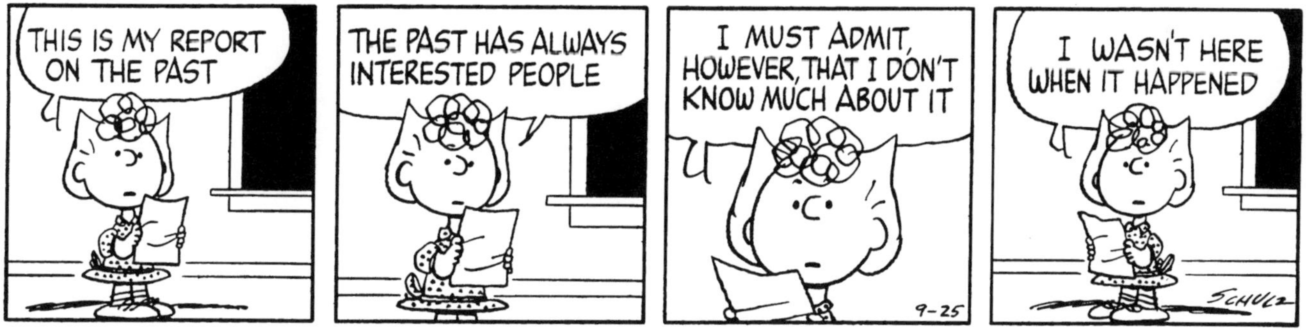
THIS IS MY REPORT ON THE PAST
THE PAST HAS ALWAYS INTERESTED PEOPLE
I MUST ADMIT, HOWEVER, THAT I DON'T KNOW MUCH ABOUT IT
9-25
I WASN'T HERE WHEN IT HAPPENED
SCHULZ

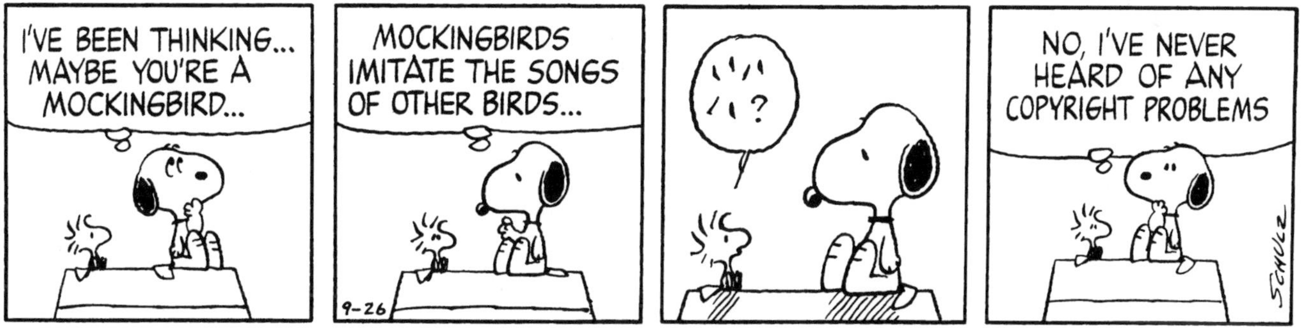
I'VE BEEN THINKING... MAYBE YOU'RE A MOCKINGBIRD...
MOCKINGBIRDS IMITATE THE SONGS OF OTHER BIRDS...
9-26
?
NO, I'VE NEVER HEARD OF ANY COPYRIGHT PROBLEMS
SCHULZ

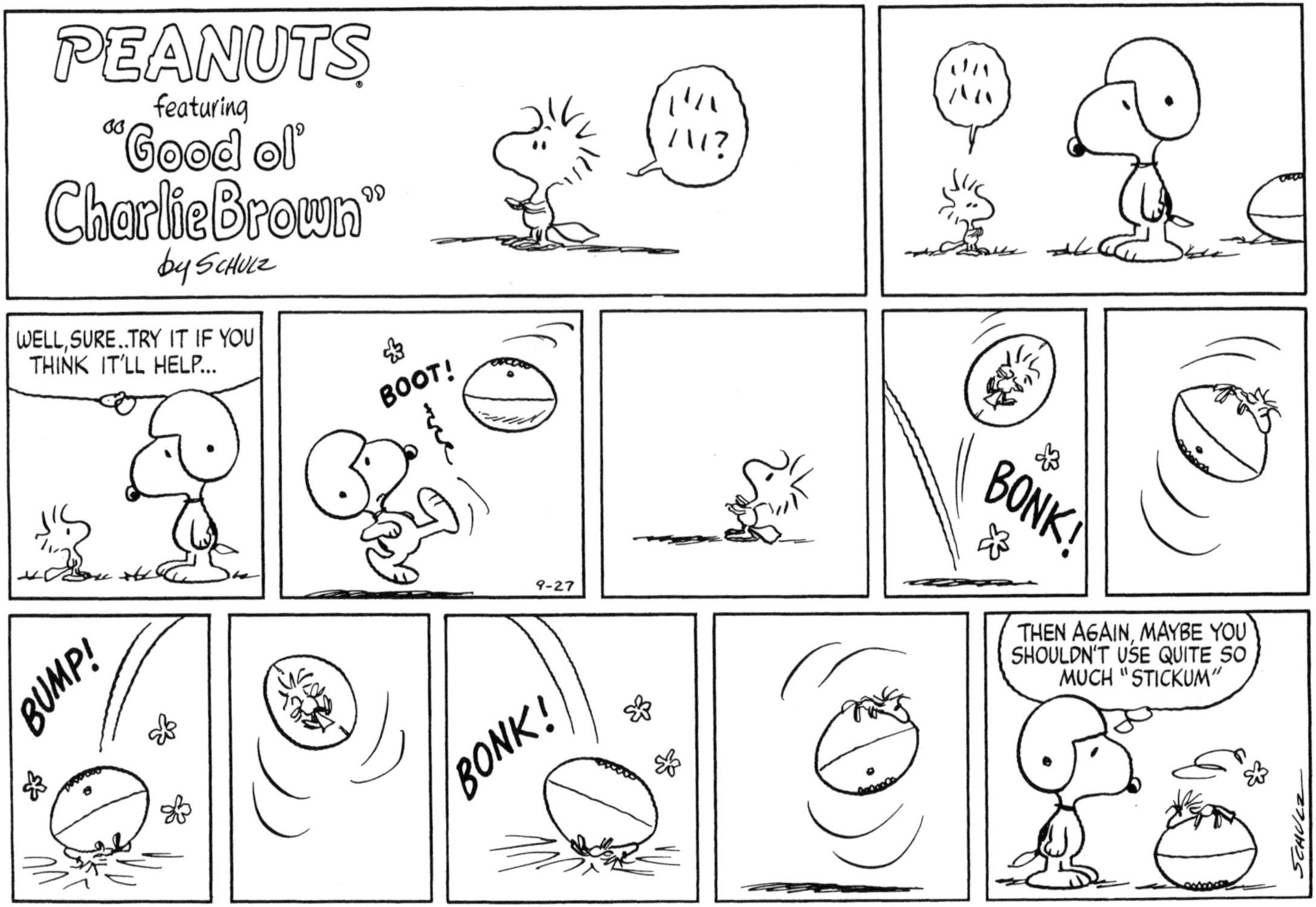
PEANUTS
featuring
"Good ol' CharlieBrown"
by SCHULZ
WELL, SURE..TRY IT IF YOU THINK IT'LL HELP...
BOOT!
9-27
BONK!
BUMP!
BONK!
THEN AGAIN, MAYBE YOU SHOULDN'T USE QUITE SO MUCH "STICKUM"
SCHULZ

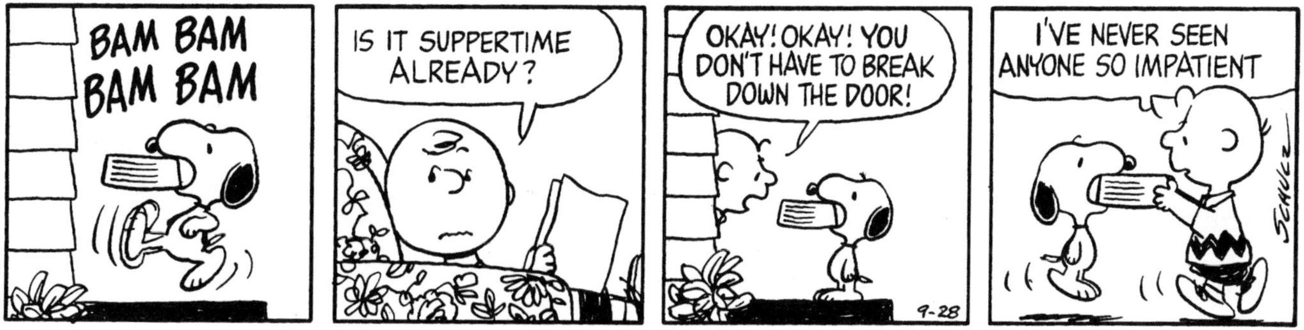
BAM BAM
BAM BAM
IS IT SUPPERTIME ALREADY?
OKAY! OKAY! YOU DON'T HAVE TO BREAK DOWN THE DOOR!
9-28
I'VE NEVER SEEN ANYONE SO IMPATIENT

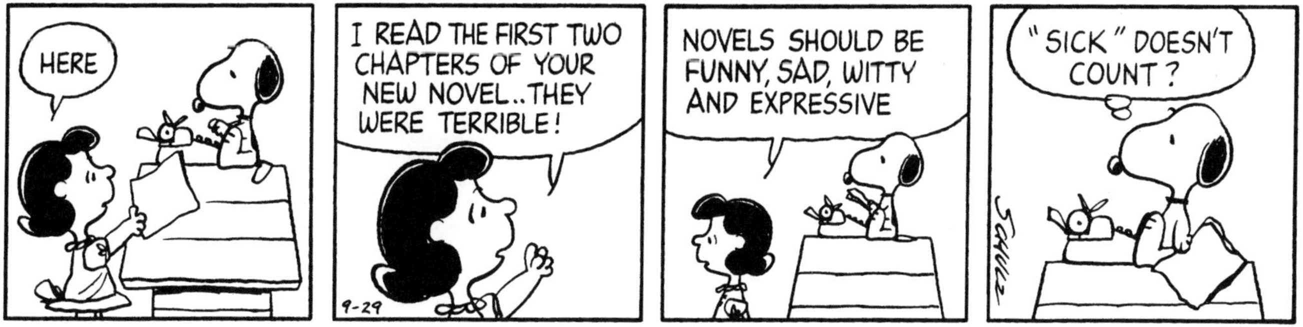
HERE
I READ THE FIRST TWO CHAPTERS OF YOUR NEW NOVEL..THEY WERE TERRIBLE!
9-29
NOVELS SHOULD BE FUNNY, SAD, WITTY AND EXPRESSIVE
"SICK" DOESN'T COUNT?

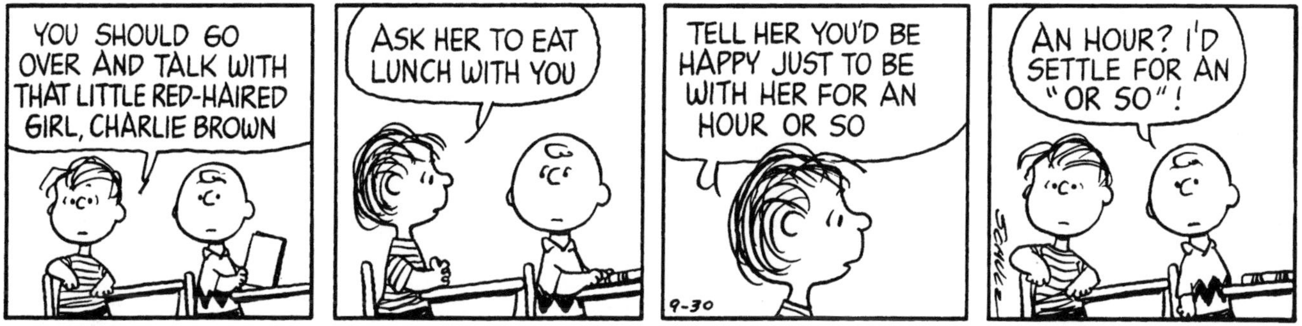
YOU SHOULD GO OVER AND TALK WITH THAT LITTLE RED-HAIRED GIRL, CHARLIE BROWN
ASK HER TO EAT LUNCH WITH YOU
TELL HER YOU'D BE HAPPY JUST TO BE WITH HER FOR AN HOUR OR SO
9-30
AN HOUR? I'D SETTLE FOR AN "OR SO"!

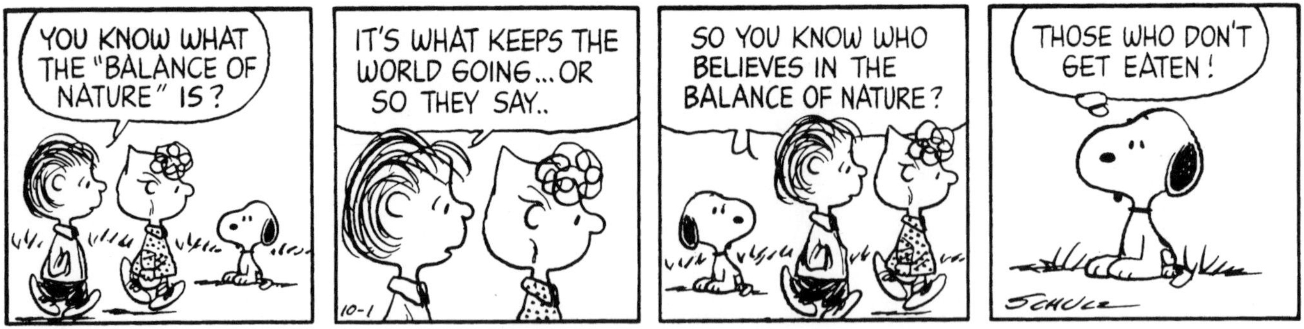
YOU KNOW WHAT THE "BALANCE OF NATURE" IS?
IT'S WHAT KEEPS THE WORLD GOING...OR SO THEY SAY..
10-1
SO YOU KNOW WHO BELIEVES IN THE BALANCE OF NATURE?
THOSE WHO DON'T GET EATEN!
SCHULZ

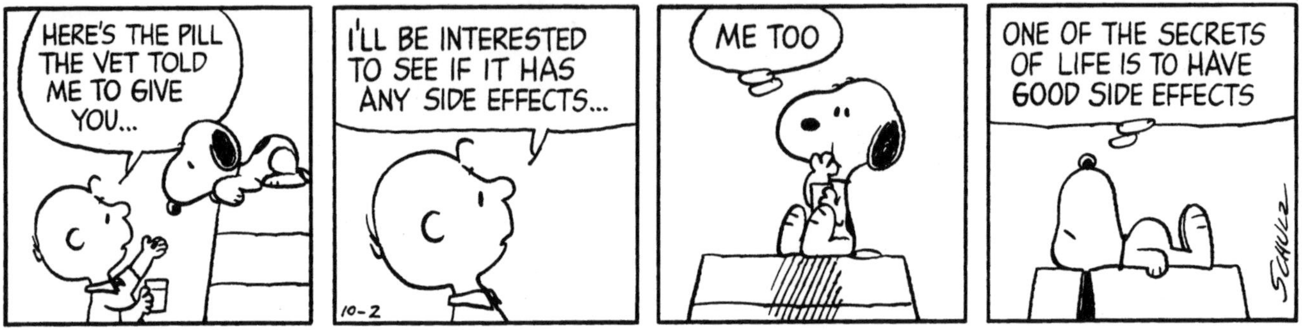
HERE'S THE PILL THE VET TOLD ME TO GIVE YOU...
I'LL BE INTERESTED TO SEE IF IT HAS ANY SIDE EFFECTS...
10-2
ME TOO
ONE OF THE SECRETS OF LIFE IS TO HAVE GOOD SIDE EFFECTS
SCHULZ

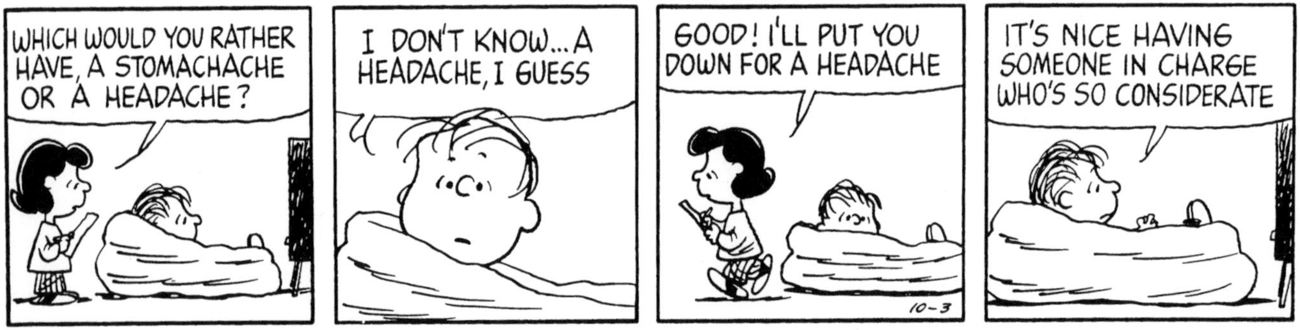
WHICH WOULD YOU RATHER HAVE, A STOMACHACHE OR A HEADACHE?
I DON'T KNOW...A HEADACHE, I GUESS
GOOD! I'LL PUT YOU DOWN FOR A HEADACHE
10-3
IT'S NICE HAVING SOMEONE IN CHARGE WHO'S SO CONSIDERATE

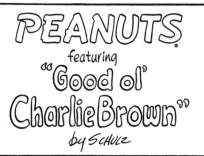

PEANUTS featuring "Good ol' Charlie Brown" by Schulz

ACE BOOK of WORLD Records

WE MADE IT! LOOK AT THAT VIEW...

OKAY, HARRIET, BREAK OUT THE CAKE

DO YOU REALIZE WE ARE ABOUT TO SET A RECORD?

WE ARE THE FIRST HIKERS EVER TO CLIMB THIS PEAK, AND THEN SIT HERE EATING ANGEL FOOD CAKE WITH SEVEN MINUTE FROSTING!

10-4

NO, OLIVIER, I DON'T WANT YOUR AUTOGRAPH!

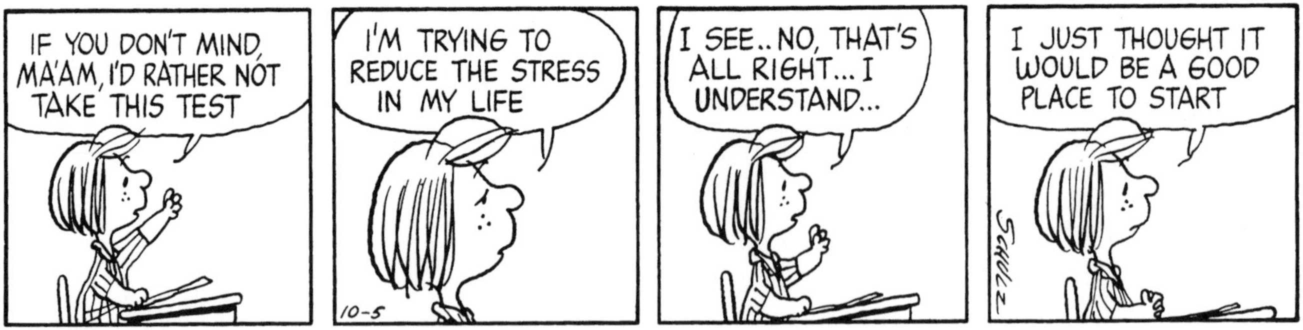
IF YOU DON'T MIND, MA'AM, I'D RATHER NOT TAKE THIS TEST
I'M TRYING TO REDUCE THE STRESS IN MY LIFE
10-5
I SEE.. NO, THAT'S ALL RIGHT... I UNDERSTAND...
I JUST THOUGHT IT WOULD BE A GOOD PLACE TO START
SCHULZ

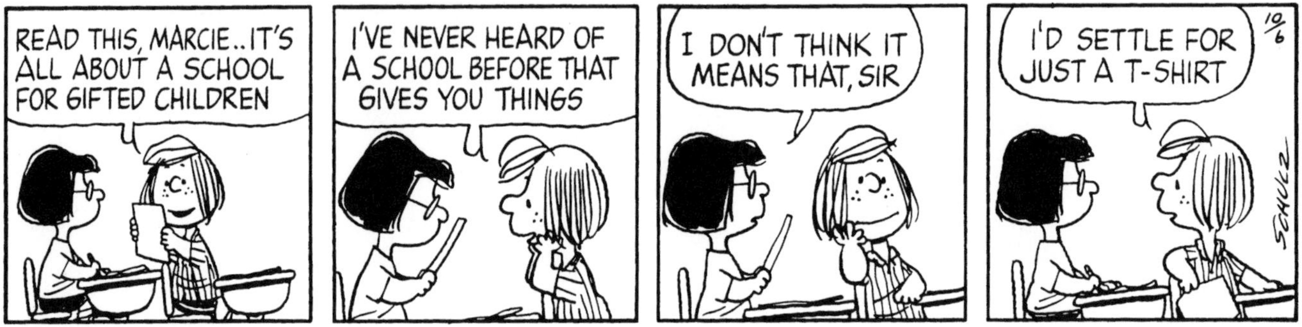
READ THIS, MARCIE.. IT'S ALL ABOUT A SCHOOL FOR GIFTED CHILDREN
I'VE NEVER HEARD OF A SCHOOL BEFORE THAT GIVES YOU THINGS
I DON'T THINK IT MEANS THAT, SIR
I'D SETTLE FOR JUST A T-SHIRT
10/6
SCHULZ

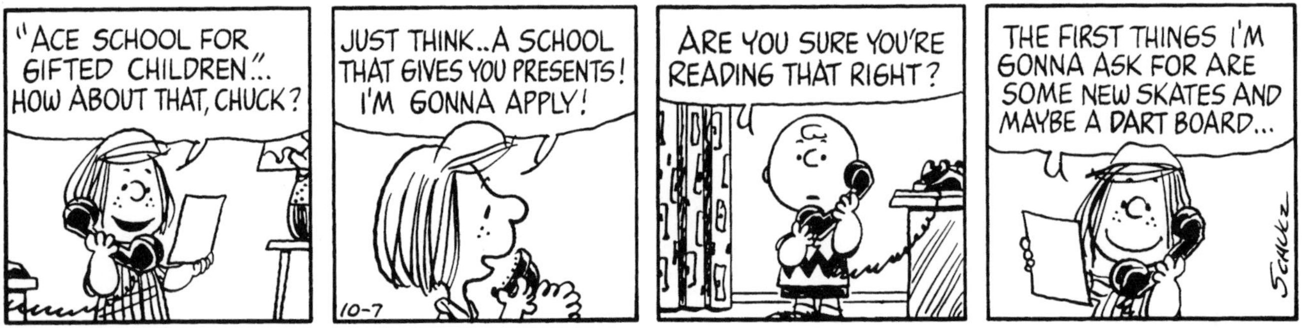
"ACE SCHOOL FOR GIFTED CHILDREN".. HOW ABOUT THAT, CHUCK?
JUST THINK.. A SCHOOL THAT GIVES YOU PRESENTS! I'M GONNA APPLY!
10-7
ARE YOU SURE YOU'RE READING THAT RIGHT?
THE FIRST THINGS I'M GONNA ASK FOR ARE SOME NEW SKATES AND MAYBE A DART BOARD...
SCHULZ

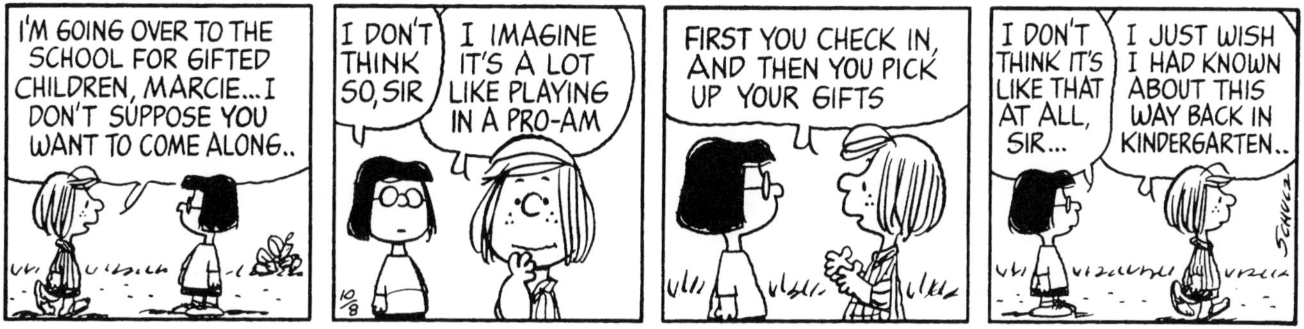
I'M GOING OVER TO THE SCHOOL FOR GIFTED CHILDREN, MARCIE...I DON'T SUPPOSE YOU WANT TO COME ALONG..
I IMAGINE IT'S A LOT LIKE PLAYING IN A PRO-AM
I DON'T THINK SO, SIR
10/8
FIRST YOU CHECK IN, AND THEN YOU PICK UP YOUR GIFTS
I DON'T THINK IT'S LIKE THAT AT ALL, SIR...
I JUST WISH I HAD KNOWN ABOUT THIS WAY BACK IN KINDERGARTEN..
SCHULZ

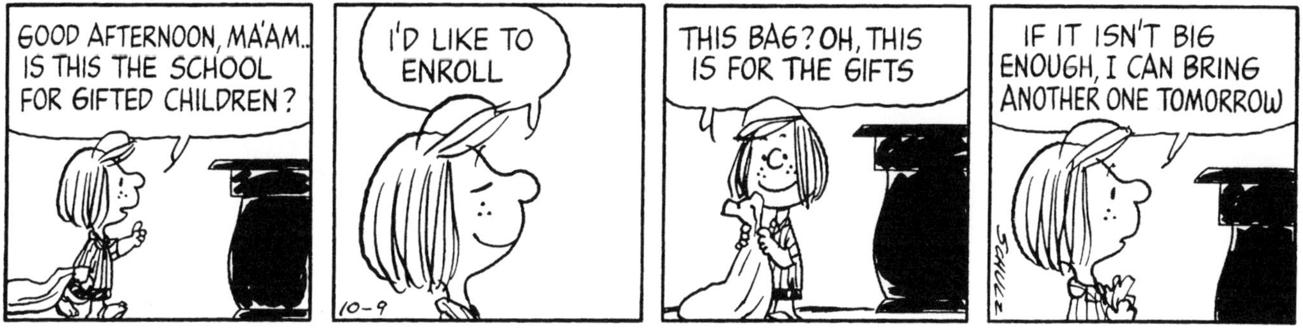
GOOD AFTERNOON, MA'AM.. IS THIS THE SCHOOL FOR GIFTED CHILDREN?
I'D LIKE TO ENROLL
10-9
THIS BAG? OH, THIS IS FOR THE GIFTS
IF IT ISN'T BIG ENOUGH, I CAN BRING ANOTHER ONE TOMORROW
SCHULZ

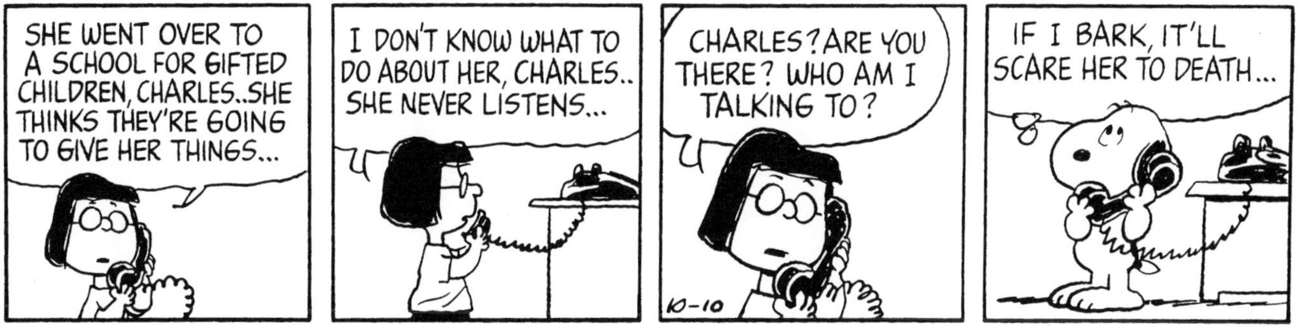
SHE WENT OVER TO A SCHOOL FOR GIFTED CHILDREN, CHARLES..SHE THINKS THEY'RE GOING TO GIVE HER THINGS...
I DON'T KNOW WHAT TO DO ABOUT HER, CHARLES.. SHE NEVER LISTENS...
CHARLES? ARE YOU THERE? WHO AM I TALKING TO?
10-10
IF I BARK, IT'LL SCARE HER TO DEATH...

PEANUTS
featuring
"Good ol' Charlie Brown"
by SCHULZ

CHARLIE BROWN, HAS ANYONE EVER TOLD YOU THAT YOU WALK FUNNY?

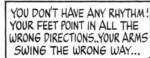

YOU DON'T HAVE ANY RHYTHM! YOUR FEET POINT IN ALL THE WRONG DIRECTIONS..YOUR ARMS SWING THE WRONG WAY...

STAND UP STRAIGHT..NOW MOVE FORWARD...WALK THE WAY I TOLD YOU...

10-11

KLUNK!

I STILL THINK IT'S A MATTER OF RHYTHM..TRY IT AGAIN...

BONK!

HOW AM I GOING TO GET HOME?

KEEP WORKING AT IT.. I'VE DONE ALL I CAN

WHAT IN THE WORLD ARE YOU DOING?

THIS IS CALLED, "STARTING OVER RIGHT FROM THE BEGINNING"

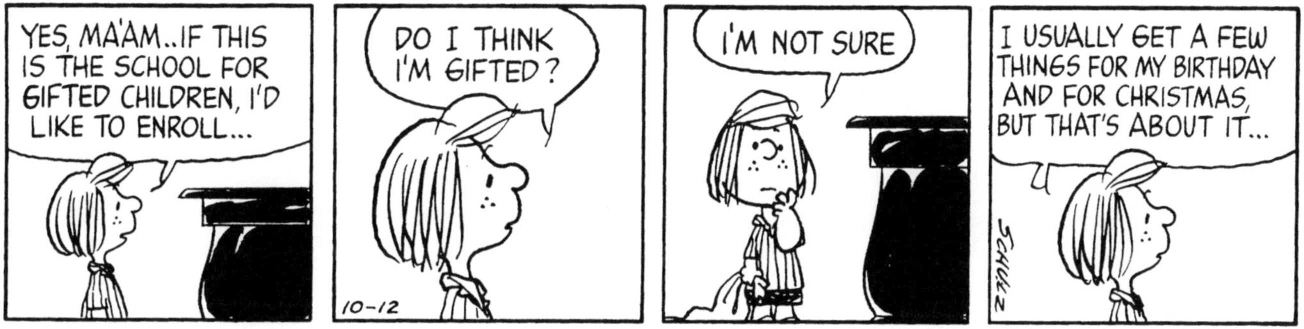
YES, MA'AM..IF THIS IS THE SCHOOL FOR GIFTED CHILDREN, I'D LIKE TO ENROLL...
DO I THINK I'M GIFTED?
10-12
I'M NOT SURE
I USUALLY GET A FEW THINGS FOR MY BIRTHDAY AND FOR CHRISTMAS, BUT THAT'S ABOUT IT...
SCHULZ

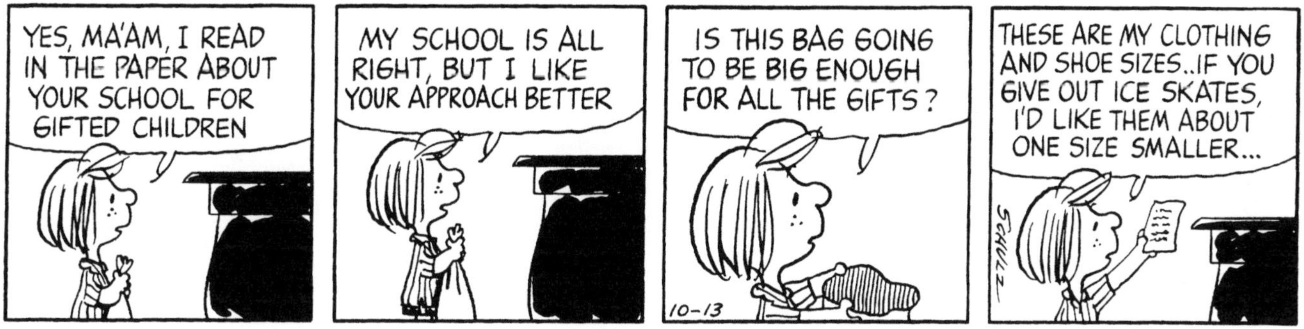
YES, MA'AM, I READ IN THE PAPER ABOUT YOUR SCHOOL FOR GIFTED CHILDREN
MY SCHOOL IS ALL RIGHT, BUT I LIKE YOUR APPROACH BETTER
IS THIS BAG GOING TO BE BIG ENOUGH FOR ALL THE GIFTS?
10-13
THESE ARE MY CLOTHING AND SHOE SIZES..IF YOU GIVE OUT ICE SKATES, I'D LIKE THEM ABOUT ONE SIZE SMALLER...
SCHULZ

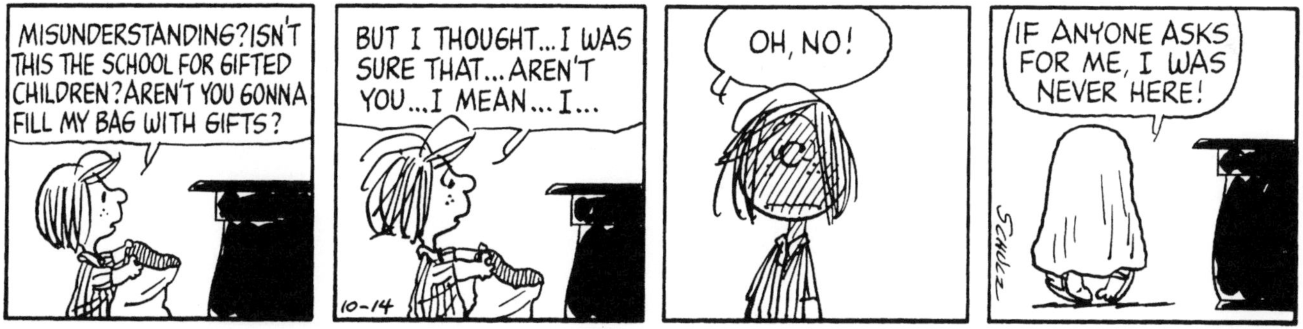
MISUNDERSTANDING? ISN'T THIS THE SCHOOL FOR GIFTED CHILDREN? AREN'T YOU GONNA FILL MY BAG WITH GIFTS?
BUT I THOUGHT...I WAS SURE THAT...AREN'T YOU...I MEAN... I...
10-14
OH, NO!
IF ANYONE ASKS FOR ME, I WAS NEVER HERE!
SCHULZ

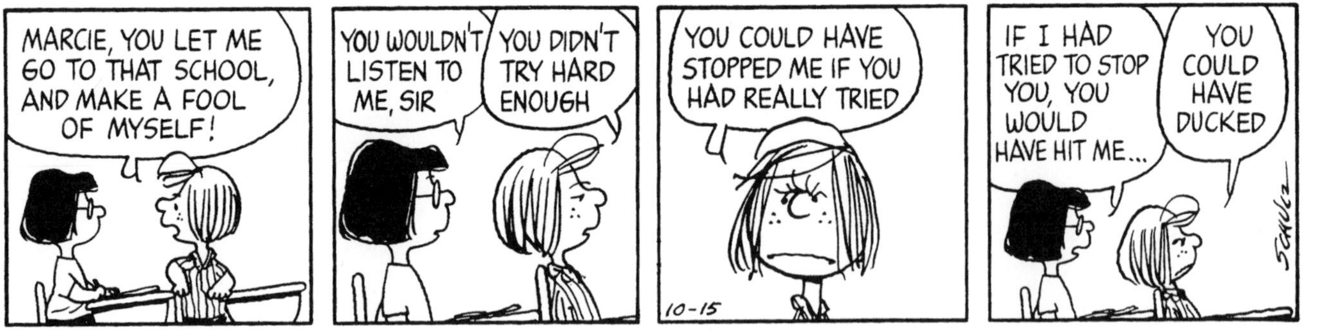
MARCIE, YOU LET ME GO TO THAT SCHOOL, AND MAKE A FOOL OF MYSELF!
YOU WOULDN'T LISTEN TO ME, SIR
YOU DIDN'T TRY HARD ENOUGH
YOU COULD HAVE STOPPED ME IF YOU HAD REALLY TRIED
10-15
IF I HAD TRIED TO STOP YOU, YOU WOULD HAVE HIT ME...
YOU COULD HAVE DUCKED
SCHULZ

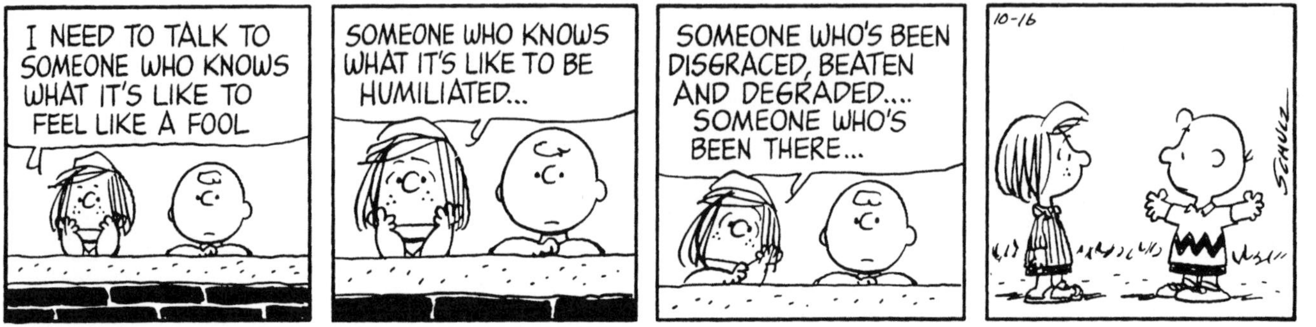
I NEED TO TALK TO SOMEONE WHO KNOWS WHAT IT'S LIKE TO FEEL LIKE A FOOL
SOMEONE WHO KNOWS WHAT IT'S LIKE TO BE HUMILIATED...
SOMEONE WHO'S BEEN DISGRACED, BEATEN AND DEGRADED.... SOMEONE WHO'S BEEN THERE...
10-16
SCHULZ

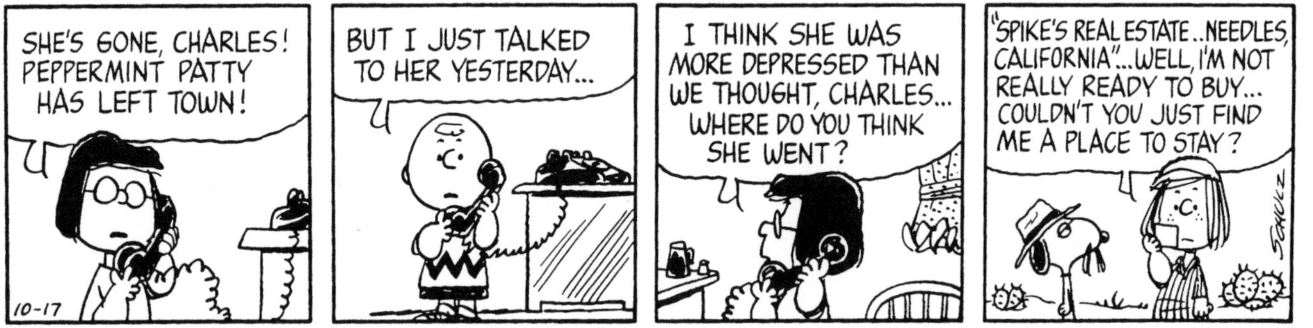
SHE'S GONE, CHARLES! PEPPERMINT PATTY HAS LEFT TOWN!
10-17
BUT I JUST TALKED TO HER YESTERDAY...
I THINK SHE WAS MORE DEPRESSED THAN WE THOUGHT, CHARLES... WHERE DO YOU THINK SHE WENT?
"SPIKE'S REAL ESTATE...NEEDLES, CALIFORNIA"...WELL, I'M NOT REALLY READY TO BUY... COULDN'T YOU JUST FIND ME A PLACE TO STAY?
SCHULZ

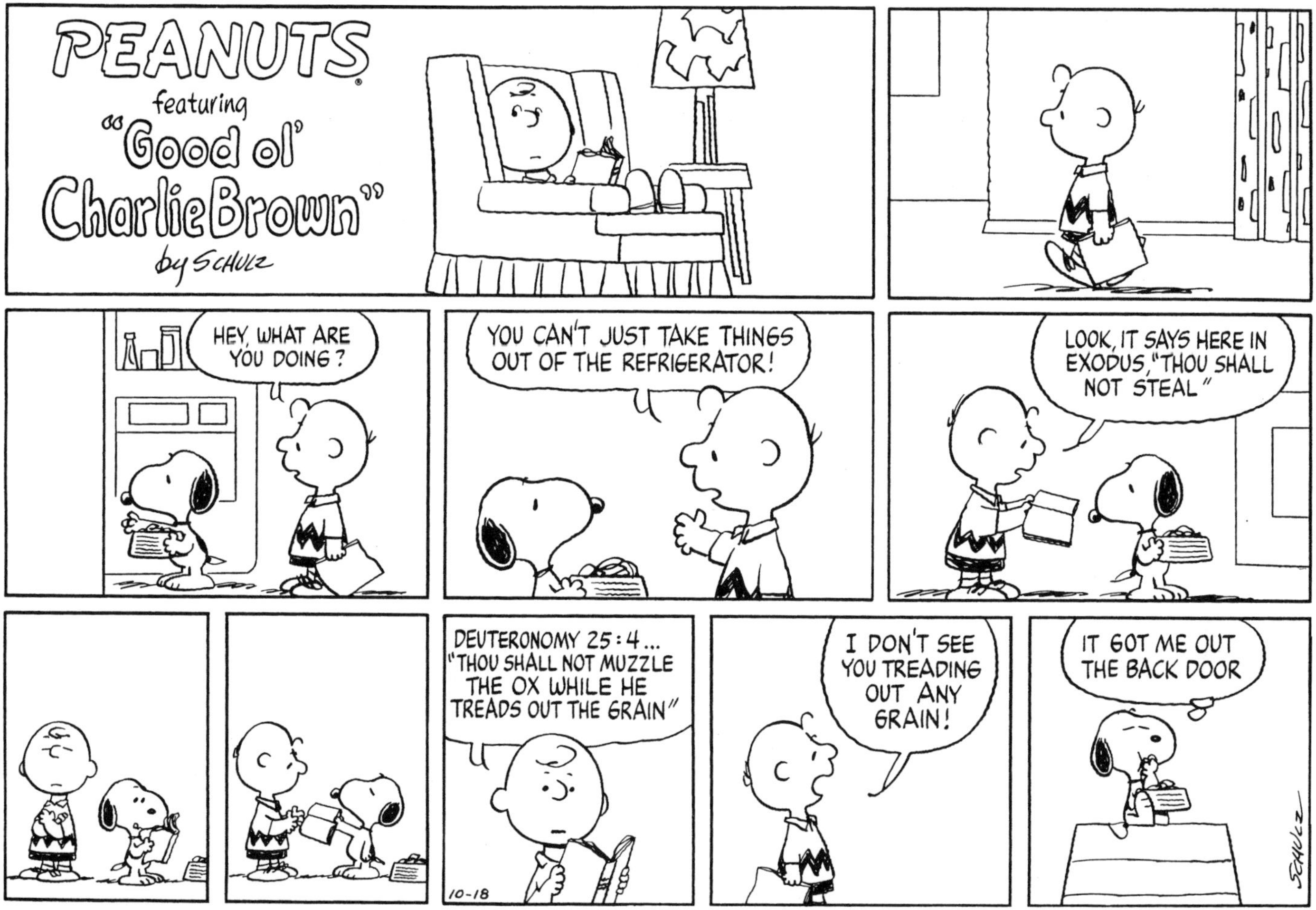
PEANUTS
featuring
"Good ol' Charlie Brown"
by SCHULZ
HEY, WHAT ARE YOU DOING?
YOU CAN'T JUST TAKE THINGS OUT OF THE REFRIGERATOR!
LOOK, IT SAYS HERE IN EXODUS, "THOU SHALL NOT STEAL"
DEUTERONOMY 25:4... "THOU SHALL NOT MUZZLE THE OX WHILE HE TREADS OUT THE GRAIN"
10-18
I DON'T SEE YOU TREADING OUT ANY GRAIN!
IT GOT ME OUT THE BACK DOOR
SCHULZ

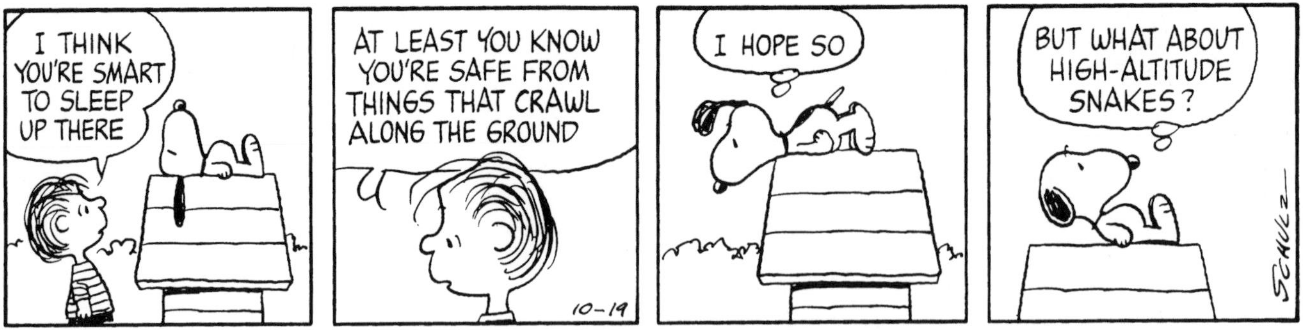
I THINK YOU'RE SMART TO SLEEP UP THERE
AT LEAST YOU KNOW YOU'RE SAFE FROM THINGS THAT CRAWL ALONG THE GROUND
10-19
I HOPE SO
BUT WHAT ABOUT HIGH-ALTITUDE SNAKES?
SCHULZ

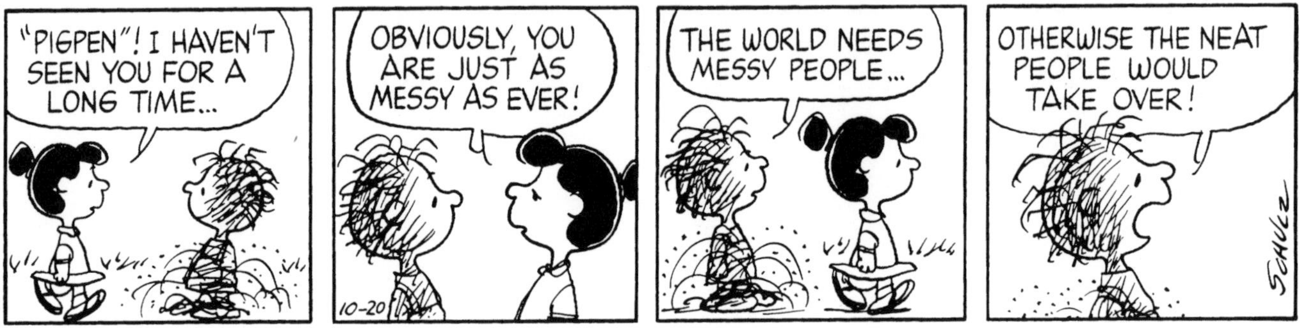
"PIGPEN"! I HAVEN'T SEEN YOU FOR A LONG TIME...
OBVIOUSLY, YOU ARE JUST AS MESSY AS EVER!
10-20
THE WORLD NEEDS MESSY PEOPLE...
OTHERWISE THE NEAT PEOPLE WOULD TAKE OVER!
SCHULZ

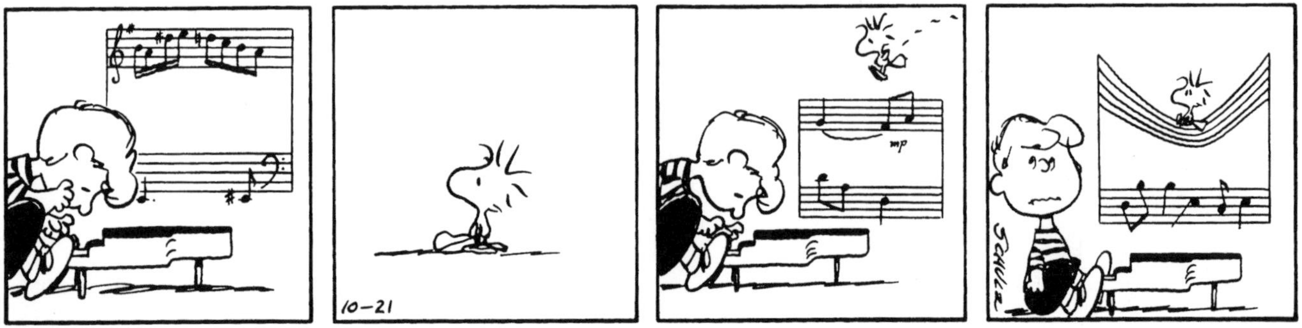
10-21
SCHULZ

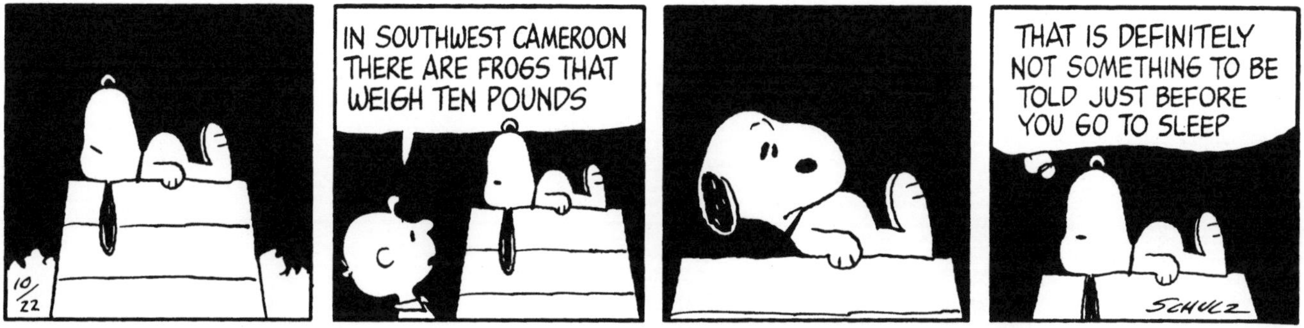
10/22
IN SOUTHWEST CAMEROON THERE ARE FROGS THAT WEIGH TEN POUNDS
THAT IS DEFINITELY NOT SOMETHING TO BE TOLD JUST BEFORE YOU GO TO SLEEP
SCHULZ

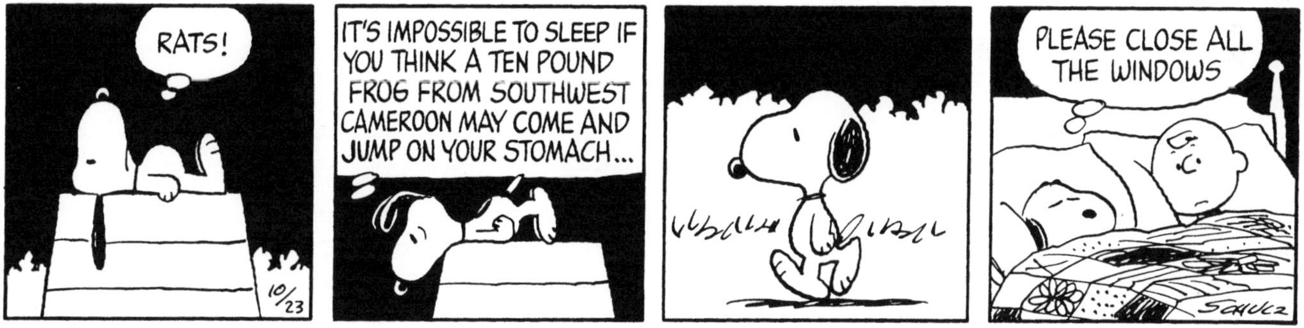
RATS!
10/23
IT'S IMPOSSIBLE TO SLEEP IF YOU THINK A TEN POUND FROG FROM SOUTHWEST CAMEROON MAY COME AND JUMP ON YOUR STOMACH...
PLEASE CLOSE ALL THE WINDOWS
SCHULZ

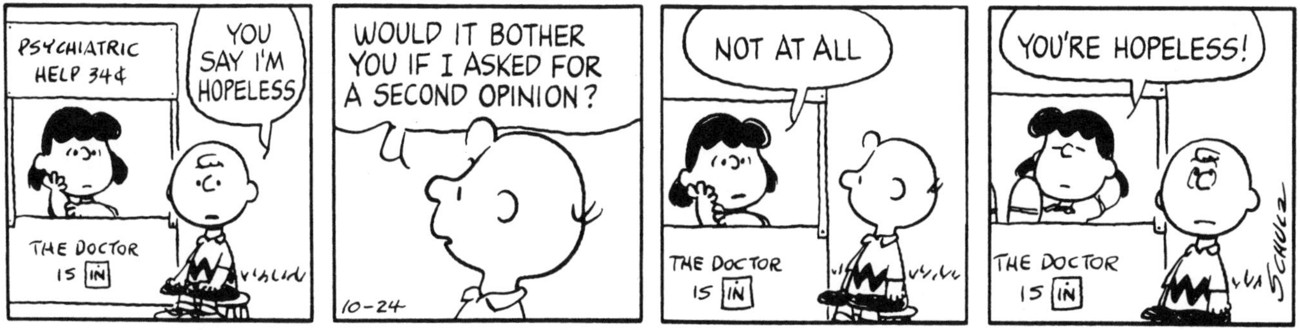
PSYCHIATRIC HELP 34¢
YOU SAY I'M HOPELESS
THE DOCTOR IS IN
WOULD IT BOTHER YOU IF I ASKED FOR A SECOND OPINION?
10-24
NOT AT ALL
THE DOCTOR IS IN
YOU'RE HOPELESS!
THE DOCTOR IS IN
SCHULZ

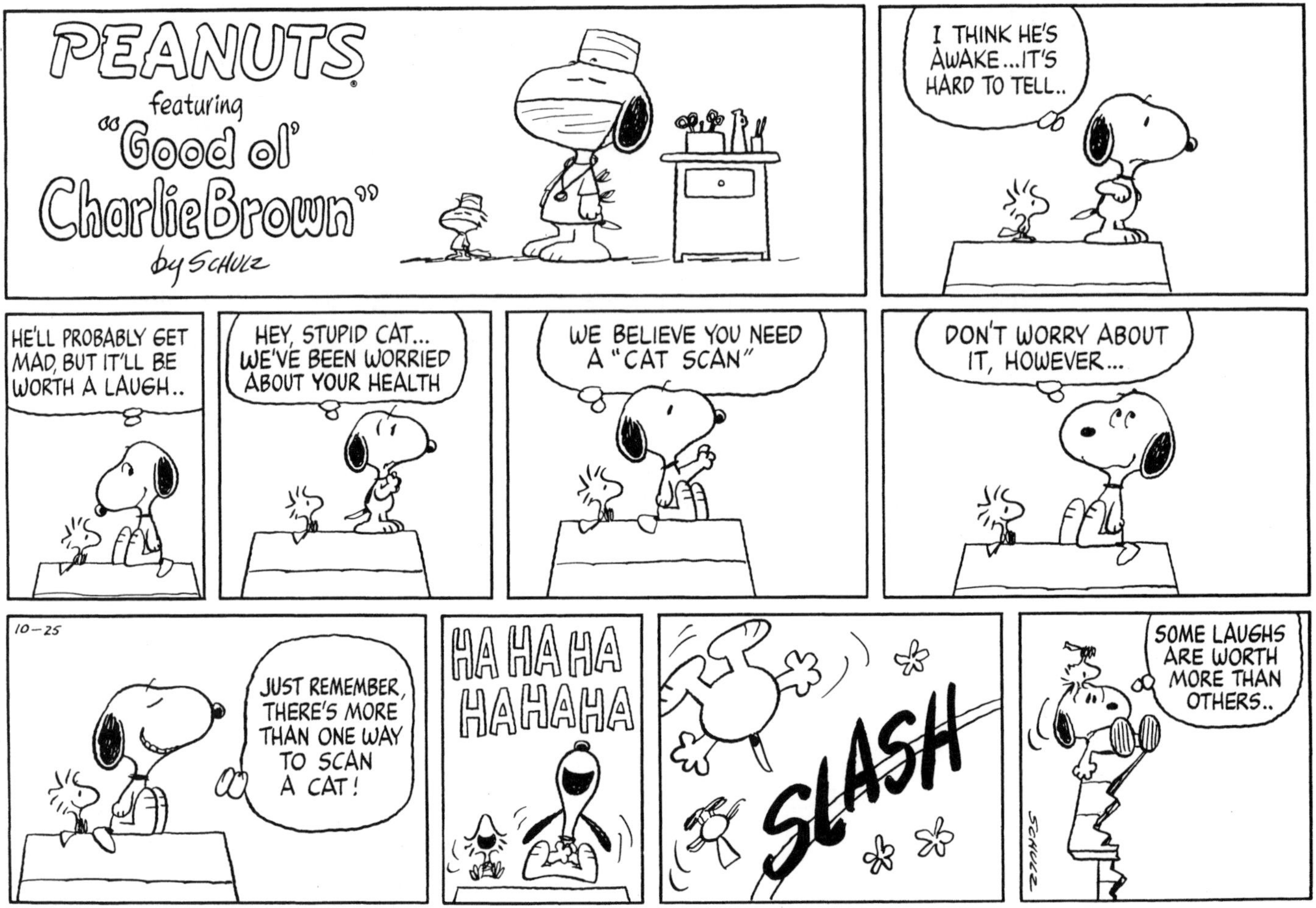
PEANUTS
featuring
"Good ol' Charlie Brown"
by SCHULZ
I THINK HE'S AWAKE...IT'S HARD TO TELL..
HE'LL PROBABLY GET MAD, BUT IT'LL BE WORTH A LAUGH..
HEY, STUPID CAT... WE'VE BEEN WORRIED ABOUT YOUR HEALTH
WE BELIEVE YOU NEED A "CAT SCAN"
DON'T WORRY ABOUT IT, HOWEVER...
10-25
JUST REMEMBER, THERE'S MORE THAN ONE WAY TO SCAN A CAT!
HA HA HA HA HAHAHA
SLASH
SCHULZ
SOME LAUGHS ARE WORTH MORE THAN OTHERS..

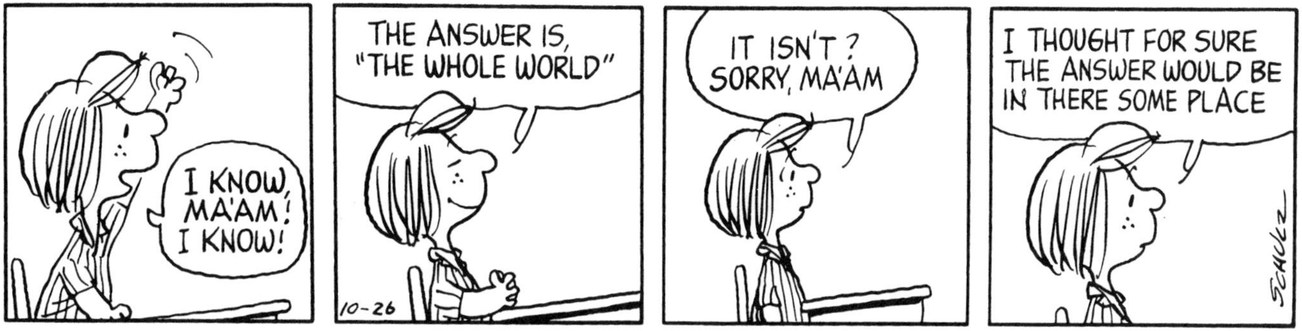
I KNOW, MA'AM! I KNOW!
THE ANSWER IS, "THE WHOLE WORLD"
10-26
IT ISN'T? SORRY, MA'AM
I THOUGHT FOR SURE THE ANSWER WOULD BE IN THERE SOME PLACE
SCHULZ

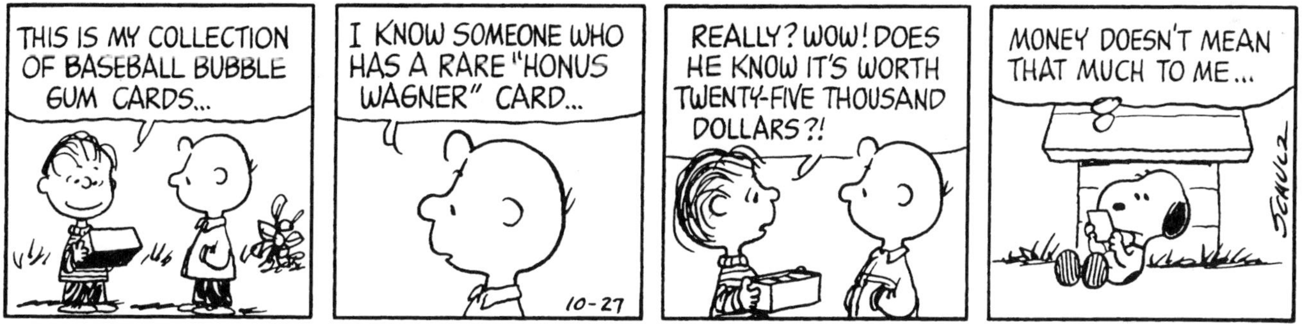
THIS IS MY COLLECTION OF BASEBALL BUBBLE GUM CARDS...
I KNOW SOMEONE WHO HAS A RARE "HONUS WAGNER" CARD...
10-27
REALLY? WOW! DOES HE KNOW IT'S WORTH TWENTY-FIVE THOUSAND DOLLARS?!
MONEY DOESN'T MEAN THAT MUCH TO ME...
SCHULZ

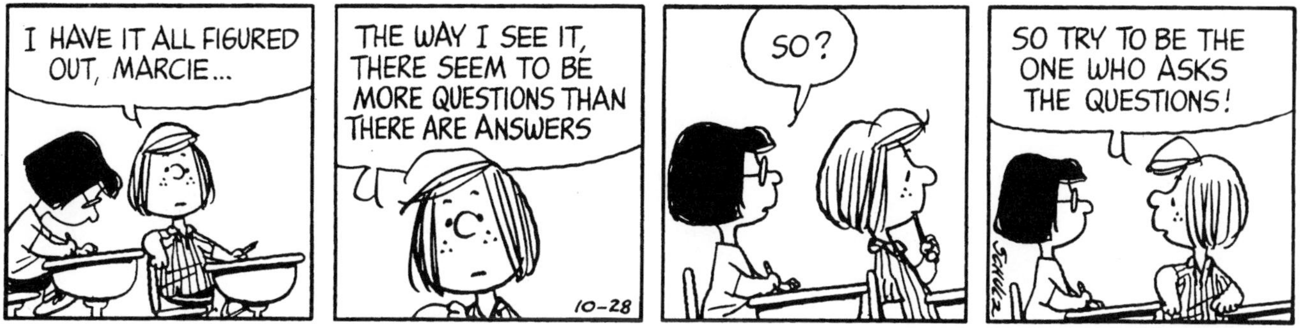
I HAVE IT ALL FIGURED OUT, MARCIE...
THE WAY I SEE IT, THERE SEEM TO BE MORE QUESTIONS THAN THERE ARE ANSWERS
10-28
SO?
SO TRY TO BE THE ONE WHO ASKS THE QUESTIONS!
SCHULZ

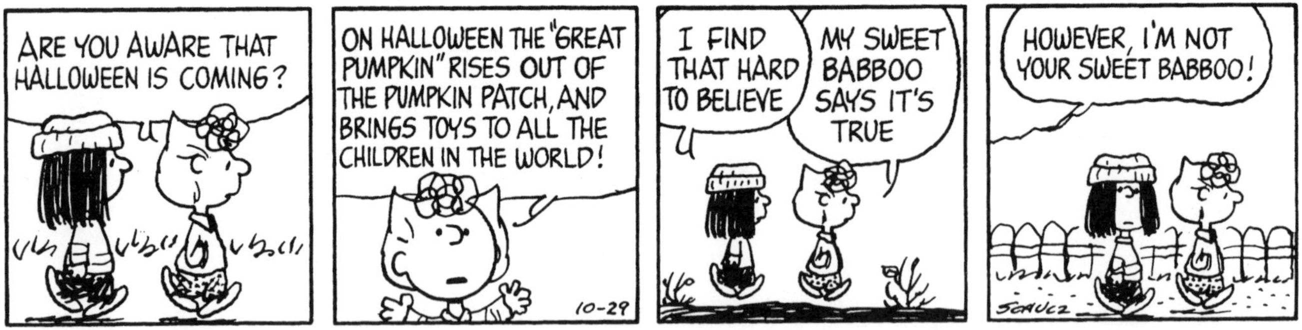
ARE YOU AWARE THAT HALLOWEEN IS COMING?
ON HALLOWEEN THE "GREAT PUMPKIN" RISES OUT OF THE PUMPKIN PATCH, AND BRINGS TOYS TO ALL THE CHILDREN IN THE WORLD!
10-29
I FIND THAT HARD TO BELIEVE
MY SWEET BABBOO SAYS IT'S TRUE
HOWEVER, I'M NOT YOUR SWEET BABBOO!

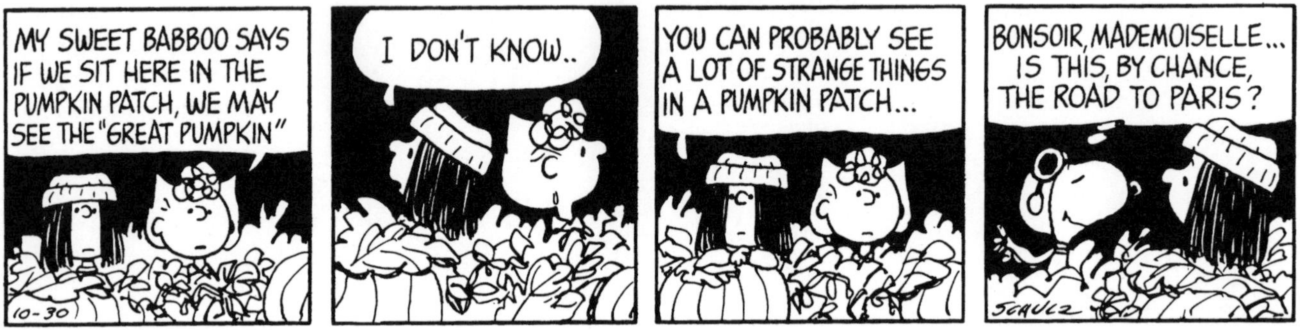
MY SWEET BABBOO SAYS IF WE SIT HERE IN THE PUMPKIN PATCH, WE MAY SEE THE "GREAT PUMPKIN"
10-30
I DON'T KNOW..
YOU CAN PROBABLY SEE A LOT OF STRANGE THINGS IN A PUMPKIN PATCH...
BONSOIR, MADEMOISELLE... IS THIS, BY CHANCE, THE ROAD TO PARIS?

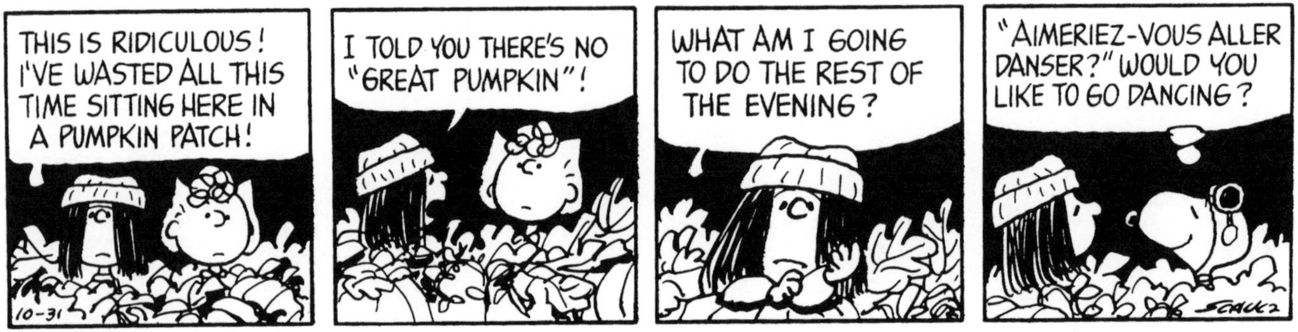
THIS IS RIDICULOUS! I'VE WASTED ALL THIS TIME SITTING HERE IN A PUMPKIN PATCH!
10-31
I TOLD YOU THERE'S NO "GREAT PUMPKIN"!
WHAT AM I GOING TO DO THE REST OF THE EVENING?
"AIMERIEZ-VOUS ALLER DANSER?" WOULD YOU LIKE TO GO DANCING?

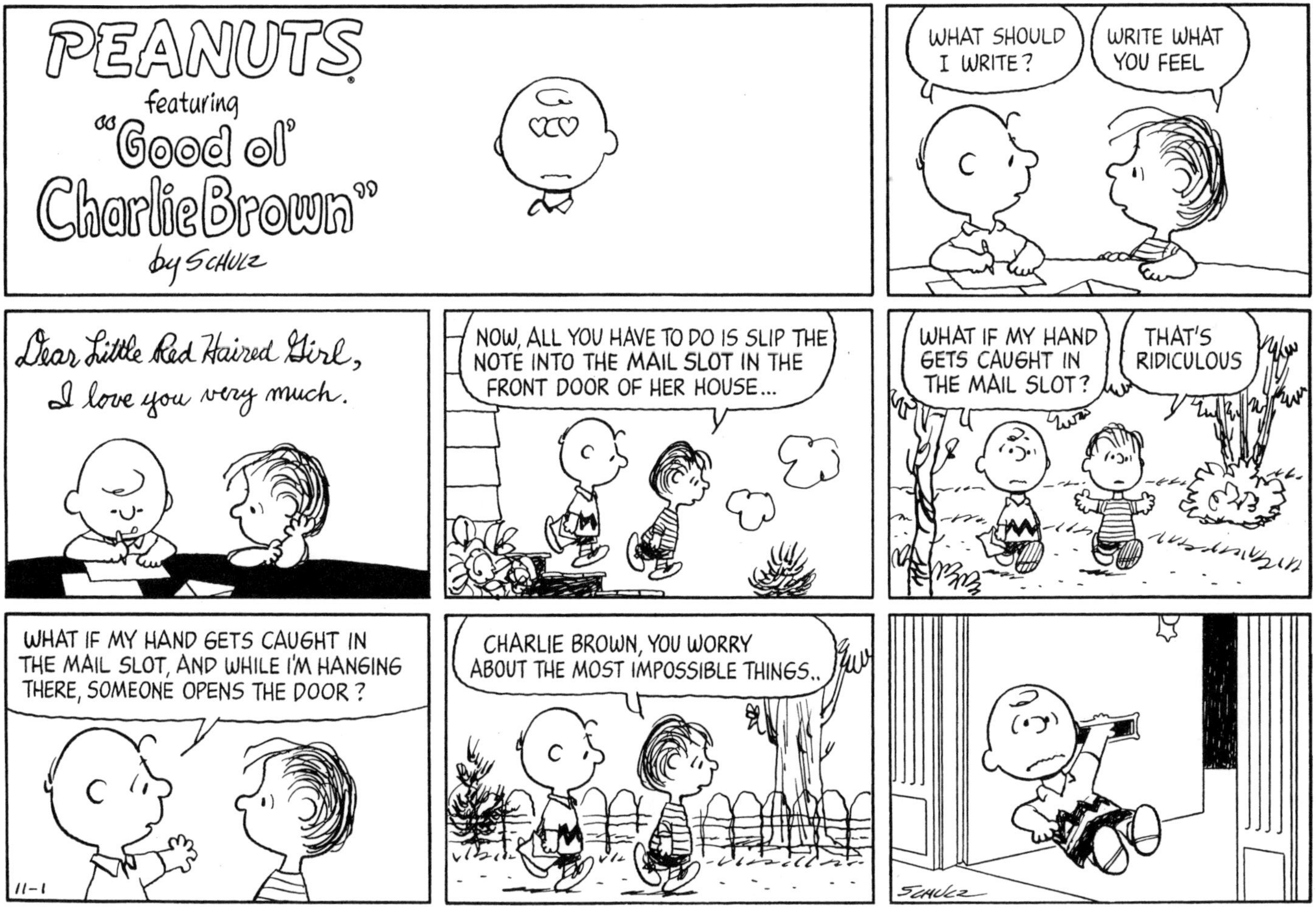
PEANUTS
featuring
"Good ol' Charlie Brown"
by SCHULZ
WHAT SHOULD I WRITE?
WRITE WHAT YOU FEEL
Dear Little Red Haired Girl,
I love you very much.
NOW, ALL YOU HAVE TO DO IS SLIP THE NOTE INTO THE MAIL SLOT IN THE FRONT DOOR OF HER HOUSE...
WHAT IF MY HAND GETS CAUGHT IN THE MAIL SLOT?
THAT'S RIDICULOUS
WHAT IF MY HAND GETS CAUGHT IN THE MAIL SLOT, AND WHILE I'M HANGING THERE, SOMEONE OPENS THE DOOR?
11-1
CHARLIE BROWN, YOU WORRY ABOUT THE MOST IMPOSSIBLE THINGS..
SCHULZ

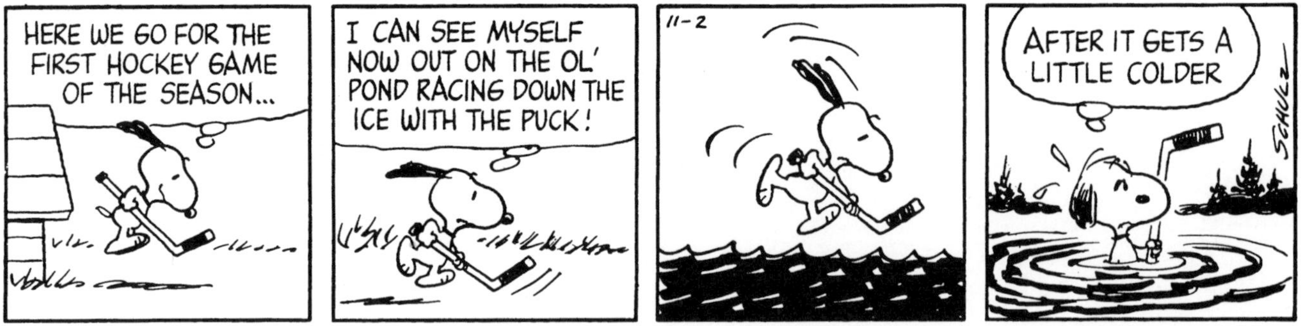
HERE WE GO FOR THE FIRST HOCKEY GAME OF THE SEASON...
I CAN SEE MYSELF NOW OUT ON THE OL' POND RACING DOWN THE ICE WITH THE PUCK!
11-2
AFTER IT GETS A LITTLE COLDER
SCHULZ

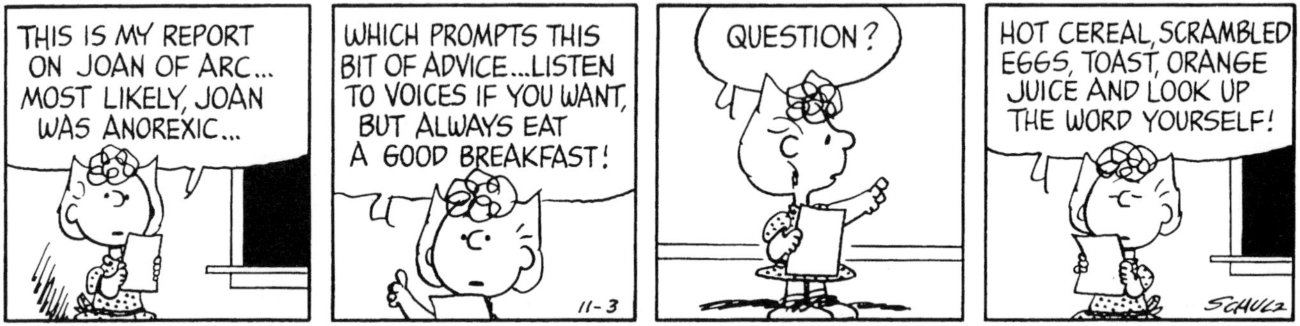
THIS IS MY REPORT ON JOAN OF ARC... MOST LIKELY, JOAN WAS ANOREXIC...
WHICH PROMPTS THIS BIT OF ADVICE...LISTEN TO VOICES IF YOU WANT, BUT ALWAYS EAT A GOOD BREAKFAST!
11-3
QUESTION?
HOT CEREAL, SCRAMBLED EGGS, TOAST, ORANGE JUICE AND LOOK UP THE WORD YOURSELF!
SCHULZ

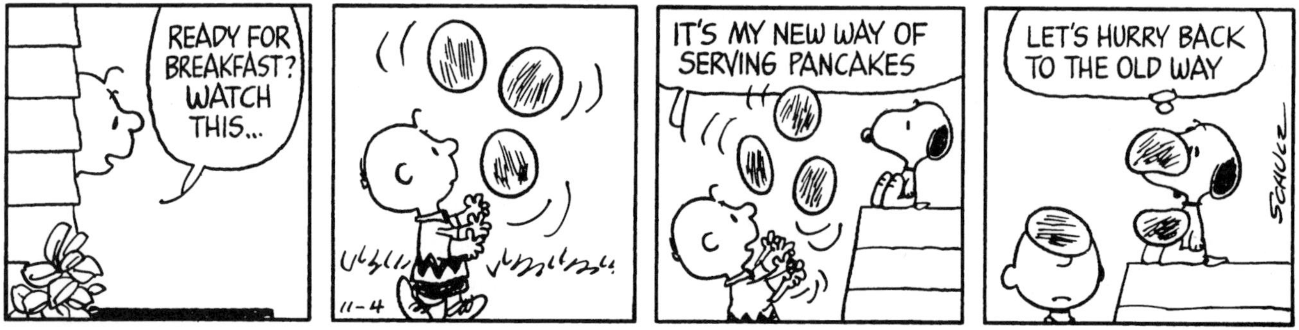
READY FOR BREAKFAST? WATCH THIS...
11-4
IT'S MY NEW WAY OF SERVING PANCAKES
LET'S HURRY BACK TO THE OLD WAY
SCHULZ

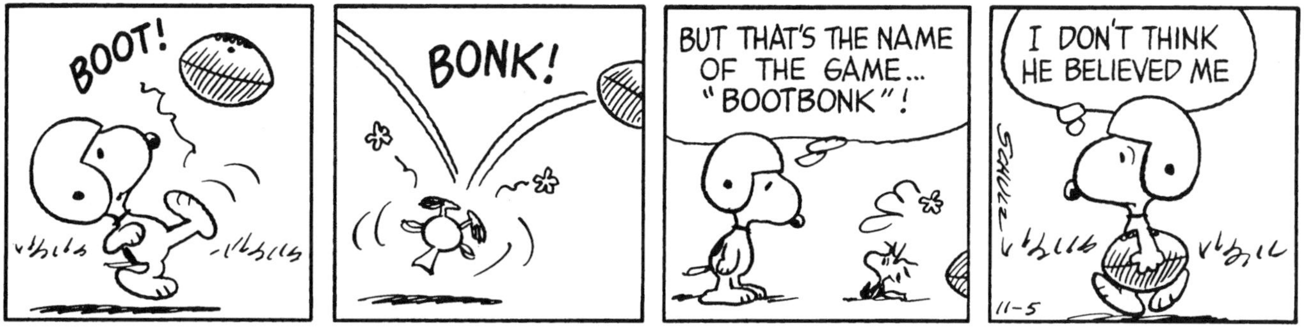
BOOT!
BONK!
BUT THAT'S THE NAME OF THE GAME... "BOOTBONK"!
I DON'T THINK HE BELIEVED ME
11-5

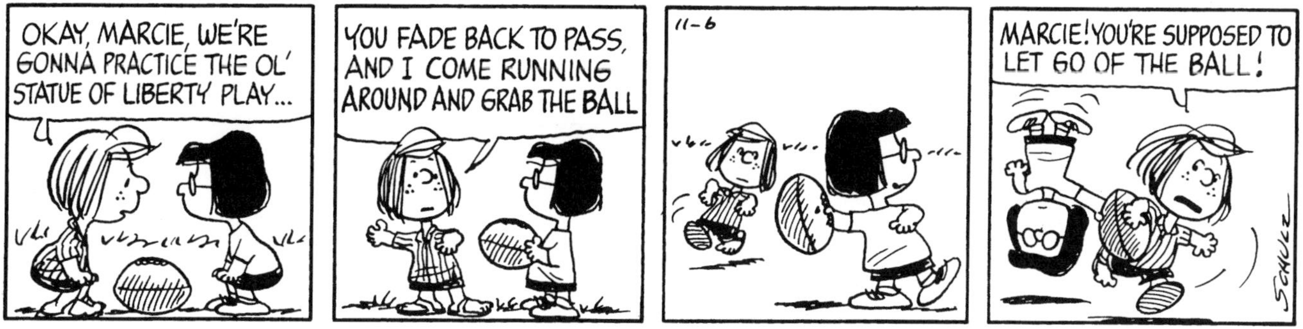
OKAY, MARCIE, WE'RE GONNA PRACTICE THE OL' STATUE OF LIBERTY PLAY...
YOU FADE BACK TO PASS, AND I COME RUNNING AROUND AND GRAB THE BALL
11-6
MARCIE! YOU'RE SUPPOSED TO LET GO OF THE BALL!

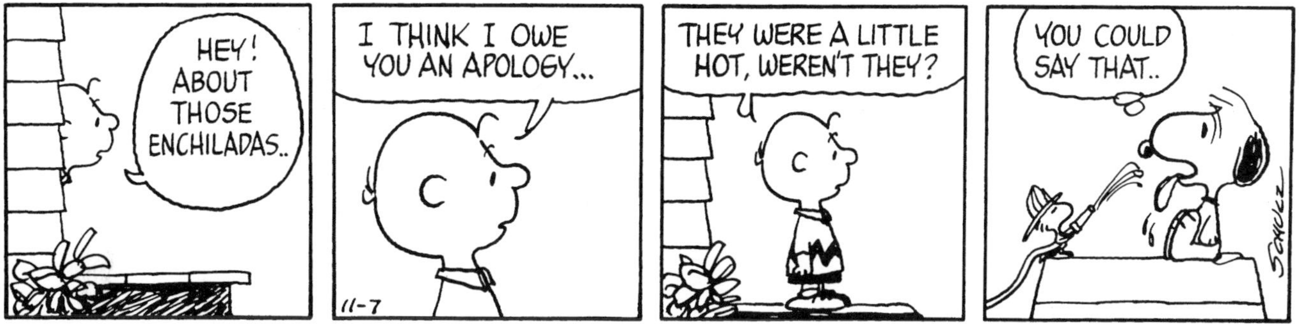
HEY! ABOUT THOSE ENCHILADAS..
I THINK I OWE YOU AN APOLOGY...
11-7
THEY WERE A LITTLE HOT, WEREN'T THEY?
YOU COULD SAY THAT..

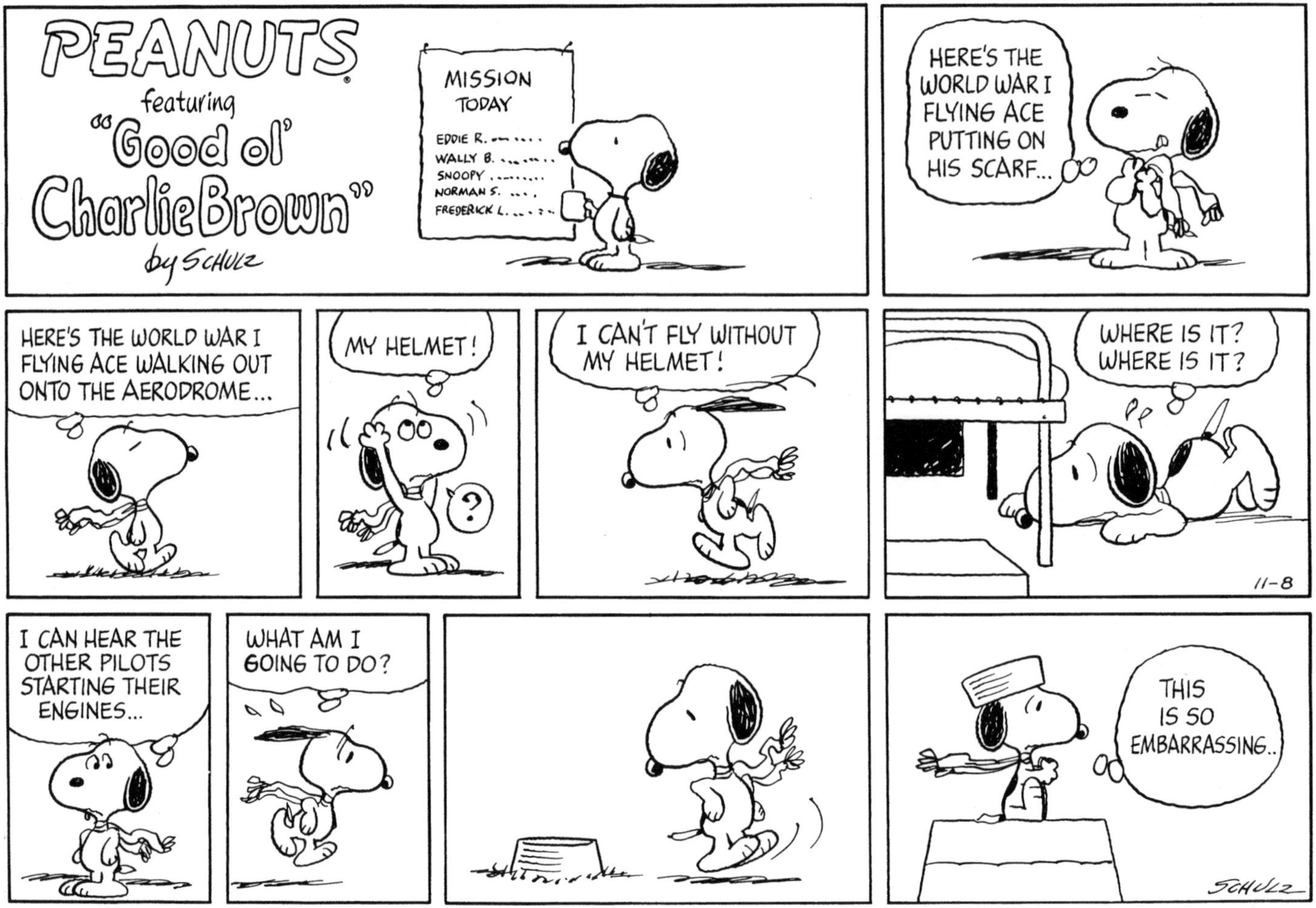
PEANUTS
featuring
"Good ol' Charlie Brown"
by SCHULZ
MISSION TODAY
EDDIE R.
WALLY B.
SNOOPY
NORMAN S.
FREDERICK L.
HERE'S THE WORLD WAR I FLYING ACE PUTTING ON HIS SCARF...
HERE'S THE WORLD WAR I FLYING ACE WALKING OUT ONTO THE AERODROME...
MY HELMET!
?
I CAN'T FLY WITHOUT MY HELMET!
WHERE IS IT? WHERE IS IT?
11-8
I CAN HEAR THE OTHER PILOTS STARTING THEIR ENGINES...
WHAT AM I GOING TO DO?
THIS IS SO EMBARRASSING..
SCHULZ

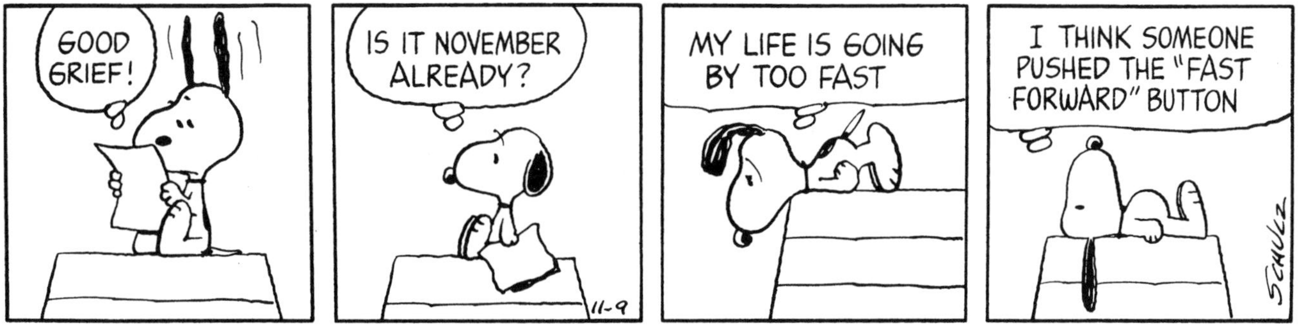
GOOD GRIEF!
IS IT NOVEMBER ALREADY?
11-9
MY LIFE IS GOING BY TOO FAST
I THINK SOMEONE PUSHED THE "FAST FORWARD" BUTTON
SCHULZ

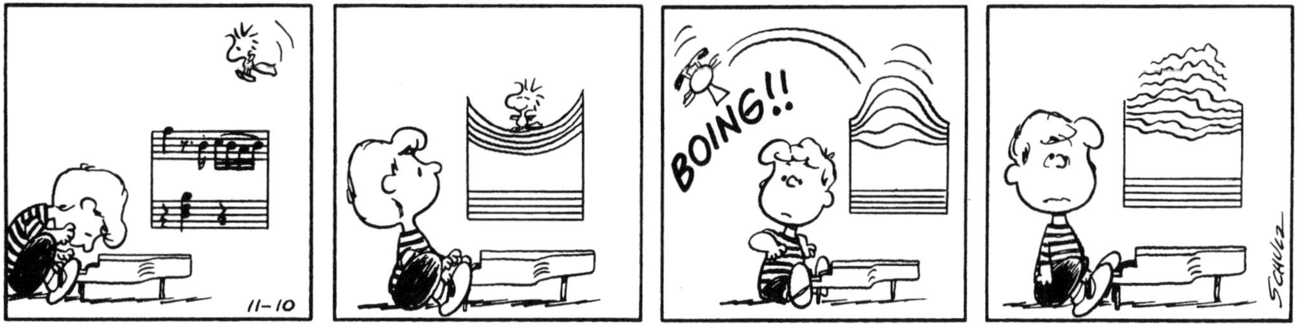
11-10
BOING!!
SCHULZ

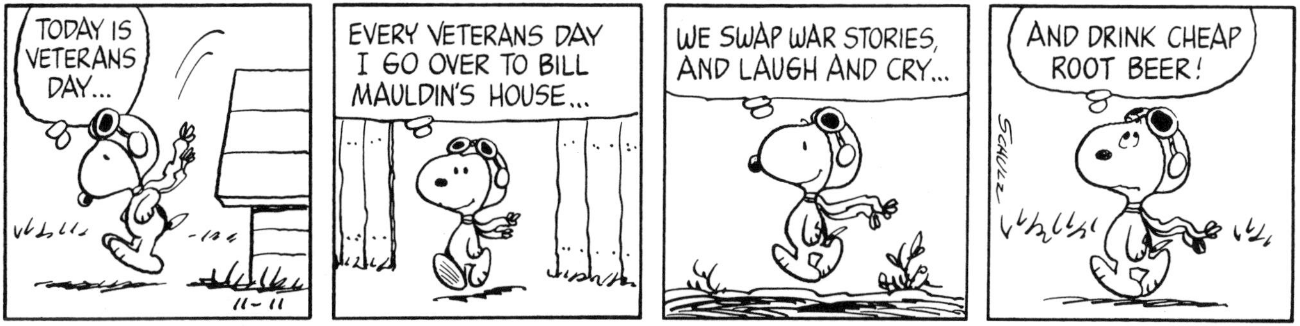
TODAY IS VETERANS DAY...
11-11
EVERY VETERANS DAY I GO OVER TO BILL MAULDIN'S HOUSE...
WE SWAP WAR STORIES, AND LAUGH AND CRY...
SCHULZ
AND DRINK CHEAP ROOT BEER!

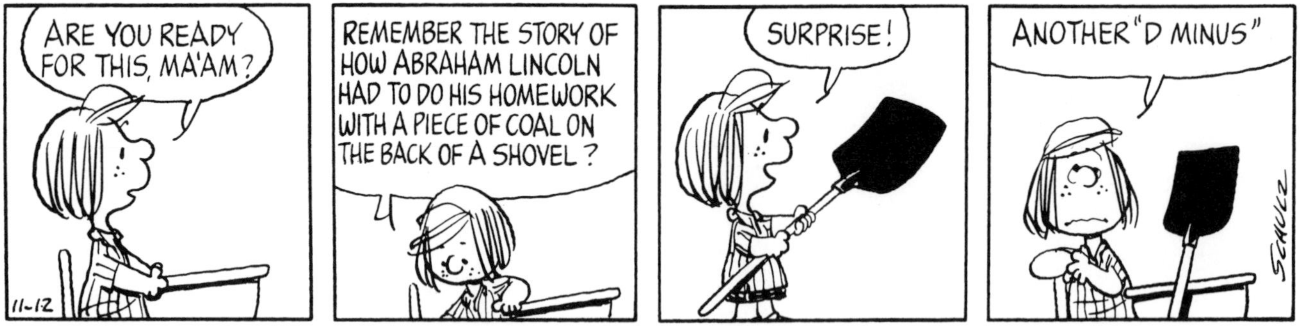
ARE YOU READY FOR THIS, MA'AM?
REMEMBER THE STORY OF HOW ABRAHAM LINCOLN HAD TO DO HIS HOMEWORK WITH A PIECE OF COAL ON THE BACK OF A SHOVEL?
SURPRISE!
ANOTHER "D MINUS"

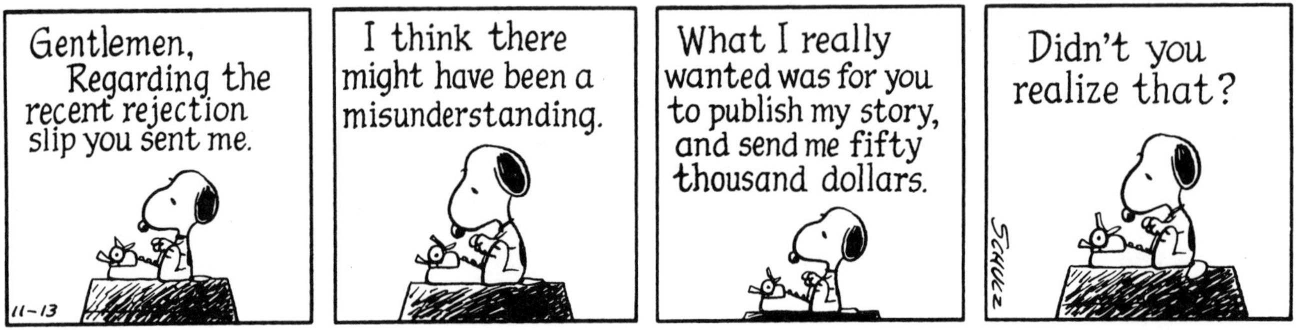
Gentlemen,
Regarding the recent rejection slip you sent me.
I think there might have been a misunderstanding.
What I really wanted was for you to publish my story, and send me fifty thousand dollars.
Didn't you realize that?

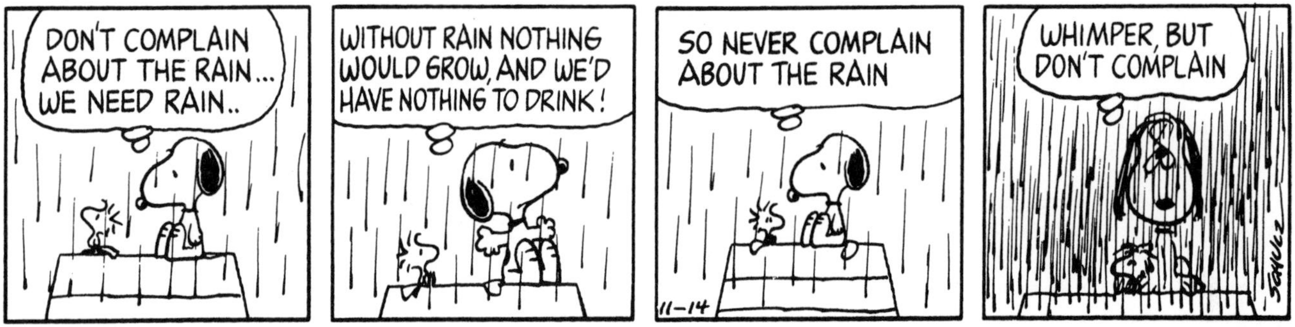
DON'T COMPLAIN ABOUT THE RAIN... WE NEED RAIN..
WITHOUT RAIN NOTHING WOULD GROW, AND WE'D HAVE NOTHING TO DRINK!
SO NEVER COMPLAIN ABOUT THE RAIN
WHIMPER, BUT DON'T COMPLAIN

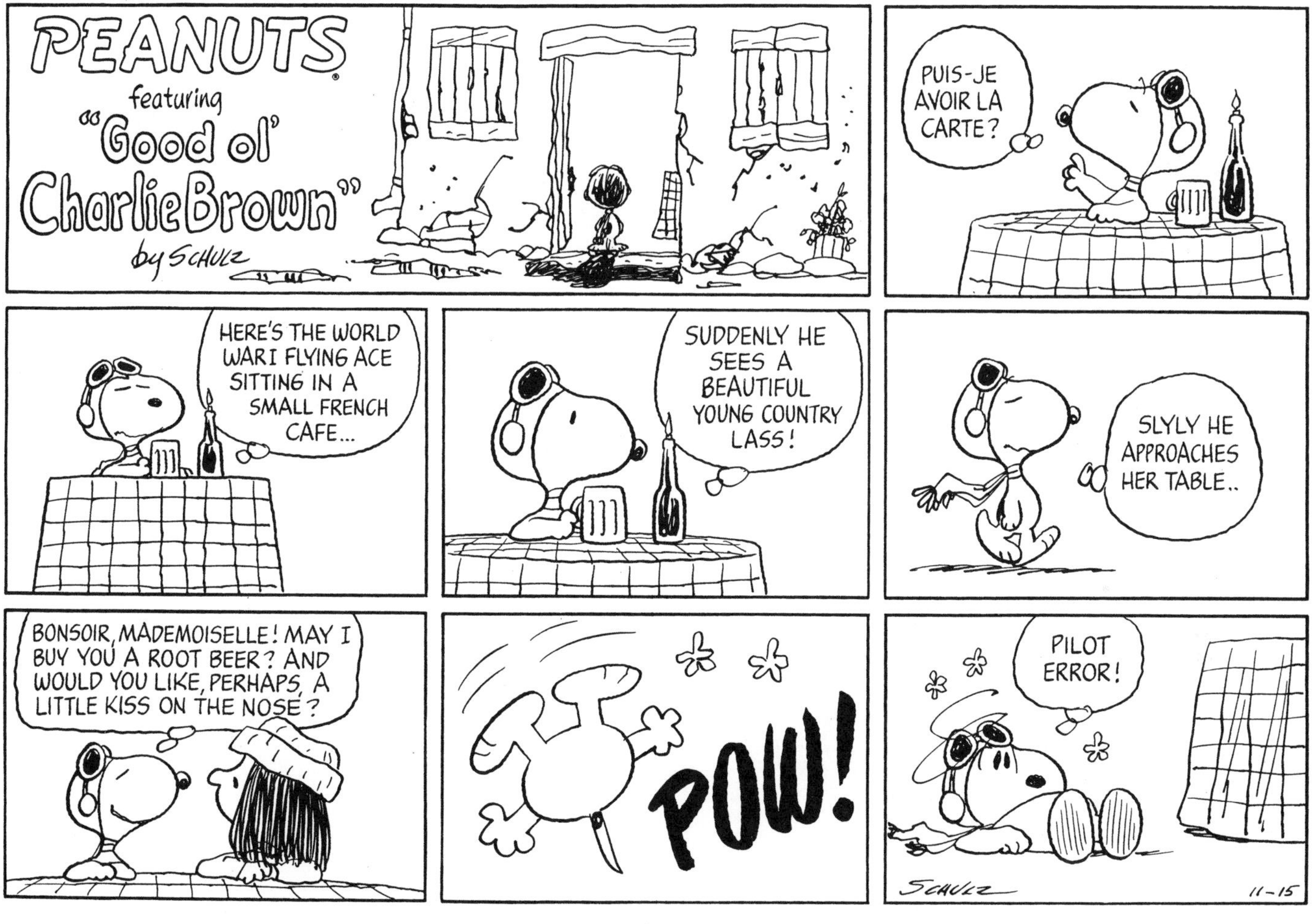
PEANUTS
featuring
"Good ol' CharlieBrown"
by SCHULZ
PUIS-JE AVOIR LA CARTE?
HERE'S THE WORLD WAR I FLYING ACE SITTING IN A SMALL FRENCH CAFE...
SUDDENLY HE SEES A BEAUTIFUL YOUNG COUNTRY LASS!
SLYLY HE APPROACHES HER TABLE..
BONSOIR, MADEMOISELLE! MAY I BUY YOU A ROOT BEER? AND WOULD YOU LIKE, PERHAPS, A LITTLE KISS ON THE NOSE?
POW!
PILOT ERROR!
SCHULZ
11-15

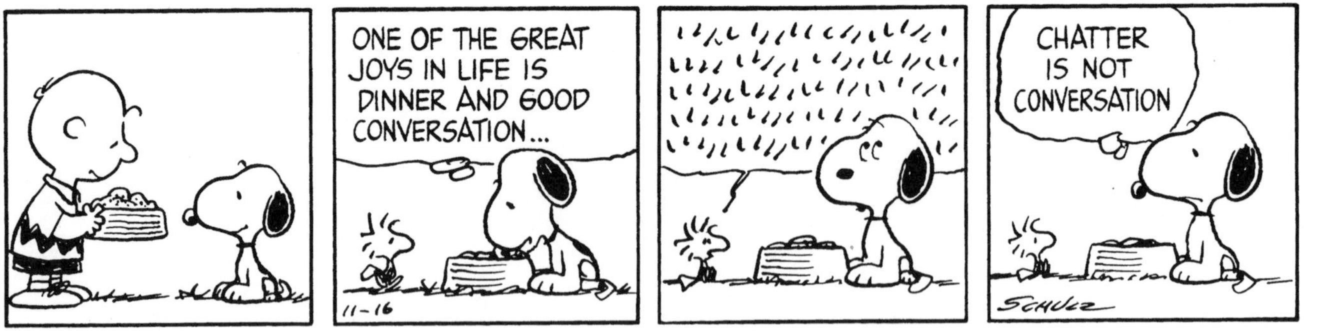
ONE OF THE GREAT JOYS IN LIFE IS DINNER AND GOOD CONVERSATION...
CHATTER IS NOT CONVERSATION

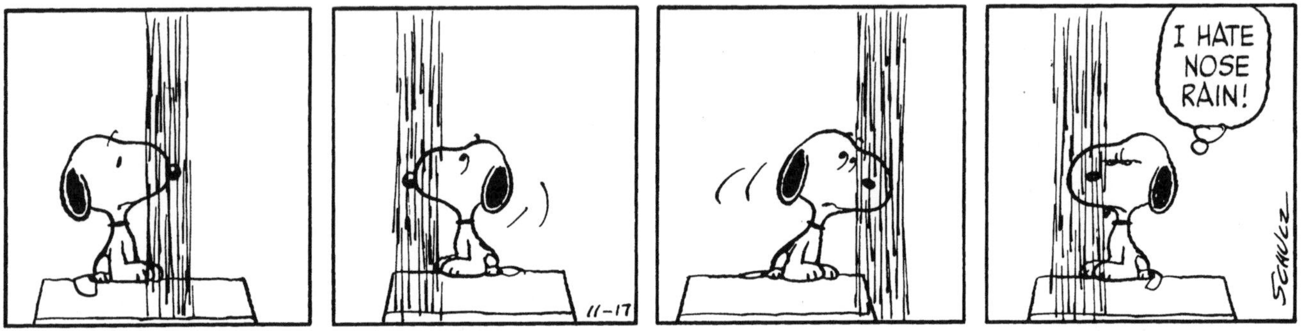
I HATE NOSE RAIN!

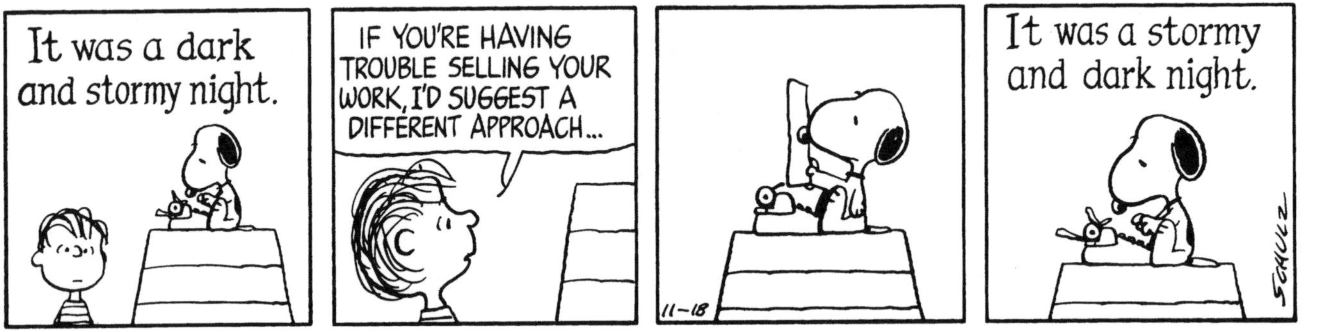
It was a dark and stormy night.
IF YOU'RE HAVING TROUBLE SELLING YOUR WORK, I'D SUGGEST A DIFFERENT APPROACH...
It was a stormy and dark night.

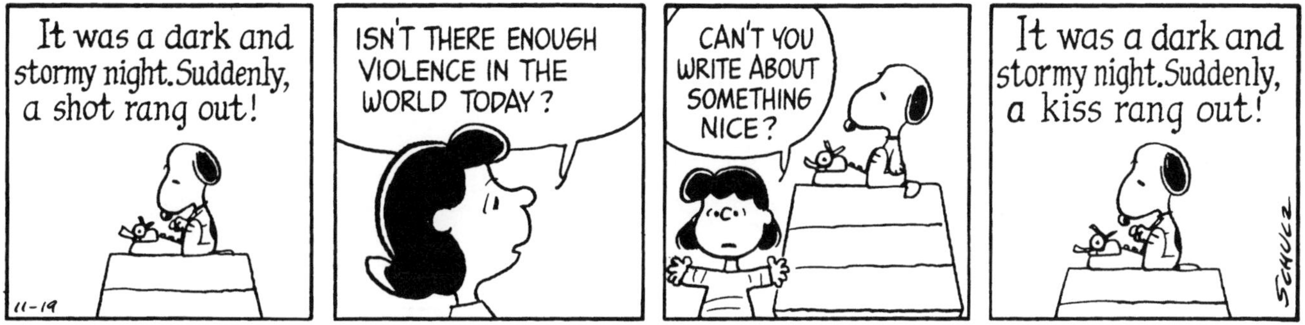
It was a dark and stormy night. Suddenly, a shot rang out!
ISN'T THERE ENOUGH VIOLENCE IN THE WORLD TODAY?
CAN'T YOU WRITE ABOUT SOMETHING NICE?
It was a dark and stormy night. Suddenly, a kiss rang out!

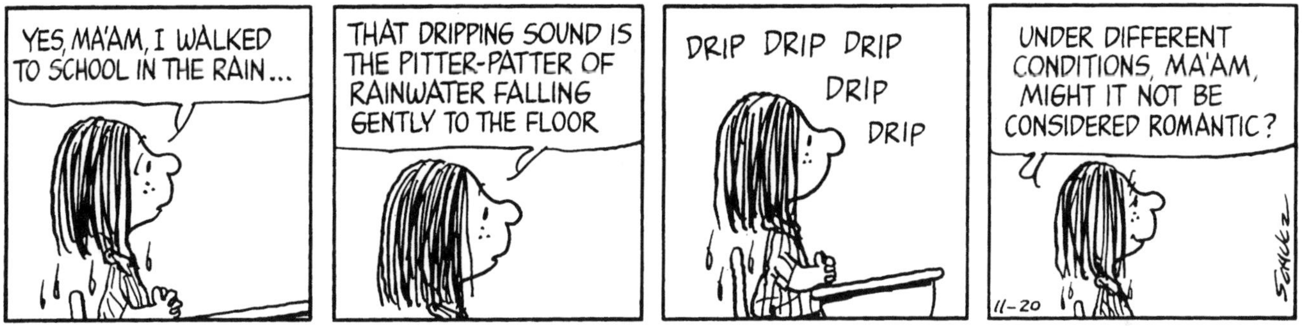
YES, MA'AM, I WALKED TO SCHOOL IN THE RAIN...
THAT DRIPPING SOUND IS THE PITTER-PATTER OF RAINWATER FALLING GENTLY TO THE FLOOR
DRIP DRIP DRIP
DRIP
DRIP
UNDER DIFFERENT CONDITIONS, MA'AM, MIGHT IT NOT BE CONSIDERED ROMANTIC?

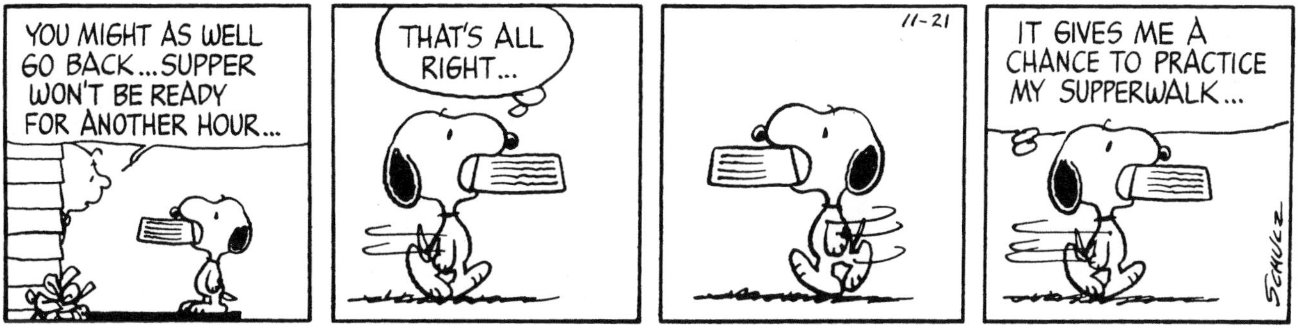
YOU MIGHT AS WELL GO BACK...SUPPER WON'T BE READY FOR ANOTHER HOUR...
THAT'S ALL RIGHT...
IT GIVES ME A CHANCE TO PRACTICE MY SUPPERWALK...

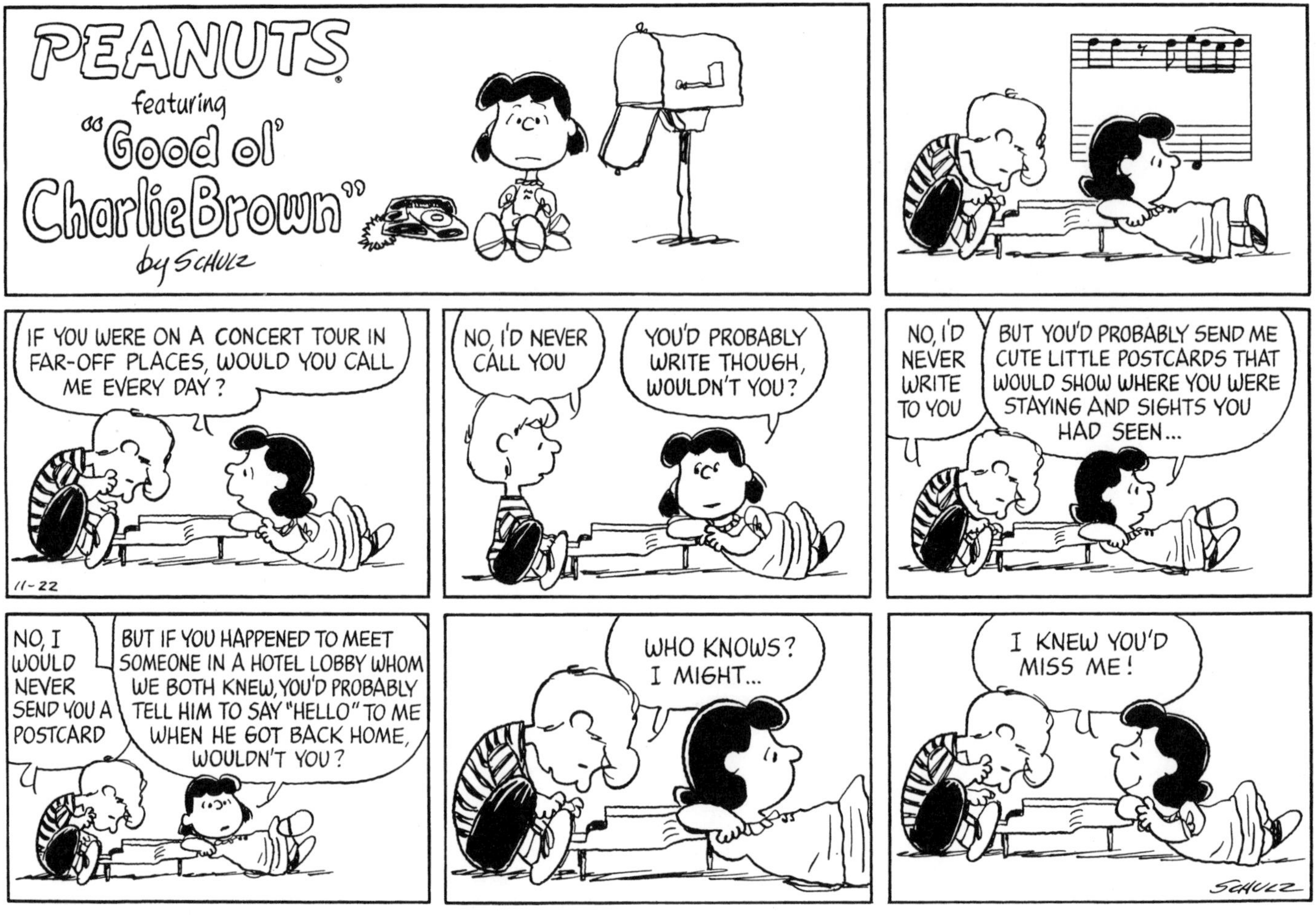
PEANUTS
featuring
"Good ol' Charlie Brown"
by SCHULZ
IF YOU WERE ON A CONCERT TOUR IN FAR-OFF PLACES, WOULD YOU CALL ME EVERY DAY?
11-22
NO, I'D NEVER CALL YOU
YOU'D PROBABLY WRITE THOUGH, WOULDN'T YOU?
NO, I'D NEVER WRITE TO YOU
BUT YOU'D PROBABLY SEND ME CUTE LITTLE POSTCARDS THAT WOULD SHOW WHERE YOU WERE STAYING AND SIGHTS YOU HAD SEEN...
NO, I WOULD NEVER SEND YOU A POSTCARD
BUT IF YOU HAPPENED TO MEET SOMEONE IN A HOTEL LOBBY WHOM WE BOTH KNEW, YOU'D PROBABLY TELL HIM TO SAY "HELLO" TO ME WHEN HE GOT BACK HOME, WOULDN'T YOU?
WHO KNOWS? I MIGHT...
I KNEW YOU'D MISS ME!
SCHULZ

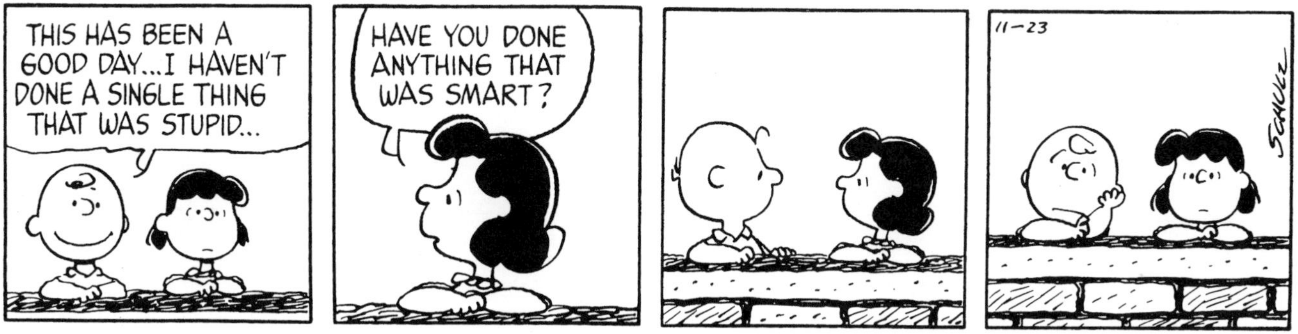
THIS HAS BEEN A GOOD DAY...I HAVEN'T DONE A SINGLE THING THAT WAS STUPID...
HAVE YOU DONE ANYTHING THAT WAS SMART?
11-23
SCHULZ

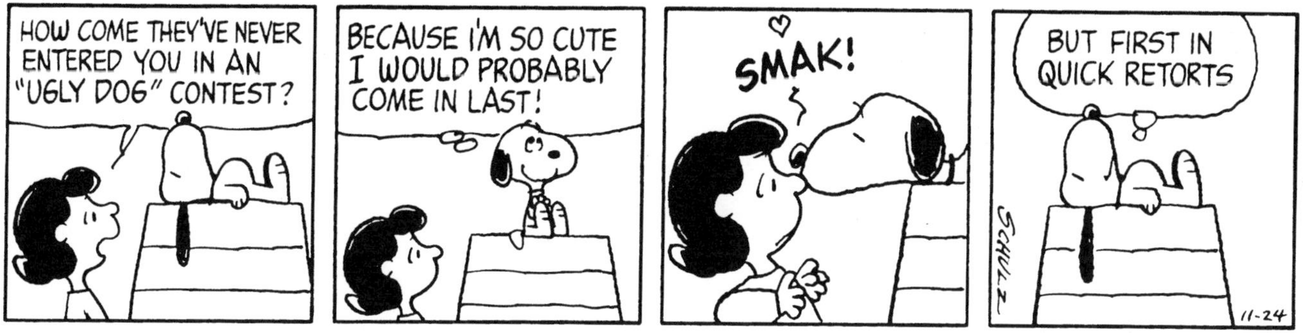
HOW COME THEY'VE NEVER ENTERED YOU IN AN "UGLY DOG" CONTEST?
BECAUSE I'M SO CUTE I WOULD PROBABLY COME IN LAST!
SMAK!
BUT FIRST IN QUICK RETORTS
SCHULZ
11-24

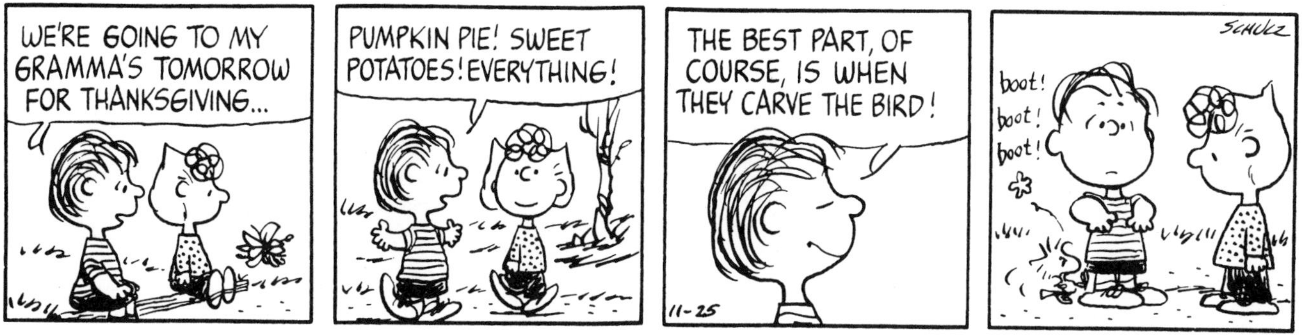
WE'RE GOING TO MY GRAMMA'S TOMORROW FOR THANKSGIVING...
PUMPKIN PIE! SWEET POTATOES! EVERYTHING!
THE BEST PART, OF COURSE, IS WHEN THEY CARVE THE BIRD!
11-25
SCHULZ
boot!
boot!
boot!

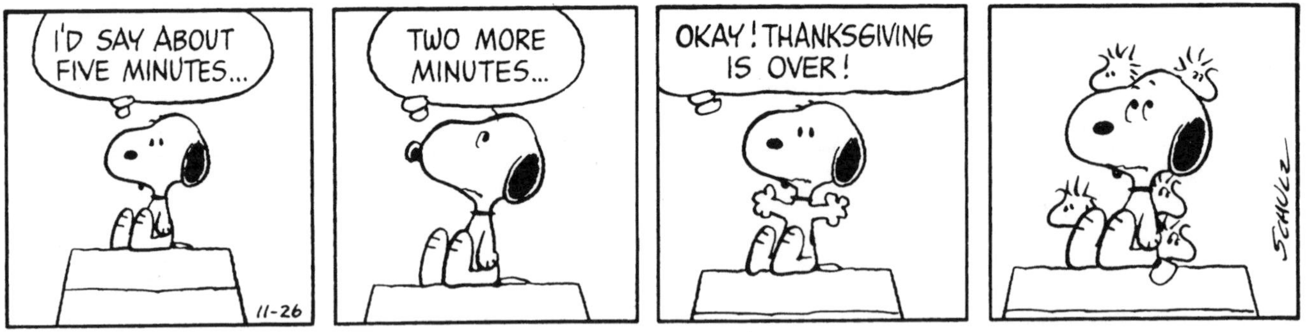
I'D SAY ABOUT FIVE MINUTES...
11-26
TWO MORE MINUTES...
OKAY! THANKSGIVING IS OVER!
SCHULZ

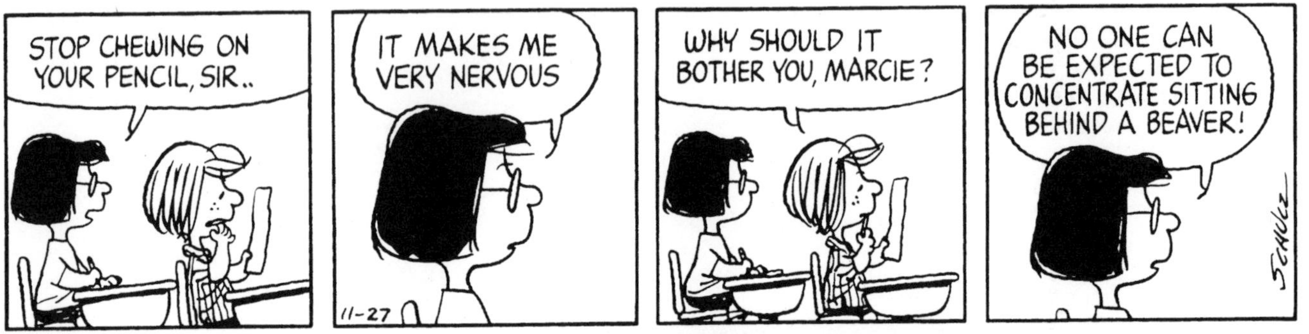
STOP CHEWING ON YOUR PENCIL, SIR..
IT MAKES ME VERY NERVOUS
11-27
WHY SHOULD IT BOTHER YOU, MARCIE?
NO ONE CAN BE EXPECTED TO CONCENTRATE SITTING BEHIND A BEAVER!
SCHULZ

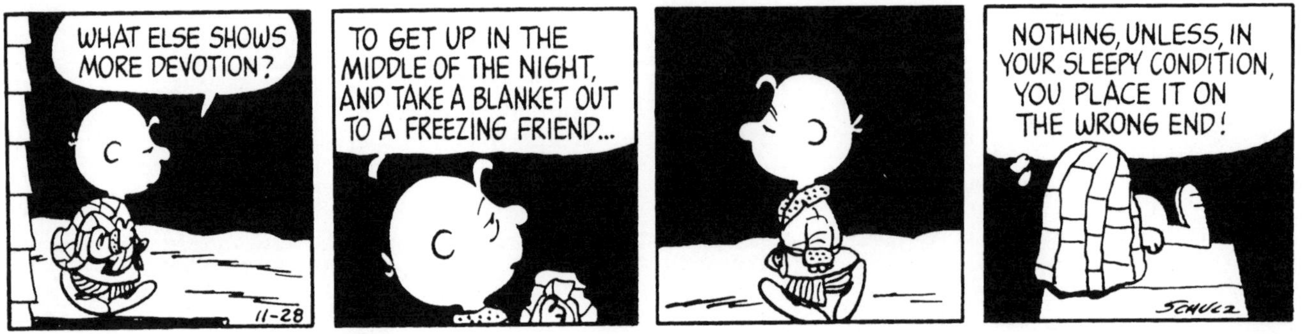
WHAT ELSE SHOWS MORE DEVOTION?
11-28
TO GET UP IN THE MIDDLE OF THE NIGHT, AND TAKE A BLANKET OUT TO A FREEZING FRIEND...
NOTHING, UNLESS, IN YOUR SLEEPY CONDITION, YOU PLACE IT ON THE WRONG END!
SCHULZ

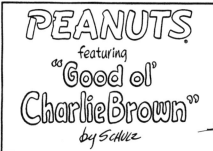

PEANUTS
featuring
"Good ol' Charlie Brown"
by Schulz

OVER HERE! I'M OVER HERE!

I CAN'T BELIEVE IT...

NOT AGAIN!

DOES SHE REALLY THINK I'M SUCH A FOOL? NOT AGAIN!

AM I DUMB ENOUGH TO THINK SHE'S GOING TO LET ME KICK THAT FOOTBALL? I CAN'T BELIEVE IT! NOT AGAIN!

AM I REALLY GOING TO TRY IT? NOT AGAIN!

I CAN'T BELIEVE I'M TRYING IT! IS IT REALLY HAPPENING AGAIN?

11-29

AAUGH!

WUMP!

AGAIN, CHARLIE BROWN... AND AGAIN, AND AGAIN AND AGAIN

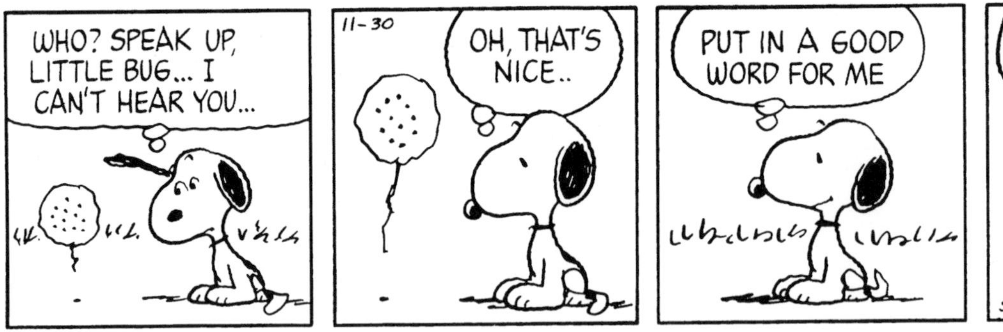
11-30
WHO? SPEAK UP, LITTLE BUG... I CAN'T HEAR YOU...
OH, THAT'S NICE..
PUT IN A GOOD WORD FOR ME
"SANTA BUG" IS COMING TO TOWN!
SCHULZ

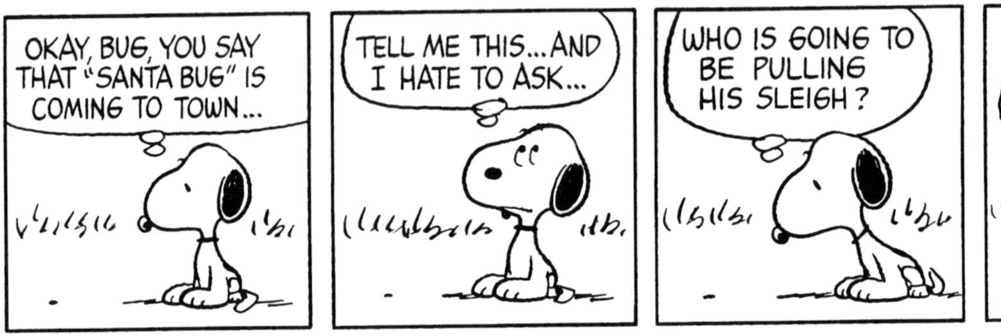
OKAY, BUG, YOU SAY THAT "SANTA BUG" IS COMING TO TOWN...
TELL ME THIS...AND I HATE TO ASK...
WHO IS GOING TO BE PULLING HIS SLEIGH?
EIGHT TINY REINBUGS?
SCHULZ
12-1

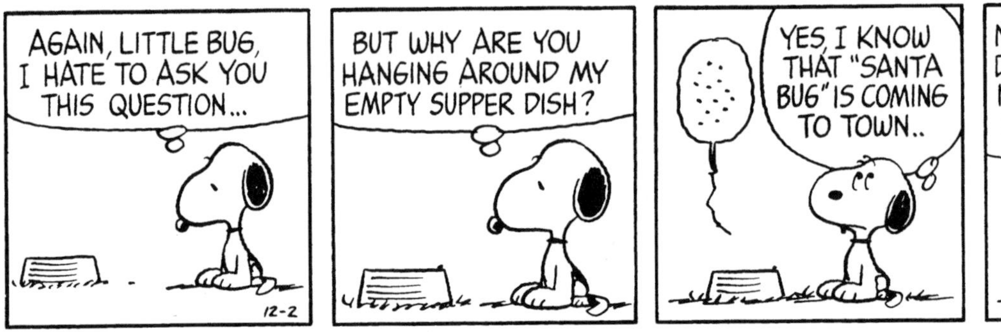
AGAIN, LITTLE BUG, I HATE TO ASK YOU THIS QUESTION...
12-2
BUT WHY ARE YOU HANGING AROUND MY EMPTY SUPPER DISH?
YES, I KNOW THAT "SANTA BUG" IS COMING TO TOWN..
NO, THIS IS MY SUPPER DISH..IT IS DEFINITELY NOT "MENDELSON'S DEPARTMENT STORE"!
SCHULZ

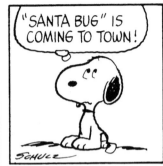

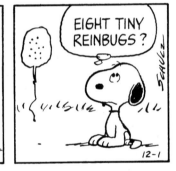

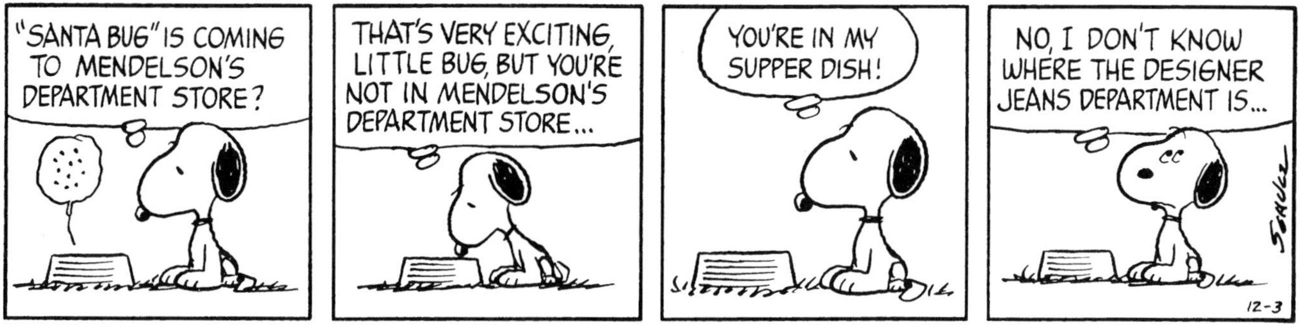
"SANTA BUG" IS COMING TO MENDELSON'S DEPARTMENT STORE?
THAT'S VERY EXCITING, LITTLE BUG, BUT YOU'RE NOT IN MENDELSON'S DEPARTMENT STORE...
YOU'RE IN MY SUPPER DISH!
NO, I DON'T KNOW WHERE THE DESIGNER JEANS DEPARTMENT IS...
SCHULZ
12-3

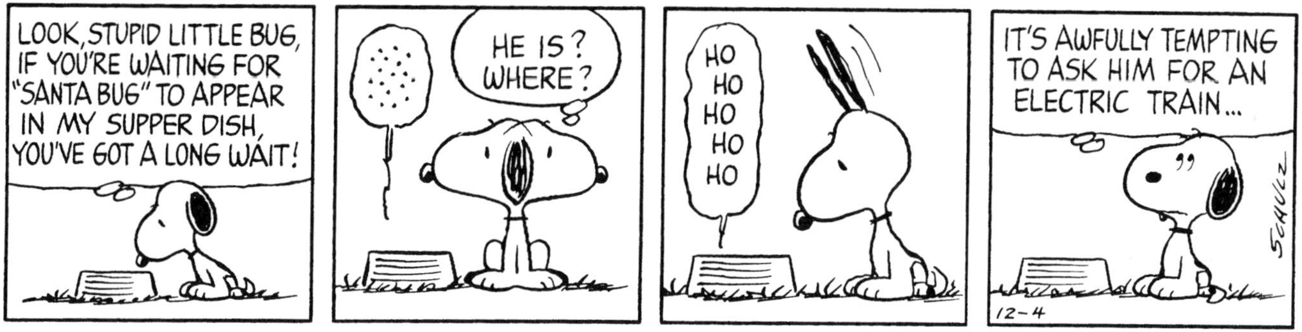
LOOK, STUPID LITTLE BUG, IF YOU'RE WAITING FOR "SANTA BUG" TO APPEAR IN MY SUPPER DISH, YOU'VE GOT A LONG WAIT!
HE IS? WHERE?
HO HO HO HO HO
IT'S AWFULLY TEMPTING TO ASK HIM FOR AN ELECTRIC TRAIN...
SCHULZ
12-4

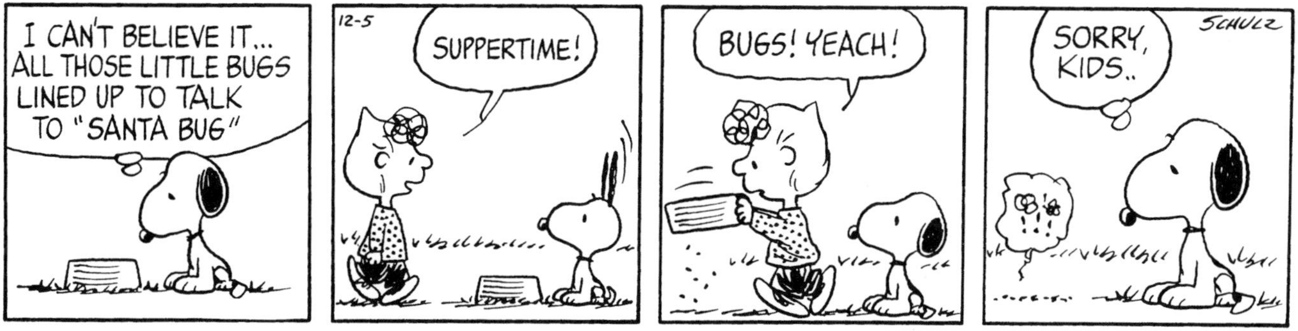
I CAN'T BELIEVE IT... ALL THOSE LITTLE BUGS LINED UP TO TALK TO "SANTA BUG"
12-5
SUPPERTIME!
BUGS! YEACH!
SCHULZ
SORRY, KIDS..

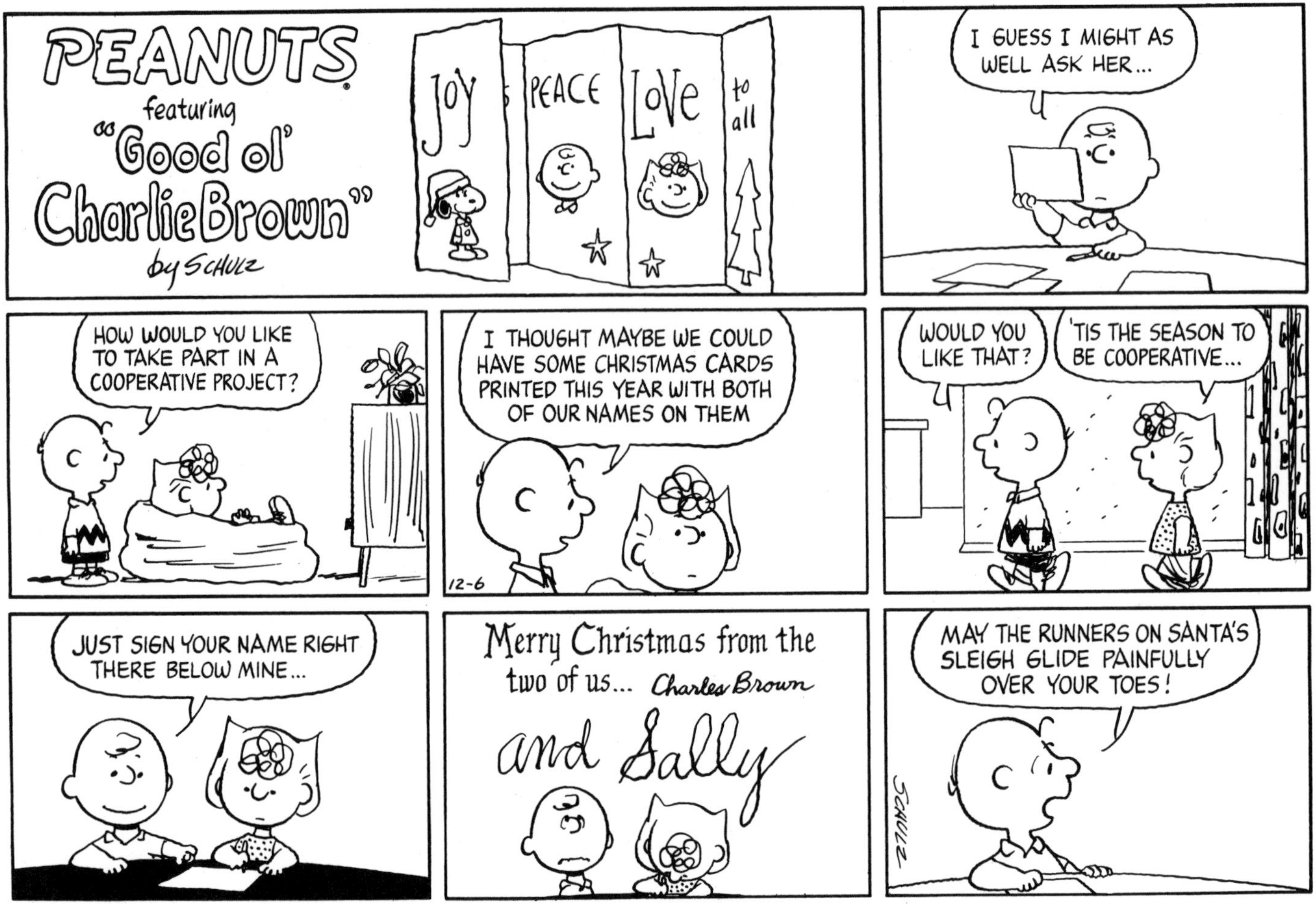
PEANUTS
featuring
"Good ol' Charlie Brown"
by SCHULZ
JOY
PEACE
LOVE
to all
I GUESS I MIGHT AS WELL ASK HER...
HOW WOULD YOU LIKE TO TAKE PART IN A COOPERATIVE PROJECT?
I THOUGHT MAYBE WE COULD HAVE SOME CHRISTMAS CARDS PRINTED THIS YEAR WITH BOTH OF OUR NAMES ON THEM
12-6
WOULD YOU LIKE THAT?
'TIS THE SEASON TO BE COOPERATIVE...
JUST SIGN YOUR NAME RIGHT THERE BELOW MINE...
Merry Christmas from the two of us... Charles Brown
and Sally
MAY THE RUNNERS ON SANTA'S SLEIGH GLIDE PAINFULLY OVER YOUR TOES!
SCHULZ

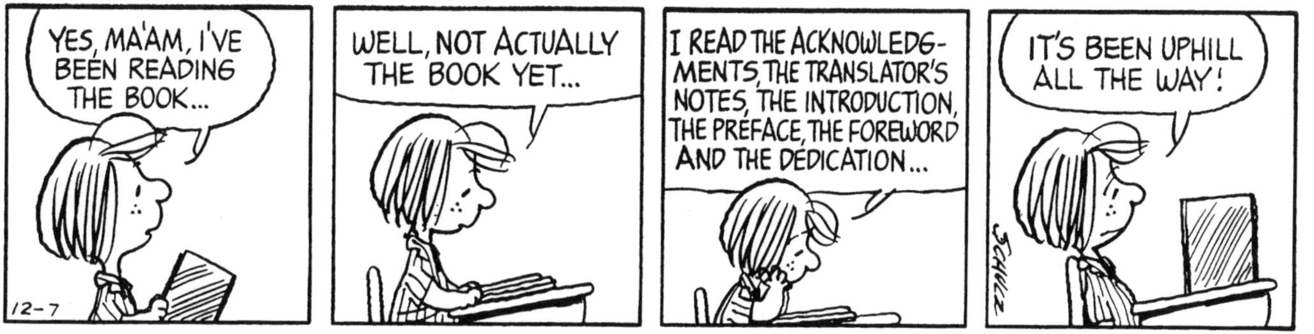
YES, MA'AM, I'VE BEEN READING THE BOOK...
12-7
WELL, NOT ACTUALLY THE BOOK YET...
I READ THE ACKNOWLEDGMENTS, THE TRANSLATOR'S NOTES, THE INTRODUCTION, THE PREFACE, THE FOREWORD AND THE DEDICATION...
IT'S BEEN UPHILL ALL THE WAY!

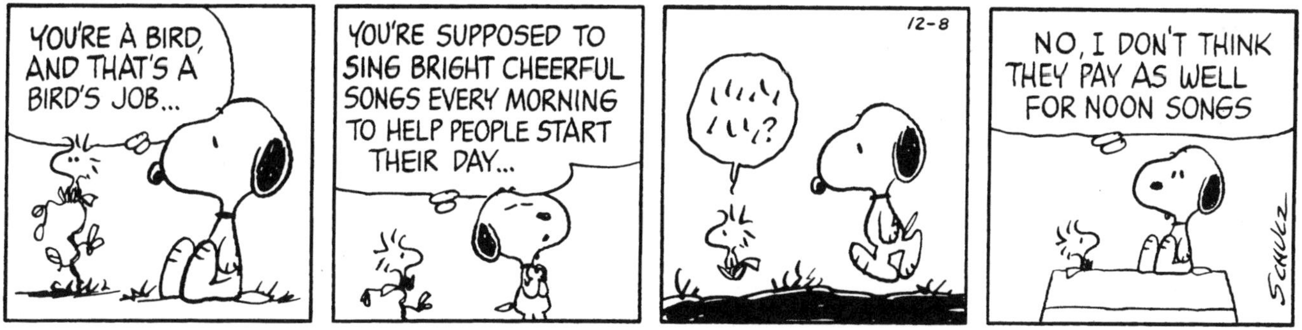
YOU'RE A BIRD, AND THAT'S A BIRD'S JOB...
YOU'RE SUPPOSED TO SING BRIGHT CHEERFUL SONGS EVERY MORNING TO HELP PEOPLE START THEIR DAY...
12-8
?
NO, I DON'T THINK THEY PAY AS WELL FOR NOON SONGS

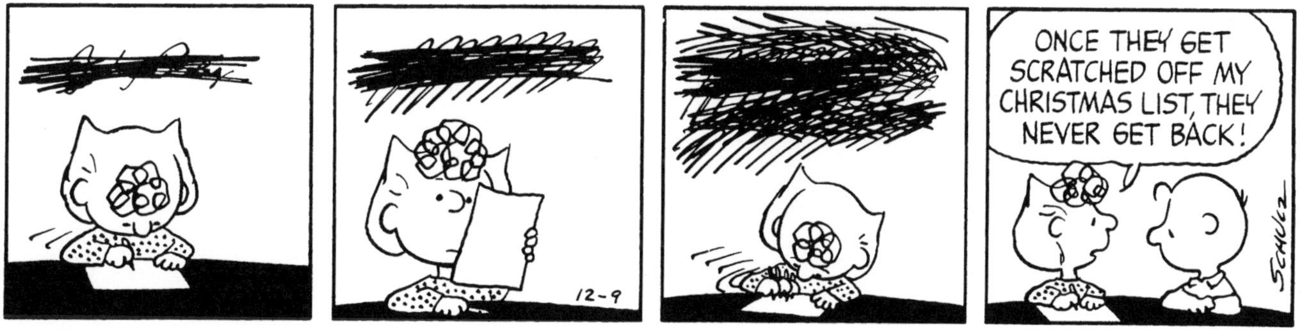
12-9
ONCE THEY GET SCRATCHED OFF MY CHRISTMAS LIST, THEY NEVER GET BACK!

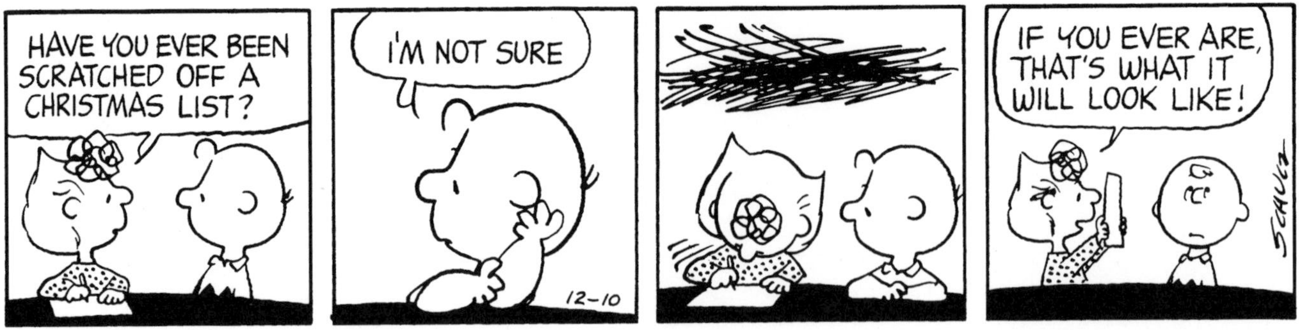
HAVE YOU EVER BEEN SCRATCHED OFF A CHRISTMAS LIST?
I'M NOT SURE
IF YOU EVER ARE, THAT'S WHAT IT WILL LOOK LIKE!

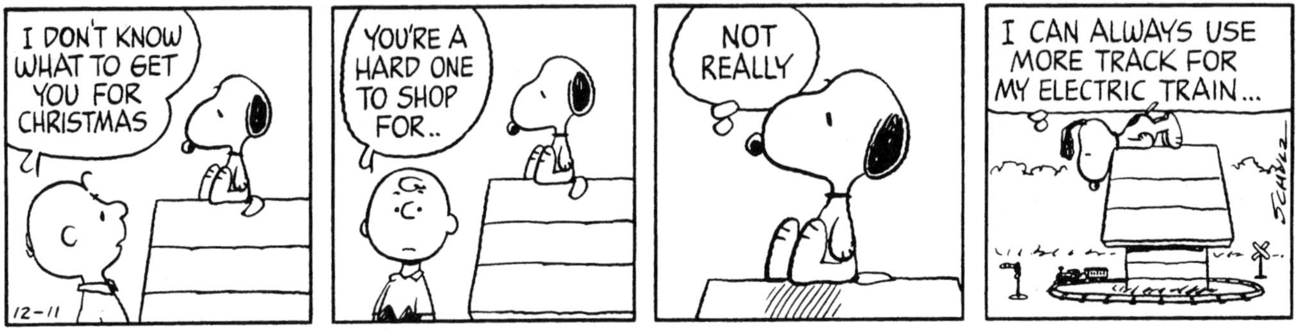
I DON'T KNOW WHAT TO GET YOU FOR CHRISTMAS
YOU'RE A HARD ONE TO SHOP FOR..
NOT REALLY
I CAN ALWAYS USE MORE TRACK FOR MY ELECTRIC TRAIN...

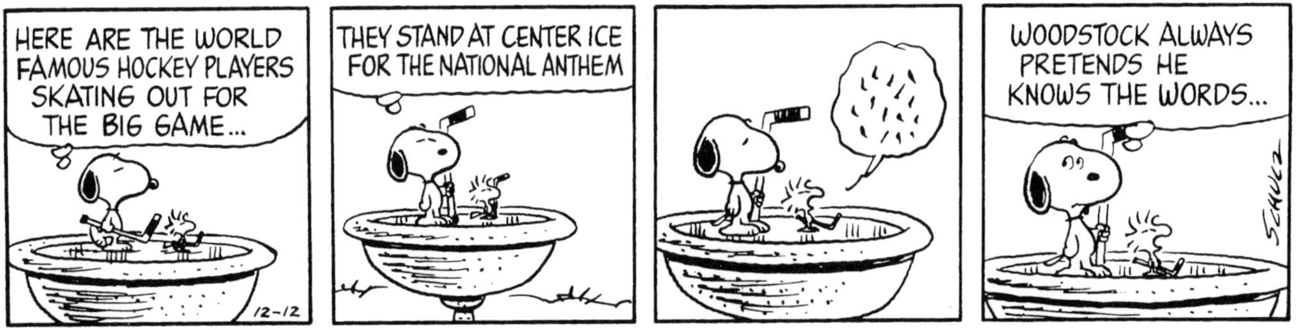
HERE ARE THE WORLD FAMOUS HOCKEY PLAYERS SKATING OUT FOR THE BIG GAME...
THEY STAND AT CENTER ICE FOR THE NATIONAL ANTHEM
WOODSTOCK ALWAYS PRETENDS HE KNOWS THE WORDS...

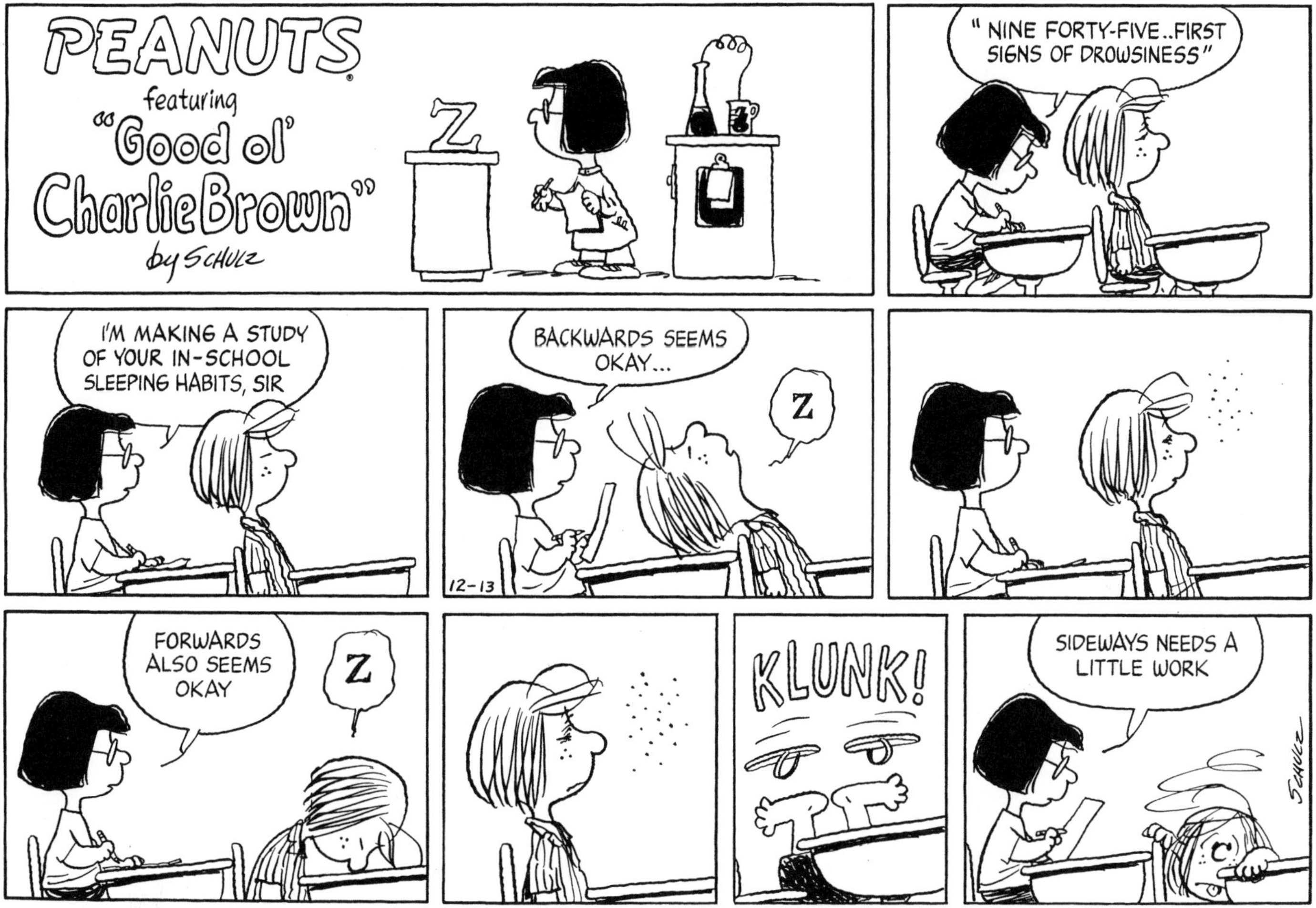
PEANUTS
featuring
"Good ol' CharlieBrown"
by SCHULZ
Z
" NINE FORTY-FIVE..FIRST SIGNS OF DROWSINESS"
I'M MAKING A STUDY OF YOUR IN-SCHOOL SLEEPING HABITS, SIR
BACKWARDS SEEMS OKAY...
Z
12-13
FORWARDS ALSO SEEMS OKAY
Z
KLUNK!
SIDEWAYS NEEDS A LITTLE WORK
SCHULZ

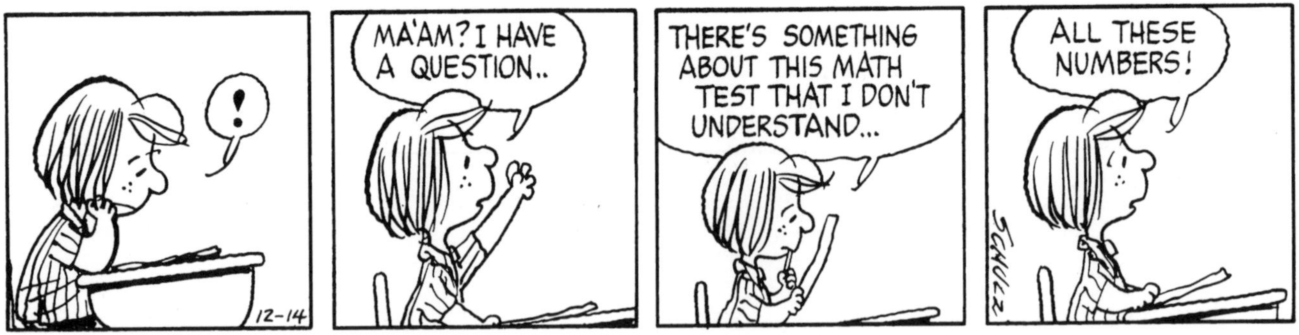
!
MA'AM? I HAVE A QUESTION..
THERE'S SOMETHING ABOUT THIS MATH TEST THAT I DON'T UNDERSTAND...
ALL THESE NUMBERS!
SCHULZ
12-14

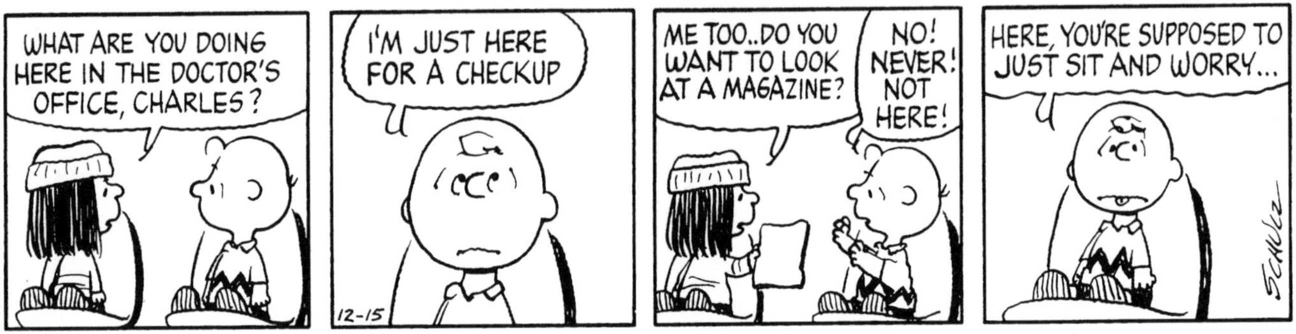
WHAT ARE YOU DOING HERE IN THE DOCTOR'S OFFICE, CHARLES?
I'M JUST HERE FOR A CHECKUP
12-15
ME TOO..DO YOU WANT TO LOOK AT A MAGAZINE?
NO! NEVER! NOT HERE!
HERE, YOU'RE SUPPOSED TO JUST SIT AND WORRY...
SCHULZ

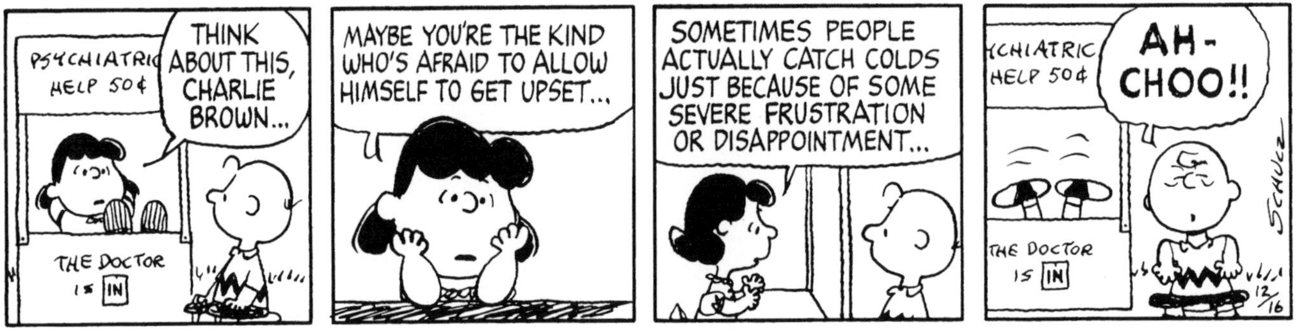
PSYCHIATRIC HELP 50¢
THE DOCTOR IS IN
THINK ABOUT THIS, CHARLIE BROWN...
MAYBE YOU'RE THE KIND WHO'S AFRAID TO ALLOW HIMSELF TO GET UPSET...
SOMETIMES PEOPLE ACTUALLY CATCH COLDS JUST BECAUSE OF SOME SEVERE FRUSTRATION OR DISAPPOINTMENT...
AH-CHOO!!
SCHULZ
12/16

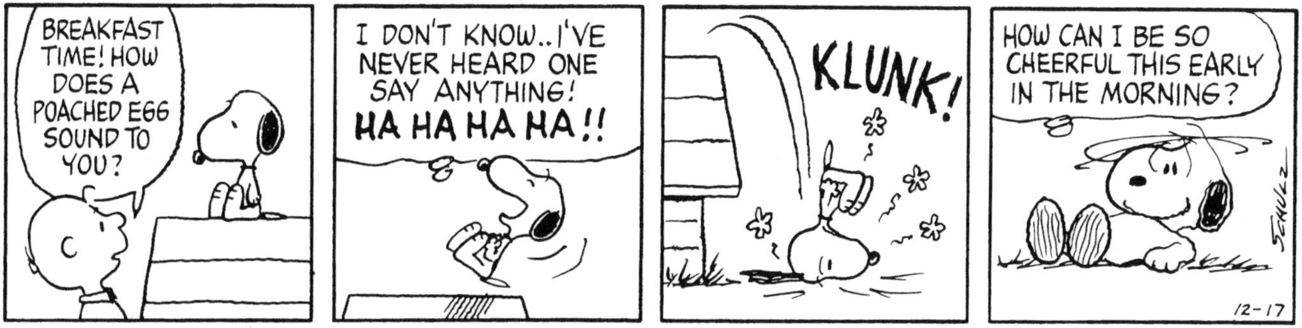
BREAKFAST TIME! HOW DOES A POACHED EGG SOUND TO YOU?
I DON'T KNOW.. I'VE NEVER HEARD ONE SAY ANYTHING! HA HA HA HA!!
KLUNK!
HOW CAN I BE SO CHEERFUL THIS EARLY IN THE MORNING?
SCHULZ
12-17

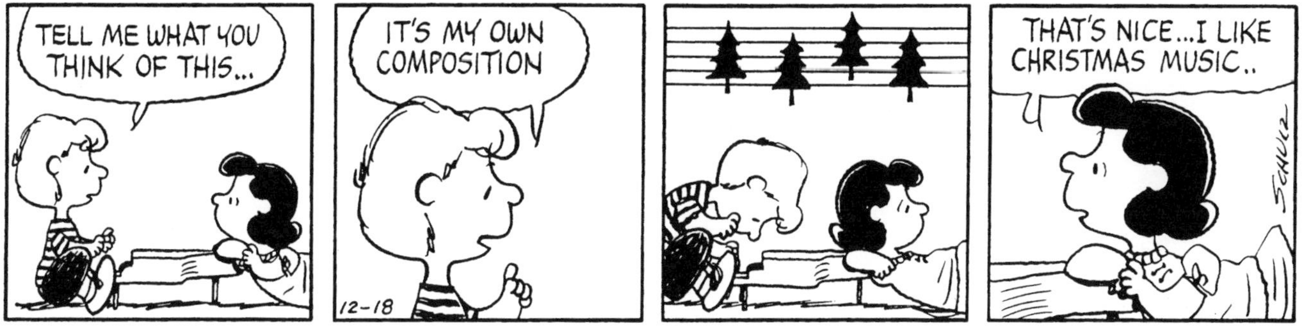
TELL ME WHAT YOU THINK OF THIS...
IT'S MY OWN COMPOSITION
12-18
THAT'S NICE...I LIKE CHRISTMAS MUSIC..
SCHULZ

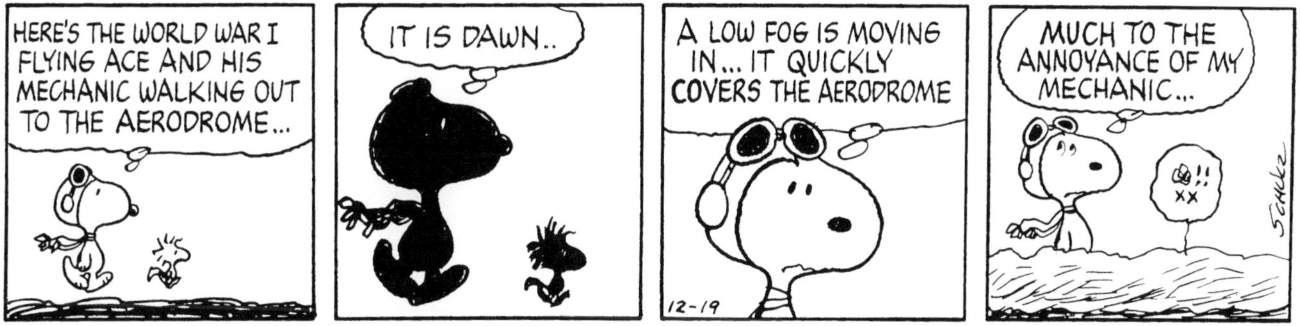
HERE'S THE WORLD WAR I FLYING ACE AND HIS MECHANIC WALKING OUT TO THE AERODROME...
IT IS DAWN..
A LOW FOG IS MOVING IN... IT QUICKLY COVERS THE AERODROME
12-19
MUCH TO THE ANNOYANCE OF MY MECHANIC...
SCHULZ

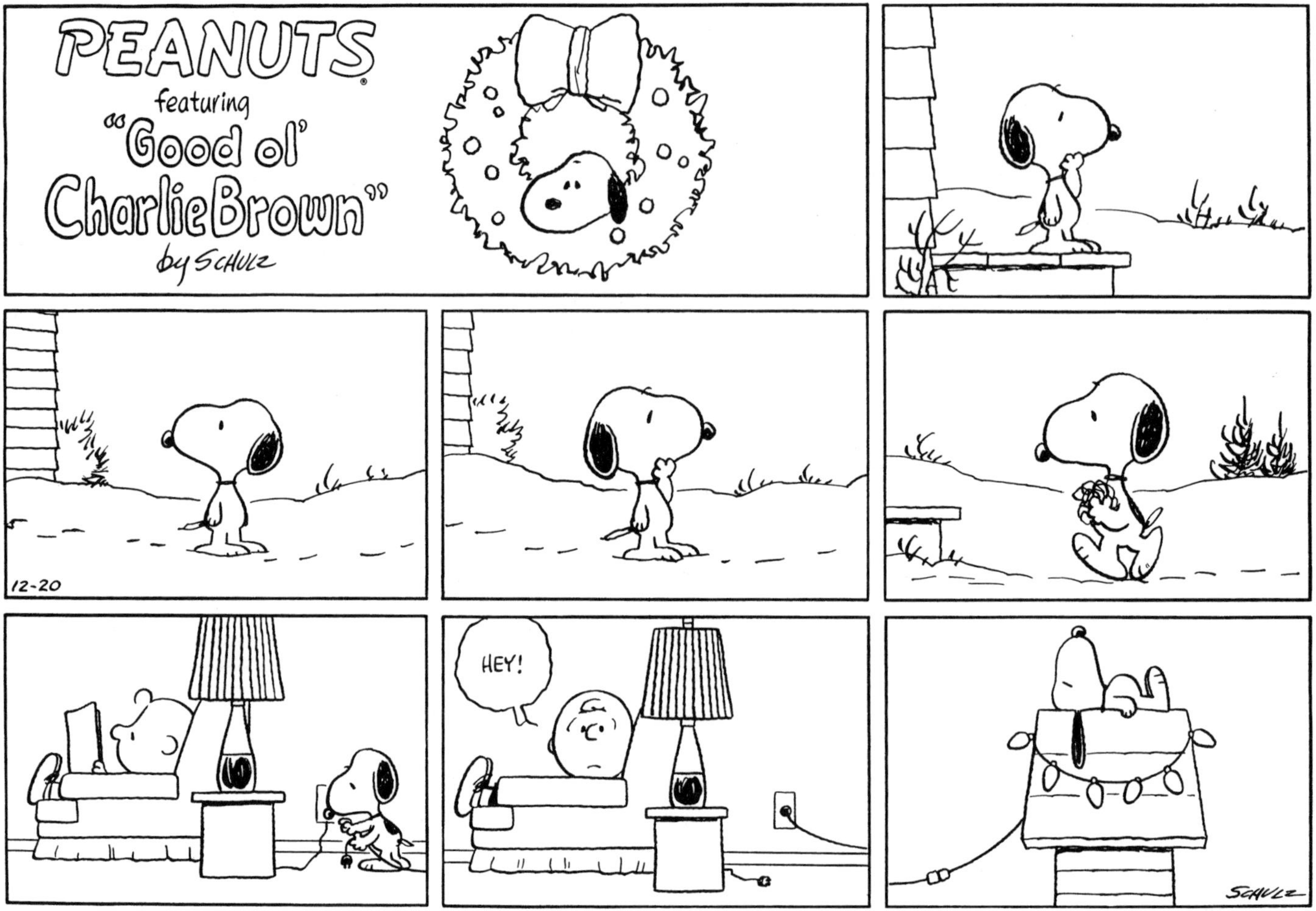
PEANUTS
featuring
"Good ol' Charlie Brown"
by SCHULZ
12-20
HEY!
SCHULZ

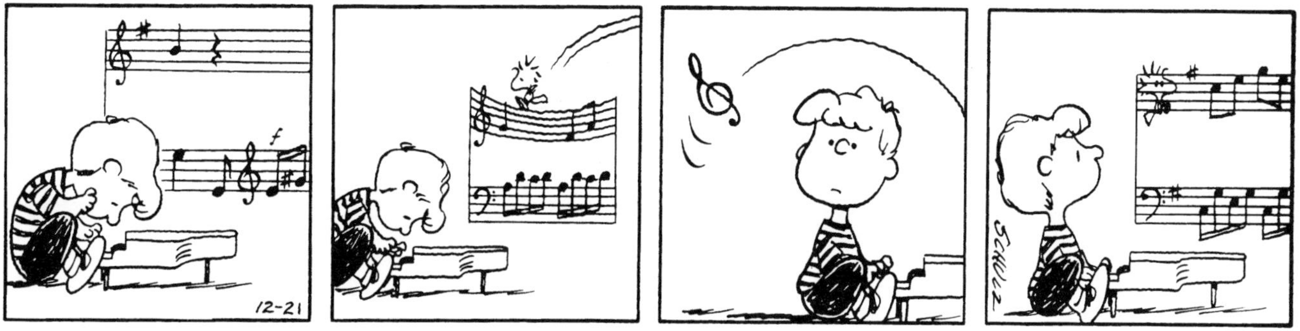
12-21
SCHULZ

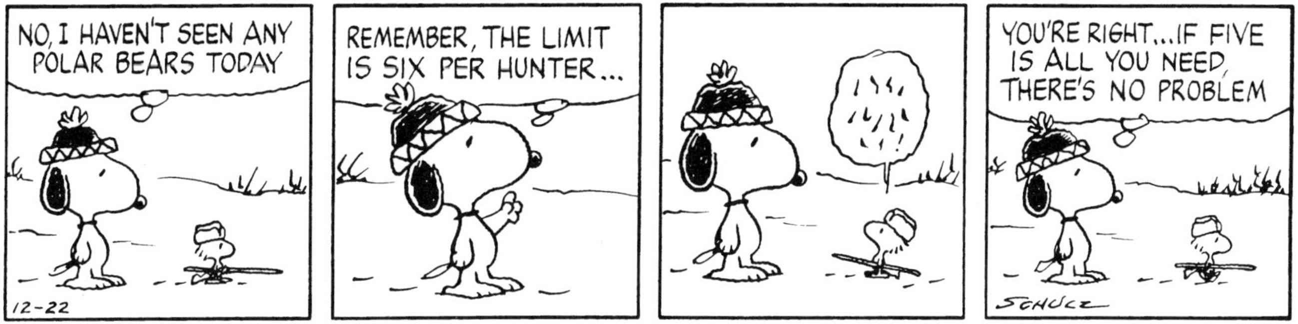
NO, I HAVEN'T SEEN ANY POLAR BEARS TODAY
12-22
REMEMBER, THE LIMIT IS SIX PER HUNTER...
YOU'RE RIGHT...IF FIVE IS ALL YOU NEED, THERE'S NO PROBLEM
SCHULZ

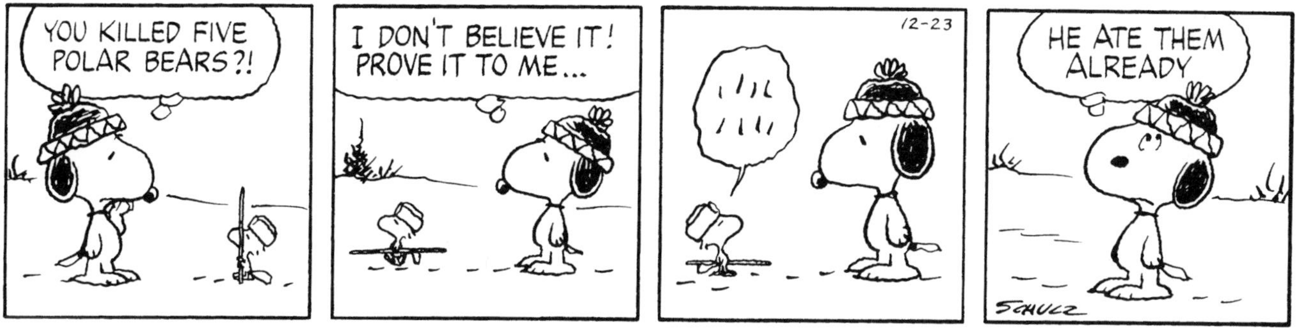
YOU KILLED FIVE POLAR BEARS?!
I DON'T BELIEVE IT! PROVE IT TO ME...
12-23
HE ATE THEM ALREADY
SCHULZ

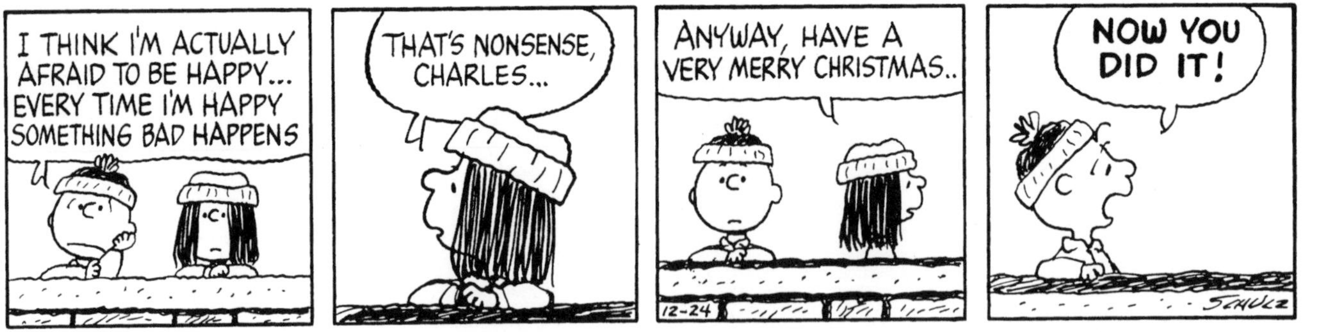
I THINK I'M ACTUALLY AFRAID TO BE HAPPY... EVERY TIME I'M HAPPY SOMETHING BAD HAPPENS
THAT'S NONSENSE, CHARLES...
ANYWAY, HAVE A VERY MERRY CHRISTMAS..
12-24
NOW YOU DID IT!

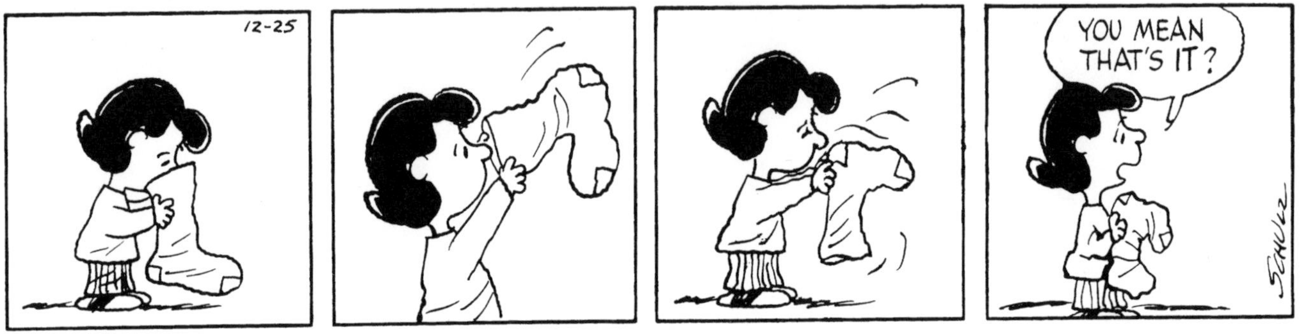
12-25
YOU MEAN THAT'S IT?

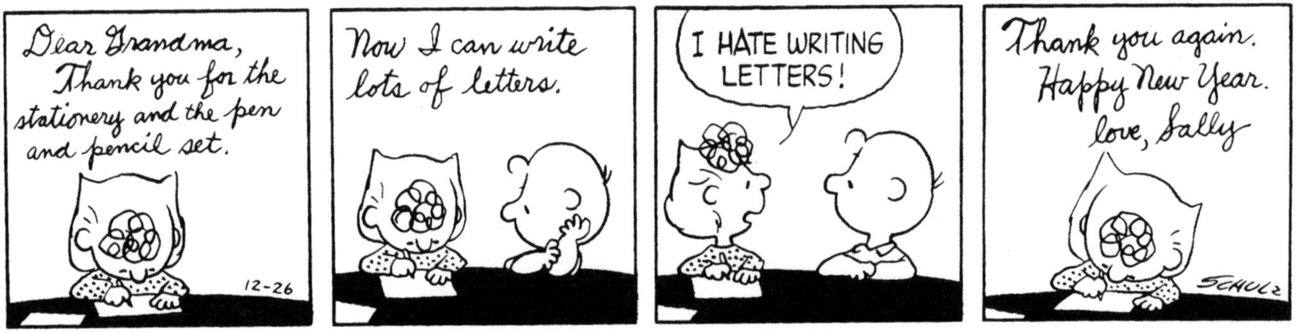
Dear Grandma, Thank you for the stationery and the pen and pencil set.
12-26
Now I can write lots of letters.
I HATE WRITING LETTERS!
Thank you again. Happy New Year. love, Sally

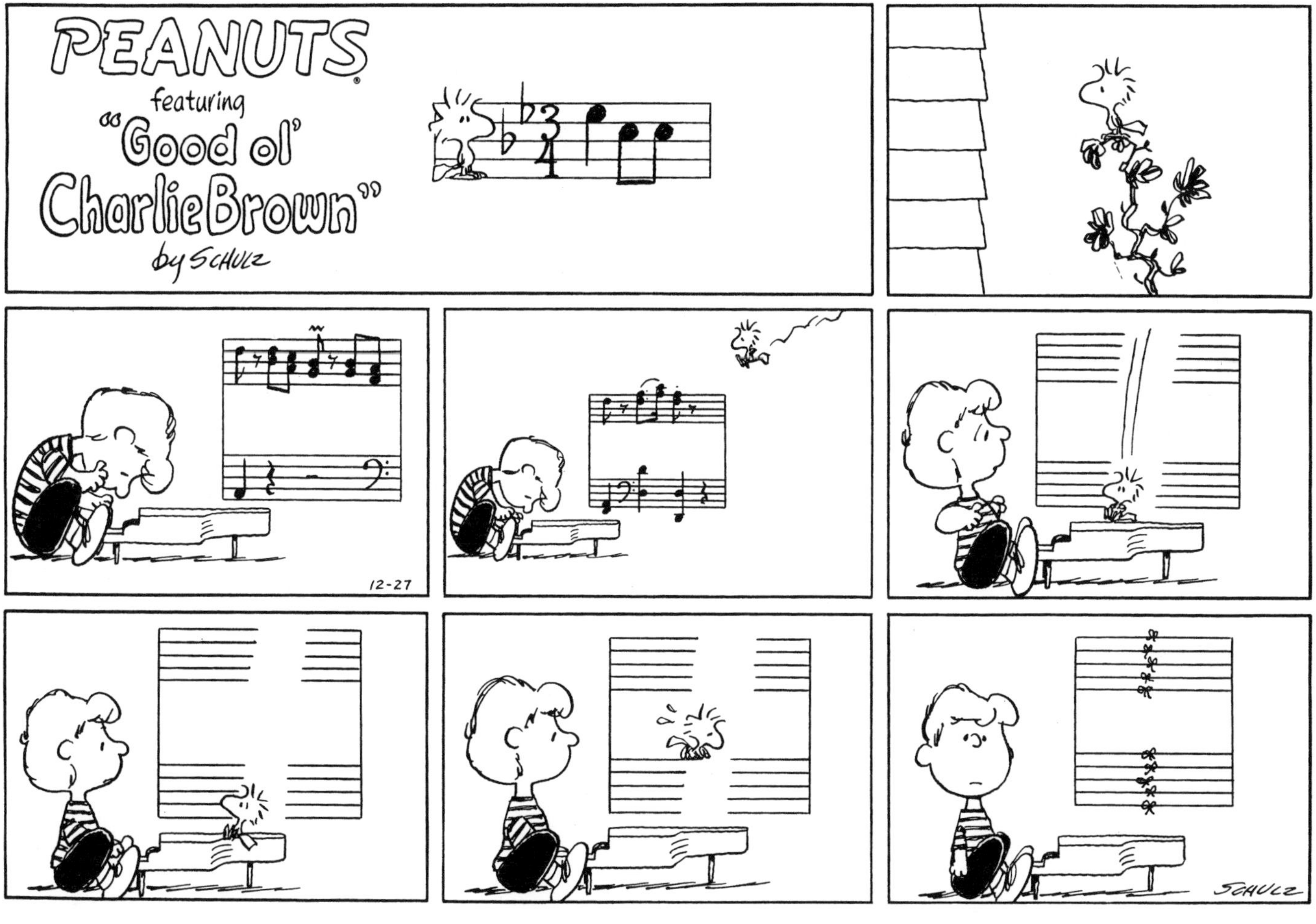
PEANUTS
featuring
"Good ol' Charlie Brown"
by SCHULZ
12-27
SCHULZ

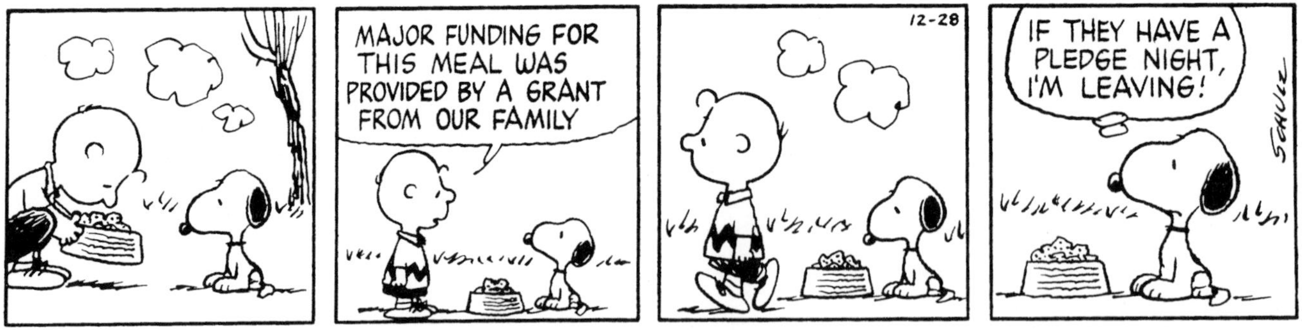
MAJOR FUNDING FOR THIS MEAL WAS PROVIDED BY A GRANT FROM OUR FAMILY
12-28
IF THEY HAVE A PLEDGE NIGHT, I'M LEAVING!
SCHULZ

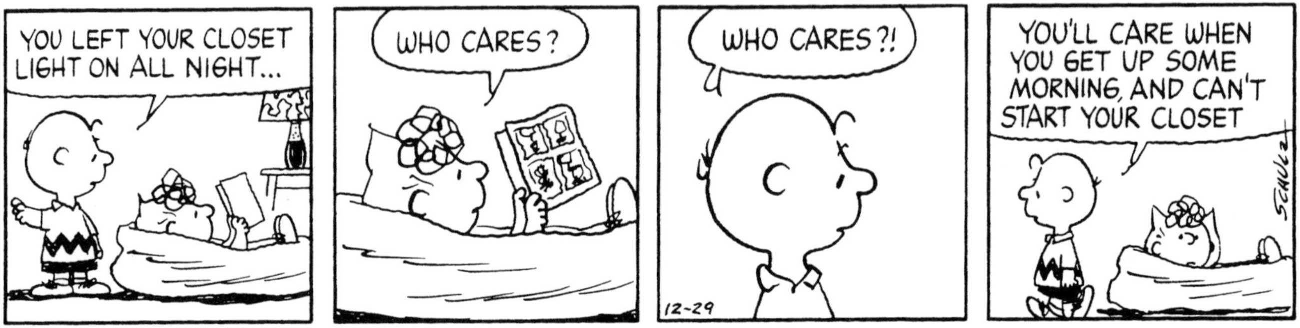
YOU LEFT YOUR CLOSET LIGHT ON ALL NIGHT...
WHO CARES?
WHO CARES?!
12-29
YOU'LL CARE WHEN YOU GET UP SOME MORNING, AND CAN'T START YOUR CLOSET
SCHULZ

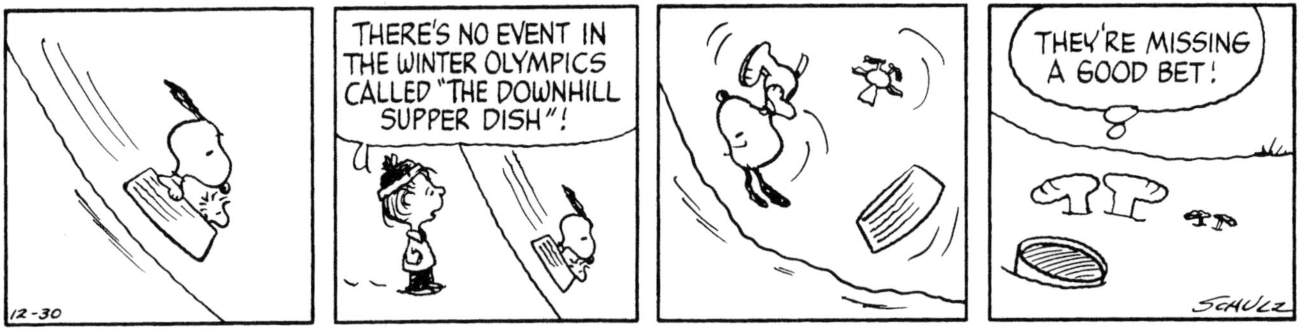
12-30
THERE'S NO EVENT IN THE WINTER OLYMPICS CALLED "THE DOWNHILL SUPPER DISH"!
THEY'RE MISSING A GOOD BET!
SCHULZ

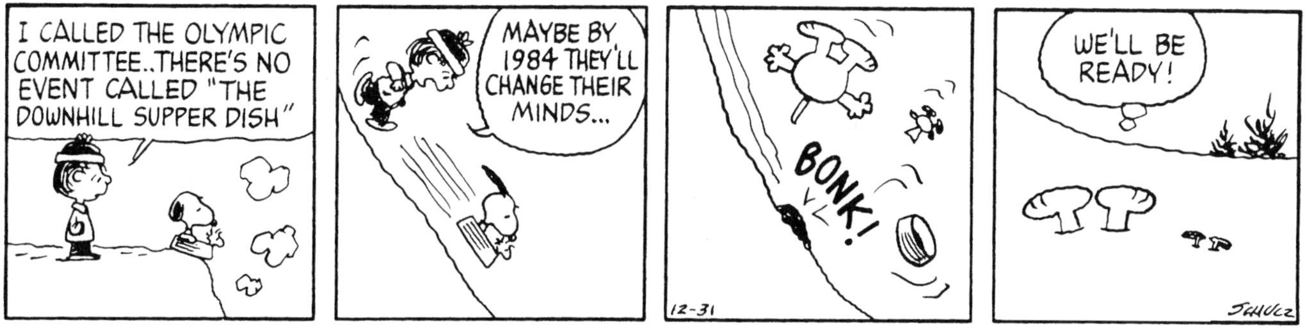
I CALLED THE OLYMPIC COMMITTEE..THERE'S NO EVENT CALLED "THE DOWNHILL SUPPER DISH"
MAYBE BY 1984 THEY'LL CHANGE THEIR MINDS...
BONK!
12-31
WE'LL BE READY!
SCHULZ

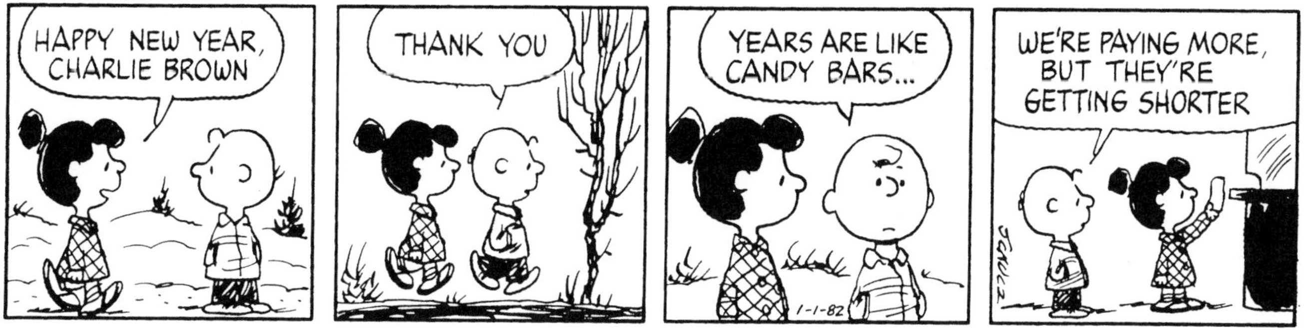
HAPPY NEW YEAR, CHARLIE BROWN
THANK YOU
YEARS ARE LIKE CANDY BARS...
1-1-82
WE'RE PAYING MORE, BUT THEY'RE GETTING SHORTER
SCHULZ

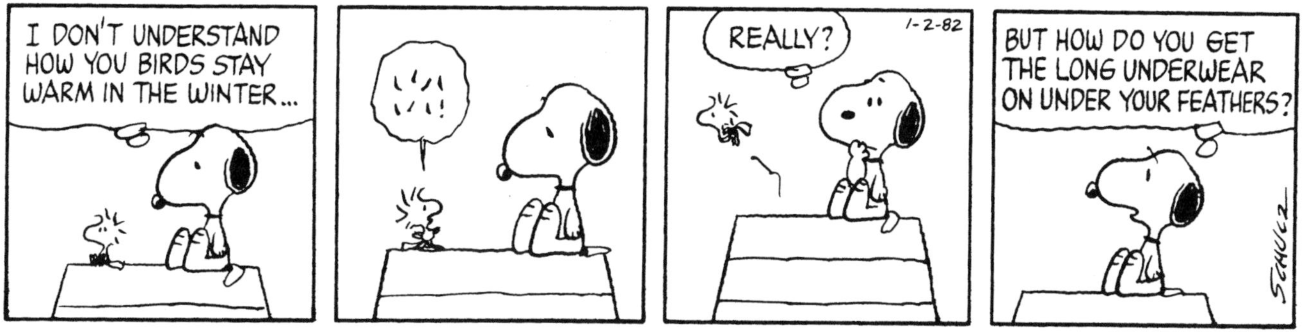
I DON'T UNDERSTAND HOW YOU BIRDS STAY WARM IN THE WINTER...
REALLY?
1-2-82
BUT HOW DO YOU GET THE LONG UNDERWEAR ON UNDER YOUR FEATHERS?
SCHULZ

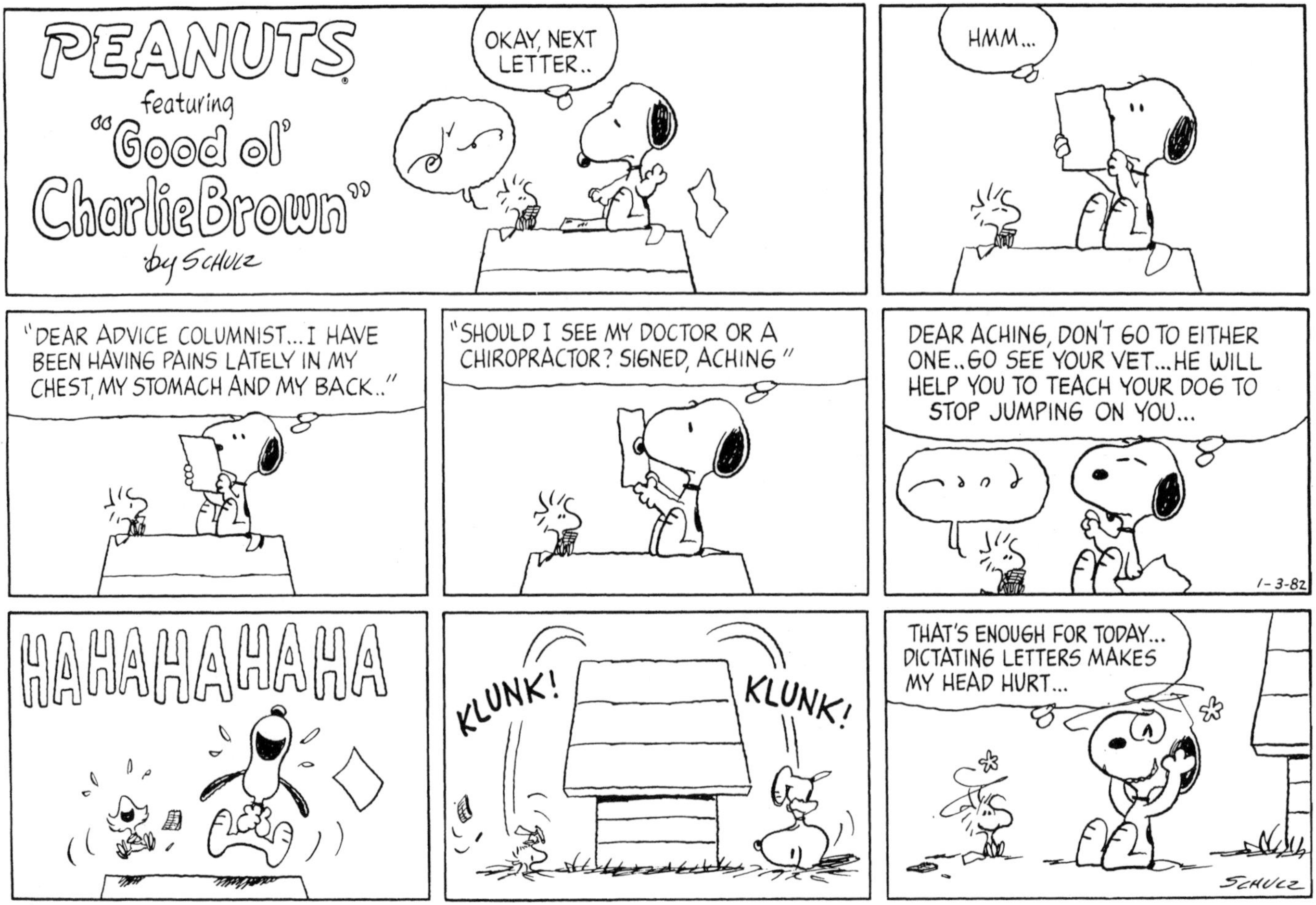
PEANUTS
featuring
"Good ol' Charlie Brown"
by SCHULZ
OKAY, NEXT LETTER..
HMM...
"DEAR ADVICE COLUMNIST...I HAVE BEEN HAVING PAINS LATELY IN MY CHEST, MY STOMACH AND MY BACK.."
"SHOULD I SEE MY DOCTOR OR A CHIROPRACTOR? SIGNED, ACHING"
DEAR ACHING, DON'T GO TO EITHER ONE..GO SEE YOUR VET...HE WILL HELP YOU TO TEACH YOUR DOG TO STOP JUMPING ON YOU...
1-3-82
HAHAHAHAHAHA
KLUNK!
KLUNK!
THAT'S ENOUGH FOR TODAY... DICTATING LETTERS MAKES MY HEAD HURT...
SCHULZ

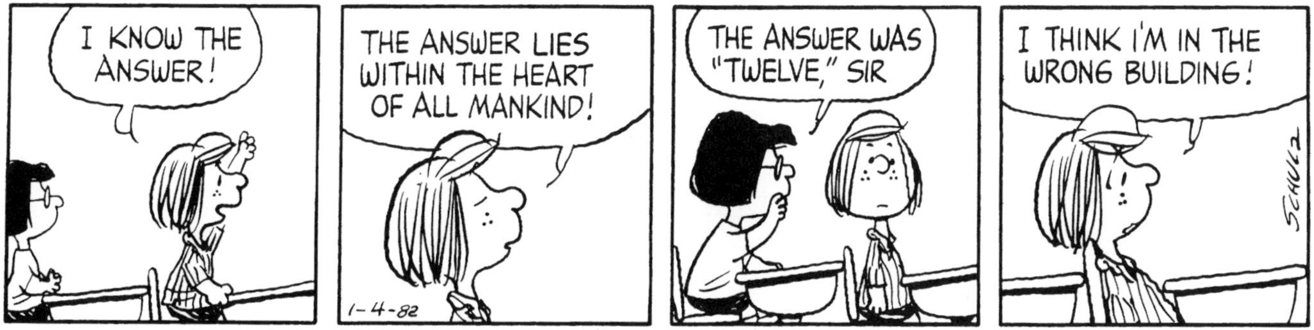
I KNOW THE ANSWER!
THE ANSWER LIES WITHIN THE HEART OF ALL MANKIND!
1-4-82
THE ANSWER WAS "TWELVE," SIR
I THINK I'M IN THE WRONG BUILDING!
SCHULZ

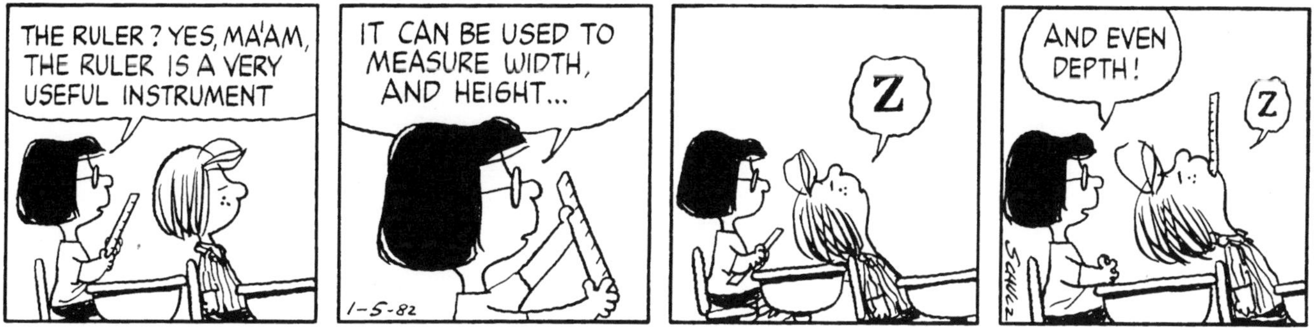
THE RULER? YES, MA'AM, THE RULER IS A VERY USEFUL INSTRUMENT
IT CAN BE USED TO MEASURE WIDTH, AND HEIGHT...
1-5-82
Z
SCHULZ
AND EVEN DEPTH!
Z

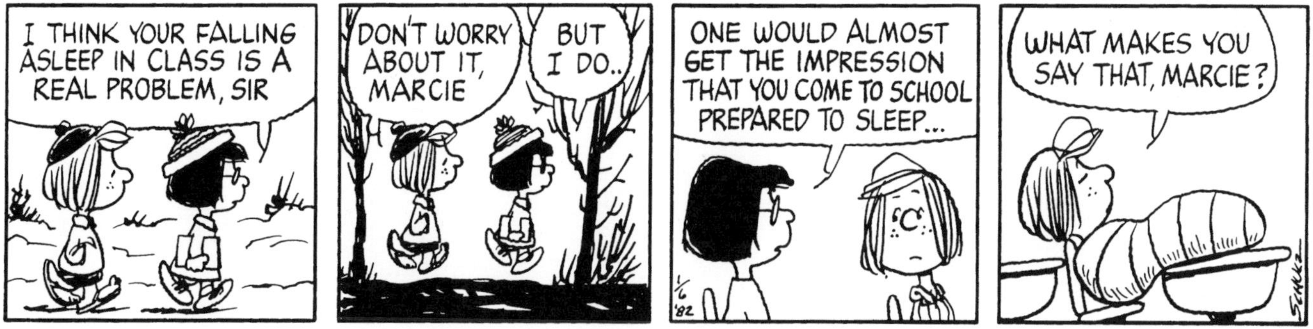
I THINK YOUR FALLING ASLEEP IN CLASS IS A REAL PROBLEM, SIR
DON'T WORRY ABOUT IT, MARCIE
BUT I DO..
ONE WOULD ALMOST GET THE IMPRESSION THAT YOU COME TO SCHOOL PREPARED TO SLEEP...
1/6 '82
WHAT MAKES YOU SAY THAT, MARCIE?
SCHULZ

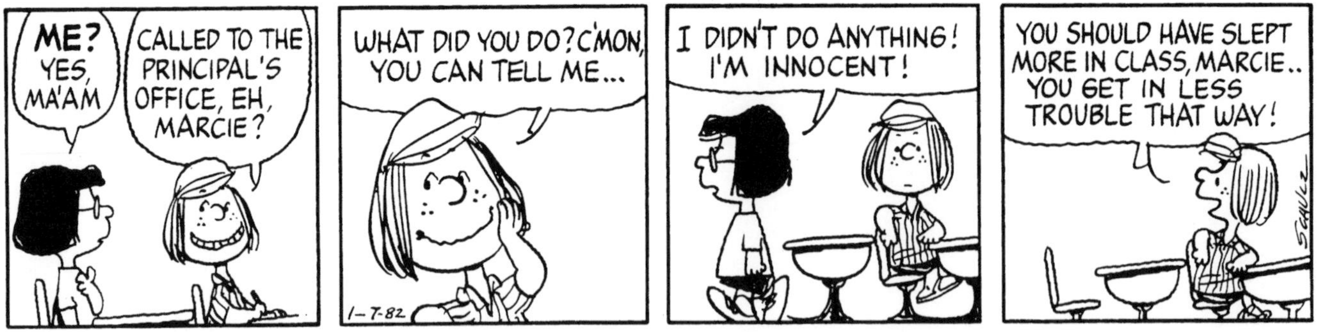
ME? YES, MA'AM
CALLED TO THE PRINCIPAL'S OFFICE, EH, MARCIE?
WHAT DID YOU DO? C'MON, YOU CAN TELL ME...
1-7-82
I DIDN'T DO ANYTHING! I'M INNOCENT!
YOU SHOULD HAVE SLEPT MORE IN CLASS, MARCIE.. YOU GET IN LESS TROUBLE THAT WAY!

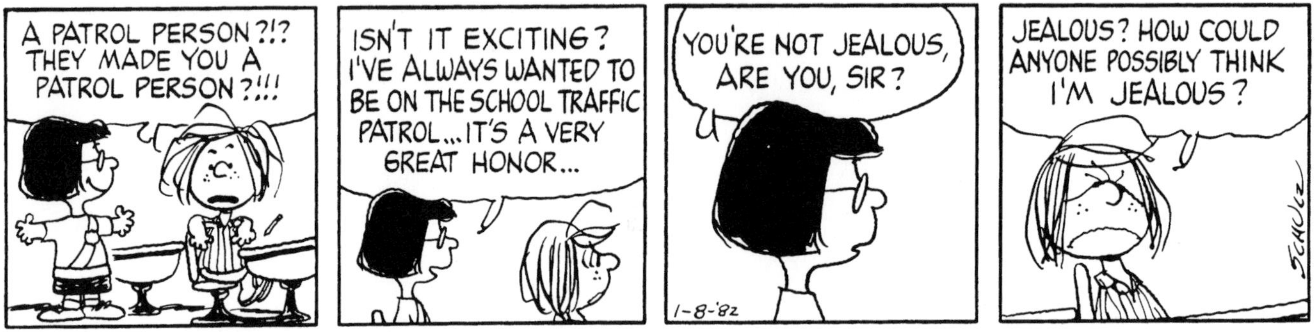
A PATROL PERSON?!? THEY MADE YOU A PATROL PERSON?!!!
ISN'T IT EXCITING? I'VE ALWAYS WANTED TO BE ON THE SCHOOL TRAFFIC PATROL... IT'S A VERY GREAT HONOR...
YOU'RE NOT JEALOUS, ARE YOU, SIR?
1-8-'82
JEALOUS? HOW COULD ANYONE POSSIBLY THINK I'M JEALOUS?

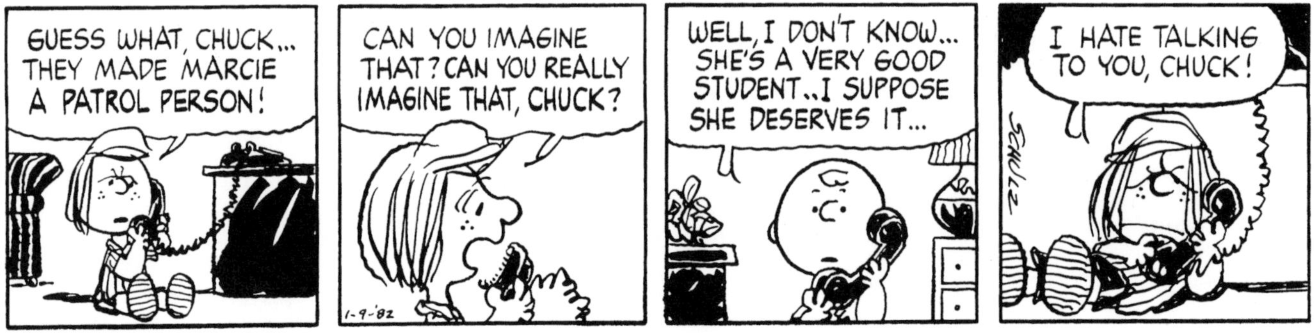
GUESS WHAT, CHUCK... THEY MADE MARCIE A PATROL PERSON!
CAN YOU IMAGINE THAT? CAN YOU REALLY IMAGINE THAT, CHUCK?
1-9-'82
WELL, I DON'T KNOW... SHE'S A VERY GOOD STUDENT..I SUPPOSE SHE DESERVES IT...
I HATE TALKING TO YOU, CHUCK!

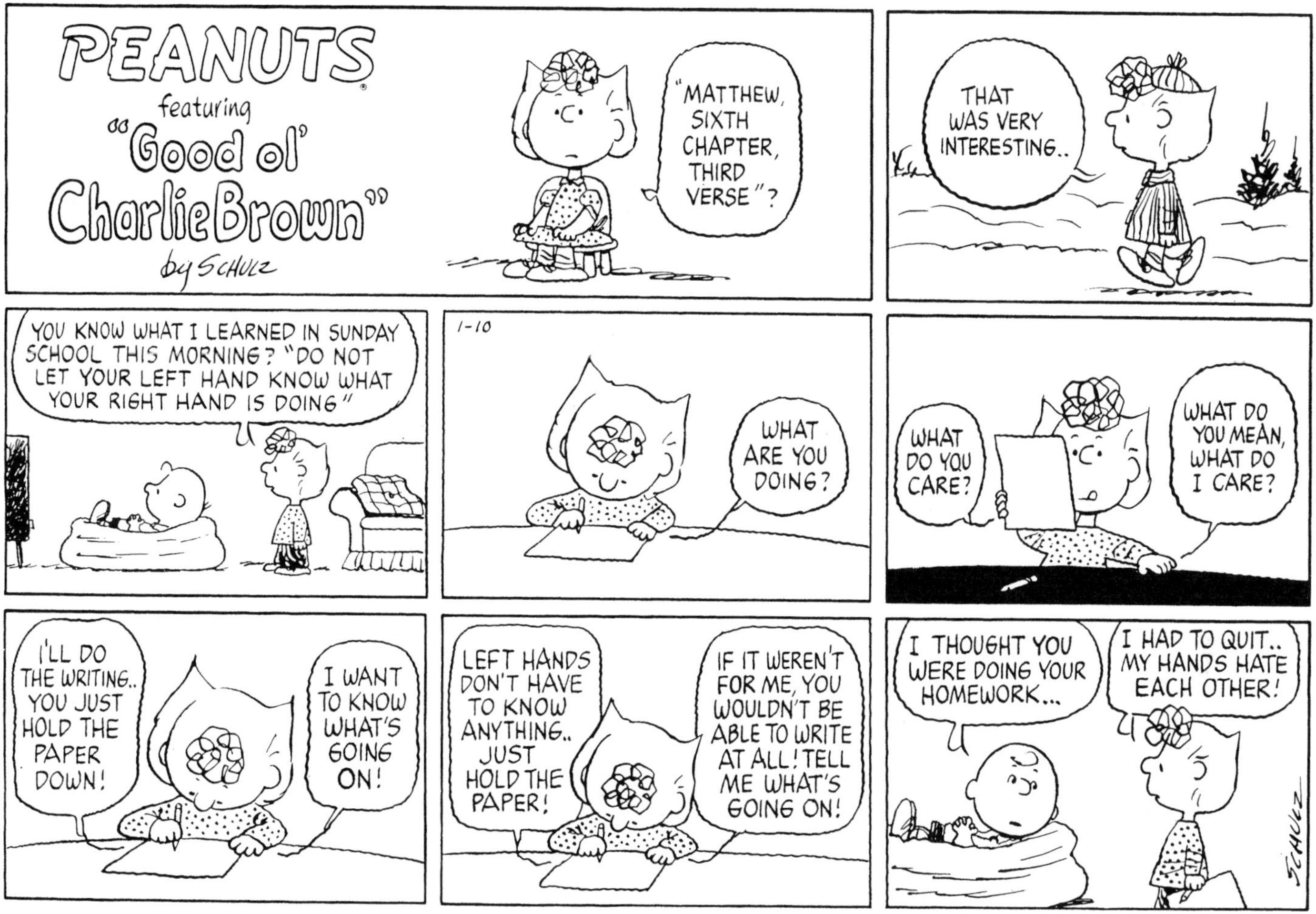
PEANUTS
featuring "Good ol' Charlie Brown"
by SCHULZ
"MATTHEW, SIXTH CHAPTER, THIRD VERSE"?
THAT WAS VERY INTERESTING..
YOU KNOW WHAT I LEARNED IN SUNDAY SCHOOL THIS MORNING? "DO NOT LET YOUR LEFT HAND KNOW WHAT YOUR RIGHT HAND IS DOING"
1-10
WHAT ARE YOU DOING?
WHAT DO YOU CARE?
WHAT DO YOU MEAN, WHAT DO I CARE?
I'LL DO THE WRITING.. YOU JUST HOLD THE PAPER DOWN!
I WANT TO KNOW WHAT'S GOING ON!
LEFT HANDS DON'T HAVE TO KNOW ANYTHING.. JUST HOLD THE PAPER!
IF IT WEREN'T FOR ME, YOU WOULDN'T BE ABLE TO WRITE AT ALL! TELL ME WHAT'S GOING ON!
I THOUGHT YOU WERE DOING YOUR HOMEWORK...
I HAD TO QUIT.. MY HANDS HATE EACH OTHER!
SCHULZ

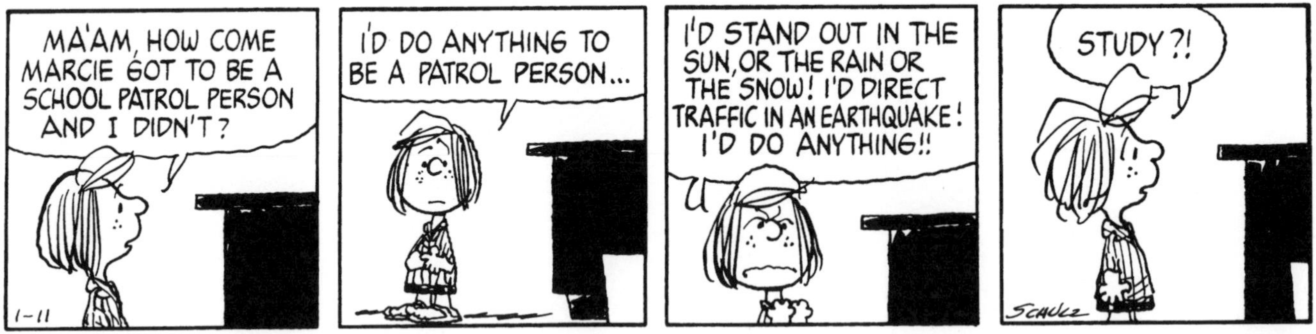
1-11
MA'AM, HOW COME MARCIE GOT TO BE A SCHOOL PATROL PERSON AND I DIDN'T?
I'D DO ANYTHING TO BE A PATROL PERSON...
I'D STAND OUT IN THE SUN, OR THE RAIN OR THE SNOW! I'D DIRECT TRAFFIC IN AN EARTHQUAKE! I'D DO ANYTHING!!
STUDY?!

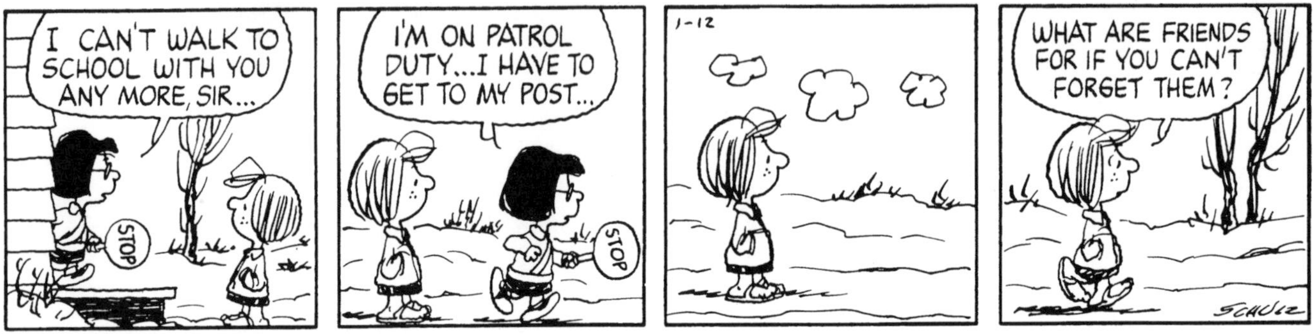
I CAN'T WALK TO SCHOOL WITH YOU ANY MORE, SIR...
STOP
I'M ON PATROL DUTY...I HAVE TO GET TO MY POST...
STOP
1-12
WHAT ARE FRIENDS FOR IF YOU CAN'T FORGET THEM?

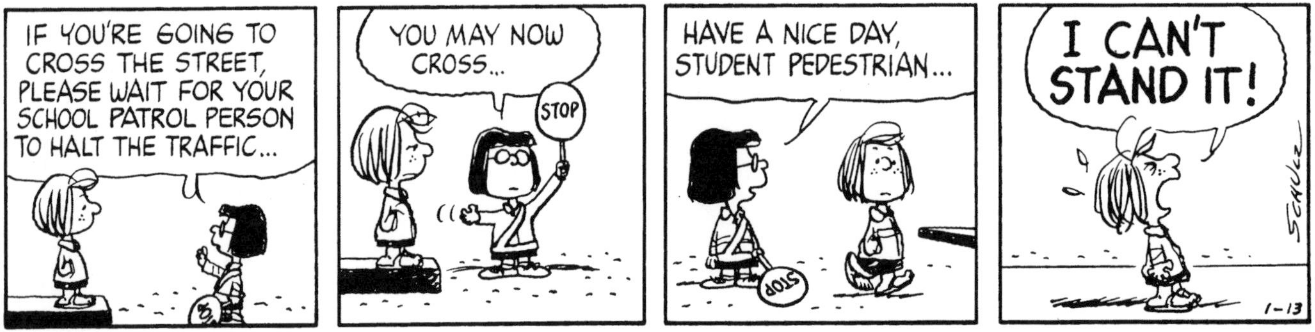
IF YOU'RE GOING TO CROSS THE STREET, PLEASE WAIT FOR YOUR SCHOOL PATROL PERSON TO HALT THE TRAFFIC...
YOU MAY NOW CROSS...
STOP
HAVE A NICE DAY, STUDENT PEDESTRIAN...
STOP
I CAN'T STAND IT!
1-13

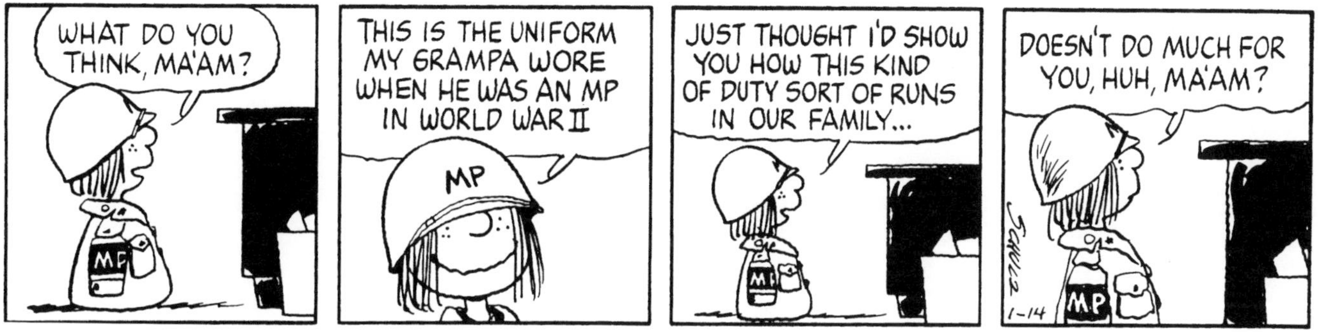
WHAT DO YOU THINK, MA'AM?
MP
THIS IS THE UNIFORM MY GRAMPA WORE WHEN HE WAS AN MP IN WORLD WAR II
MP
JUST THOUGHT I'D SHOW YOU HOW THIS KIND OF DUTY SORT OF RUNS IN OUR FAMILY...
DOESN'T DO MUCH FOR YOU, HUH, MA'AM?
1-14
MP

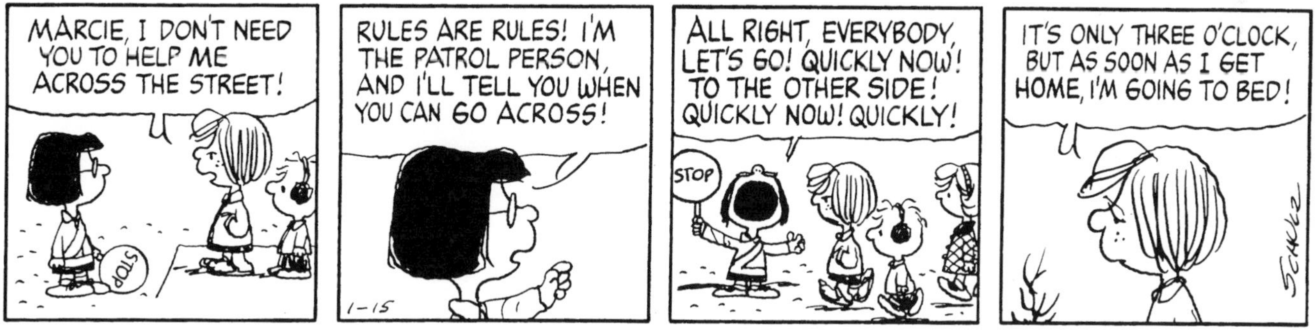
MARCIE, I DON'T NEED YOU TO HELP ME ACROSS THE STREET!
STOP
RULES ARE RULES! I'M THE PATROL PERSON, AND I'LL TELL YOU WHEN YOU CAN GO ACROSS!
1-15
ALL RIGHT, EVERYBODY, LET'S GO! QUICKLY NOW! TO THE OTHER SIDE! QUICKLY NOW! QUICKLY!
STOP
IT'S ONLY THREE O'CLOCK, BUT AS SOON AS I GET HOME, I'M GOING TO BED!

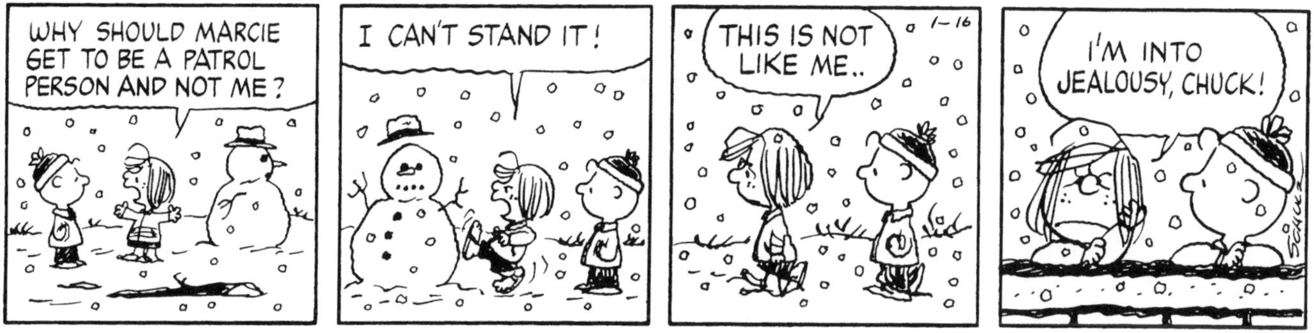
WHY SHOULD MARCIE GET TO BE A PATROL PERSON AND NOT ME?
I CAN'T STAND IT!
THIS IS NOT LIKE ME..
1-16
I'M INTO JEALOUSY, CHUCK!

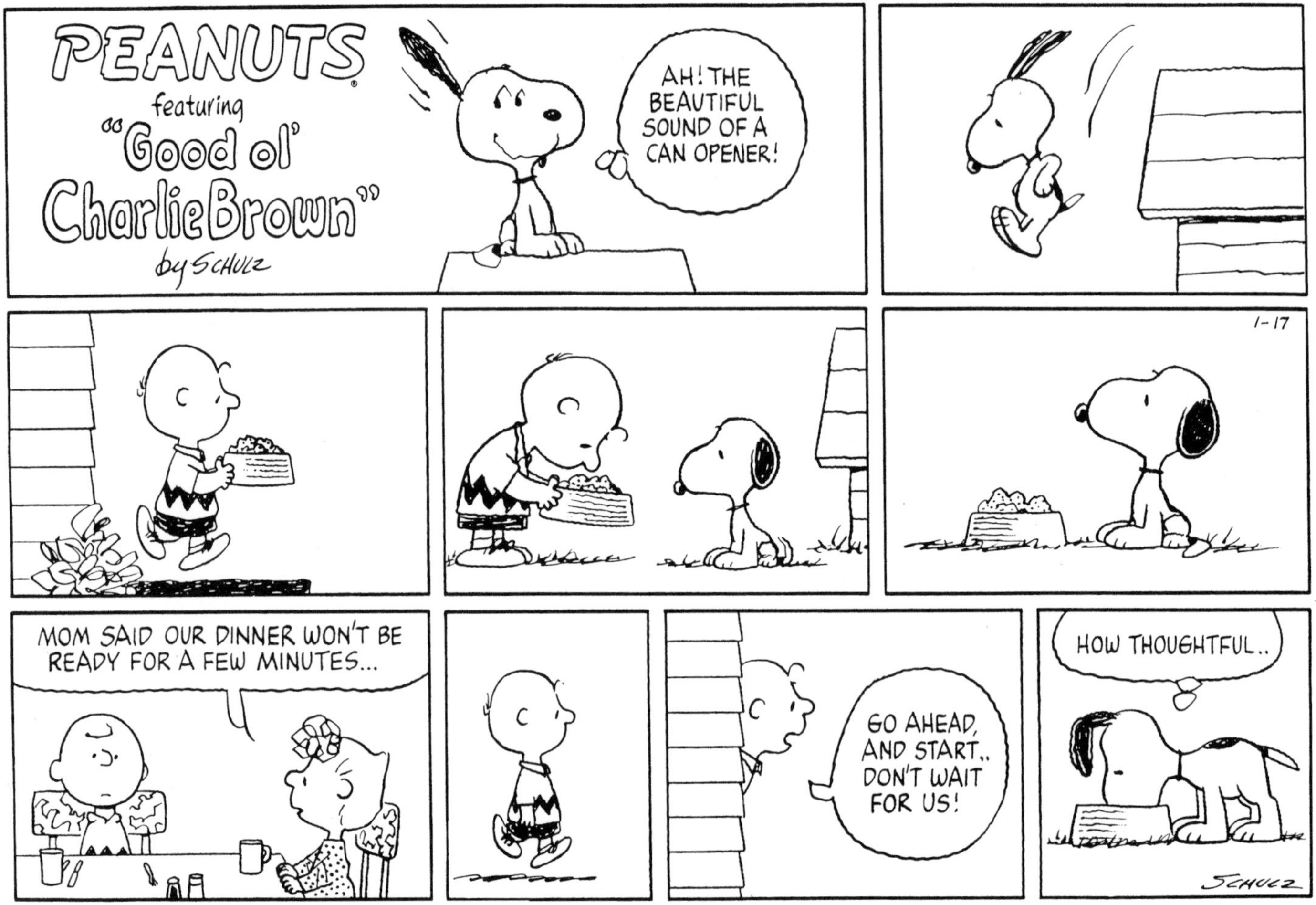
PEANUTS
featuring "Good ol' Charlie Brown"
by SCHULZ
AH! THE BEAUTIFUL SOUND OF A CAN OPENER!
1-17
MOM SAID OUR DINNER WON'T BE READY FOR A FEW MINUTES...
GO AHEAD, AND START.. DON'T WAIT FOR US!
HOW THOUGHTFUL..
SCHULZ

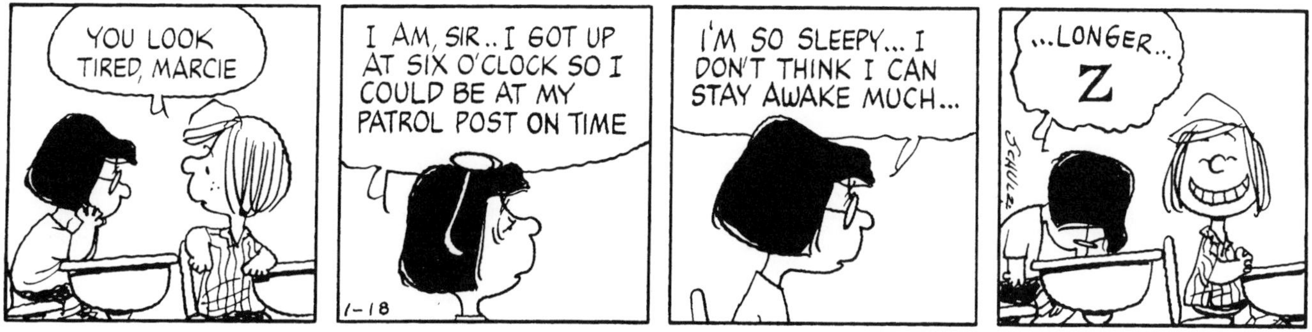
YOU LOOK TIRED, MARCIE
I AM, SIR.. I GOT UP AT SIX O'CLOCK SO I COULD BE AT MY PATROL POST ON TIME
1-18
I'M SO SLEEPY... I DON'T THINK I CAN STAY AWAKE MUCH...
...LONGER...
Z
SCHULZ

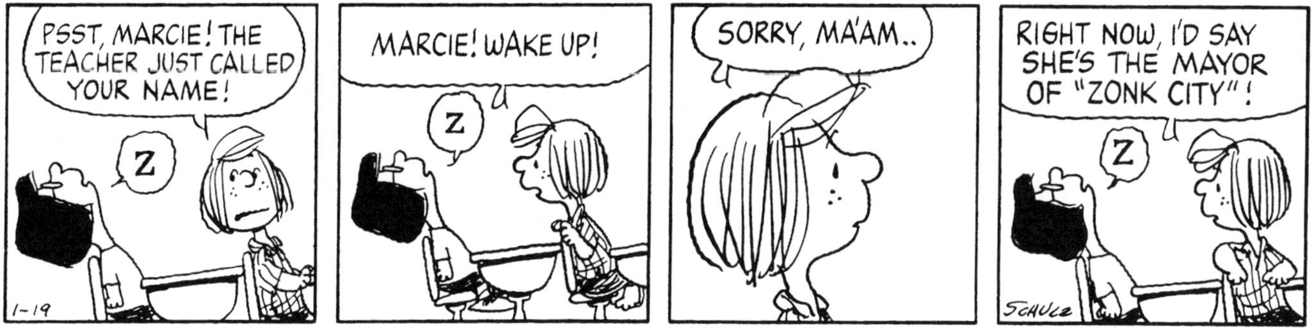
PSST, MARCIE! THE TEACHER JUST CALLED YOUR NAME!
Z
1-19
MARCIE! WAKE UP!
Z
SORRY, MA'AM..
RIGHT NOW, I'D SAY SHE'S THE MAYOR OF "ZONK CITY"!
Z
SCHULZ

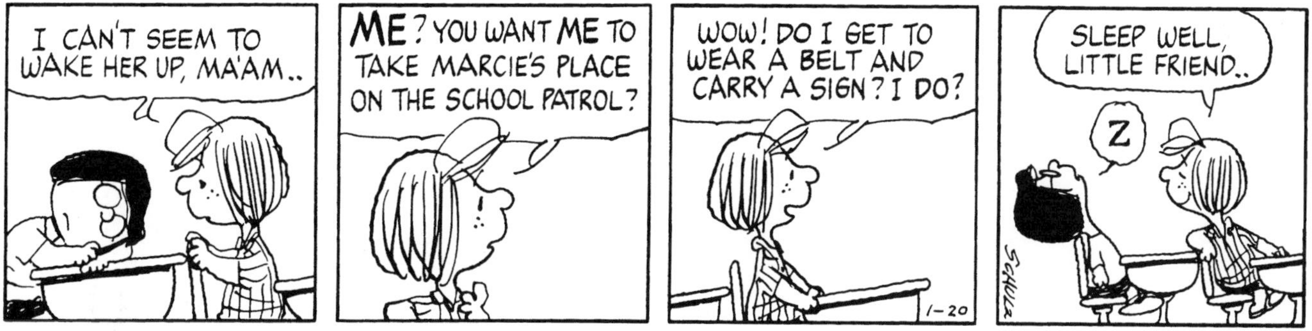
I CAN'T SEEM TO WAKE HER UP, MA'AM..
ME? YOU WANT ME TO TAKE MARCIE'S PLACE ON THE SCHOOL PATROL?
WOW! DO I GET TO WEAR A BELT AND CARRY A SIGN? I DO?
1-20
SLEEP WELL, LITTLE FRIEND..
Z
SCHULZ

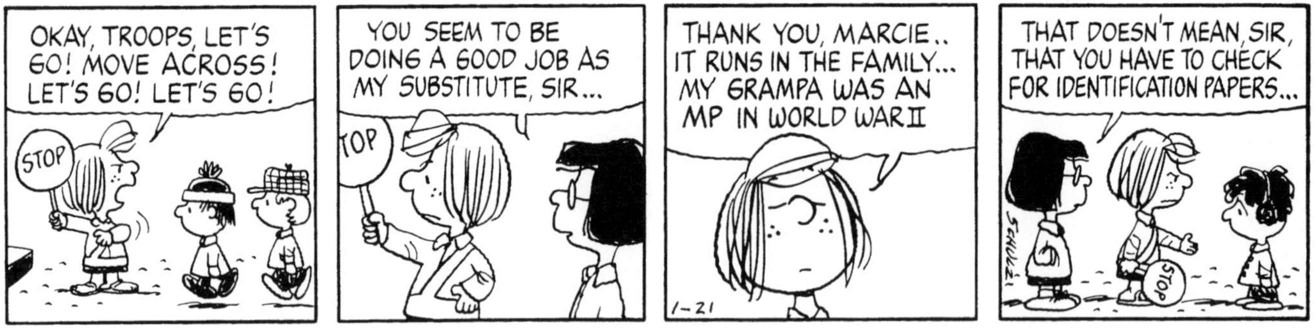
OKAY, TROOPS, LET'S GO! MOVE ACROSS! LET'S GO! LET'S GO!
STOP
YOU SEEM TO BE DOING A GOOD JOB AS MY SUBSTITUTE, SIR...
TOP
THANK YOU, MARCIE.. IT RUNS IN THE FAMILY... MY GRAMPA WAS AN MP IN WORLD WAR II
1-21
THAT DOESN'T MEAN, SIR, THAT YOU HAVE TO CHECK FOR IDENTIFICATION PAPERS...
SCHULZ
STOP

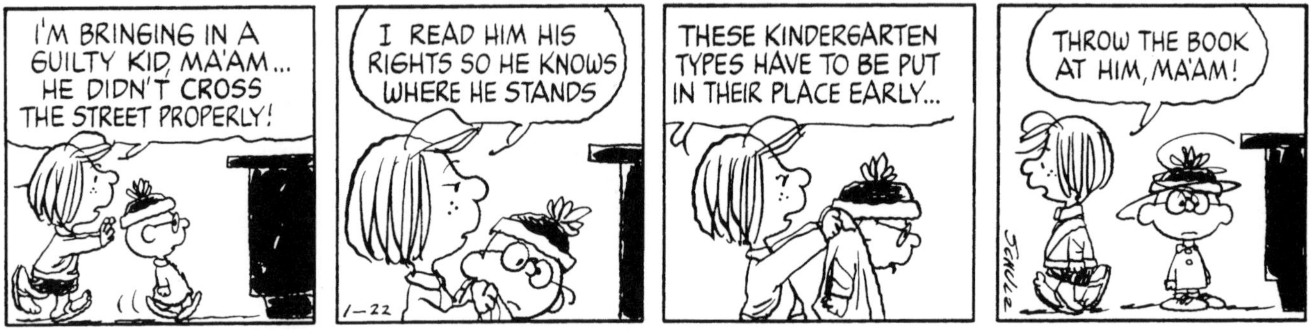
I'M BRINGING IN A GUILTY KID, MA'AM... HE DIDN'T CROSS THE STREET PROPERLY!
I READ HIM HIS RIGHTS SO HE KNOWS WHERE HE STANDS
1-22
THESE KINDERGARTEN TYPES HAVE TO BE PUT IN THEIR PLACE EARLY...
THROW THE BOOK AT HIM, MA'AM!
SCHULZ

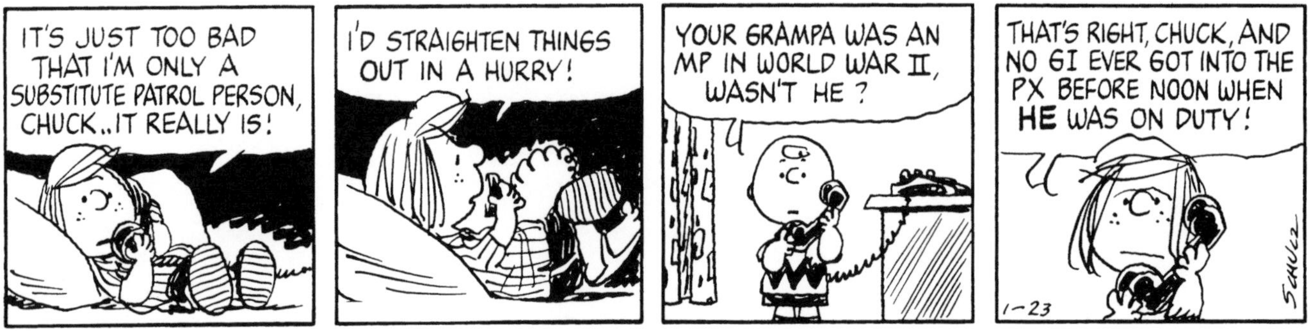
IT'S JUST TOO BAD THAT I'M ONLY A SUBSTITUTE PATROL PERSON, CHUCK..IT REALLY IS!
I'D STRAIGHTEN THINGS OUT IN A HURRY!
YOUR GRAMPA WAS AN MP IN WORLD WAR II, WASN'T HE ?
THAT'S RIGHT, CHUCK, AND NO GI EVER GOT INTO THE PX BEFORE NOON WHEN HE WAS ON DUTY!
SCHULZ
1-23

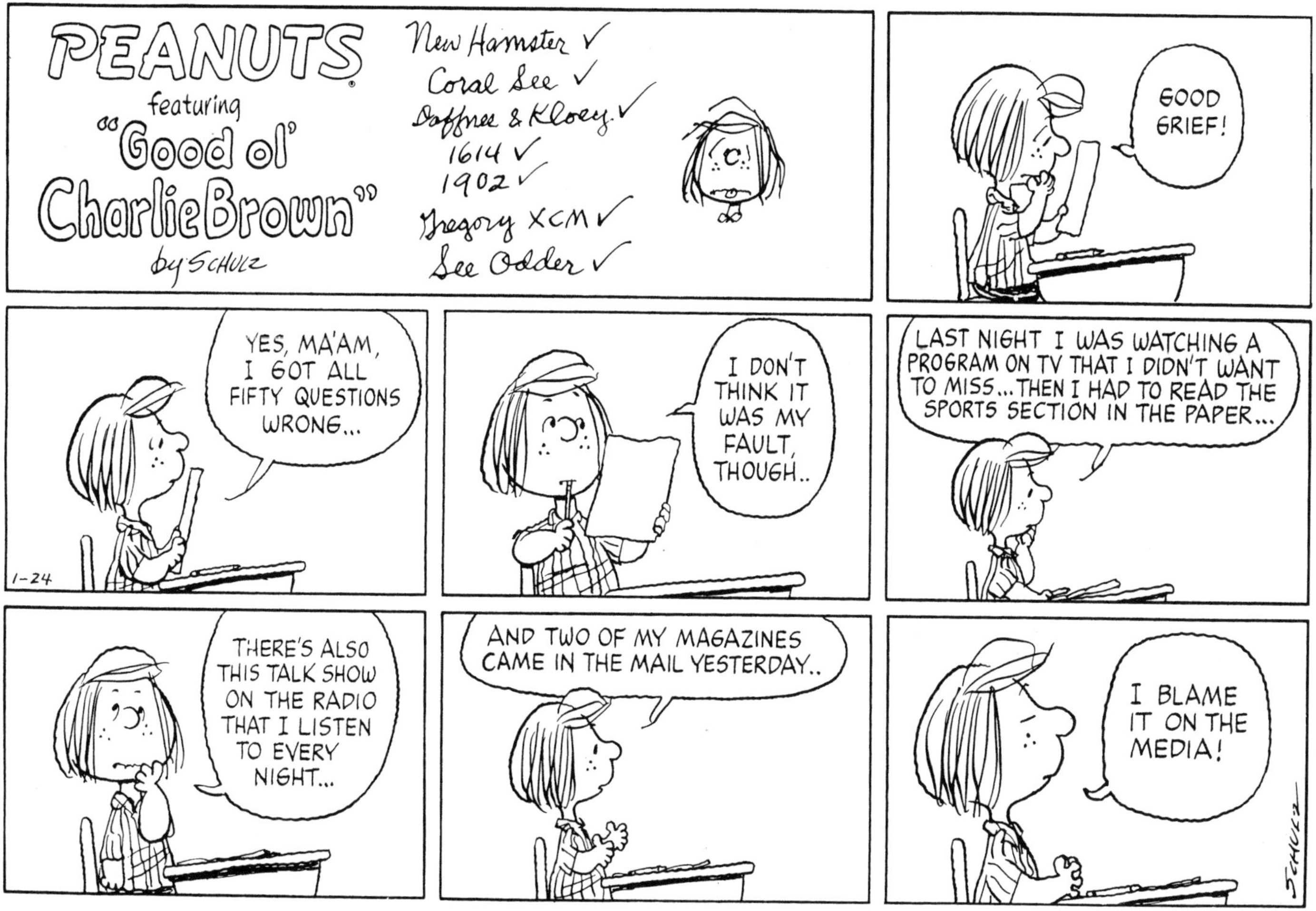
PEANUTS
featuring
"Good ol' Charlie Brown"
by SCHULZ
New Hamster ✓
Coral See ✓
Doffree & Kloey ✓
1614 ✓
1902 ✓
Gregory XCM ✓
See Odder ✓
GOOD GRIEF!
YES, MA'AM, I GOT ALL FIFTY QUESTIONS WRONG...
1-24
I DON'T THINK IT WAS MY FAULT, THOUGH..
LAST NIGHT I WAS WATCHING A PROGRAM ON TV THAT I DIDN'T WANT TO MISS...THEN I HAD TO READ THE SPORTS SECTION IN THE PAPER...
THERE'S ALSO THIS TALK SHOW ON THE RADIO THAT I LISTEN TO EVERY NIGHT...
AND TWO OF MY MAGAZINES CAME IN THE MAIL YESTERDAY..
I BLAME IT ON THE MEDIA!
SCHULZ

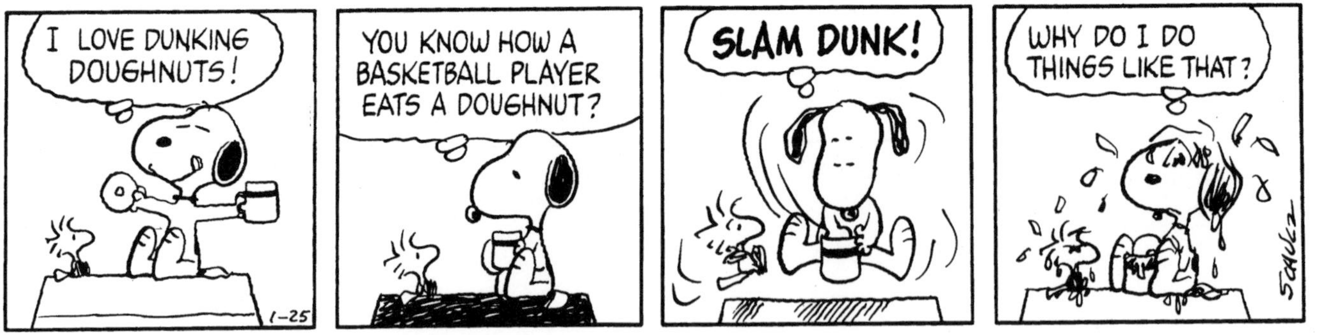
I LOVE DUNKING DOUGHNUTS!
YOU KNOW HOW A BASKETBALL PLAYER EATS A DOUGHNUT?
SLAM DUNK!
WHY DO I DO THINGS LIKE THAT?

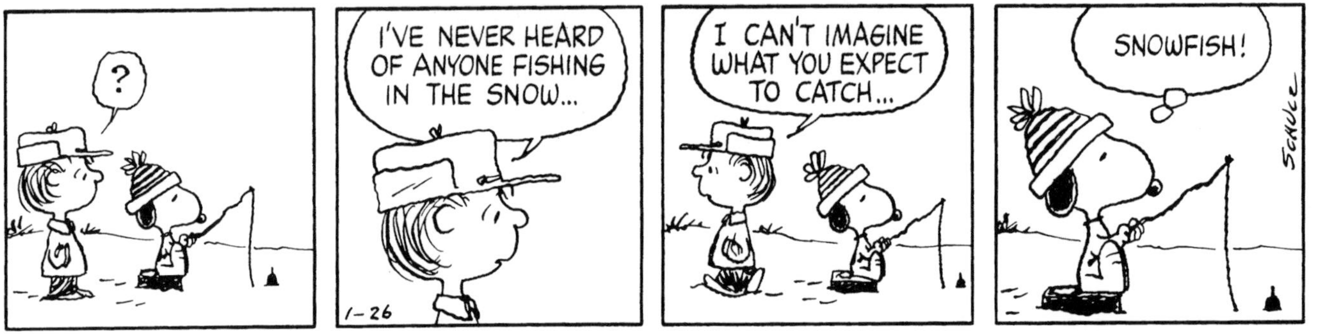
?
I'VE NEVER HEARD OF ANYONE FISHING IN THE SNOW...
I CAN'T IMAGINE WHAT YOU EXPECT TO CATCH...
SNOWFISH!

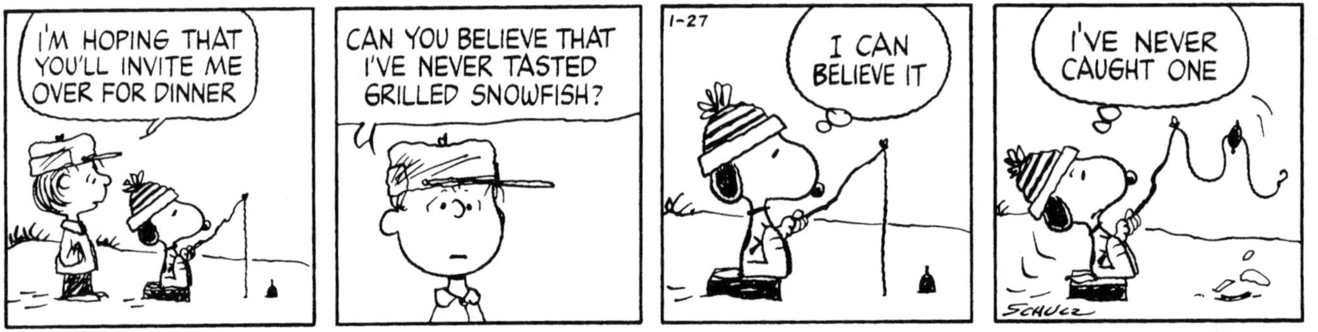
I'M HOPING THAT YOU'LL INVITE ME OVER FOR DINNER
CAN YOU BELIEVE THAT I'VE NEVER TASTED GRILLED SNOWFISH?
I CAN BELIEVE IT
I'VE NEVER CAUGHT ONE

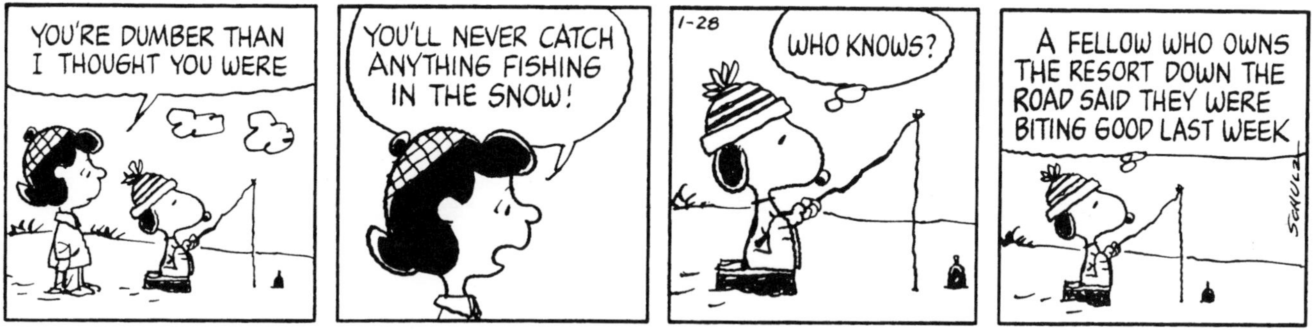
YOU'RE DUMBER THAN I THOUGHT YOU WERE
YOU'LL NEVER CATCH ANYTHING FISHING IN THE SNOW!
1-28
WHO KNOWS?
A FELLOW WHO OWNS THE RESORT DOWN THE ROAD SAID THEY WERE BITING GOOD LAST WEEK

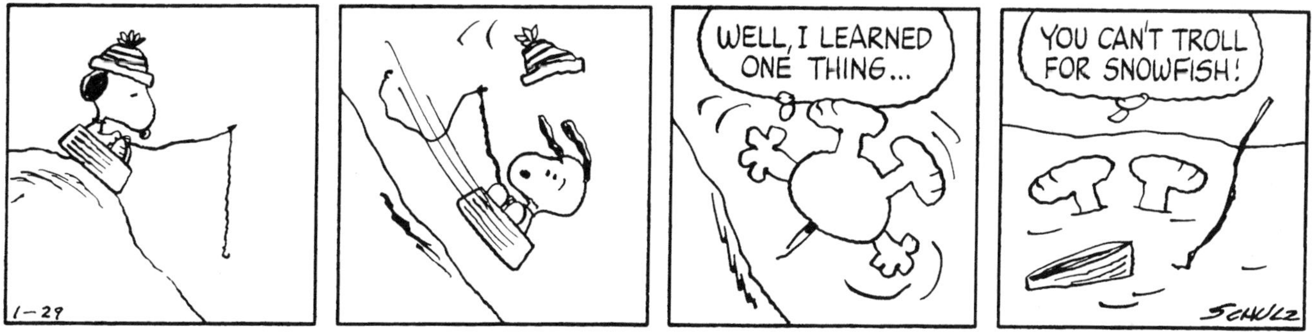
1-29
WELL, I LEARNED ONE THING...
YOU CAN'T TROLL FOR SNOWFISH!

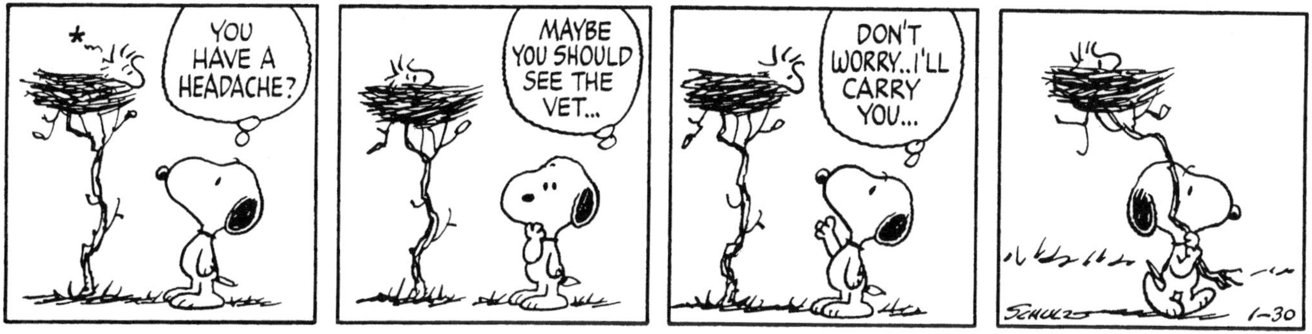
YOU HAVE A HEADACHE?
MAYBE YOU SHOULD SEE THE VET...
DON'T WORRY..I'LL CARRY YOU...
1-30

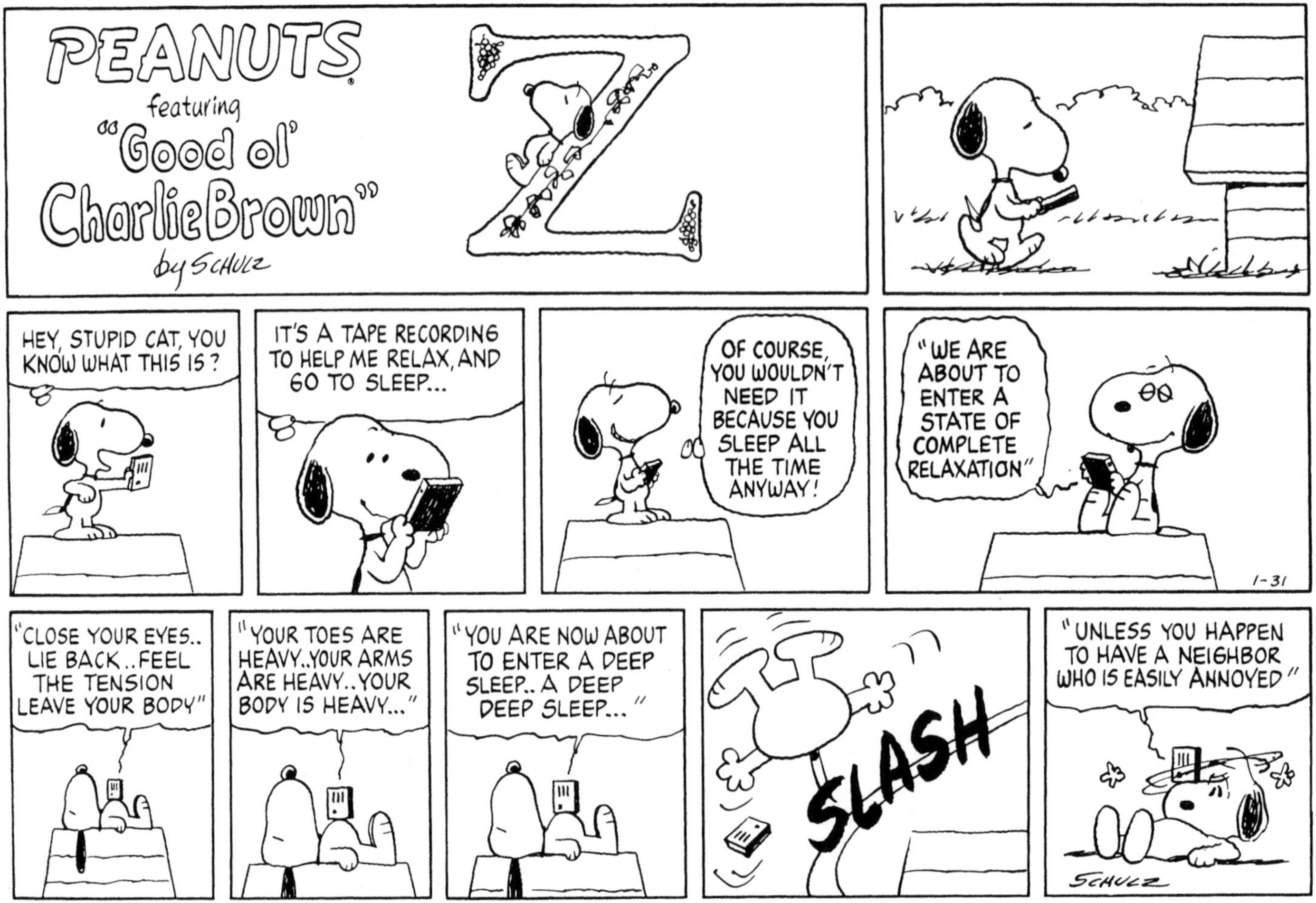
PEANUTS
featuring
"Good ol' CharlieBrown"
by SCHULZ
Z
HEY, STUPID CAT, YOU KNOW WHAT THIS IS?
IT'S A TAPE RECORDING TO HELP ME RELAX, AND GO TO SLEEP...
OF COURSE, YOU WOULDN'T NEED IT BECAUSE YOU SLEEP ALL THE TIME ANYWAY!
"WE ARE ABOUT TO ENTER A STATE OF COMPLETE RELAXATION"
1-31
"CLOSE YOUR EYES.. LIE BACK..FEEL THE TENSION LEAVE YOUR BODY"
"YOUR TOES ARE HEAVY..YOUR ARMS ARE HEAVY..YOUR BODY IS HEAVY..."
"YOU ARE NOW ABOUT TO ENTER A DEEP SLEEP.. A DEEP DEEP SLEEP..."
SLASH
"UNLESS YOU HAPPEN TO HAVE A NEIGHBOR WHO IS EASILY ANNOYED"
SCHULZ

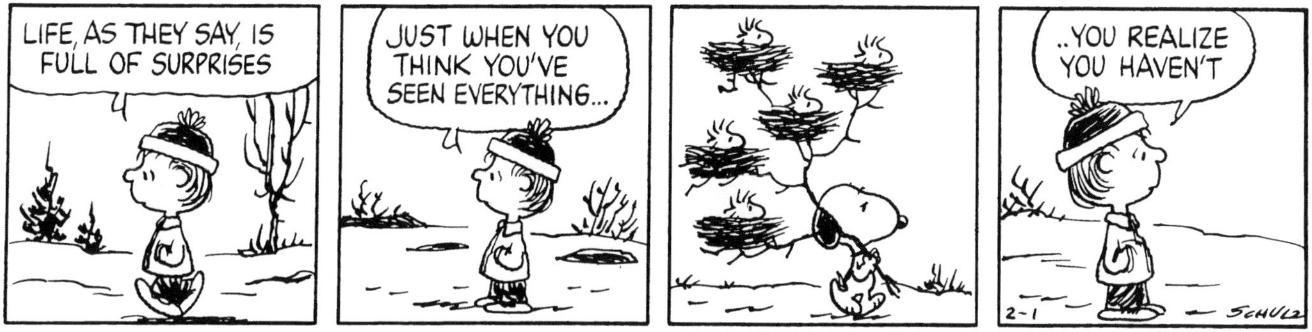
LIFE, AS THEY SAY, IS FULL OF SURPRISES
JUST WHEN YOU THINK YOU'VE SEEN EVERYTHING...
..YOU REALIZE YOU HAVEN'T
2-1
SCHULZ

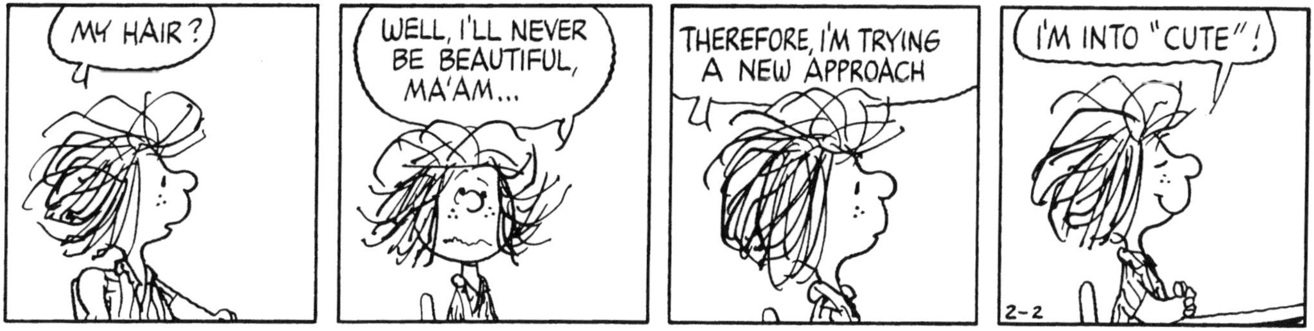
MY HAIR?
WELL, I'LL NEVER BE BEAUTIFUL, MA'AM...
THEREFORE, I'M TRYING A NEW APPROACH
I'M INTO "CUTE"!
2-2

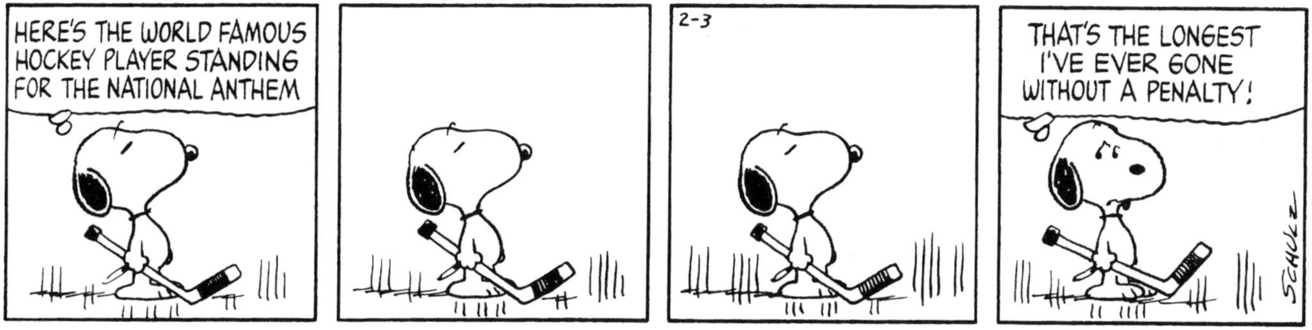
HERE'S THE WORLD FAMOUS HOCKEY PLAYER STANDING FOR THE NATIONAL ANTHEM
2-3
THAT'S THE LONGEST I'VE EVER GONE WITHOUT A PENALTY!
SCHULZ

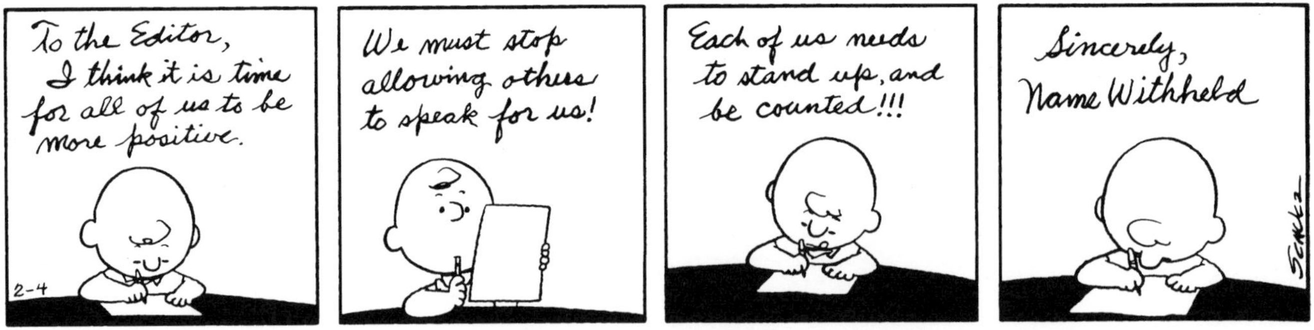
To the Editor,
I think it is time for all of us to be more positive.
2-4
We must stop allowing others to speak for us!
Each of us needs to stand up, and be counted!!!
Sincerely,
Name Withheld
SCHULZ

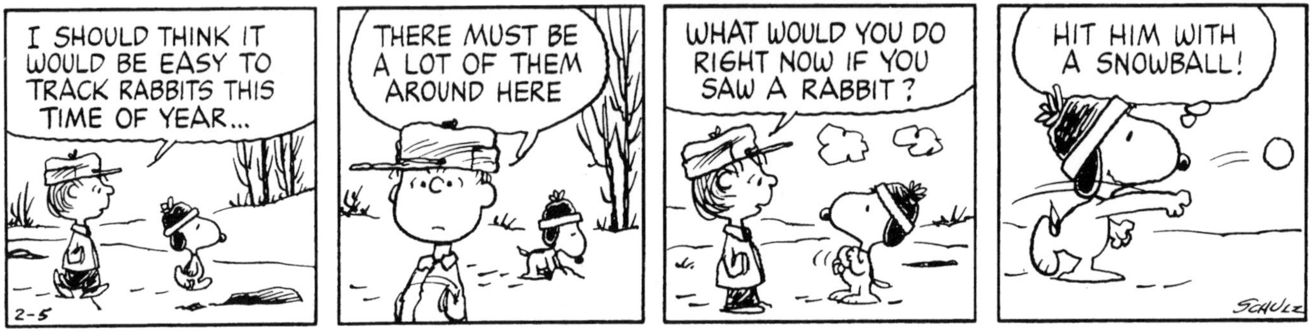
I SHOULD THINK IT WOULD BE EASY TO TRACK RABBITS THIS TIME OF YEAR...
2-5
THERE MUST BE A LOT OF THEM AROUND HERE
WHAT WOULD YOU DO RIGHT NOW IF YOU SAW A RABBIT?
HIT HIM WITH A SNOWBALL!
SCHULZ

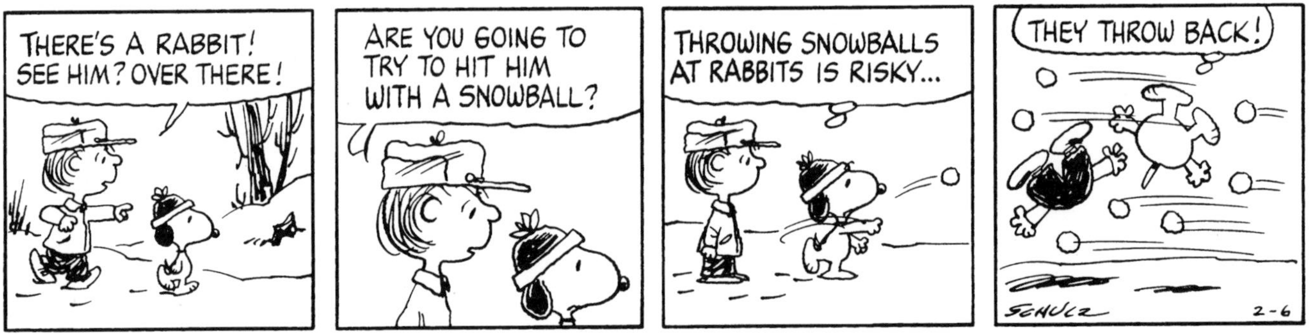
THERE'S A RABBIT! SEE HIM? OVER THERE!
ARE YOU GOING TO TRY TO HIT HIM WITH A SNOWBALL?
THROWING SNOWBALLS AT RABBITS IS RISKY...
THEY THROW BACK!
SCHULZ
2-6

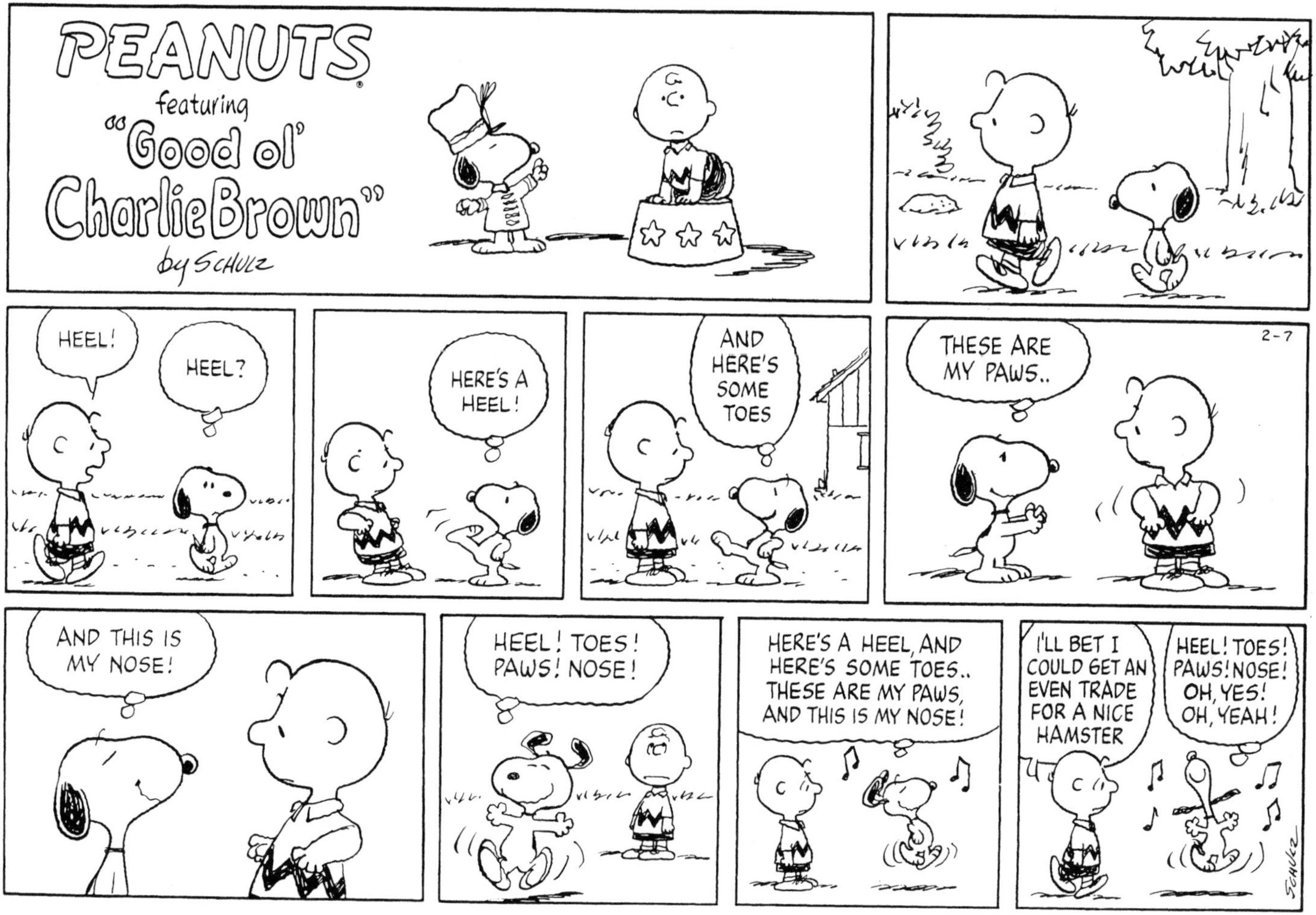
PEANUTS
featuring
"Good ol' Charlie Brown"
by SCHULZ
HEEL!
HEEL?
HERE'S A HEEL!
AND HERE'S SOME TOES
THESE ARE MY PAWS..
2-7
AND THIS IS MY NOSE!
HEEL! TOES! PAWS! NOSE!
HERE'S A HEEL, AND HERE'S SOME TOES.. THESE ARE MY PAWS, AND THIS IS MY NOSE!
I'LL BET I COULD GET AN EVEN TRADE FOR A NICE HAMSTER
HEEL! TOES! PAWS! NOSE! OH, YES! OH, YEAH!
SCHULZ

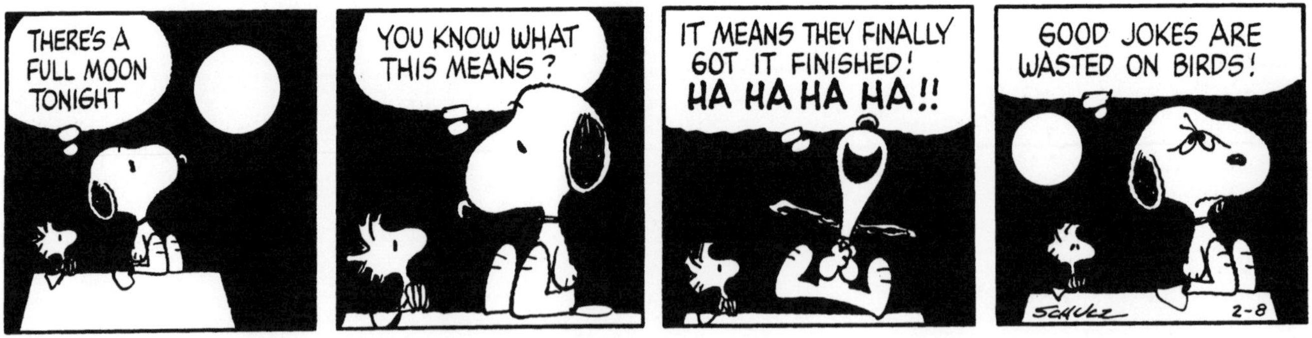
THERE'S A FULL MOON TONIGHT
YOU KNOW WHAT THIS MEANS ?
IT MEANS THEY FINALLY GOT IT FINISHED! HA HA HA HA!!
GOOD JOKES ARE WASTED ON BIRDS!
SCHULZ
2-8

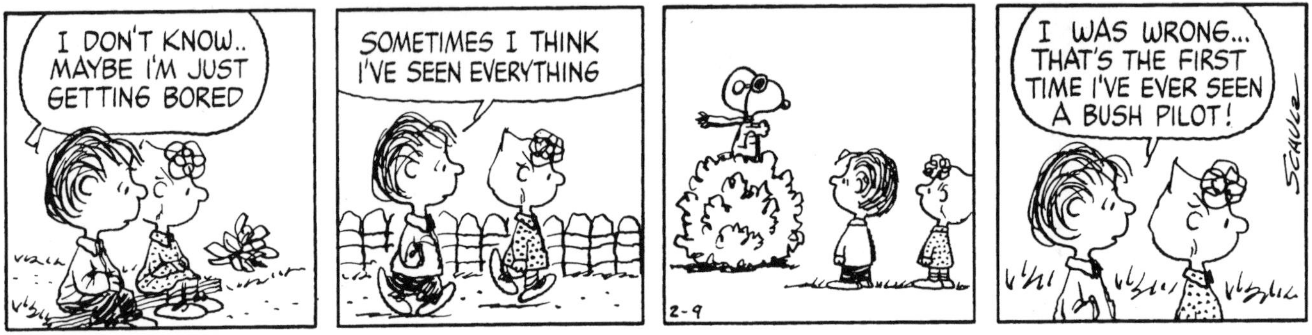
I DON'T KNOW.. MAYBE I'M JUST GETTING BORED
SOMETIMES I THINK I'VE SEEN EVERYTHING
2-9
I WAS WRONG... THAT'S THE FIRST TIME I'VE EVER SEEN A BUSH PILOT!
SCHULZ

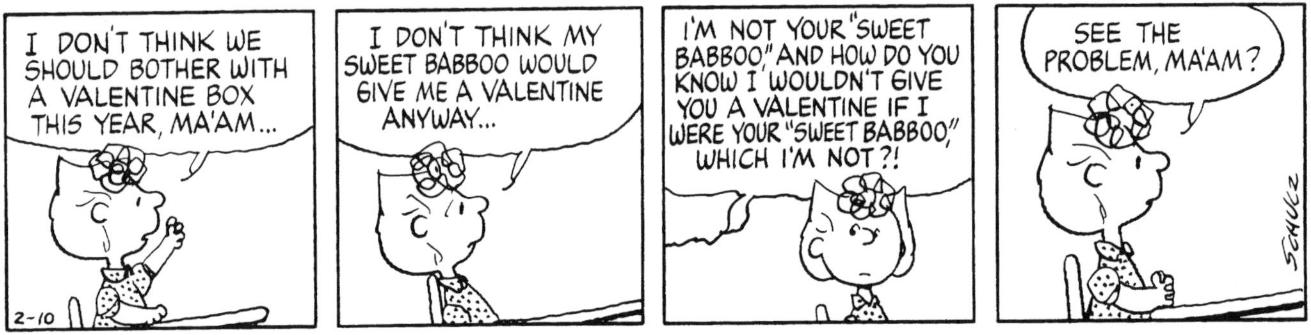
I DON'T THINK WE SHOULD BOTHER WITH A VALENTINE BOX THIS YEAR, MA'AM...
2-10
I DON'T THINK MY SWEET BABBOO WOULD GIVE ME A VALENTINE ANYWAY...
I'M NOT YOUR "SWEET BABBOO," AND HOW DO YOU KNOW I WOULDN'T GIVE YOU A VALENTINE IF I WERE YOUR "SWEET BABBOO," WHICH I'M NOT?!
SEE THE PROBLEM, MA'AM?
SCHULZ

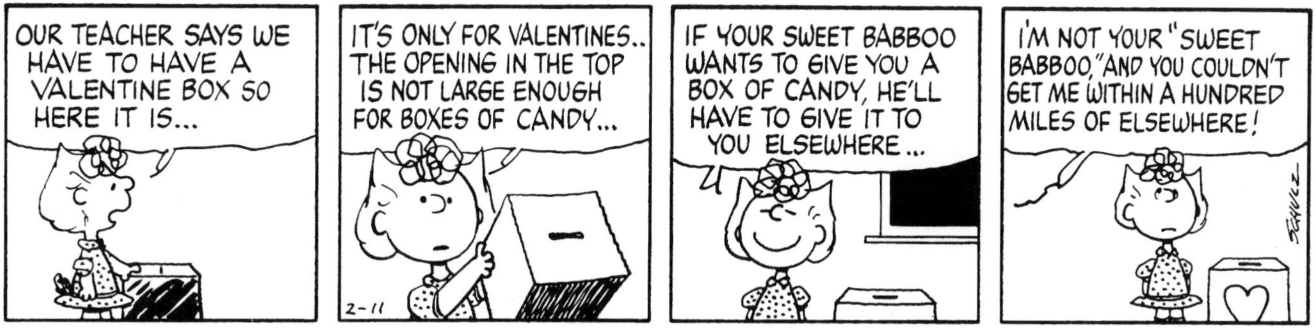
OUR TEACHER SAYS WE HAVE TO HAVE A VALENTINE BOX SO HERE IT IS...
IT'S ONLY FOR VALENTINES.. THE OPENING IN THE TOP IS NOT LARGE ENOUGH FOR BOXES OF CANDY...
2-11
IF YOUR SWEET BABBOO WANTS TO GIVE YOU A BOX OF CANDY, HE'LL HAVE TO GIVE IT TO YOU ELSEWHERE...
I'M NOT YOUR "SWEET BABBOO," AND YOU COULDN'T GET ME WITHIN A HUNDRED MILES OF ELSEWHERE!
SCHULZ

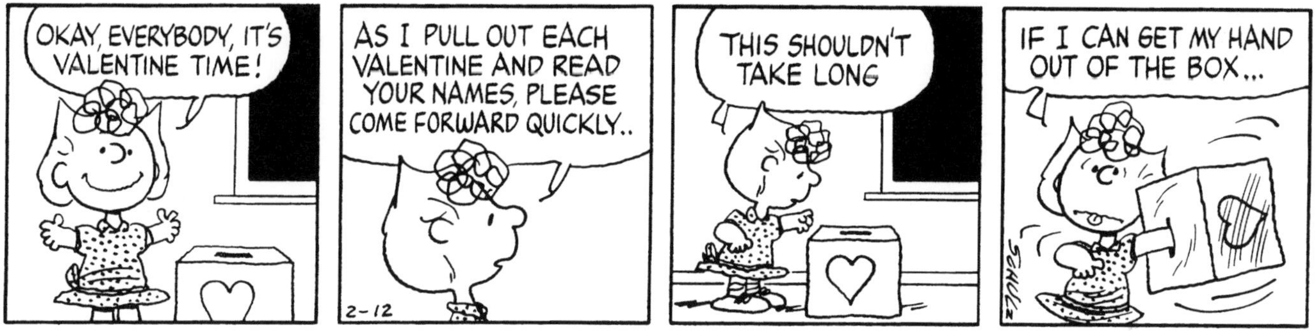
OKAY, EVERYBODY, IT'S VALENTINE TIME!
AS I PULL OUT EACH VALENTINE AND READ YOUR NAMES, PLEASE COME FORWARD QUICKLY..
2-12
THIS SHOULDN'T TAKE LONG
IF I CAN GET MY HAND OUT OF THE BOX...
SCHULZ

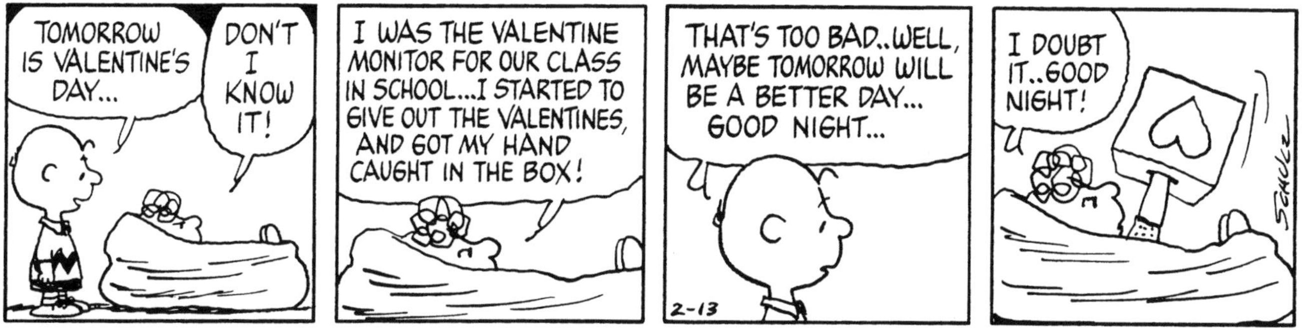
TOMORROW IS VALENTINE'S DAY...
DON'T I KNOW IT!
I WAS THE VALENTINE MONITOR FOR OUR CLASS IN SCHOOL...I STARTED TO GIVE OUT THE VALENTINES, AND GOT MY HAND CAUGHT IN THE BOX!
THAT'S TOO BAD..WELL, MAYBE TOMORROW WILL BE A BETTER DAY... GOOD NIGHT...
2-13
I DOUBT IT..GOOD NIGHT!
SCHULZ

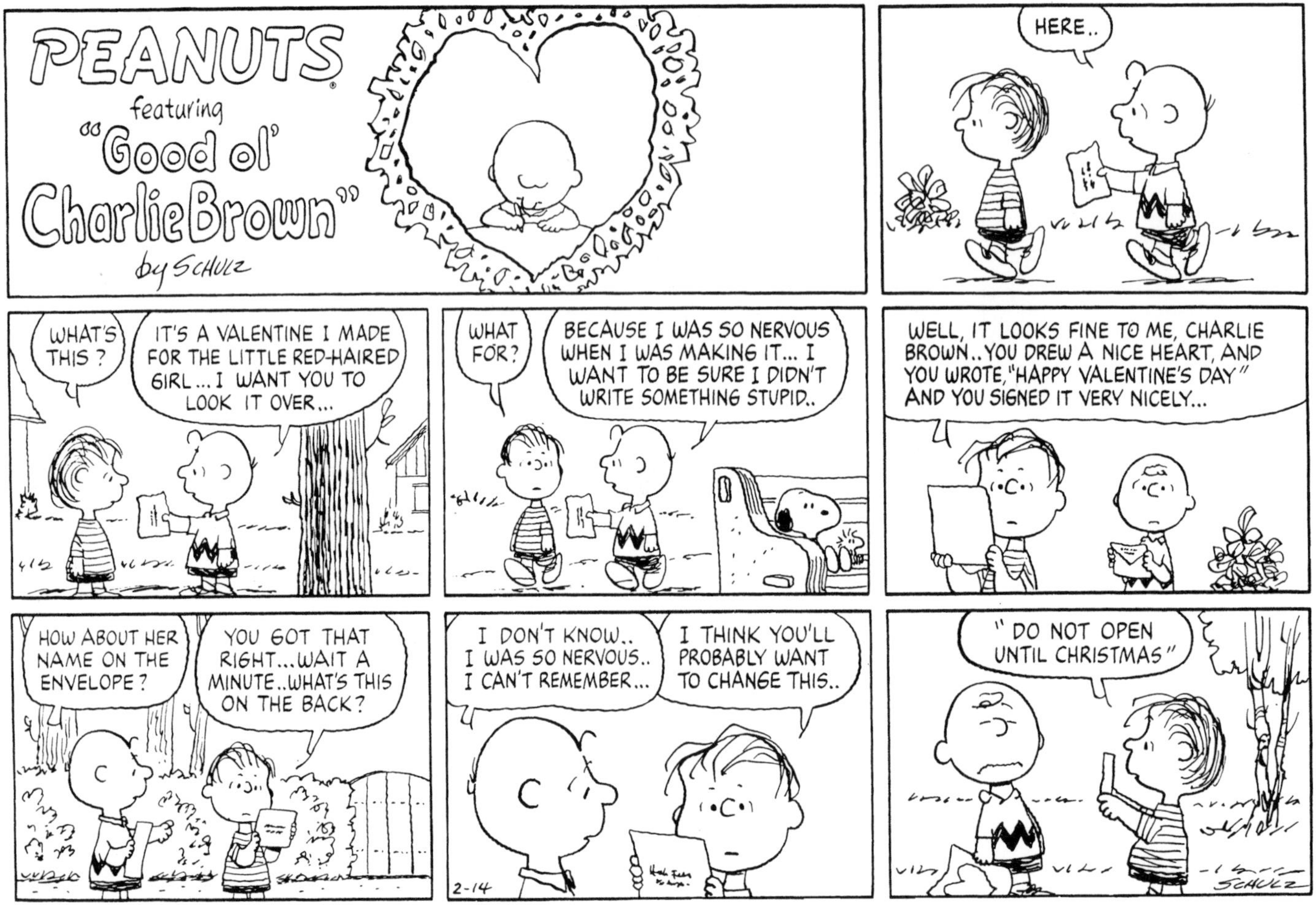
PEANUTS
featuring
"Good ol' Charlie Brown"
by SCHULZ
HERE..
WHAT'S THIS ?
IT'S A VALENTINE I MADE FOR THE LITTLE RED-HAIRED GIRL... I WANT YOU TO LOOK IT OVER...
WHAT FOR?
BECAUSE I WAS SO NERVOUS WHEN I WAS MAKING IT... I WANT TO BE SURE I DIDN'T WRITE SOMETHING STUPID..
WELL, IT LOOKS FINE TO ME, CHARLIE BROWN..YOU DREW A NICE HEART, AND YOU WROTE, "HAPPY VALENTINE'S DAY" AND YOU SIGNED IT VERY NICELY...
HOW ABOUT HER NAME ON THE ENVELOPE?
YOU GOT THAT RIGHT...WAIT A MINUTE..WHAT'S THIS ON THE BACK?
I DON'T KNOW.. I WAS SO NERVOUS.. I CAN'T REMEMBER...
I THINK YOU'LL PROBABLY WANT TO CHANGE THIS..
2-14
"DO NOT OPEN UNTIL CHRISTMAS"
SCHULZ

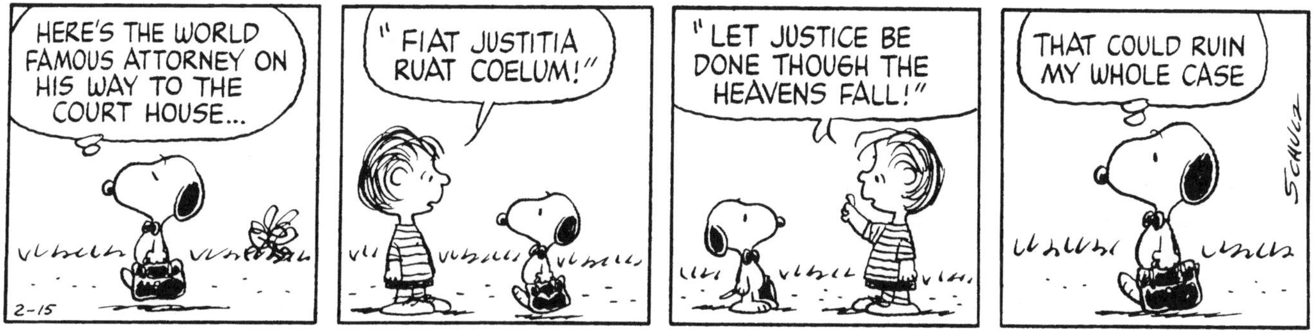
HERE'S THE WORLD FAMOUS ATTORNEY ON HIS WAY TO THE COURT HOUSE...
2-15
" FIAT JUSTITIA RUAT COELUM!"
" LET JUSTICE BE DONE THOUGH THE HEAVENS FALL!"
THAT COULD RUIN MY WHOLE CASE
SCHULZ

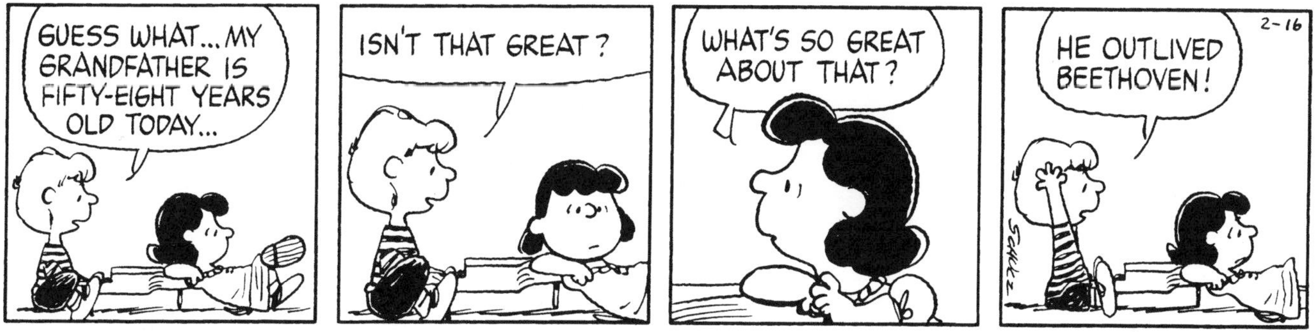
GUESS WHAT... MY GRANDFATHER IS FIFTY-EIGHT YEARS OLD TODAY...
ISN'T THAT GREAT?
WHAT'S SO GREAT ABOUT THAT?
2-16
HE OUTLIVED BEETHOVEN!
SCHULZ

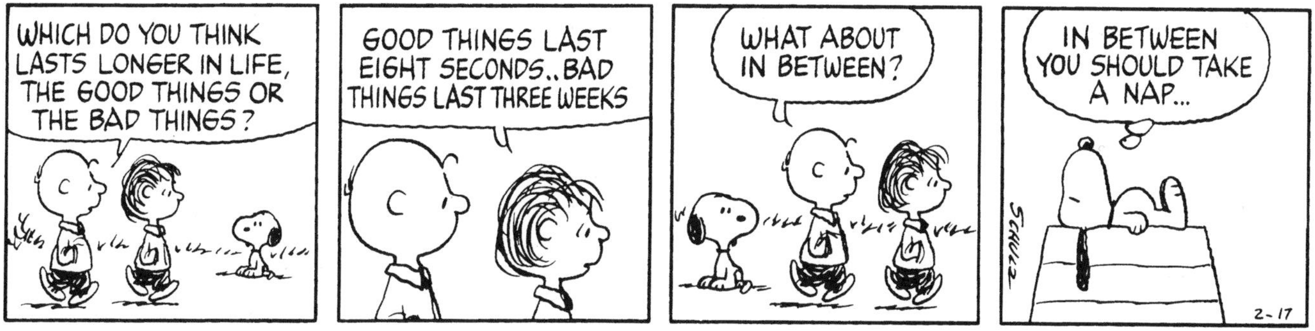
WHICH DO YOU THINK LASTS LONGER IN LIFE, THE GOOD THINGS OR THE BAD THINGS?
GOOD THINGS LAST EIGHT SECONDS.. BAD THINGS LAST THREE WEEKS
WHAT ABOUT IN BETWEEN?
IN BETWEEN YOU SHOULD TAKE A NAP...
SCHULZ
2-17

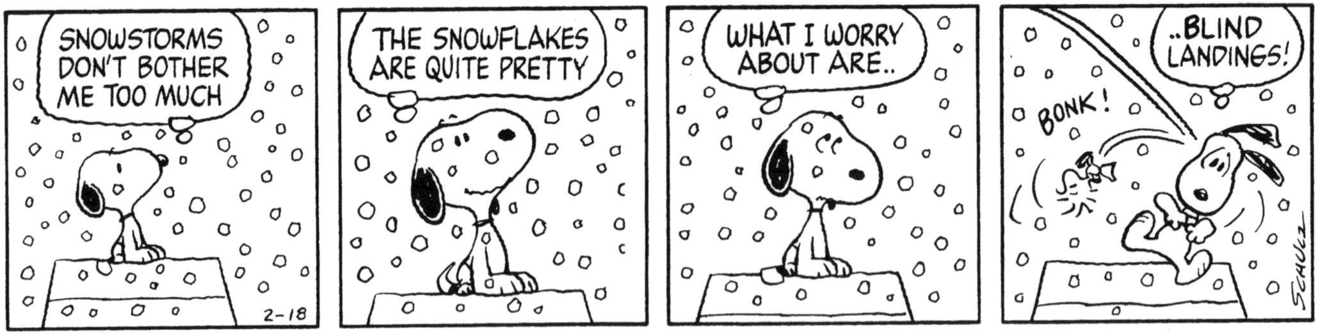
SNOWSTORMS DON'T BOTHER ME TOO MUCH
2-18
THE SNOWFLAKES ARE QUITE PRETTY
WHAT I WORRY ABOUT ARE..
BONK!
..BLIND LANDINGS!
SCHULZ

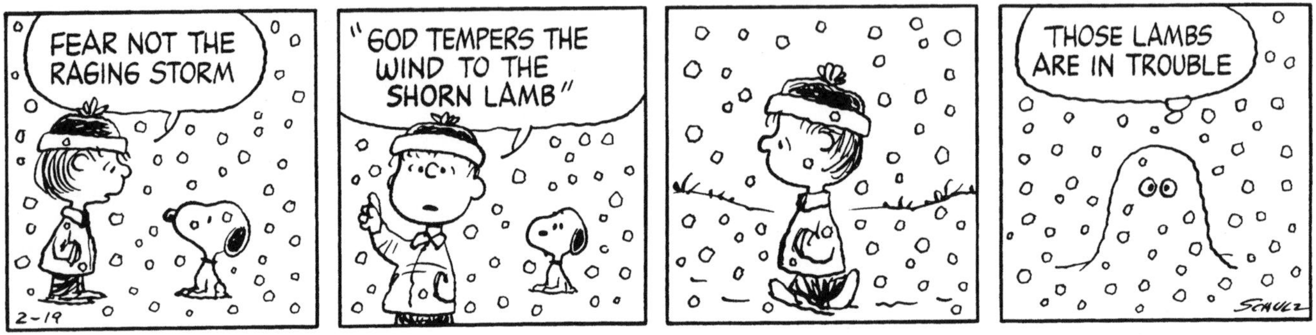
FEAR NOT THE RAGING STORM
2-19
"GOD TEMPERS THE WIND TO THE SHORN LAMB"
THOSE LAMBS ARE IN TROUBLE
SCHULZ

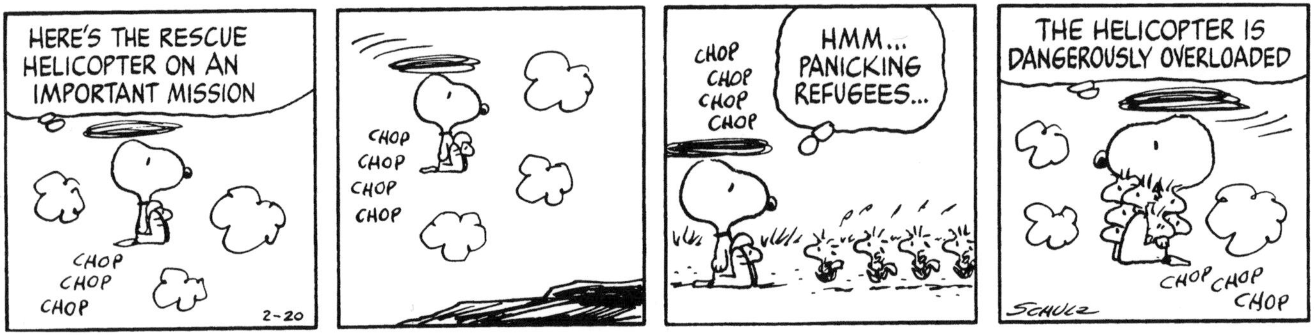
HERE'S THE RESCUE HELICOPTER ON AN IMPORTANT MISSION
CHOP
CHOP
CHOP
2-20
CHOP
CHOP
CHOP
CHOP
CHOP
CHOP
CHOP
CHOP
HMM... PANICKING REFUGEES...
THE HELICOPTER IS DANGEROUSLY OVERLOADED
CHOP CHOP
CHOP
SCHULZ

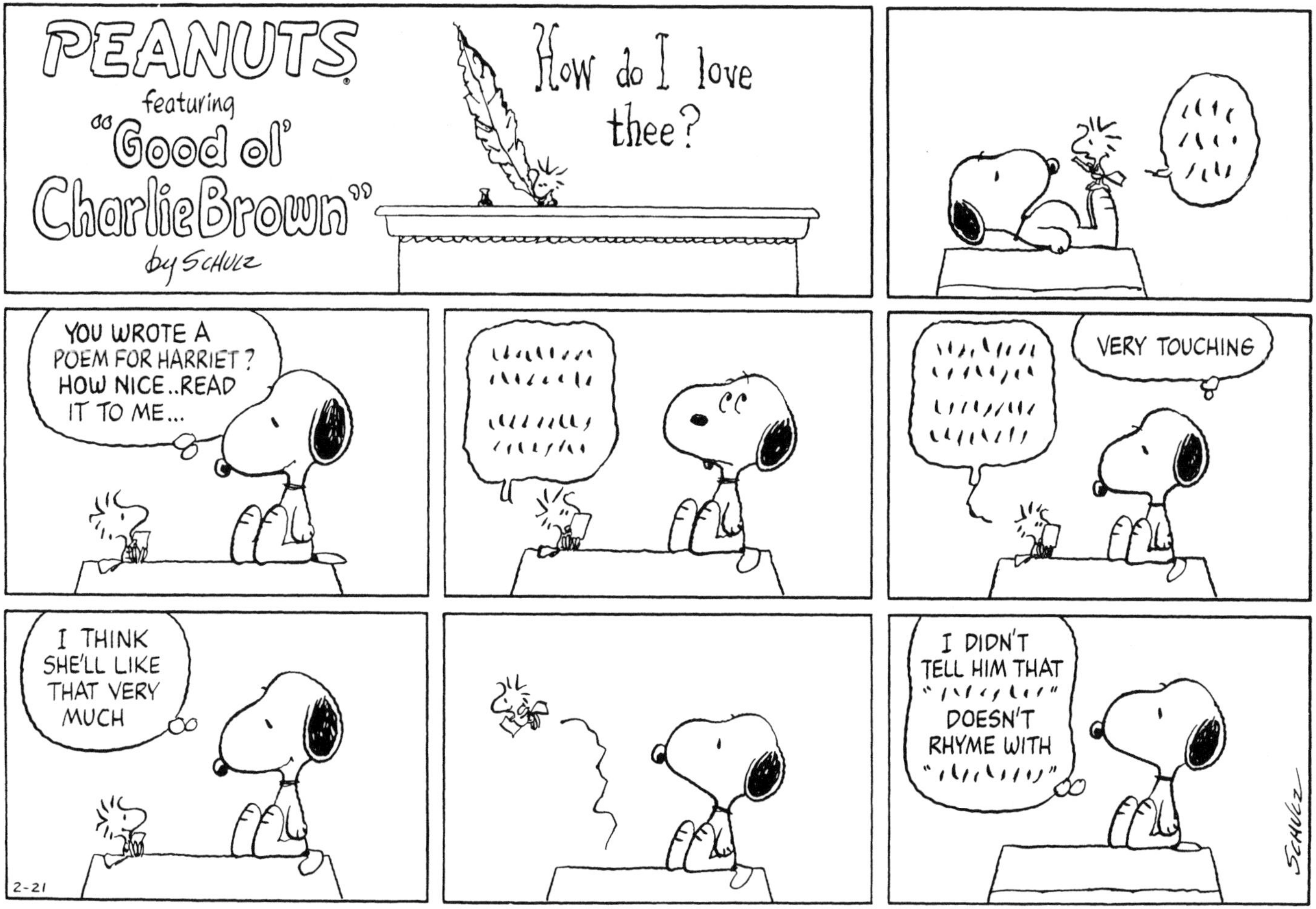
PEANUTS
featuring
"Good ol' CharlieBrown"
by SCHULZ
How do I love thee?
YOU WROTE A POEM FOR HARRIET? HOW NICE..READ IT TO ME...
VERY TOUCHING
I THINK SHE'LL LIKE THAT VERY MUCH
2-21
I DIDN'T TELL HIM THAT "" DOESN'T RHYME WITH ""
SCHULZ

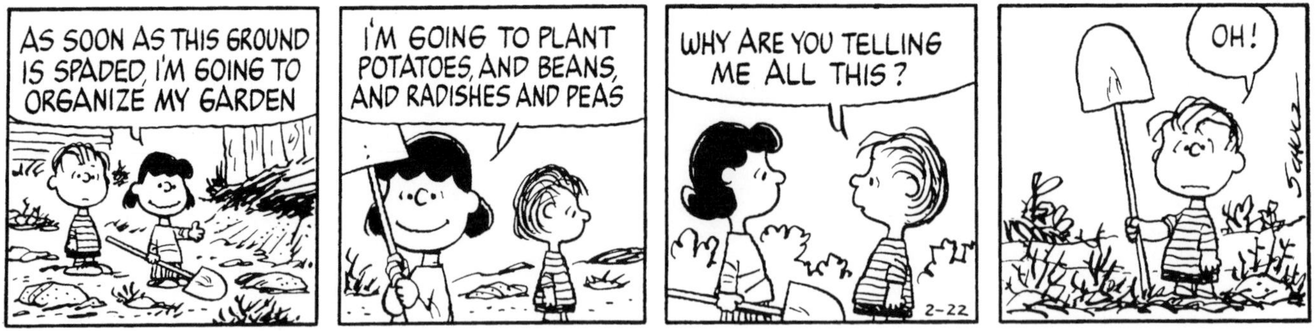
AS SOON AS THIS GROUND IS SPADED, I'M GOING TO ORGANIZE MY GARDEN
I'M GOING TO PLANT POTATOES, AND BEANS, AND RADISHES AND PEAS
WHY ARE YOU TELLING ME ALL THIS?
OH!

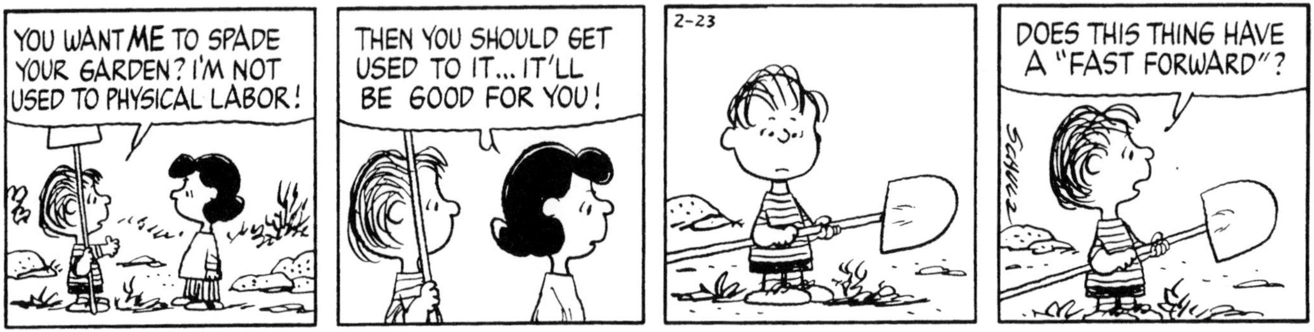
YOU WANT ME TO SPADE YOUR GARDEN? I'M NOT USED TO PHYSICAL LABOR!
THEN YOU SHOULD GET USED TO IT... IT'LL BE GOOD FOR YOU!
DOES THIS THING HAVE A "FAST FORWARD"?

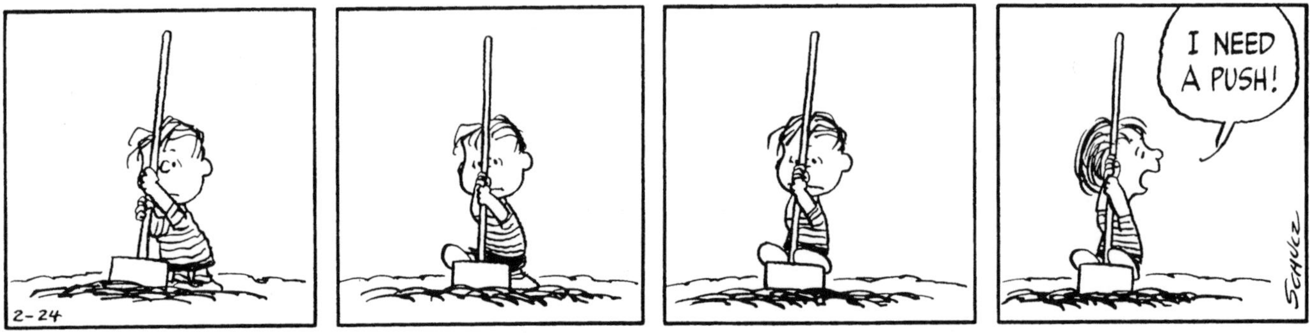
I NEED A PUSH!

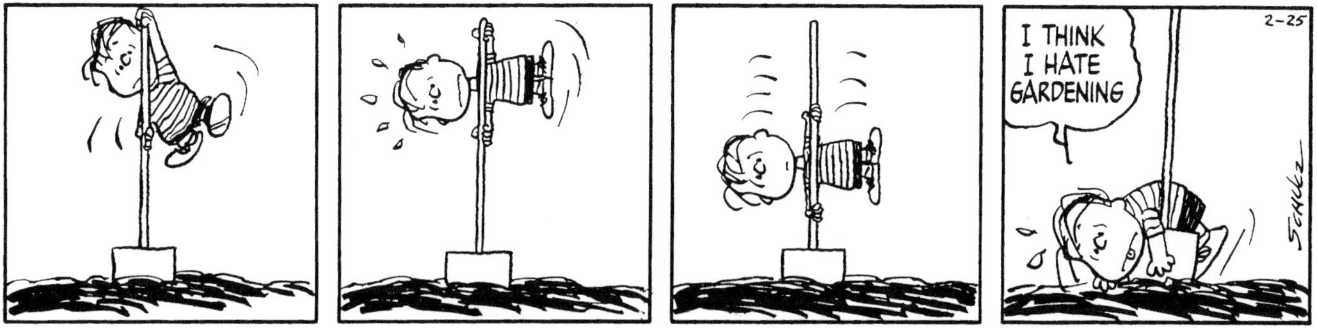
I THINK I HATE GARDENING

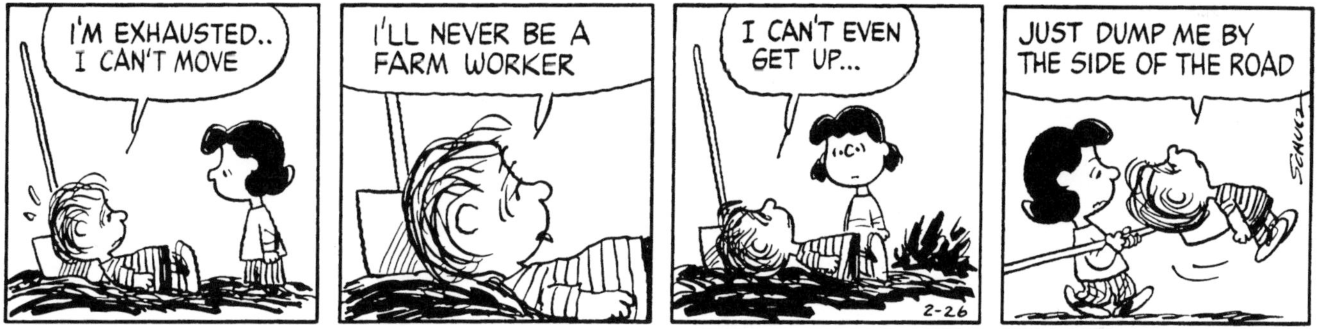
I'M EXHAUSTED.. I CAN'T MOVE
I'LL NEVER BE A FARM WORKER
I CAN'T EVEN GET UP...
JUST DUMP ME BY THE SIDE OF THE ROAD

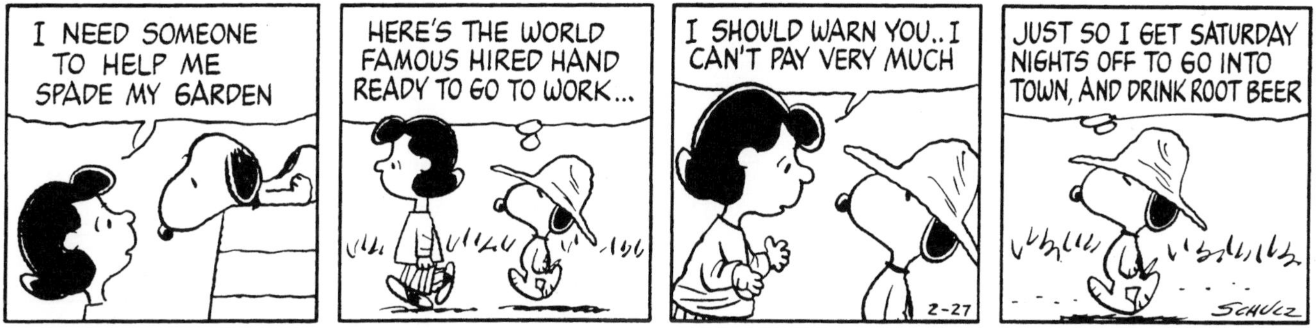
I NEED SOMEONE TO HELP ME SPADE MY GARDEN
HERE'S THE WORLD FAMOUS HIRED HAND READY TO GO TO WORK...
I SHOULD WARN YOU.. I CAN'T PAY VERY MUCH
JUST SO I GET SATURDAY NIGHTS OFF TO GO INTO TOWN, AND DRINK ROOT BEER

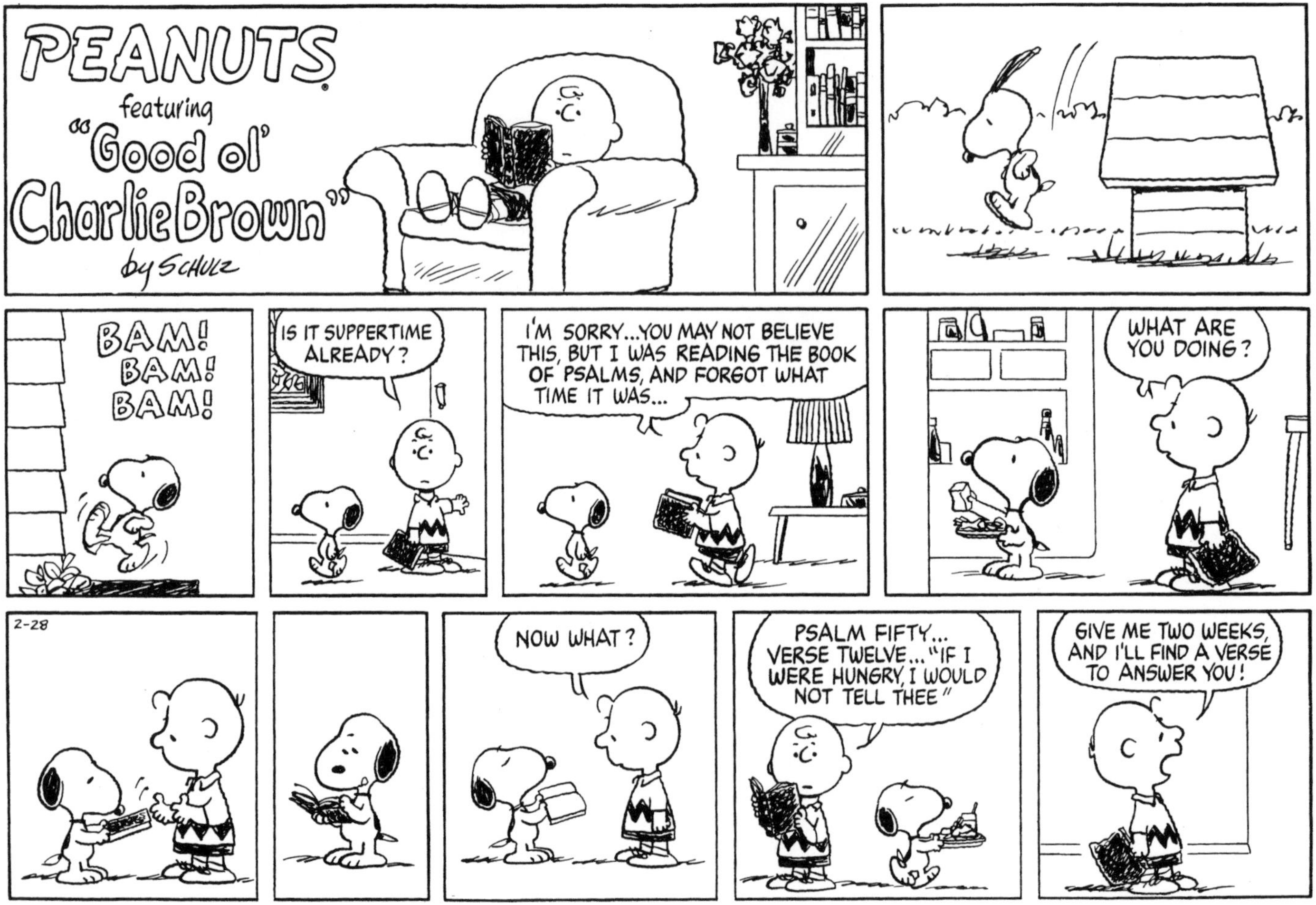
PEANUTS
featuring
"Good ol' CharlieBrown"
by SCHULZ
BAM! BAM! BAM!
IS IT SUPPERTIME ALREADY?
I'M SORRY...YOU MAY NOT BELIEVE THIS, BUT I WAS READING THE BOOK OF PSALMS, AND FORGOT WHAT TIME IT WAS...
WHAT ARE YOU DOING?
2-28
NOW WHAT?
PSALM FIFTY... VERSE TWELVE..."IF I WERE HUNGRY, I WOULD NOT TELL THEE"
GIVE ME TWO WEEKS, AND I'LL FIND A VERSE TO ANSWER YOU!

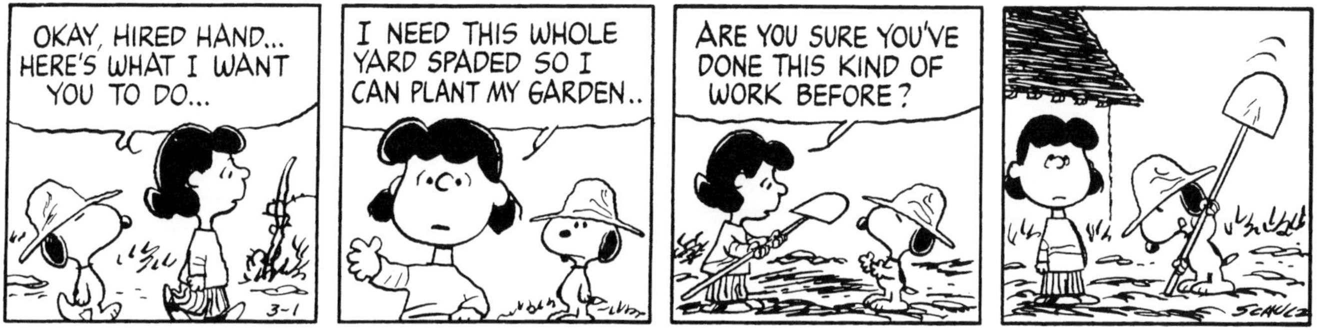
OKAY, HIRED HAND... HERE'S WHAT I WANT YOU TO DO...
3-1
I NEED THIS WHOLE YARD SPADED SO I CAN PLANT MY GARDEN..
ARE YOU SURE YOU'VE DONE THIS KIND OF WORK BEFORE?
SCHULZ

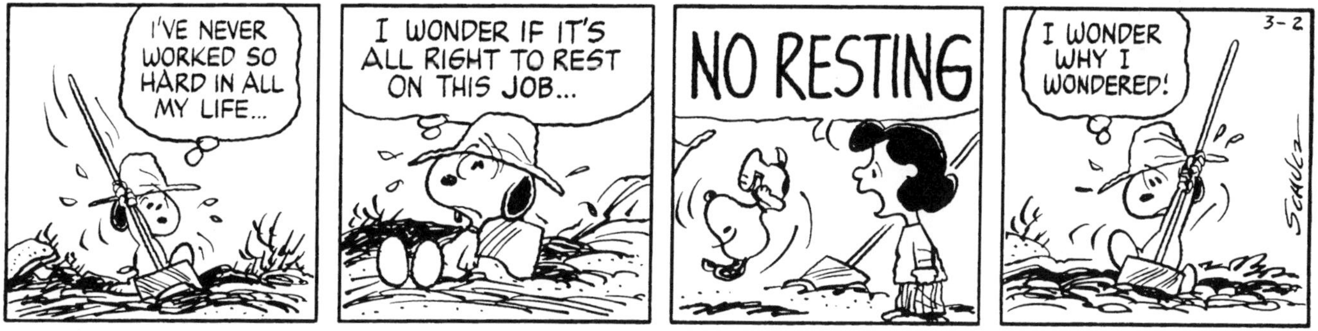
I'VE NEVER WORKED SO HARD IN ALL MY LIFE...
I WONDER IF IT'S ALL RIGHT TO REST ON THIS JOB...
NO RESTING
3-2
I WONDER WHY I WONDERED!
SCHULZ

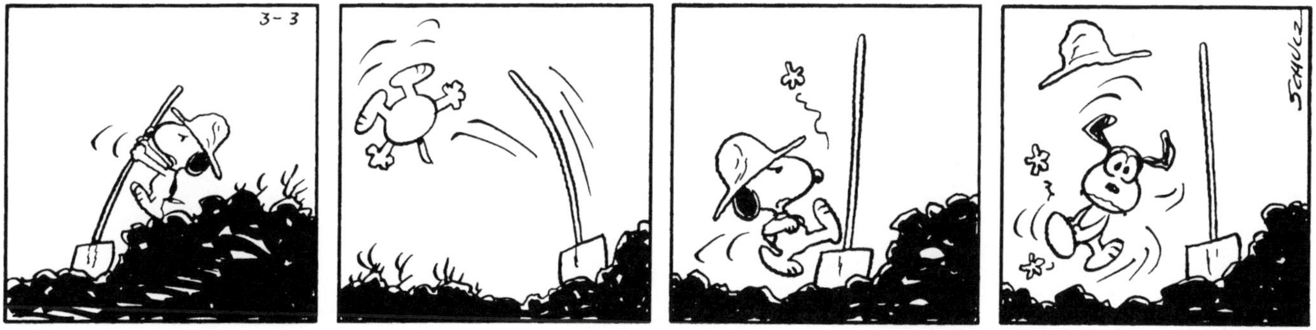
3-3
SCHULZ

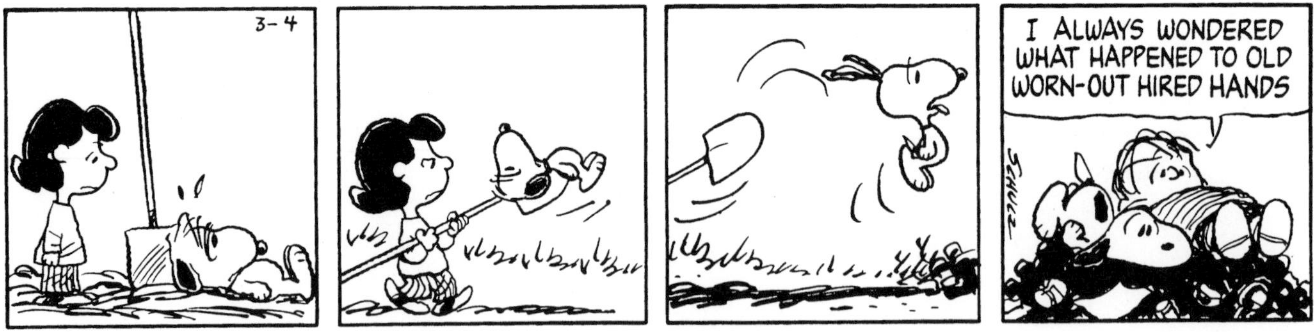
3-4
I ALWAYS WONDERED WHAT HAPPENED TO OLD WORN-OUT HIRED HANDS
SCHULZ

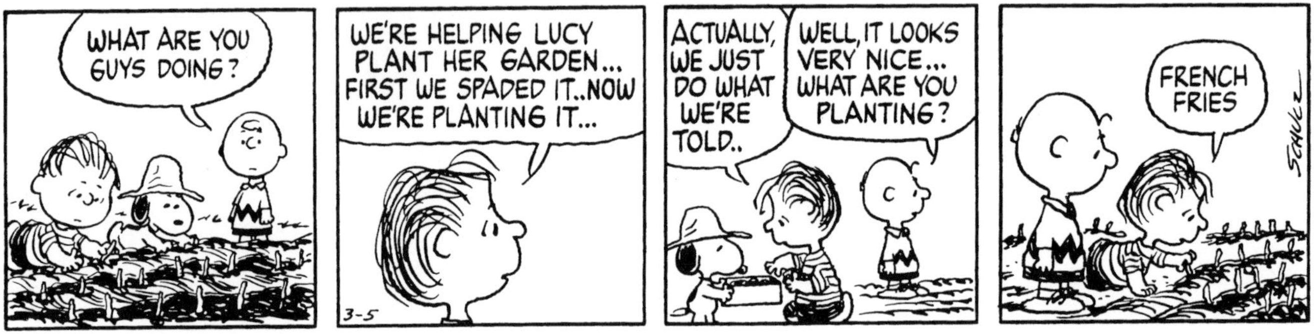
WHAT ARE YOU GUYS DOING?
WE'RE HELPING LUCY PLANT HER GARDEN... FIRST WE SPADED IT..NOW WE'RE PLANTING IT...
3-5
ACTUALLY, WE JUST DO WHAT WE'RE TOLD..
WELL, IT LOOKS VERY NICE... WHAT ARE YOU PLANTING?
FRENCH FRIES
SCHULZ

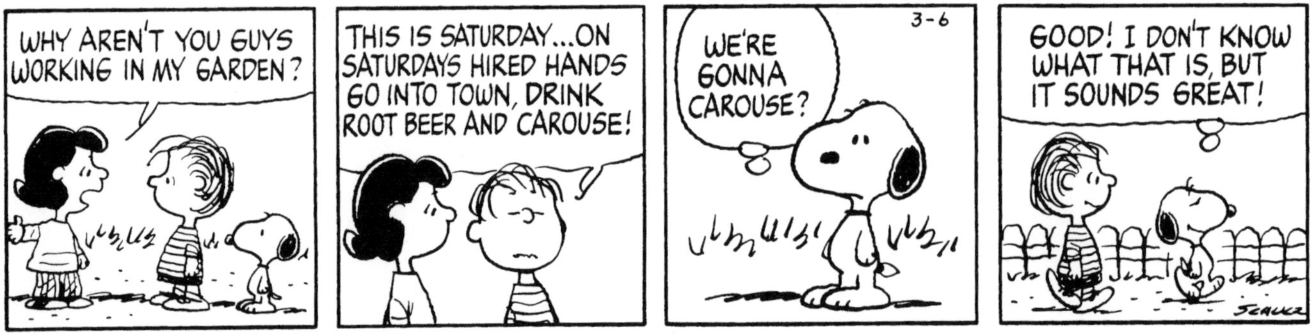
WHY AREN'T YOU GUYS WORKING IN MY GARDEN?
THIS IS SATURDAY...ON SATURDAYS HIRED HANDS GO INTO TOWN, DRINK ROOT BEER AND CAROUSE!
3-6
WE'RE GONNA CAROUSE?
GOOD! I DON'T KNOW WHAT THAT IS, BUT IT SOUNDS GREAT!
SCHULZ

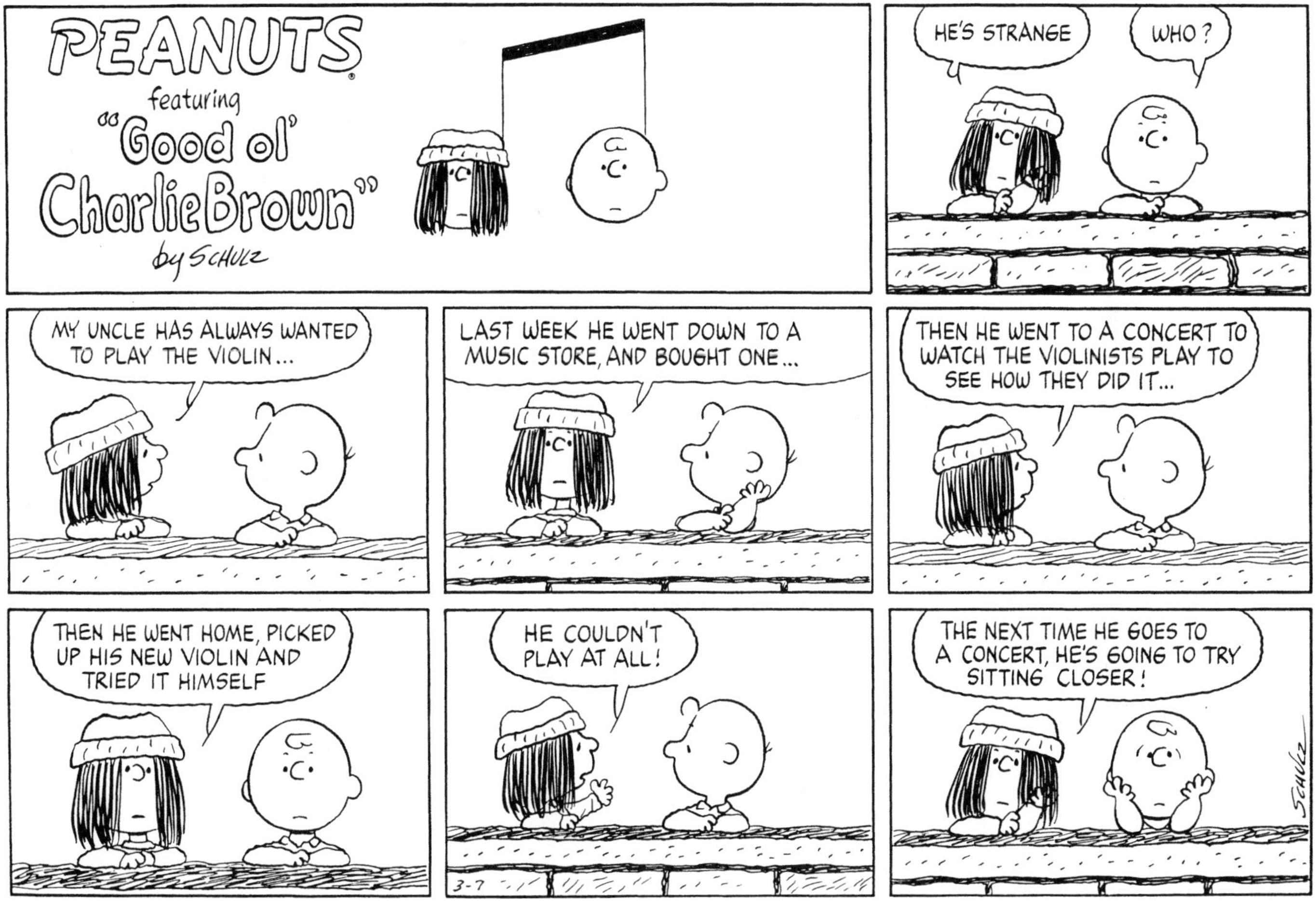
PEANUTS
featuring
"Good ol' Charlie Brown"
by SCHULZ
HE'S STRANGE
WHO?
MY UNCLE HAS ALWAYS WANTED TO PLAY THE VIOLIN...
LAST WEEK HE WENT DOWN TO A MUSIC STORE, AND BOUGHT ONE...
THEN HE WENT TO A CONCERT TO WATCH THE VIOLINISTS PLAY TO SEE HOW THEY DID IT...
THEN HE WENT HOME, PICKED UP HIS NEW VIOLIN AND TRIED IT HIMSELF
HE COULDN'T PLAY AT ALL!
THE NEXT TIME HE GOES TO A CONCERT, HE'S GOING TO TRY SITTING CLOSER!
3-7
SCHULZ

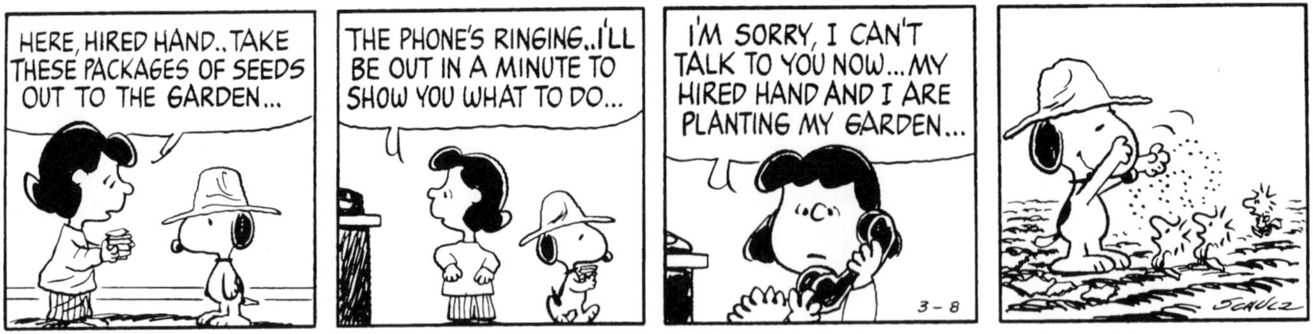
HERE, HIRED HAND.. TAKE THESE PACKAGES OF SEEDS OUT TO THE GARDEN...
THE PHONE'S RINGING..I'LL BE OUT IN A MINUTE TO SHOW YOU WHAT TO DO...
I'M SORRY, I CAN'T TALK TO YOU NOW... MY HIRED HAND AND I ARE PLANTING MY GARDEN...
3-8
SCHULZ

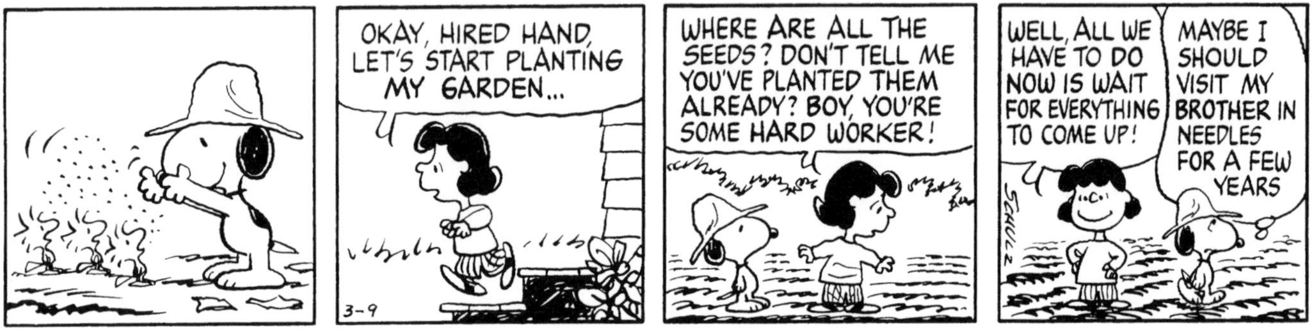
OKAY, HIRED HAND, LET'S START PLANTING MY GARDEN...
3-9
WHERE ARE ALL THE SEEDS? DON'T TELL ME YOU'VE PLANTED THEM ALREADY? BOY, YOU'RE SOME HARD WORKER!
WELL, ALL WE HAVE TO DO NOW IS WAIT FOR EVERYTHING TO COME UP!
MAYBE I SHOULD VISIT MY BROTHER IN NEEDLES FOR A FEW YEARS
SCHULZ

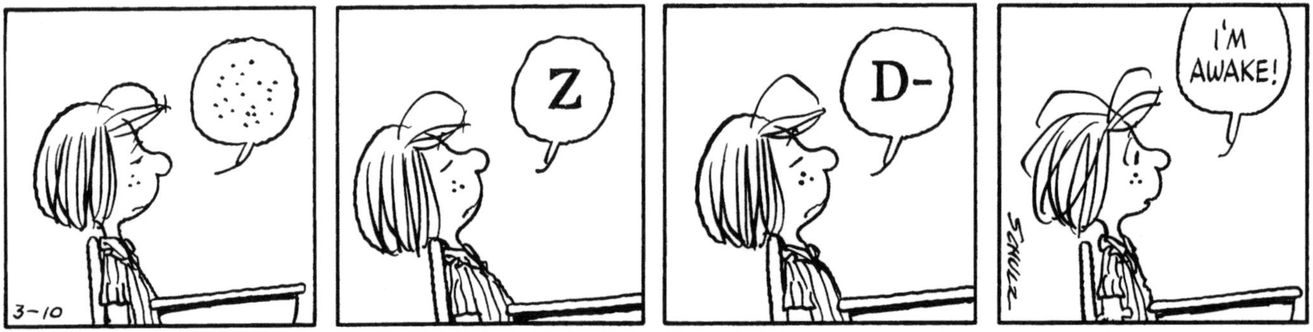
3-10
Z
D-
SCHULZ
I'M AWAKE!

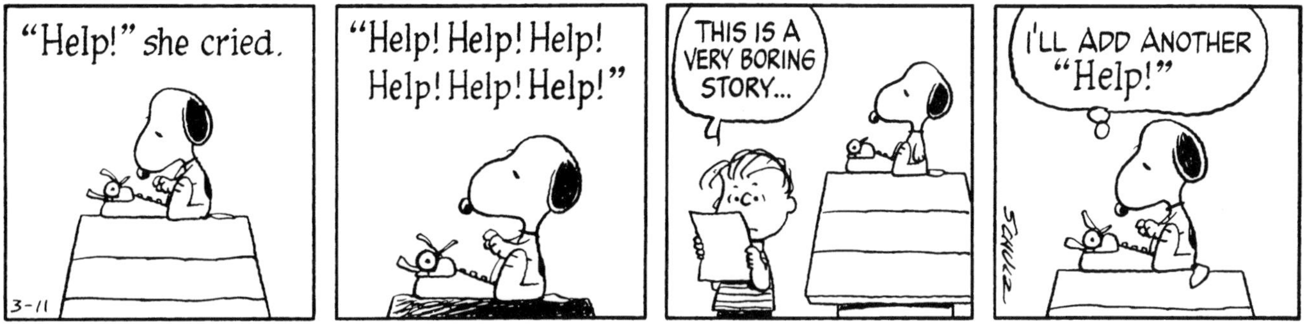
"Help!" she cried.
3-11
"Help! Help! Help!
Help! Help! Help!"
THIS IS A VERY BORING STORY...
I'LL ADD ANOTHER "Help!"

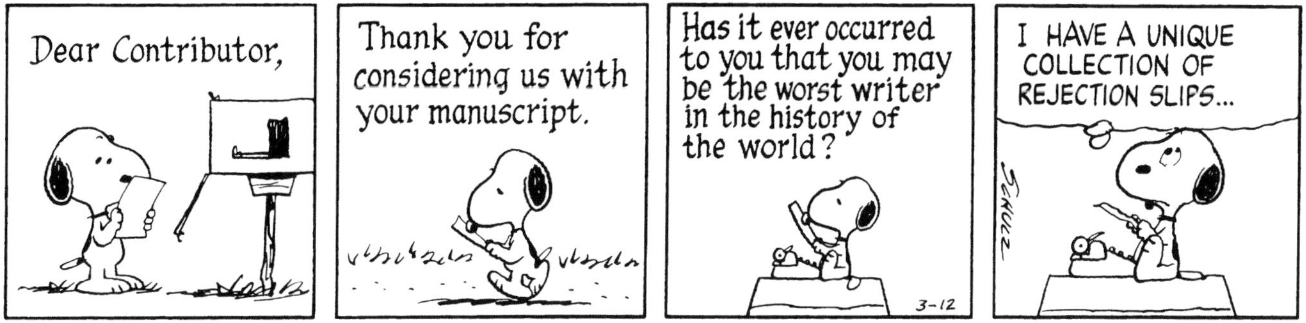
Dear Contributor,
Thank you for considering us with your manuscript.
Has it ever occurred to you that you may be the worst writer in the history of the world?
3-12
I HAVE A UNIQUE COLLECTION OF REJECTION SLIPS...

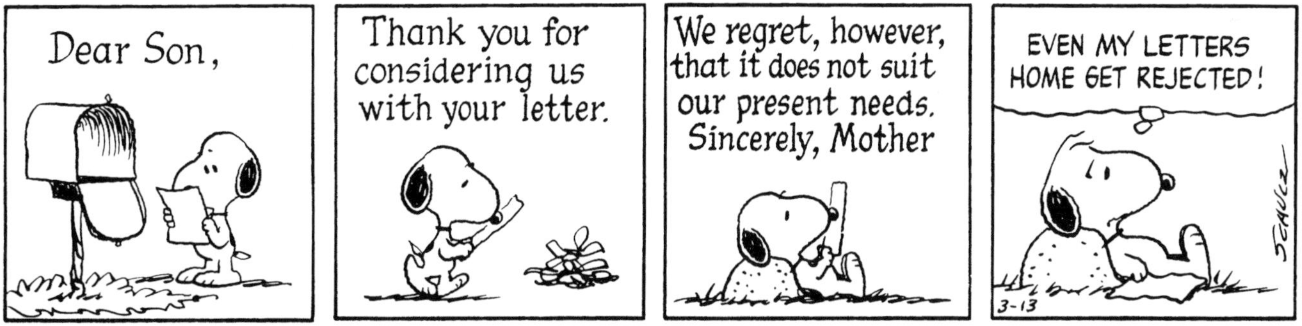
Dear Son,
Thank you for considering us with your letter.
We regret, however, that it does not suit our present needs.
Sincerely, Mother
EVEN MY LETTERS HOME GET REJECTED!
3-13

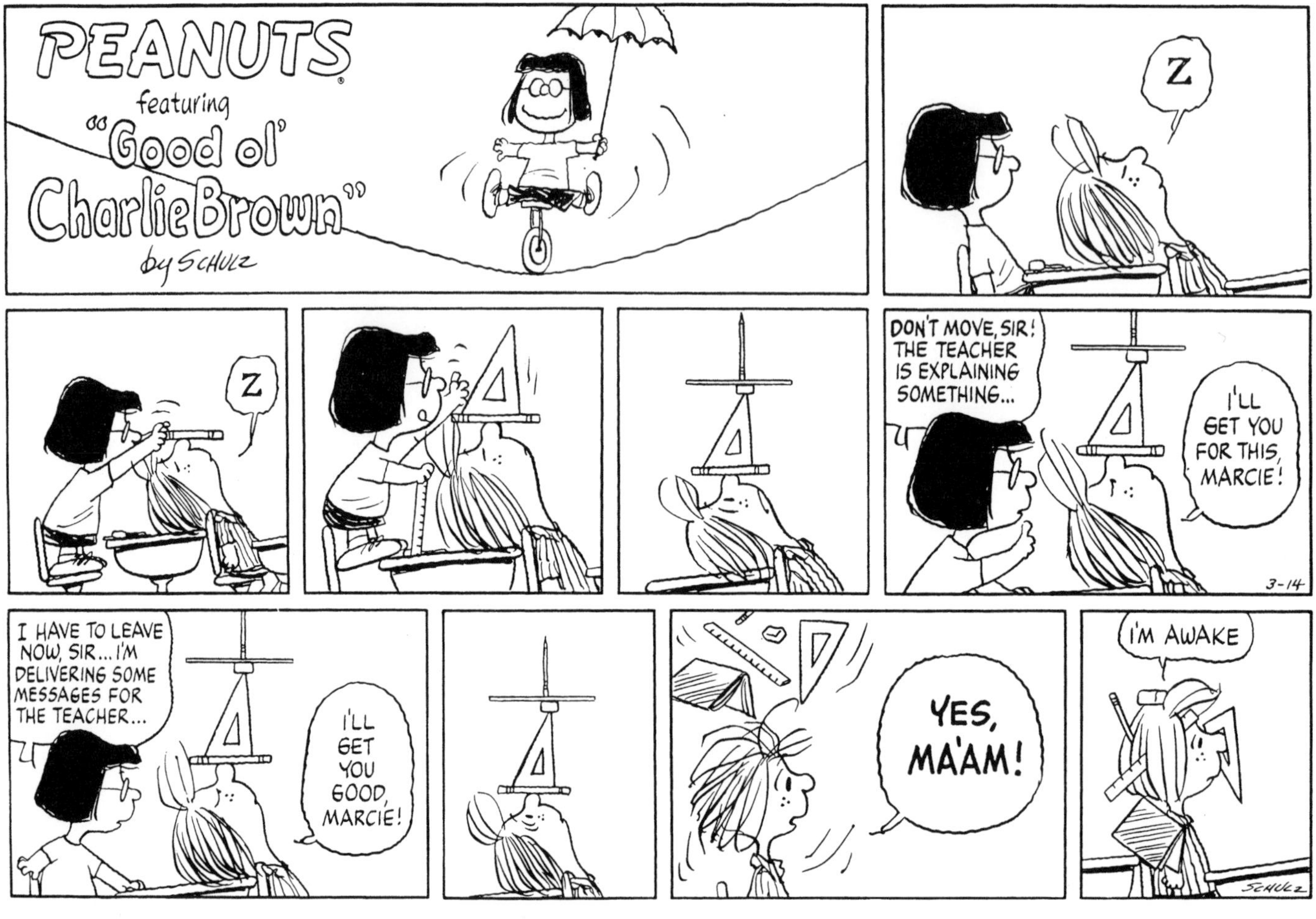
PEANUTS
featuring
"Good ol' CharlieBrown"
by SCHULZ
Z
Z
DON'T MOVE, SIR! THE TEACHER IS EXPLAINING SOMETHING...
I'LL GET YOU FOR THIS, MARCIE!
3-14
I HAVE TO LEAVE NOW, SIR... I'M DELIVERING SOME MESSAGES FOR THE TEACHER...
I'LL GET YOU GOOD, MARCIE!
YES, MA'AM!
I'M AWAKE
SCHULZ

I HATE FIELD TRIPS! I HATE RIDING ON THIS BUS!

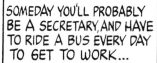
SOMEDAY YOU'LL PROBABLY BE A SECRETARY, AND HAVE TO RIDE A BUS EVERY DAY TO GET TO WORK...

NOT ME! I'LL HAVE MY OWN SPORTS CAR AND A PRIVATE PARKING PLACE!

LIFE IS A WISHBONE

I HATE THESE FIELD TRIPS!

WHAT ARE WE SUPPOSED TO BE DOING, ANYWAY?

WELL, FOR ONE THING, YOU'RE SUPPOSED TO TAKE NOTES...

GOOD! I'LL TAKE YOURS!

WHAT ARE WE SUPPOSED TO BE TAKING NOTES ON?

TREES...WE'RE SUPPOSED TO WRITE DOWN THE NAMES OF ALL THE DIFFERENT TREES WE SEE

HOW DO I KNOW WHAT THEIR NAMES ARE?

HI, TREE...MY NAME'S SALLY! WHAT'S YOUR NAME?

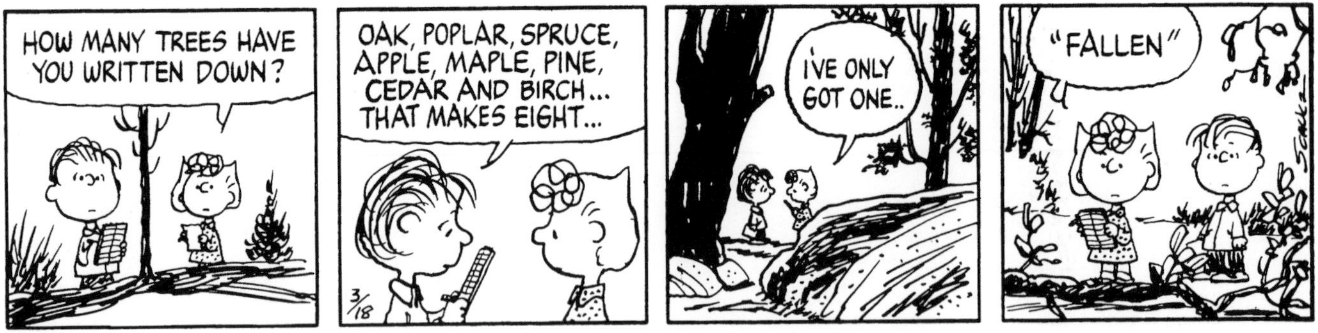
HOW MANY TREES HAVE YOU WRITTEN DOWN?
OAK, POPLAR, SPRUCE, APPLE, MAPLE, PINE, CEDAR AND BIRCH... THAT MAKES EIGHT...
3/18
I'VE ONLY GOT ONE..
"FALLEN"

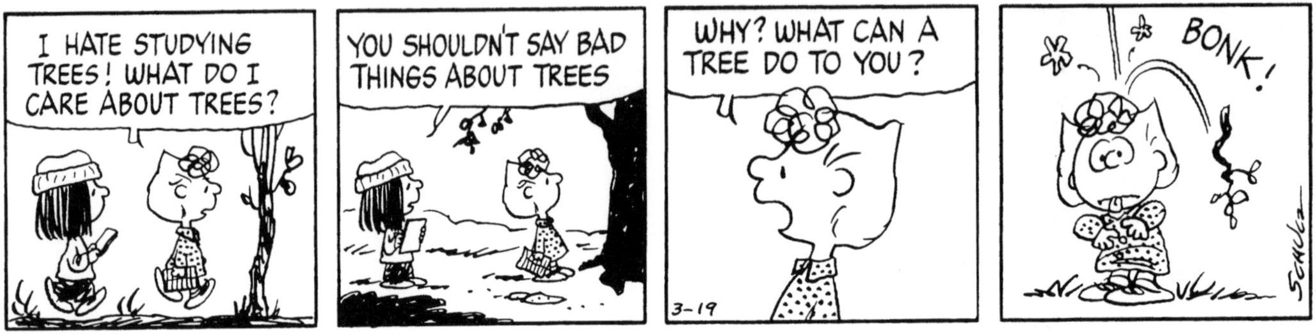
I HATE STUDYING TREES! WHAT DO I CARE ABOUT TREES?
YOU SHOULDN'T SAY BAD THINGS ABOUT TREES
WHY? WHAT CAN A TREE DO TO YOU?
3-19
BONK!

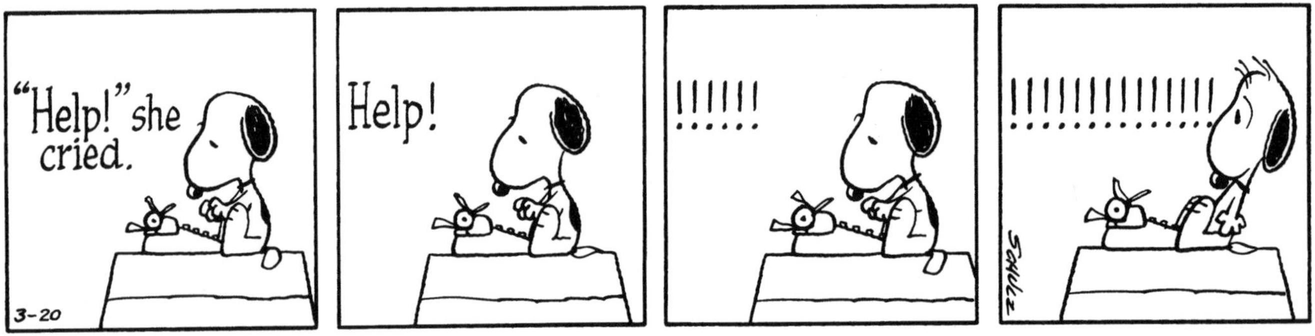
"Help!" she cried.
3-20
Help!
!!!!!!
!!!!!!!!!!!!!!

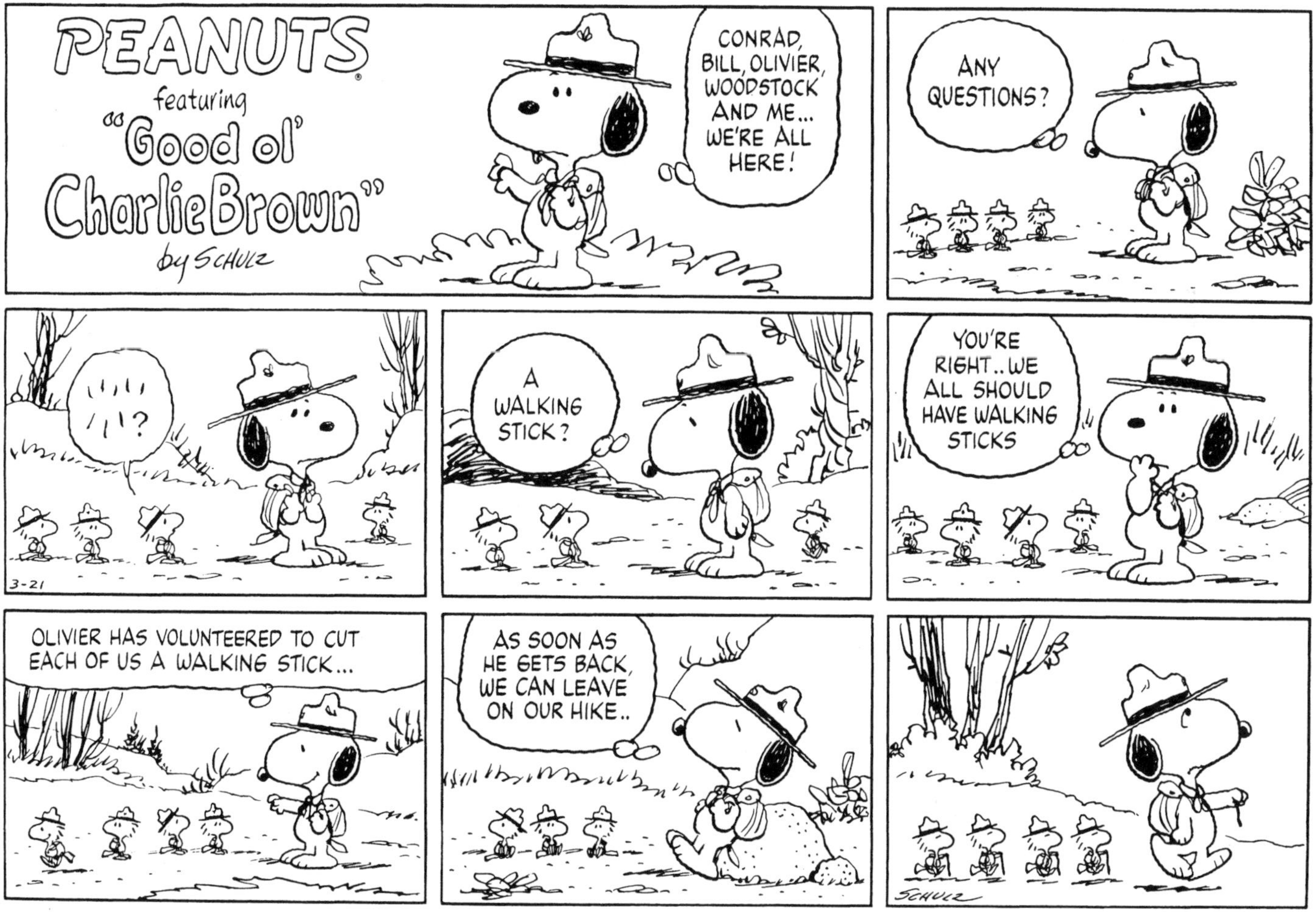
PEANUTS
featuring "Good ol' CharlieBrown"
by SCHULZ
CONRAD, BILL, OLIVIER, WOODSTOCK AND ME... WE'RE ALL HERE!
ANY QUESTIONS?
?
3-21
A WALKING STICK?
YOU'RE RIGHT.. WE ALL SHOULD HAVE WALKING STICKS
OLIVIER HAS VOLUNTEERED TO CUT EACH OF US A WALKING STICK...
AS SOON AS HE GETS BACK, WE CAN LEAVE ON OUR HIKE..
SCHULZ

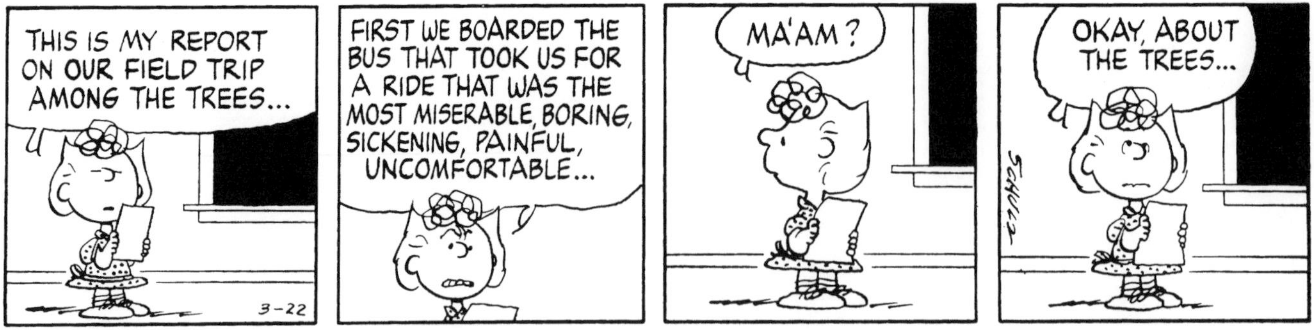
THIS IS MY REPORT ON OUR FIELD TRIP AMONG THE TREES...
3-22
FIRST WE BOARDED THE BUS THAT TOOK US FOR A RIDE THAT WAS THE MOST MISERABLE, BORING, SICKENING, PAINFUL, UNCOMFORTABLE...
MA'AM?
OKAY, ABOUT THE TREES...

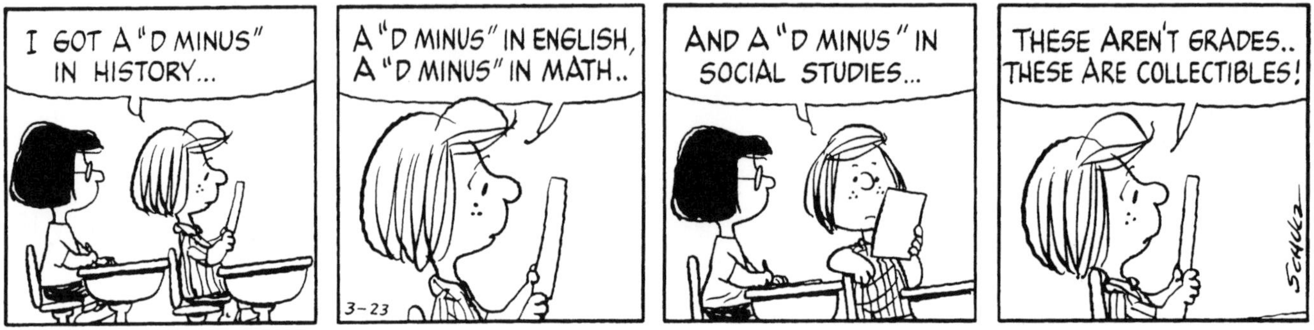
I GOT A "D MINUS" IN HISTORY...
A "D MINUS" IN ENGLISH, A "D MINUS" IN MATH..
3-23
AND A "D MINUS" IN SOCIAL STUDIES...
THESE AREN'T GRADES.. THESE ARE COLLECTIBLES!

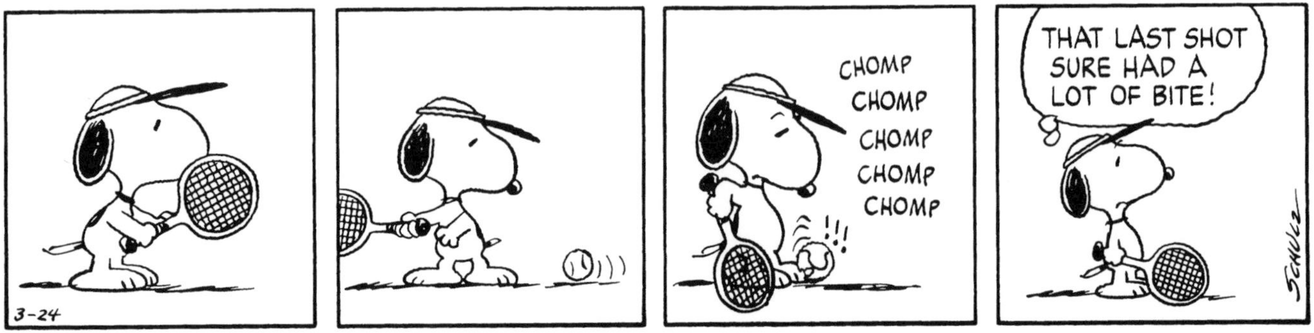
3-24
CHOMP
CHOMP
CHOMP
CHOMP
CHOMP
!!!
THAT LAST SHOT SURE HAD A LOT OF BITE!

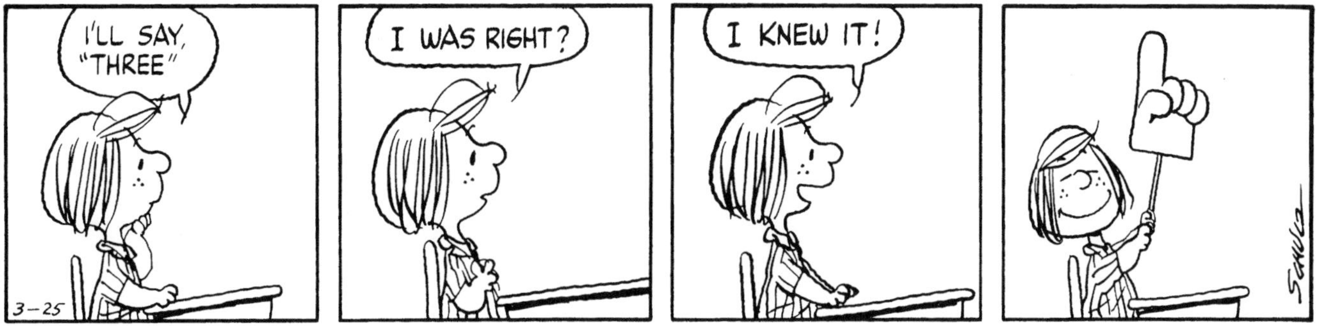
I'LL SAY, "THREE"
3-25
I WAS RIGHT?
I KNEW IT!
SCHULZ

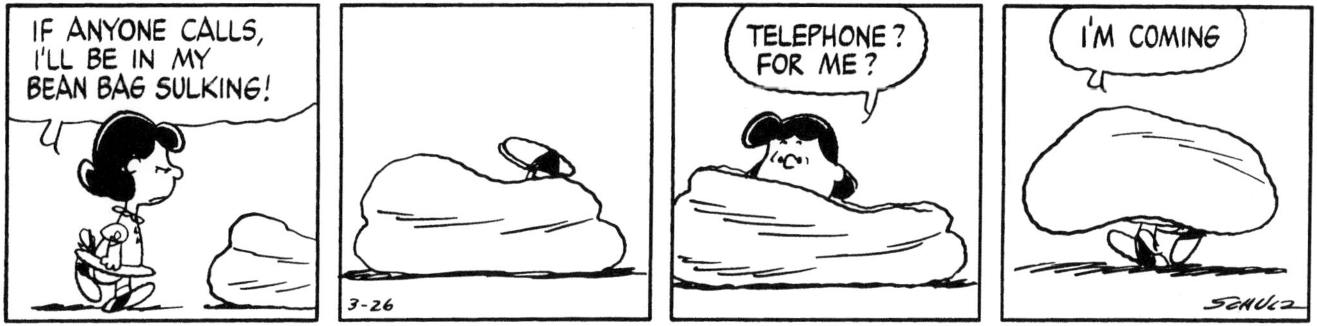
IF ANYONE CALLS, I'LL BE IN MY BEAN BAG SULKING!
3-26
TELEPHONE? FOR ME?
I'M COMING
SCHULZ

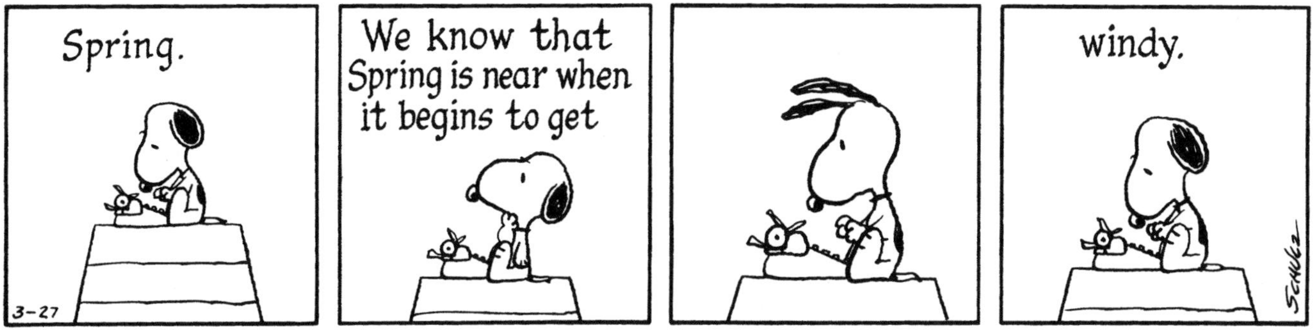
Spring.
3-27
We know that Spring is near when it begins to get
windy.
SCHULZ

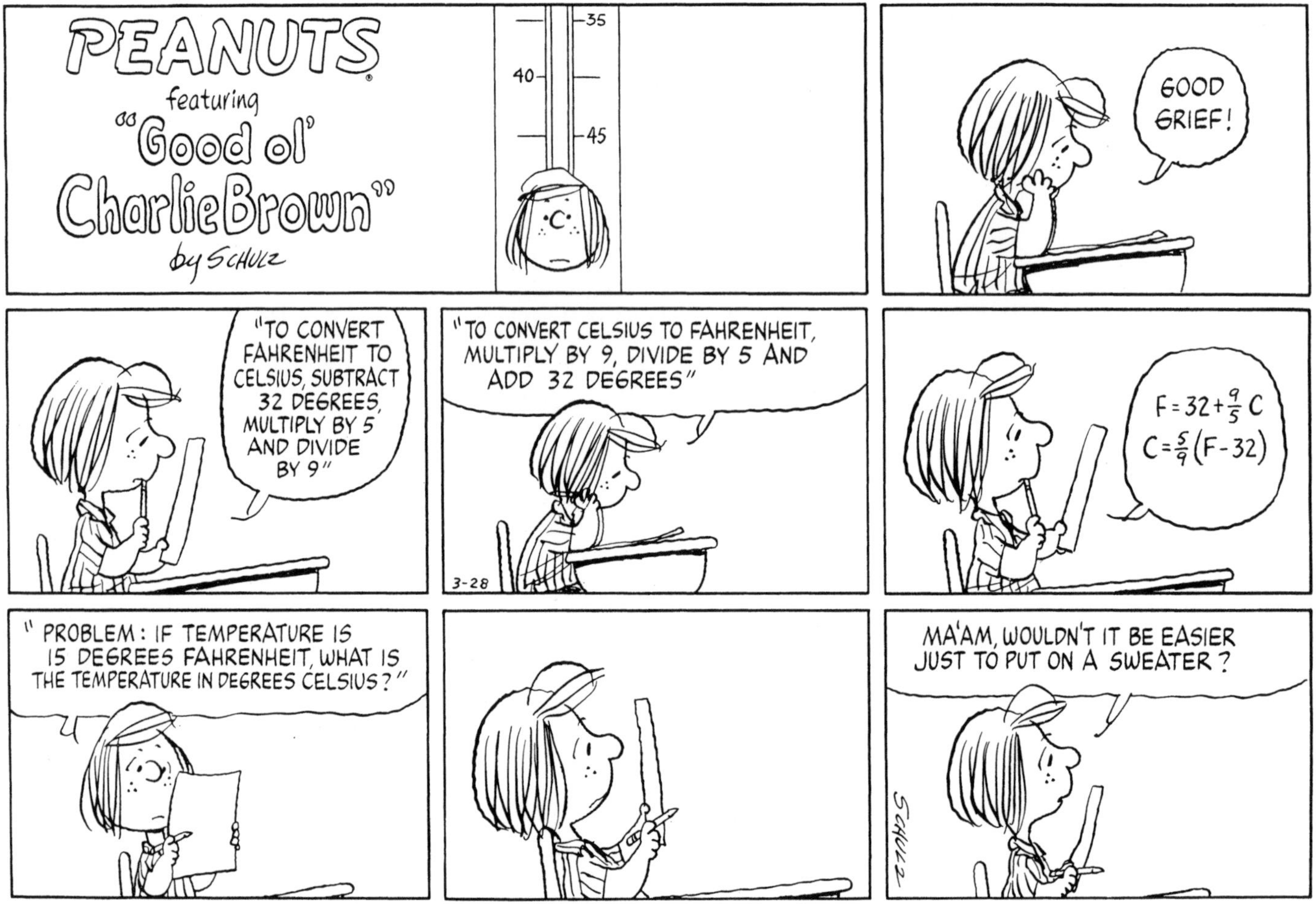
PEANUTS
featuring "Good ol' Charlie Brown"
by SCHULZ
35
40
45
GOOD GRIEF!
"TO CONVERT FAHRENHEIT TO CELSIUS, SUBTRACT 32 DEGREES, MULTIPLY BY 5 AND DIVIDE BY 9"
"TO CONVERT CELSIUS TO FAHRENHEIT, MULTIPLY BY 9, DIVIDE BY 5 AND ADD 32 DEGREES"
3-28
$F = 32 + \frac{9}{5}C$
$C = \frac{5}{9}(F - 32)$
"PROBLEM: IF TEMPERATURE IS 15 DEGREES FAHRENHEIT, WHAT IS THE TEMPERATURE IN DEGREES CELSIUS?"
MA'AM, WOULDN'T IT BE EASIER JUST TO PUT ON A SWEATER?
SCHULZ

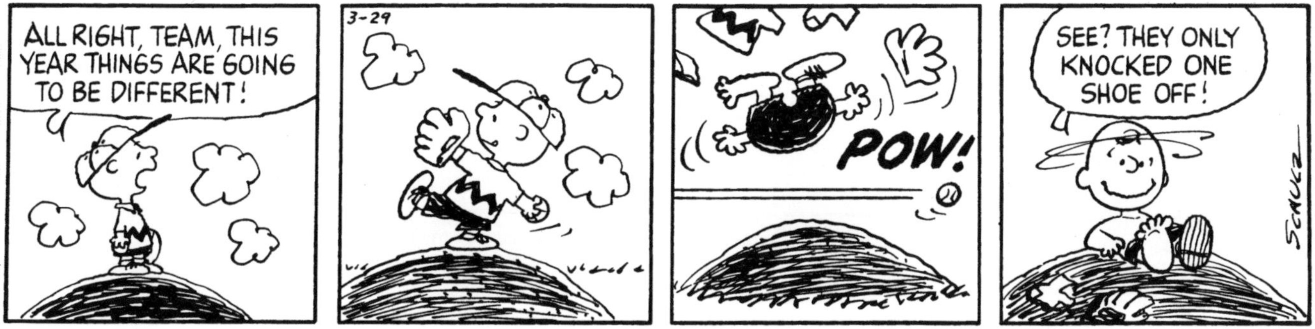
ALL RIGHT, TEAM, THIS YEAR THINGS ARE GOING TO BE DIFFERENT!
3-29
POW!
SEE? THEY ONLY KNOCKED ONE SHOE OFF!
SCHULZ

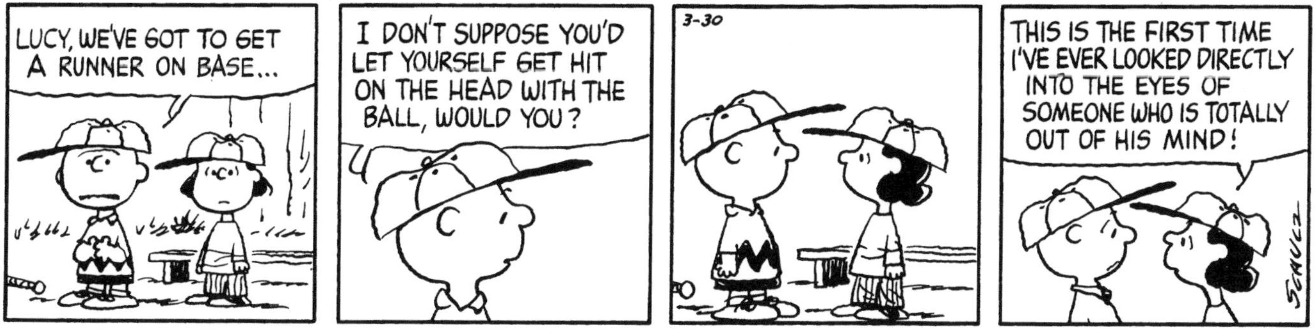
LUCY, WE'VE GOT TO GET A RUNNER ON BASE...
I DON'T SUPPOSE YOU'D LET YOURSELF GET HIT ON THE HEAD WITH THE BALL, WOULD YOU?
3-30
THIS IS THE FIRST TIME I'VE EVER LOOKED DIRECTLY INTO THE EYES OF SOMEONE WHO IS TOTALLY OUT OF HIS MIND!
SCHULZ

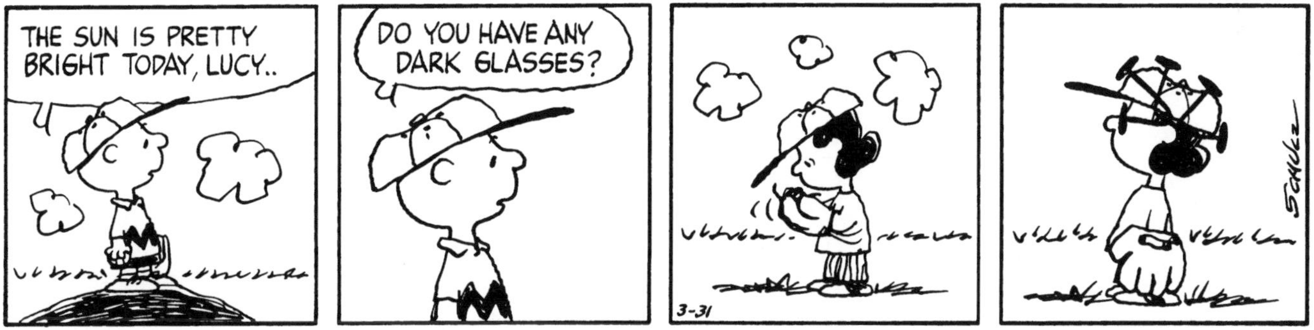
THE SUN IS PRETTY BRIGHT TODAY, LUCY..
DO YOU HAVE ANY DARK GLASSES?
3-31
SCHULZ

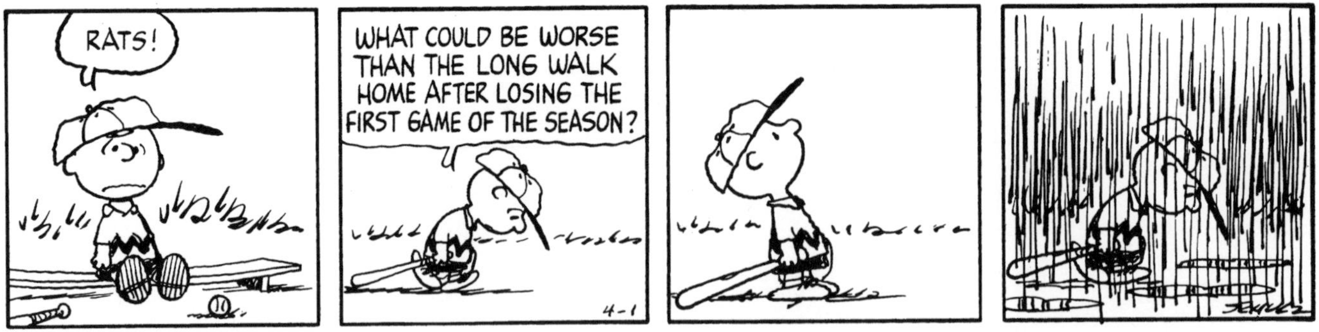
RATS!
WHAT COULD BE WORSE THAN THE LONG WALK HOME AFTER LOSING THE FIRST GAME OF THE SEASON?
4-1

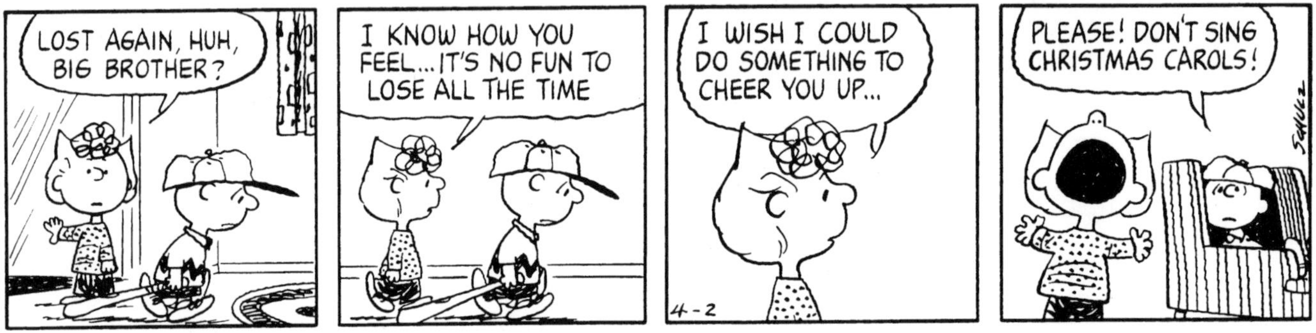
LOST AGAIN, HUH, BIG BROTHER?
I KNOW HOW YOU FEEL...IT'S NO FUN TO LOSE ALL THE TIME
I WISH I COULD DO SOMETHING TO CHEER YOU UP...
4-2
PLEASE! DON'T SING CHRISTMAS CAROLS!

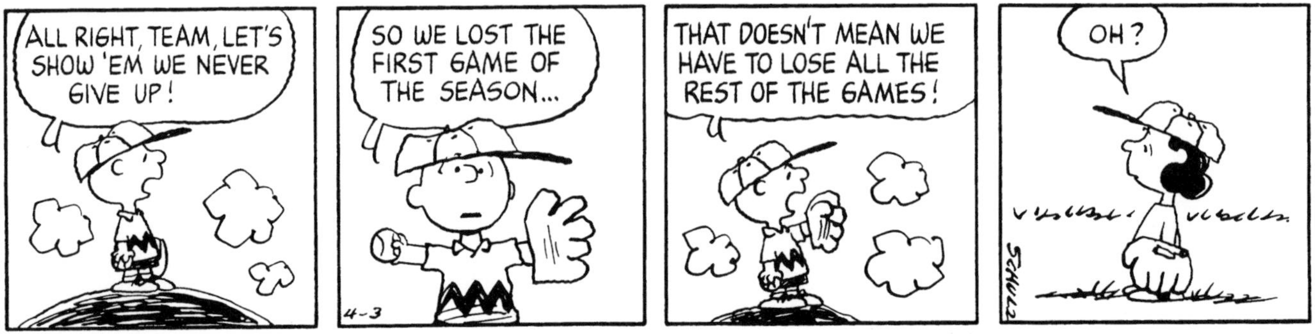
ALL RIGHT, TEAM, LET'S SHOW 'EM WE NEVER GIVE UP!
SO WE LOST THE FIRST GAME OF THE SEASON...
4-3
THAT DOESN'T MEAN WE HAVE TO LOSE ALL THE REST OF THE GAMES!
OH?

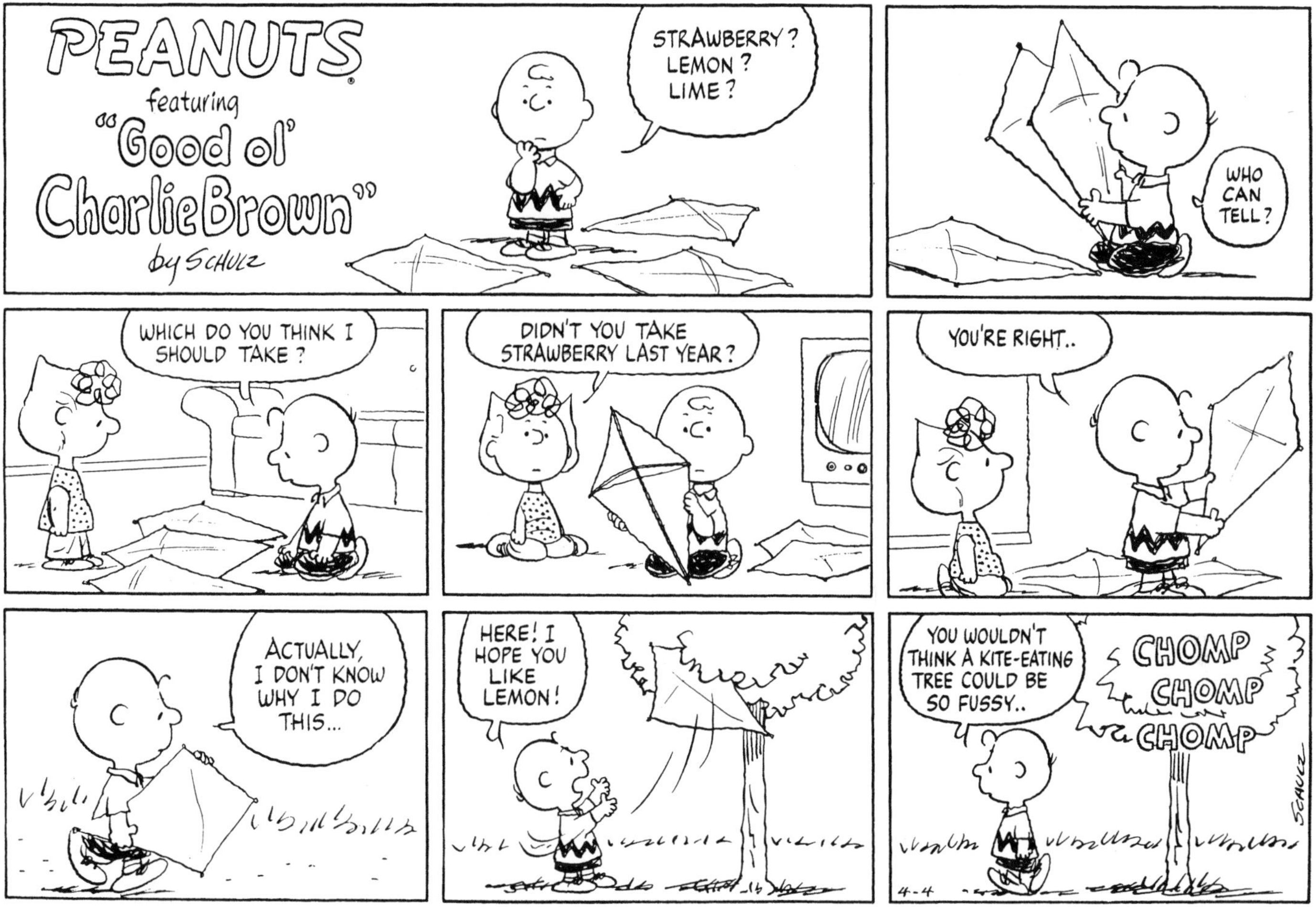
PEANUTS
featuring "Good ol' CharlieBrown"
by SCHULZ
STRAWBERRY? LEMON? LIME?
WHO CAN TELL?
WHICH DO YOU THINK I SHOULD TAKE?
DIDN'T YOU TAKE STRAWBERRY LAST YEAR?
YOU'RE RIGHT..
ACTUALLY, I DON'T KNOW WHY I DO THIS...
HERE! I HOPE YOU LIKE LEMON!
YOU WOULDN'T THINK A KITE-EATING TREE COULD BE SO FUSSY..
CHOMP
CHOMP
CHOMP
SCHULZ
4-4

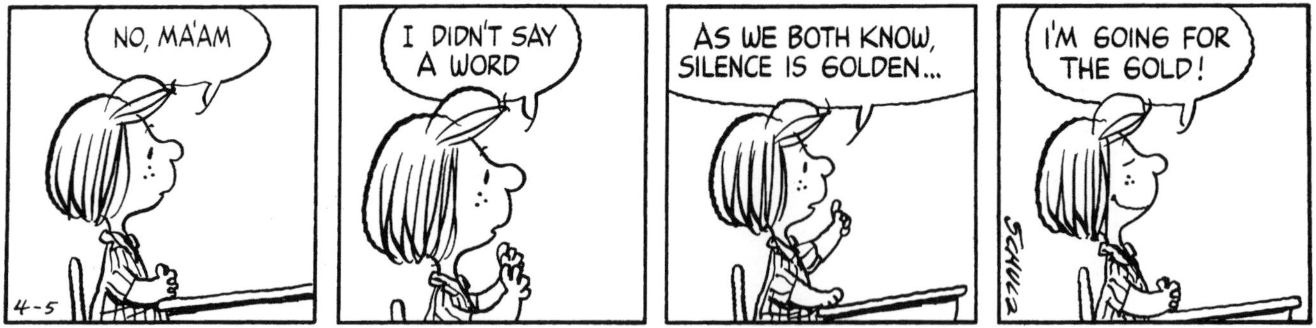
NO, MA'AM
I DIDN'T SAY A WORD
AS WE BOTH KNOW, SILENCE IS GOLDEN...
I'M GOING FOR THE GOLD!

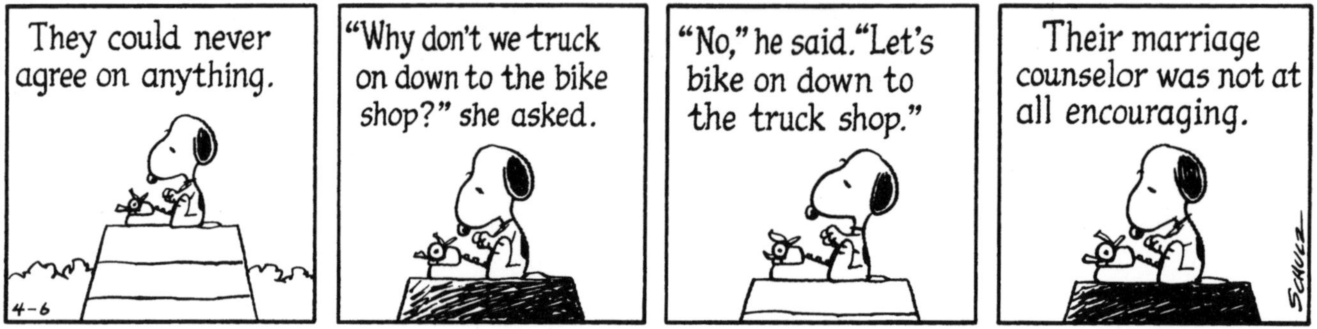
They could never agree on anything.
"Why don't we truck on down to the bike shop?" she asked.
"No," he said. "Let's bike on down to the truck shop."
Their marriage counselor was not at all encouraging.

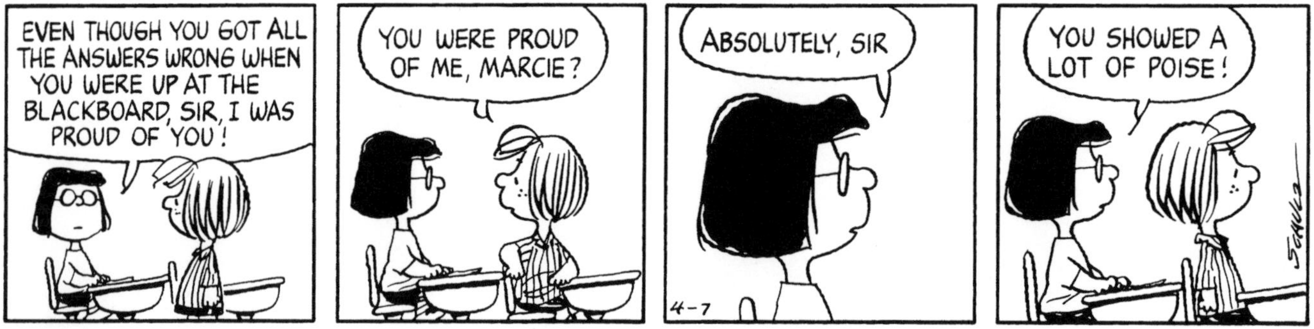
EVEN THOUGH YOU GOT ALL THE ANSWERS WRONG WHEN YOU WERE UP AT THE BLACKBOARD, SIR, I WAS PROUD OF YOU!
YOU WERE PROUD OF ME, MARCIE?
ABSOLUTELY, SIR
YOU SHOWED A LOT OF POISE!

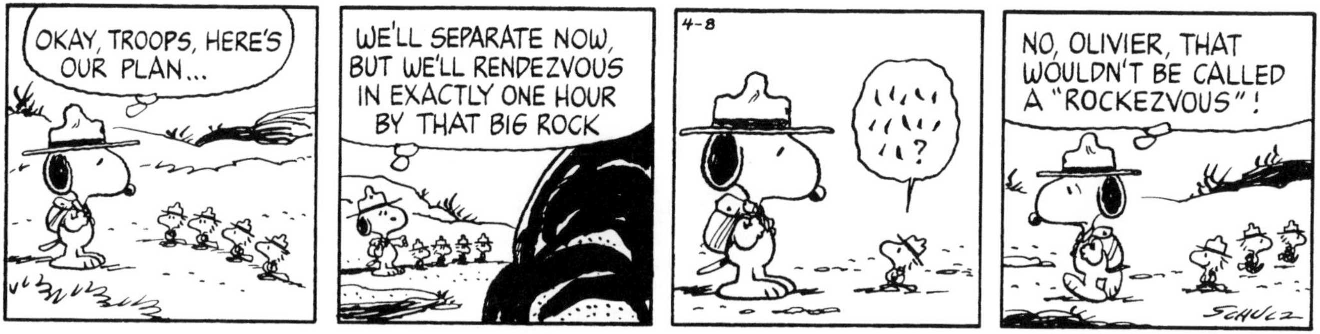
OKAY, TROOPS, HERE'S OUR PLAN...
WE'LL SEPARATE NOW, BUT WE'LL RENDEZVOUS IN EXACTLY ONE HOUR BY THAT BIG ROCK
4-8
?
NO, OLIVIER, THAT WOULDN'T BE CALLED A "ROCKEZVOUS"!
SCHULZ

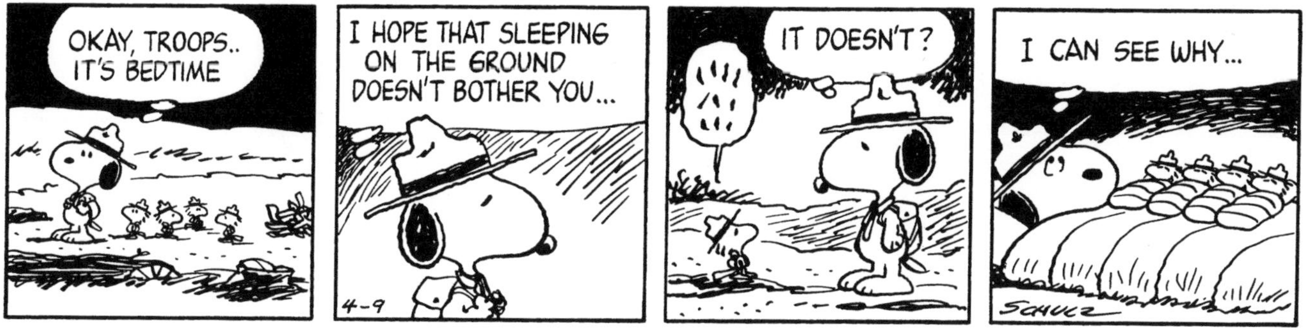
OKAY, TROOPS.. IT'S BEDTIME
I HOPE THAT SLEEPING ON THE GROUND DOESN'T BOTHER YOU...
4-9
IT DOESN'T?
I CAN SEE WHY...
SCHULZ

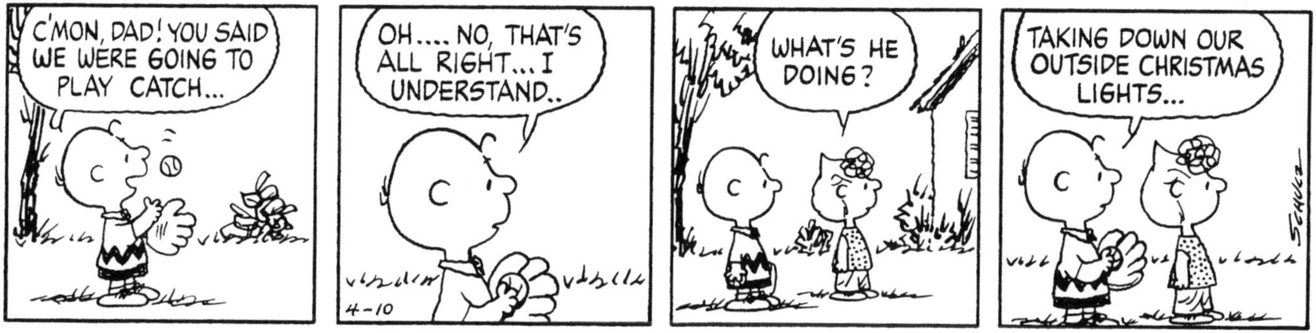
C'MON, DAD! YOU SAID WE WERE GOING TO PLAY CATCH...
OH.... NO, THAT'S ALL RIGHT... I UNDERSTAND..
4-10
WHAT'S HE DOING?
TAKING DOWN OUR OUTSIDE CHRISTMAS LIGHTS...
SCHULZ

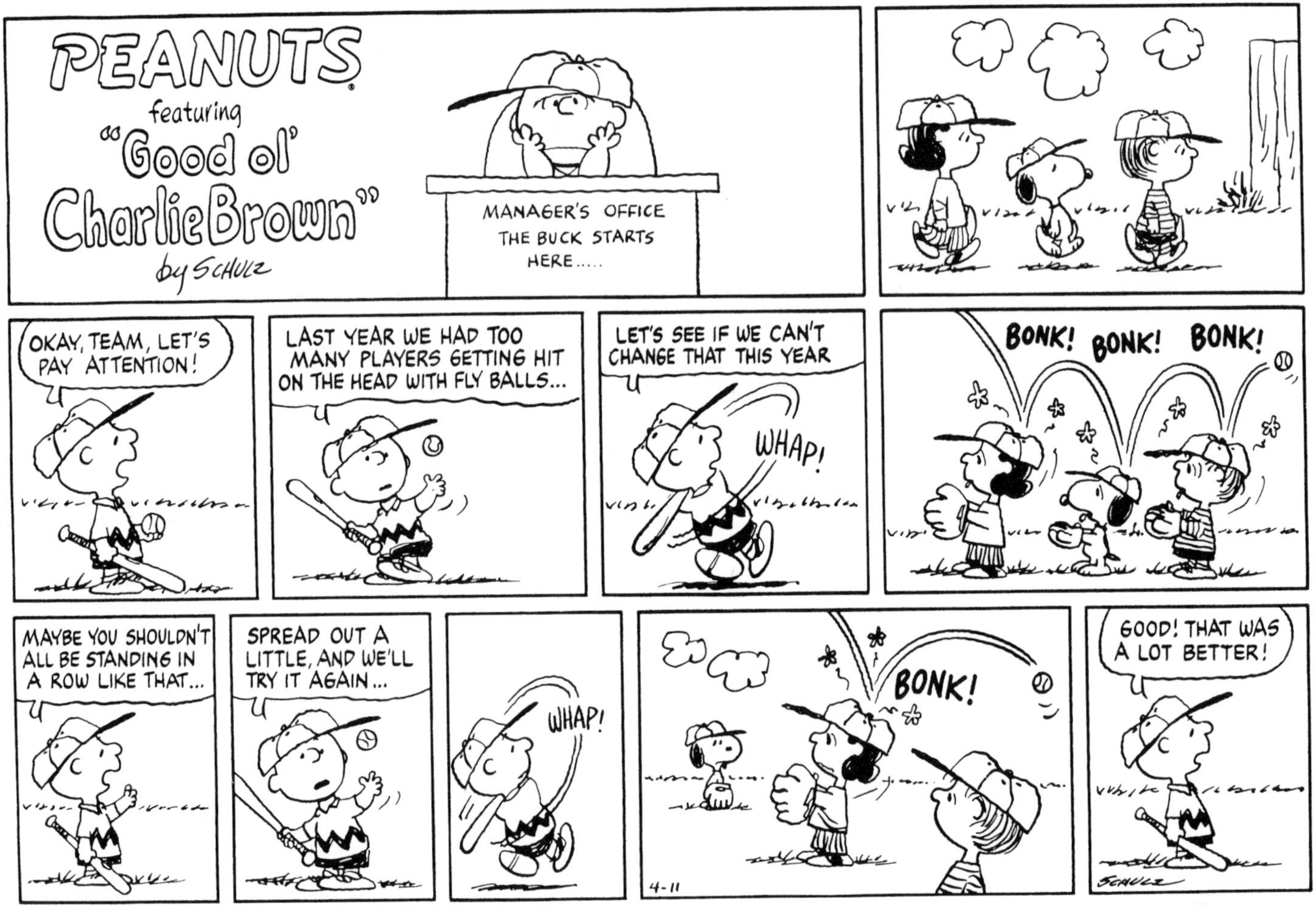
PEANUTS
featuring
"Good ol' Charlie Brown"
by SCHULZ
MANAGER'S OFFICE
THE BUCK STARTS HERE.....
OKAY, TEAM, LET'S PAY ATTENTION!
LAST YEAR WE HAD TOO MANY PLAYERS GETTING HIT ON THE HEAD WITH FLY BALLS...
LET'S SEE IF WE CAN'T CHANGE THAT THIS YEAR
WHAP!
BONK! BONK! BONK!
MAYBE YOU SHOULDN'T ALL BE STANDING IN A ROW LIKE THAT...
SPREAD OUT A LITTLE, AND WE'LL TRY IT AGAIN...
WHAP!
BONK!
4-11
GOOD! THAT WAS A LOT BETTER!
SCHULZ

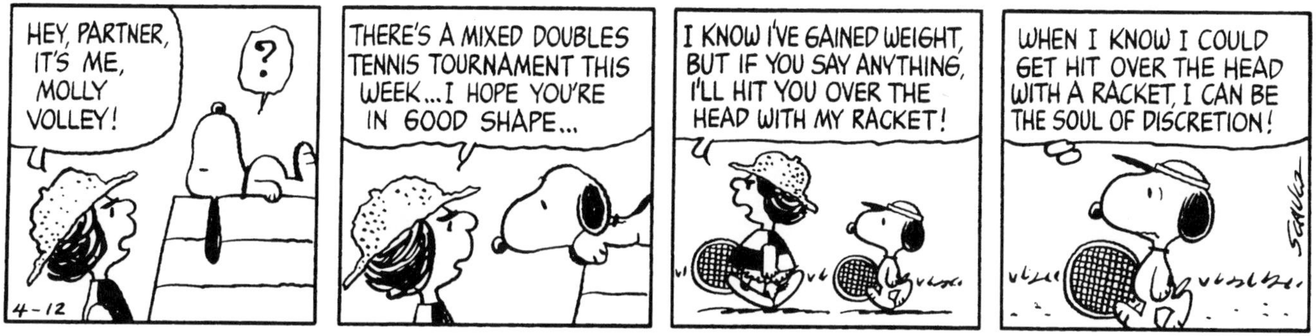
HEY, PARTNER, IT'S ME, MOLLY VOLLEY!
?
4-12
THERE'S A MIXED DOUBLES TENNIS TOURNAMENT THIS WEEK...I HOPE YOU'RE IN GOOD SHAPE...
I KNOW I'VE GAINED WEIGHT, BUT IF YOU SAY ANYTHING, I'LL HIT YOU OVER THE HEAD WITH MY RACKET!
WHEN I KNOW I COULD GET HIT OVER THE HEAD WITH A RACKET, I CAN BE THE SOUL OF DISCRETION!
SCHULZ

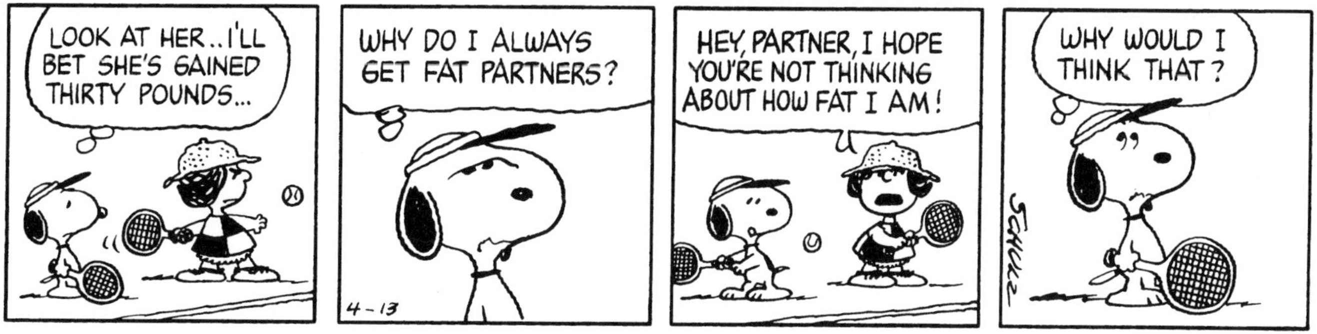
LOOK AT HER..I'LL BET SHE'S GAINED THIRTY POUNDS...
WHY DO I ALWAYS GET FAT PARTNERS?
4-13
HEY, PARTNER, I HOPE YOU'RE NOT THINKING ABOUT HOW FAT I AM!
WHY WOULD I THINK THAT?
SCHULZ

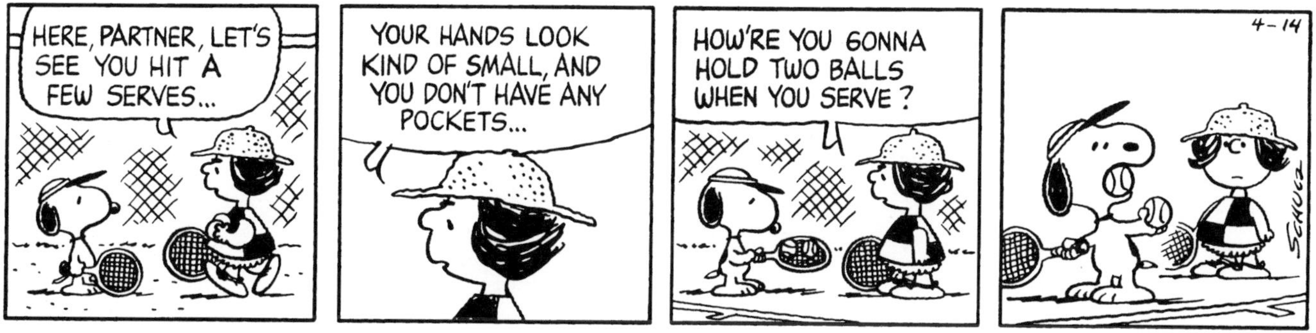
HERE, PARTNER, LET'S SEE YOU HIT A FEW SERVES...
YOUR HANDS LOOK KIND OF SMALL, AND YOU DON'T HAVE ANY POCKETS...
HOW'RE YOU GONNA HOLD TWO BALLS WHEN YOU SERVE?
4-14
SCHULZ

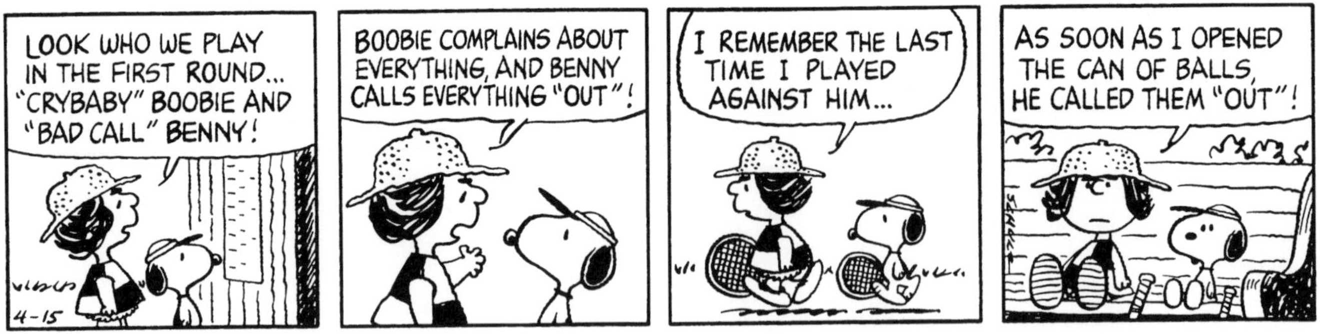
LOOK WHO WE PLAY IN THE FIRST ROUND... "CRYBABY" BOOBIE AND "BAD CALL" BENNY!
4-15
BOOBIE COMPLAINS ABOUT EVERYTHING, AND BENNY CALLS EVERYTHING "OUT"!
I REMEMBER THE LAST TIME I PLAYED AGAINST HIM...
AS SOON AS I OPENED THE CAN OF BALLS, HE CALLED THEM "OUT"!
SCHULZ

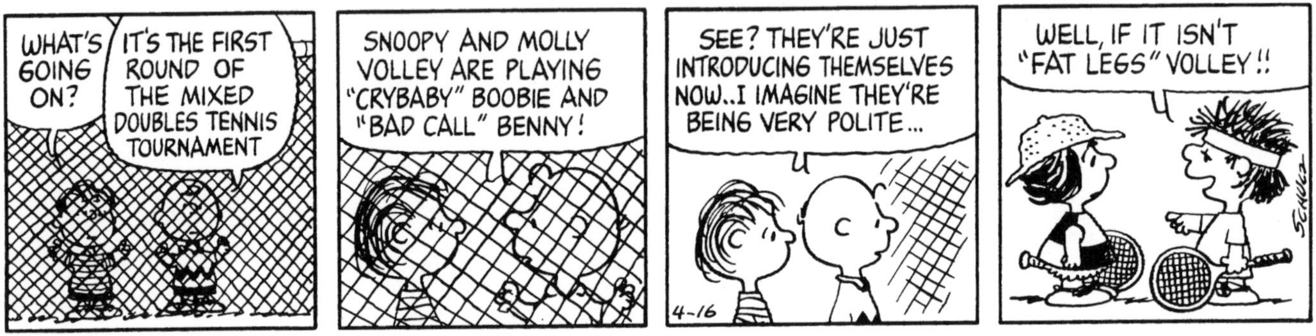
WHAT'S GOING ON?
IT'S THE FIRST ROUND OF THE MIXED DOUBLES TENNIS TOURNAMENT
SNOOPY AND MOLLY VOLLEY ARE PLAYING "CRYBABY" BOOBIE AND "BAD CALL" BENNY!
SEE? THEY'RE JUST INTRODUCING THEMSELVES NOW..I IMAGINE THEY'RE BEING VERY POLITE...
4-16
WELL, IF IT ISN'T "FAT LEGS" VOLLEY!!
SCHULZ

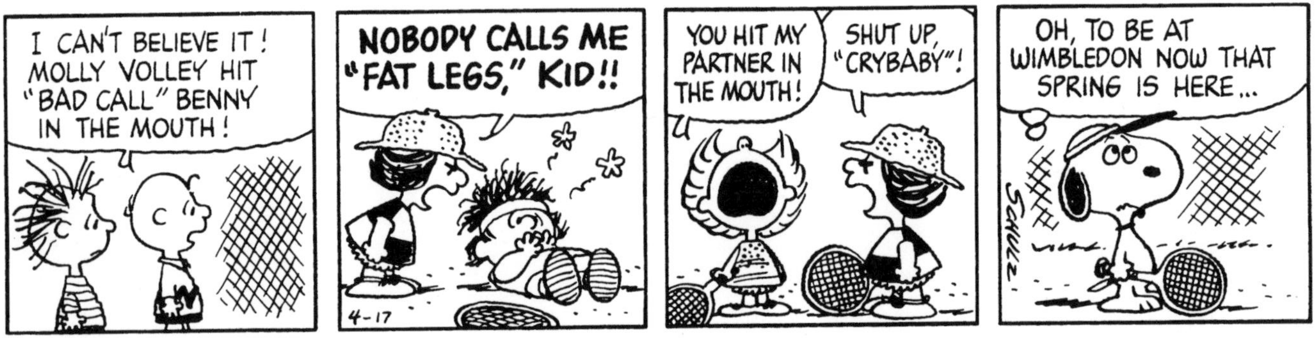
I CAN'T BELIEVE IT! MOLLY VOLLEY HIT "BAD CALL" BENNY IN THE MOUTH!
NOBODY CALLS ME "FAT LEGS," KID!!
4-17
YOU HIT MY PARTNER IN THE MOUTH!
SHUT UP, "CRYBABY"!
OH, TO BE AT WIMBLEDON NOW THAT SPRING IS HERE...
SCHULZ

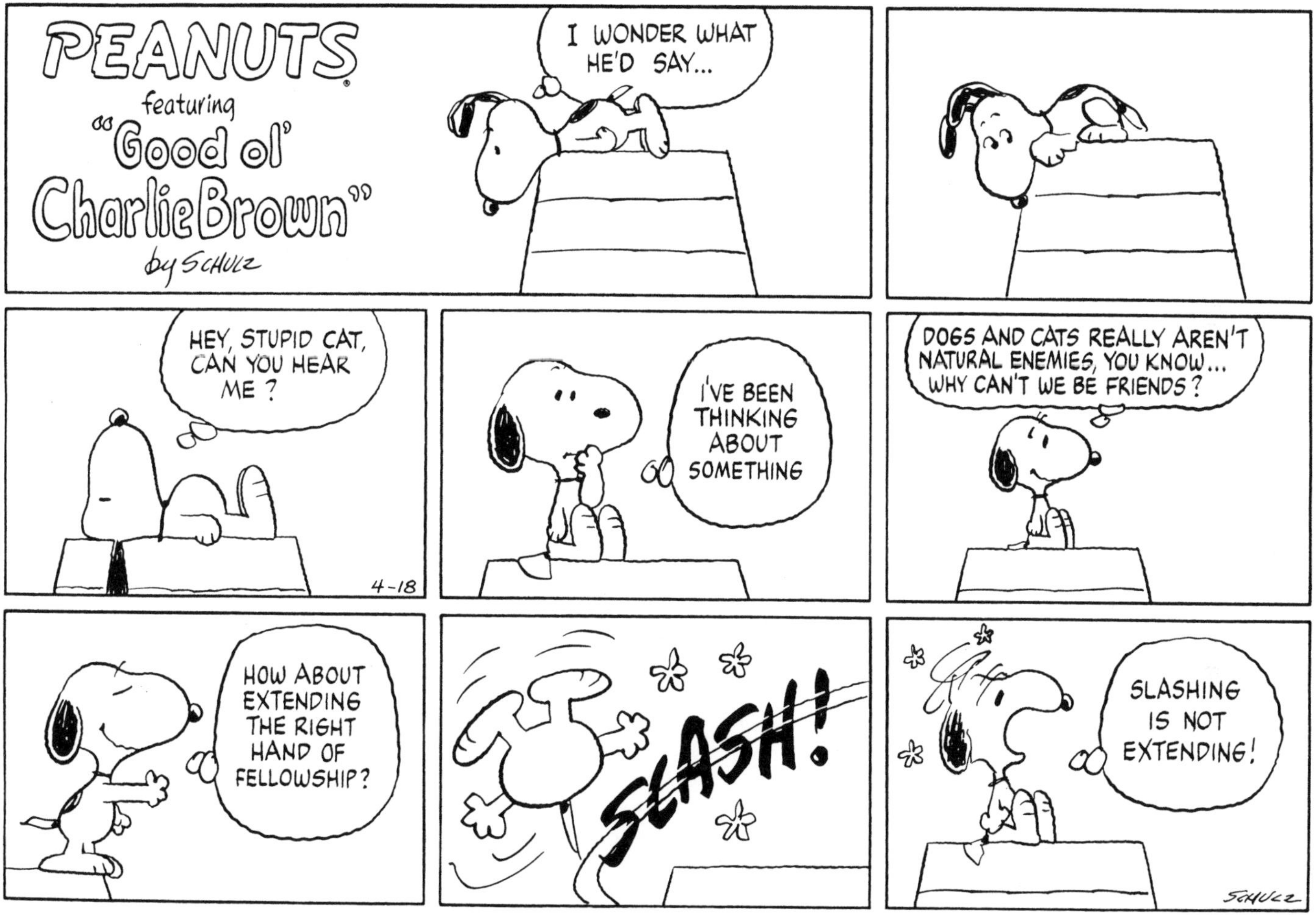
PEANUTS
featuring "Good ol' Charlie Brown"
by SCHULZ
I WONDER WHAT HE'D SAY...
HEY, STUPID CAT, CAN YOU HEAR ME ?
4-18
I'VE BEEN THINKING ABOUT SOMETHING
DOGS AND CATS REALLY AREN'T NATURAL ENEMIES, YOU KNOW... WHY CAN'T WE BE FRIENDS ?
HOW ABOUT EXTENDING THE RIGHT HAND OF FELLOWSHIP?
SLASH!
SLASHING IS NOT EXTENDING!
SCHULZ

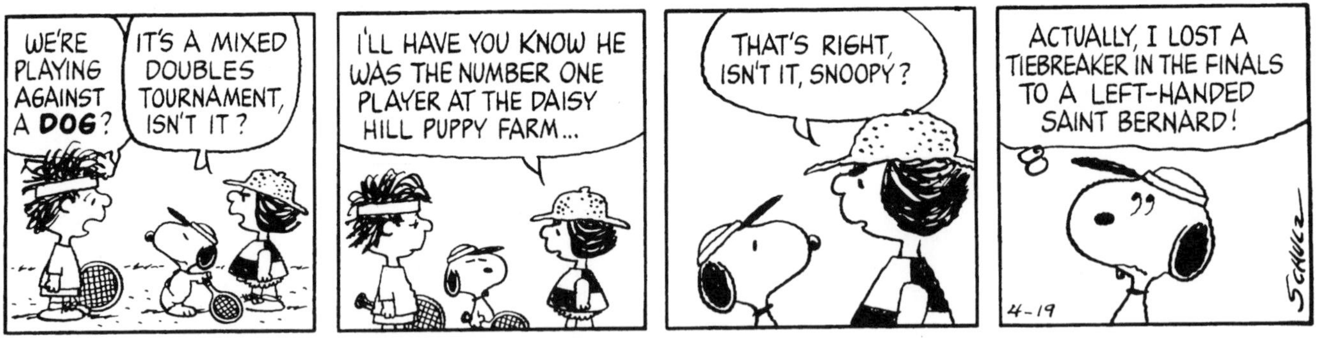
WE'RE PLAYING AGAINST A **DOG**?
IT'S A MIXED DOUBLES TOURNAMENT, ISN'T IT?
I'LL HAVE YOU KNOW HE WAS THE NUMBER ONE PLAYER AT THE DAISY HILL PUPPY FARM...
THAT'S RIGHT, ISN'T IT, SNOOPY?
ACTUALLY, I LOST A TIEBREAKER IN THE FINALS TO A LEFT-HANDED SAINT BERNARD!
SCHULZ
4-19

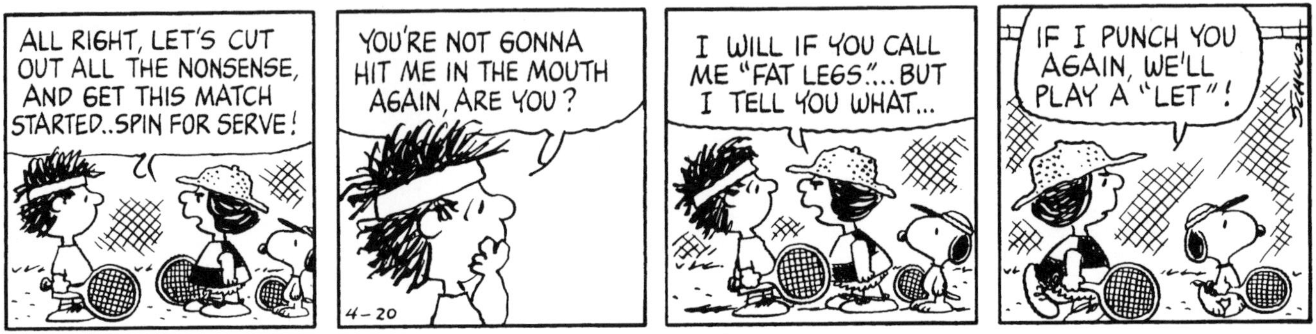
ALL RIGHT, LET'S CUT OUT ALL THE NONSENSE, AND GET THIS MATCH STARTED..SPIN FOR SERVE!
YOU'RE NOT GONNA HIT ME IN THE MOUTH AGAIN, ARE YOU?
4-20
I WILL IF YOU CALL ME "FAT LEGS"... BUT I TELL YOU WHAT...
IF I PUNCH YOU AGAIN, WE'LL PLAY A "LET"!
SCHULZ

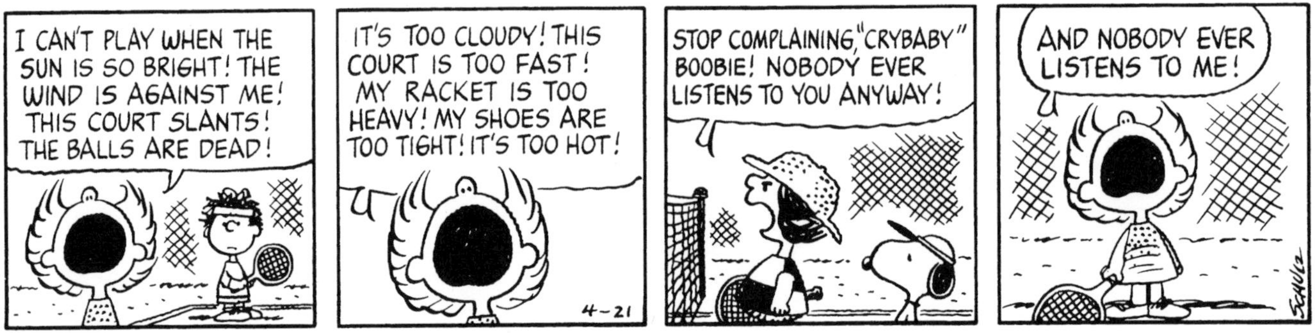
I CAN'T PLAY WHEN THE SUN IS SO BRIGHT! THE WIND IS AGAINST ME! THIS COURT SLANTS! THE BALLS ARE DEAD!
IT'S TOO CLOUDY! THIS COURT IS TOO FAST! MY RACKET IS TOO HEAVY! MY SHOES ARE TOO TIGHT! IT'S TOO HOT!
4-21
STOP COMPLAINING, "CRYBABY" BOOBIE! NOBODY EVER LISTENS TO YOU ANYWAY!
AND NOBODY EVER LISTENS TO ME!
SCHULZ

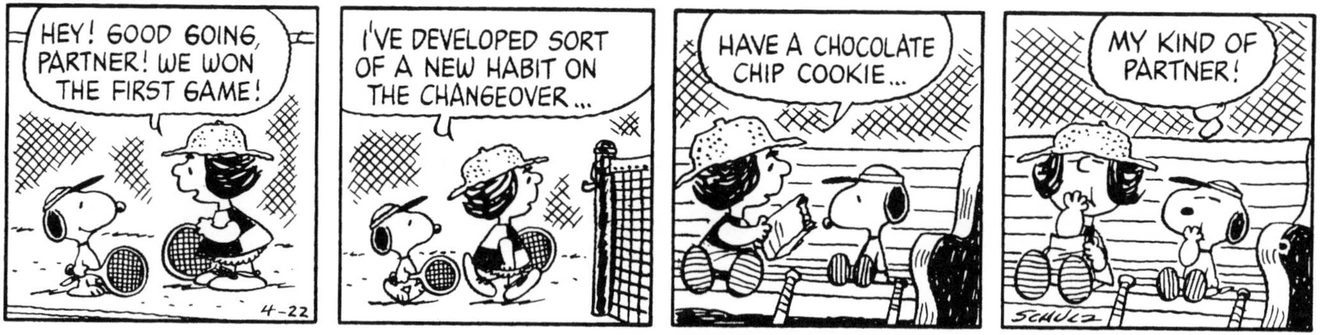
HEY! GOOD GOING, PARTNER! WE WON THE FIRST GAME!
I'VE DEVELOPED SORT OF A NEW HABIT ON THE CHANGEOVER...
HAVE A CHOCOLATE CHIP COOKIE...
MY KIND OF PARTNER!

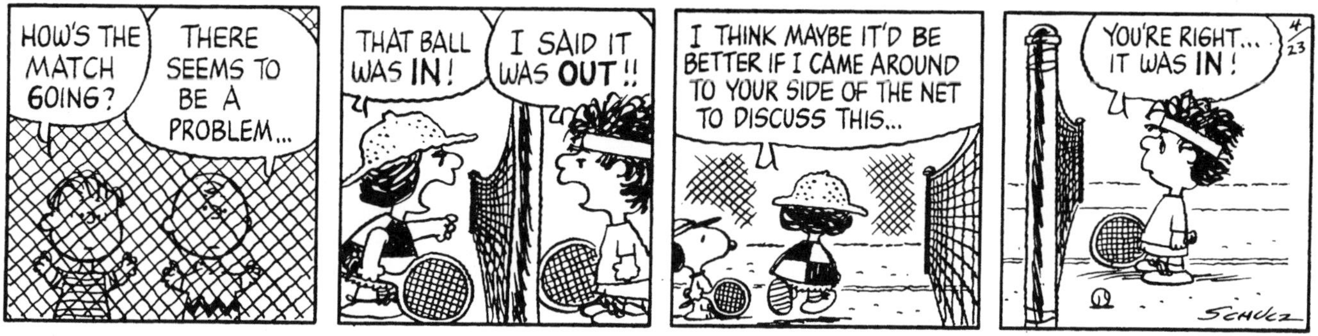
HOW'S THE MATCH GOING?
THERE SEEMS TO BE A PROBLEM...
THAT BALL WAS **IN**!
I SAID IT WAS **OUT**!!
I THINK MAYBE IT'D BE BETTER IF I CAME AROUND TO YOUR SIDE OF THE NET TO DISCUSS THIS...
YOU'RE RIGHT... IT WAS **IN**!

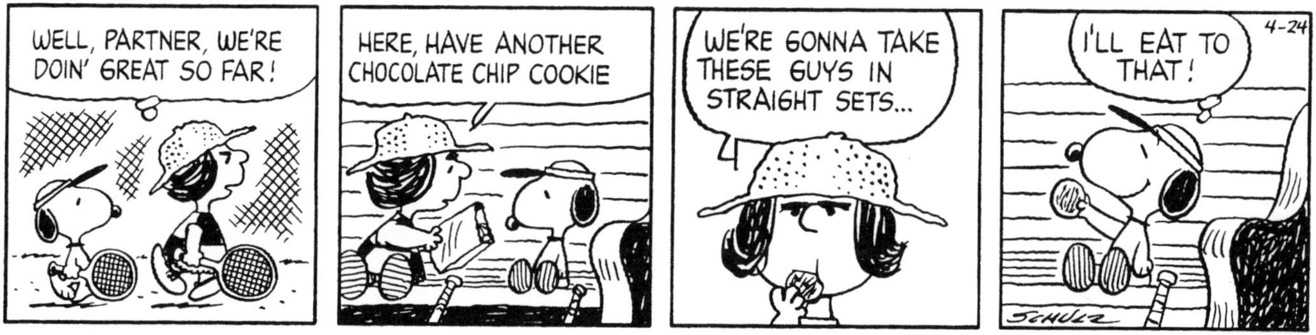
WELL, PARTNER, WE'RE DOIN' GREAT SO FAR!
HERE, HAVE ANOTHER CHOCOLATE CHIP COOKIE
WE'RE GONNA TAKE THESE GUYS IN STRAIGHT SETS...
I'LL EAT TO THAT!

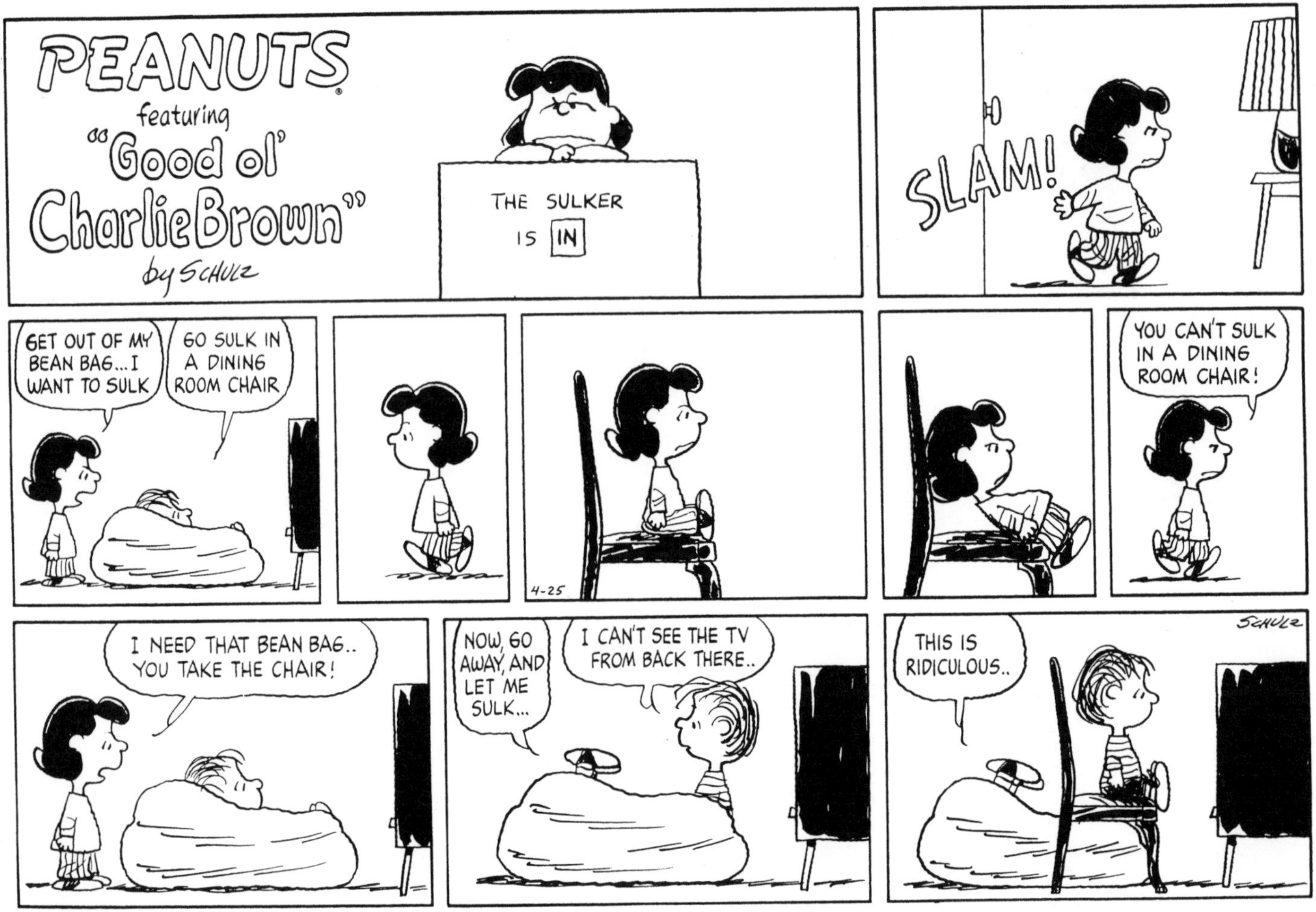
PEANUTS
featuring
"Good ol' Charlie Brown"
by SCHULZ
THE SULKER IS IN
SLAM!
GET OUT OF MY BEAN BAG...I WANT TO SULK
GO SULK IN A DINING ROOM CHAIR
4-25
YOU CAN'T SULK IN A DINING ROOM CHAIR!
I NEED THAT BEAN BAG.. YOU TAKE THE CHAIR!
NOW, GO AWAY, AND LET ME SULK...
I CAN'T SEE THE TV FROM BACK THERE..
SCHULZ
THIS IS RIDICULOUS..

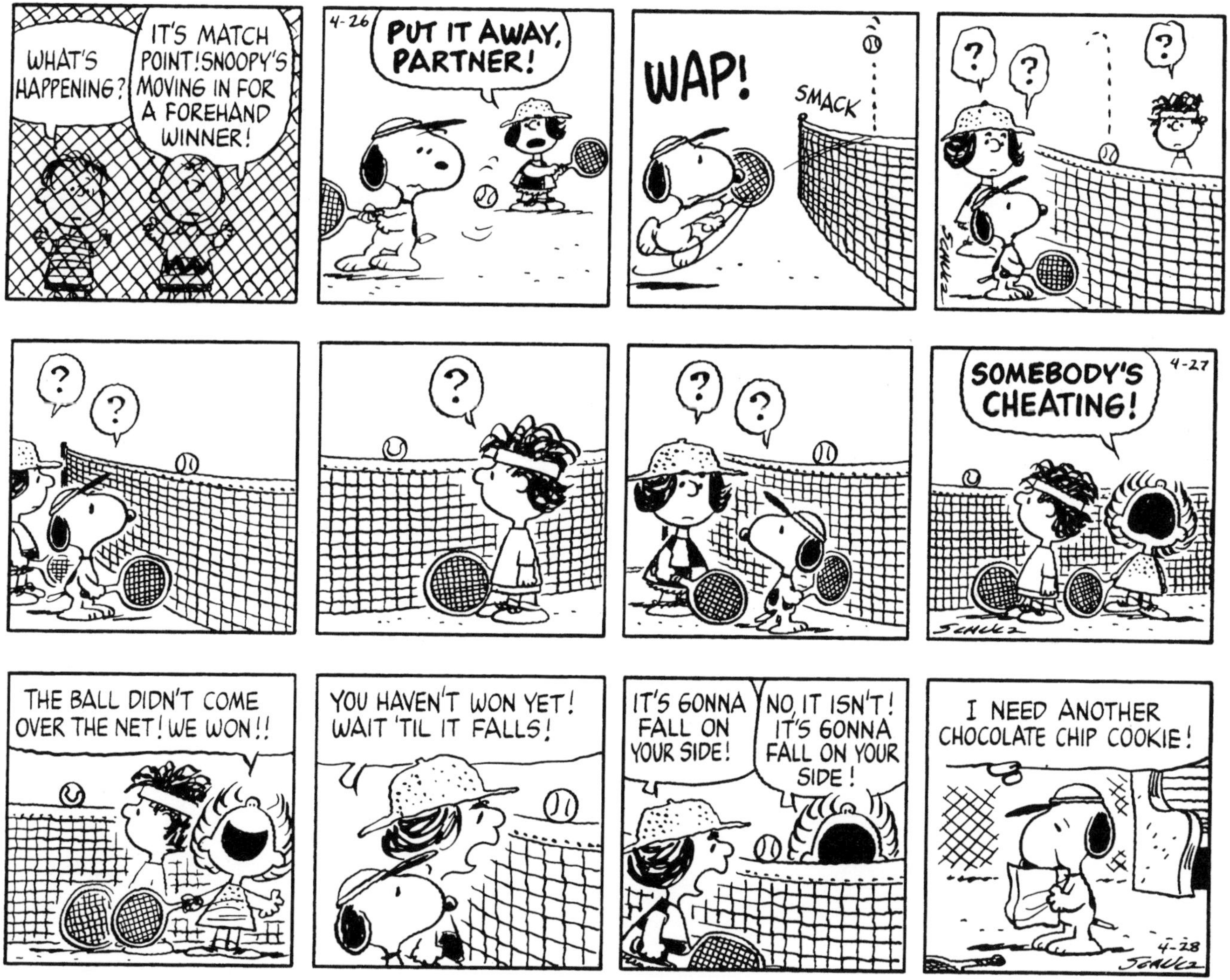
WHAT'S HAPPENING?
IT'S MATCH POINT! SNOOPY'S MOVING IN FOR A FOREHAND WINNER!
4-26
PUT IT AWAY, PARTNER!
WAP!
SMACK
?
?
?
?
?
?
?
?
SOMEBODY'S CHEATING!
4-27
SCHULZ
THE BALL DIDN'T COME OVER THE NET! WE WON!!
YOU HAVEN'T WON YET! WAIT 'TIL IT FALLS!
IT'S GONNA FALL ON YOUR SIDE!
NO, IT ISN'T! IT'S GONNA FALL ON YOUR SIDE!
I NEED ANOTHER CHOCOLATE CHIP COOKIE!
4-28
SCHULZ

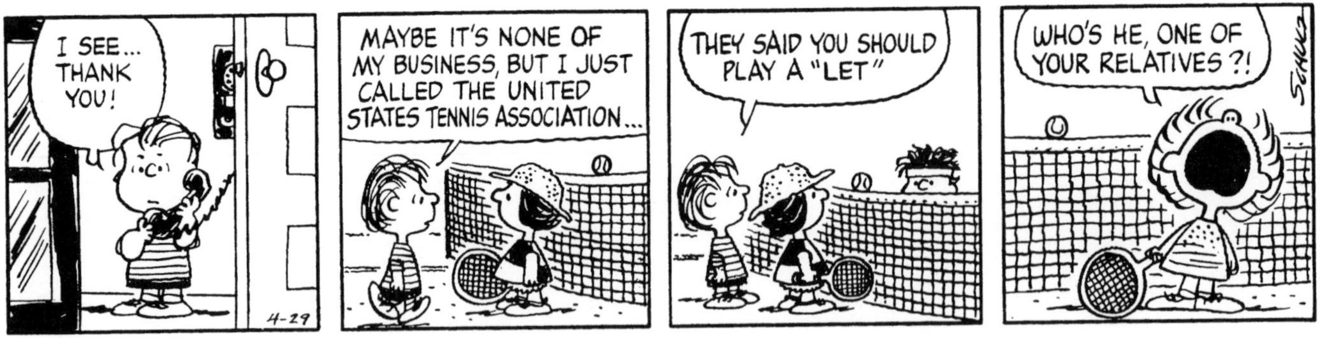
I SEE... THANK YOU!
MAYBE IT'S NONE OF MY BUSINESS, BUT I JUST CALLED THE UNITED STATES TENNIS ASSOCIATION...
THEY SAID YOU SHOULD PLAY A "LET"
WHO'S HE, ONE OF YOUR RELATIVES?!
4-29

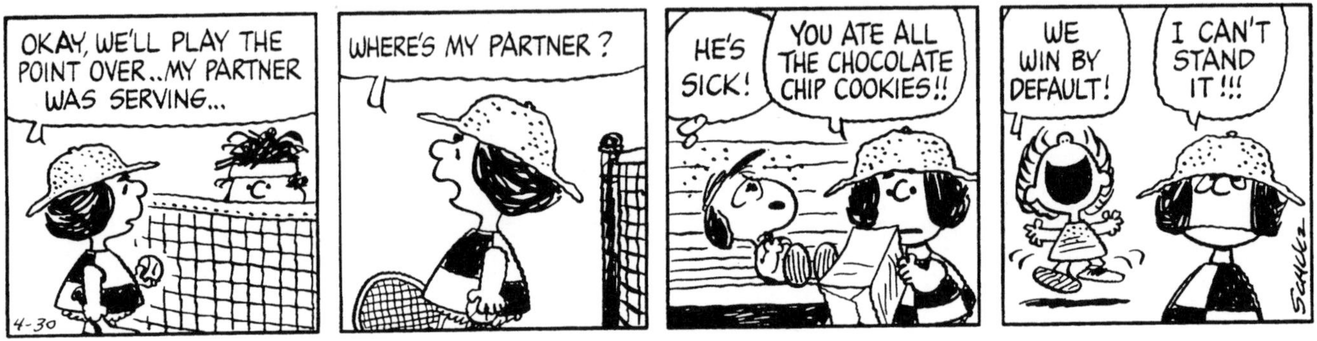
OKAY, WE'LL PLAY THE POINT OVER..MY PARTNER WAS SERVING...
WHERE'S MY PARTNER?
HE'S SICK!
YOU ATE ALL THE CHOCOLATE CHIP COOKIES!!
WE WIN BY DEFAULT!
I CAN'T STAND IT!!!
4-30

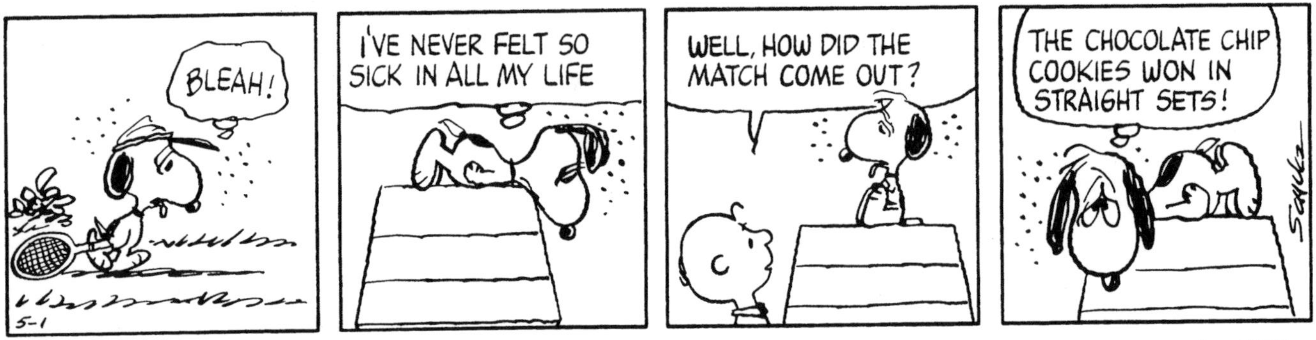
BLEAH!
I'VE NEVER FELT SO SICK IN ALL MY LIFE
WELL, HOW DID THE MATCH COME OUT?
THE CHOCOLATE CHIP COOKIES WON IN STRAIGHT SETS!
5-1

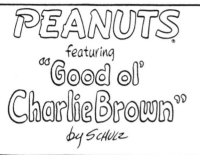

Peanuts featuring **"Good ol' CharlieBrown"** by Schulz

?

YOU'RE LOOKING FOR YOUR PIANO, RIGHT?

GUESS WHAT.. I WASHED IT!

YOU **WHAT**?

I'LL BET THAT PIANO HASN'T BEEN CLEANED IN TWO YEARS... I PUT IT IN THE WASHER..

YOU CAN'T PUT A PIANO IN THE WASHER!

DON'T GET SO EXCITED! IT CAME OUT FINE...

FROM A **WASHER**?!!

I WILL ADMIT ONE THING, HOWEVER...

I DON'T THINK I SHOULD HAVE PUT IT IN THE DRYER..

5-2

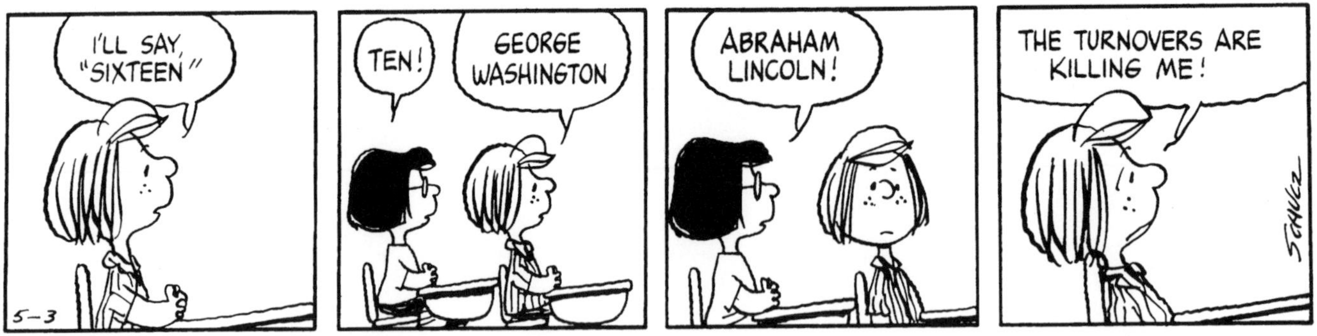
5-3
I'LL SAY, "SIXTEEN"
TEN!
GEORGE WASHINGTON
ABRAHAM LINCOLN!
THE TURNOVERS ARE KILLING ME!
SCHULZ

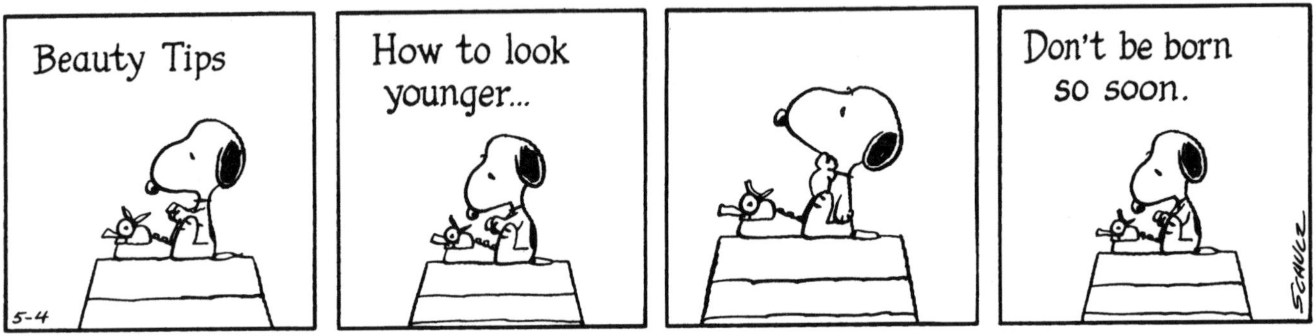
5-4
Beauty Tips
How to look younger...
Don't be born so soon.
SCHULZ

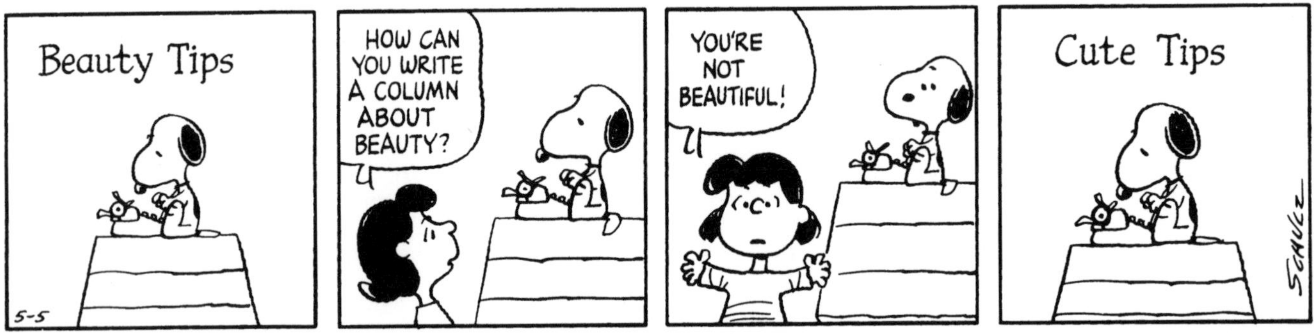
5-5
Beauty Tips
HOW CAN YOU WRITE A COLUMN ABOUT BEAUTY?
YOU'RE NOT BEAUTIFUL!
Cute Tips
SCHULZ

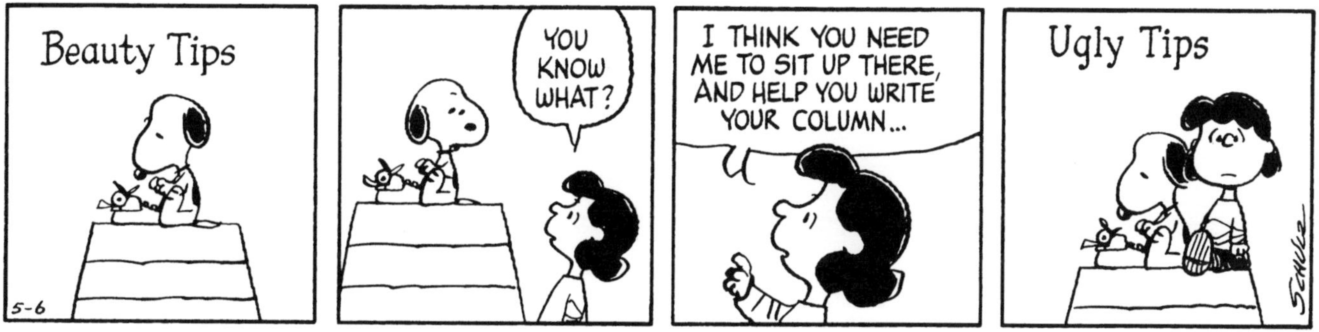
Beauty Tips
5-6
YOU KNOW WHAT?
I THINK YOU NEED ME TO SIT UP THERE, AND HELP YOU WRITE YOUR COLUMN...
Ugly Tips
SCHULZ

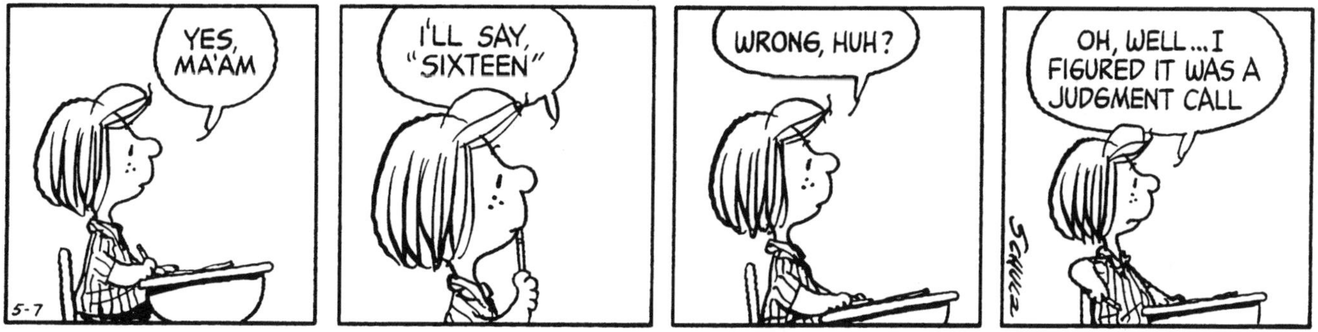
YES, MA'AM
5-7
I'LL SAY, "SIXTEEN"
WRONG, HUH?
OH, WELL... I FIGURED IT WAS A JUDGMENT CALL
SCHULZ

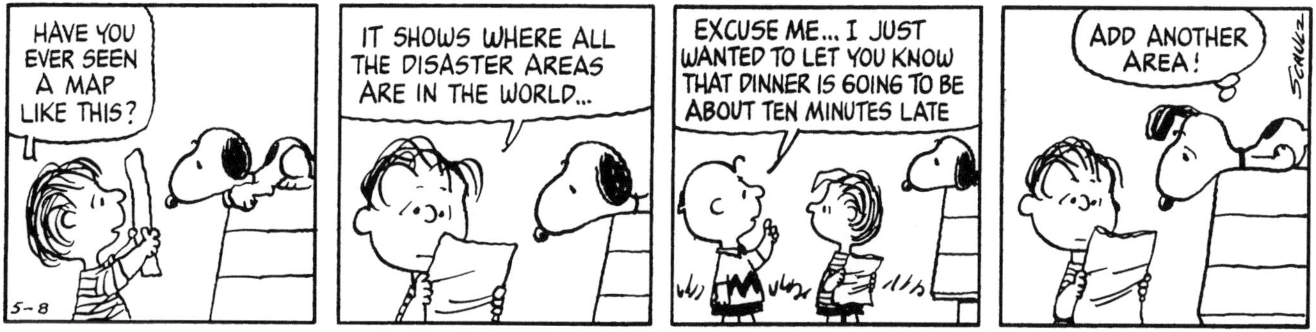
HAVE YOU EVER SEEN A MAP LIKE THIS?
5-8
IT SHOWS WHERE ALL THE DISASTER AREAS ARE IN THE WORLD...
EXCUSE ME... I JUST WANTED TO LET YOU KNOW THAT DINNER IS GOING TO BE ABOUT TEN MINUTES LATE
ADD ANOTHER AREA!
SCHULZ

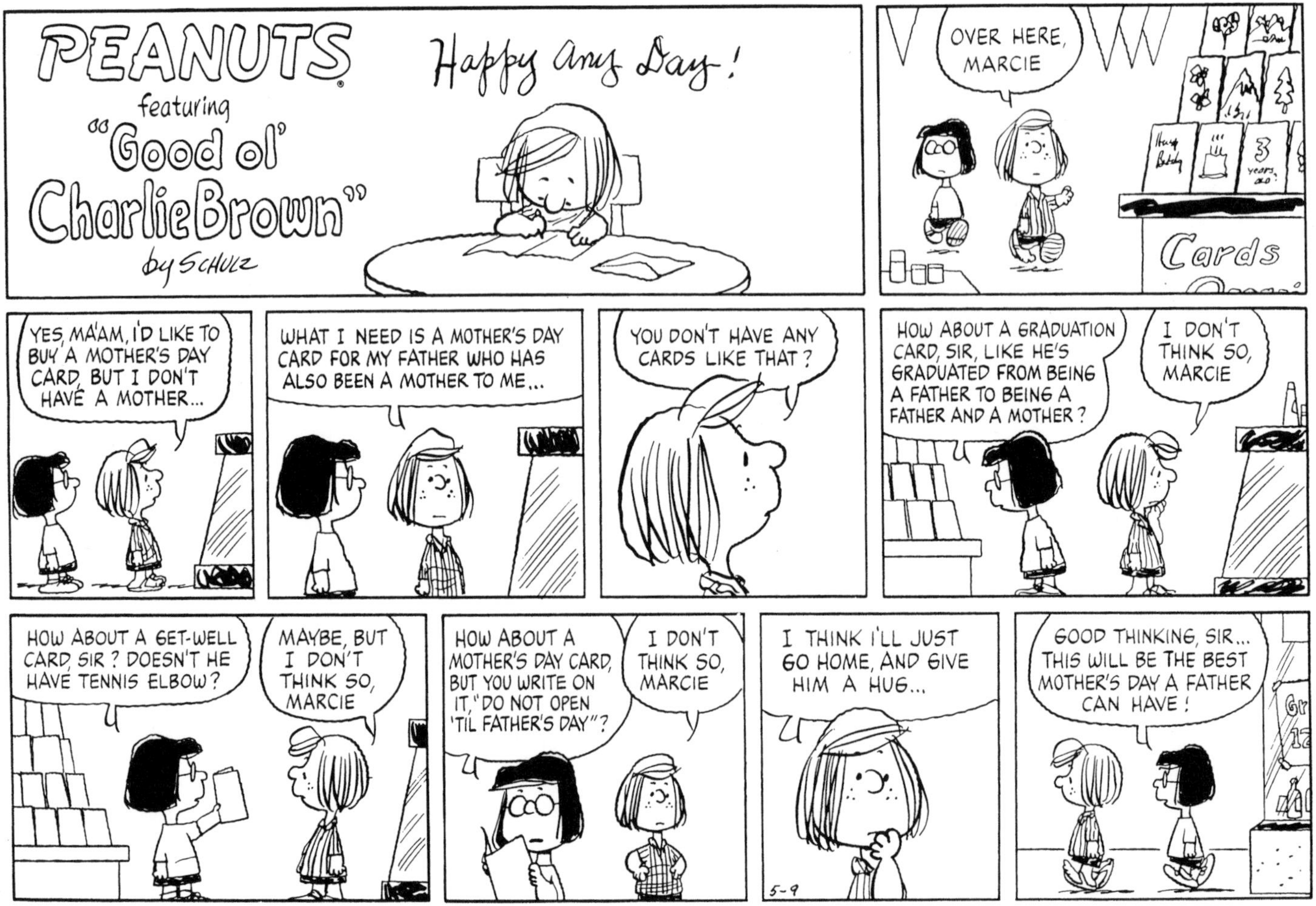
PEANUTS
featuring "Good ol' Charlie Brown"
by SCHULZ
Happy Any Day!
OVER HERE, MARCIE
Cards
YES, MA'AM, I'D LIKE TO BUY A MOTHER'S DAY CARD, BUT I DON'T HAVE A MOTHER...
WHAT I NEED IS A MOTHER'S DAY CARD FOR MY FATHER WHO HAS ALSO BEEN A MOTHER TO ME...
YOU DON'T HAVE ANY CARDS LIKE THAT?
HOW ABOUT A GRADUATION CARD, SIR, LIKE HE'S GRADUATED FROM BEING A FATHER TO BEING A FATHER AND A MOTHER?
I DON'T THINK SO, MARCIE
HOW ABOUT A GET-WELL CARD, SIR? DOESN'T HE HAVE TENNIS ELBOW?
MAYBE, BUT I DON'T THINK SO, MARCIE
HOW ABOUT A MOTHER'S DAY CARD, BUT YOU WRITE ON IT, "DO NOT OPEN 'TIL FATHER'S DAY"?
I DON'T THINK SO, MARCIE
I THINK I'LL JUST GO HOME, AND GIVE HIM A HUG...
5-9
GOOD THINKING, SIR... THIS WILL BE THE BEST MOTHER'S DAY A FATHER CAN HAVE!

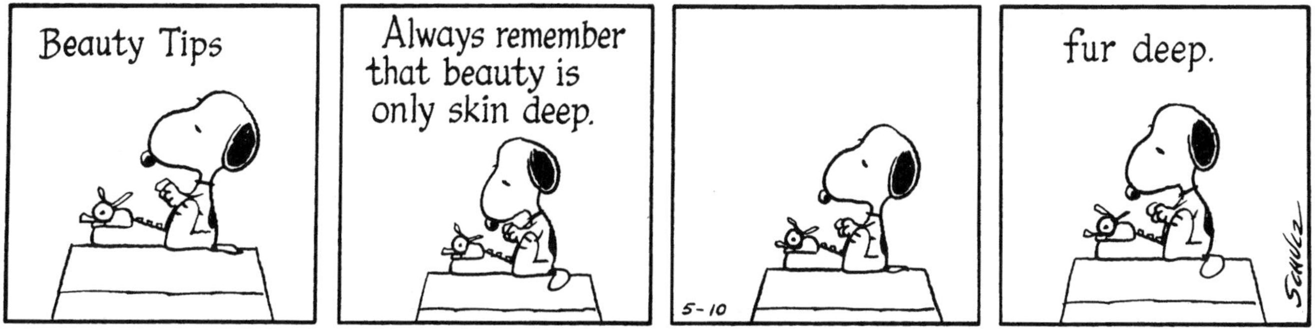
Beauty Tips
Always remember that beauty is only skin deep.
5-10
fur deep.
SCHULZ

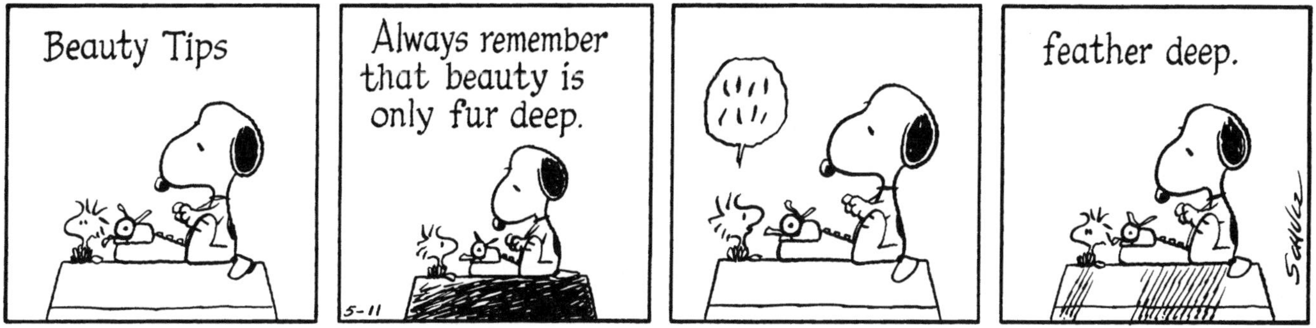
Beauty Tips
Always remember that beauty is only fur deep.
5-11
feather deep.
SCHULZ

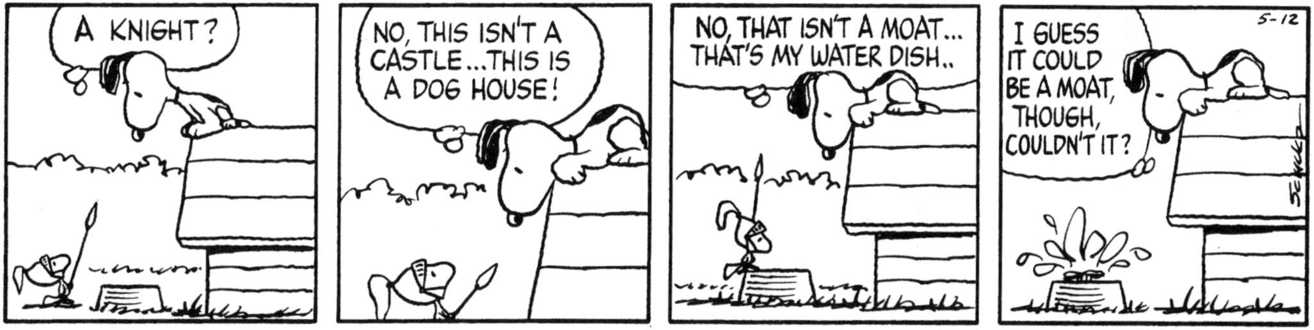
A KNIGHT?
NO, THIS ISN'T A CASTLE...THIS IS A DOG HOUSE!
NO, THAT ISN'T A MOAT... THAT'S MY WATER DISH..
5-12
I GUESS IT COULD BE A MOAT, THOUGH, COULDN'T IT?

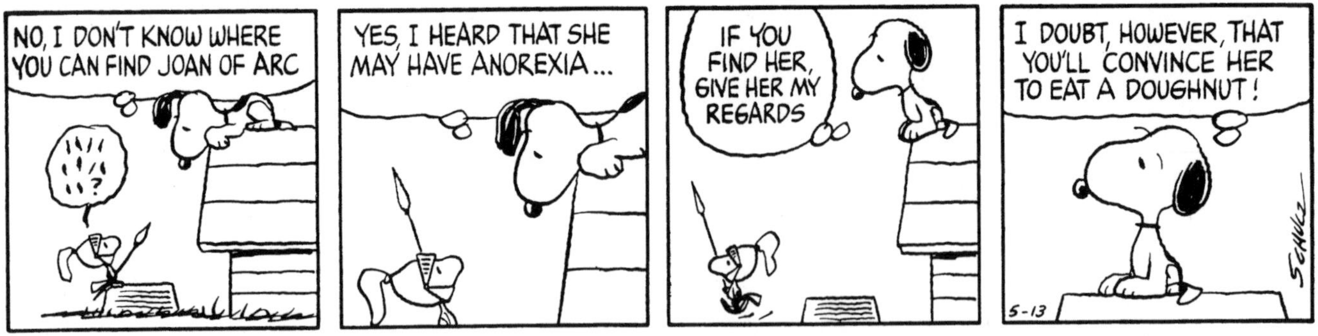
NO, I DON'T KNOW WHERE YOU CAN FIND JOAN OF ARC
?
YES, I HEARD THAT SHE MAY HAVE ANOREXIA...
IF YOU FIND HER, GIVE HER MY REGARDS
I DOUBT, HOWEVER, THAT YOU'LL CONVINCE HER TO EAT A DOUGHNUT!
5-13

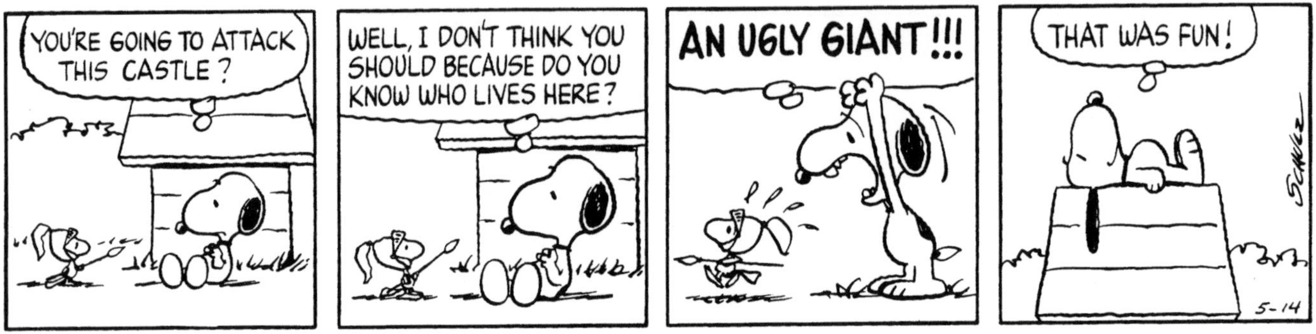
YOU'RE GOING TO ATTACK THIS CASTLE?
WELL, I DON'T THINK YOU SHOULD BECAUSE DO YOU KNOW WHO LIVES HERE?
AN UGLY GIANT!!!
THAT WAS FUN!
5-14

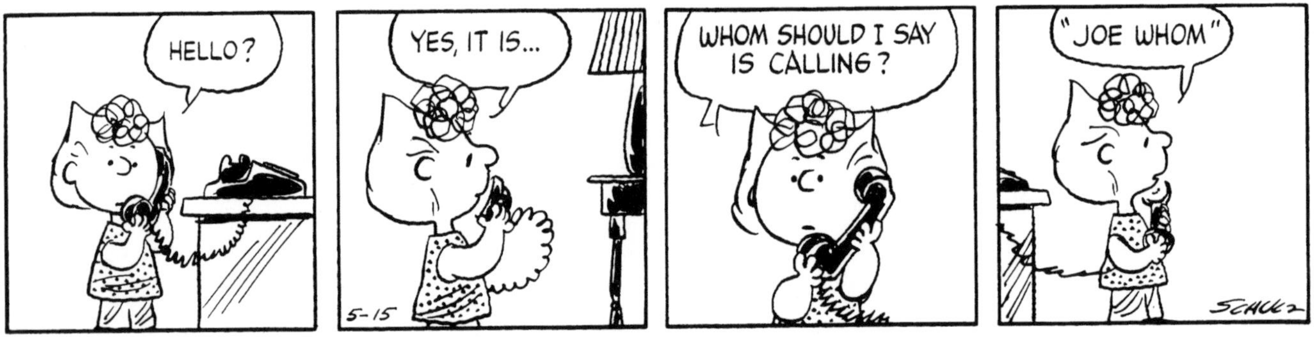
HELLO?
YES, IT IS...
5-15
WHOM SHOULD I SAY IS CALLING?
"JOE WHOM"

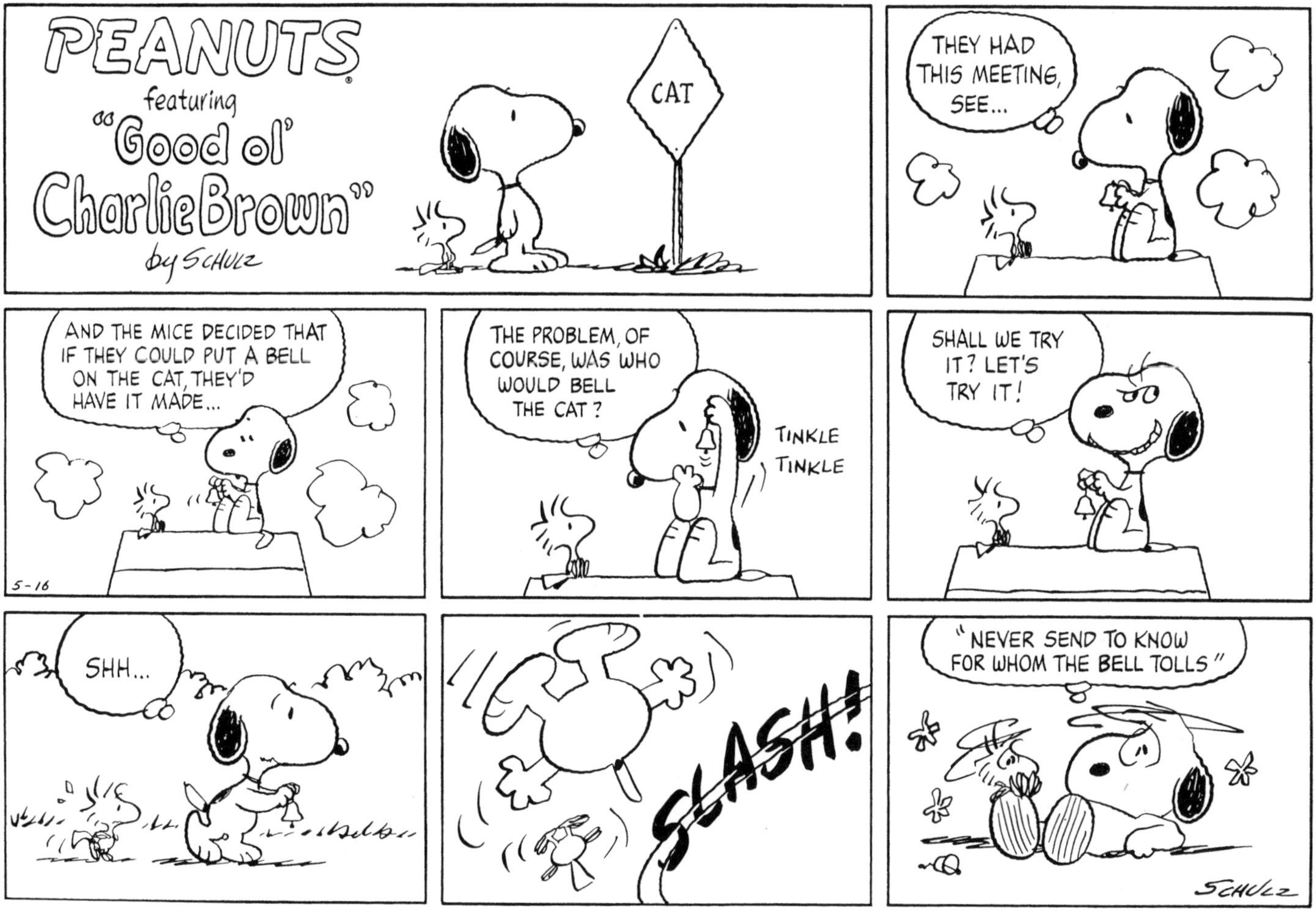
PEANUTS
featuring
"Good ol' CharlieBrown"
by SCHULZ
CAT
THEY HAD THIS MEETING, SEE...
AND THE MICE DECIDED THAT IF THEY COULD PUT A BELL ON THE CAT, THEY'D HAVE IT MADE...
5-16
THE PROBLEM, OF COURSE, WAS WHO WOULD BELL THE CAT?
TINKLE
TINKLE
SHALL WE TRY IT? LET'S TRY IT!
SHH...
SLASH!
"NEVER SEND TO KNOW FOR WHOM THE BELL TOLLS"
SCHULZ

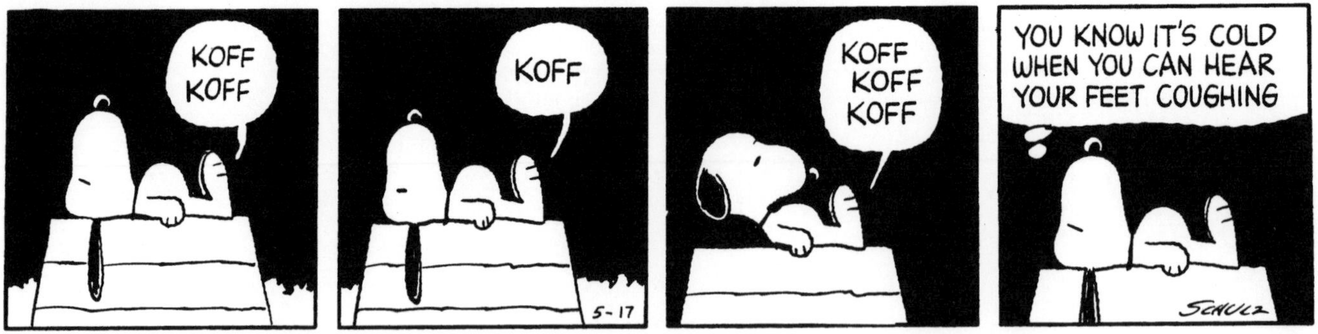
KOFF KOFF
KOFF
5-17
KOFF KOFF KOFF
YOU KNOW IT'S COLD WHEN YOU CAN HEAR YOUR FEET COUGHING

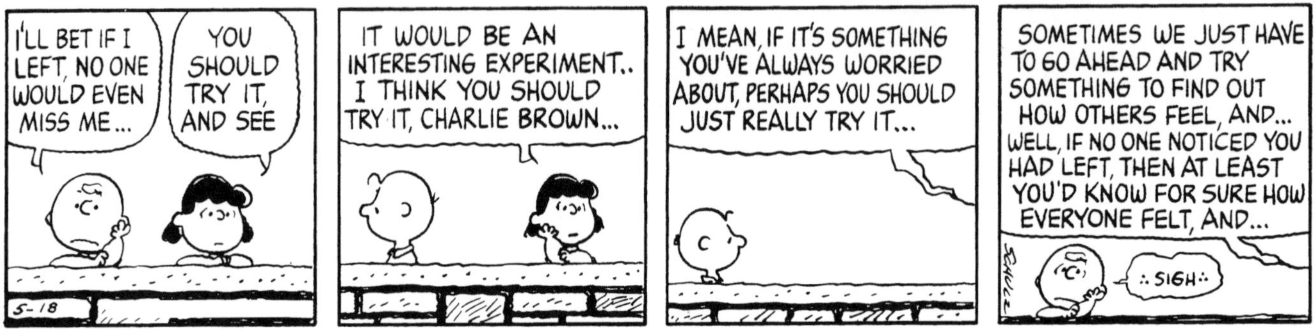
I'LL BET IF I LEFT, NO ONE WOULD EVEN MISS ME...
YOU SHOULD TRY IT, AND SEE
5-18
IT WOULD BE AN INTERESTING EXPERIMENT.. I THINK YOU SHOULD TRY IT, CHARLIE BROWN...
I MEAN, IF IT'S SOMETHING YOU'VE ALWAYS WORRIED ABOUT, PERHAPS YOU SHOULD JUST REALLY TRY IT...
SOMETIMES WE JUST HAVE TO GO AHEAD AND TRY SOMETHING TO FIND OUT HOW OTHERS FEEL, AND... WELL, IF NO ONE NOTICED YOU HAD LEFT, THEN AT LEAST YOU'D KNOW FOR SURE HOW EVERYONE FELT, AND...
SIGH

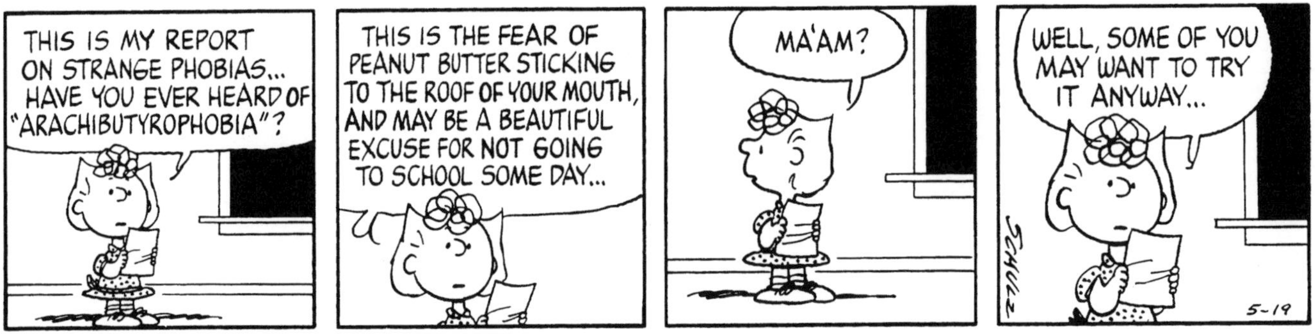
THIS IS MY REPORT ON STRANGE PHOBIAS... HAVE YOU EVER HEARD OF "ARACHIBUTYROPHOBIA"?
THIS IS THE FEAR OF PEANUT BUTTER STICKING TO THE ROOF OF YOUR MOUTH, AND MAY BE A BEAUTIFUL EXCUSE FOR NOT GOING TO SCHOOL SOME DAY...
MA'AM?
WELL, SOME OF YOU MAY WANT TO TRY IT ANYWAY...
5-19

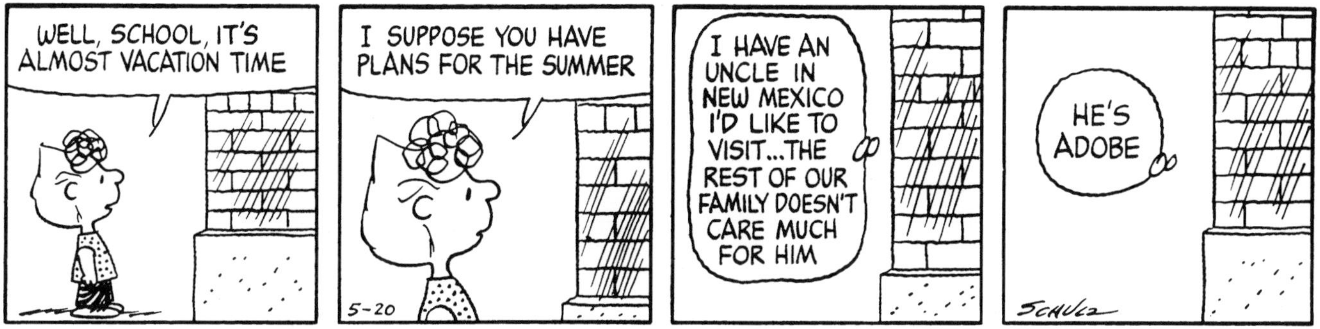
WELL, SCHOOL, IT'S ALMOST VACATION TIME
I SUPPOSE YOU HAVE PLANS FOR THE SUMMER
5-20
I HAVE AN UNCLE IN NEW MEXICO I'D LIKE TO VISIT...THE REST OF OUR FAMILY DOESN'T CARE MUCH FOR HIM
HE'S ADOBE
SCHULZ

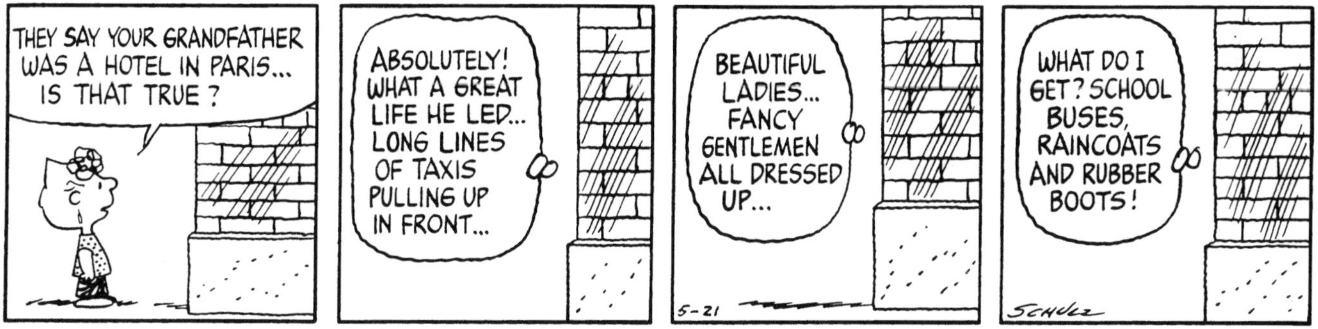
THEY SAY YOUR GRANDFATHER WAS A HOTEL IN PARIS... IS THAT TRUE ?
ABSOLUTELY! WHAT A GREAT LIFE HE LED... LONG LINES OF TAXIS PULLING UP IN FRONT...
BEAUTIFUL LADIES... FANCY GENTLEMEN ALL DRESSED UP...
5-21
WHAT DO I GET? SCHOOL BUSES, RAINCOATS AND RUBBER BOOTS!
SCHULZ

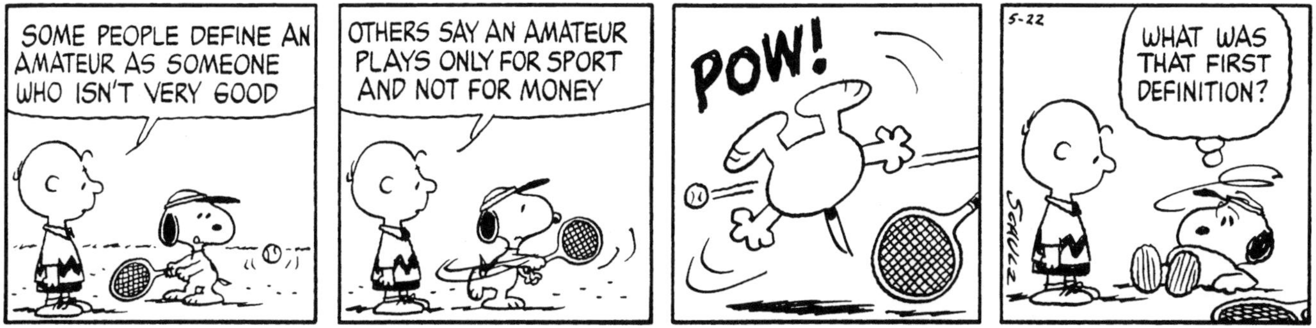
SOME PEOPLE DEFINE AN AMATEUR AS SOMEONE WHO ISN'T VERY GOOD
OTHERS SAY AN AMATEUR PLAYS ONLY FOR SPORT AND NOT FOR MONEY
POW!
5-22
WHAT WAS THAT FIRST DEFINITION?
SCHULZ

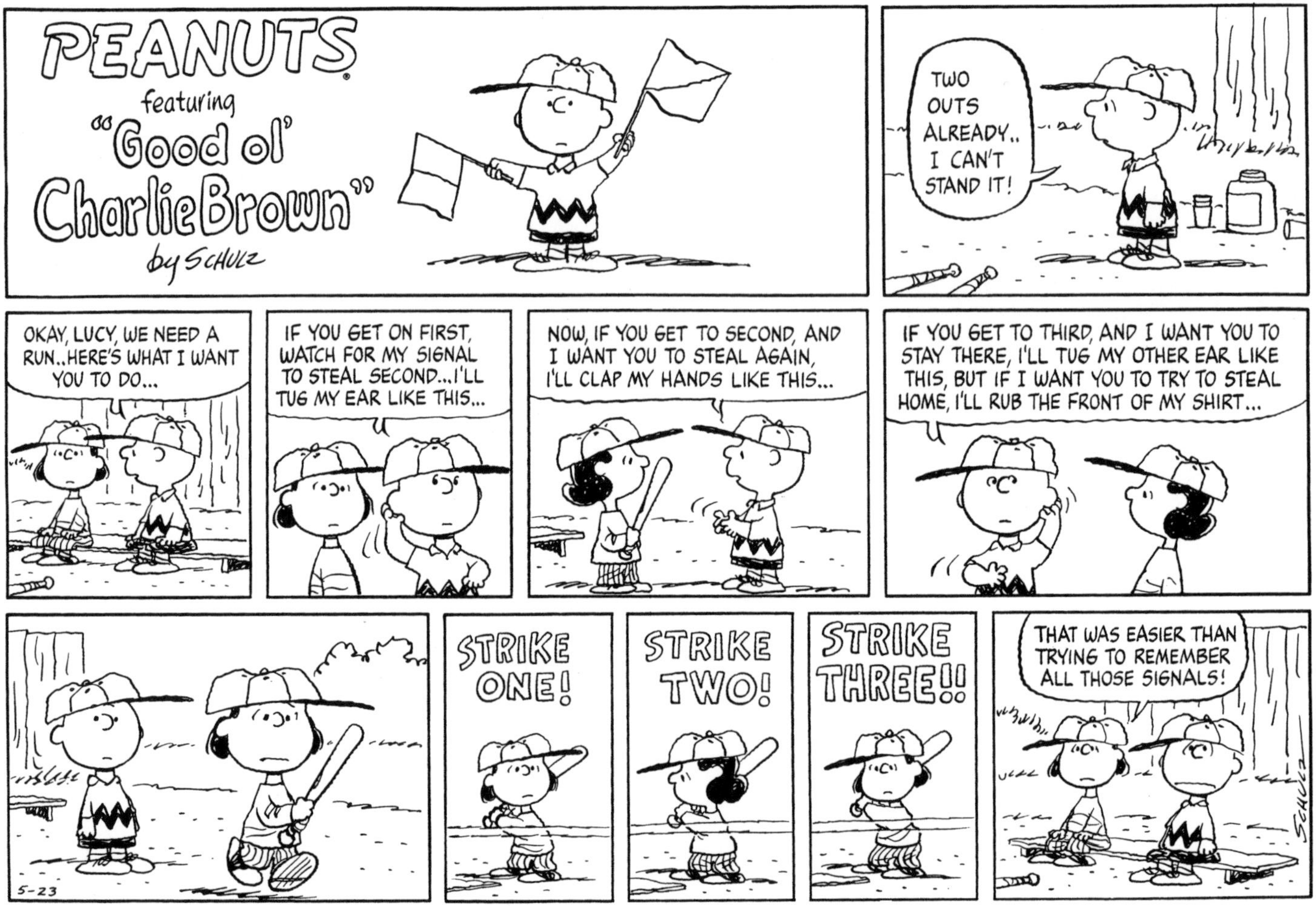
PEANUTS
featuring
"Good ol' CharlieBrown"
by SCHULZ
TWO OUTS ALREADY.. I CAN'T STAND IT!
OKAY, LUCY, WE NEED A RUN..HERE'S WHAT I WANT YOU TO DO...
IF YOU GET ON FIRST, WATCH FOR MY SIGNAL TO STEAL SECOND...I'LL TUG MY EAR LIKE THIS...
NOW, IF YOU GET TO SECOND, AND I WANT YOU TO STEAL AGAIN, I'LL CLAP MY HANDS LIKE THIS...
IF YOU GET TO THIRD, AND I WANT YOU TO STAY THERE, I'LL TUG MY OTHER EAR LIKE THIS, BUT IF I WANT YOU TO TRY TO STEAL HOME, I'LL RUB THE FRONT OF MY SHIRT...
5-23
STRIKE ONE!
STRIKE TWO!
STRIKE THREE!!
THAT WAS EASIER THAN TRYING TO REMEMBER ALL THOSE SIGNALS!
SCHULZ

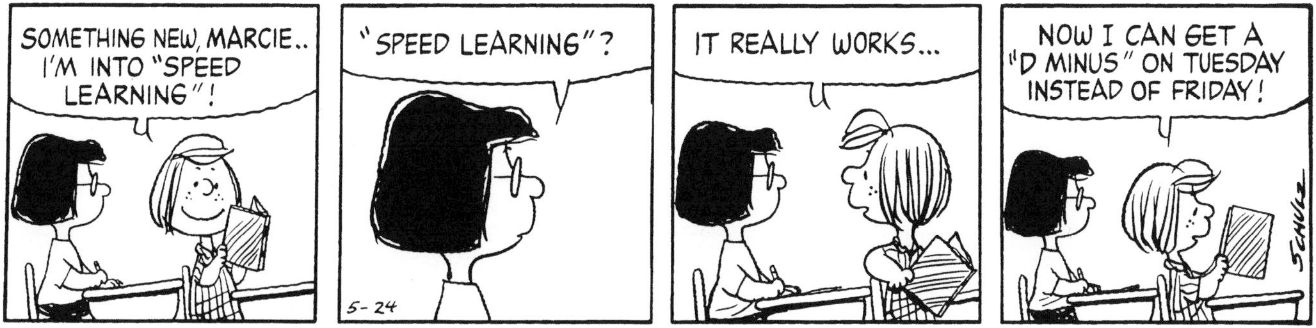
SOMETHING NEW, MARCIE.. I'M INTO "SPEED LEARNING"!
"SPEED LEARNING"?
5-24
IT REALLY WORKS...
NOW I CAN GET A "D MINUS" ON TUESDAY INSTEAD OF FRIDAY!
SCHULZ

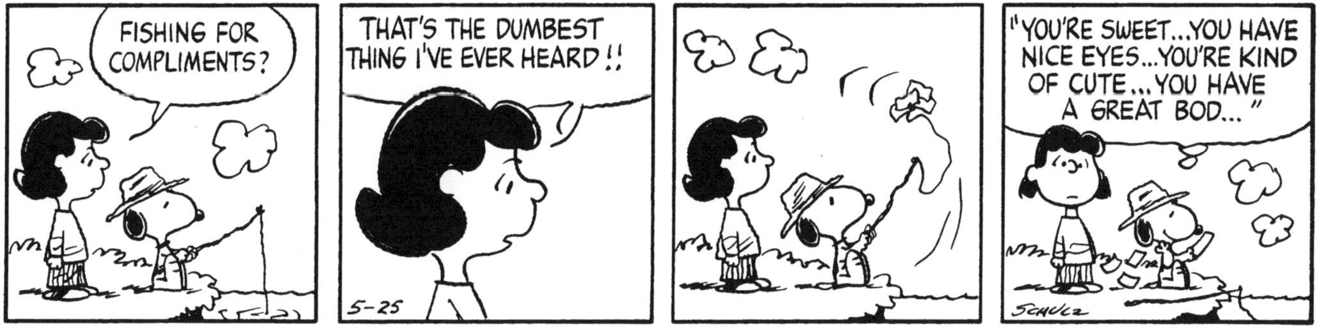
FISHING FOR COMPLIMENTS?
THAT'S THE DUMBEST THING I'VE EVER HEARD!!
5-25
"YOU'RE SWEET...YOU HAVE NICE EYES...YOU'RE KIND OF CUTE...YOU HAVE A GREAT BOD..."
SCHULZ

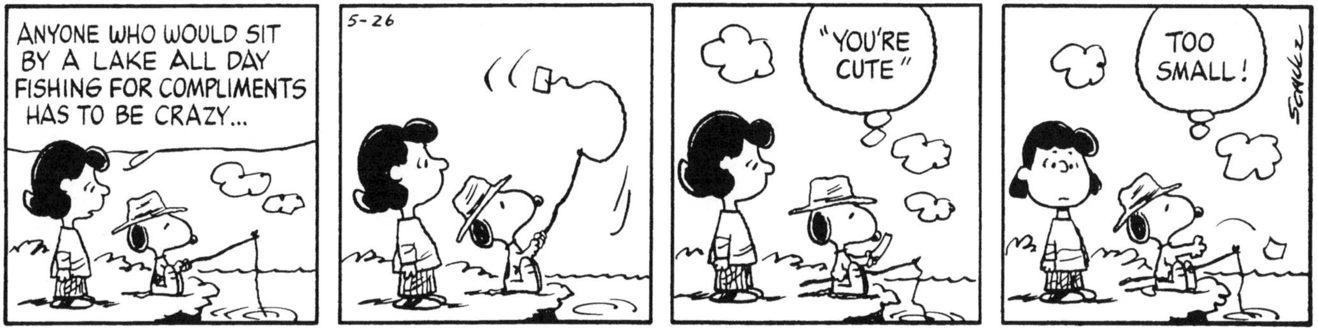
ANYONE WHO WOULD SIT BY A LAKE ALL DAY FISHING FOR COMPLIMENTS HAS TO BE CRAZY...
5-26
"YOU'RE CUTE"
TOO SMALL!
SCHULZ

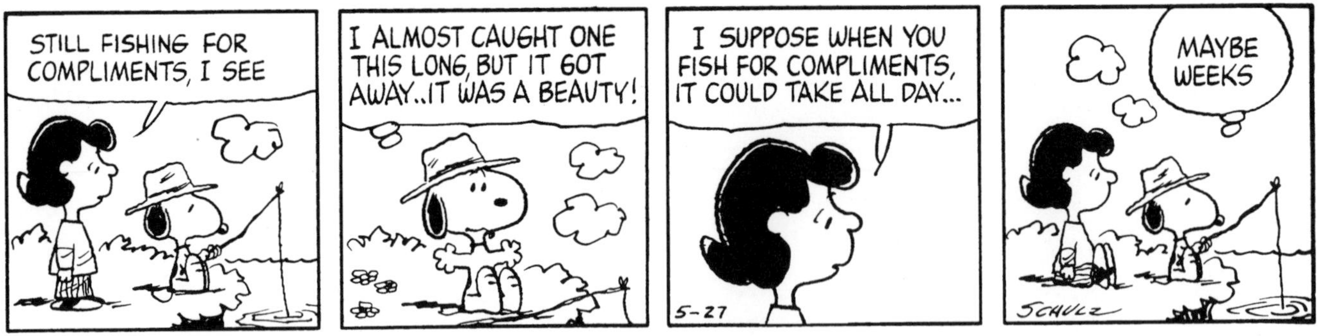
STILL FISHING FOR COMPLIMENTS, I SEE
I ALMOST CAUGHT ONE THIS LONG, BUT IT GOT AWAY..IT WAS A BEAUTY!
I SUPPOSE WHEN YOU FISH FOR COMPLIMENTS, IT COULD TAKE ALL DAY...
5-27
MAYBE WEEKS
SCHULZ

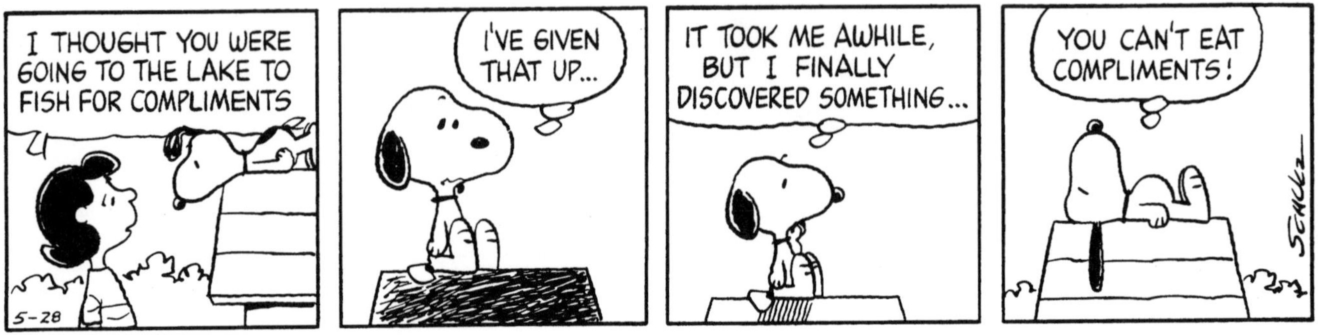
I THOUGHT YOU WERE GOING TO THE LAKE TO FISH FOR COMPLIMENTS
5-28
I'VE GIVEN THAT UP...
IT TOOK ME AWHILE, BUT I FINALLY DISCOVERED SOMETHING...
YOU CAN'T EAT COMPLIMENTS!
SCHULZ

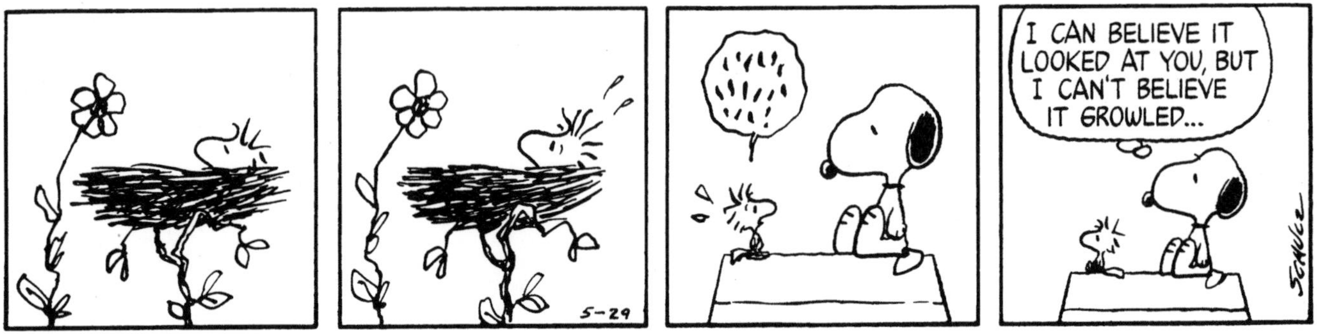
5-29
I CAN BELIEVE IT LOOKED AT YOU, BUT I CAN'T BELIEVE IT GROWLED...
SCHULZ

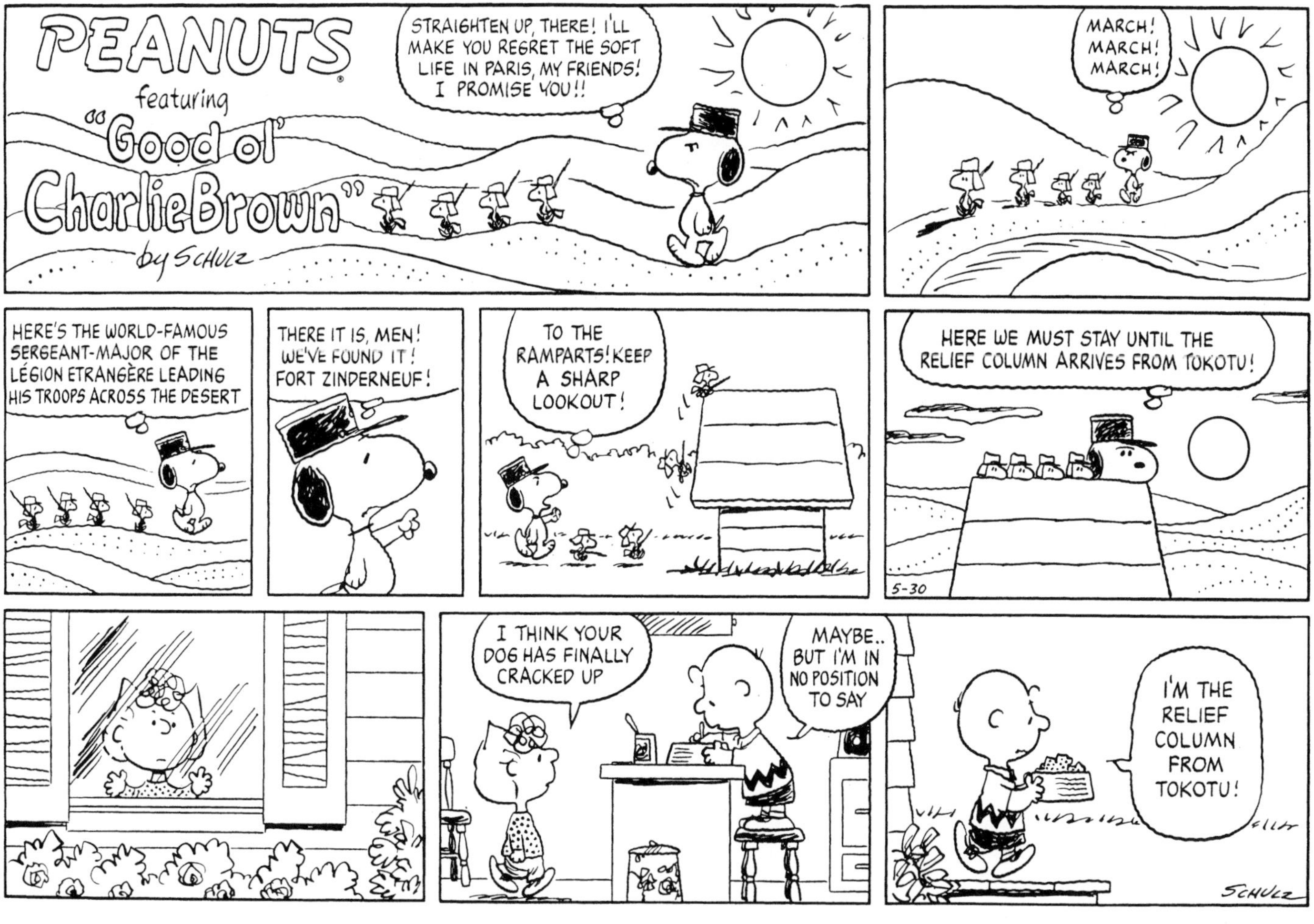
PEANUTS
featuring "Good ol' Charlie Brown"
by SCHULZ
STRAIGHTEN UP, THERE! I'LL MAKE YOU REGRET THE SOFT LIFE IN PARIS, MY FRIENDS! I PROMISE YOU!!
MARCH! MARCH! MARCH!
HERE'S THE WORLD-FAMOUS SERGEANT-MAJOR OF THE LÉGION ETRANGÈRE LEADING HIS TROOPS ACROSS THE DESERT
THERE IT IS, MEN! WE'VE FOUND IT! FORT ZINDERNEUF!
TO THE RAMPARTS! KEEP A SHARP LOOKOUT!
HERE WE MUST STAY UNTIL THE RELIEF COLUMN ARRIVES FROM TOKOTU!
5-30
I THINK YOUR DOG HAS FINALLY CRACKED UP
MAYBE.. BUT I'M IN NO POSITION TO SAY
I'M THE RELIEF COLUMN FROM TOKOTU!
SCHULZ

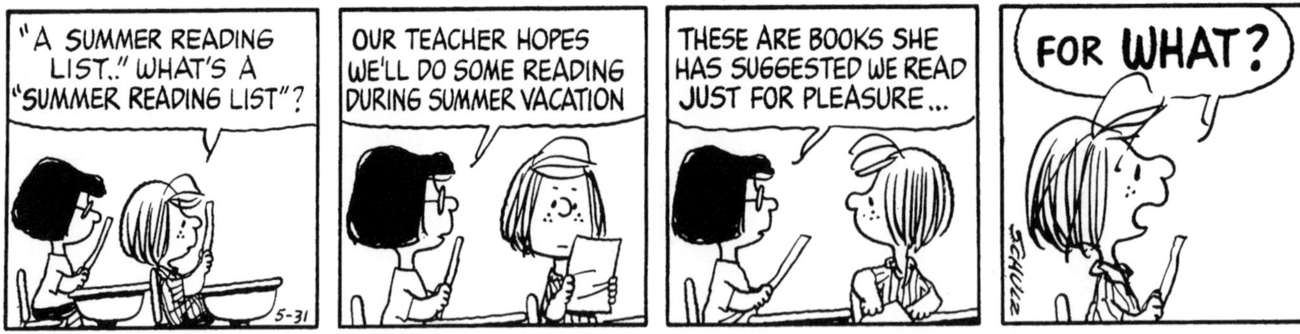
"A SUMMER READING LIST.." WHAT'S A "SUMMER READING LIST"?
5-31
OUR TEACHER HOPES WE'LL DO SOME READING DURING SUMMER VACATION
THESE ARE BOOKS SHE HAS SUGGESTED WE READ JUST FOR PLEASURE...
FOR WHAT?
SCHULZ

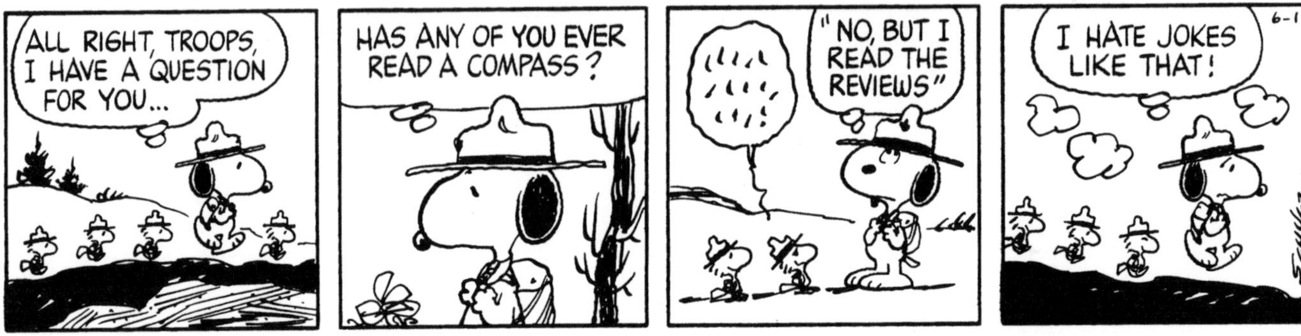
ALL RIGHT, TROOPS, I HAVE A QUESTION FOR YOU...
HAS ANY OF YOU EVER READ A COMPASS?
"NO, BUT I READ THE REVIEWS"
6-1
I HATE JOKES LIKE THAT!
SCHULZ

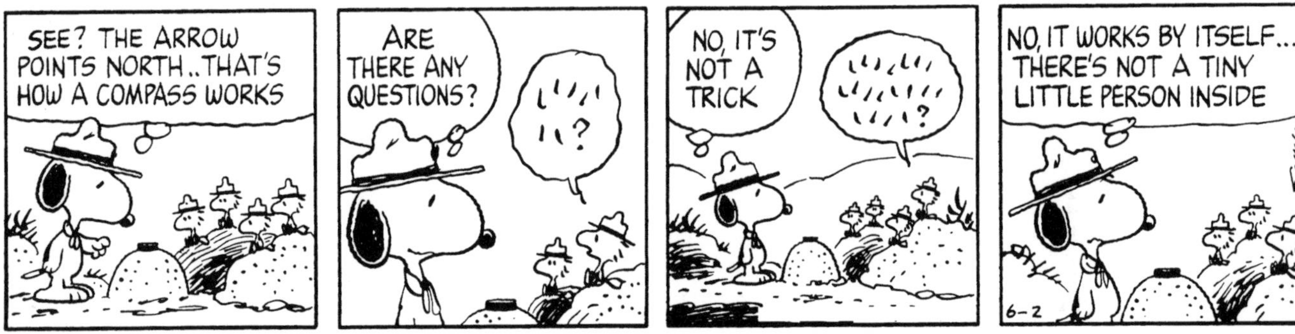
SEE? THE ARROW POINTS NORTH..THAT'S HOW A COMPASS WORKS
ARE THERE ANY QUESTIONS?
?
NO, IT'S NOT A TRICK
?
NO, IT WORKS BY ITSELF... THERE'S NOT A TINY LITTLE PERSON INSIDE
SCHULZ
6-2

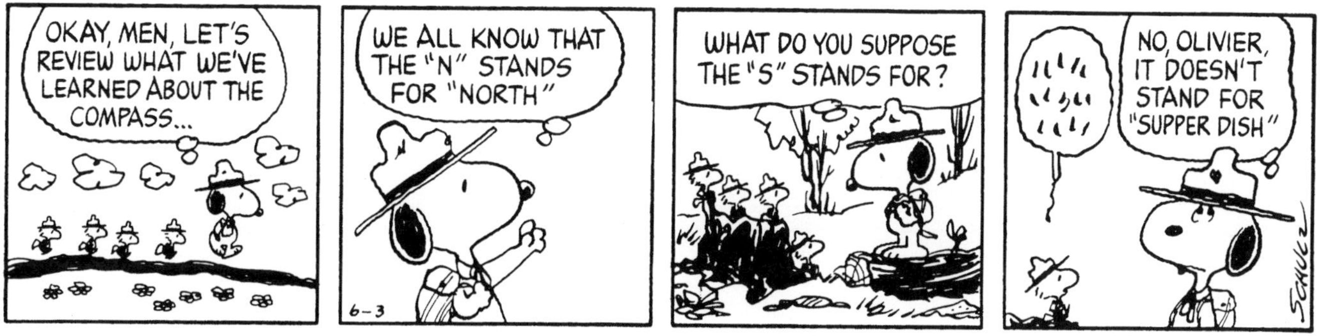
OKAY, MEN, LET'S REVIEW WHAT WE'VE LEARNED ABOUT THE COMPASS...
WE ALL KNOW THAT THE "N" STANDS FOR "NORTH"
6-3
WHAT DO YOU SUPPOSE THE "S" STANDS FOR?
NO, OLIVIER, IT DOESN'T STAND FOR "SUPPER DISH"
SCHULZ

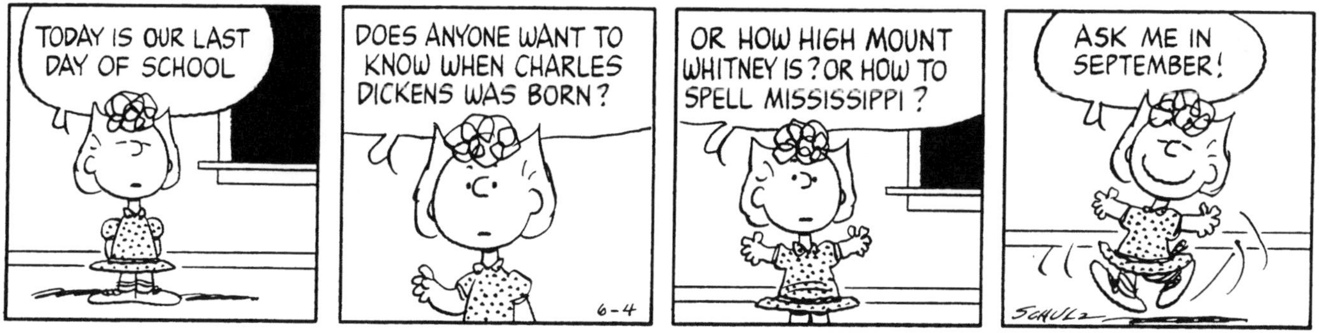
TODAY IS OUR LAST DAY OF SCHOOL
DOES ANYONE WANT TO KNOW WHEN CHARLES DICKENS WAS BORN?
6-4
OR HOW HIGH MOUNT WHITNEY IS? OR HOW TO SPELL MISSISSIPPI?
ASK ME IN SEPTEMBER!
SCHULZ

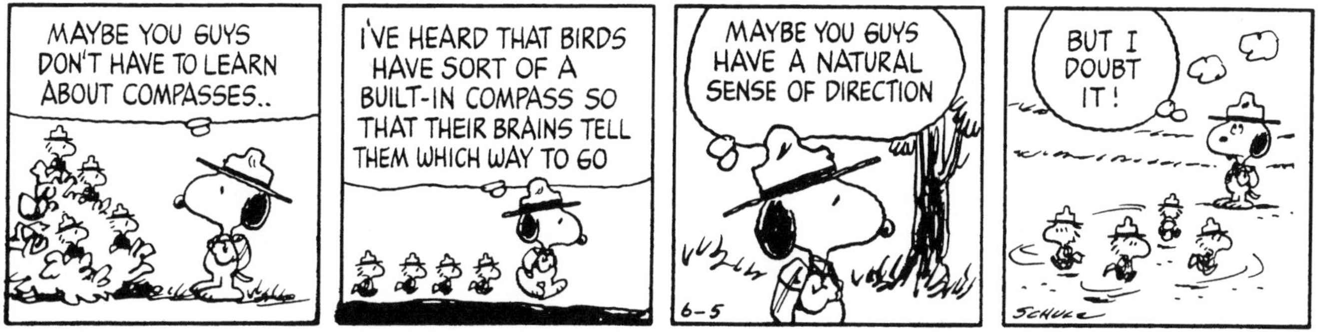
MAYBE YOU GUYS DON'T HAVE TO LEARN ABOUT COMPASSES..
I'VE HEARD THAT BIRDS HAVE SORT OF A BUILT-IN COMPASS SO THAT THEIR BRAINS TELL THEM WHICH WAY TO GO
MAYBE YOU GUYS HAVE A NATURAL SENSE OF DIRECTION
6-5
BUT I DOUBT IT!
SCHULZ

Peanuts featuring "Good ol' CharlieBrown" by Schulz

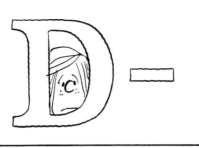

GO AHEAD, SIR..IT CAN'T HURT TO ASK...

MA'AM, ABOUT THIS "D MINUS" ON MY REPORT CARD...

6-6

"D" IS CERTAINLY A WONDERFUL LETTER.. IT'S PROBABLY ONE OF THE MOST IMPORTANT LETTERS IN OUR ALPHABET..BY ITSELF, IT HAS DIGNITY...

WHEN YOU PUT A "MINUS" IN FRONT OF IT, HOWEVER, IT LOSES THAT DIGNITY...IT APPEARS DRAINED..

PUT A "PLUS" IN FRONT OF THAT "D," MA'AM, AND IT CHANGES COMPLETELY! YOU'VE PLACED A SWORD IN ITS HAND THAT GIVES IT POWER AND STRENGTH!!!

I SEE...NO, THAT'S ALL RIGHT.. I UNDERSTAND...

SHE SAID SHE COULDN'T CHANGE MY GRADE...

BUT SHE SAID IF SHE'S EVER ON TRIAL FOR HER LIFE, SHE'D WANT ME FOR HER ATTORNEY...

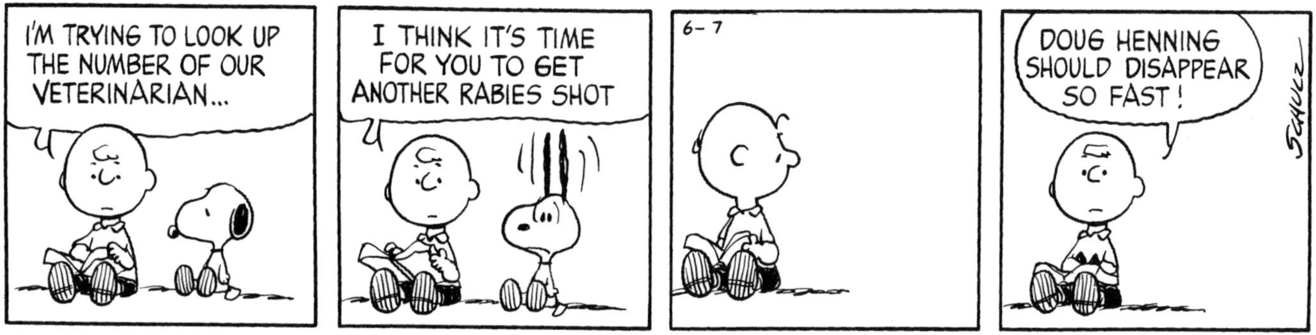
I'M TRYING TO LOOK UP THE NUMBER OF OUR VETERINARIAN...
I THINK IT'S TIME FOR YOU TO GET ANOTHER RABIES SHOT
DOUG HENNING SHOULD DISAPPEAR SO FAST!

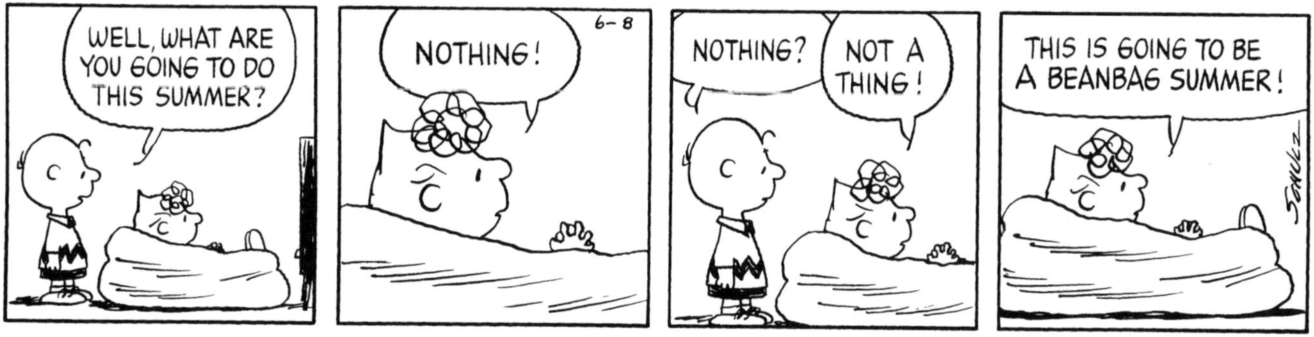
WELL, WHAT ARE YOU GOING TO DO THIS SUMMER?
NOTHING!
NOTHING?
NOT A THING!
THIS IS GOING TO BE A BEANBAG SUMMER!

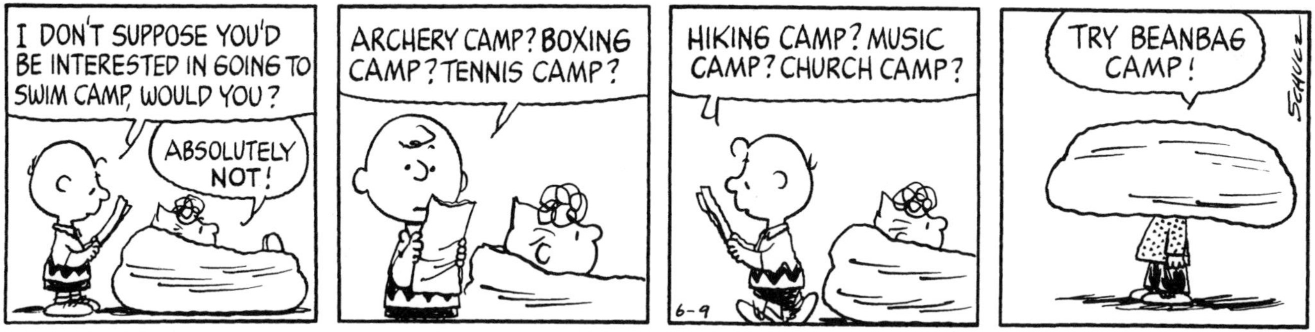
I DON'T SUPPOSE YOU'D BE INTERESTED IN GOING TO SWIM CAMP, WOULD YOU?
ABSOLUTELY NOT!
ARCHERY CAMP? BOXING CAMP? TENNIS CAMP?
HIKING CAMP? MUSIC CAMP? CHURCH CAMP?
TRY BEANBAG CAMP!

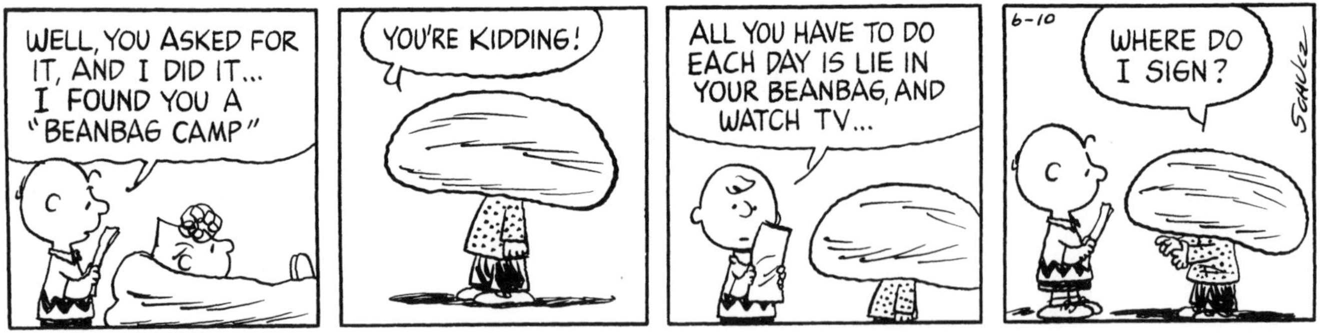
WELL, YOU ASKED FOR IT, AND I DID IT... I FOUND YOU A "BEANBAG CAMP"
YOU'RE KIDDING!
ALL YOU HAVE TO DO EACH DAY IS LIE IN YOUR BEANBAG, AND WATCH TV...
6-10
WHERE DO I SIGN?
SCHULZ

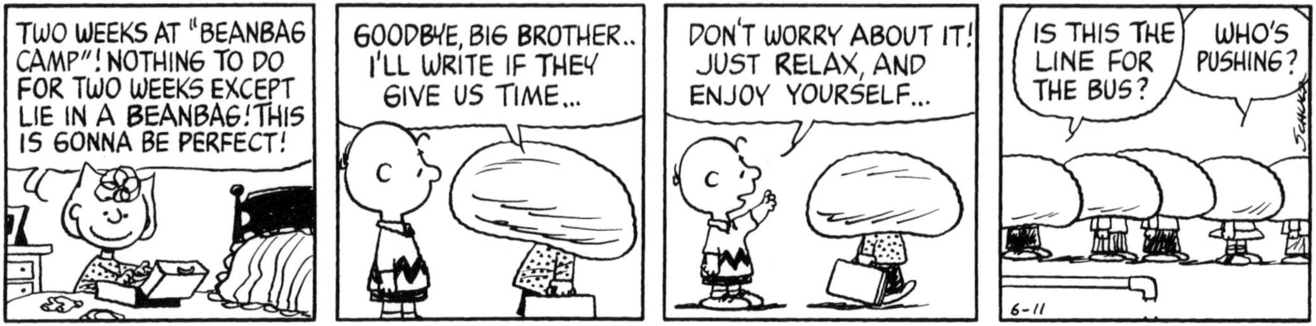
TWO WEEKS AT "BEANBAG CAMP"! NOTHING TO DO FOR TWO WEEKS EXCEPT LIE IN A BEANBAG! THIS IS GONNA BE PERFECT!
GOODBYE, BIG BROTHER.. I'LL WRITE IF THEY GIVE US TIME...
DON'T WORRY ABOUT IT! JUST RELAX, AND ENJOY YOURSELF...
IS THIS THE LINE FOR THE BUS?
WHO'S PUSHING?
SCHULZ
6-11

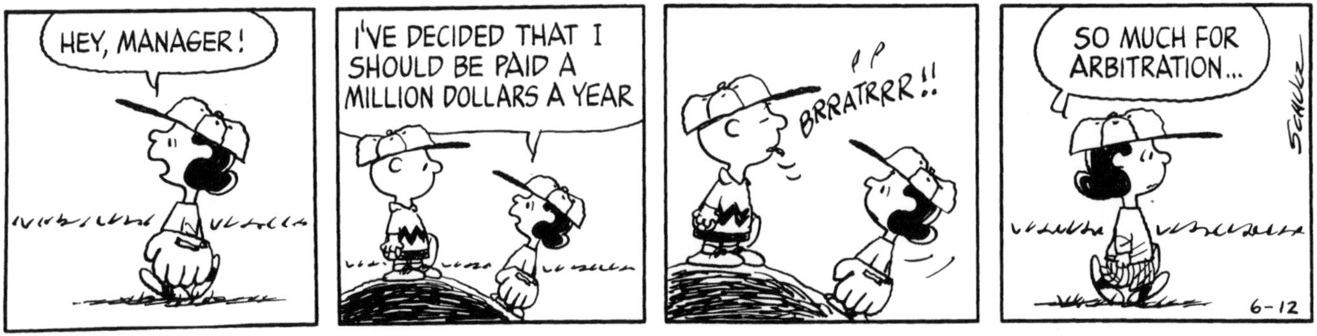
HEY, MANAGER!
I'VE DECIDED THAT I SHOULD BE PAID A MILLION DOLLARS A YEAR
BRRATRRR!!
SO MUCH FOR ARBITRATION...
SCHULZ
6-12

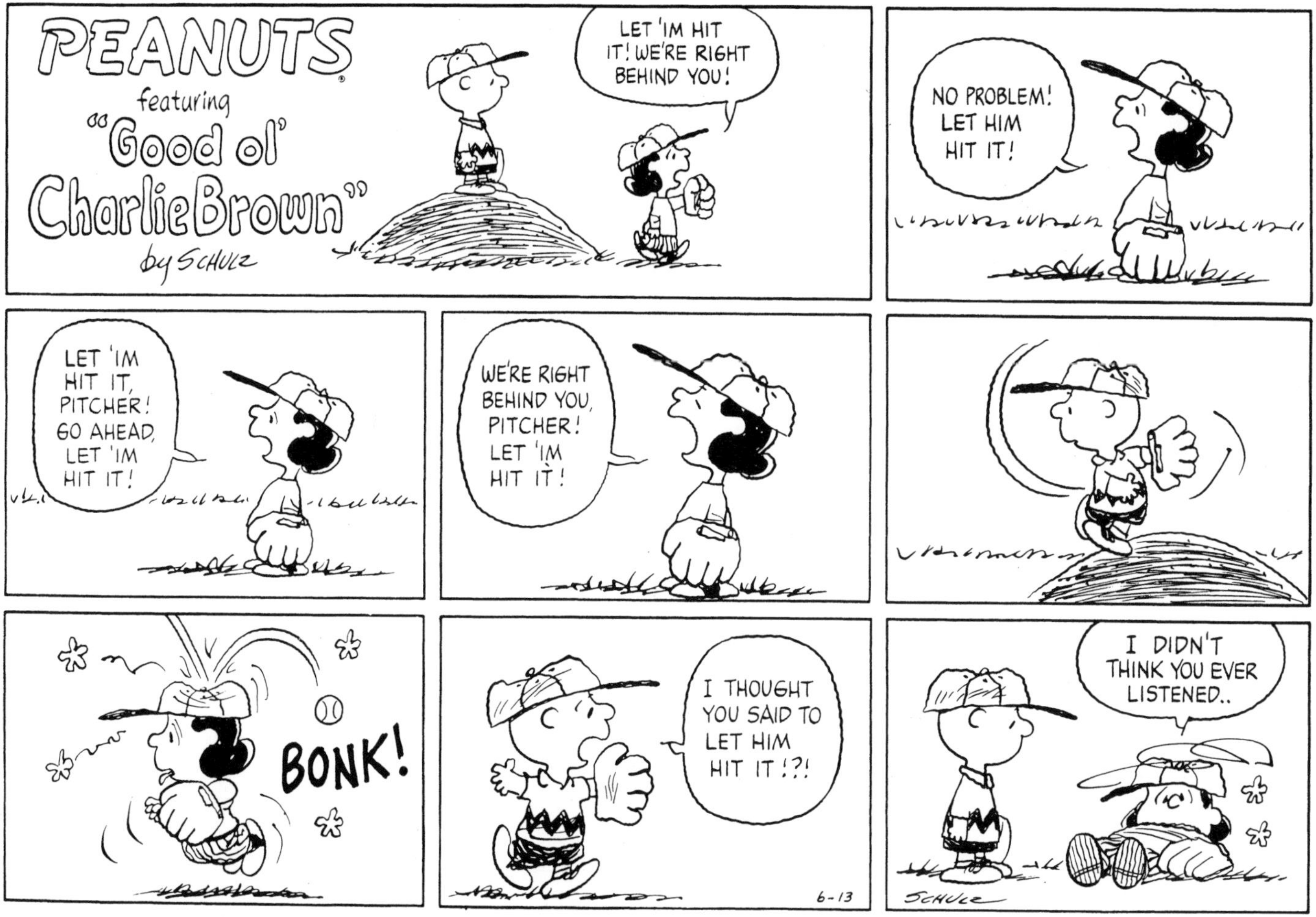
PEANUTS
featuring
"Good ol' Charlie Brown"
by SCHULZ
LET 'IM HIT IT! WE'RE RIGHT BEHIND YOU!
NO PROBLEM! LET HIM HIT IT!
LET 'IM HIT IT, PITCHER! GO AHEAD, LET 'IM HIT IT!
WE'RE RIGHT BEHIND YOU, PITCHER! LET 'IM HIT IT!
BONK!
I THOUGHT YOU SAID TO LET HIM HIT IT!?!
6-13
I DIDN'T THINK YOU EVER LISTENED..
SCHULZ

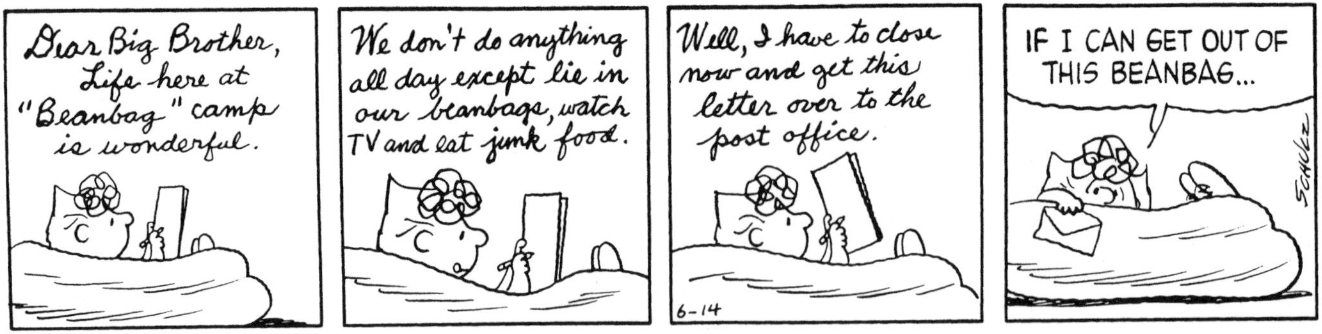
Dear Big Brother,
Life here at "Beanbag" camp is wonderful.
We don't do anything all day except lie in our beanbags, watch TV and eat junk food.
Well, I have to close now and get this letter over to the post office.
6-14
IF I CAN GET OUT OF THIS BEANBAG...
SCHULZ

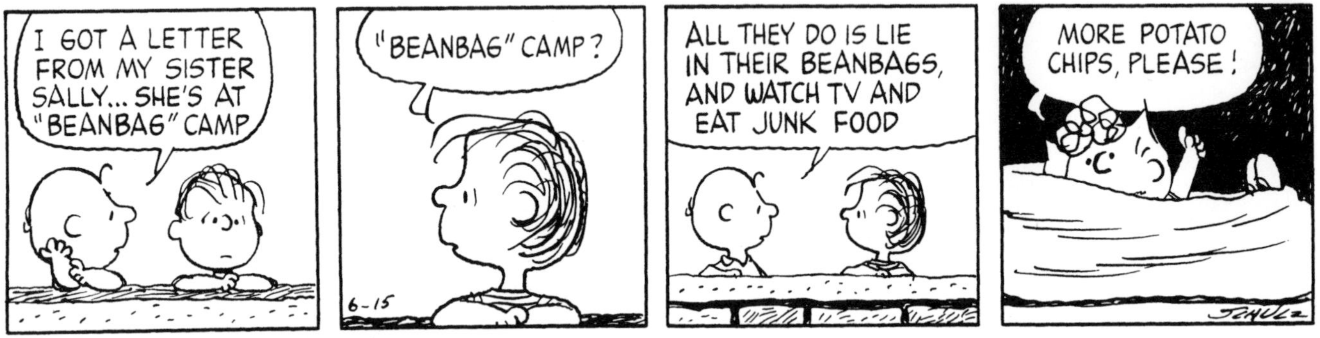
I GOT A LETTER FROM MY SISTER SALLY... SHE'S AT "BEANBAG" CAMP
"BEANBAG" CAMP?
6-15
ALL THEY DO IS LIE IN THEIR BEANBAGS, AND WATCH TV AND EAT JUNK FOOD
MORE POTATO CHIPS, PLEASE!
SCHULZ

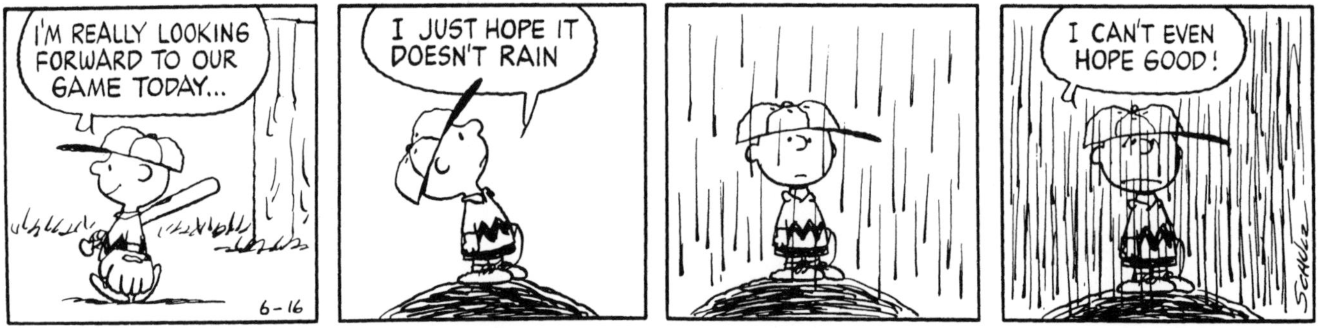
I'M REALLY LOOKING FORWARD TO OUR GAME TODAY...
6-16
I JUST HOPE IT DOESN'T RAIN
I CAN'T EVEN HOPE GOOD!
SCHULZ

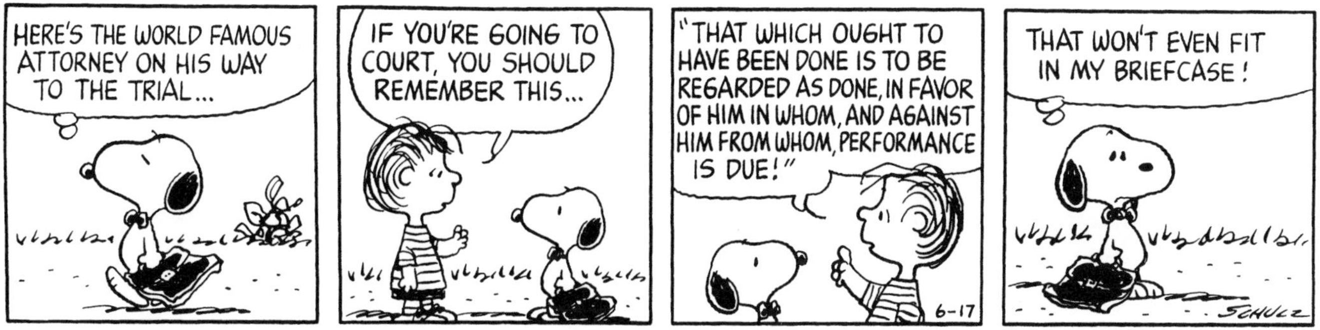
HERE'S THE WORLD FAMOUS ATTORNEY ON HIS WAY TO THE TRIAL...
IF YOU'RE GOING TO COURT, YOU SHOULD REMEMBER THIS...
"THAT WHICH OUGHT TO HAVE BEEN DONE IS TO BE REGARDED AS DONE, IN FAVOR OF HIM IN WHOM, AND AGAINST HIM FROM WHOM, PERFORMANCE IS DUE!"
6-17
THAT WON'T EVEN FIT IN MY BRIEFCASE!
SCHULZ

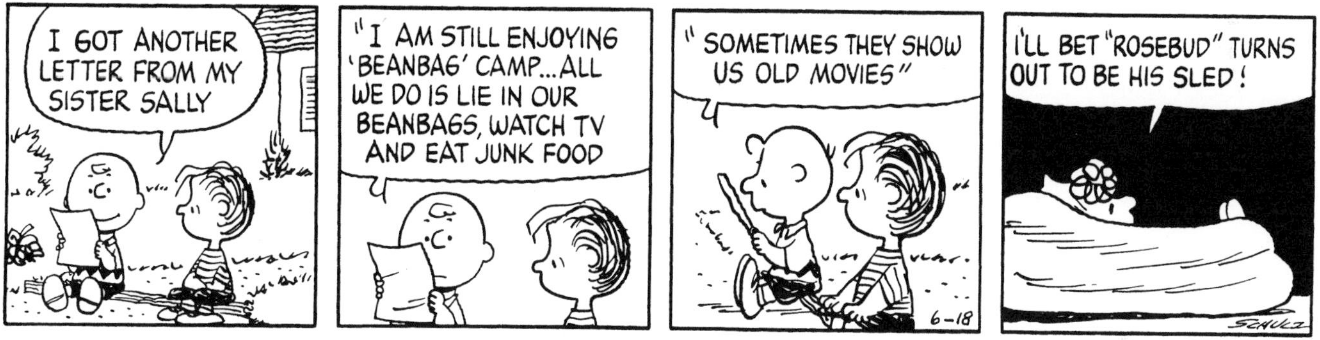
I GOT ANOTHER LETTER FROM MY SISTER SALLY
"I AM STILL ENJOYING 'BEANBAG' CAMP...ALL WE DO IS LIE IN OUR BEANBAGS, WATCH TV AND EAT JUNK FOOD
" SOMETIMES THEY SHOW US OLD MOVIES"
6-18
I'LL BET "ROSEBUD" TURNS OUT TO BE HIS SLED!
SCHULZ

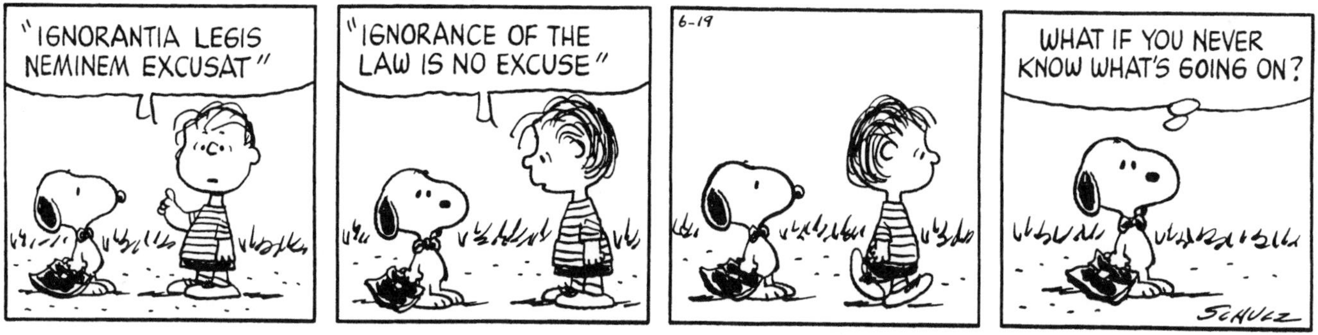
"IGNORANTIA LEGIS NEMINEM EXCUSAT"
"IGNORANCE OF THE LAW IS NO EXCUSE"
6-19
WHAT IF YOU NEVER KNOW WHAT'S GOING ON?
SCHULZ

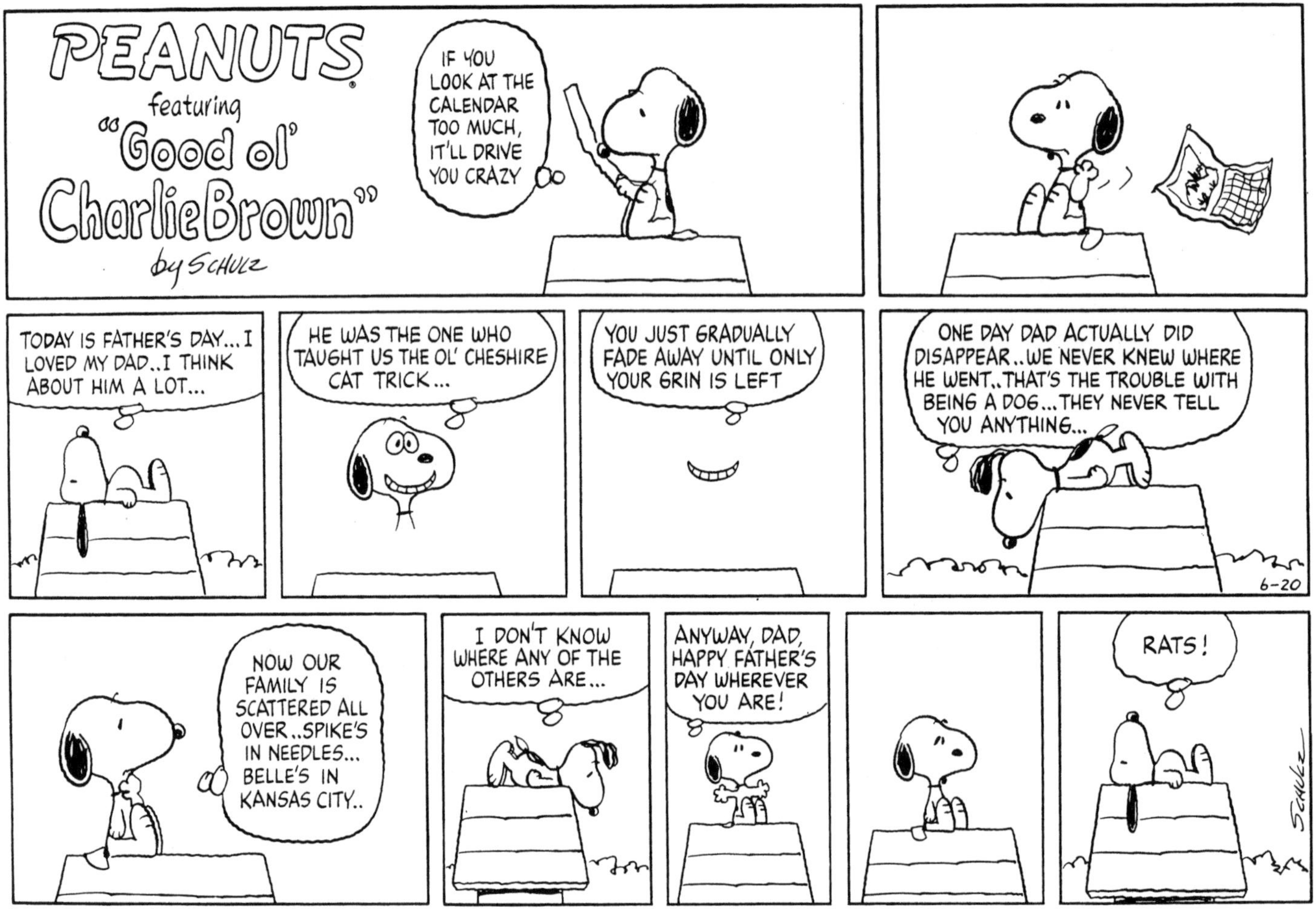
PEANUTS
featuring "Good ol' CharlieBrown"
by SCHULZ
IF YOU LOOK AT THE CALENDAR TOO MUCH, IT'LL DRIVE YOU CRAZY
TODAY IS FATHER'S DAY... I LOVED MY DAD.. I THINK ABOUT HIM A LOT...
HE WAS THE ONE WHO TAUGHT US THE OL' CHESHIRE CAT TRICK...
YOU JUST GRADUALLY FADE AWAY UNTIL ONLY YOUR GRIN IS LEFT
ONE DAY DAD ACTUALLY DID DISAPPEAR.. WE NEVER KNEW WHERE HE WENT.. THAT'S THE TROUBLE WITH BEING A DOG... THEY NEVER TELL YOU ANYTHING...
6-20
NOW OUR FAMILY IS SCATTERED ALL OVER.. SPIKE'S IN NEEDLES... BELLE'S IN KANSAS CITY..
I DON'T KNOW WHERE ANY OF THE OTHERS ARE...
ANYWAY, DAD, HAPPY FATHER'S DAY WHEREVER YOU ARE!
RATS!
SCHULZ

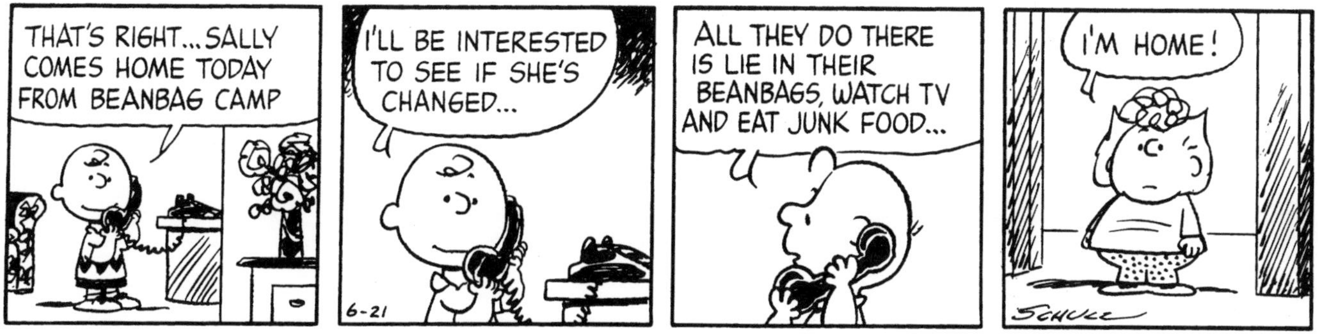
THAT'S RIGHT...SALLY COMES HOME TODAY FROM BEANBAG CAMP
I'LL BE INTERESTED TO SEE IF SHE'S CHANGED...
6-21
ALL THEY DO THERE IS LIE IN THEIR BEANBAGS, WATCH TV AND EAT JUNK FOOD...
I'M HOME!
SCHULZ

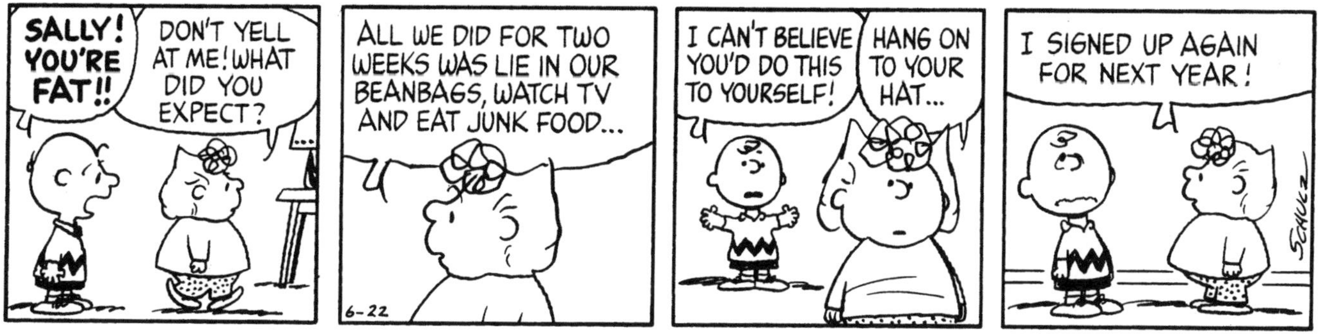
SALLY! YOU'RE FAT!!
DON'T YELL AT ME! WHAT DID YOU EXPECT?
ALL WE DID FOR TWO WEEKS WAS LIE IN OUR BEANBAGS, WATCH TV AND EAT JUNK FOOD...
6-22
I CAN'T BELIEVE YOU'D DO THIS TO YOURSELF!
HANG ON TO YOUR HAT...
I SIGNED UP AGAIN FOR NEXT YEAR!
SCHULZ

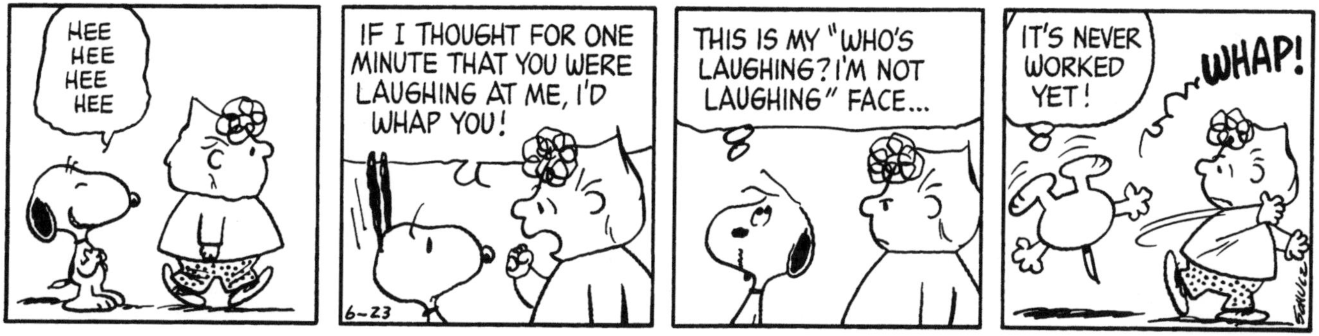
HEE HEE HEE HEE
IF I THOUGHT FOR ONE MINUTE THAT YOU WERE LAUGHING AT ME, I'D WHAP YOU!
6-23
THIS IS MY "WHO'S LAUGHING? I'M NOT LAUGHING" FACE...
IT'S NEVER WORKED YET!
WHAP!
SCHULZ

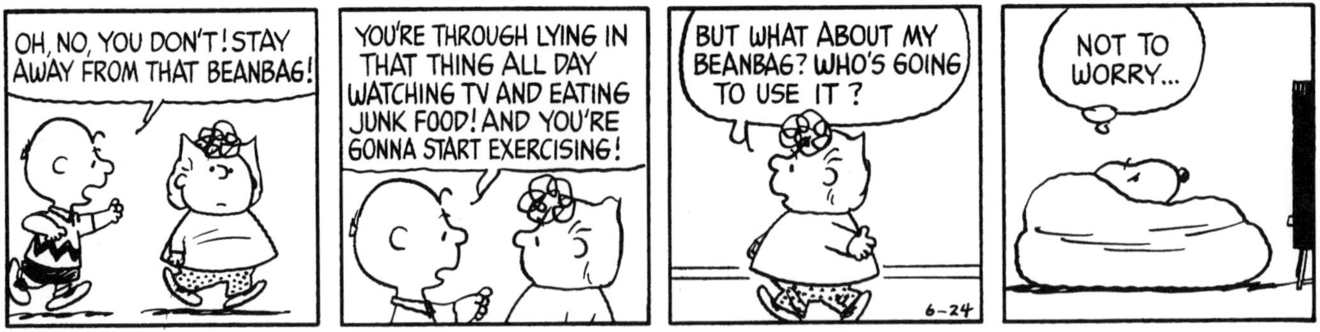
OH, NO, YOU DON'T! STAY AWAY FROM THAT BEANBAG!
YOU'RE THROUGH LYING IN THAT THING ALL DAY WATCHING TV AND EATING JUNK FOOD! AND YOU'RE GONNA START EXERCISING!
BUT WHAT ABOUT MY BEANBAG? WHO'S GOING TO USE IT ?
NOT TO WORRY...

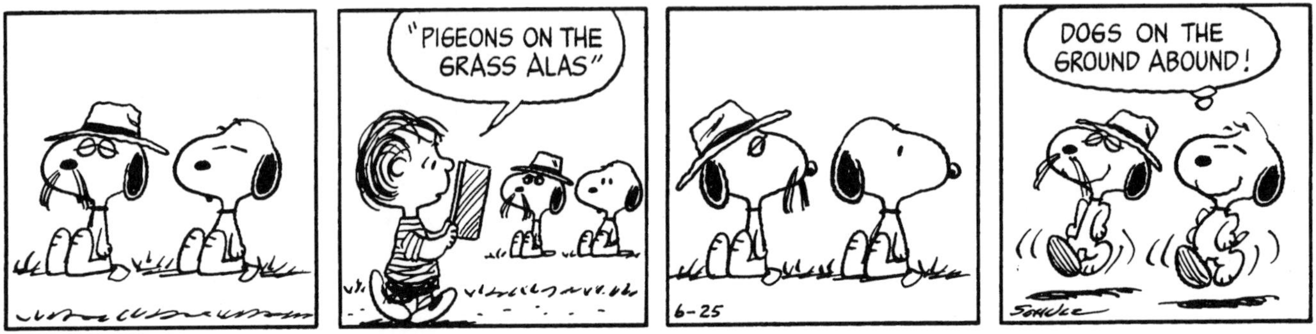
"PIGEONS ON THE GRASS ALAS"
DOGS ON THE GROUND ABOUND!

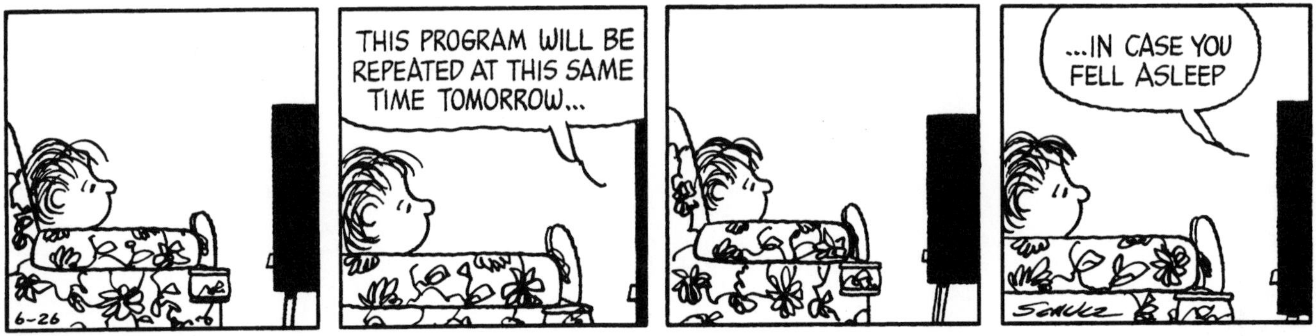
THIS PROGRAM WILL BE REPEATED AT THIS SAME TIME TOMORROW...
...IN CASE YOU FELL ASLEEP

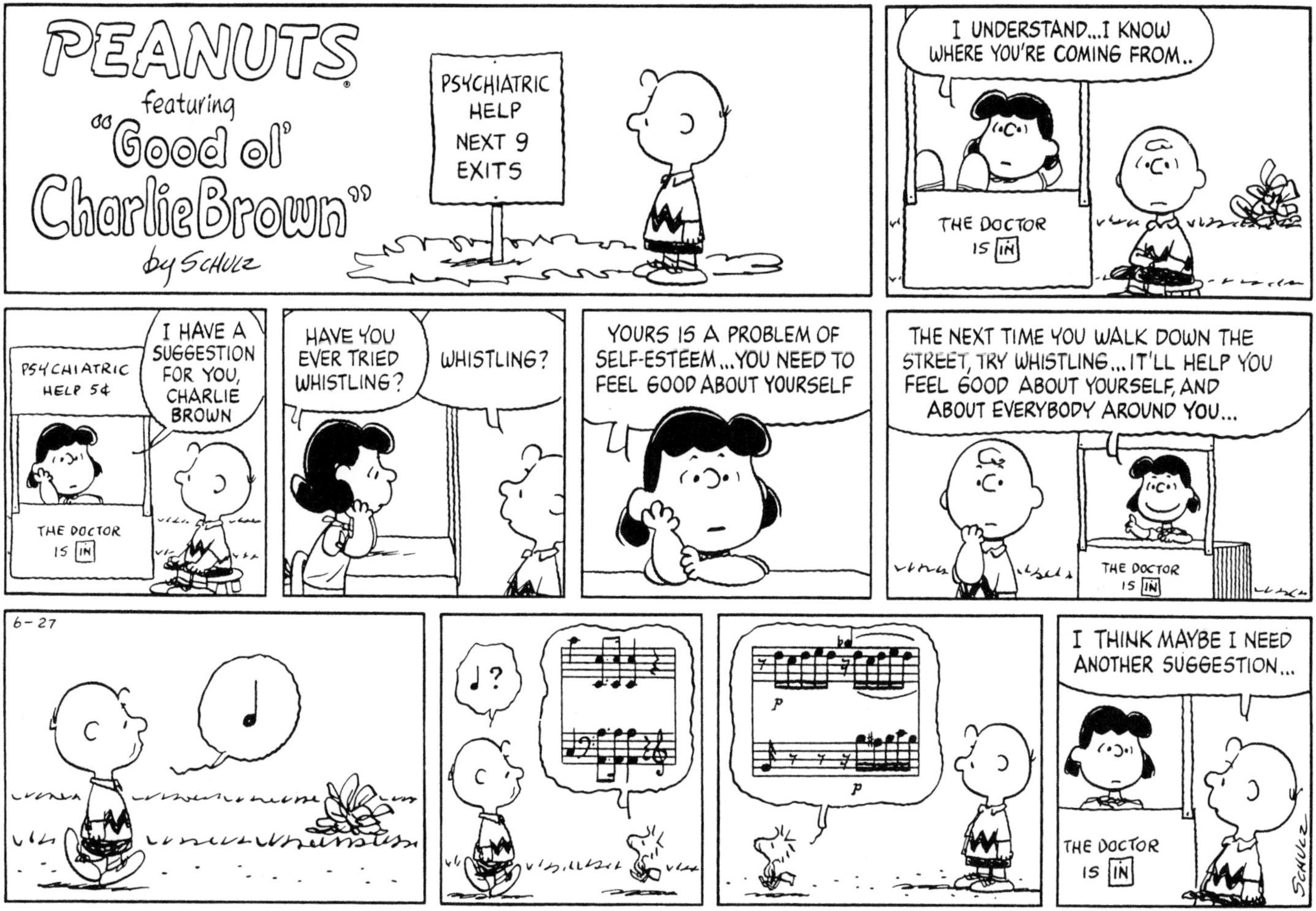
PEANUTS
featuring
"Good ol' Charlie Brown"
by SCHULZ
PSYCHIATRIC HELP NEXT 9 EXITS
I UNDERSTAND...I KNOW WHERE YOU'RE COMING FROM..
THE DOCTOR IS IN
PSYCHIATRIC HELP 5¢
I HAVE A SUGGESTION FOR YOU, CHARLIE BROWN
THE DOCTOR IS IN
HAVE YOU EVER TRIED WHISTLING?
WHISTLING?
YOURS IS A PROBLEM OF SELF-ESTEEM...YOU NEED TO FEEL GOOD ABOUT YOURSELF
THE NEXT TIME YOU WALK DOWN THE STREET, TRY WHISTLING... IT'LL HELP YOU FEEL GOOD ABOUT YOURSELF, AND ABOUT EVERYBODY AROUND YOU...
THE DOCTOR IS IN
6-27
?
p
p
I THINK MAYBE I NEED ANOTHER SUGGESTION...
THE DOCTOR IS IN
SCHULZ

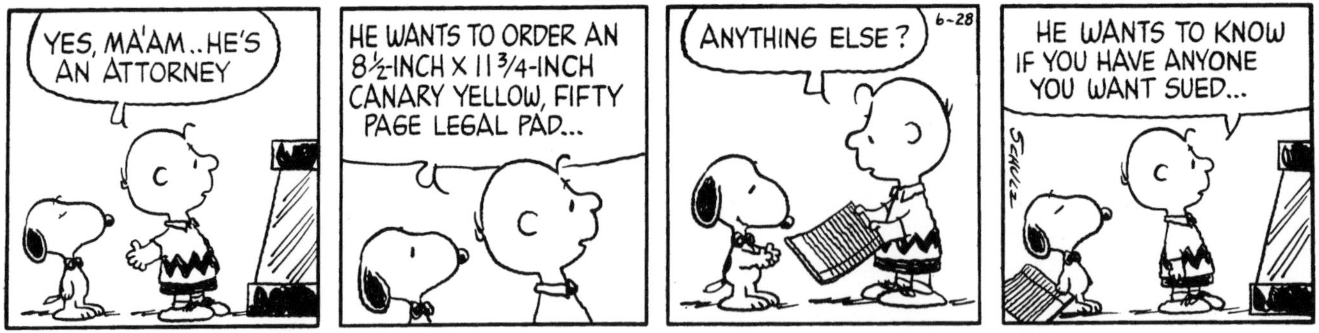
YES, MA'AM..HE'S AN ATTORNEY
HE WANTS TO ORDER AN 8½-INCH X 11¾-INCH CANARY YELLOW, FIFTY PAGE LEGAL PAD...
6-28
ANYTHING ELSE?
HE WANTS TO KNOW IF YOU HAVE ANYONE YOU WANT SUED...
SCHULZ

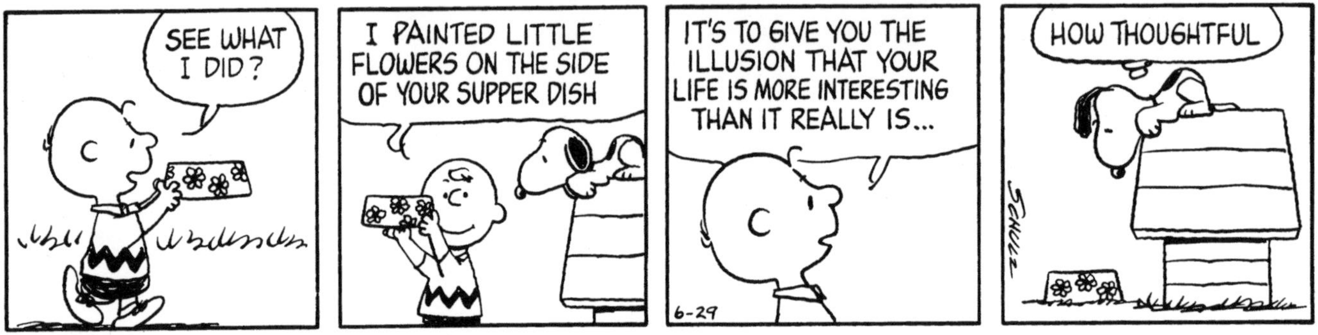
SEE WHAT I DID?
I PAINTED LITTLE FLOWERS ON THE SIDE OF YOUR SUPPER DISH
IT'S TO GIVE YOU THE ILLUSION THAT YOUR LIFE IS MORE INTERESTING THAN IT REALLY IS...
6-29
HOW THOUGHTFUL
SCHULZ

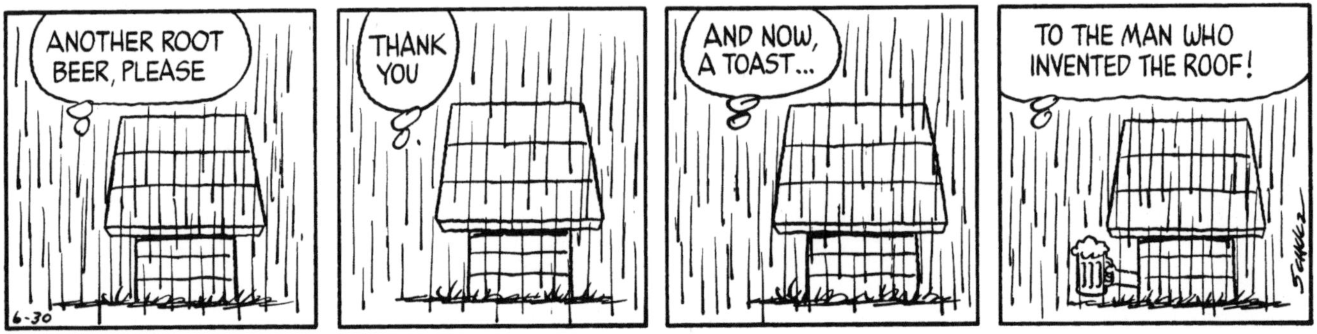
ANOTHER ROOT BEER, PLEASE
6-30
THANK YOU
AND NOW, A TOAST...
TO THE MAN WHO INVENTED THE ROOF!
SCHULZ

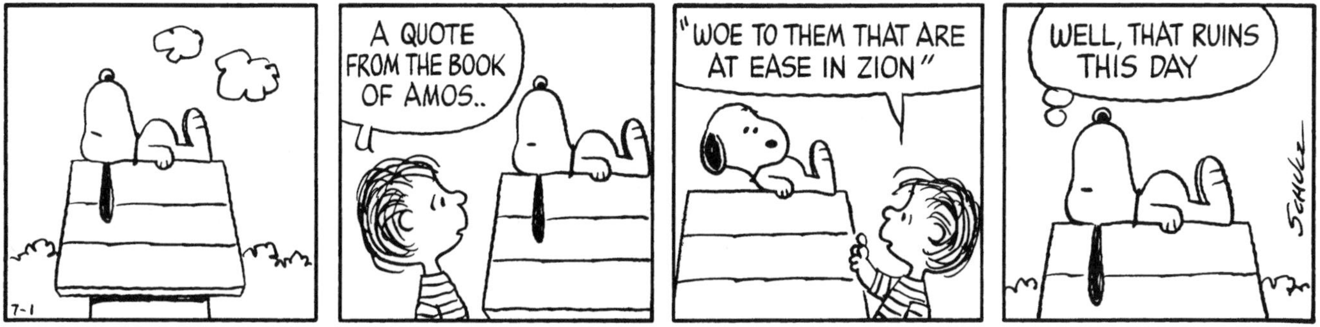
A QUOTE FROM THE BOOK OF AMOS..
"WOE TO THEM THAT ARE AT EASE IN ZION"
WELL, THAT RUINS THIS DAY

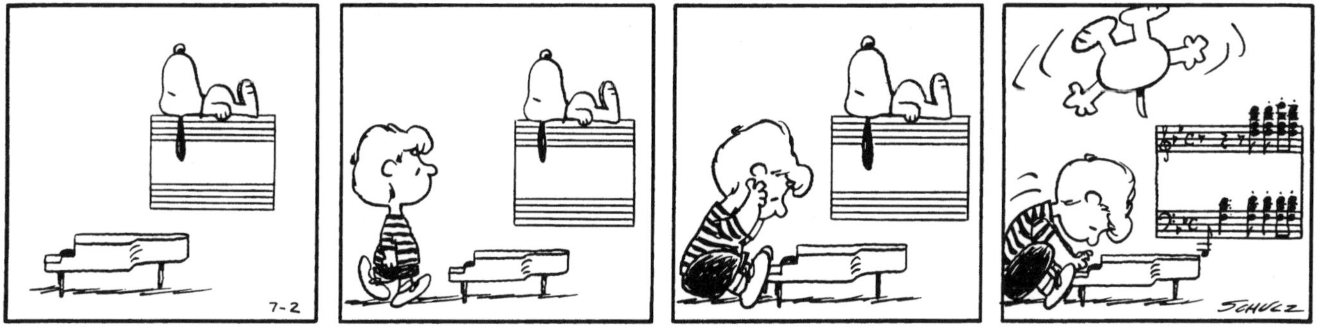

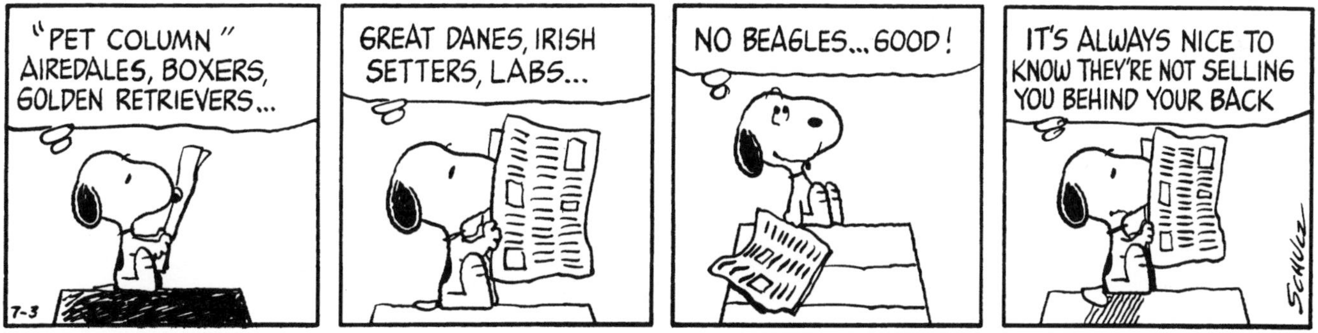
"PET COLUMN" AIREDALES, BOXERS, GOLDEN RETRIEVERS...
GREAT DANES, IRISH SETTERS, LABS...
NO BEAGLES... GOOD!
IT'S ALWAYS NICE TO KNOW THEY'RE NOT SELLING YOU BEHIND YOUR BACK

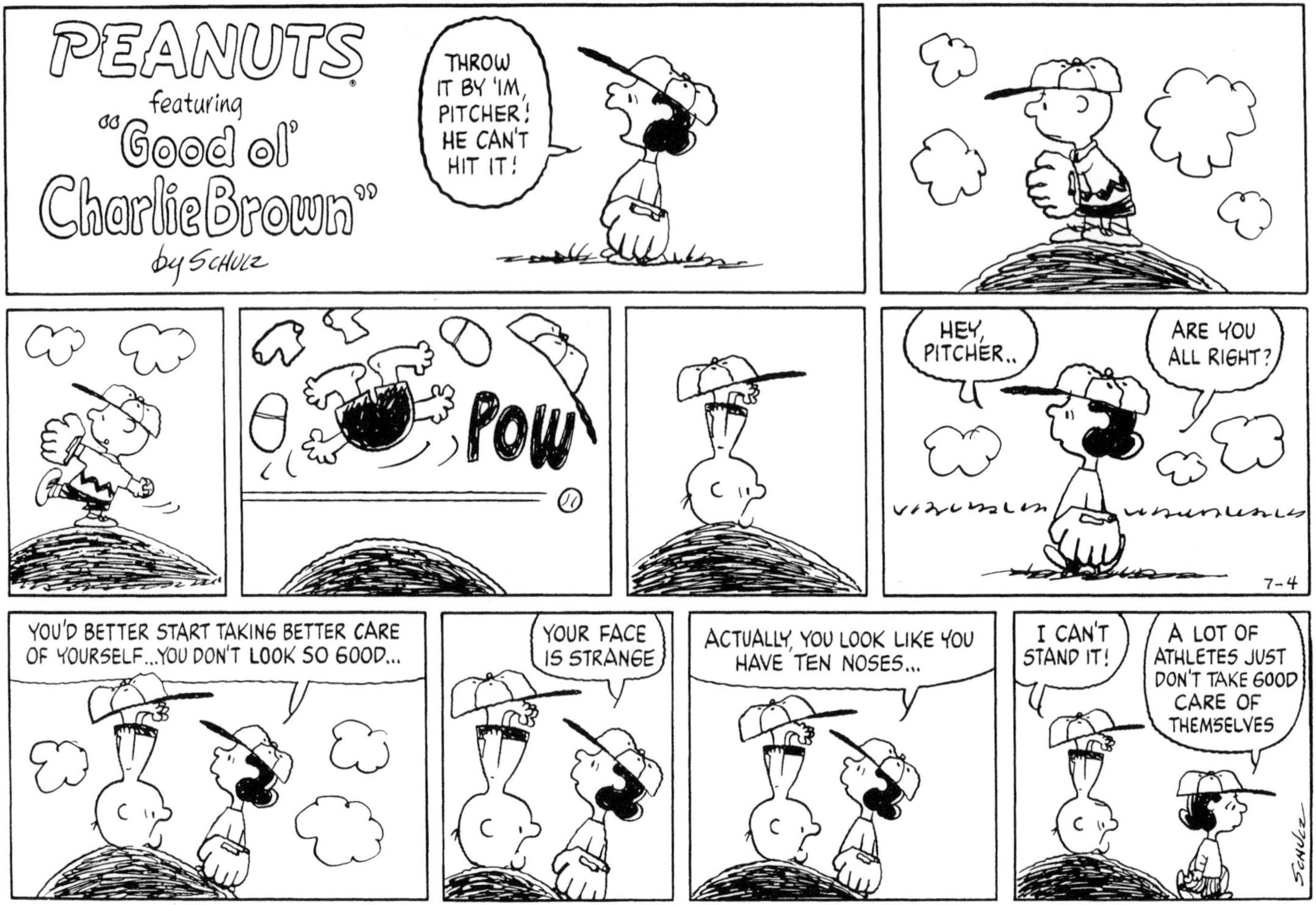
PEANUTS
featuring "Good ol' Charlie Brown"
by SCHULZ
THROW IT BY 'IM, PITCHER! HE CAN'T HIT IT!
POW
HEY, PITCHER..
ARE YOU ALL RIGHT?
7-4
YOU'D BETTER START TAKING BETTER CARE OF YOURSELF...YOU DON'T LOOK SO GOOD...
YOUR FACE IS STRANGE
ACTUALLY, YOU LOOK LIKE YOU HAVE TEN NOSES...
I CAN'T STAND IT!
A LOT OF ATHLETES JUST DON'T TAKE GOOD CARE OF THEMSELVES
SCHULZ

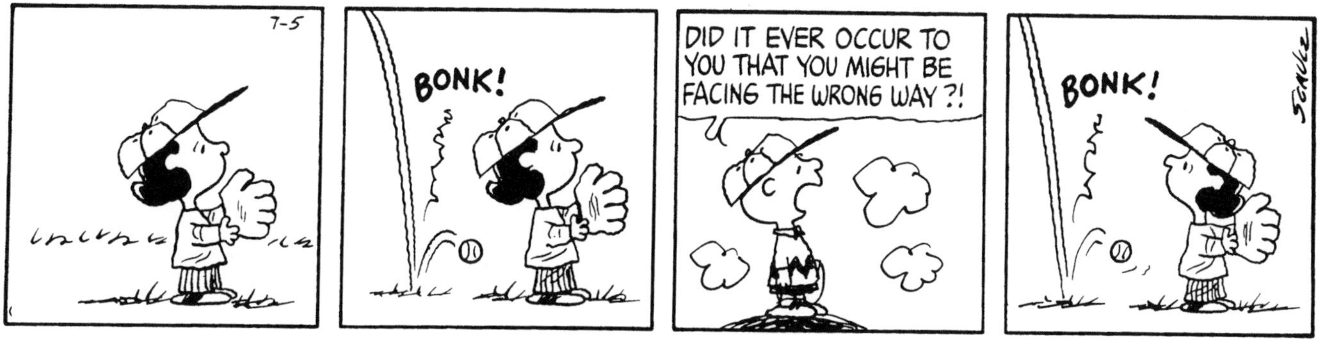
BONK!
DID IT EVER OCCUR TO YOU THAT YOU MIGHT BE FACING THE WRONG WAY ?!
BONK!

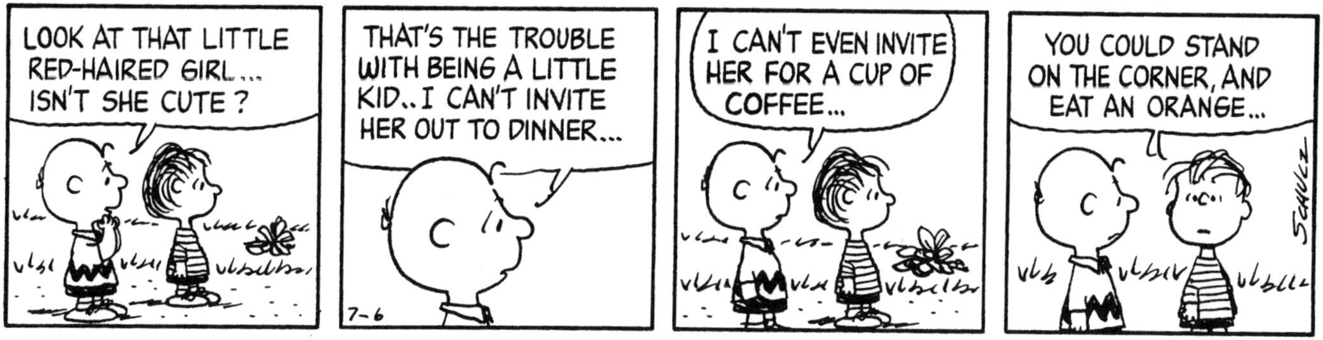
LOOK AT THAT LITTLE RED-HAIRED GIRL... ISN'T SHE CUTE ?
THAT'S THE TROUBLE WITH BEING A LITTLE KID.. I CAN'T INVITE HER OUT TO DINNER...
I CAN'T EVEN INVITE HER FOR A CUP OF COFFEE...
YOU COULD STAND ON THE CORNER, AND EAT AN ORANGE...

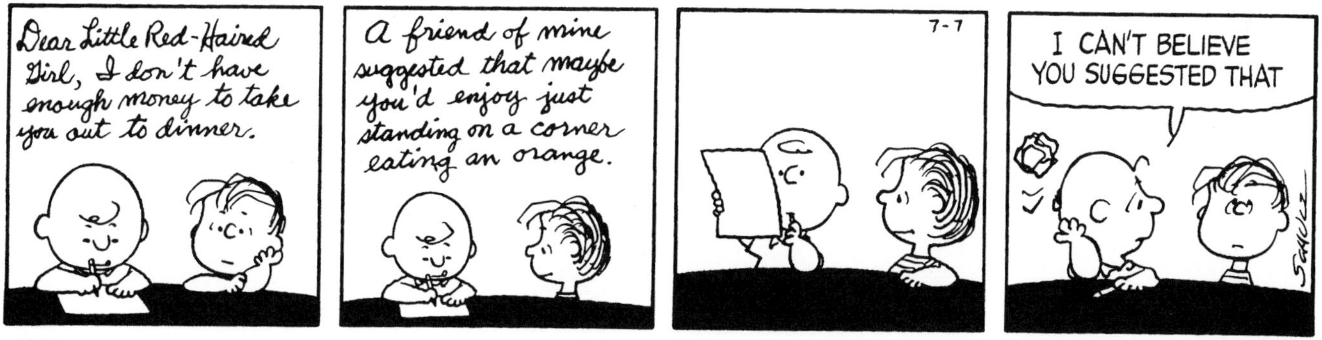
Dear Little Red-Haired Girl, I don't have enough money to take you out to dinner.
A friend of mine suggested that maybe you'd enjoy just standing on a corner eating an orange.
I CAN'T BELIEVE YOU SUGGESTED THAT

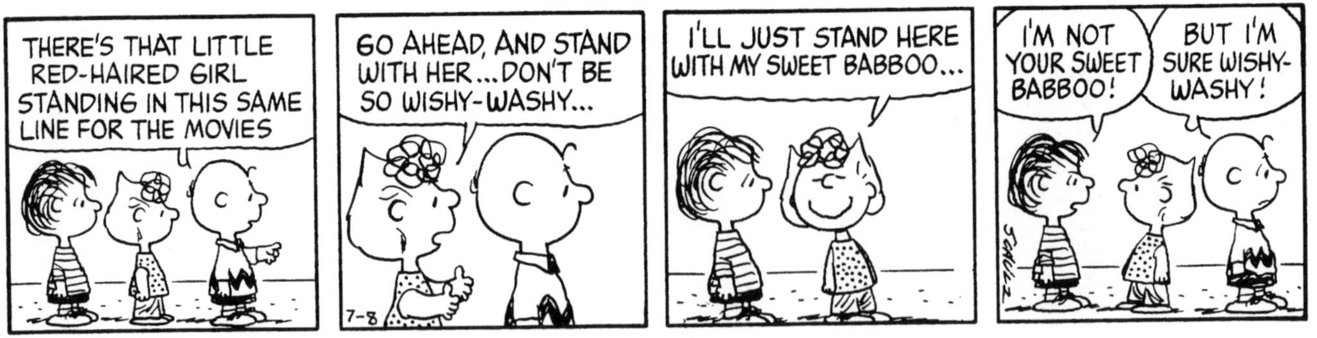
THERE'S THAT LITTLE RED-HAIRED GIRL STANDING IN THIS SAME LINE FOR THE MOVIES
GO AHEAD, AND STAND WITH HER...DON'T BE SO WISHY-WASHY...
7-8
I'LL JUST STAND HERE WITH MY SWEET BABBOO...
I'M NOT YOUR SWEET BABBOO!
BUT I'M SURE WISHY-WASHY!
SCHULZ

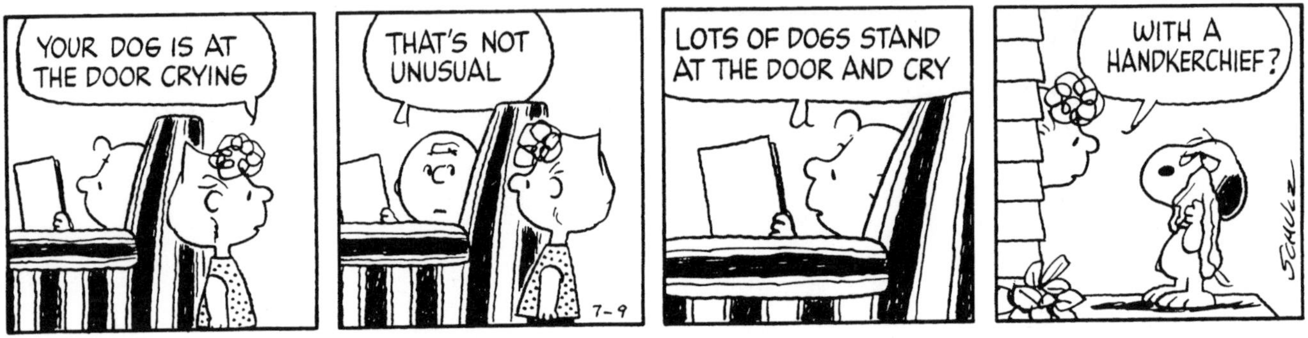
YOUR DOG IS AT THE DOOR CRYING
THAT'S NOT UNUSUAL
7-9
LOTS OF DOGS STAND AT THE DOOR AND CRY
WITH A HANDKERCHIEF?
SCHULZ

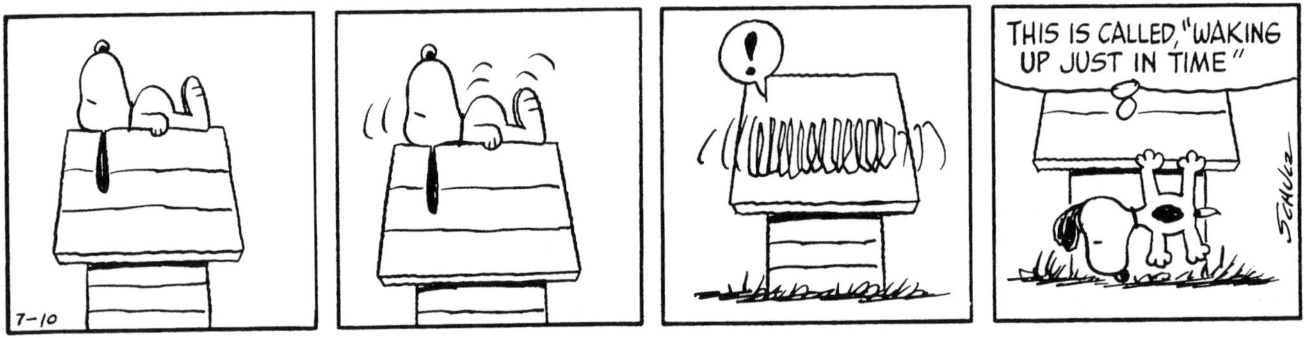
7-10
!
THIS IS CALLED, "WAKING UP JUST IN TIME"
SCHULZ

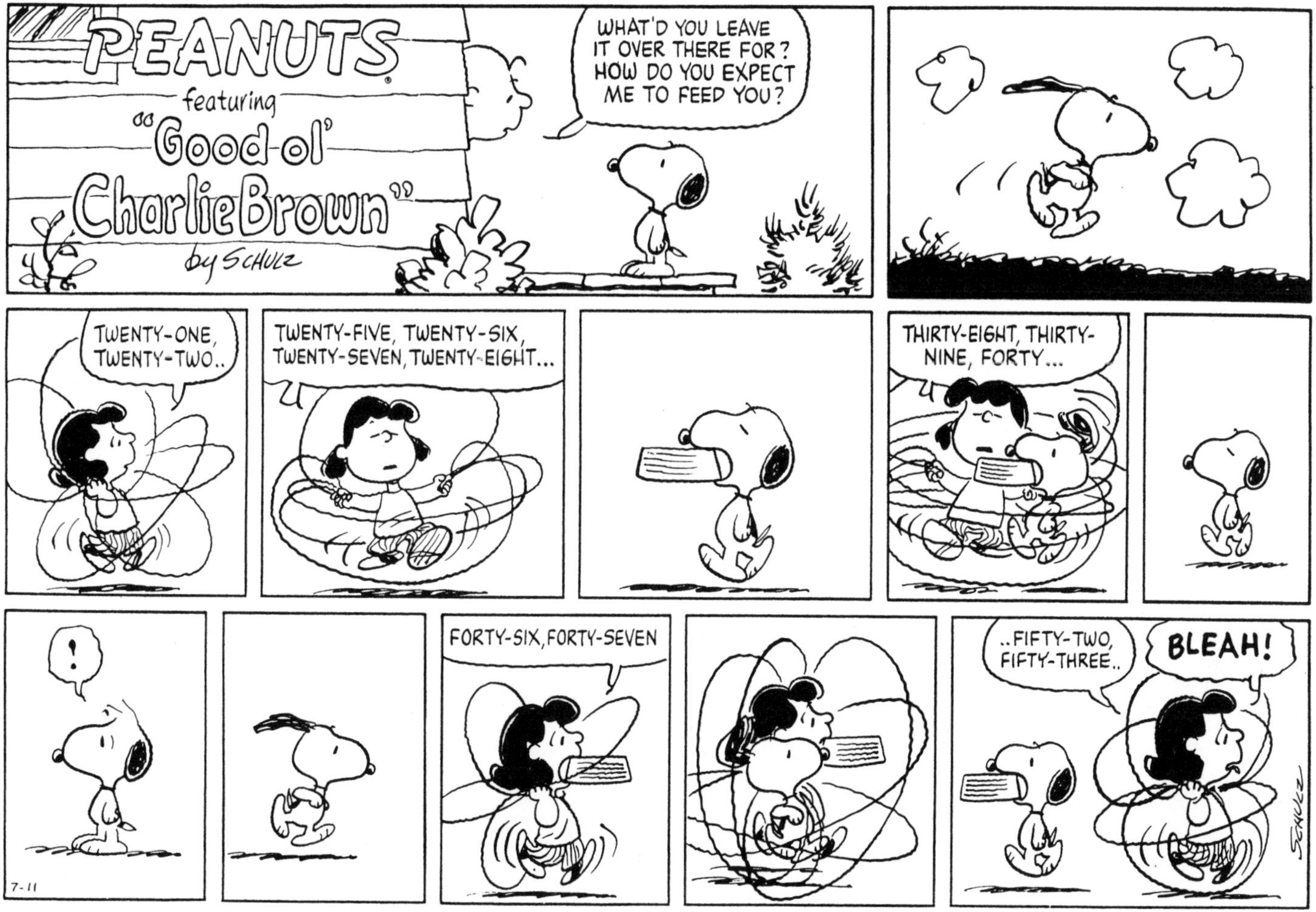
PEANUTS
featuring
"Good ol' Charlie Brown"
by SCHULZ
WHAT'D YOU LEAVE IT OVER THERE FOR? HOW DO YOU EXPECT ME TO FEED YOU?
TWENTY-ONE, TWENTY-TWO..
TWENTY-FIVE, TWENTY-SIX, TWENTY-SEVEN, TWENTY-EIGHT...
THIRTY-EIGHT, THIRTY-NINE, FORTY...
!
FORTY-SIX, FORTY-SEVEN
..FIFTY-TWO, FIFTY-THREE..
BLEAH!
SCHULZ
7-11

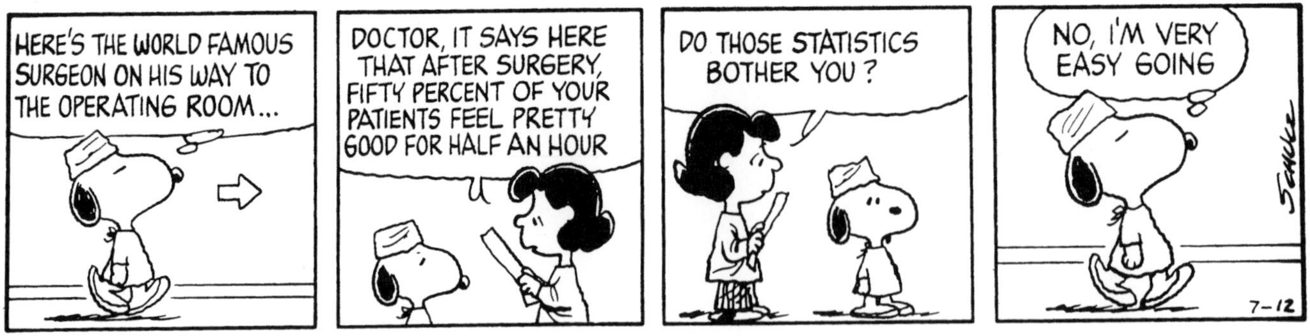
HERE'S THE WORLD FAMOUS SURGEON ON HIS WAY TO THE OPERATING ROOM...
DOCTOR, IT SAYS HERE THAT AFTER SURGERY, FIFTY PERCENT OF YOUR PATIENTS FEEL PRETTY GOOD FOR HALF AN HOUR
DO THOSE STATISTICS BOTHER YOU ?
NO, I'M VERY EASY GOING
SCHULZ
7-12

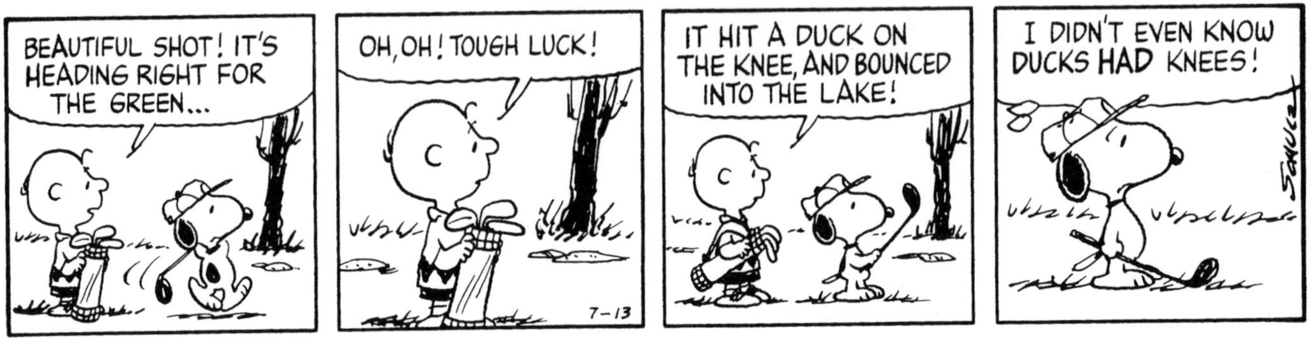
BEAUTIFUL SHOT! IT'S HEADING RIGHT FOR THE GREEN...
OH, OH! TOUGH LUCK!
7-13
IT HIT A DUCK ON THE KNEE, AND BOUNCED INTO THE LAKE!
I DIDN'T EVEN KNOW DUCKS HAD KNEES!
SCHULZ

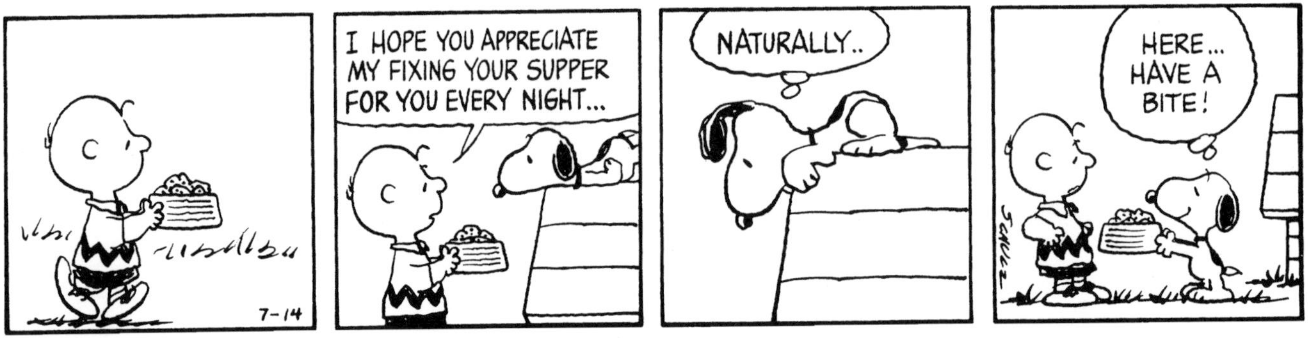
7-14
I HOPE YOU APPRECIATE MY FIXING YOUR SUPPER FOR YOU EVERY NIGHT...
NATURALLY..
HERE... HAVE A BITE!
SCHULZ

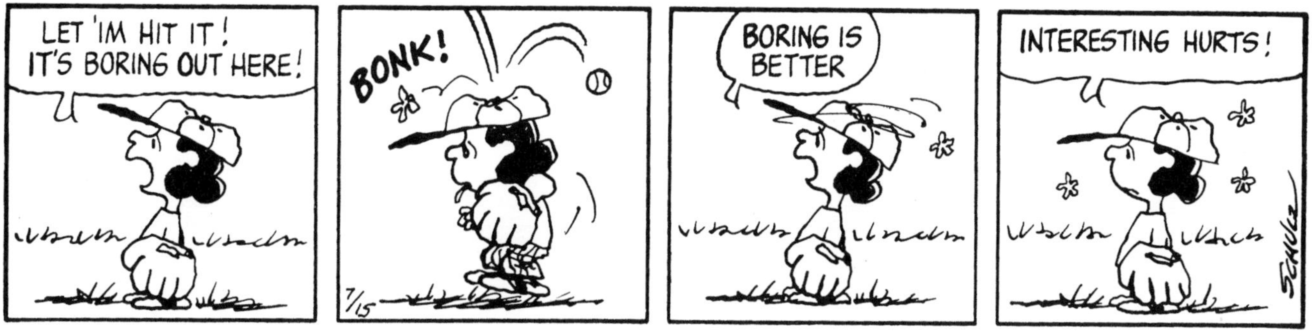
LET 'IM HIT IT! IT'S BORING OUT HERE!
BONK!
7/15
BORING IS BETTER
INTERESTING HURTS!
SCHULZ

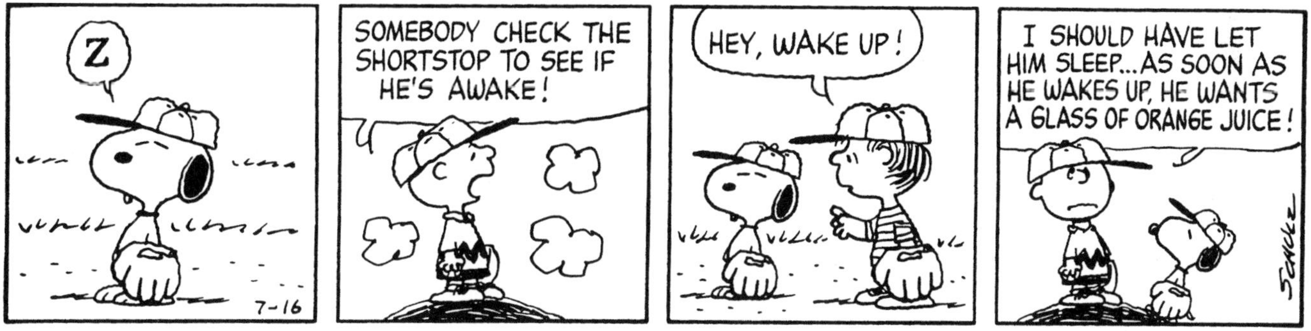
Z
7-16
SOMEBODY CHECK THE SHORTSTOP TO SEE IF HE'S AWAKE!
HEY, WAKE UP!
I SHOULD HAVE LET HIM SLEEP...AS SOON AS HE WAKES UP, HE WANTS A GLASS OF ORANGE JUICE!
SCHULZ

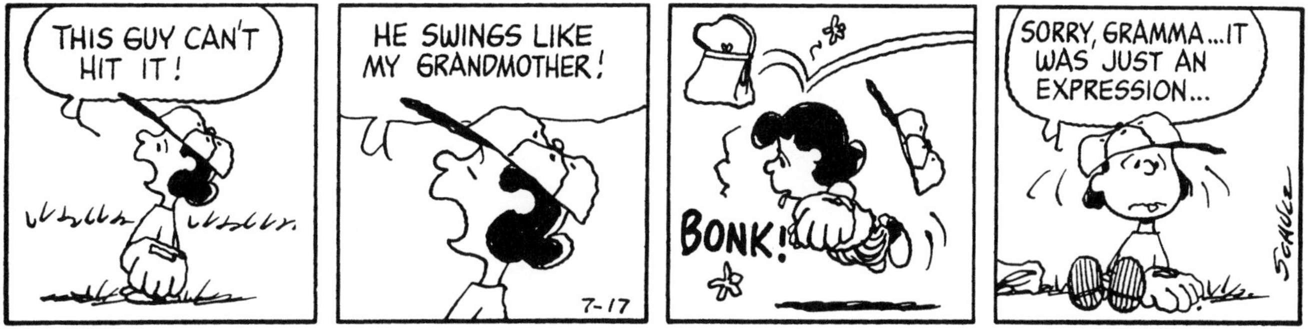
THIS GUY CAN'T HIT IT!
HE SWINGS LIKE MY GRANDMOTHER!
7-17
BONK!
SORRY, GRAMMA...IT WAS JUST AN EXPRESSION...
SCHULZ

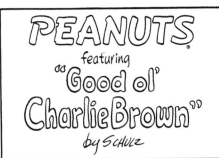

PEANUTS
featuring
"Good ol'
Charlie Brown"
by Schulz

I DON'T UNDERSTAND

ALL RIGHT, CHARLIE BROWN, LET'S PUT IT ANOTHER WAY..

PSYCHIATRIC HELP 5¢

THE DOCTOR IS IN

LIFE IS LIKE A GROCERY CART!

A GROCERY CART?

EACH OF US HAS A GROCERY CART, AND THE WORLD IS OUR SUPERMARKET!

7-18

THE WORLD IS FILLED WITH WONDERFUL THINGS...PUSH YOUR CART DOWN THE AISLES, CHARLIE BROWN!

THE DOCTOR

THAT GROCERY CART IS YOUR LIFE! PUSH IT, CHARLIE BROWN! PUSH IT RIGHT UP TO THE CHECK-OUT COUNTER!

WHICH ONE?

PSYCHIATRIC HELP 5¢

THE DOCTOR IS IN

I THINK I HAVE SIX ITEMS OR LESS!

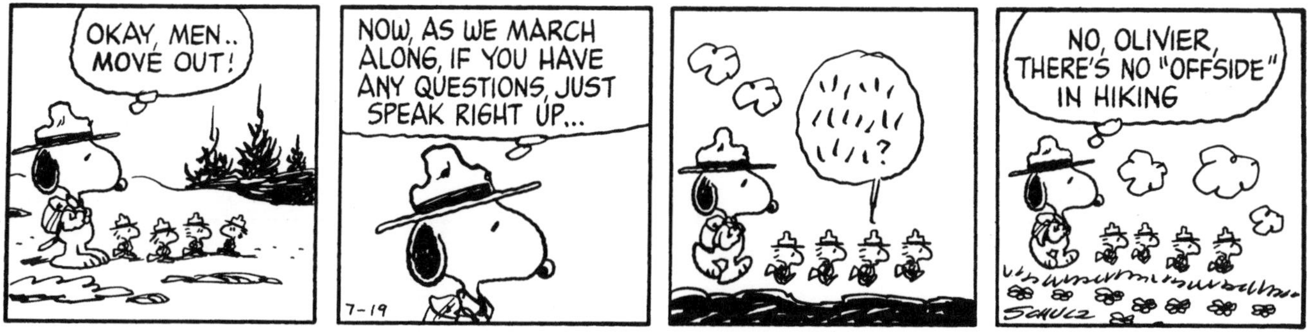
OKAY, MEN.. MOVE OUT!
NOW, AS WE MARCH ALONG, IF YOU HAVE ANY QUESTIONS, JUST SPEAK RIGHT UP...
7-19
?
NO, OLIVIER, THERE'S NO "OFFSIDE" IN HIKING
SCHULZ

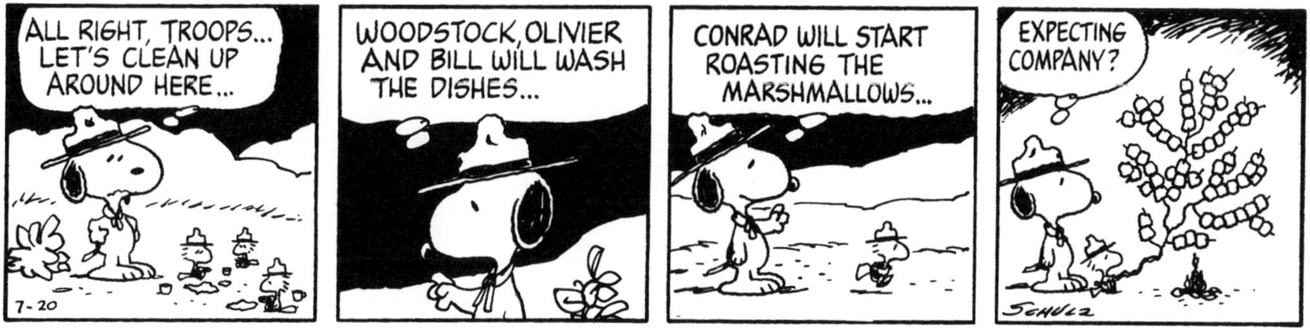
ALL RIGHT, TROOPS... LET'S CLEAN UP AROUND HERE...
7-20
WOODSTOCK, OLIVIER AND BILL WILL WASH THE DISHES...
CONRAD WILL START ROASTING THE MARSHMALLOWS...
EXPECTING COMPANY?
SCHULZ

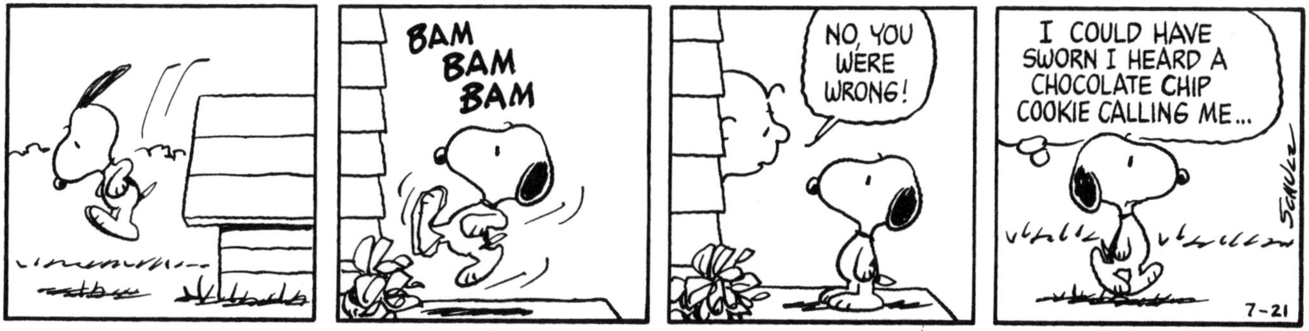
BAM
BAM
BAM
NO, YOU WERE WRONG!
I COULD HAVE SWORN I HEARD A CHOCOLATE CHIP COOKIE CALLING ME...
SCHULZ
7-21

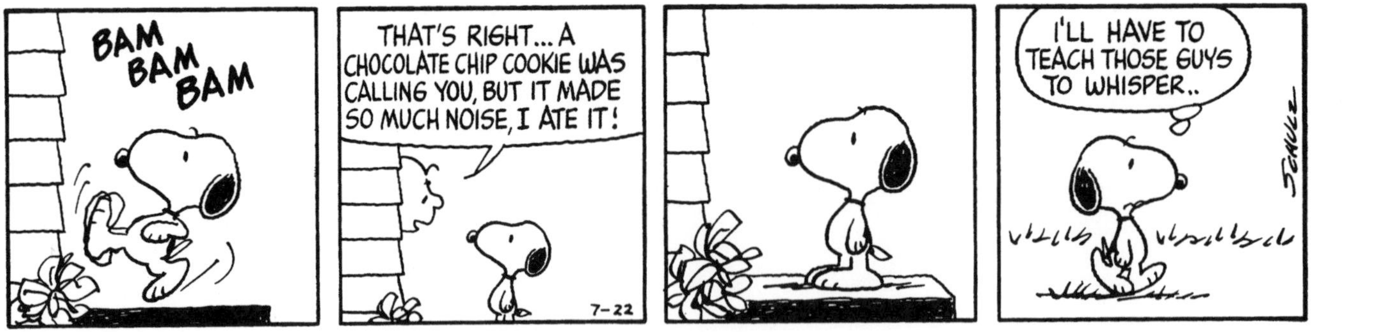
BAM BAM BAM
THAT'S RIGHT... A CHOCOLATE CHIP COOKIE WAS CALLING YOU, BUT IT MADE SO MUCH NOISE, I ATE IT!
7-22
I'LL HAVE TO TEACH THOSE GUYS TO WHISPER..
SCHULZ

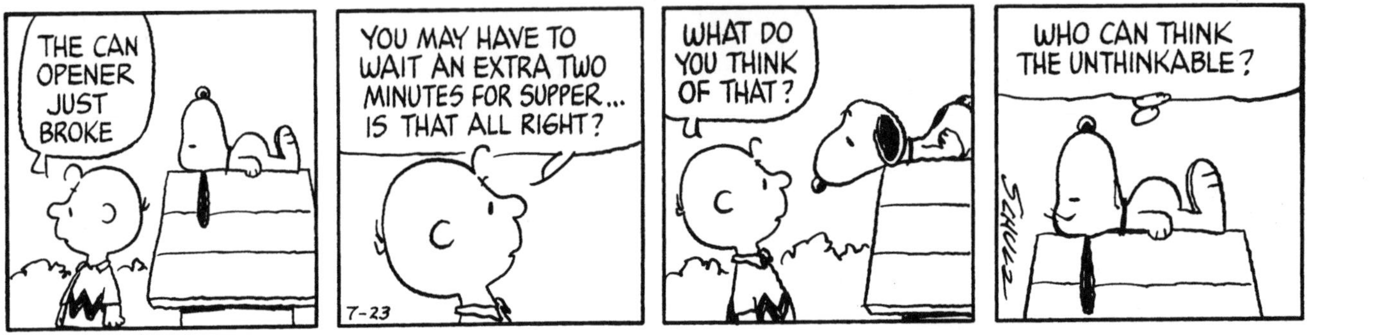
THE CAN OPENER JUST BROKE
YOU MAY HAVE TO WAIT AN EXTRA TWO MINUTES FOR SUPPER... IS THAT ALL RIGHT?
7-23
WHAT DO YOU THINK OF THAT?
WHO CAN THINK THE UNTHINKABLE?
SCHULZ

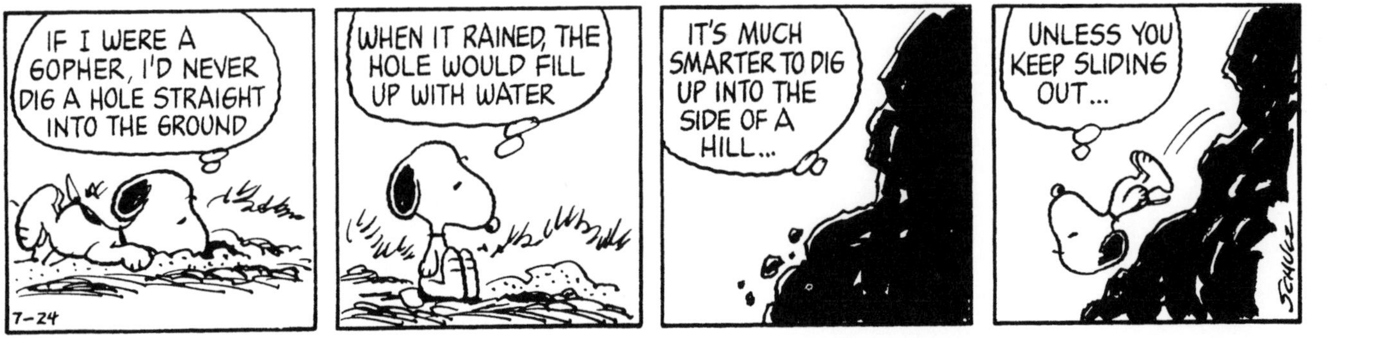
IF I WERE A GOPHER, I'D NEVER DIG A HOLE STRAIGHT INTO THE GROUND
7-24
WHEN IT RAINED, THE HOLE WOULD FILL UP WITH WATER
IT'S MUCH SMARTER TO DIG UP INTO THE SIDE OF A HILL...
UNLESS YOU KEEP SLIDING OUT...
SCHULZ

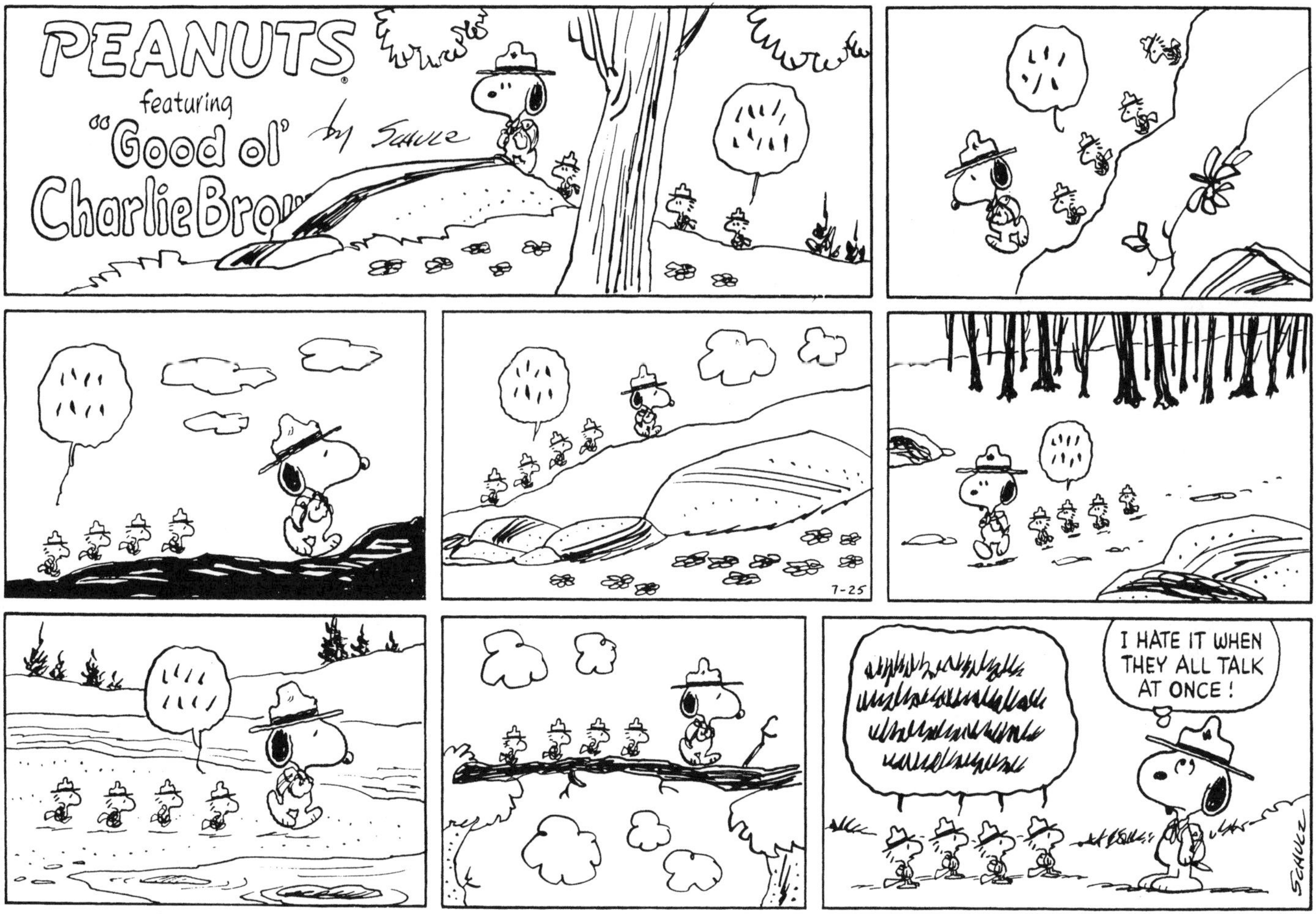
PEANUTS
featuring
"Good ol' CharlieBrown"
I HATE IT WHEN THEY ALL TALK AT ONCE!

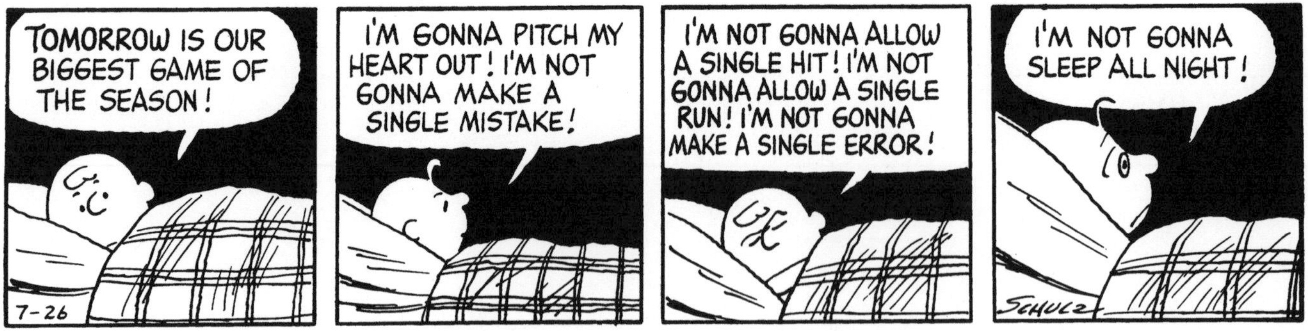
TOMORROW IS OUR BIGGEST GAME OF THE SEASON!
7-26
I'M GONNA PITCH MY HEART OUT! I'M NOT GONNA MAKE A SINGLE MISTAKE!
I'M NOT GONNA ALLOW A SINGLE HIT! I'M NOT GONNA ALLOW A SINGLE RUN! I'M NOT GONNA MAKE A SINGLE ERROR!
I'M NOT GONNA SLEEP ALL NIGHT!
SCHULZ

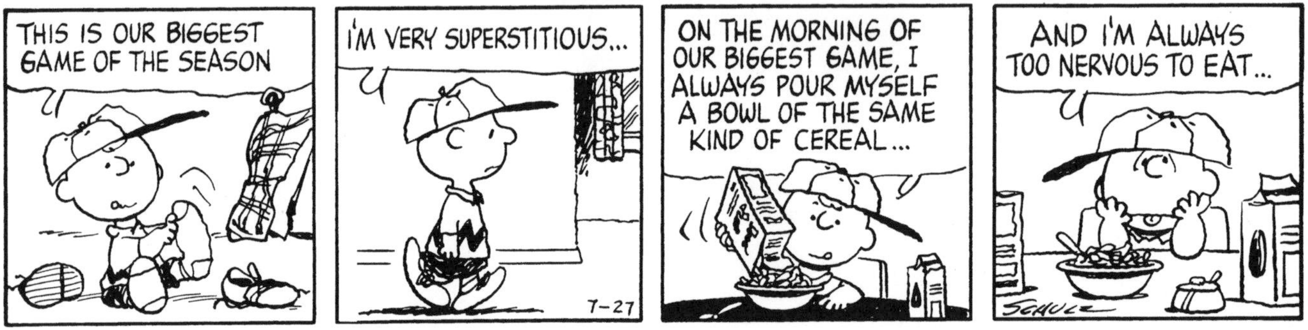
THIS IS OUR BIGGEST GAME OF THE SEASON
I'M VERY SUPERSTITIOUS...
7-27
ON THE MORNING OF OUR BIGGEST GAME, I ALWAYS POUR MYSELF A BOWL OF THE SAME KIND OF CEREAL...
AND I'M ALWAYS TOO NERVOUS TO EAT...
SCHULZ

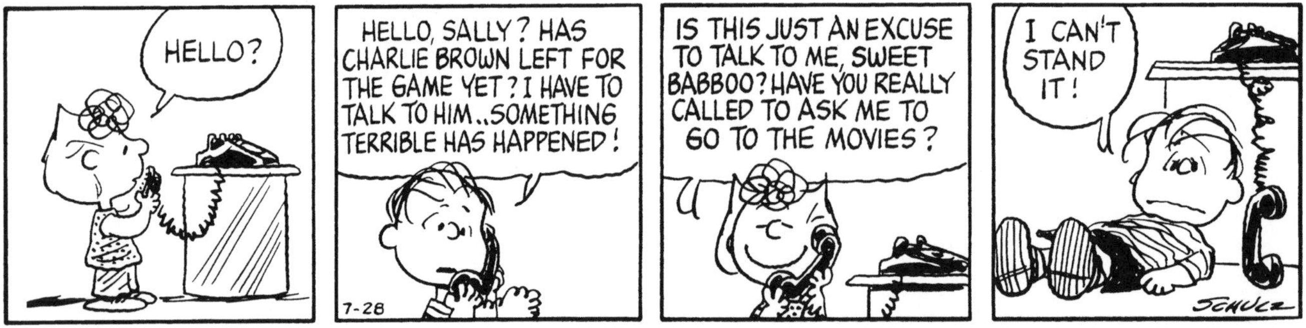
HELLO?
HELLO, SALLY? HAS CHARLIE BROWN LEFT FOR THE GAME YET? I HAVE TO TALK TO HIM..SOMETHING TERRIBLE HAS HAPPENED!
7-28
IS THIS JUST AN EXCUSE TO TALK TO ME, SWEET BABBOO? HAVE YOU REALLY CALLED TO ASK ME TO GO TO THE MOVIES?
I CAN'T STAND IT!
SCHULZ

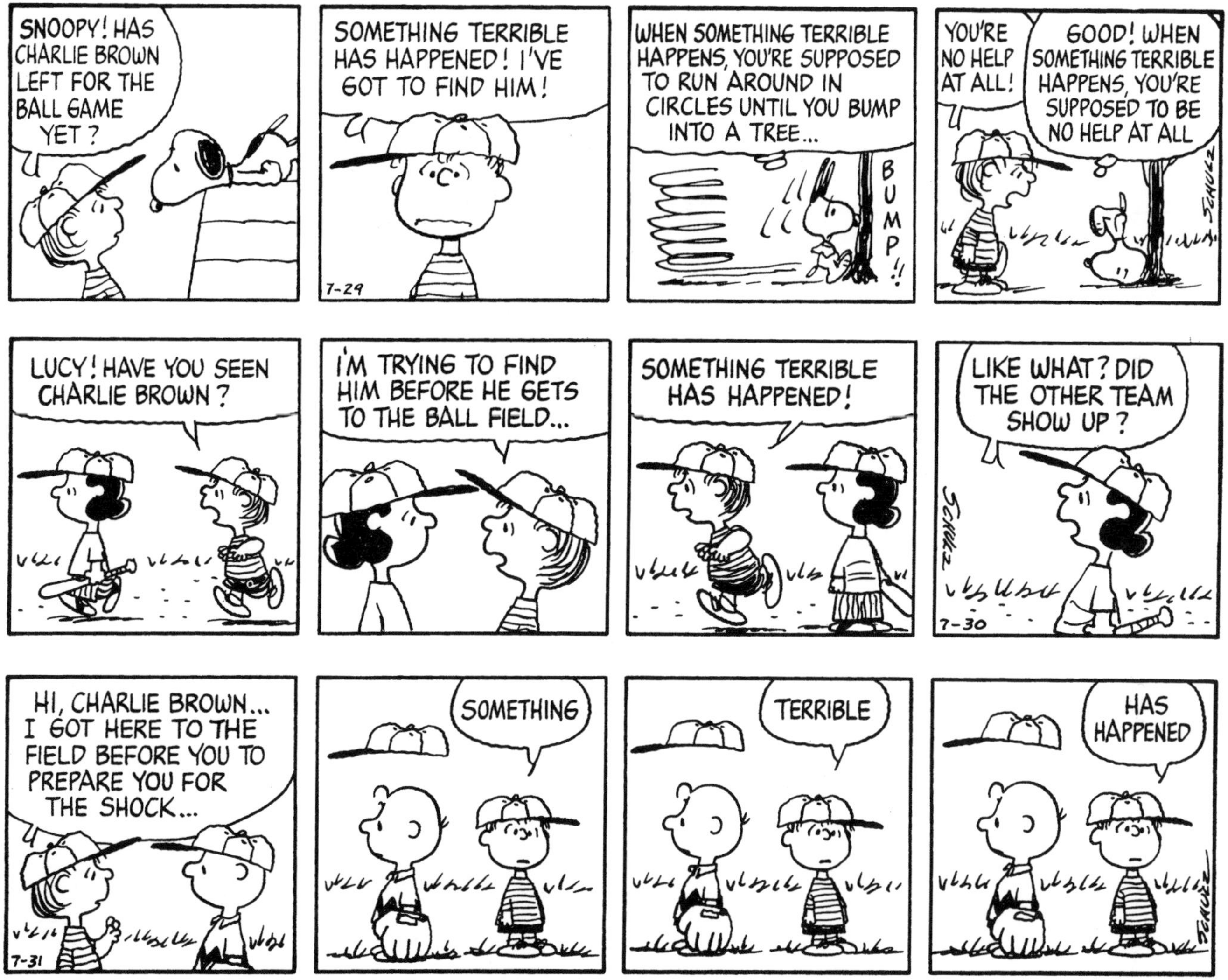
SNOOPY! HAS CHARLIE BROWN LEFT FOR THE BALL GAME YET?
SOMETHING TERRIBLE HAS HAPPENED! I'VE GOT TO FIND HIM!
7-29
WHEN SOMETHING TERRIBLE HAPPENS, YOU'RE SUPPOSED TO RUN AROUND IN CIRCLES UNTIL YOU BUMP INTO A TREE...
BUMP!!
YOU'RE NO HELP AT ALL!
GOOD! WHEN SOMETHING TERRIBLE HAPPENS, YOU'RE SUPPOSED TO BE NO HELP AT ALL
SCHULZ
LUCY! HAVE YOU SEEN CHARLIE BROWN?
I'M TRYING TO FIND HIM BEFORE HE GETS TO THE BALL FIELD...
SOMETHING TERRIBLE HAS HAPPENED!
LIKE WHAT? DID THE OTHER TEAM SHOW UP?
SCHULZ
7-30
HI, CHARLIE BROWN... I GOT HERE TO THE FIELD BEFORE YOU TO PREPARE YOU FOR THE SHOCK...
7-31
SOMETHING
TERRIBLE
HAS HAPPENED
SCHULZ

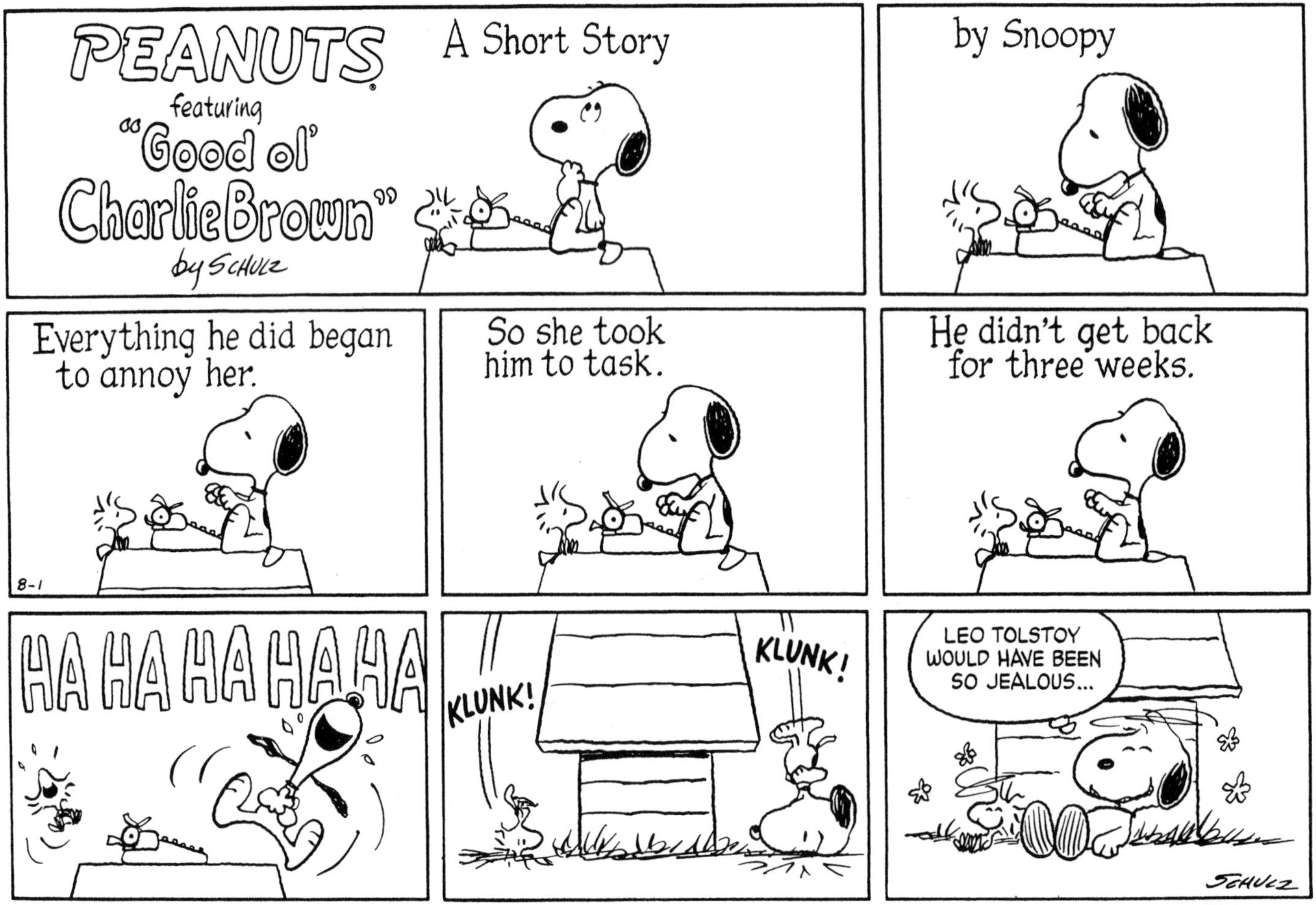
PEANUTS
featuring
"Good ol' Charlie Brown"
by SCHULZ
A Short Story
by Snoopy
Everything he did began to annoy her.
8-1
So she took him to task.
He didn't get back for three weeks.
HA HA HA HA HA HA
KLUNK!
KLUNK!
LEO TOLSTOY WOULD HAVE BEEN SO JEALOUS...
SCHULZ

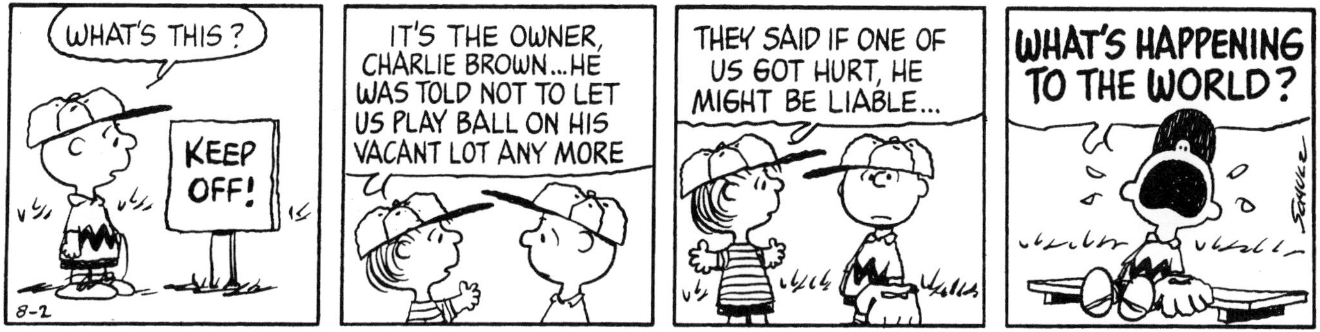
WHAT'S THIS ?
KEEP OFF!
IT'S THE OWNER, CHARLIE BROWN...HE WAS TOLD NOT TO LET US PLAY BALL ON HIS VACANT LOT ANY MORE
THEY SAID IF ONE OF US GOT HURT, HE MIGHT BE LIABLE...
WHAT'S HAPPENING TO THE WORLD?
8-2
SCHULZ

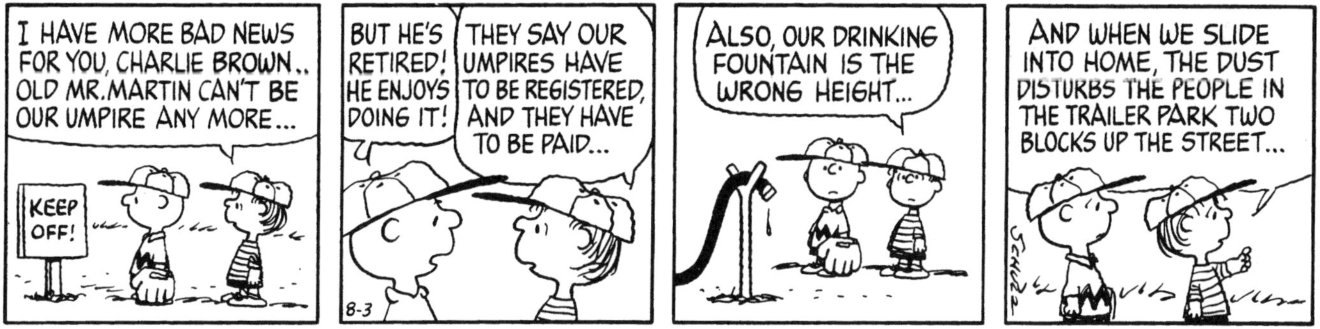
I HAVE MORE BAD NEWS FOR YOU, CHARLIE BROWN.. OLD MR.MARTIN CAN'T BE OUR UMPIRE ANY MORE...
KEEP OFF!
BUT HE'S RETIRED! HE ENJOYS DOING IT!
THEY SAY OUR UMPIRES HAVE TO BE REGISTERED, AND THEY HAVE TO BE PAID...
ALSO, OUR DRINKING FOUNTAIN IS THE WRONG HEIGHT...
AND WHEN WE SLIDE INTO HOME, THE DUST DISTURBS THE PEOPLE IN THE TRAILER PARK TWO BLOCKS UP THE STREET...
8-3
SCHULZ

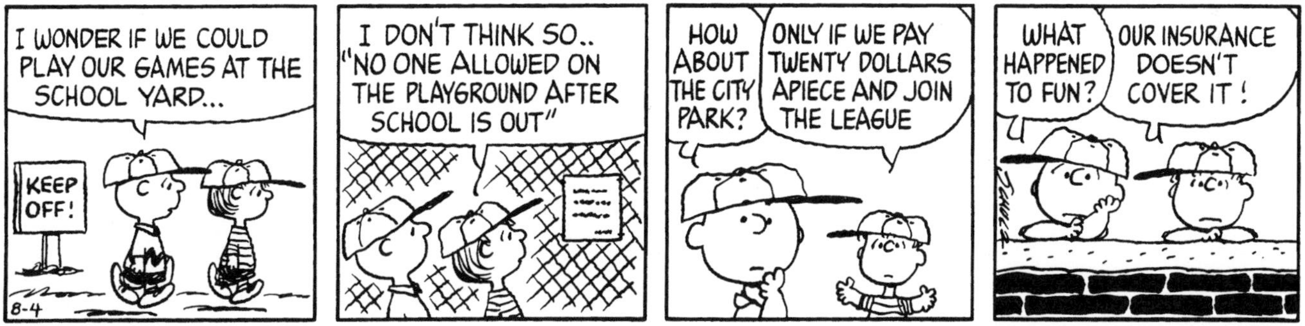
I WONDER IF WE COULD PLAY OUR GAMES AT THE SCHOOL YARD...
KEEP OFF!
I DON'T THINK SO.. "NO ONE ALLOWED ON THE PLAYGROUND AFTER SCHOOL IS OUT"
HOW ABOUT THE CITY PARK?
ONLY IF WE PAY TWENTY DOLLARS APIECE AND JOIN THE LEAGUE
WHAT HAPPENED TO FUN?
OUR INSURANCE DOESN'T COVER IT !
8-4
SCHULZ

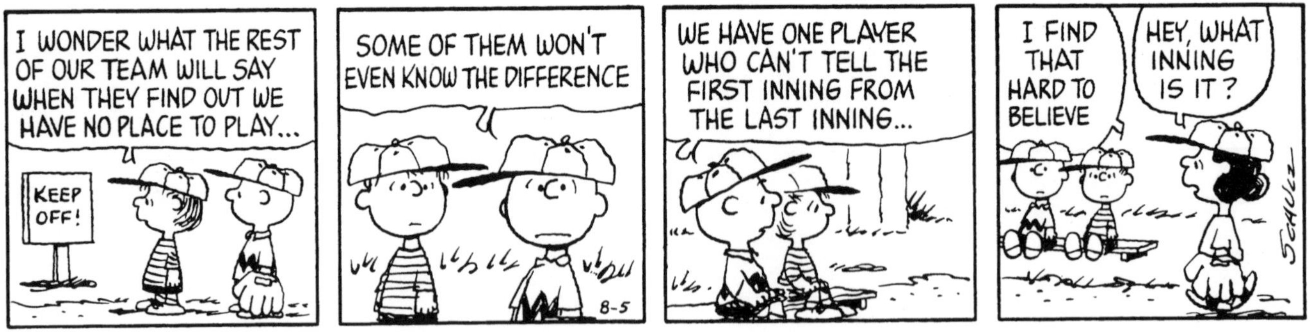
I WONDER WHAT THE REST OF OUR TEAM WILL SAY WHEN THEY FIND OUT WE HAVE NO PLACE TO PLAY...
KEEP OFF!
SOME OF THEM WON'T EVEN KNOW THE DIFFERENCE
8-5
WE HAVE ONE PLAYER WHO CAN'T TELL THE FIRST INNING FROM THE LAST INNING...
I FIND THAT HARD TO BELIEVE
HEY, WHAT INNING IS IT?
SCHULZ

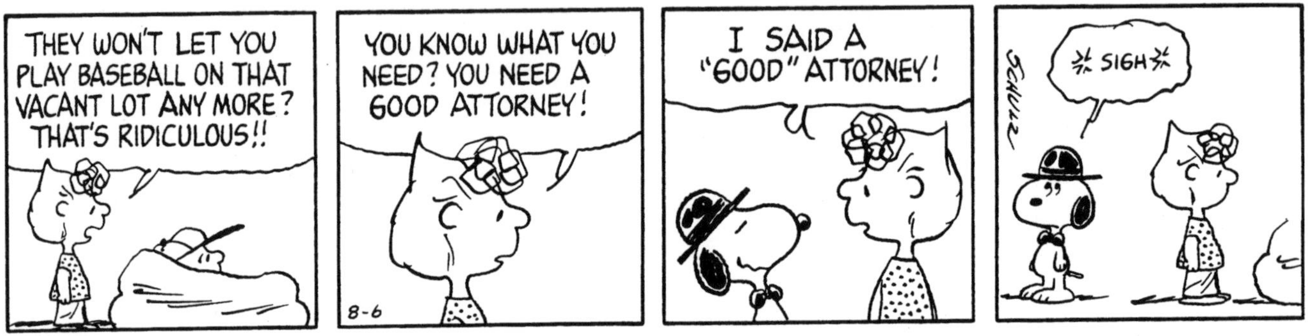
THEY WON'T LET YOU PLAY BASEBALL ON THAT VACANT LOT ANY MORE? THAT'S RIDICULOUS!!
YOU KNOW WHAT YOU NEED? YOU NEED A GOOD ATTORNEY!
8-6
I SAID A "GOOD" ATTORNEY!
SCHULZ
SIGH

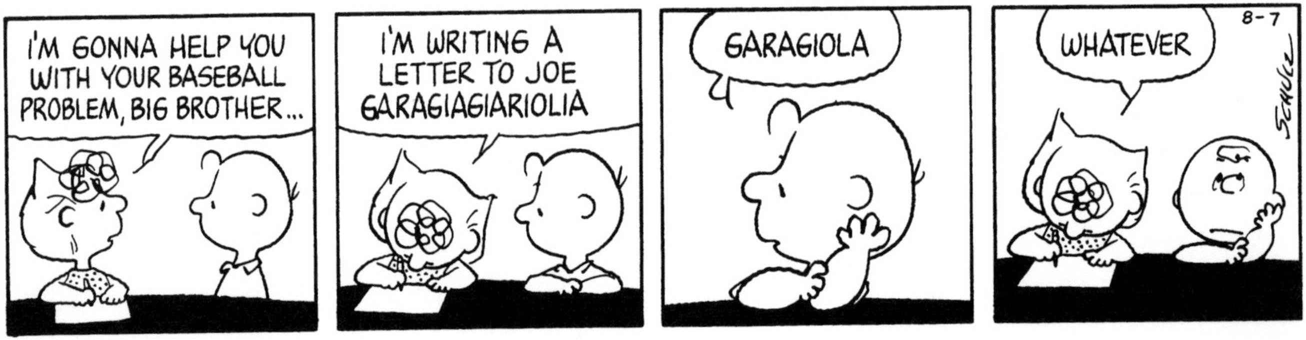
I'M GONNA HELP YOU WITH YOUR BASEBALL PROBLEM, BIG BROTHER...
I'M WRITING A LETTER TO JOE GARAGIAGIARIOLIA
GARAGIOLA
WHATEVER
8-7
SCHULZ

PEANUTS featuring "Good ol' Charlie Brown" *by Schulz*

"JOHNNY MILLER ALL THE WAY"

"...FOUR TO THREE IN TEN INNINGS"

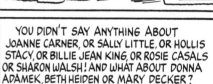

"AND THAT'S SPORTS FOR TONIGHT"

THAT'S SPORTS?!! WHAT DO YOU MEAN, THAT'S SPORTS?!!

ALL YOU TOLD US ABOUT WERE MEN! WHAT ABOUT WOMEN IN SPORTS?!!!

YOU DIDN'T SAY ANYTHING ABOUT JOANNE CARNER, OR SALLY LITTLE, OR HOLLIS STACY, OR BILLIE JEAN KING, OR ROSIE CASALS OR SHARON WALSH! AND WHAT ABOUT DONNA ADAMEK, BETH HEIDEN OR MARY DECKER?

DID YOU TELL US WHAT CONNI PLACE HAS BEEN DOING? AND HOW ABOUT ALISON ROWE, AND TRACY CAULKINS, AND KAREN ROGERS, AND EVELYN ASHFORD, AND ANN MEYERS, AND JUDY SLADKY AND SARAH DOCTER?!

DID YOU SAY ANYTHING ABOUT JENNIFER HARDING OR SHIRLEY MULDOWNEY? WHAT DO YOU MEAN, "THAT'S SPORTS"?!!

WHAT DO YOU WANT TO WATCH NEXT, SIR? THERE'RE SOME OLD MOVIES ON THE OTHER CHANNELS..

"THE MEN," "A MAN FOR ALL SEASONS" AND "ALL THE KING'S MEN"

I CAN'T STAND IT...

8-8

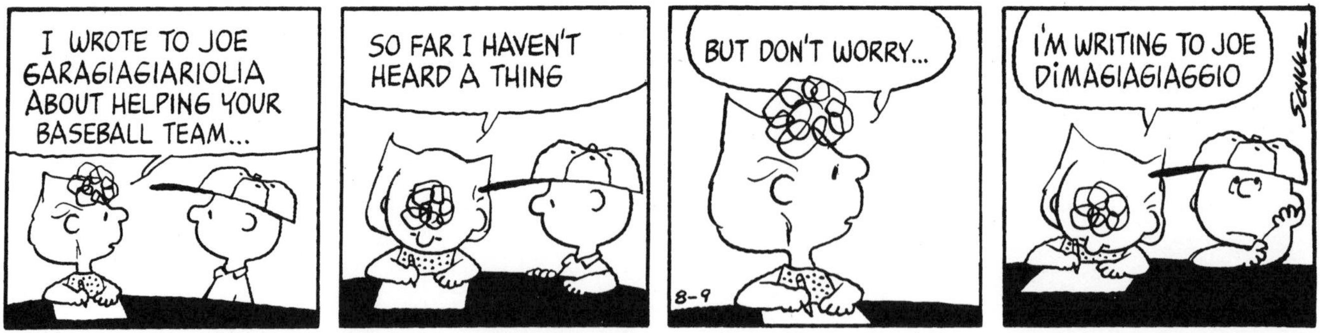
I WROTE TO JOE GARAGIAGIARIOLIA ABOUT HELPING YOUR BASEBALL TEAM...
SO FAR I HAVEN'T HEARD A THING
BUT DON'T WORRY...
I'M WRITING TO JOE DIMAGIAGIAGGIO
8-9
SCHULZ

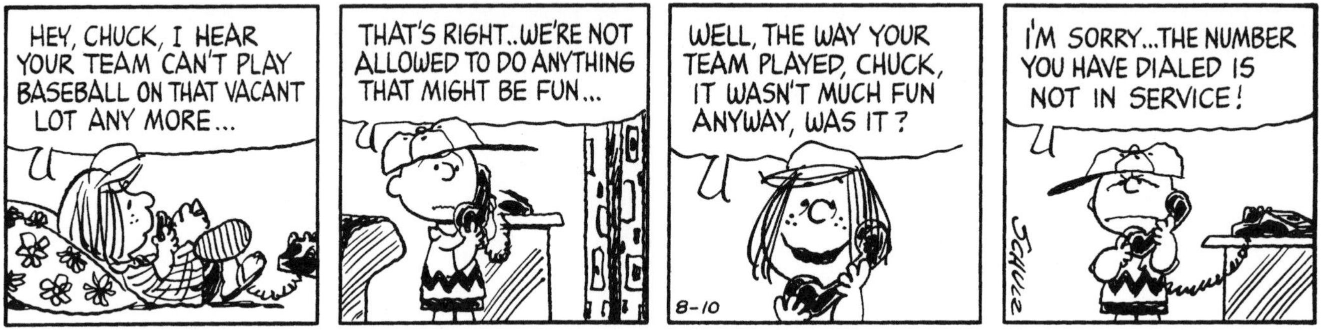
HEY, CHUCK, I HEAR YOUR TEAM CAN'T PLAY BASEBALL ON THAT VACANT LOT ANY MORE...
THAT'S RIGHT..WE'RE NOT ALLOWED TO DO ANYTHING THAT MIGHT BE FUN...
WELL, THE WAY YOUR TEAM PLAYED, CHUCK, IT WASN'T MUCH FUN ANYWAY, WAS IT?
I'M SORRY...THE NUMBER YOU HAVE DIALED IS NOT IN SERVICE!
8-10
SCHULZ

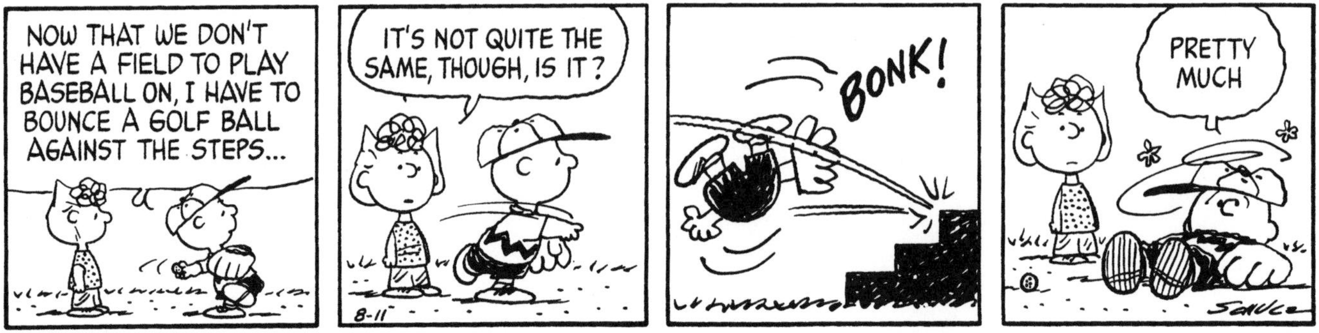
NOW THAT WE DON'T HAVE A FIELD TO PLAY BASEBALL ON, I HAVE TO BOUNCE A GOLF BALL AGAINST THE STEPS...
IT'S NOT QUITE THE SAME, THOUGH, IS IT?
BONK!
PRETTY MUCH
8-11
SCHULZ

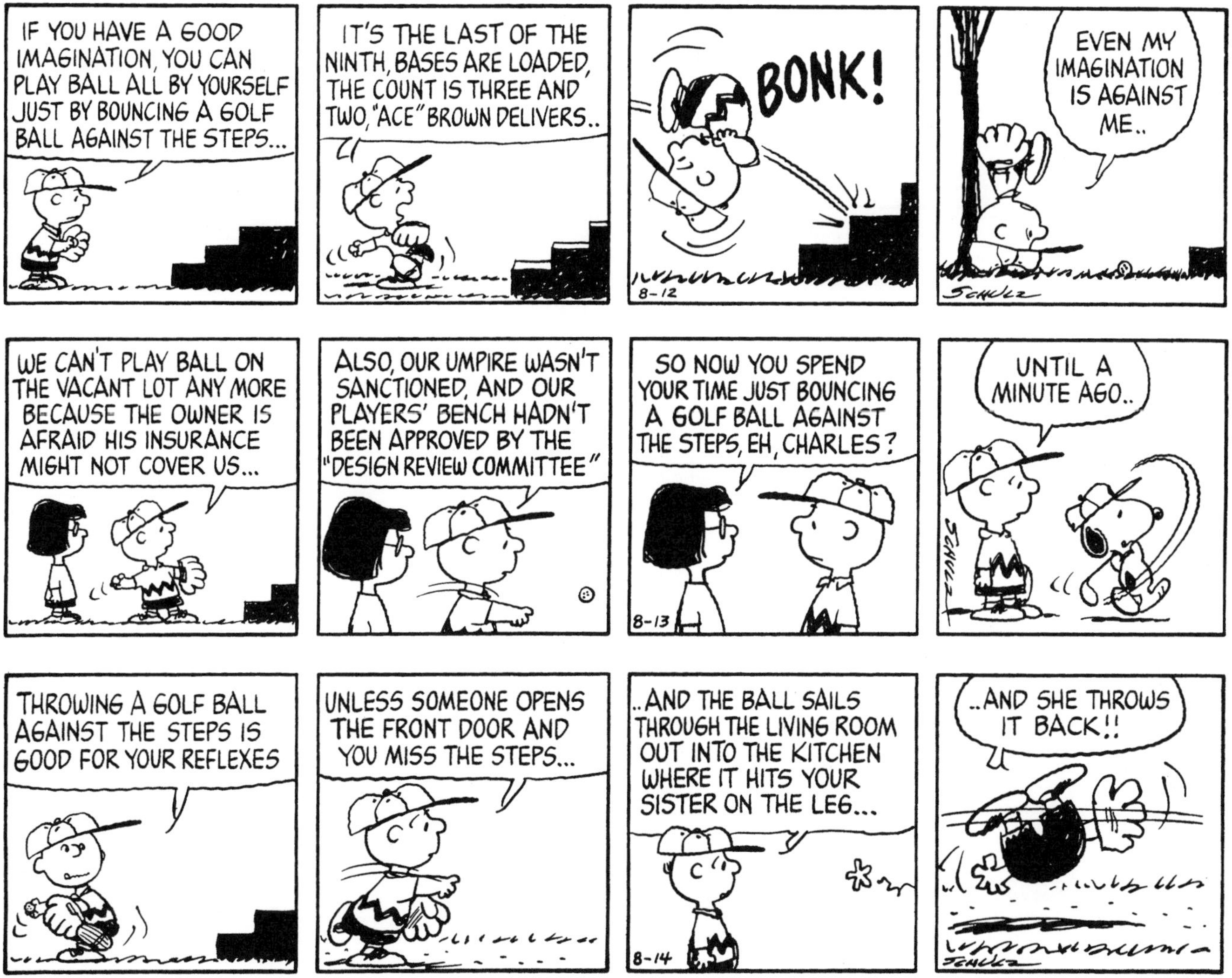

IF YOU HAVE A GOOD IMAGINATION, YOU CAN PLAY BALL ALL BY YOURSELF JUST BY BOUNCING A GOLF BALL AGAINST THE STEPS...
IT'S THE LAST OF THE NINTH, BASES ARE LOADED, THE COUNT IS THREE AND TWO, "ACE" BROWN DELIVERS..
BONK!
8-12
EVEN MY IMAGINATION IS AGAINST ME..
SCHULZ
WE CAN'T PLAY BALL ON THE VACANT LOT ANY MORE BECAUSE THE OWNER IS AFRAID HIS INSURANCE MIGHT NOT COVER US...
ALSO, OUR UMPIRE WASN'T SANCTIONED, AND OUR PLAYERS' BENCH HADN'T BEEN APPROVED BY THE "DESIGN REVIEW COMMITTEE"
SO NOW YOU SPEND YOUR TIME JUST BOUNCING A GOLF BALL AGAINST THE STEPS, EH, CHARLES?
8-13
UNTIL A MINUTE AGO..
SCHULZ
THROWING A GOLF BALL AGAINST THE STEPS IS GOOD FOR YOUR REFLEXES
UNLESS SOMEONE OPENS THE FRONT DOOR AND YOU MISS THE STEPS...
..AND THE BALL SAILS THROUGH THE LIVING ROOM OUT INTO THE KITCHEN WHERE IT HITS YOUR SISTER ON THE LEG...
8-14
..AND SHE THROWS IT BACK!!
SCHULZ

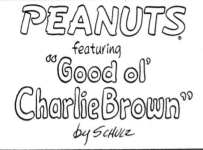

PEANUTS
featuring
"Good ol'
Charlie Brown"
by SCHULZ

8-15

ALL PACKED, HUH?

WELL, YOU'LL HAVE A GOOD TIME...

IF YOU GET A CHANCE, SEND ME A POSTCARD

SO LONG, LITTLE FRIEND...

I HATE LONG GOODBYES

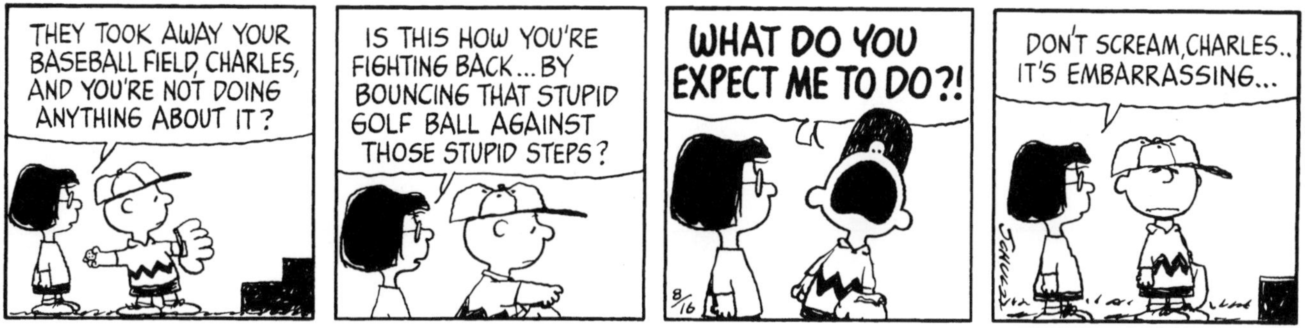
THEY TOOK AWAY YOUR BASEBALL FIELD, CHARLES, AND YOU'RE NOT DOING ANYTHING ABOUT IT?
IS THIS HOW YOU'RE FIGHTING BACK... BY BOUNCING THAT STUPID GOLF BALL AGAINST THOSE STUPID STEPS?
WHAT DO YOU EXPECT ME TO DO?!
DON'T SCREAM, CHARLES.. IT'S EMBARRASSING...

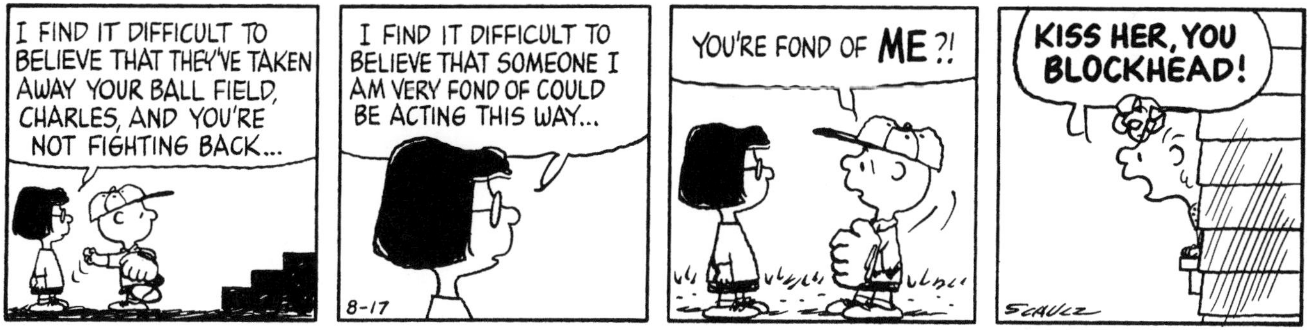
I FIND IT DIFFICULT TO BELIEVE THAT THEY'VE TAKEN AWAY YOUR BALL FIELD, CHARLES, AND YOU'RE NOT FIGHTING BACK...
I FIND IT DIFFICULT TO BELIEVE THAT SOMEONE I AM VERY FOND OF COULD BE ACTING THIS WAY...
YOU'RE FOND OF ME?!
KISS HER, YOU BLOCKHEAD!

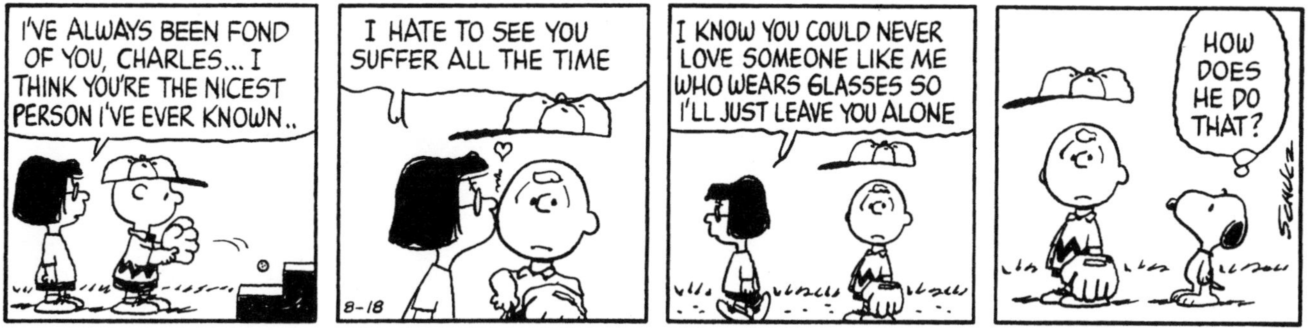
I'VE ALWAYS BEEN FOND OF YOU, CHARLES... I THINK YOU'RE THE NICEST PERSON I'VE EVER KNOWN..
I HATE TO SEE YOU SUFFER ALL THE TIME
I KNOW YOU COULD NEVER LOVE SOMEONE LIKE ME WHO WEARS GLASSES SO I'LL JUST LEAVE YOU ALONE
HOW DOES HE DO THAT?

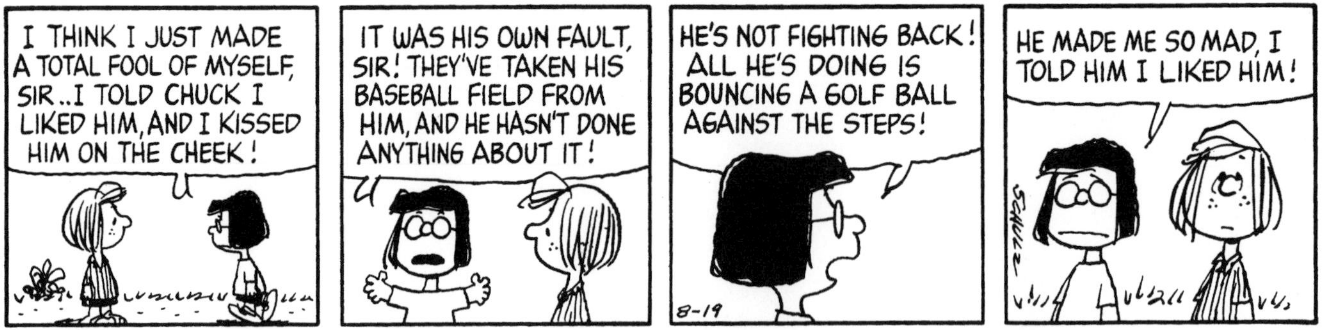
I THINK I JUST MADE A TOTAL FOOL OF MYSELF, SIR..I TOLD CHUCK I LIKED HIM, AND I KISSED HIM ON THE CHEEK!
IT WAS HIS OWN FAULT, SIR! THEY'VE TAKEN HIS BASEBALL FIELD FROM HIM, AND HE HASN'T DONE ANYTHING ABOUT IT!
HE'S NOT FIGHTING BACK! ALL HE'S DOING IS BOUNCING A GOLF BALL AGAINST THE STEPS!
8-19
HE MADE ME SO MAD, I TOLD HIM I LIKED HIM!
SCHULZ

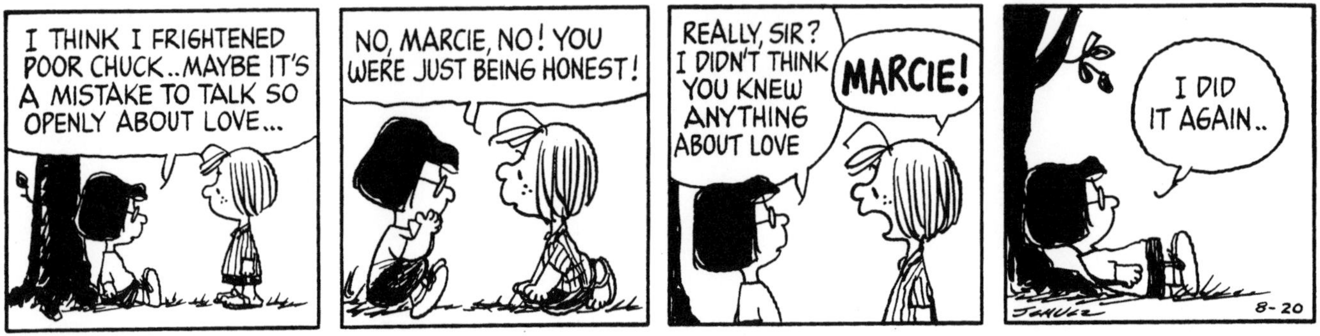
I THINK I FRIGHTENED POOR CHUCK..MAYBE IT'S A MISTAKE TO TALK SO OPENLY ABOUT LOVE...
NO, MARCIE, NO! YOU WERE JUST BEING HONEST!
REALLY, SIR? I DIDN'T THINK YOU KNEW ANYTHING ABOUT LOVE
MARCIE!
I DID IT AGAIN..
SCHULZ
8-20

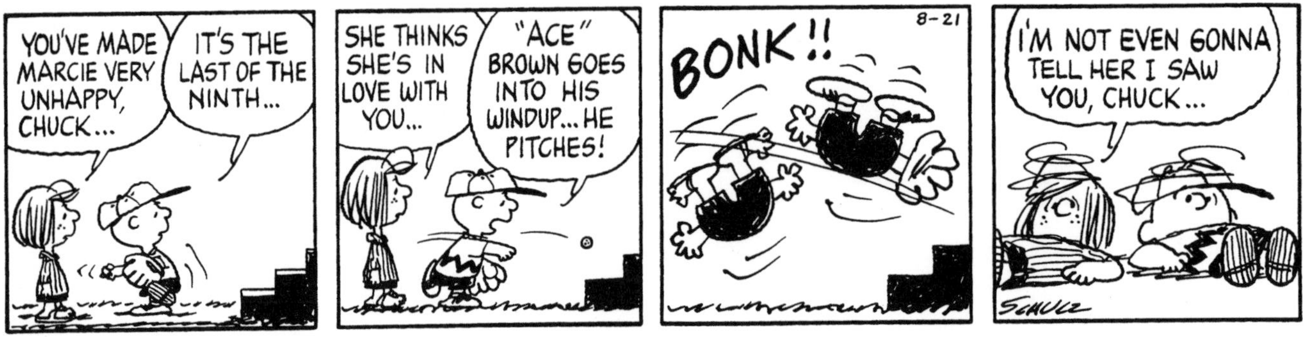
YOU'VE MADE MARCIE VERY UNHAPPY, CHUCK...
IT'S THE LAST OF THE NINTH...
SHE THINKS SHE'S IN LOVE WITH YOU...
"ACE" BROWN GOES INTO HIS WINDUP... HE PITCHES!
8-21
BONK!!
I'M NOT EVEN GONNA TELL HER I SAW YOU, CHUCK...
SCHULZ

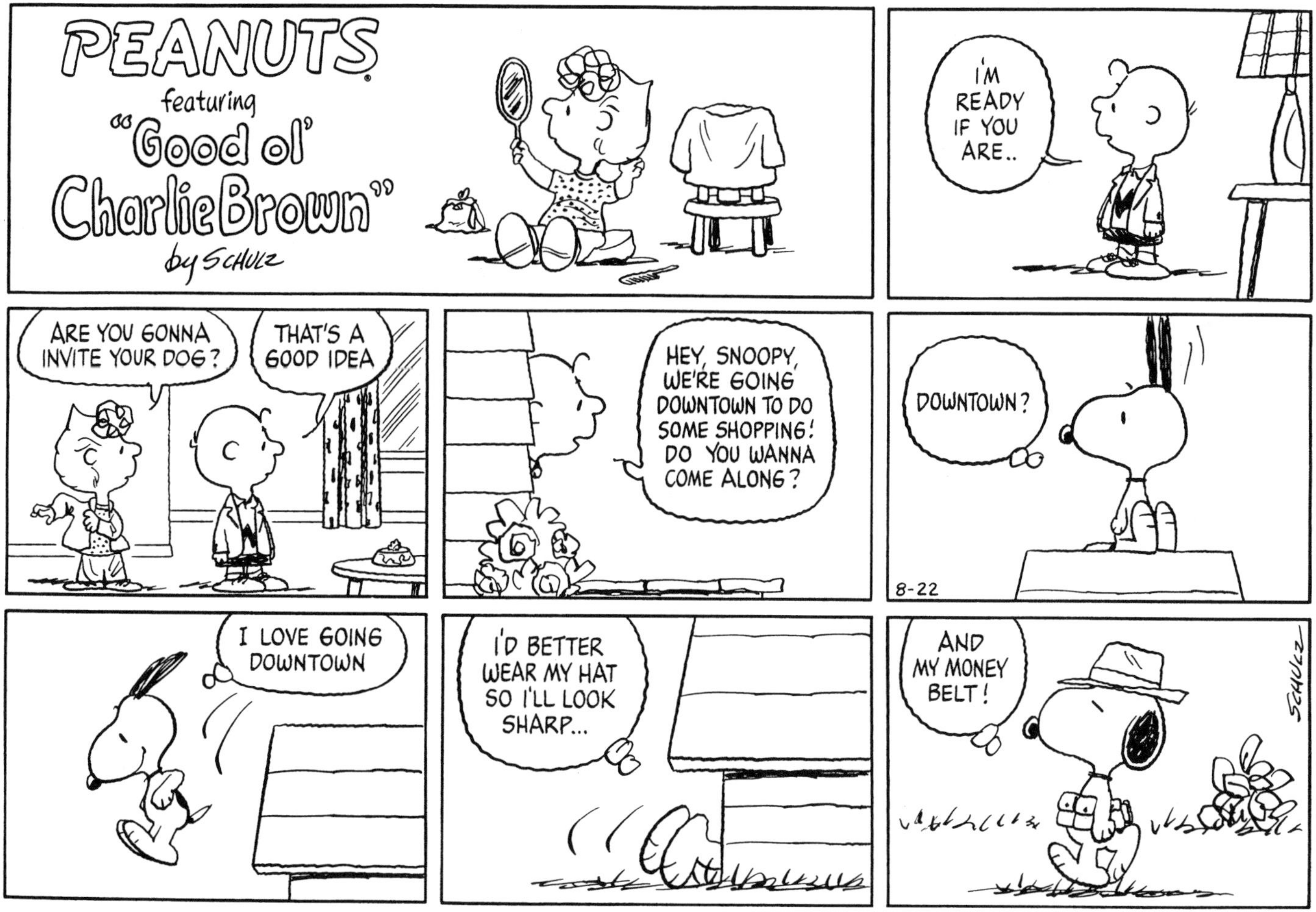
PEANUTS
featuring "Good ol' Charlie Brown"
by SCHULZ
I'M READY IF YOU ARE..
ARE YOU GONNA INVITE YOUR DOG?
THAT'S A GOOD IDEA
HEY, SNOOPY, WE'RE GOING DOWNTOWN TO DO SOME SHOPPING! DO YOU WANNA COME ALONG?
DOWNTOWN?
8-22
I LOVE GOING DOWNTOWN
I'D BETTER WEAR MY HAT SO I'LL LOOK SHARP...
AND MY MONEY BELT!
SCHULZ

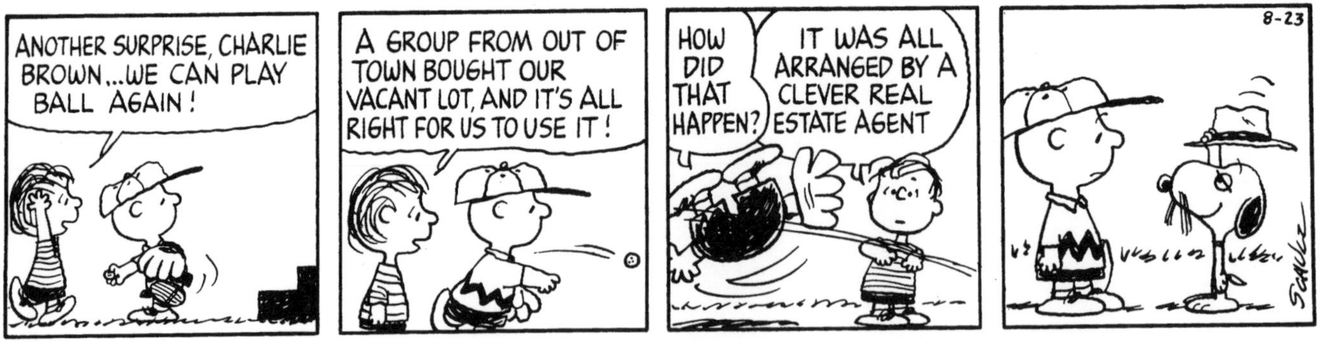
ANOTHER SURPRISE, CHARLIE BROWN...WE CAN PLAY BALL AGAIN!
A GROUP FROM OUT OF TOWN BOUGHT OUR VACANT LOT, AND IT'S ALL RIGHT FOR US TO USE IT!
HOW DID THAT HAPPEN?
IT WAS ALL ARRANGED BY A CLEVER REAL ESTATE AGENT
8-23
SCHULZ

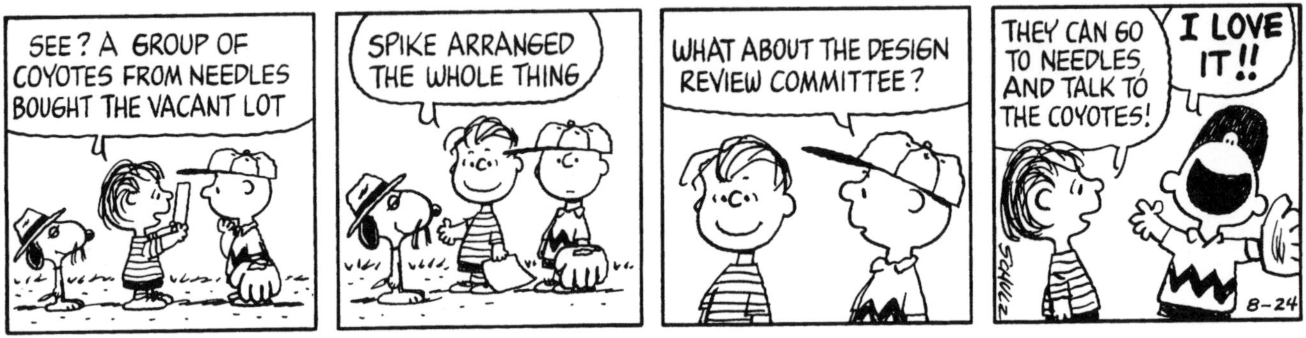
SEE? A GROUP OF COYOTES FROM NEEDLES BOUGHT THE VACANT LOT
SPIKE ARRANGED THE WHOLE THING
WHAT ABOUT THE DESIGN REVIEW COMMITTEE?
THEY CAN GO TO NEEDLES, AND TALK TO THE COYOTES!
I LOVE IT!!
SCHULZ
8-24

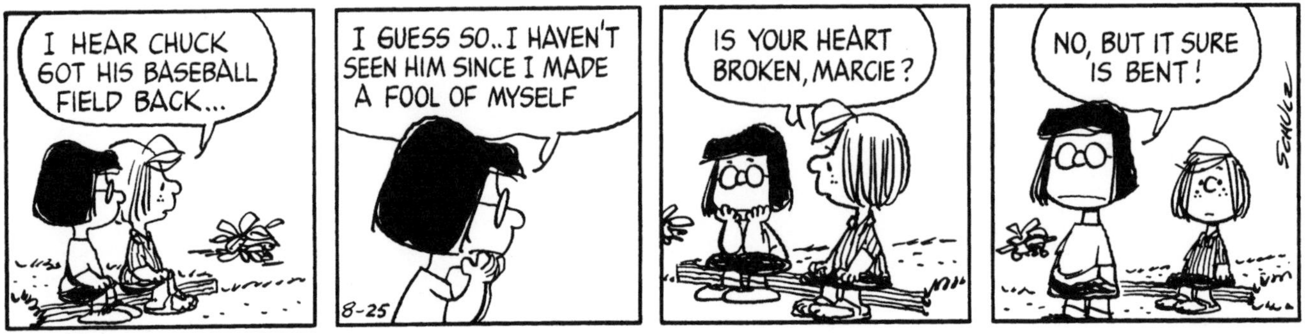
I HEAR CHUCK GOT HIS BASEBALL FIELD BACK...
I GUESS SO..I HAVEN'T SEEN HIM SINCE I MADE A FOOL OF MYSELF
8-25
IS YOUR HEART BROKEN, MARCIE?
NO, BUT IT SURE IS BENT!
SCHULZ

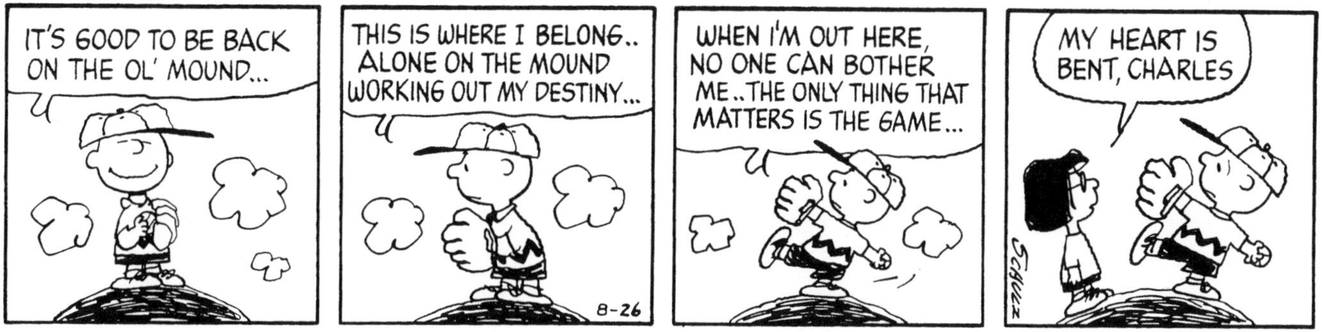
IT'S GOOD TO BE BACK ON THE OL' MOUND...
THIS IS WHERE I BELONG.. ALONE ON THE MOUND WORKING OUT MY DESTINY...
8-26
WHEN I'M OUT HERE, NO ONE CAN BOTHER ME..THE ONLY THING THAT MATTERS IS THE GAME...
MY HEART IS BENT, CHARLES
SCHULZ

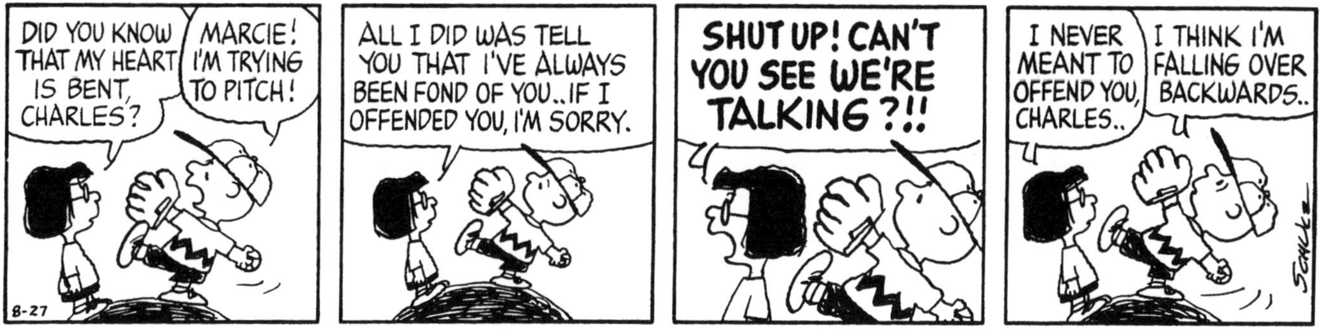
DID YOU KNOW THAT MY HEART IS BENT, CHARLES?
MARCIE! I'M TRYING TO PITCH!
8-27
ALL I DID WAS TELL YOU THAT I'VE ALWAYS BEEN FOND OF YOU..IF I OFFENDED YOU, I'M SORRY.
SHUT UP! CAN'T YOU SEE WE'RE TALKING?!!
I NEVER MEANT TO OFFEND YOU, CHARLES..
I THINK I'M FALLING OVER BACKWARDS..
SCHULZ

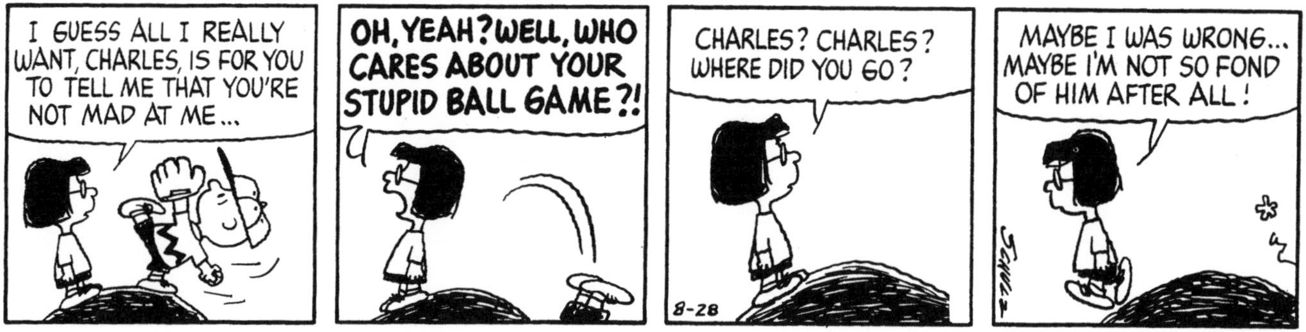
I GUESS ALL I REALLY WANT, CHARLES, IS FOR YOU TO TELL ME THAT YOU'RE NOT MAD AT ME...
OH, YEAH? WELL, WHO CARES ABOUT YOUR STUPID BALL GAME?!
CHARLES? CHARLES? WHERE DID YOU GO?
8-28
MAYBE I WAS WRONG... MAYBE I'M NOT SO FOND OF HIM AFTER ALL!
SCHULZ

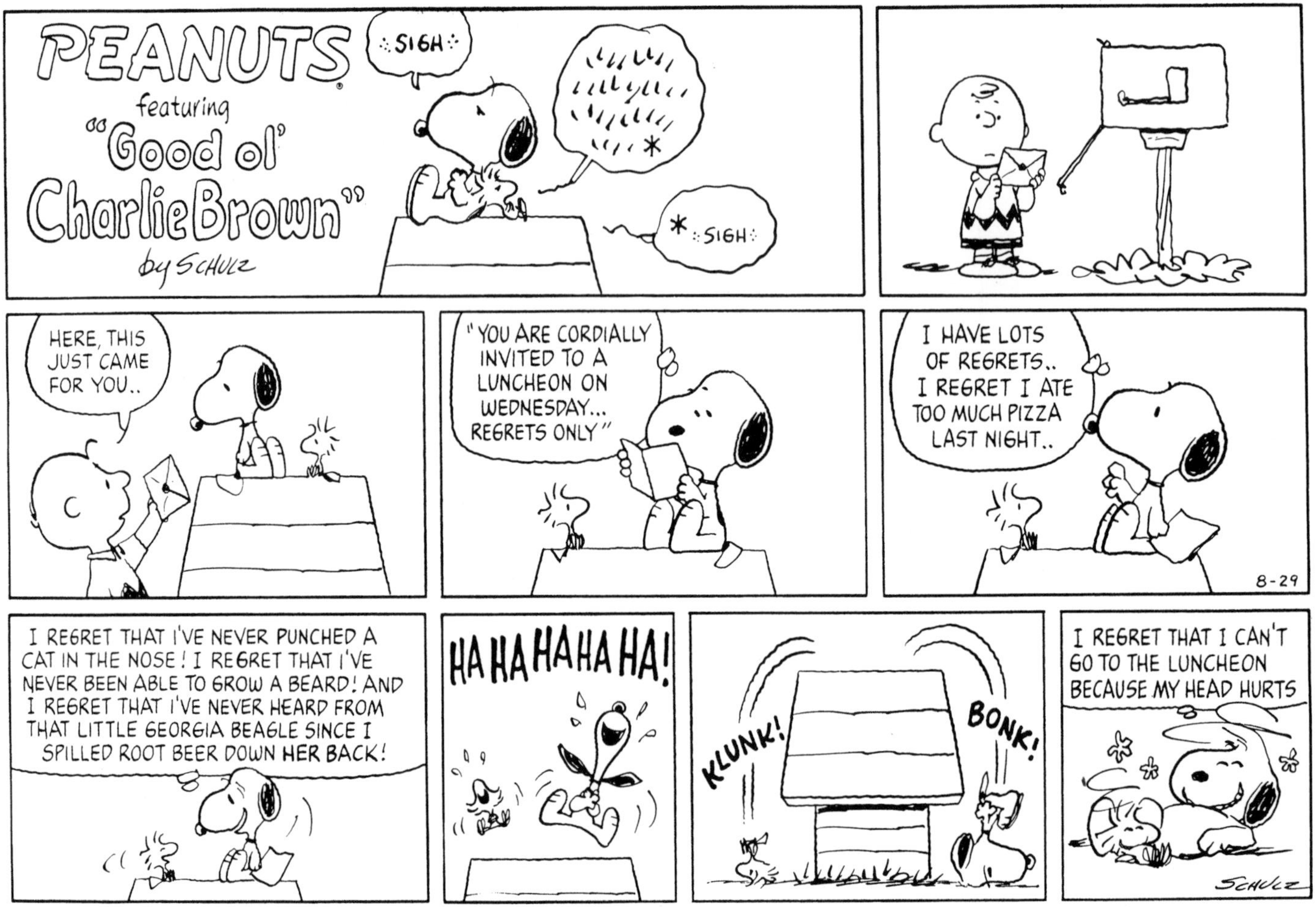
PEANUTS
featuring "Good ol' Charlie Brown"
by SCHULZ
SIGH
SIGH
HERE, THIS JUST CAME FOR YOU..
"YOU ARE CORDIALLY INVITED TO A LUNCHEON ON WEDNESDAY... REGRETS ONLY"
I HAVE LOTS OF REGRETS.. I REGRET I ATE TOO MUCH PIZZA LAST NIGHT..
8-29
I REGRET THAT I'VE NEVER PUNCHED A CAT IN THE NOSE! I REGRET THAT I'VE NEVER BEEN ABLE TO GROW A BEARD! AND I REGRET THAT I'VE NEVER HEARD FROM THAT LITTLE GEORGIA BEAGLE SINCE I SPILLED ROOT BEER DOWN HER BACK!
HA HA HA HA HA HA!
KLUNK!
BONK!
I REGRET THAT I CAN'T GO TO THE LUNCHEON BECAUSE MY HEAD HURTS
SCHULZ

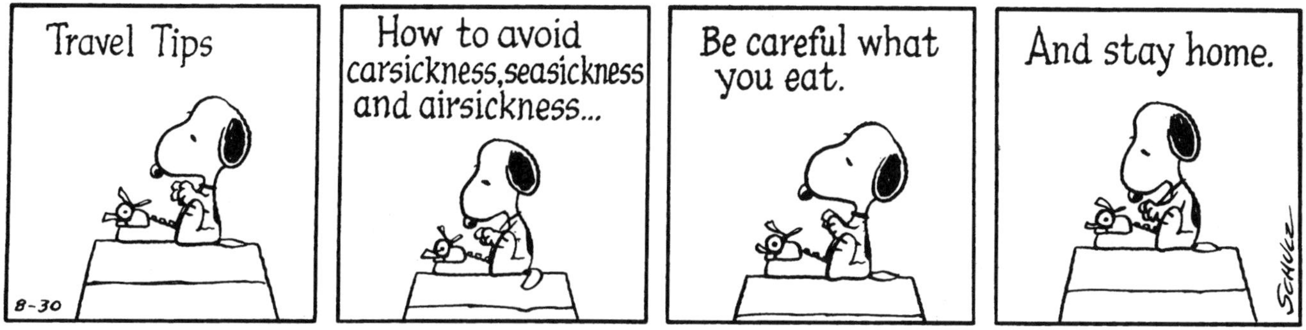
Travel Tips
8-30
How to avoid carsickness,seasickness and airsickness...
Be careful what you eat.
And stay home.

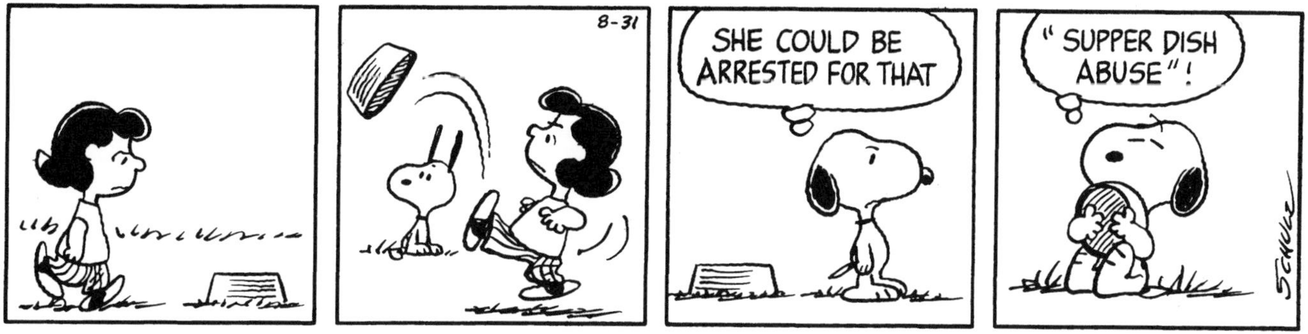
8-31
SHE COULD BE ARRESTED FOR THAT
" SUPPER DISH ABUSE " !

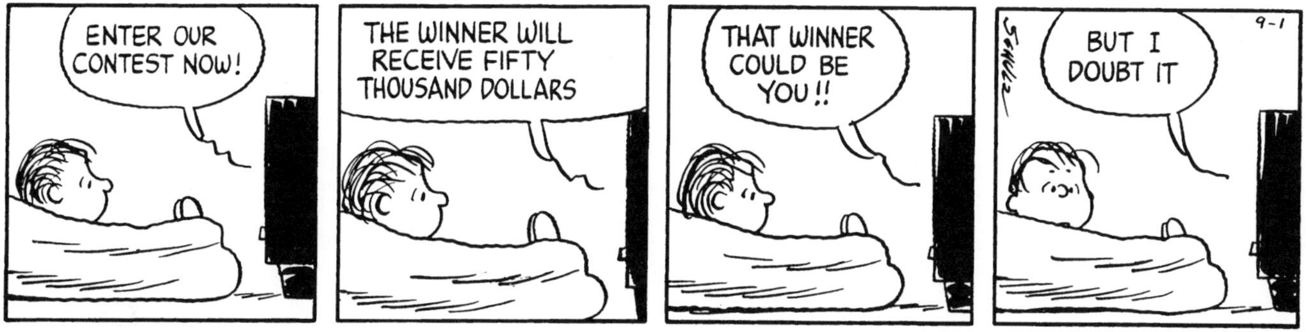
ENTER OUR CONTEST NOW!
THE WINNER WILL RECEIVE FIFTY THOUSAND DOLLARS
THAT WINNER COULD BE YOU!!
9-1
BUT I DOUBT IT

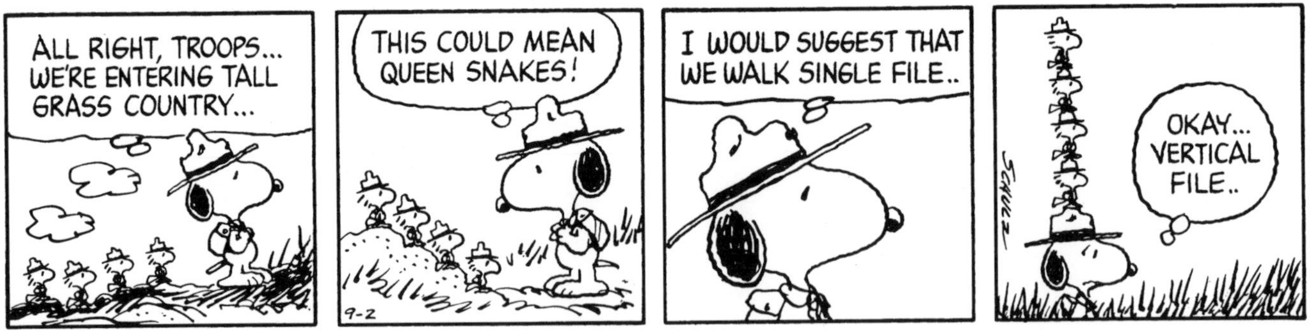
ALL RIGHT, TROOPS... WE'RE ENTERING TALL GRASS COUNTRY...
THIS COULD MEAN QUEEN SNAKES!
9-2
I WOULD SUGGEST THAT WE WALK SINGLE FILE..
OKAY... VERTICAL FILE..
SCHULZ

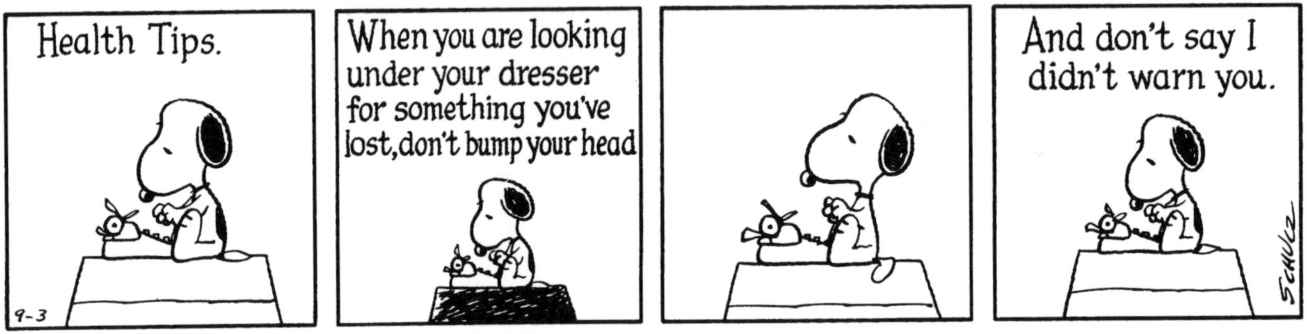
Health Tips.
9-3
When you are looking under your dresser for something you've lost, don't bump your head
And don't say I didn't warn you.
SCHULZ

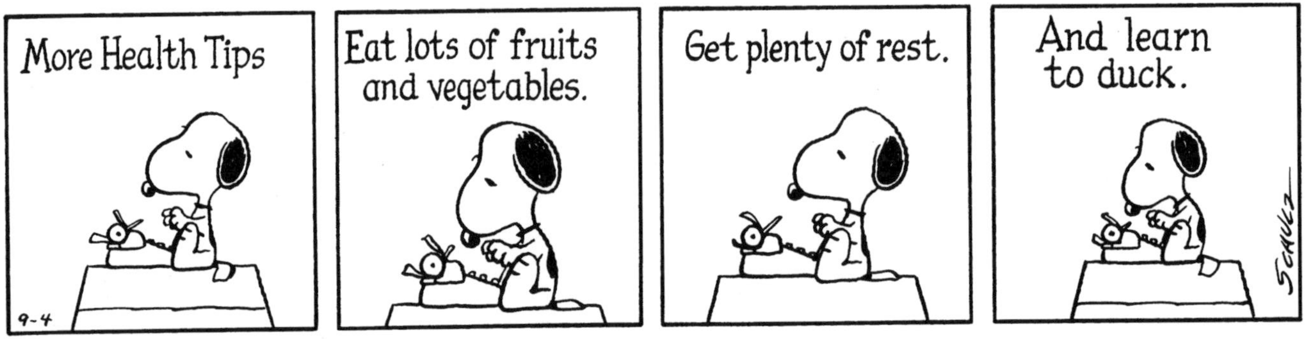
More Health Tips
9-4
Eat lots of fruits and vegetables.
Get plenty of rest.
And learn to duck.
SCHULZ

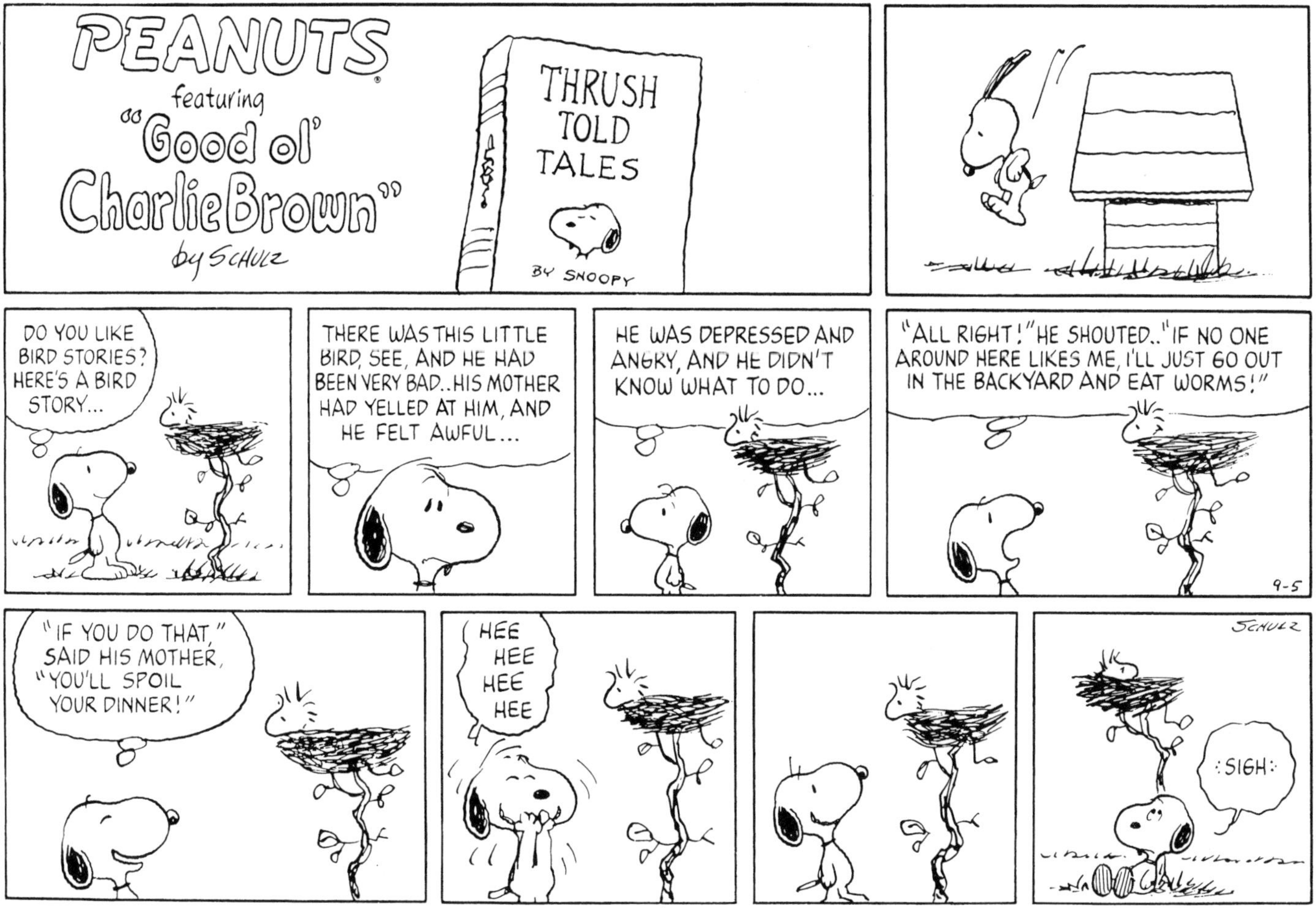
PEANUTS
featuring
"Good ol' Charlie Brown"
by SCHULZ
THRUSH TOLD TALES
BY SNOOPY
DO YOU LIKE BIRD STORIES? HERE'S A BIRD STORY...
THERE WAS THIS LITTLE BIRD, SEE, AND HE HAD BEEN VERY BAD..HIS MOTHER HAD YELLED AT HIM, AND HE FELT AWFUL...
HE WAS DEPRESSED AND ANGRY, AND HE DIDN'T KNOW WHAT TO DO...
"ALL RIGHT!" HE SHOUTED.."IF NO ONE AROUND HERE LIKES ME, I'LL JUST GO OUT IN THE BACKYARD AND EAT WORMS!"
9-5
"IF YOU DO THAT," SAID HIS MOTHER, "YOU'LL SPOIL YOUR DINNER!"
HEE HEE HEE HEE
SCHULZ
:SIGH:

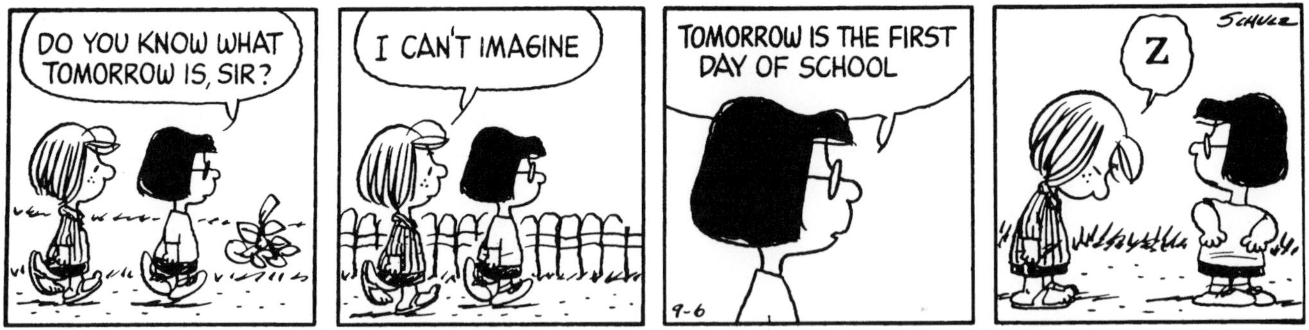
DO YOU KNOW WHAT TOMORROW IS, SIR?
I CAN'T IMAGINE
TOMORROW IS THE FIRST DAY OF SCHOOL
9-6
Z
SCHULZ

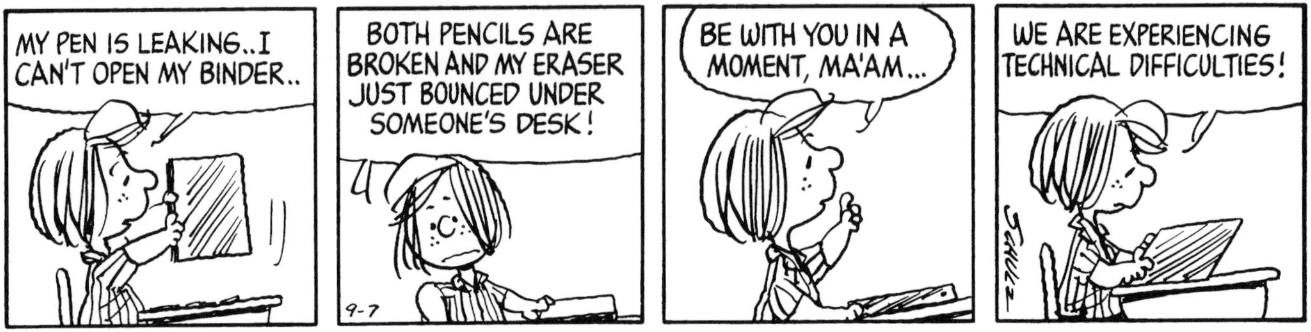
MY PEN IS LEAKING..I CAN'T OPEN MY BINDER..
BOTH PENCILS ARE BROKEN AND MY ERASER JUST BOUNCED UNDER SOMEONE'S DESK!
9-7
BE WITH YOU IN A MOMENT, MA'AM...
WE ARE EXPERIENCING TECHNICAL DIFFICULTIES!
SCHULZ

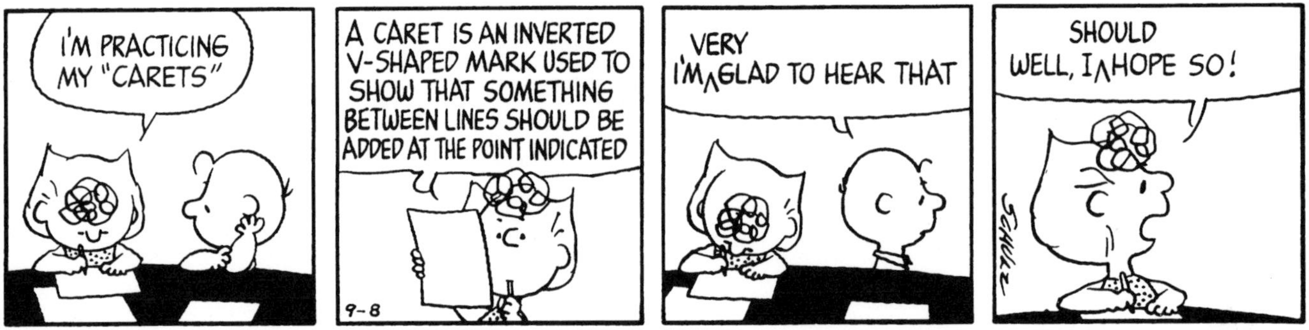
I'M PRACTICING MY "CARETS"
A CARET IS AN INVERTED V-SHAPED MARK USED TO SHOW THAT SOMETHING BETWEEN LINES SHOULD BE ADDED AT THE POINT INDICATED
9-8
VERY
I'M∧GLAD TO HEAR THAT
SHOULD
WELL, I∧HOPE SO!
SCHULZ

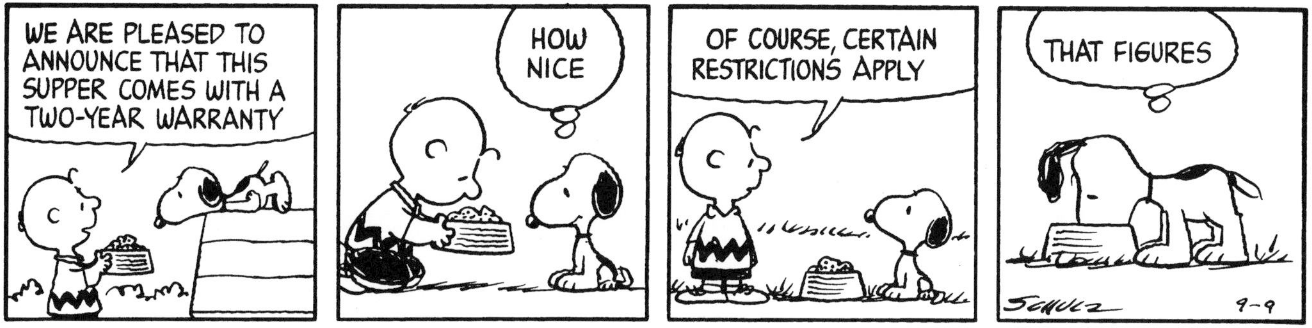
WE ARE PLEASED TO ANNOUNCE THAT THIS SUPPER COMES WITH A TWO-YEAR WARRANTY
HOW NICE
OF COURSE, CERTAIN RESTRICTIONS APPLY
THAT FIGURES
SCHULZ
9-9

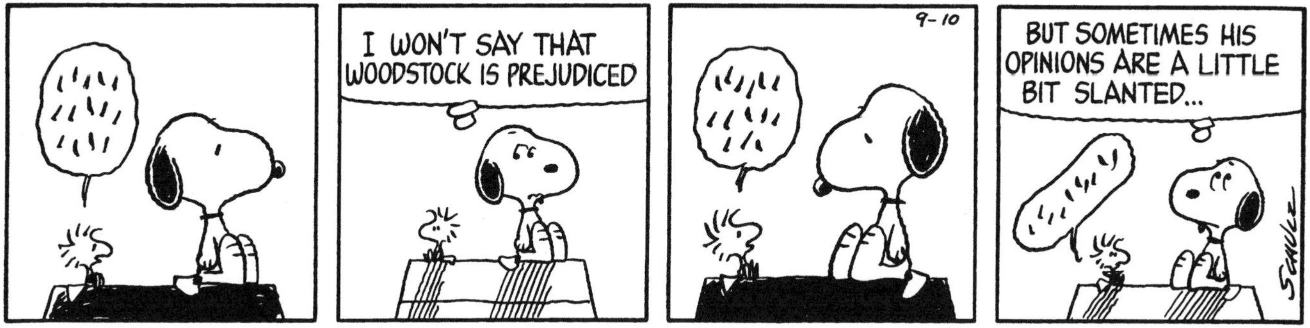
I WON'T SAY THAT WOODSTOCK IS PREJUDICED
9-10
BUT SOMETIMES HIS OPINIONS ARE A LITTLE BIT SLANTED...
SCHULZ

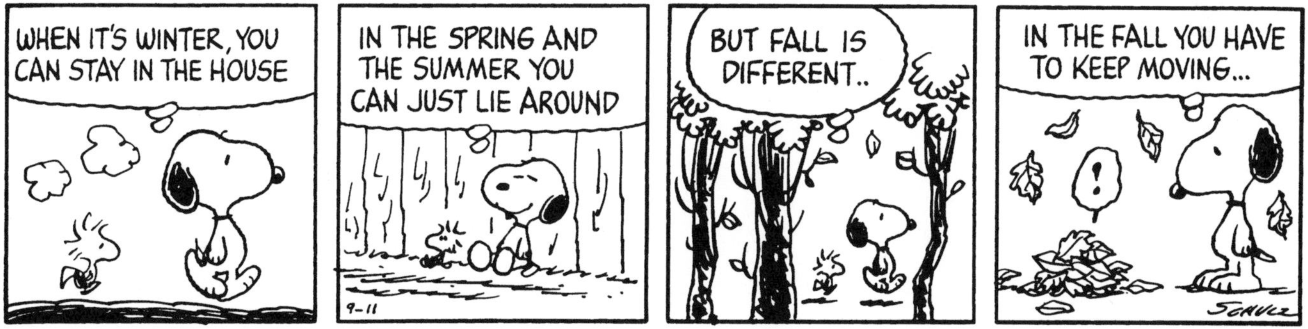
WHEN IT'S WINTER, YOU CAN STAY IN THE HOUSE
IN THE SPRING AND THE SUMMER YOU CAN JUST LIE AROUND
9-11
BUT FALL IS DIFFERENT..
IN THE FALL YOU HAVE TO KEEP MOVING...
!
SCHULZ

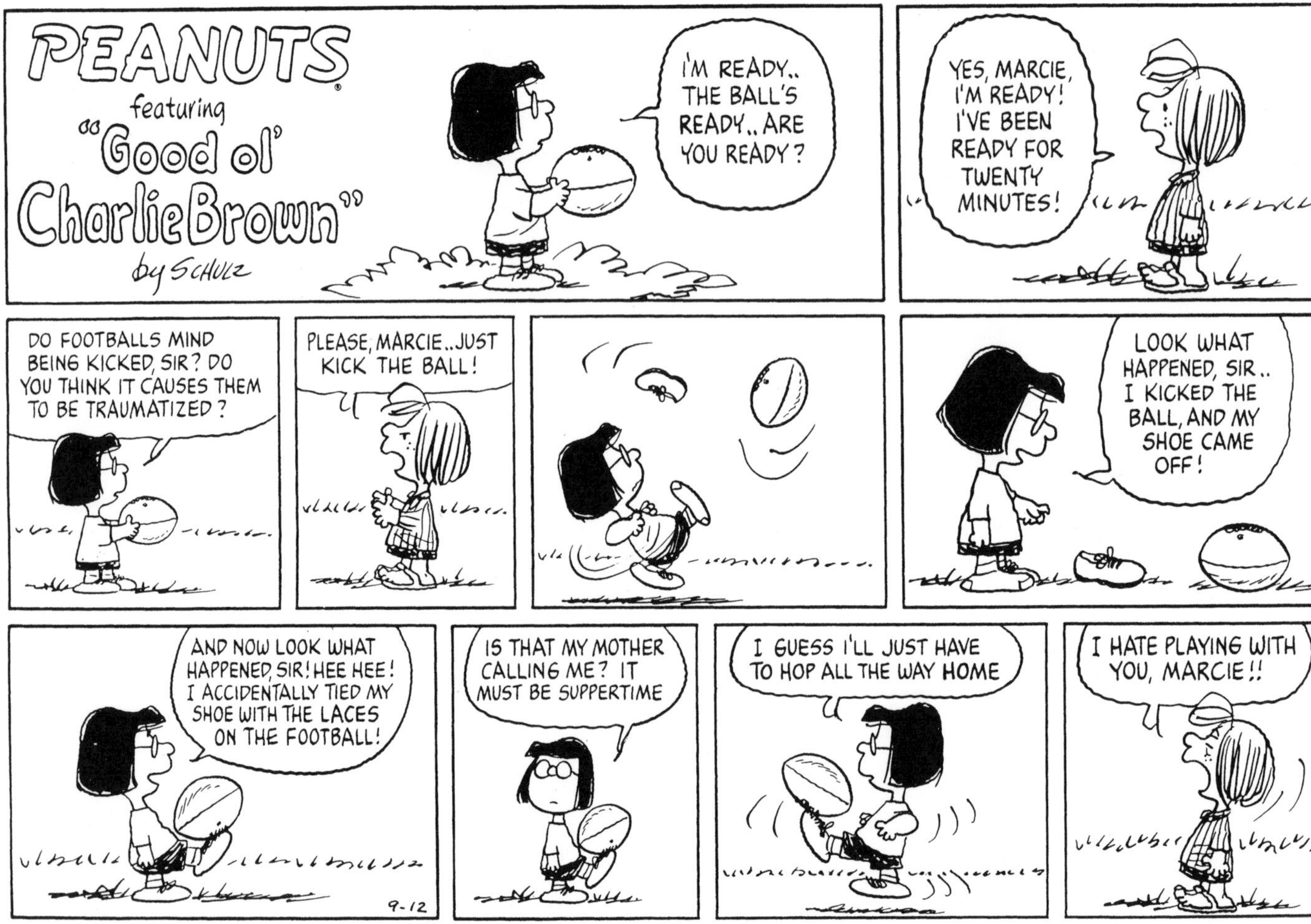
PEANUTS
featuring "Good ol' CharlieBrown"
by SCHULZ
I'M READY.. THE BALL'S READY.. ARE YOU READY?
YES, MARCIE, I'M READY! I'VE BEEN READY FOR TWENTY MINUTES!
DO FOOTBALLS MIND BEING KICKED, SIR? DO YOU THINK IT CAUSES THEM TO BE TRAUMATIZED?
PLEASE, MARCIE..JUST KICK THE BALL!
LOOK WHAT HAPPENED, SIR.. I KICKED THE BALL, AND MY SHOE CAME OFF!
AND NOW LOOK WHAT HAPPENED, SIR! HEE HEE! I ACCIDENTALLY TIED MY SHOE WITH THE LACES ON THE FOOTBALL!
9-12
IS THAT MY MOTHER CALLING ME? IT MUST BE SUPPERTIME
I GUESS I'LL JUST HAVE TO HOP ALL THE WAY HOME
I HATE PLAYING WITH YOU, MARCIE!!
SCHULZ

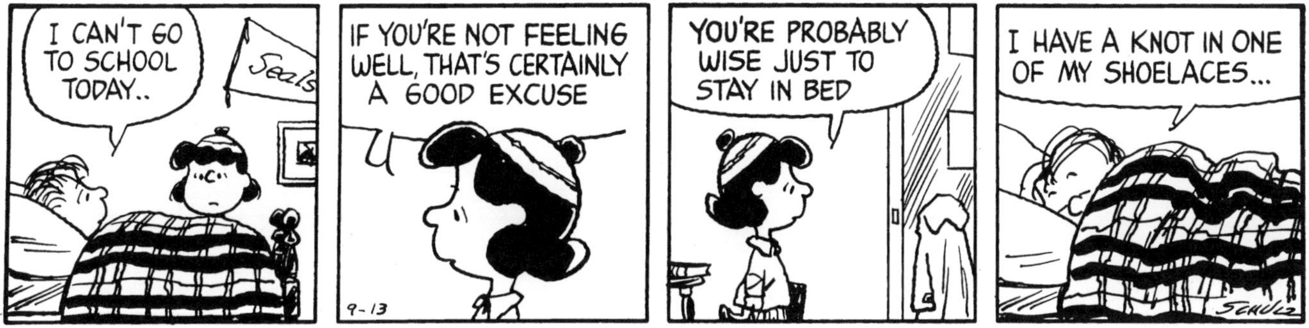
I CAN'T GO TO SCHOOL TODAY..
IF YOU'RE NOT FEELING WELL, THAT'S CERTAINLY A GOOD EXCUSE
9-13
YOU'RE PROBABLY WISE JUST TO STAY IN BED
I HAVE A KNOT IN ONE OF MY SHOELACES...
SCHULZ

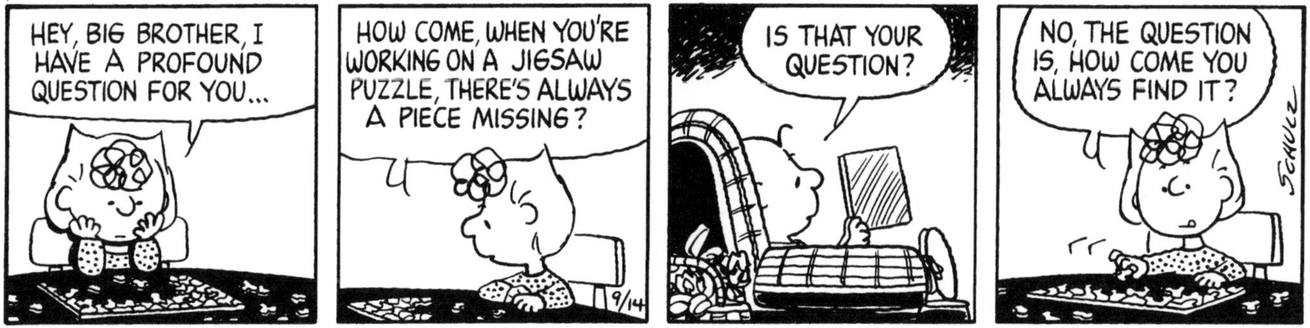
HEY, BIG BROTHER, I HAVE A PROFOUND QUESTION FOR YOU...
HOW COME, WHEN YOU'RE WORKING ON A JIGSAW PUZZLE, THERE'S ALWAYS A PIECE MISSING?
9/14
IS THAT YOUR QUESTION?
NO, THE QUESTION IS, HOW COME YOU ALWAYS FIND IT?
SCHULZ

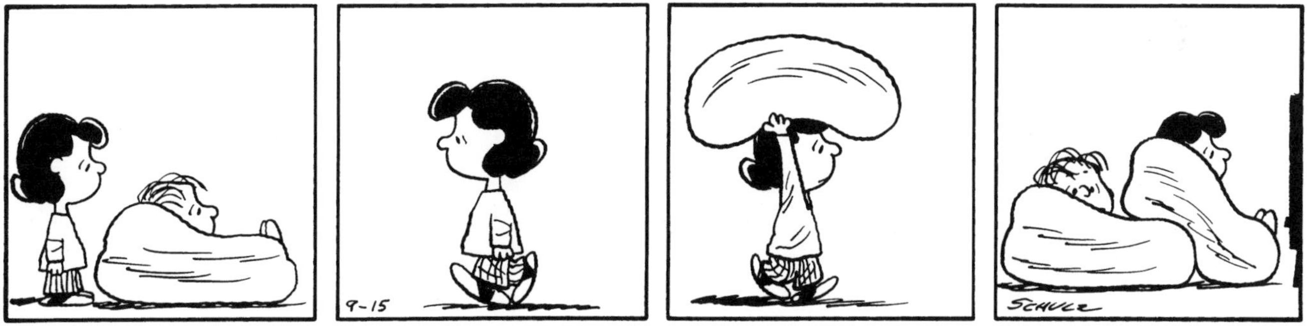
9-15
SCHULZ

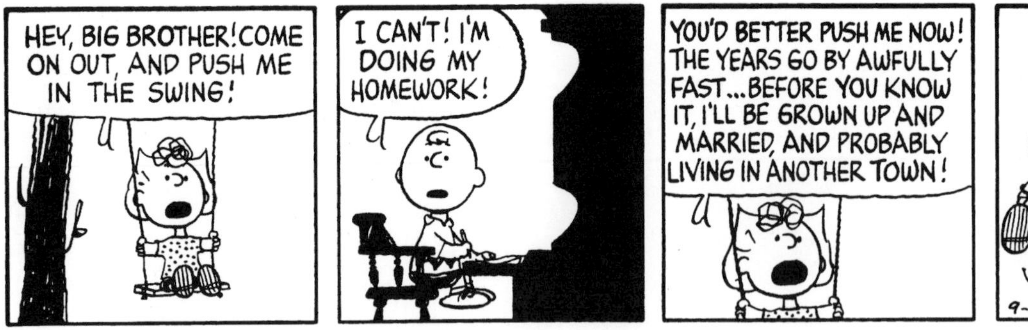
HEY, BIG BROTHER! COME ON OUT, AND PUSH ME IN THE SWING!
I CAN'T! I'M DOING MY HOMEWORK!
YOU'D BETTER PUSH ME NOW! THE YEARS GO BY AWFULLY FAST...BEFORE YOU KNOW IT, I'LL BE GROWN UP AND MARRIED, AND PROBABLY LIVING IN ANOTHER TOWN!
:SIGH:
SCHULZ
9-16

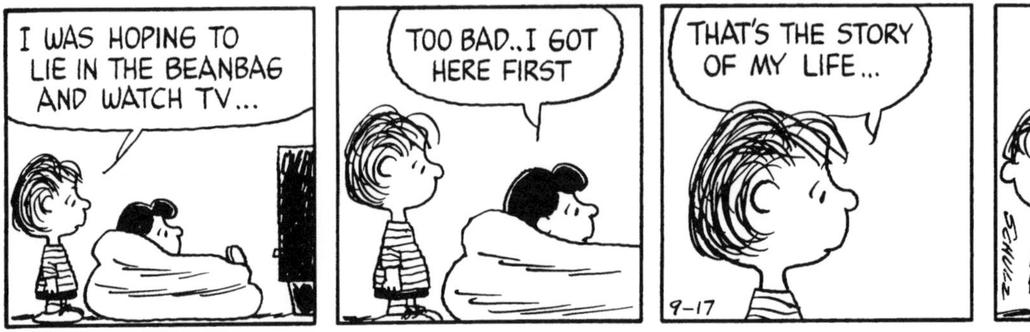
I WAS HOPING TO LIE IN THE BEANBAG AND WATCH TV...
TOO BAD..I GOT HERE FIRST
THAT'S THE STORY OF MY LIFE...
9-17
LOW MAN ON THE BEANBAG!
SCHULZ

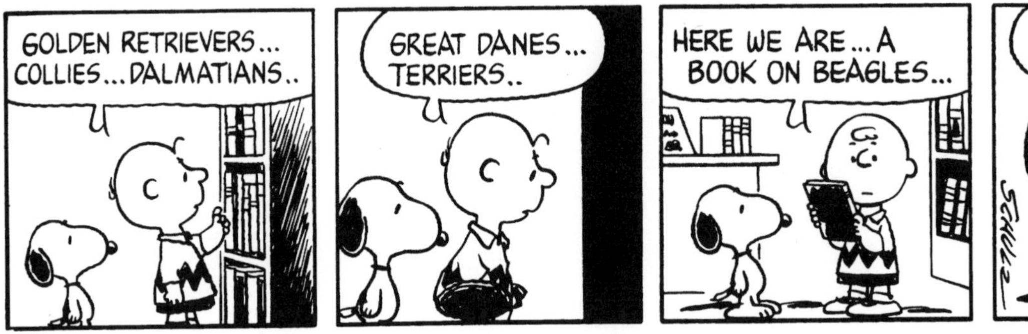
GOLDEN RETRIEVERS... COLLIES...DALMATIANS..
GREAT DANES... TERRIERS..
HERE WE ARE...A BOOK ON BEAGLES...
MY PEOPLE!
SCHULZ
9-18

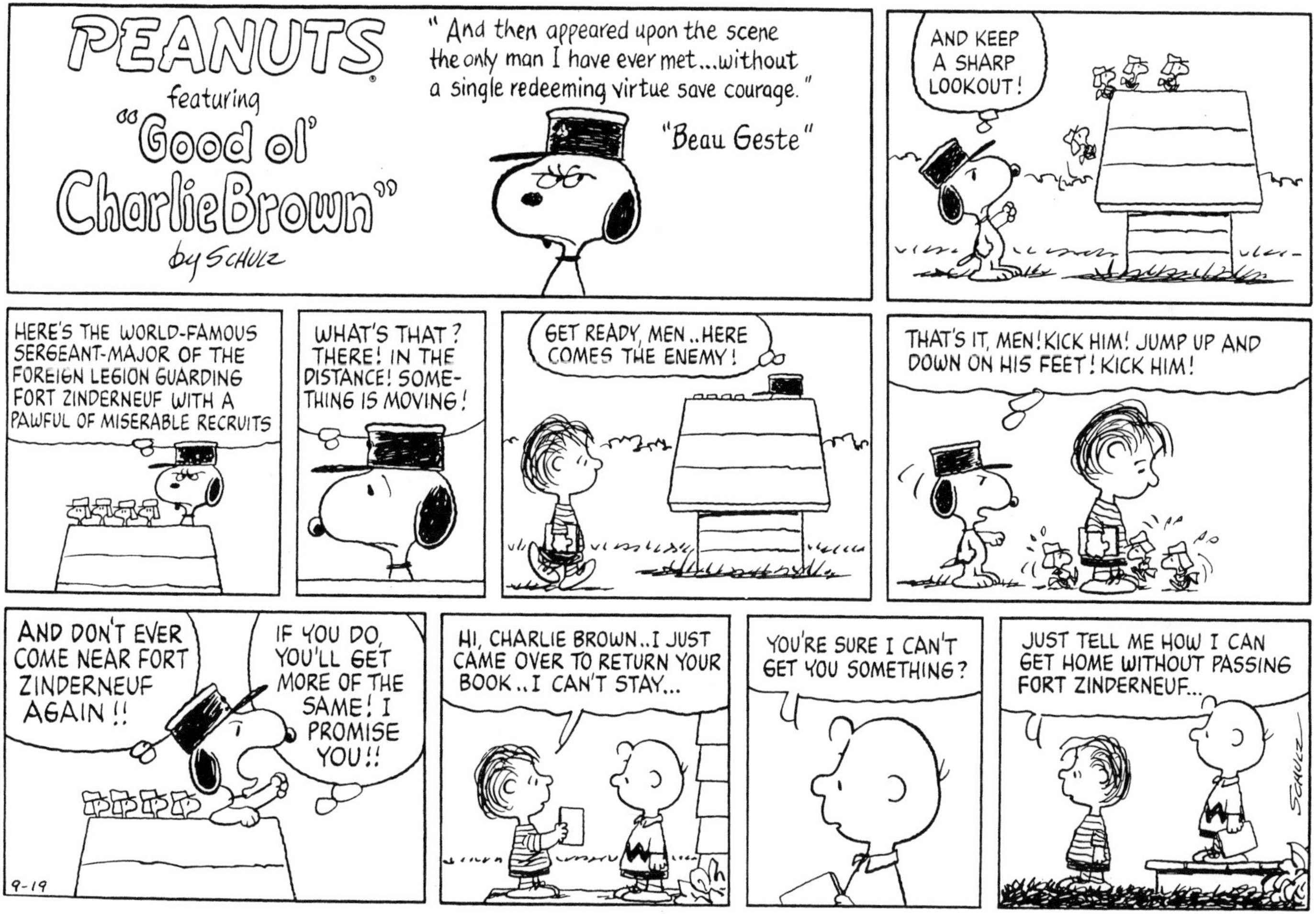
PEANUTS
featuring
"Good ol' Charlie Brown"
by SCHULZ
"And then appeared upon the scene the only man I have ever met...without a single redeeming virtue save courage."
"Beau Geste"
AND KEEP A SHARP LOOKOUT!
HERE'S THE WORLD-FAMOUS SERGEANT-MAJOR OF THE FOREIGN LEGION GUARDING FORT ZINDERNEUF WITH A PAWFUL OF MISERABLE RECRUITS
WHAT'S THAT? THERE! IN THE DISTANCE! SOMETHING IS MOVING!
GET READY, MEN..HERE COMES THE ENEMY!
THAT'S IT, MEN! KICK HIM! JUMP UP AND DOWN ON HIS FEET! KICK HIM!
AND DON'T EVER COME NEAR FORT ZINDERNEUF AGAIN!!
IF YOU DO, YOU'LL GET MORE OF THE SAME! I PROMISE YOU!!
9-19
HI, CHARLIE BROWN..I JUST CAME OVER TO RETURN YOUR BOOK..I CAN'T STAY...
YOU'RE SURE I CAN'T GET YOU SOMETHING?
JUST TELL ME HOW I CAN GET HOME WITHOUT PASSING FORT ZINDERNEUF...
SCHULZ

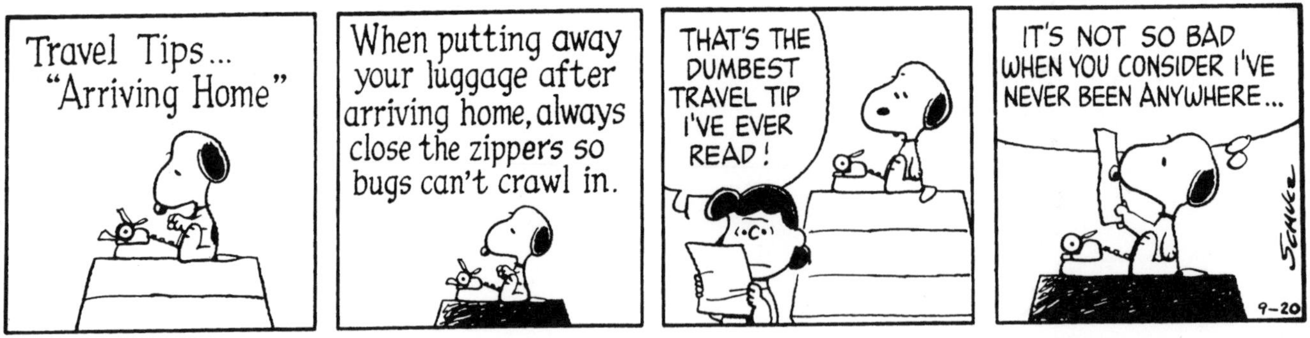
Travel Tips...
"Arriving Home"
When putting away your luggage after arriving home, always close the zippers so bugs can't crawl in.
THAT'S THE DUMBEST TRAVEL TIP I'VE EVER READ!
IT'S NOT SO BAD WHEN YOU CONSIDER I'VE NEVER BEEN ANYWHERE...
SCHULZ
9-20

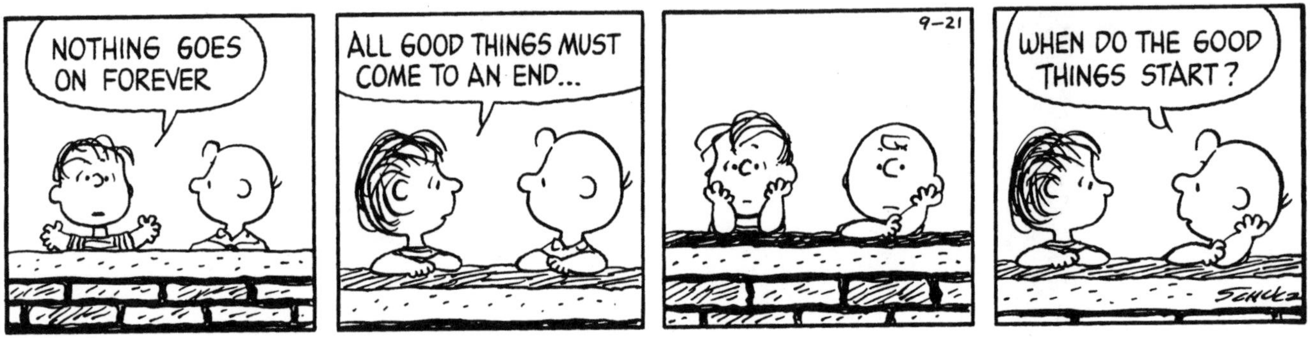
NOTHING GOES ON FOREVER
ALL GOOD THINGS MUST COME TO AN END...
9-21
WHEN DO THE GOOD THINGS START?
SCHULZ

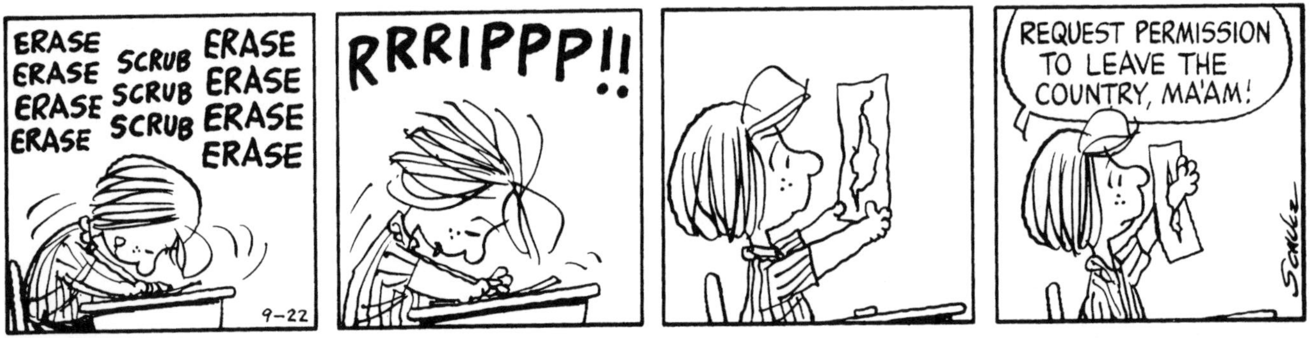
ERASE ERASE ERASE ERASE
SCRUB SCRUB SCRUB
ERASE ERASE ERASE ERASE
9-22
RRRIPPP!!
REQUEST PERMISSION TO LEAVE THE COUNTRY, MA'AM!
SCHULZ

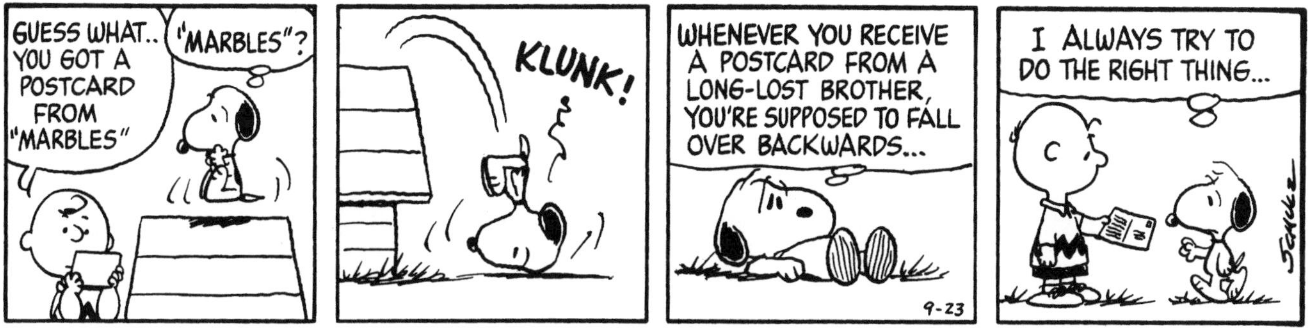
GUESS WHAT.. YOU GOT A POSTCARD FROM "MARBLES"
"MARBLES"?
KLUNK!
WHENEVER YOU RECEIVE A POSTCARD FROM A LONG-LOST BROTHER, YOU'RE SUPPOSED TO FALL OVER BACKWARDS...
9-23
I ALWAYS TRY TO DO THE RIGHT THING...
SCHULZ

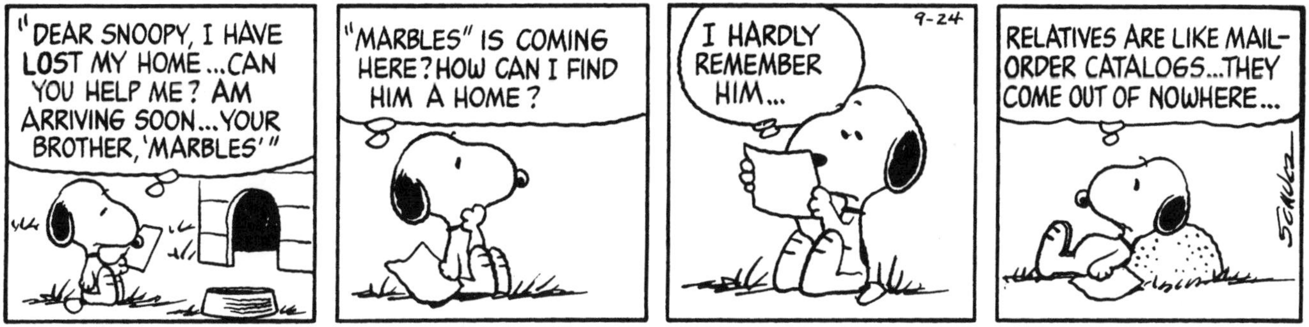
"DEAR SNOOPY, I HAVE LOST MY HOME...CAN YOU HELP ME? AM ARRIVING SOON...YOUR BROTHER, 'MARBLES'"
"MARBLES" IS COMING HERE? HOW CAN I FIND HIM A HOME?
I HARDLY REMEMBER HIM...
9-24
RELATIVES ARE LIKE MAIL-ORDER CATALOGS...THEY COME OUT OF NOWHERE...
SCHULZ

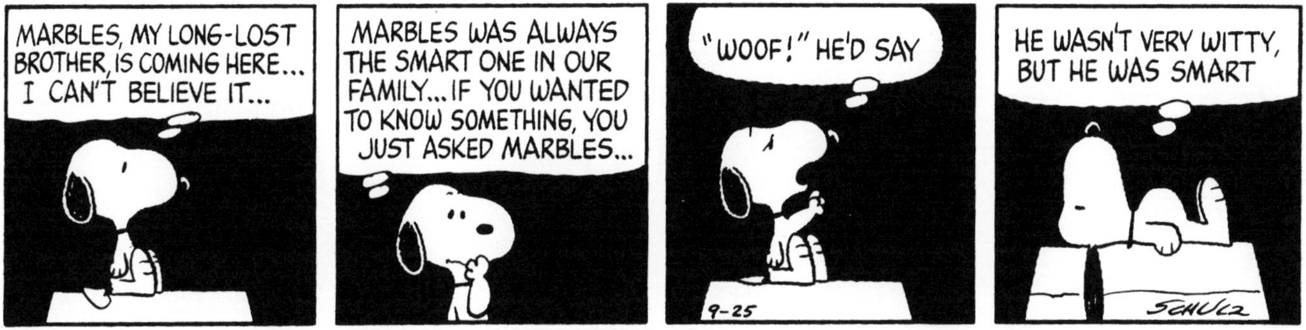
MARBLES, MY LONG-LOST BROTHER, IS COMING HERE... I CAN'T BELIEVE IT...
MARBLES WAS ALWAYS THE SMART ONE IN OUR FAMILY...IF YOU WANTED TO KNOW SOMETHING, YOU JUST ASKED MARBLES...
"WOOF!" HE'D SAY
9-25
HE WASN'T VERY WITTY, BUT HE WAS SMART
SCHULZ

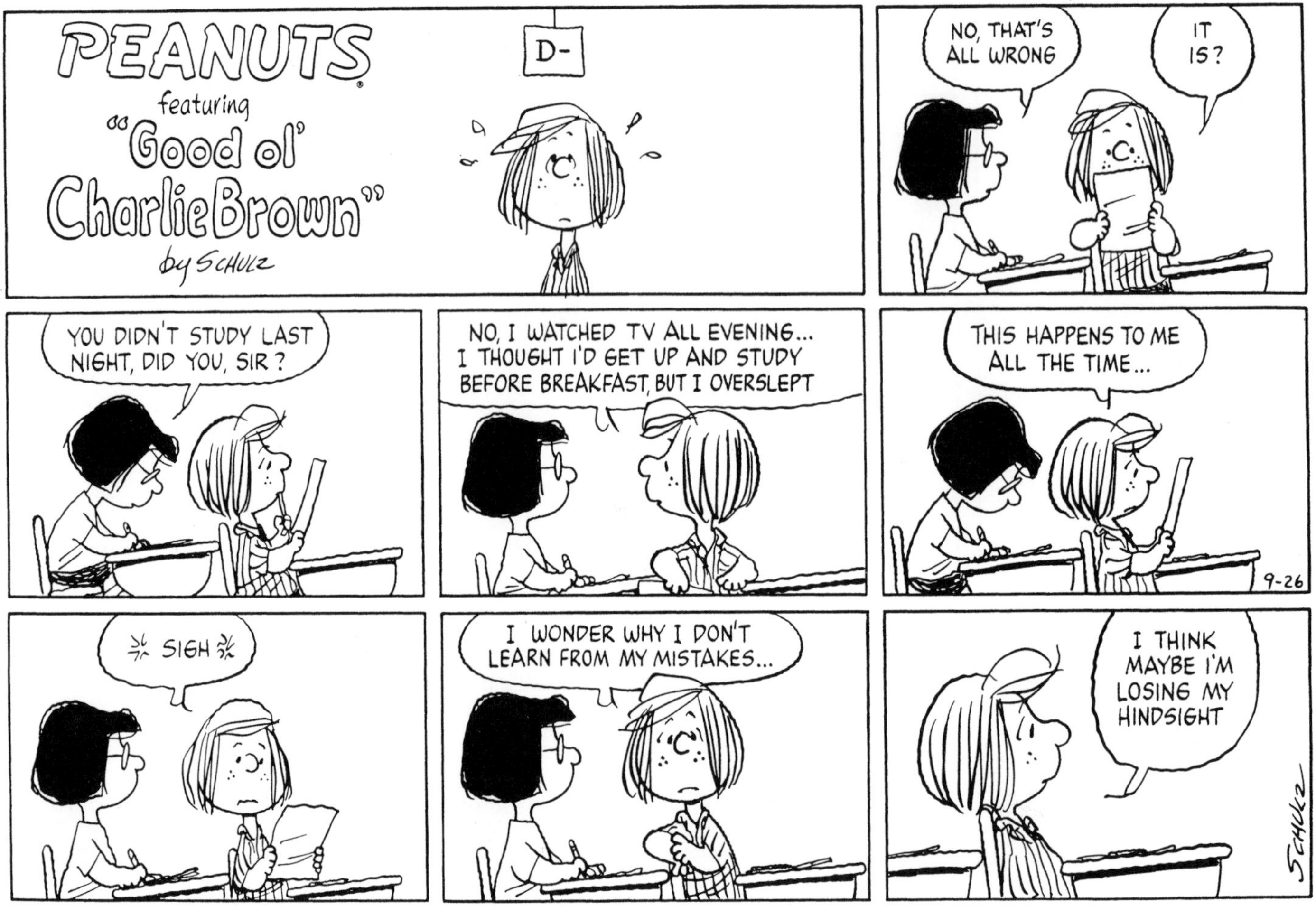
PEANUTS
featuring "Good ol' Charlie Brown"
by SCHULZ
D-
NO, THAT'S ALL WRONG
IT IS?
YOU DIDN'T STUDY LAST NIGHT, DID YOU, SIR?
NO, I WATCHED TV ALL EVENING... I THOUGHT I'D GET UP AND STUDY BEFORE BREAKFAST, BUT I OVERSLEPT
THIS HAPPENS TO ME ALL THE TIME...
9-26
SIGH
I WONDER WHY I DON'T LEARN FROM MY MISTAKES...
I THINK MAYBE I'M LOSING MY HINDSIGHT
SCHULZ

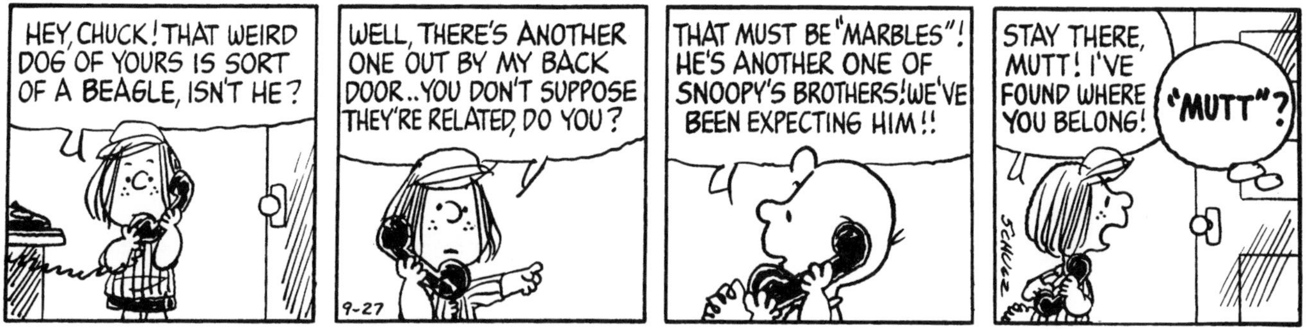
HEY, CHUCK! THAT WEIRD DOG OF YOURS IS SORT OF A BEAGLE, ISN'T HE?
WELL, THERE'S ANOTHER ONE OUT BY MY BACK DOOR.. YOU DON'T SUPPOSE THEY'RE RELATED, DO YOU?
9-27
THAT MUST BE "MARBLES"! HE'S ANOTHER ONE OF SNOOPY'S BROTHERS! WE'VE BEEN EXPECTING HIM!!
STAY THERE, MUTT! I'VE FOUND WHERE YOU BELONG!
"MUTT"?

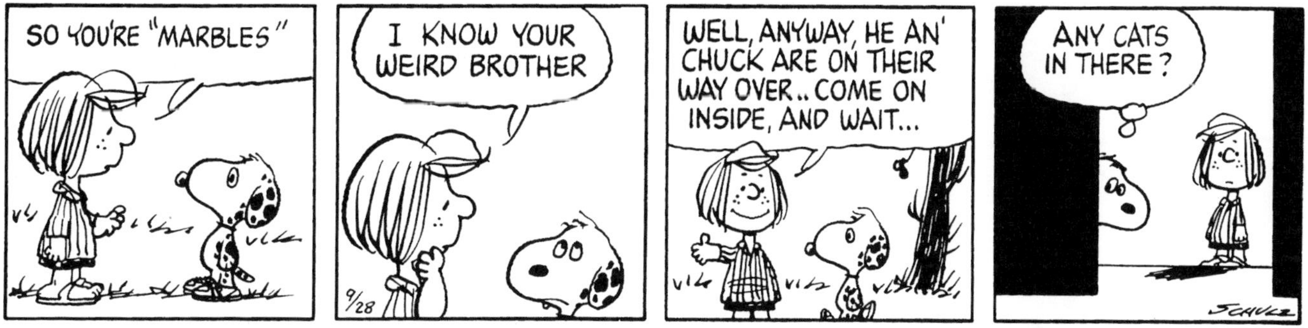
SO YOU'RE "MARBLES"
I KNOW YOUR WEIRD BROTHER
9/28
WELL, ANYWAY, HE AN' CHUCK ARE ON THEIR WAY OVER.. COME ON INSIDE, AND WAIT...
ANY CATS IN THERE?

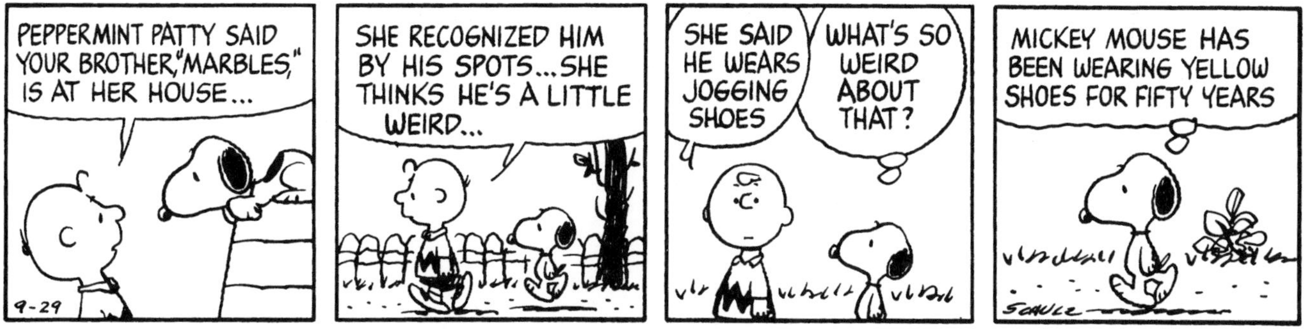
PEPPERMINT PATTY SAID YOUR BROTHER, "MARBLES," IS AT HER HOUSE...
9-29
SHE RECOGNIZED HIM BY HIS SPOTS... SHE THINKS HE'S A LITTLE WEIRD...
SHE SAID HE WEARS JOGGING SHOES
WHAT'S SO WEIRD ABOUT THAT?
MICKEY MOUSE HAS BEEN WEARING YELLOW SHOES FOR FIFTY YEARS

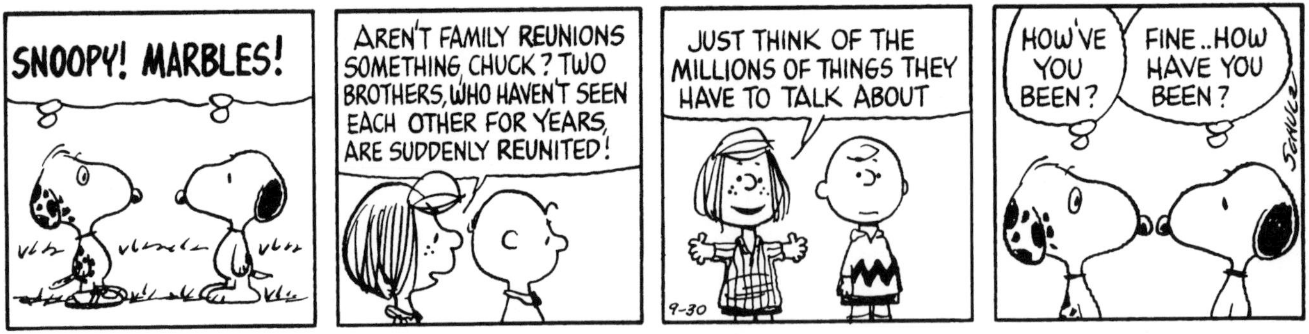
SNOOPY! MARBLES!
AREN'T FAMILY REUNIONS SOMETHING, CHUCK? TWO BROTHERS, WHO HAVEN'T SEEN EACH OTHER FOR YEARS, ARE SUDDENLY REUNITED!
JUST THINK OF THE MILLIONS OF THINGS THEY HAVE TO TALK ABOUT
9-30
HOW'VE YOU BEEN?
FINE..HOW HAVE YOU BEEN?
SCHULZ

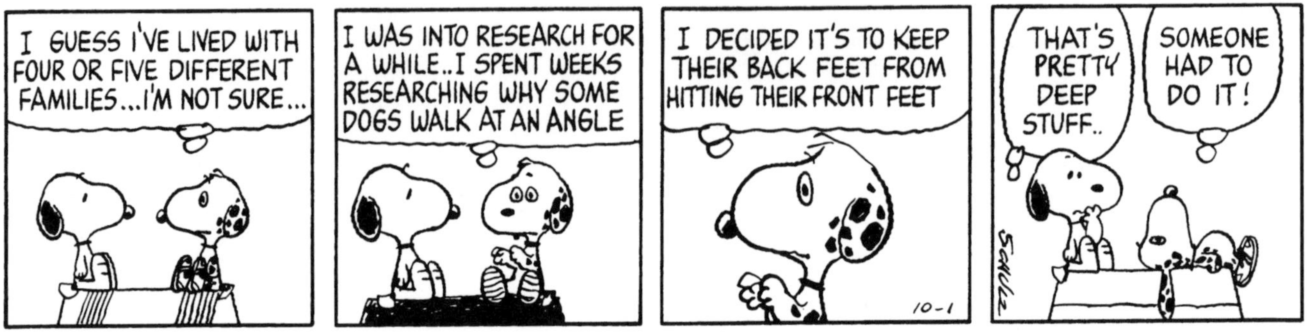
I GUESS I'VE LIVED WITH FOUR OR FIVE DIFFERENT FAMILIES...I'M NOT SURE...
I WAS INTO RESEARCH FOR A WHILE..I SPENT WEEKS RESEARCHING WHY SOME DOGS WALK AT AN ANGLE
I DECIDED IT'S TO KEEP THEIR BACK FEET FROM HITTING THEIR FRONT FEET
10-1
THAT'S PRETTY DEEP STUFF..
SOMEONE HAD TO DO IT!
SCHULZ

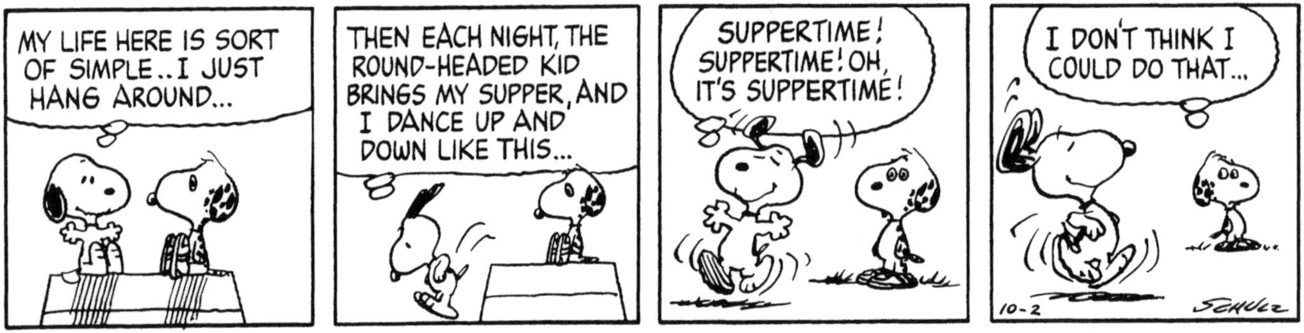
MY LIFE HERE IS SORT OF SIMPLE..I JUST HANG AROUND...
THEN EACH NIGHT, THE ROUND-HEADED KID BRINGS MY SUPPER, AND I DANCE UP AND DOWN LIKE THIS...
SUPPERTIME! SUPPERTIME! OH, IT'S SUPPERTIME!
I DON'T THINK I COULD DO THAT...
10-2
SCHULZ

PEANUTS featuring "Good ol' Charlie Brown" by Schulz

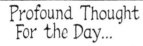

Profound Thought For the Day...

BAD NEWS..

WE'RE ALL OUT OF THE KIND OF DOG FOOD THAT YOU LIKE...

WE GOT ANOTHER BRAND, BUT I'M AFRAID IT'S NOT YOUR FAVORITE

10-3

Bad News Can Be a Depressant.

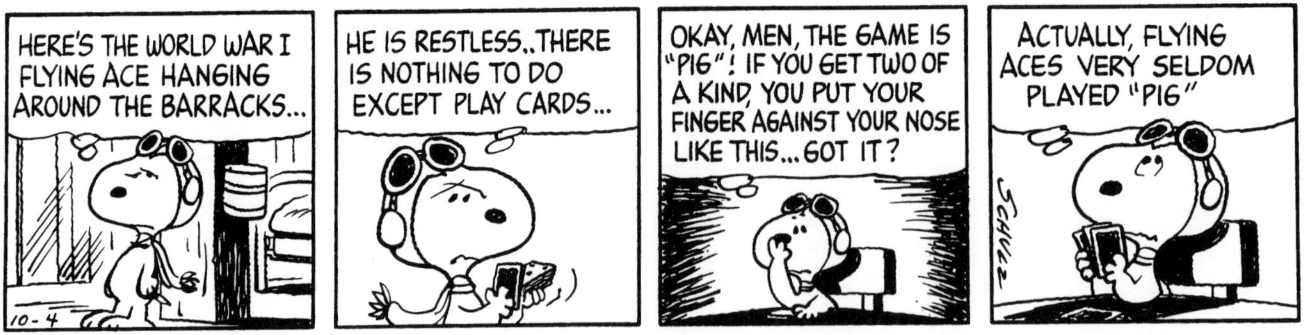
HERE'S THE WORLD WAR I FLYING ACE HANGING AROUND THE BARRACKS...
10-4
HE IS RESTLESS..THERE IS NOTHING TO DO EXCEPT PLAY CARDS...
OKAY, MEN, THE GAME IS "PIG"! IF YOU GET TWO OF A KIND, YOU PUT YOUR FINGER AGAINST YOUR NOSE LIKE THIS...GOT IT?
ACTUALLY, FLYING ACES VERY SELDOM PLAYED "PIG"

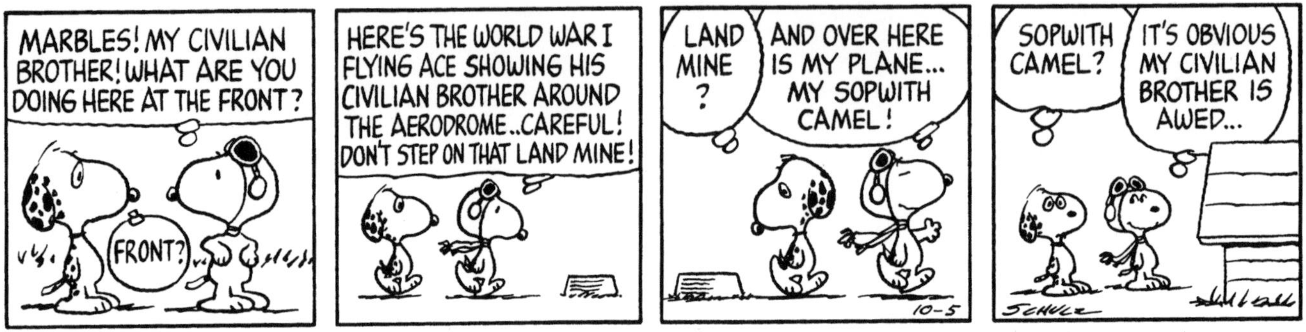
MARBLES! MY CIVILIAN BROTHER! WHAT ARE YOU DOING HERE AT THE FRONT?
FRONT?
HERE'S THE WORLD WAR I FLYING ACE SHOWING HIS CIVILIAN BROTHER AROUND THE AERODROME..CAREFUL! DON'T STEP ON THAT LAND MINE!
LAND MINE ?
AND OVER HERE IS MY PLANE... MY SOPWITH CAMEL!
10-5
SOPWITH CAMEL?
IT'S OBVIOUS MY CIVILIAN BROTHER IS AWED...

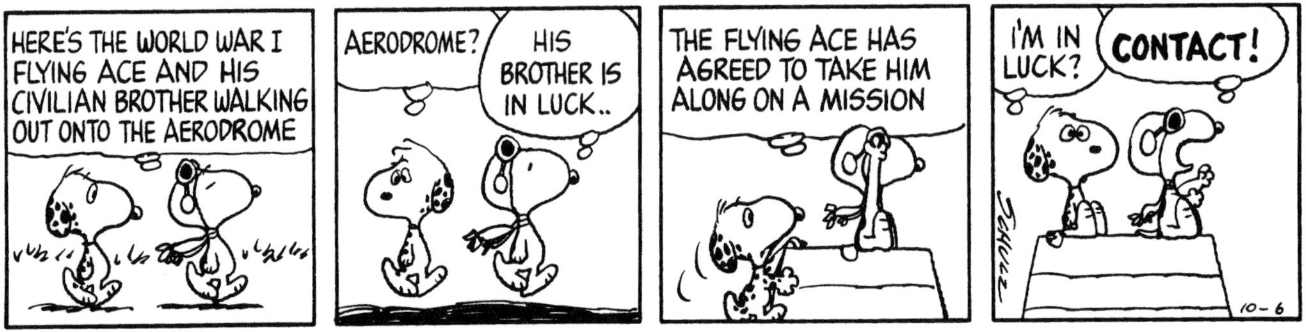
HERE'S THE WORLD WAR I FLYING ACE AND HIS CIVILIAN BROTHER WALKING OUT ONTO THE AERODROME
AERODROME?
HIS BROTHER IS IN LUCK..
THE FLYING ACE HAS AGREED TO TAKE HIM ALONG ON A MISSION
I'M IN LUCK?
CONTACT!
10-6

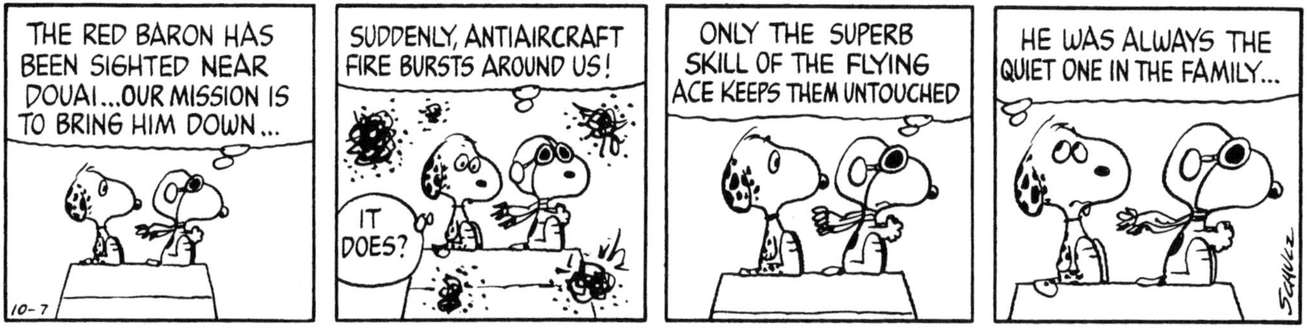
THE RED BARON HAS BEEN SIGHTED NEAR DOUAI...OUR MISSION IS TO BRING HIM DOWN...
10-7
SUDDENLY, ANTIAIRCRAFT FIRE BURSTS AROUND US!
IT DOES?
ONLY THE SUPERB SKILL OF THE FLYING ACE KEEPS THEM UNTOUCHED
HE WAS ALWAYS THE QUIET ONE IN THE FAMILY...
SCHULZ

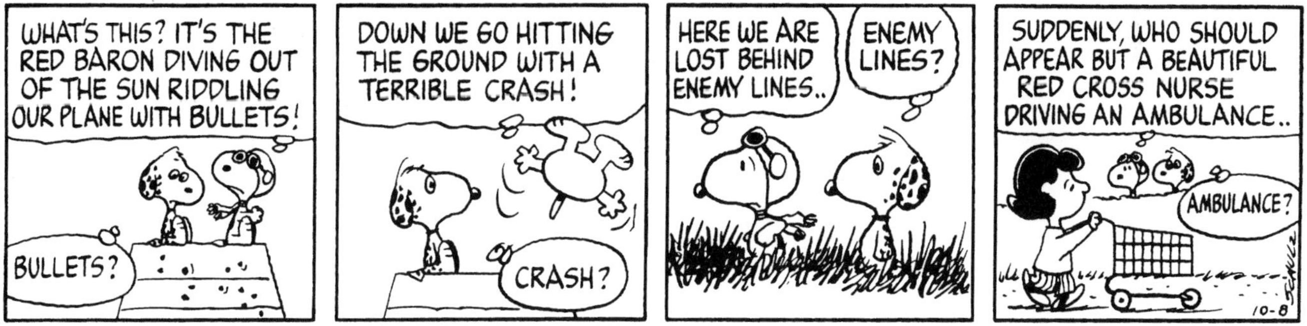
WHAT'S THIS? IT'S THE RED BARON DIVING OUT OF THE SUN RIDDLING OUR PLANE WITH BULLETS!
BULLETS?
DOWN WE GO HITTING THE GROUND WITH A TERRIBLE CRASH!
CRASH?
HERE WE ARE LOST BEHIND ENEMY LINES..
ENEMY LINES?
SUDDENLY, WHO SHOULD APPEAR BUT A BEAUTIFUL RED CROSS NURSE DRIVING AN AMBULANCE..
AMBULANCE?
SCHULZ
10-8

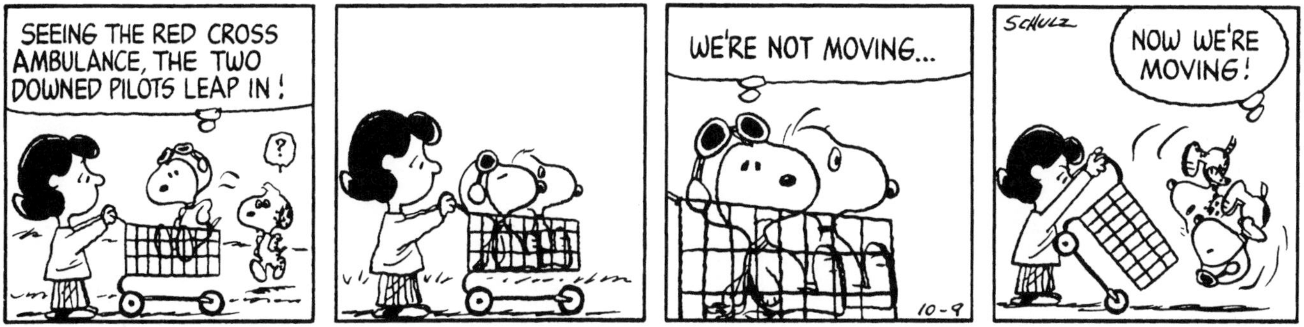
SEEING THE RED CROSS AMBULANCE, THE TWO DOWNED PILOTS LEAP IN!
?
WE'RE NOT MOVING...
10-9
SCHULZ
NOW WE'RE MOVING!

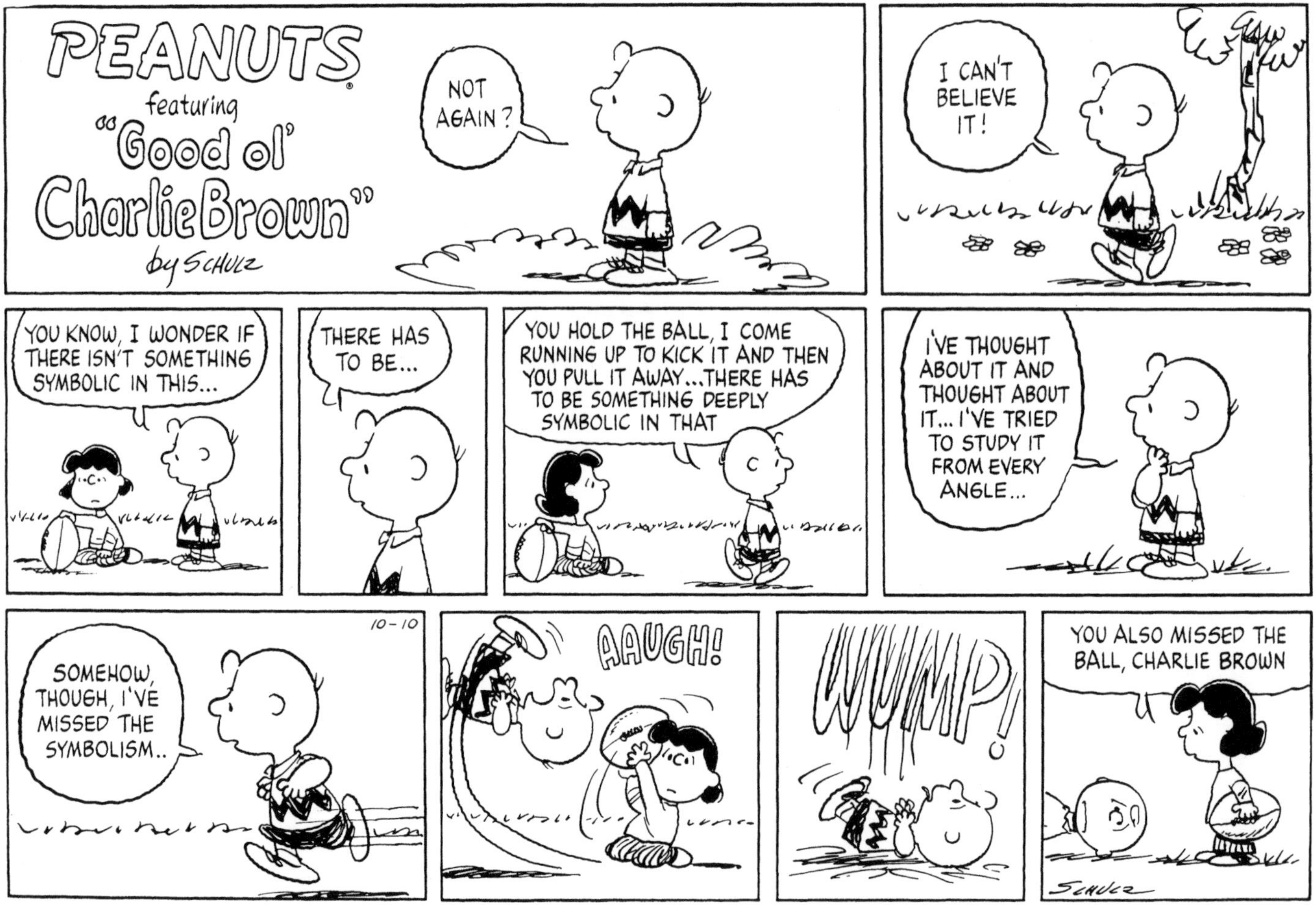
PEANUTS®
featuring "Good ol' Charlie Brown"
by SCHULZ
NOT AGAIN?
I CAN'T BELIEVE IT!
YOU KNOW, I WONDER IF THERE ISN'T SOMETHING SYMBOLIC IN THIS...
THERE HAS TO BE...
YOU HOLD THE BALL, I COME RUNNING UP TO KICK IT AND THEN YOU PULL IT AWAY...THERE HAS TO BE SOMETHING DEEPLY SYMBOLIC IN THAT
I'VE THOUGHT ABOUT IT AND THOUGHT ABOUT IT... I'VE TRIED TO STUDY IT FROM EVERY ANGLE...
10-10
SOMEHOW, THOUGH, I'VE MISSED THE SYMBOLISM..
AAUGH!
WUMP!
YOU ALSO MISSED THE BALL, CHARLIE BROWN
SCHULZ

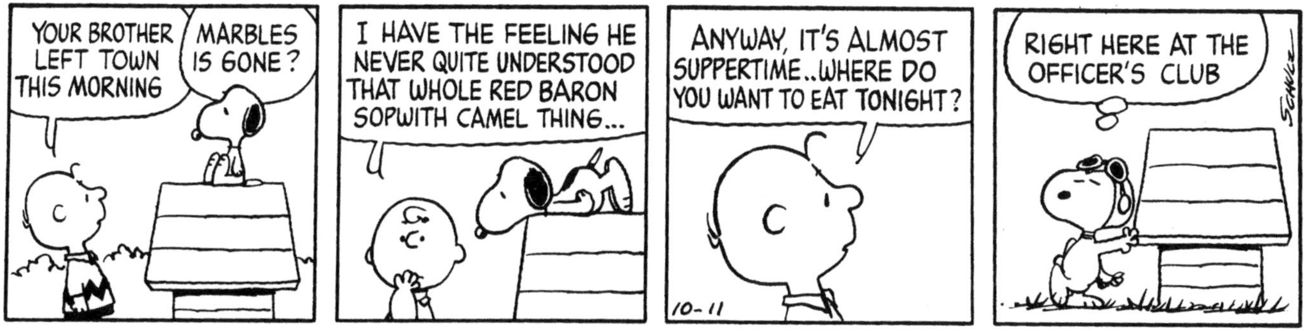
YOUR BROTHER LEFT TOWN THIS MORNING
MARBLES IS GONE ?
I HAVE THE FEELING HE NEVER QUITE UNDERSTOOD THAT WHOLE RED BARON SOPWITH CAMEL THING...
ANYWAY, IT'S ALMOST SUPPERTIME..WHERE DO YOU WANT TO EAT TONIGHT ?
10-11
RIGHT HERE AT THE OFFICER'S CLUB
SCHULZ

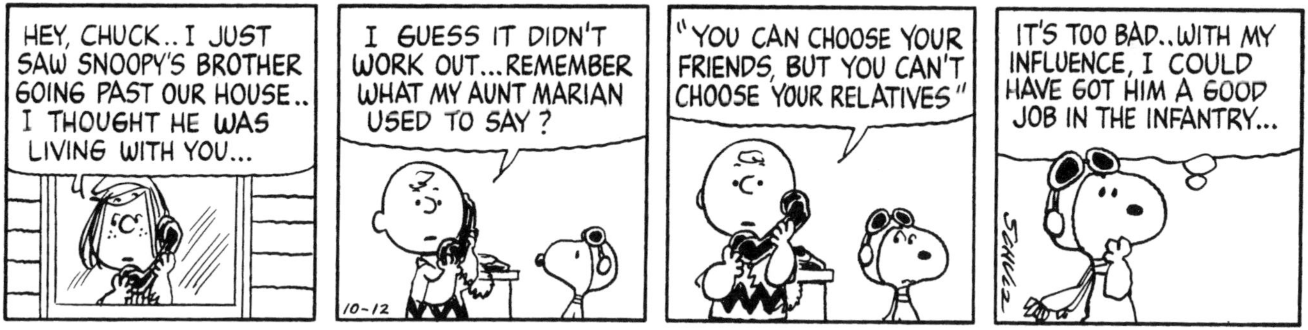
HEY, CHUCK.. I JUST SAW SNOOPY'S BROTHER GOING PAST OUR HOUSE.. I THOUGHT HE WAS LIVING WITH YOU...
I GUESS IT DIDN'T WORK OUT...REMEMBER WHAT MY AUNT MARIAN USED TO SAY ?
10-12
"YOU CAN CHOOSE YOUR FRIENDS, BUT YOU CAN'T CHOOSE YOUR RELATIVES"
IT'S TOO BAD..WITH MY INFLUENCE, I COULD HAVE GOT HIM A GOOD JOB IN THE INFANTRY...
SCHULZ

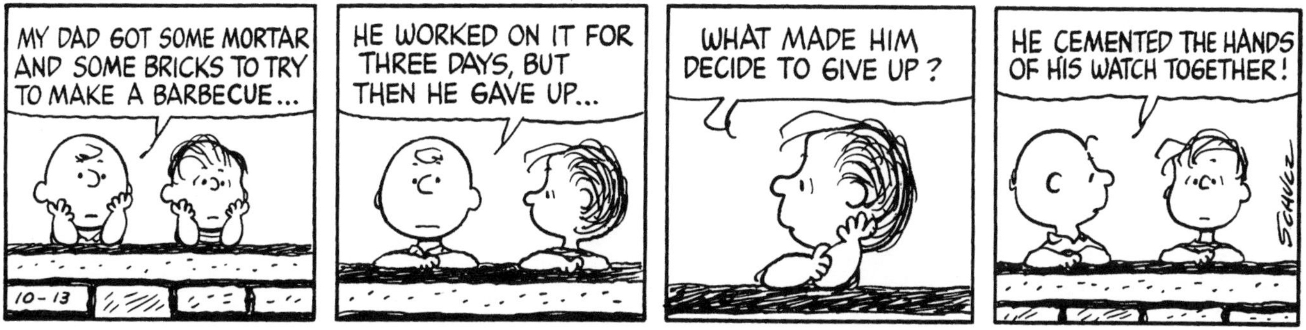
MY DAD GOT SOME MORTAR AND SOME BRICKS TO TRY TO MAKE A BARBECUE...
10-13
HE WORKED ON IT FOR THREE DAYS, BUT THEN HE GAVE UP...
WHAT MADE HIM DECIDE TO GIVE UP ?
HE CEMENTED THE HANDS OF HIS WATCH TOGETHER !
SCHULZ

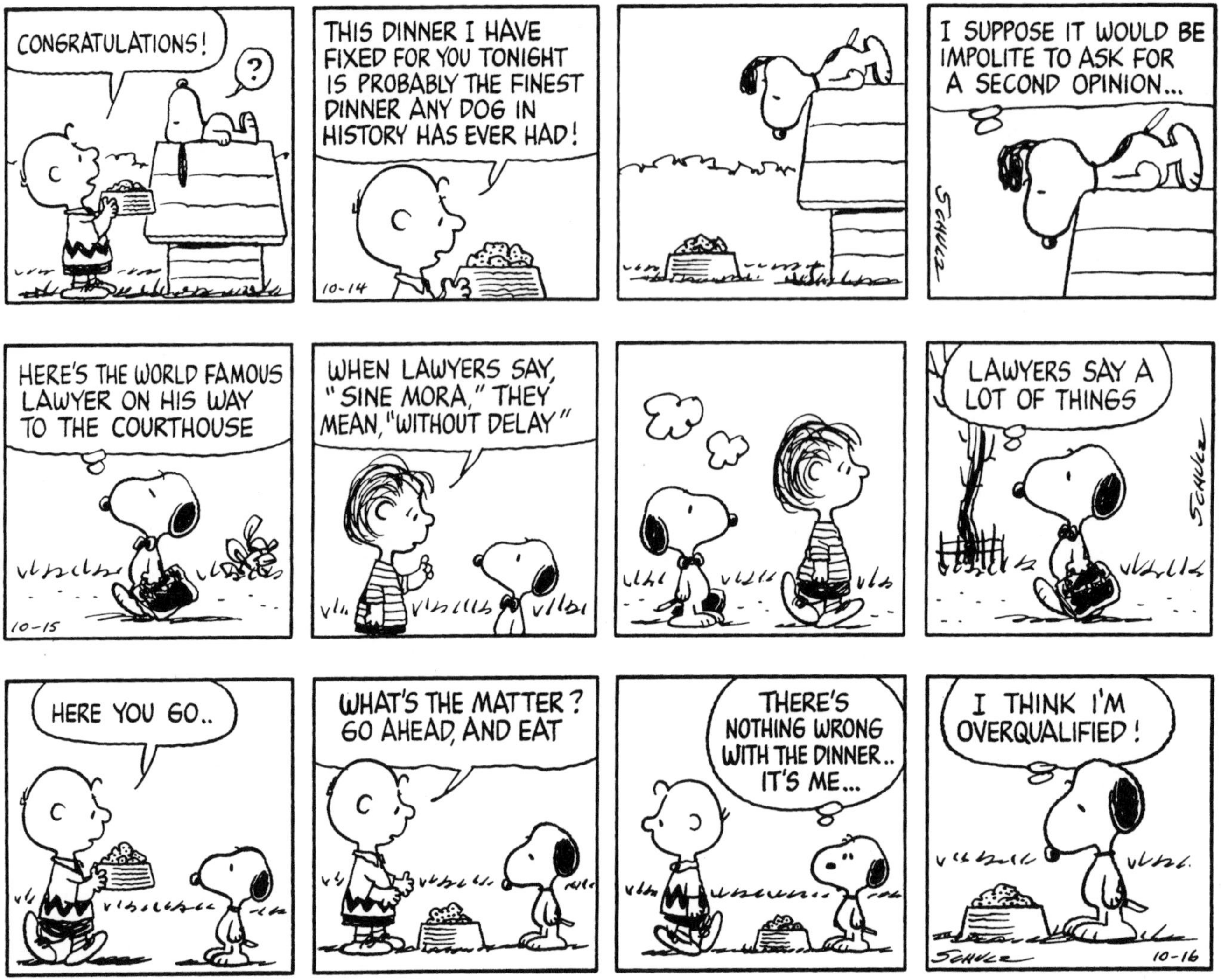
CONGRATULATIONS!
?
THIS DINNER I HAVE FIXED FOR YOU TONIGHT IS PROBABLY THE FINEST DINNER ANY DOG IN HISTORY HAS EVER HAD!
10-14
I SUPPOSE IT WOULD BE IMPOLITE TO ASK FOR A SECOND OPINION...
SCHULZ
HERE'S THE WORLD FAMOUS LAWYER ON HIS WAY TO THE COURTHOUSE
10-15
WHEN LAWYERS SAY, "SINE MORA," THEY MEAN, "WITHOUT DELAY"
LAWYERS SAY A LOT OF THINGS
SCHULZ
HERE YOU GO..
WHAT'S THE MATTER? GO AHEAD, AND EAT
THERE'S NOTHING WRONG WITH THE DINNER.. IT'S ME...
I THINK I'M OVERQUALIFIED!
SCHULZ
10-16

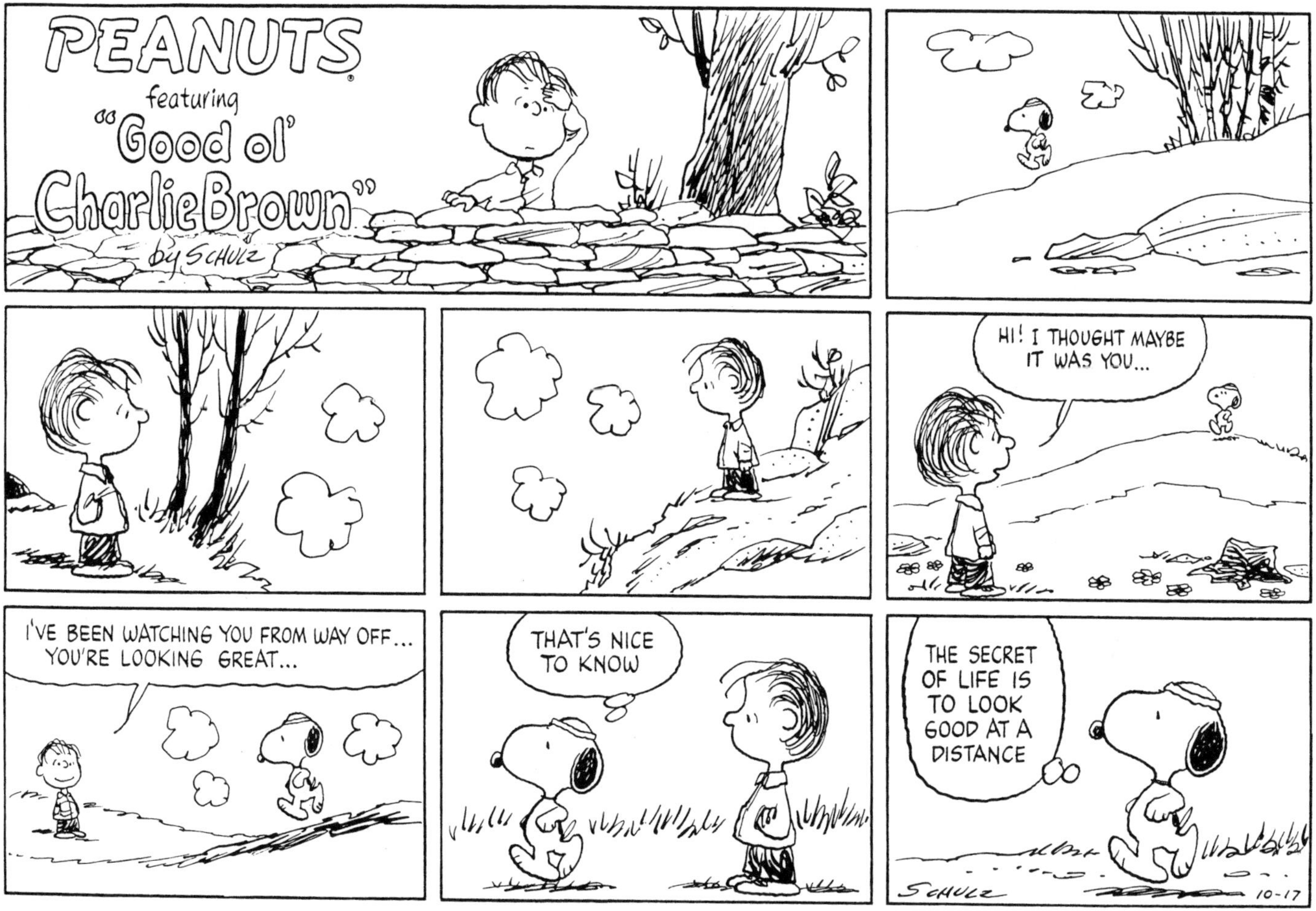
PEANUTS
featuring
"Good ol' Charlie Brown"
by SCHULZ
HI! I THOUGHT MAYBE IT WAS YOU...
I'VE BEEN WATCHING YOU FROM WAY OFF... YOU'RE LOOKING GREAT...
THAT'S NICE TO KNOW
THE SECRET OF LIFE IS TO LOOK GOOD AT A DISTANCE
SCHULZ
10-17

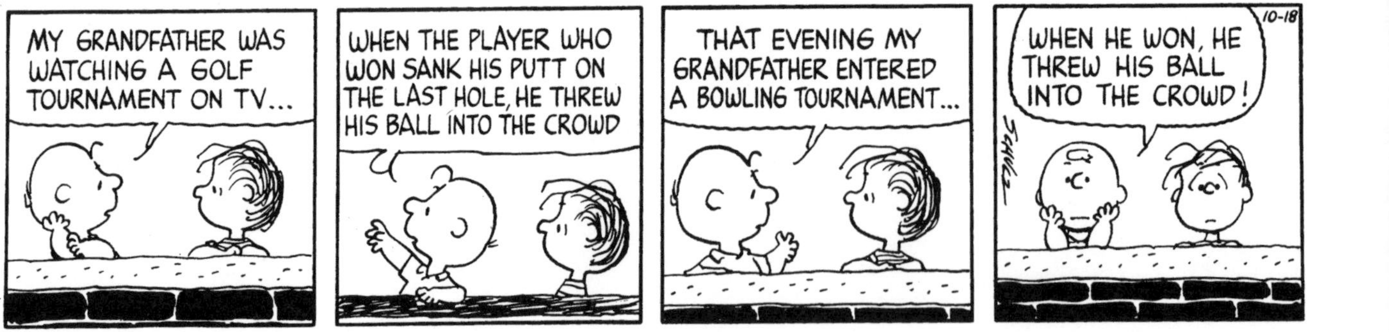
MY GRANDFATHER WAS WATCHING A GOLF TOURNAMENT ON TV...
WHEN THE PLAYER WHO WON SANK HIS PUTT ON THE LAST HOLE, HE THREW HIS BALL INTO THE CROWD
THAT EVENING MY GRANDFATHER ENTERED A BOWLING TOURNAMENT...
10-18
WHEN HE WON, HE THREW HIS BALL INTO THE CROWD!
SCHULZ

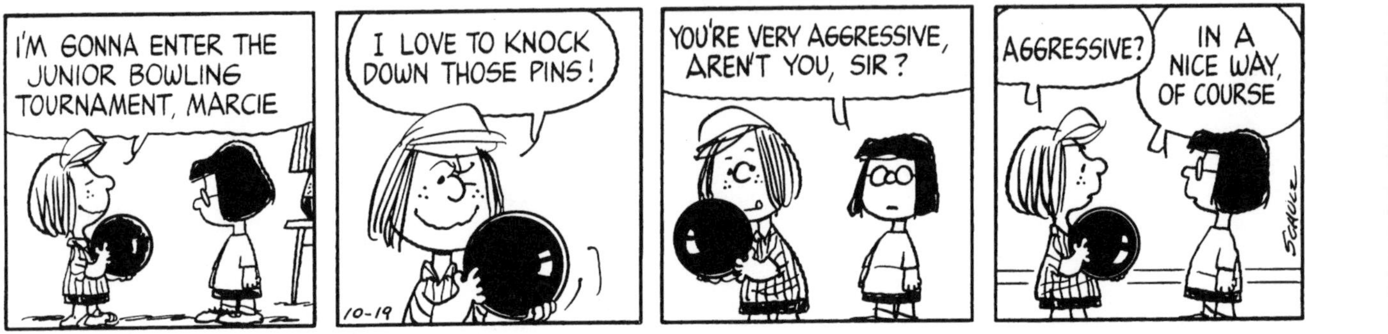
I'M GONNA ENTER THE JUNIOR BOWLING TOURNAMENT, MARCIE
I LOVE TO KNOCK DOWN THOSE PINS!
10-19
YOU'RE VERY AGGRESSIVE, AREN'T YOU, SIR?
AGGRESSIVE?
IN A NICE WAY, OF COURSE
SCHULZ

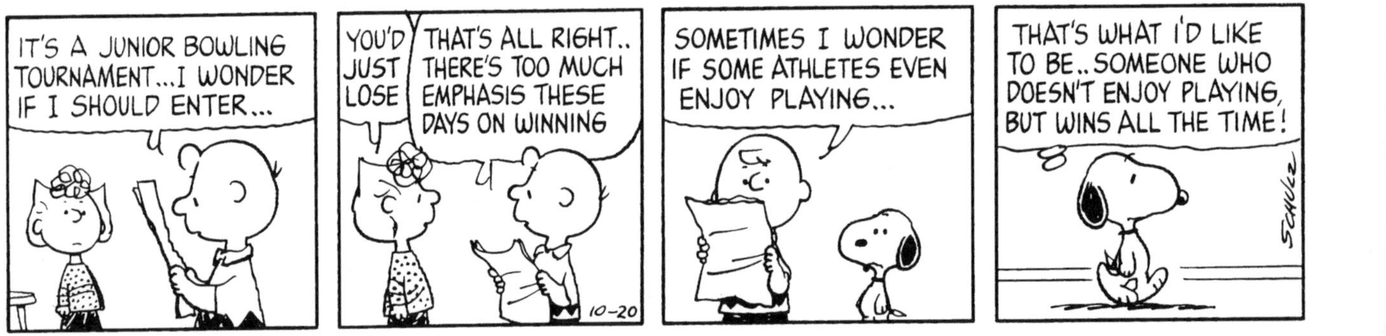
IT'S A JUNIOR BOWLING TOURNAMENT...I WONDER IF I SHOULD ENTER...
YOU'D JUST LOSE
THAT'S ALL RIGHT.. THERE'S TOO MUCH EMPHASIS THESE DAYS ON WINNING
10-20
SOMETIMES I WONDER IF SOME ATHLETES EVEN ENJOY PLAYING...
THAT'S WHAT I'D LIKE TO BE..SOMEONE WHO DOESN'T ENJOY PLAYING, BUT WINS ALL THE TIME!
SCHULZ

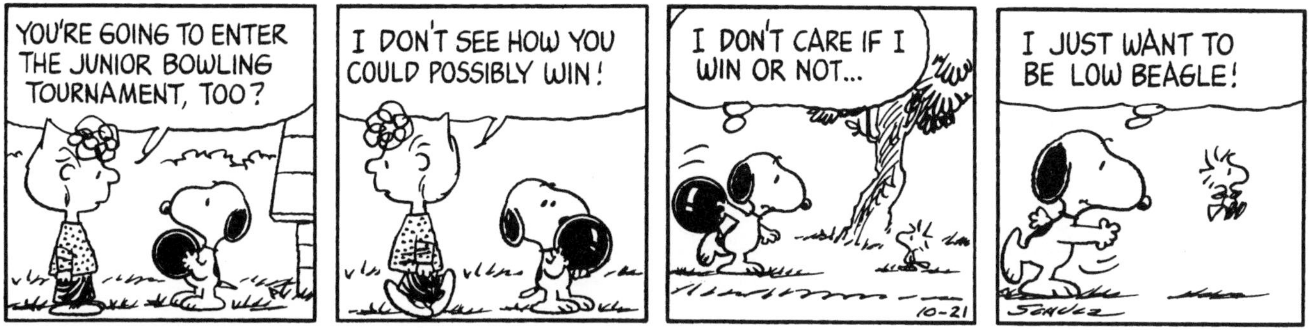
YOU'RE GOING TO ENTER THE JUNIOR BOWLING TOURNAMENT, TOO?
I DON'T SEE HOW YOU COULD POSSIBLY WIN!
I DON'T CARE IF I WIN OR NOT...
10-21
I JUST WANT TO BE LOW BEAGLE!
SCHULZ

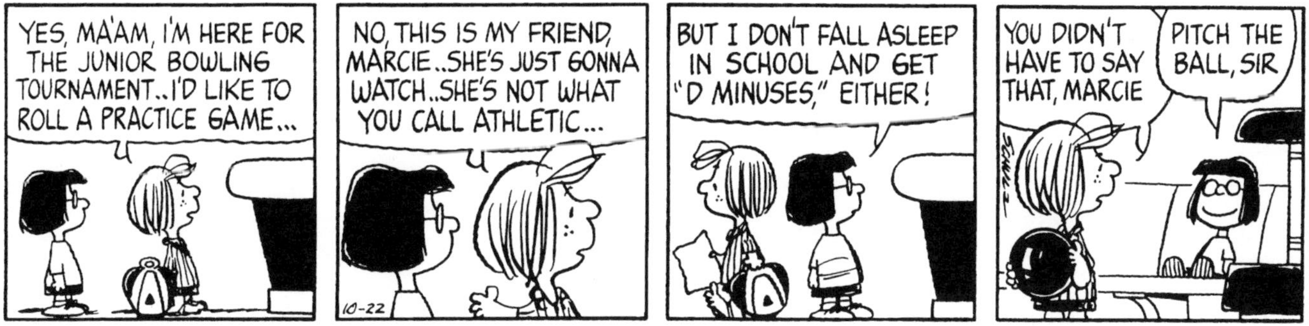
YES, MA'AM, I'M HERE FOR THE JUNIOR BOWLING TOURNAMENT..I'D LIKE TO ROLL A PRACTICE GAME...
NO, THIS IS MY FRIEND, MARCIE..SHE'S JUST GONNA WATCH..SHE'S NOT WHAT YOU CALL ATHLETIC...
10-22
BUT I DON'T FALL ASLEEP IN SCHOOL AND GET "D MINUSES," EITHER!
YOU DIDN'T HAVE TO SAY THAT, MARCIE
PITCH THE BALL, SIR
SCHULZ

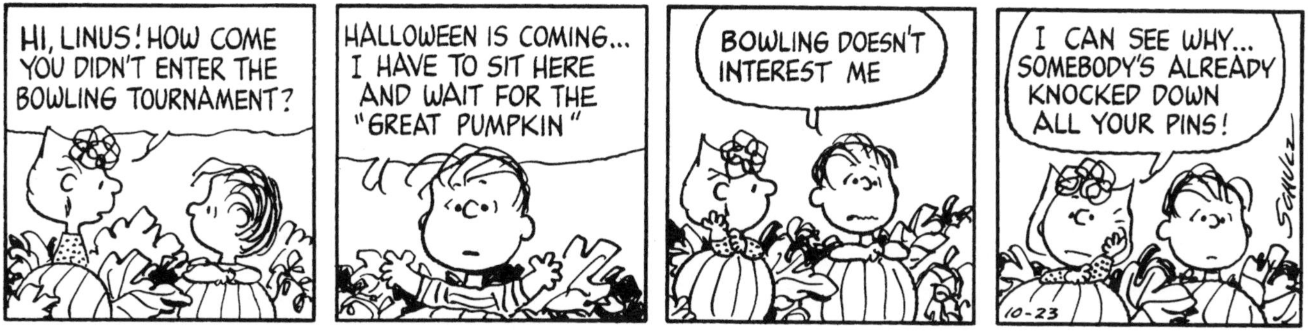
HI, LINUS! HOW COME YOU DIDN'T ENTER THE BOWLING TOURNAMENT?
HALLOWEEN IS COMING... I HAVE TO SIT HERE AND WAIT FOR THE "GREAT PUMPKIN"
BOWLING DOESN'T INTEREST ME
I CAN SEE WHY... SOMEBODY'S ALREADY KNOCKED DOWN ALL YOUR PINS!
SCHULZ
10-23

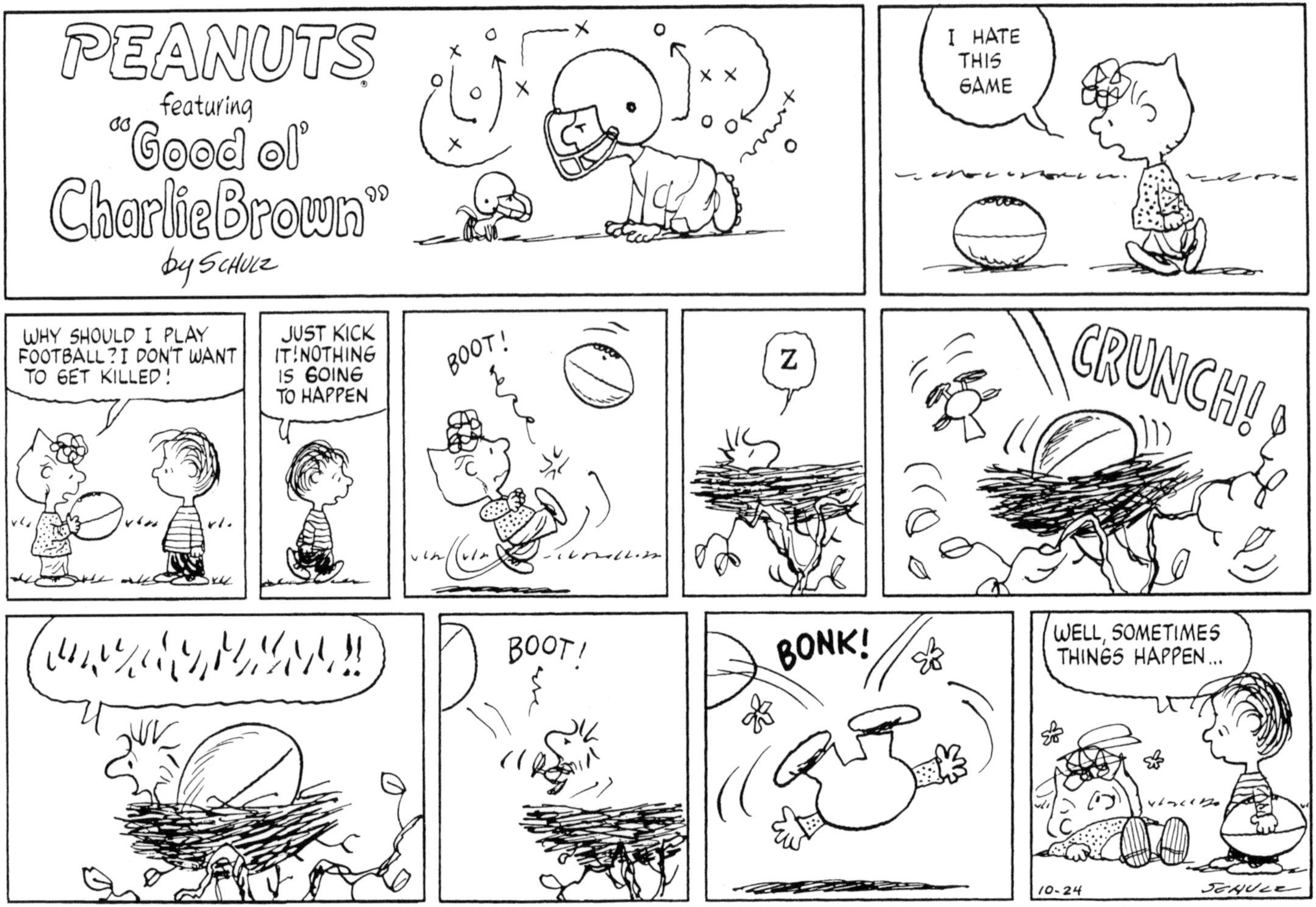

PEANUTS
featuring
"Good ol' Charlie Brown"
by SCHULZ
I HATE THIS GAME
WHY SHOULD I PLAY FOOTBALL? I DON'T WANT TO GET KILLED!
JUST KICK IT! NOTHING IS GOING TO HAPPEN
BOOT!
Z
CRUNCH!
BOOT!
BONK!
WELL, SOMETIMES THINGS HAPPEN...
10-24
SCHULZ

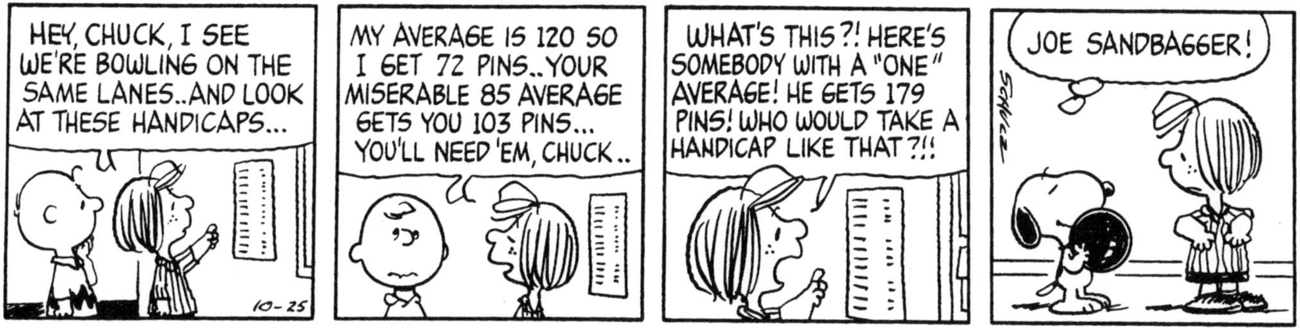
HEY, CHUCK, I SEE WE'RE BOWLING ON THE SAME LANES..AND LOOK AT THESE HANDICAPS...
10-25
MY AVERAGE IS 120 SO I GET 72 PINS..YOUR MISERABLE 85 AVERAGE GETS YOU 103 PINS... YOU'LL NEED 'EM, CHUCK..
WHAT'S THIS?! HERE'S SOMEBODY WITH A "ONE" AVERAGE! HE GETS 179 PINS! WHO WOULD TAKE A HANDICAP LIKE THAT?!!
JOE SANDBAGGER!
SCHULZ

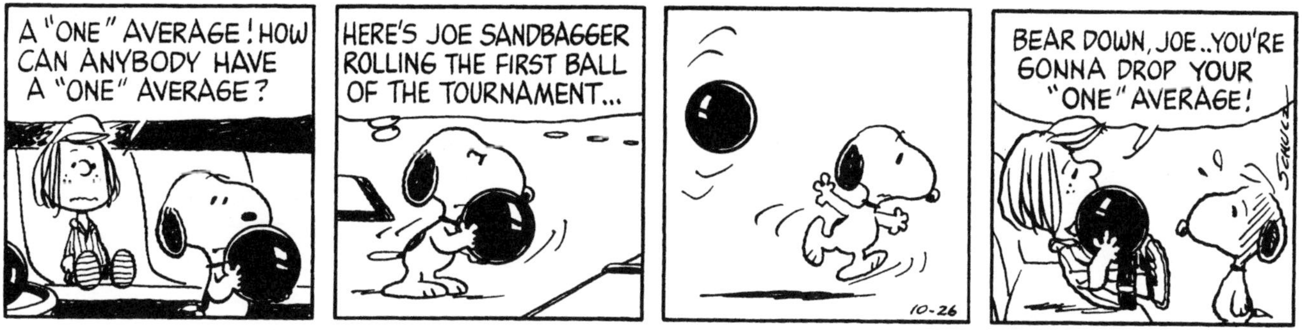
A "ONE" AVERAGE! HOW CAN ANYBODY HAVE A "ONE" AVERAGE?
HERE'S JOE SANDBAGGER ROLLING THE FIRST BALL OF THE TOURNAMENT...
10-26
BEAR DOWN, JOE..YOU'RE GONNA DROP YOUR "ONE" AVERAGE!
SCHULZ

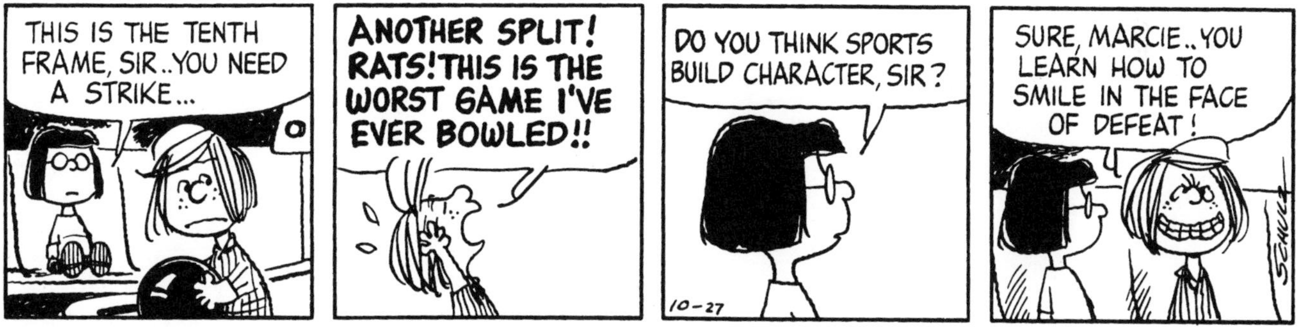
THIS IS THE TENTH FRAME, SIR..YOU NEED A STRIKE...
ANOTHER SPLIT! RATS! THIS IS THE WORST GAME I'VE EVER BOWLED!!
DO YOU THINK SPORTS BUILD CHARACTER, SIR?
10-27
SURE, MARCIE..YOU LEARN HOW TO SMILE IN THE FACE OF DEFEAT!
SCHULZ

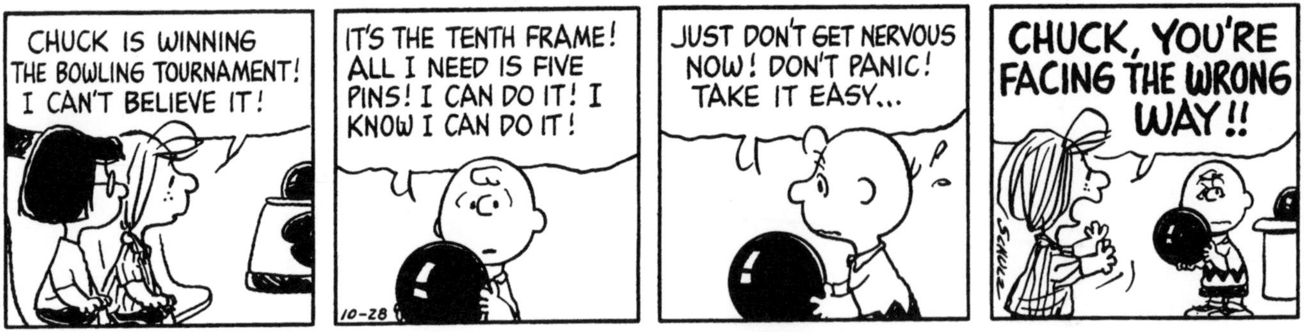
CHUCK IS WINNING THE BOWLING TOURNAMENT! I CAN'T BELIEVE IT!
IT'S THE TENTH FRAME! ALL I NEED IS FIVE PINS! I CAN DO IT! I KNOW I CAN DO IT!
10-28
JUST DON'T GET NERVOUS NOW! DON'T PANIC! TAKE IT EASY...
CHUCK, YOU'RE FACING THE WRONG WAY!!

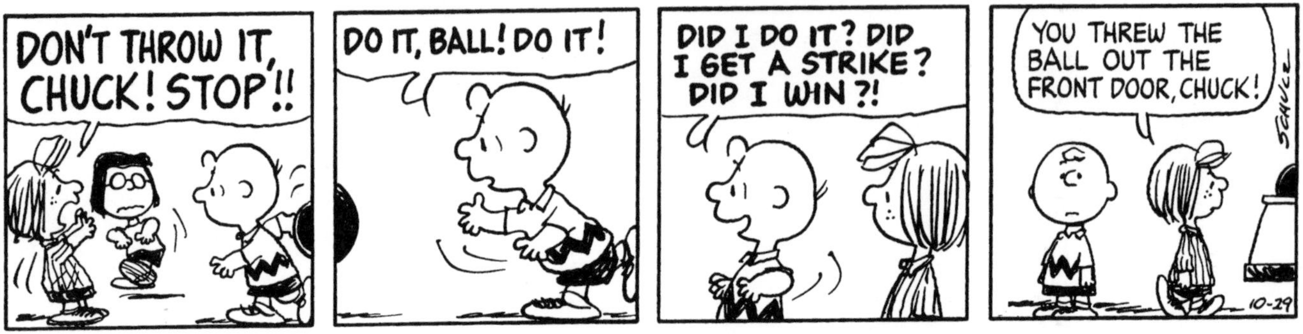
DON'T THROW IT, CHUCK! STOP!!
DO IT, BALL! DO IT!
DID I DO IT? DID I GET A STRIKE? DID I WIN?!
YOU THREW THE BALL OUT THE FRONT DOOR, CHUCK!
10-29

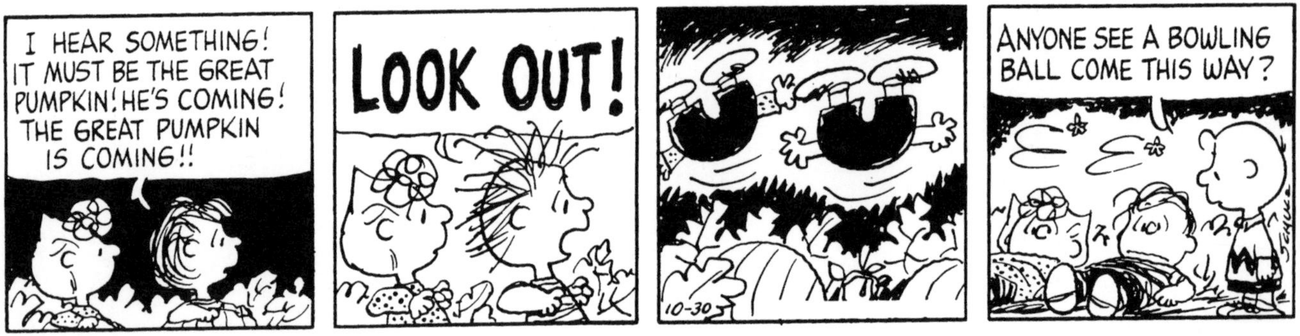
I HEAR SOMETHING! IT MUST BE THE GREAT PUMPKIN! HE'S COMING! THE GREAT PUMPKIN IS COMING!!
LOOK OUT!
10-30
ANYONE SEE A BOWLING BALL COME THIS WAY?

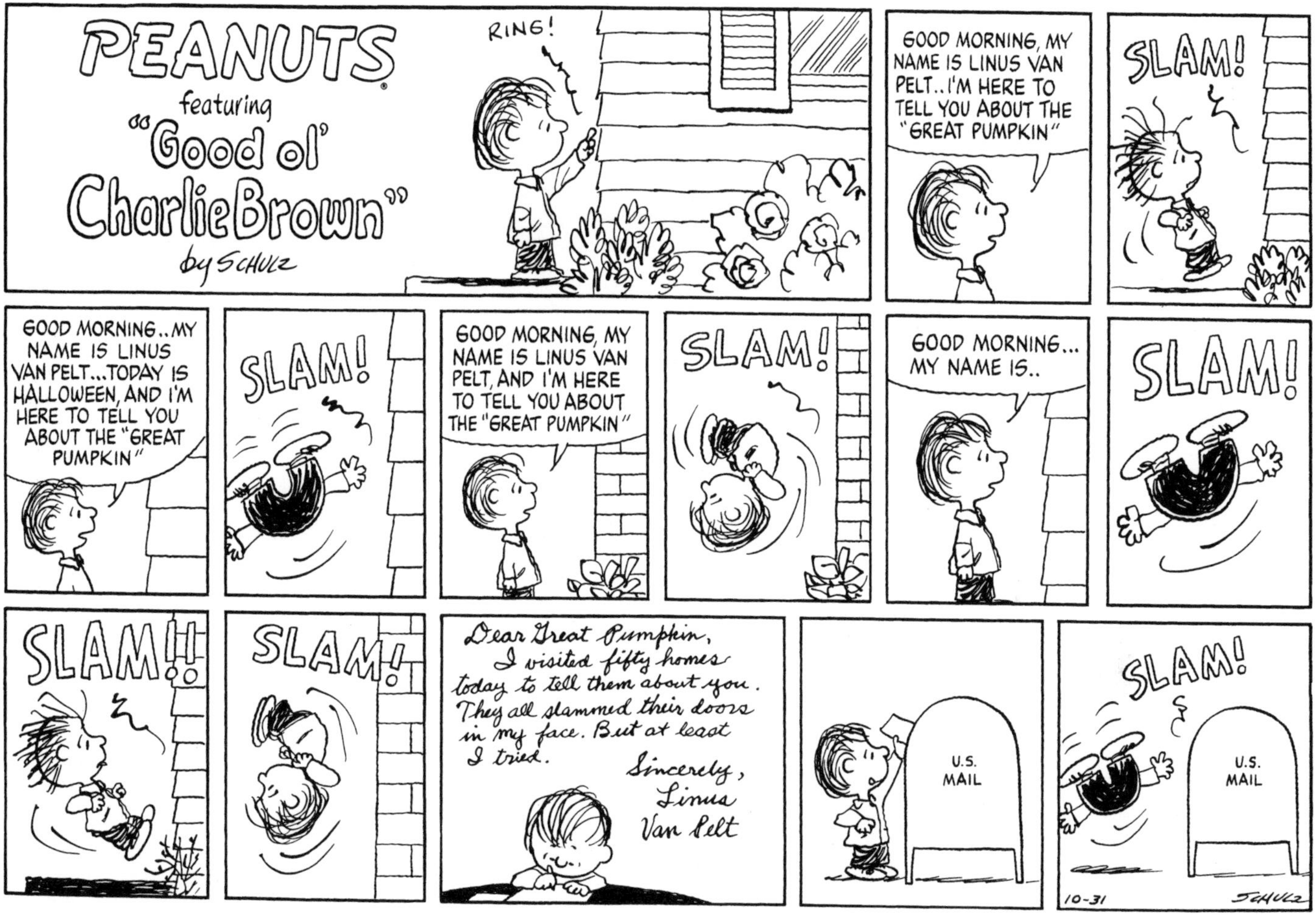
PEANUTS
featuring
"Good ol' Charlie Brown"
by SCHULZ
RING!
GOOD MORNING, MY NAME IS LINUS VAN PELT..I'M HERE TO TELL YOU ABOUT THE "GREAT PUMPKIN"
SLAM!
GOOD MORNING..MY NAME IS LINUS VAN PELT...TODAY IS HALLOWEEN, AND I'M HERE TO TELL YOU ABOUT THE "GREAT PUMPKIN"
SLAM!
GOOD MORNING, MY NAME IS LINUS VAN PELT, AND I'M HERE TO TELL YOU ABOUT THE "GREAT PUMPKIN"
SLAM!
GOOD MORNING... MY NAME IS..
SLAM!
SLAM!!
SLAM!
Dear Great Pumpkin,
I visited fifty homes today to tell them about you. They all slammed their doors in my face. But at least I tried.
Sincerely,
Linus Van Pelt
U.S. MAIL
U.S. MAIL
SLAM!
10-31
SCHULZ

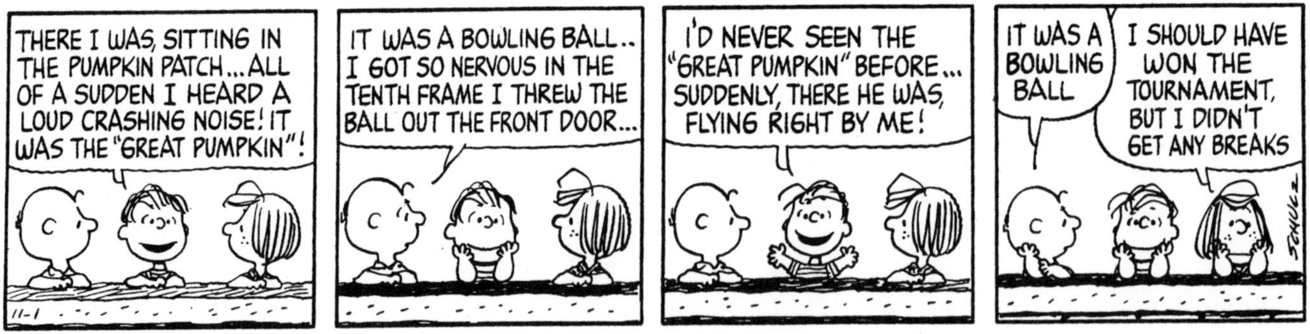
THERE I WAS, SITTING IN THE PUMPKIN PATCH... ALL OF A SUDDEN I HEARD A LOUD CRASHING NOISE! IT WAS THE "GREAT PUMPKIN"!
11-1
IT WAS A BOWLING BALL.. I GOT SO NERVOUS IN THE TENTH FRAME I THREW THE BALL OUT THE FRONT DOOR...
I'D NEVER SEEN THE "GREAT PUMPKIN" BEFORE... SUDDENLY, THERE HE WAS, FLYING RIGHT BY ME!
IT WAS A BOWLING BALL
I SHOULD HAVE WON THE TOURNAMENT, BUT I DIDN'T GET ANY BREAKS

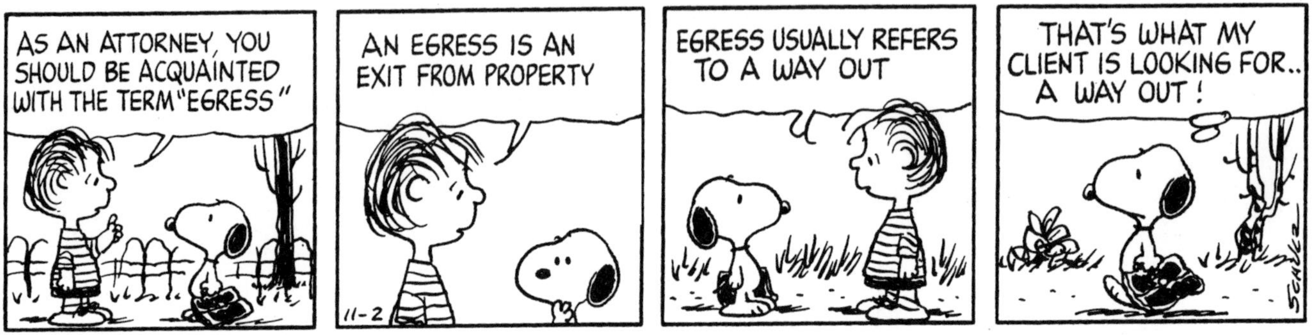
AS AN ATTORNEY, YOU SHOULD BE ACQUAINTED WITH THE TERM "EGRESS"
AN EGRESS IS AN EXIT FROM PROPERTY
11-2
EGRESS USUALLY REFERS TO A WAY OUT
THAT'S WHAT MY CLIENT IS LOOKING FOR.. A WAY OUT!

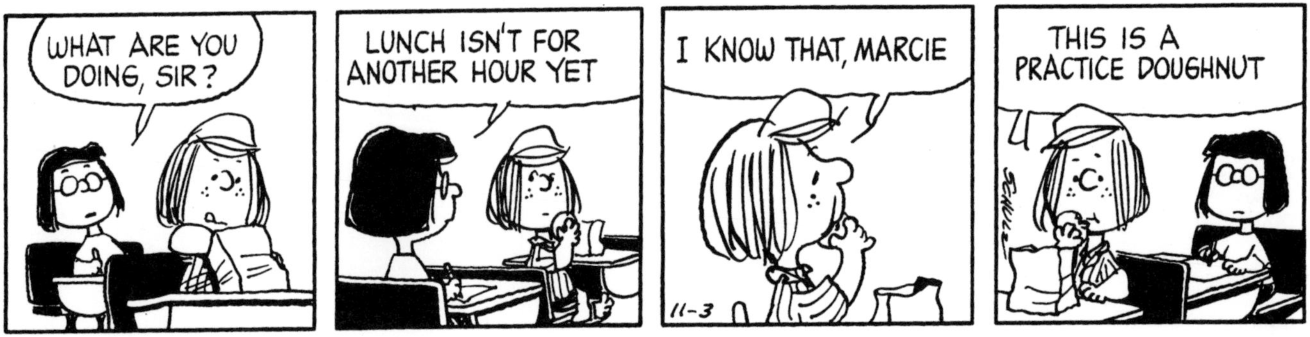
WHAT ARE YOU DOING, SIR?
LUNCH ISN'T FOR ANOTHER HOUR YET
I KNOW THAT, MARCIE
11-3
THIS IS A PRACTICE DOUGHNUT

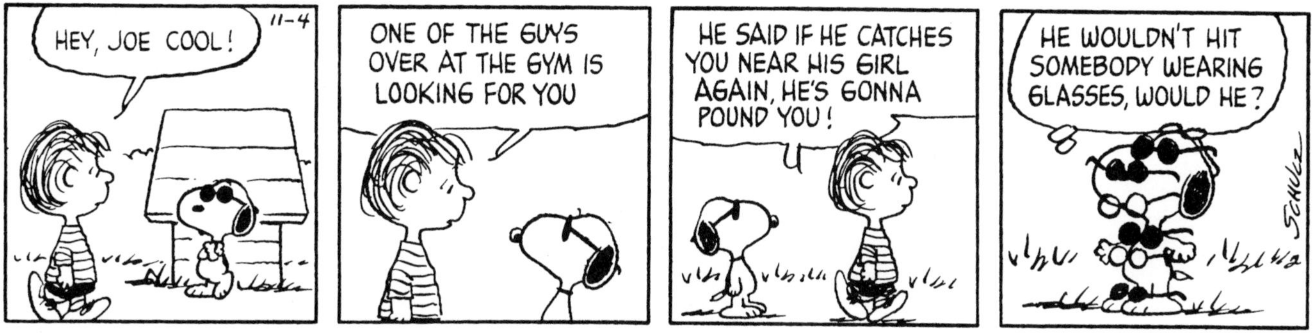
11-4
HEY, JOE COOL!
ONE OF THE GUYS OVER AT THE GYM IS LOOKING FOR YOU
HE SAID IF HE CATCHES YOU NEAR HIS GIRL AGAIN, HE'S GONNA POUND YOU!
HE WOULDN'T HIT SOMEBODY WEARING GLASSES, WOULD HE?
SCHULZ

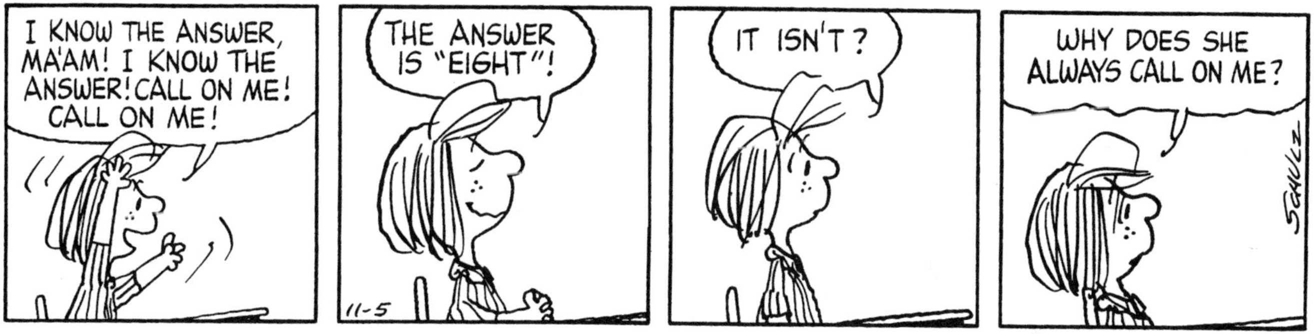
I KNOW THE ANSWER, MA'AM! I KNOW THE ANSWER! CALL ON ME! CALL ON ME!
THE ANSWER IS "EIGHT"!
11-5
IT ISN'T?
WHY DOES SHE ALWAYS CALL ON ME?
SCHULZ

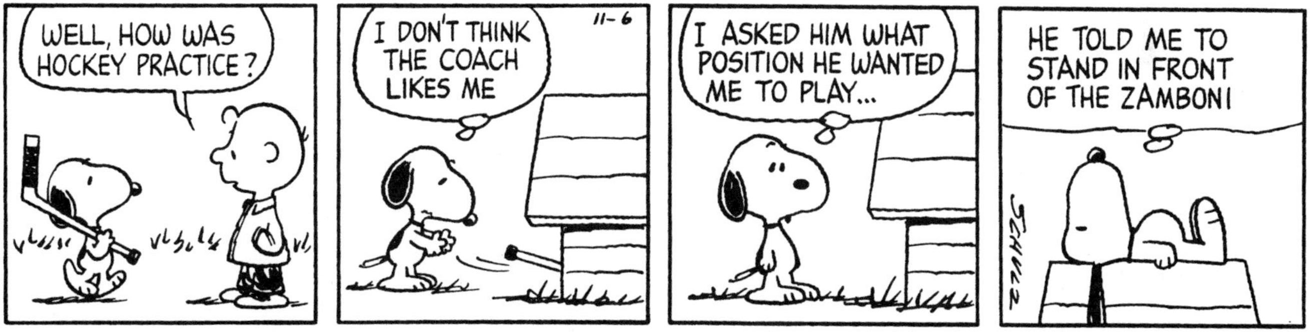
WELL, HOW WAS HOCKEY PRACTICE?
11-6
I DON'T THINK THE COACH LIKES ME
I ASKED HIM WHAT POSITION HE WANTED ME TO PLAY...
HE TOLD ME TO STAND IN FRONT OF THE ZAMBONI
SCHULZ

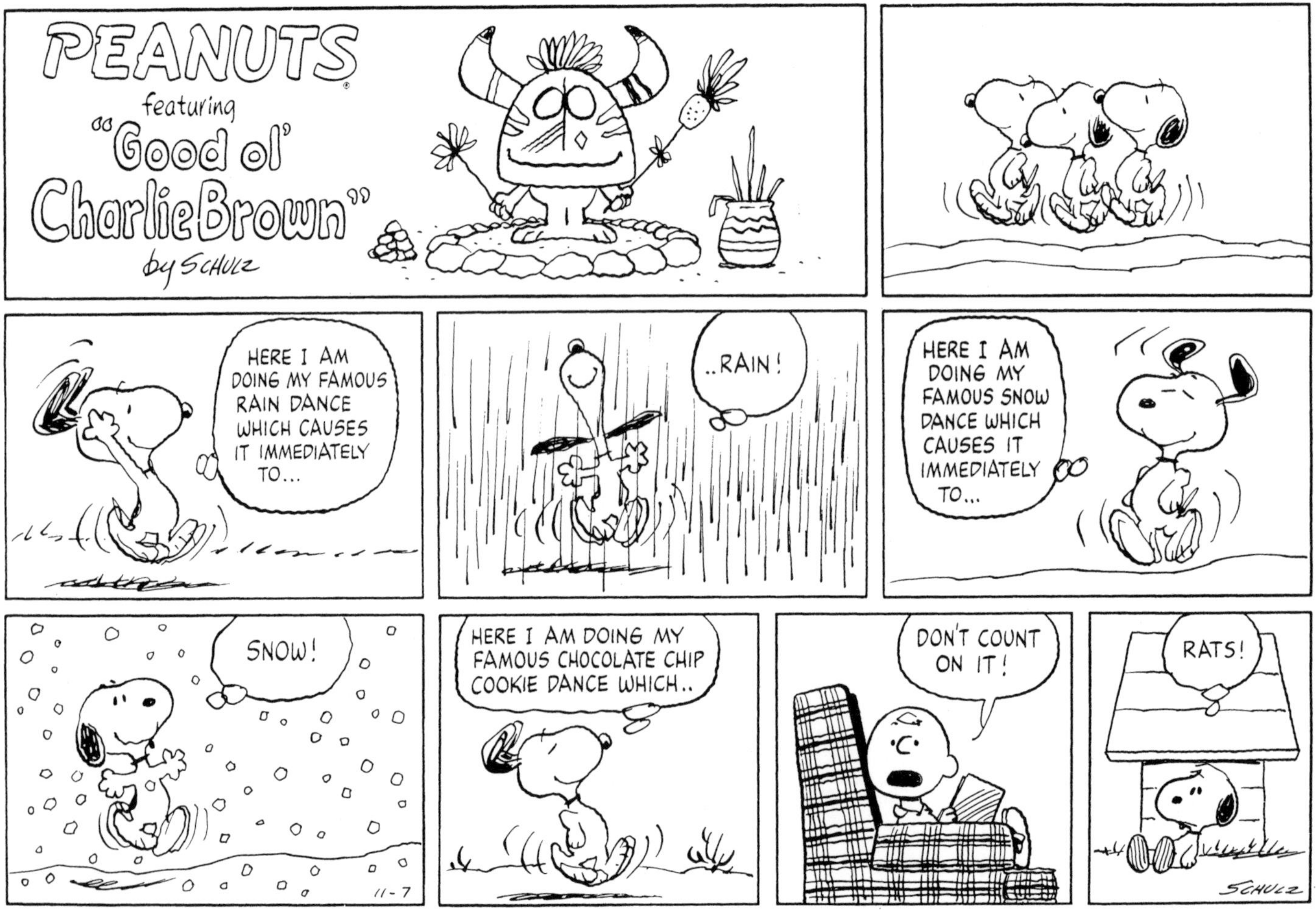
PEANUTS
featuring "Good ol' Charlie Brown"
by SCHULZ
HERE I AM DOING MY FAMOUS RAIN DANCE WHICH CAUSES IT IMMEDIATELY TO...
..RAIN!
HERE I AM DOING MY FAMOUS SNOW DANCE WHICH CAUSES IT IMMEDIATELY TO...
SNOW!
11-7
HERE I AM DOING MY FAMOUS CHOCOLATE CHIP COOKIE DANCE WHICH..
DON'T COUNT ON IT!
RATS!
SCHULZ

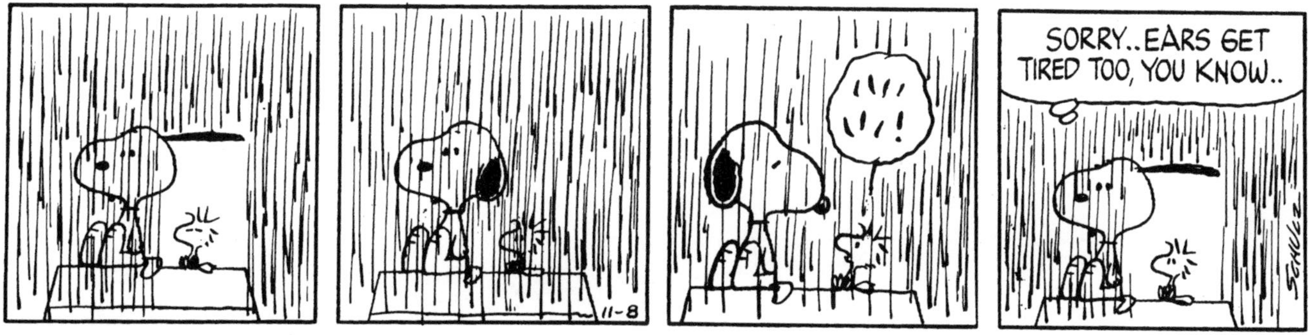
11-8
SORRY..EARS GET TIRED TOO, YOU KNOW..

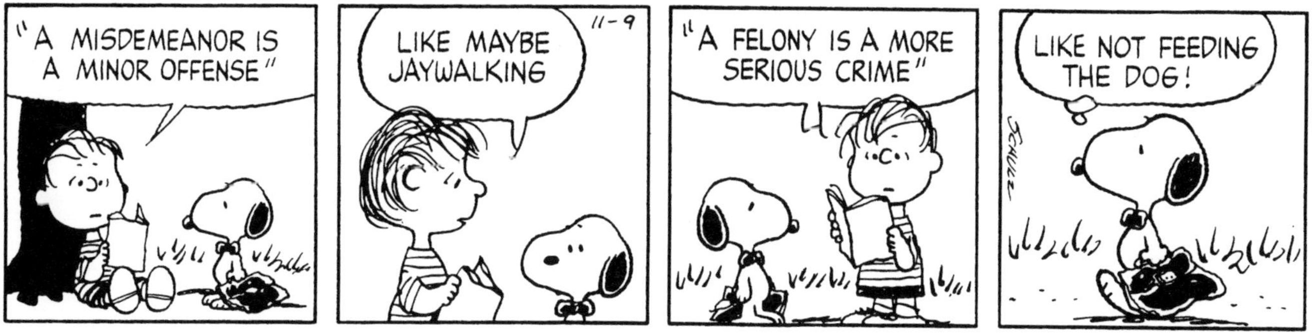
"A MISDEMEANOR IS A MINOR OFFENSE"
11-9
LIKE MAYBE JAYWALKING
"A FELONY IS A MORE SERIOUS CRIME"
LIKE NOT FEEDING THE DOG!

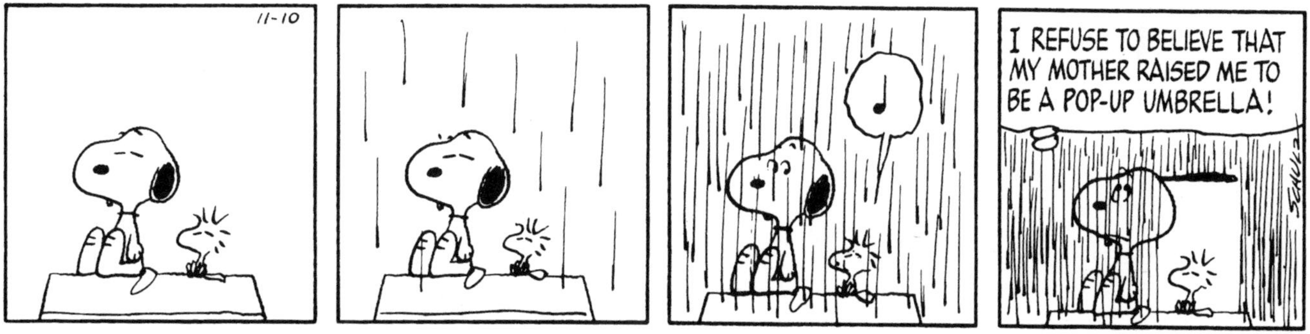
11-10
I REFUSE TO BELIEVE THAT MY MOTHER RAISED ME TO BE A POP-UP UMBRELLA!

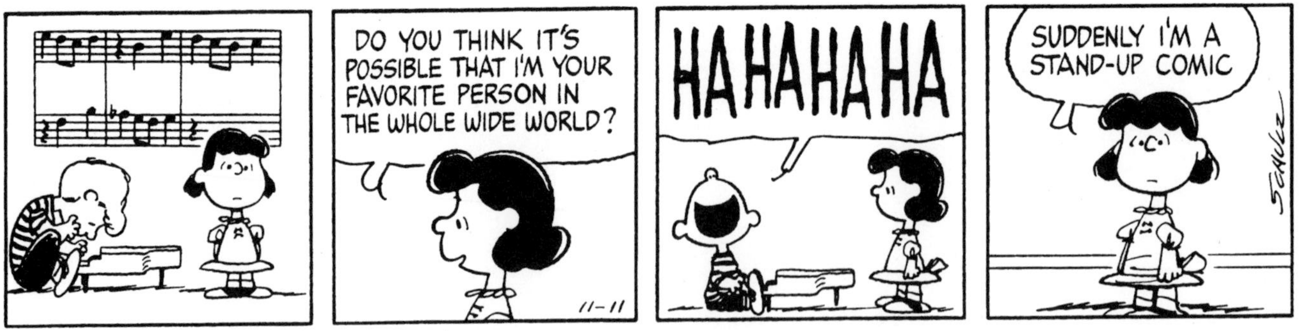
DO YOU THINK IT'S POSSIBLE THAT I'M YOUR FAVORITE PERSON IN THE WHOLE WIDE WORLD?
11-11
HAHAHAHA
SUDDENLY I'M A STAND-UP COMIC
SCHULZ

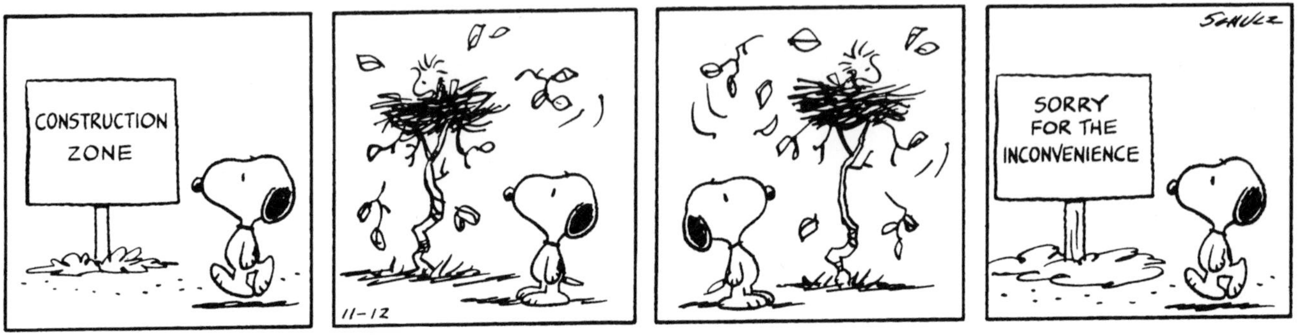
CONSTRUCTION ZONE
11-12
SCHULZ
SORRY FOR THE INCONVENIENCE

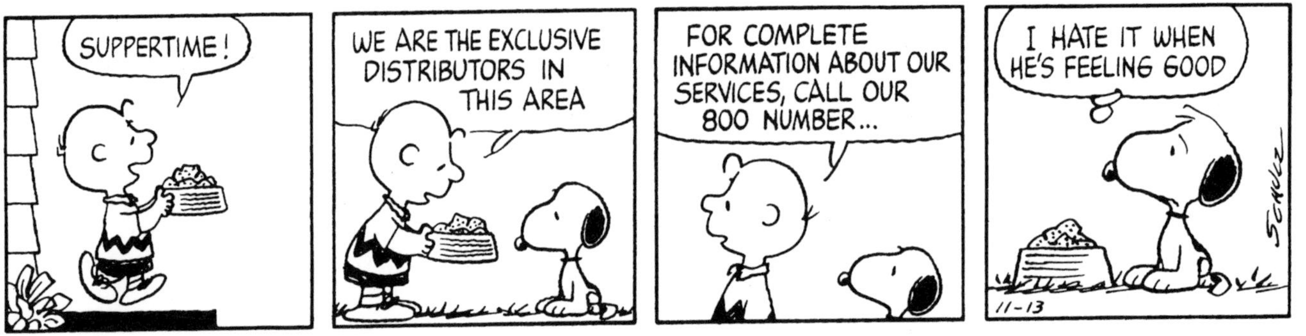
SUPPERTIME!
WE ARE THE EXCLUSIVE DISTRIBUTORS IN THIS AREA
FOR COMPLETE INFORMATION ABOUT OUR SERVICES, CALL OUR 800 NUMBER...
I HATE IT WHEN HE'S FEELING GOOD
SCHULZ
11-13

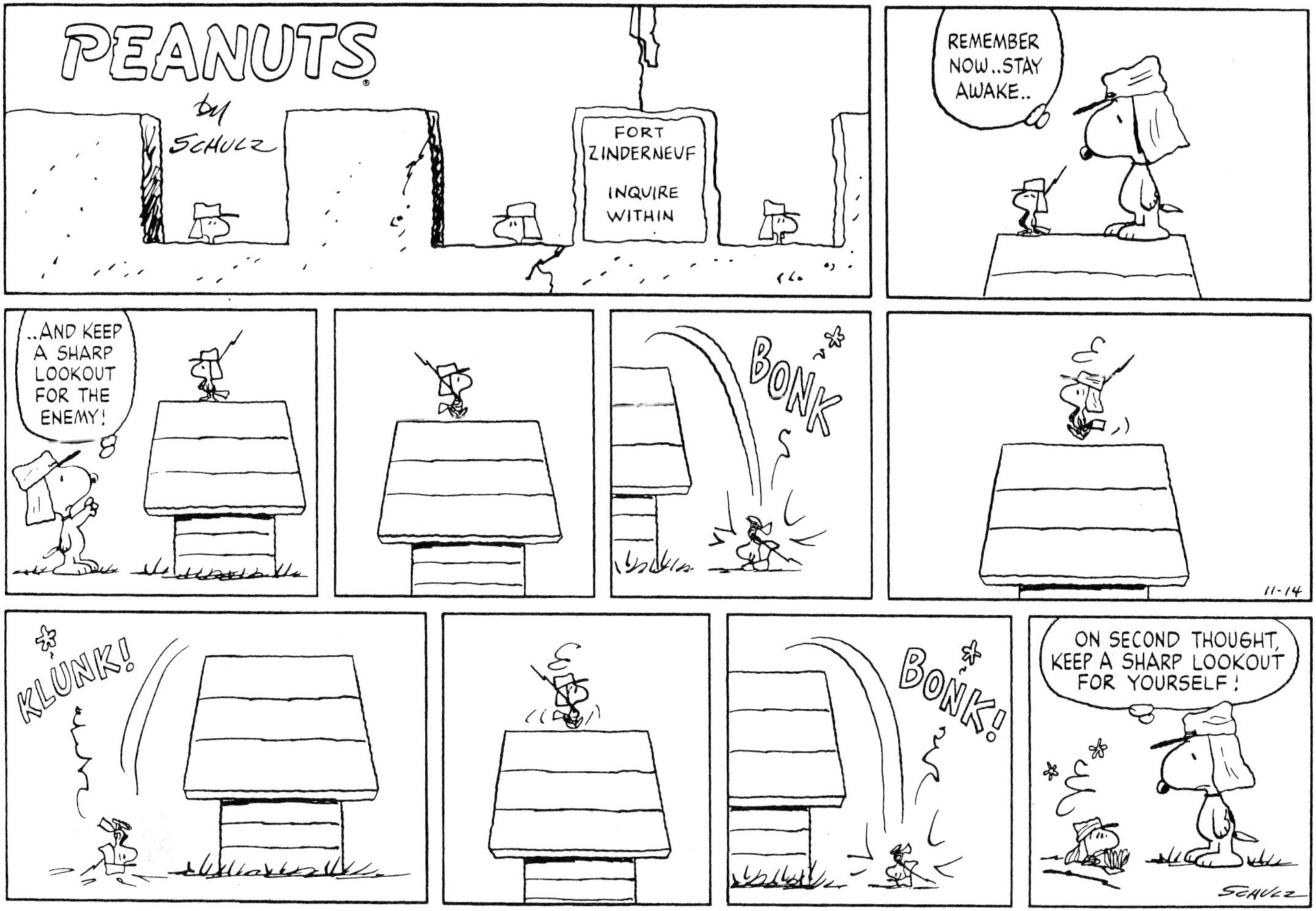
PEANUTS
by SCHULZ
FORT ZINDERNEUF
INQUIRE WITHIN
REMEMBER NOW..STAY AWAKE..
..AND KEEP A SHARP LOOKOUT FOR THE ENEMY!
BONK
11-14
KLUNK!
BONK!
ON SECOND THOUGHT, KEEP A SHARP LOOKOUT FOR YOURSELF!
SCHULZ

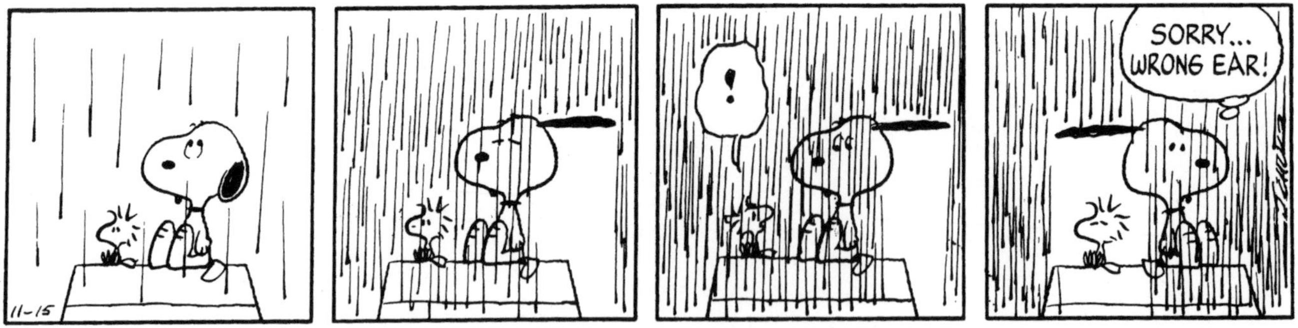
11-15
!
SORRY... WRONG EAR!
SCHULZ

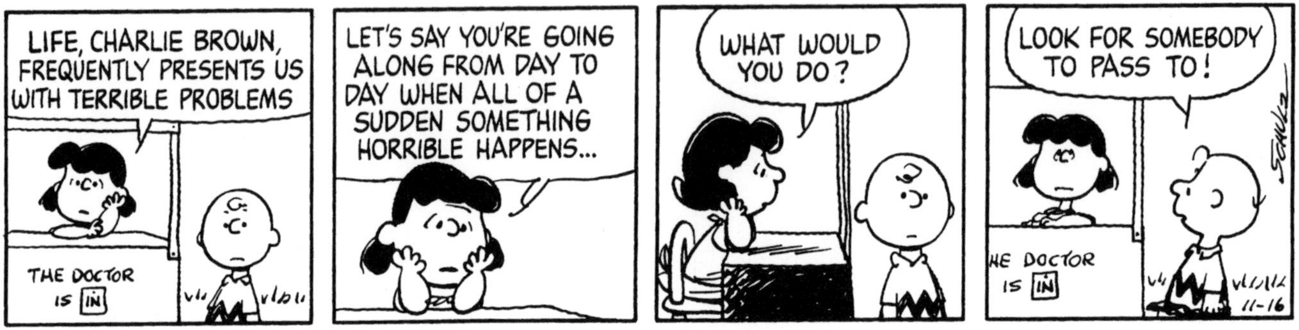
LIFE, CHARLIE BROWN, FREQUENTLY PRESENTS US WITH TERRIBLE PROBLEMS
THE DOCTOR IS IN
LET'S SAY YOU'RE GOING ALONG FROM DAY TO DAY WHEN ALL OF A SUDDEN SOMETHING HORRIBLE HAPPENS...
WHAT WOULD YOU DO?
LOOK FOR SOMEBODY TO PASS TO!
HE DOCTOR IS IN
SCHULZ
11-16

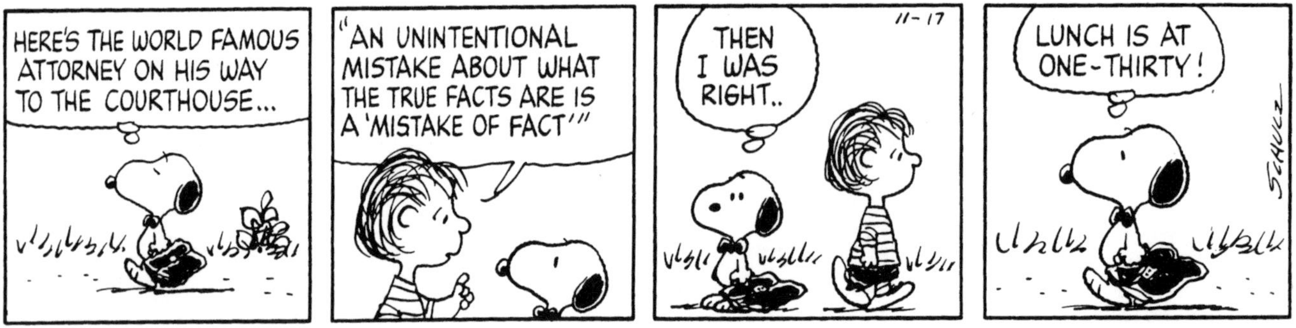
HERE'S THE WORLD FAMOUS ATTORNEY ON HIS WAY TO THE COURTHOUSE...
"AN UNINTENTIONAL MISTAKE ABOUT WHAT THE TRUE FACTS ARE IS A 'MISTAKE OF FACT'"
11-17
THEN I WAS RIGHT..
LUNCH IS AT ONE-THIRTY!
SCHULZ

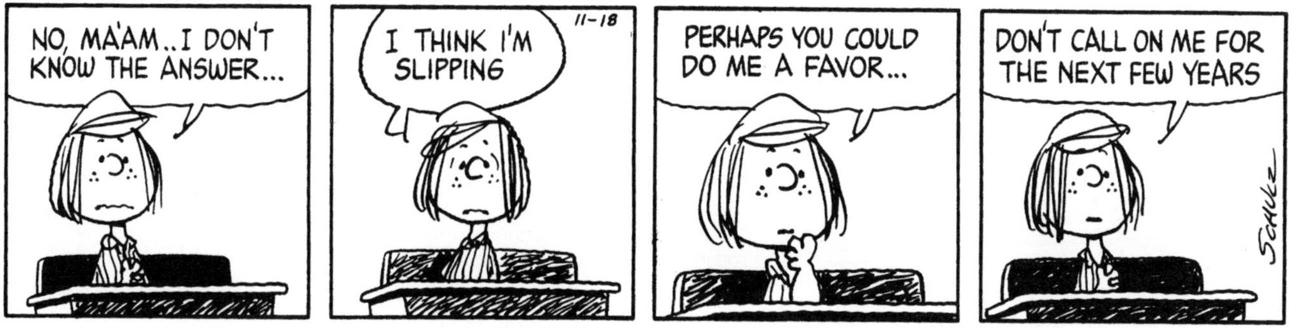
NO, MA'AM..I DON'T KNOW THE ANSWER...
11-18
I THINK I'M SLIPPING
PERHAPS YOU COULD DO ME A FAVOR...
DON'T CALL ON ME FOR THE NEXT FEW YEARS
SCHULZ

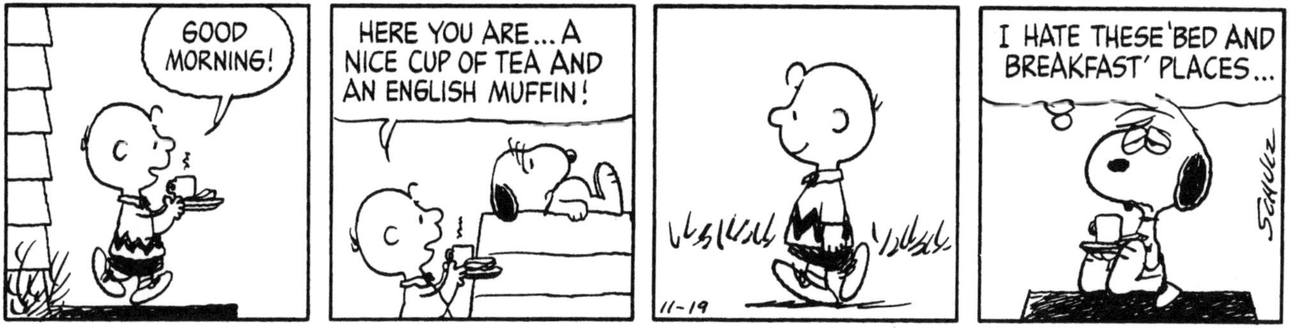
GOOD MORNING!
HERE YOU ARE... A NICE CUP OF TEA AND AN ENGLISH MUFFIN!
11-19
I HATE THESE 'BED AND BREAKFAST' PLACES...
SCHULZ

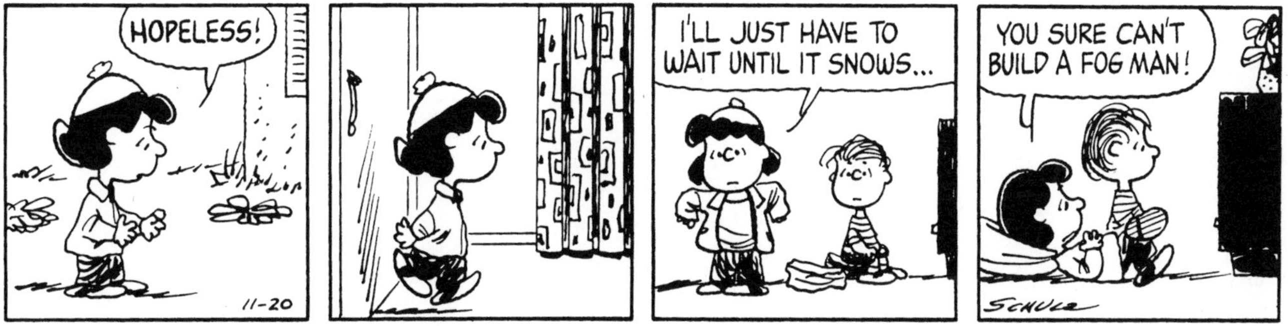
HOPELESS!
11-20
I'LL JUST HAVE TO WAIT UNTIL IT SNOWS...
YOU SURE CAN'T BUILD A FOG MAN!
SCHULZ

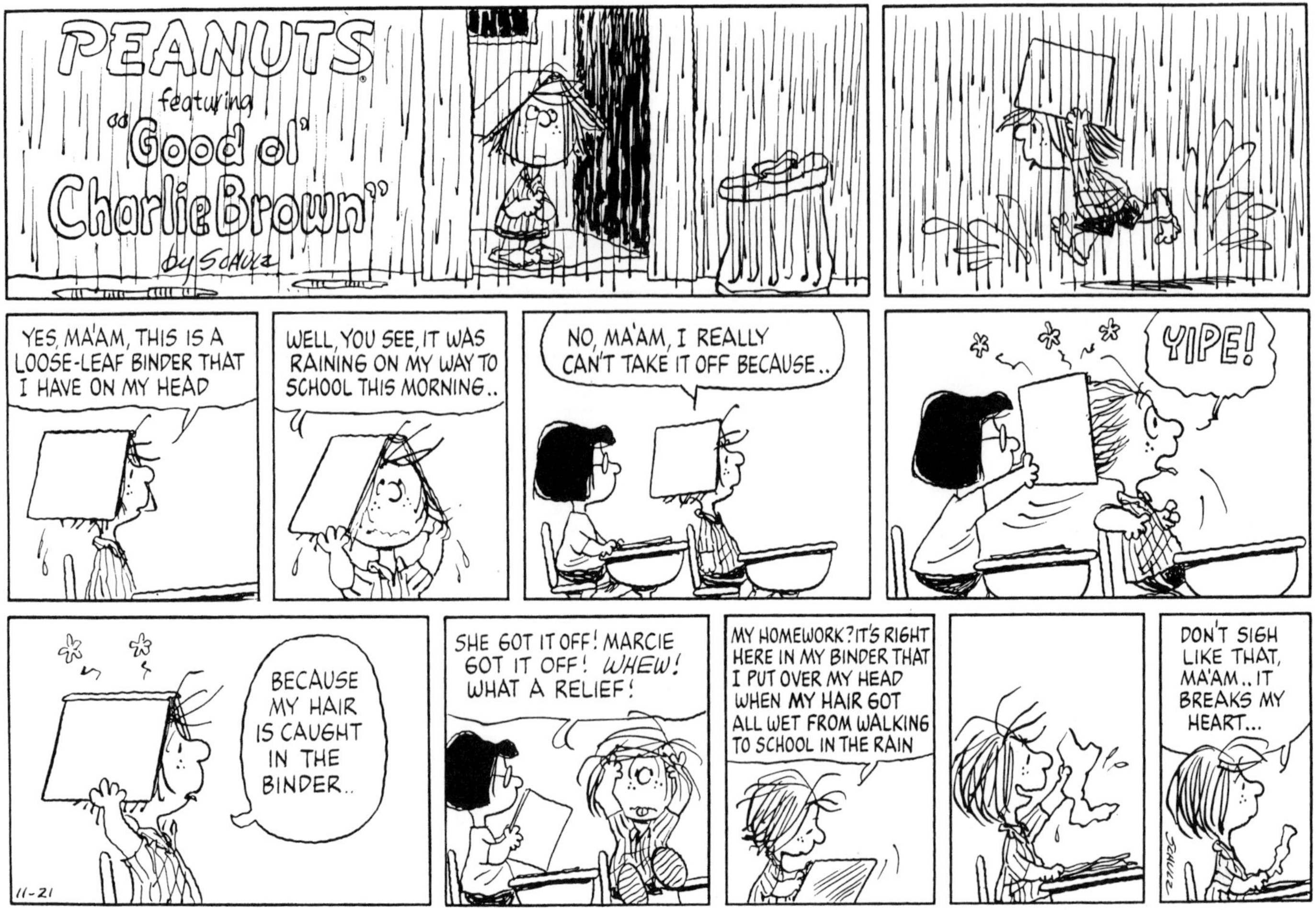
PEANUTS featuring "Good ol' Charlie Brown" by SCHULZ
YES, MA'AM, THIS IS A LOOSE-LEAF BINDER THAT I HAVE ON MY HEAD
WELL, YOU SEE, IT WAS RAINING ON MY WAY TO SCHOOL THIS MORNING..
NO, MA'AM, I REALLY CAN'T TAKE IT OFF BECAUSE..
YIPE!
BECAUSE MY HAIR IS CAUGHT IN THE BINDER..
SHE GOT IT OFF! MARCIE GOT IT OFF! WHEW! WHAT A RELIEF!
MY HOMEWORK? IT'S RIGHT HERE IN MY BINDER THAT I PUT OVER MY HEAD WHEN MY HAIR GOT ALL WET FROM WALKING TO SCHOOL IN THE RAIN
DON'T SIGH LIKE THAT, MA'AM.. IT BREAKS MY HEART...
11-21

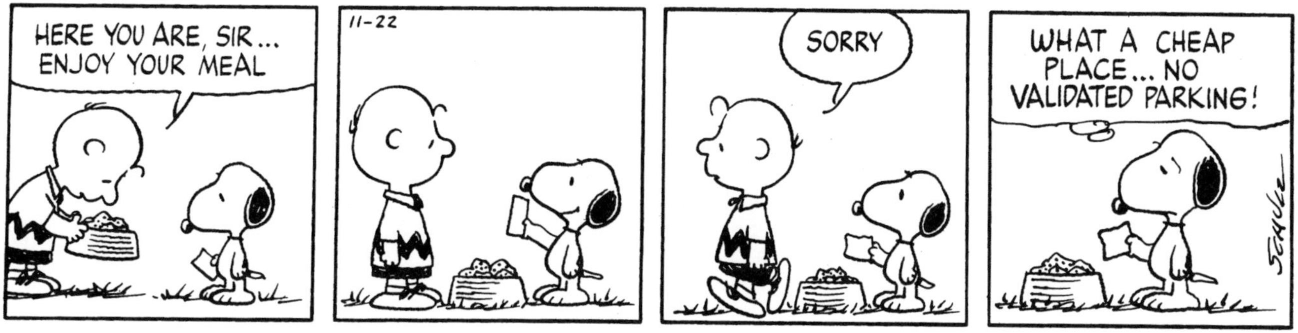

HERE YOU ARE, SIR... ENJOY YOUR MEAL
11-22
SORRY
WHAT A CHEAP PLACE... NO VALIDATED PARKING!
SCHULZ

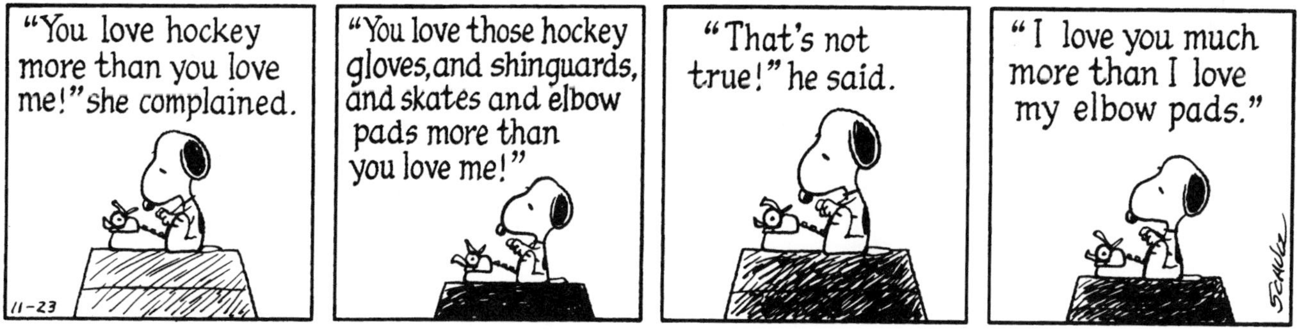

"You love hockey more than you love me!" she complained.
11-23
"You love those hockey gloves, and shinguards, and skates and elbow pads more than you love me!"
"That's not true!" he said.
"I love you much more than I love my elbow pads."
SCHULZ

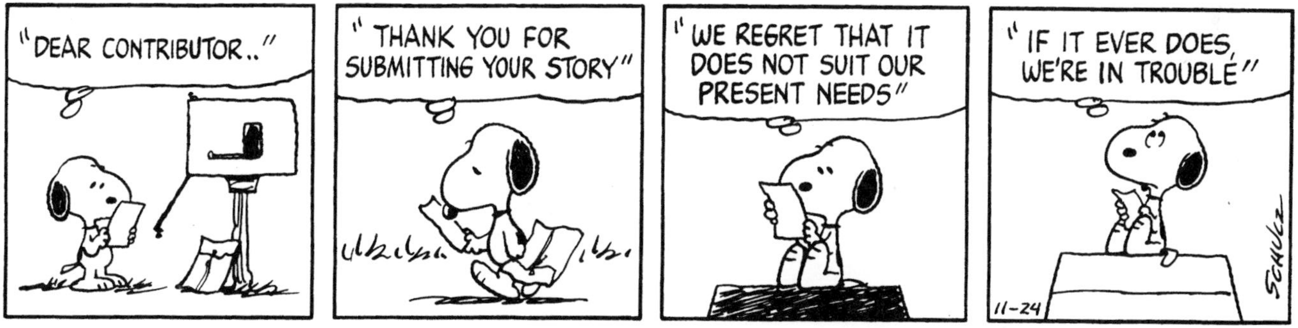

"DEAR CONTRIBUTOR.."
"THANK YOU FOR SUBMITTING YOUR STORY"
"WE REGRET THAT IT DOES NOT SUIT OUR PRESENT NEEDS"
"IF IT EVER DOES, WE'RE IN TROUBLE"
11-24
SCHULZ

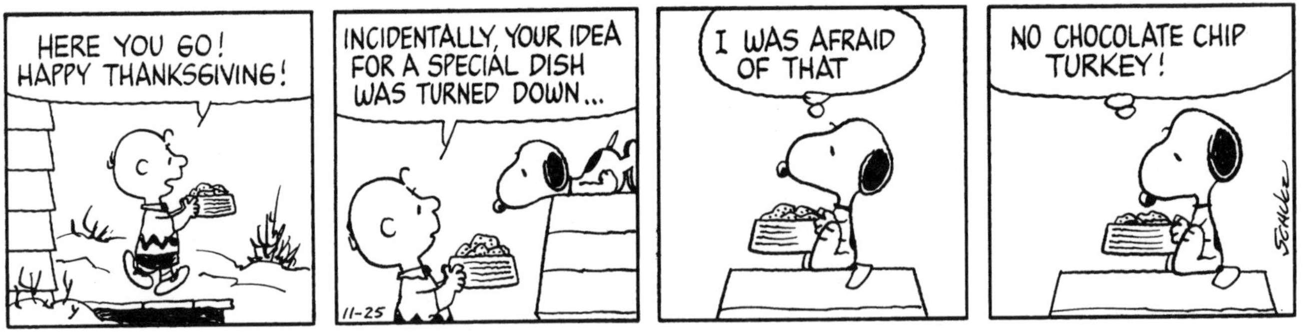
HERE YOU GO! HAPPY THANKSGIVING!
INCIDENTALLY, YOUR IDEA FOR A SPECIAL DISH WAS TURNED DOWN...
11-25
I WAS AFRAID OF THAT
NO CHOCOLATE CHIP TURKEY!
SCHULZ

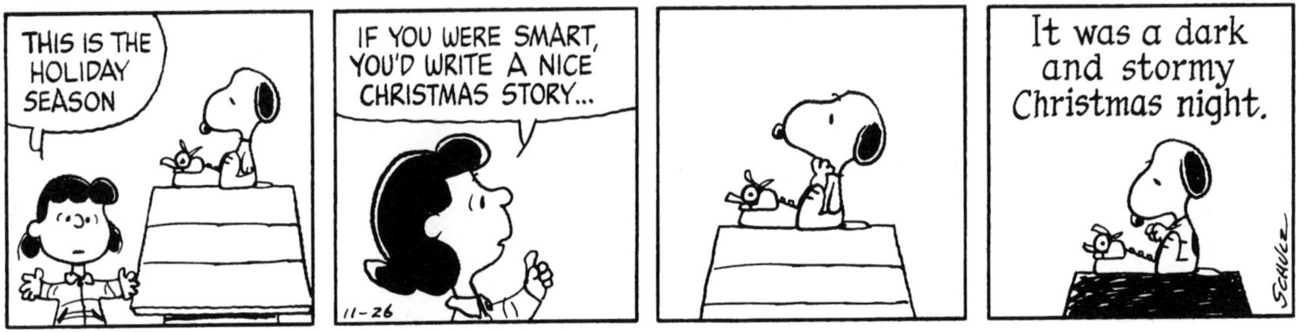
THIS IS THE HOLIDAY SEASON
IF YOU WERE SMART, YOU'D WRITE A NICE CHRISTMAS STORY...
11-26
It was a dark and stormy Christmas night.
SCHULZ

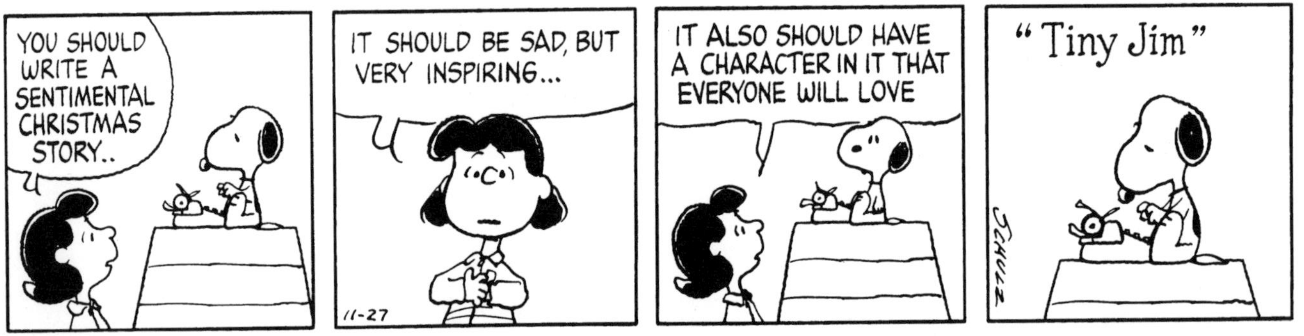
YOU SHOULD WRITE A SENTIMENTAL CHRISTMAS STORY..
IT SHOULD BE SAD, BUT VERY INSPIRING...
11-27
IT ALSO SHOULD HAVE A CHARACTER IN IT THAT EVERYONE WILL LOVE
"Tiny Jim"
SCHULZ

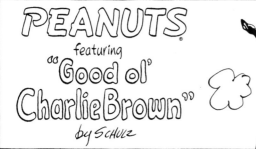

PEANUTS featuring "Good ol' Charlie Brown" by Schulz

11-28

I'M COMING! I'M COMING!

BAM! BAM! BAM!

AGAIN? YOU MUST HAVE GOOD EARS..

I NEVER HEARD A THING...

HERE YOU GO..

FOUR? HOW COME YOU'RE TAKING FOUR?

I CAN'T BELIEVE HE WAS CALLED BY A QUARTET OF COOKIES

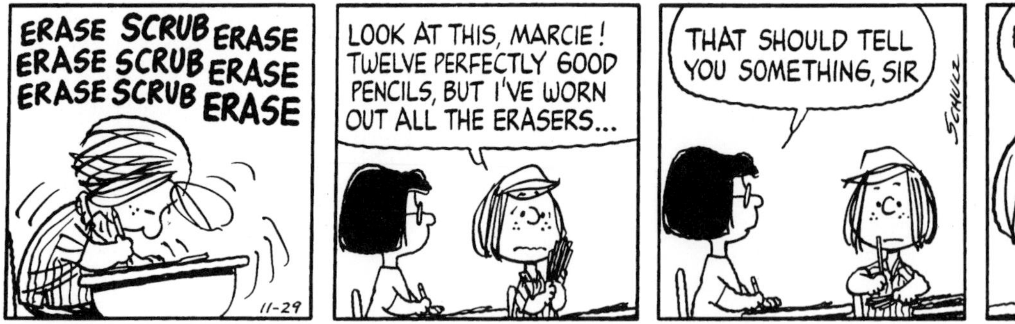
ERASE SCRUB ERASE
ERASE SCRUB ERASE
ERASE SCRUB ERASE
11-29
LOOK AT THIS, MARCIE! TWELVE PERFECTLY GOOD PENCILS, BUT I'VE WORN OUT ALL THE ERASERS...
THAT SHOULD TELL YOU SOMETHING, SIR
SCHULZ
EVEN MY PENCILS CRITICIZE ME

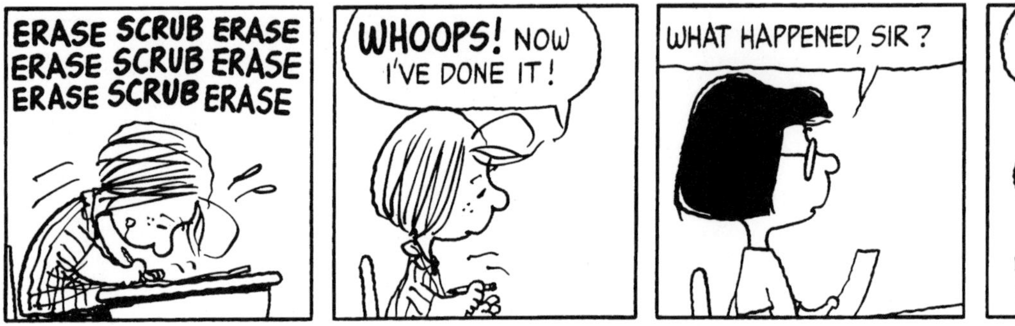
ERASE SCRUB ERASE
ERASE SCRUB ERASE
ERASE SCRUB ERASE
WHOOPS! NOW I'VE DONE IT!
WHAT HAPPENED, SIR?
11-30
I ERASED MY WHOLE DESK!
SCHULZ

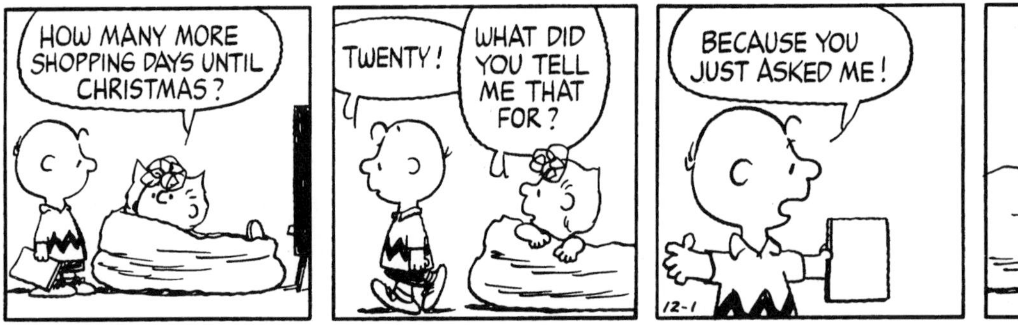
HOW MANY MORE SHOPPING DAYS UNTIL CHRISTMAS?
TWENTY!
WHAT DID YOU TELL ME THAT FOR?
BECAUSE YOU JUST ASKED ME!
12-1
I REALLY DIDN'T WANT TO KNOW
SCHULZ

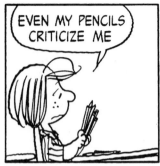

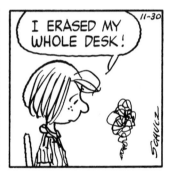

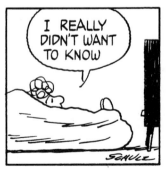

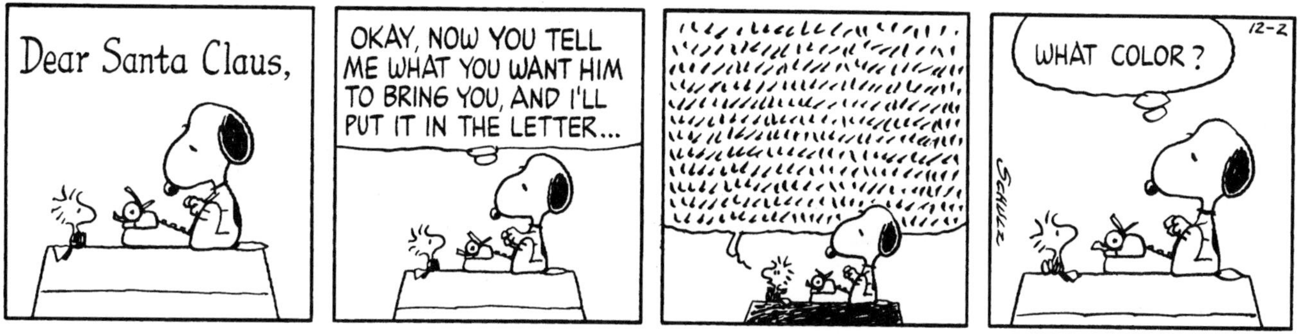
Dear Santa Claus,
OKAY, NOW YOU TELL ME WHAT YOU WANT HIM TO BRING YOU, AND I'LL PUT IT IN THE LETTER...
12-2
WHAT COLOR?
SCHULZ

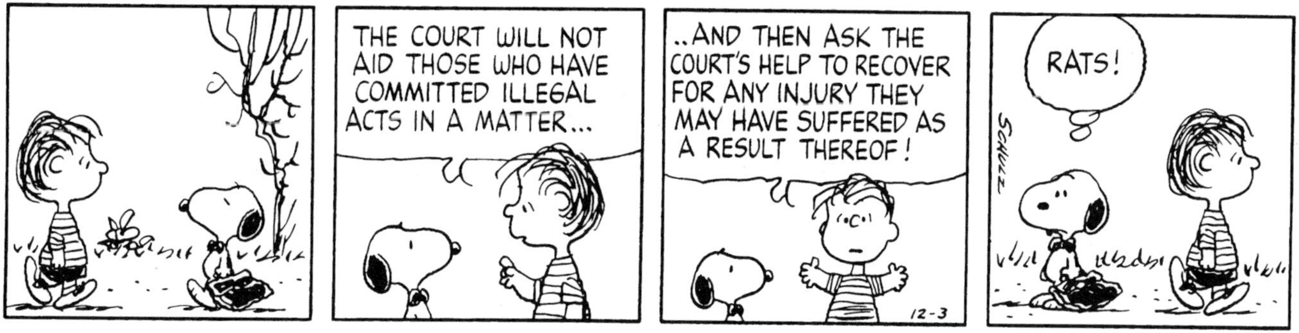
THE COURT WILL NOT AID THOSE WHO HAVE COMMITTED ILLEGAL ACTS IN A MATTER...
..AND THEN ASK THE COURT'S HELP TO RECOVER FOR ANY INJURY THEY MAY HAVE SUFFERED AS A RESULT THEREOF!
12-3
RATS!
SCHULZ

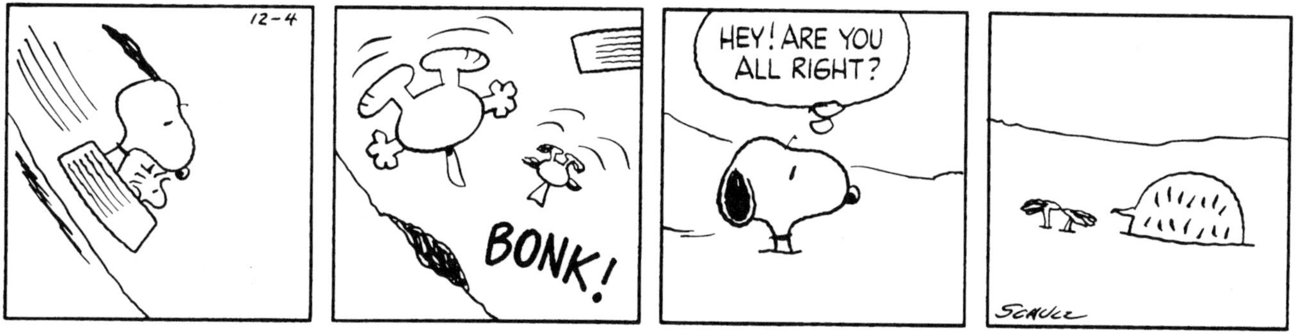
12-4
BONK!
HEY! ARE YOU ALL RIGHT?
SCHULZ

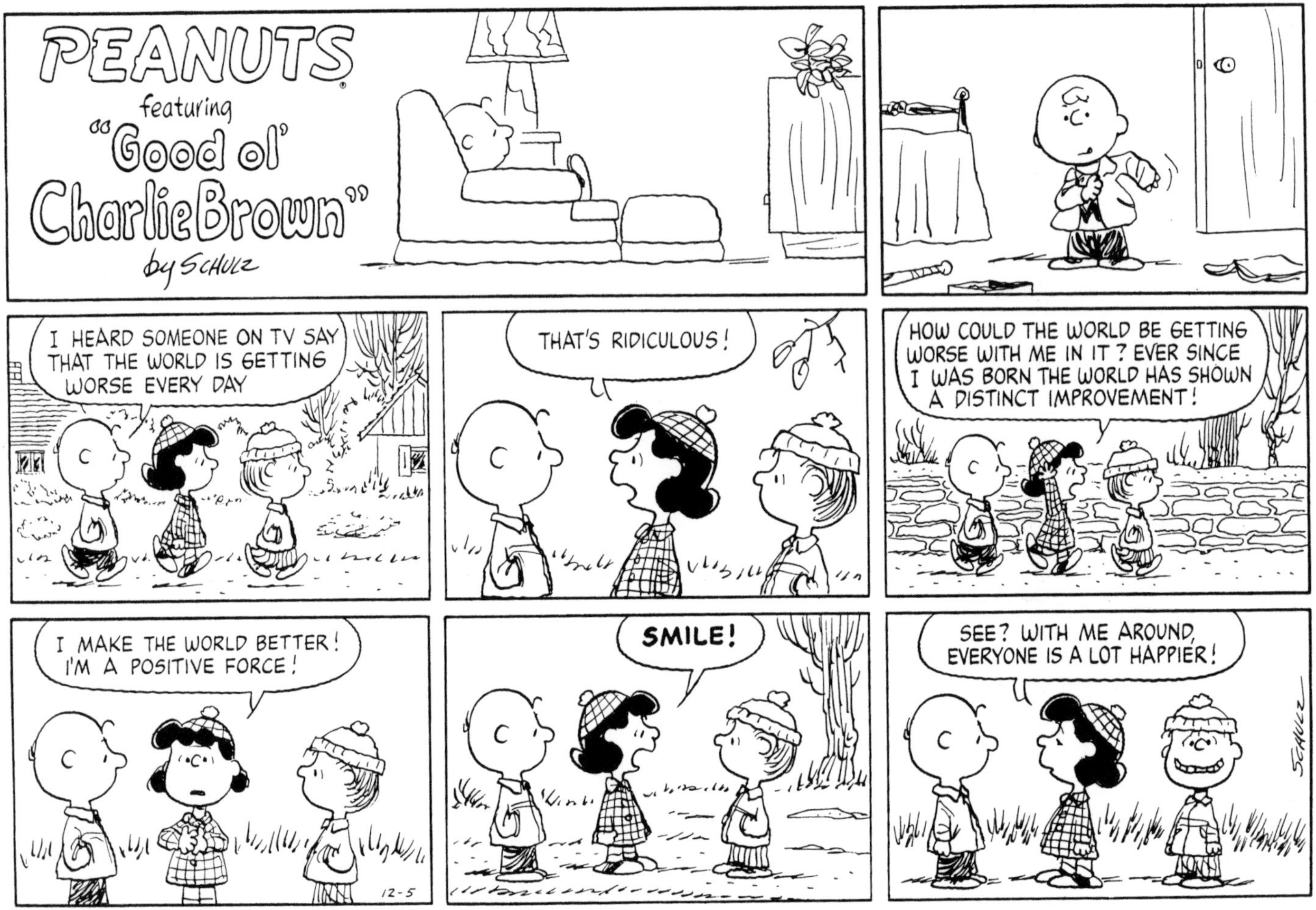
PEANUTS
featuring
"Good ol' Charlie Brown"
by SCHULZ
I HEARD SOMEONE ON TV SAY THAT THE WORLD IS GETTING WORSE EVERY DAY
THAT'S RIDICULOUS!
HOW COULD THE WORLD BE GETTING WORSE WITH ME IN IT? EVER SINCE I WAS BORN THE WORLD HAS SHOWN A DISTINCT IMPROVEMENT!
I MAKE THE WORLD BETTER! I'M A POSITIVE FORCE!
12-5
SMILE!
SEE? WITH ME AROUND, EVERYONE IS A LOT HAPPIER!
SCHULZ

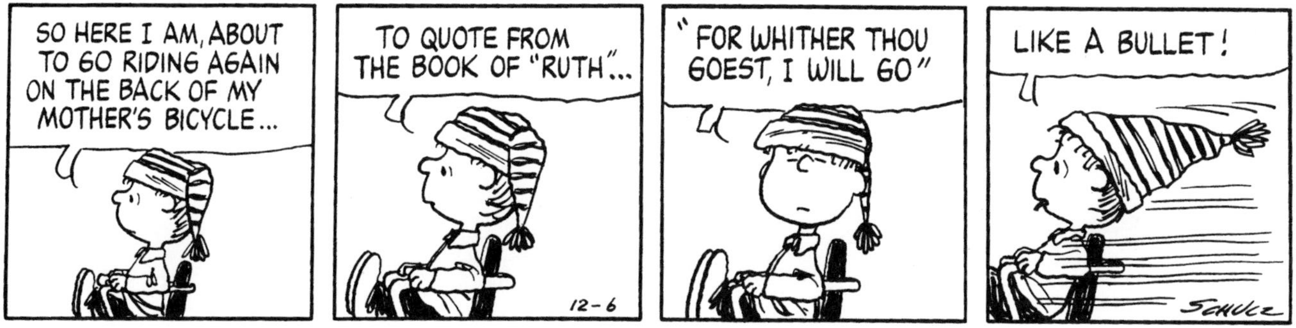
SO HERE I AM, ABOUT TO GO RIDING AGAIN ON THE BACK OF MY MOTHER'S BICYCLE...
TO QUOTE FROM THE BOOK OF "RUTH"...
12-6
"FOR WHITHER THOU GOEST, I WILL GO"
LIKE A BULLET!
SCHULZ

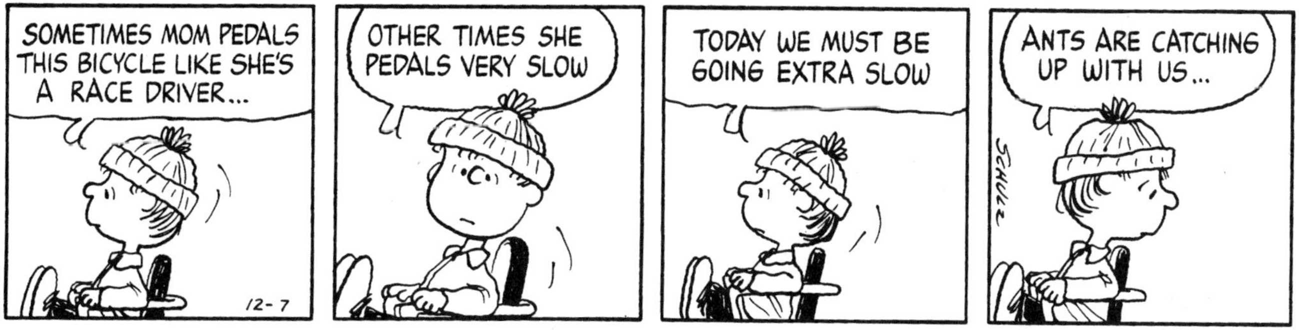
SOMETIMES MOM PEDALS THIS BICYCLE LIKE SHE'S A RACE DRIVER...
12-7
OTHER TIMES SHE PEDALS VERY SLOW
TODAY WE MUST BE GOING EXTRA SLOW
ANTS ARE CATCHING UP WITH US...
SCHULZ

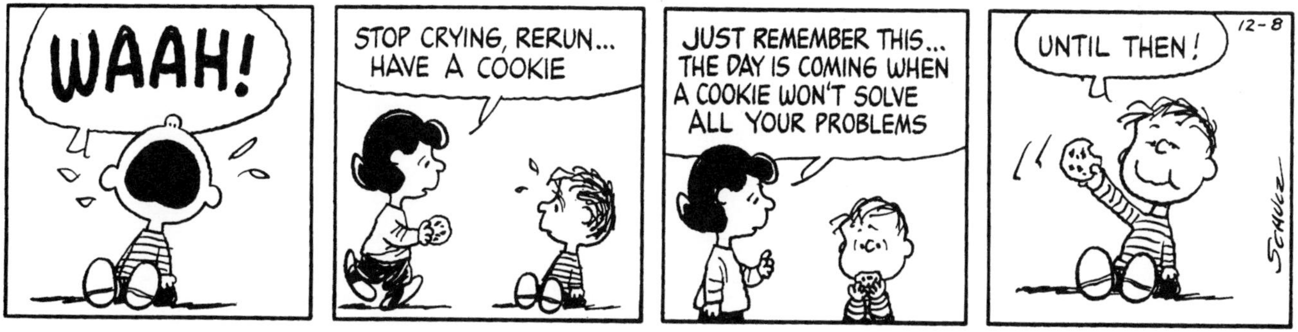
WAAH!
STOP CRYING, RERUN... HAVE A COOKIE
JUST REMEMBER THIS... THE DAY IS COMING WHEN A COOKIE WON'T SOLVE ALL YOUR PROBLEMS
UNTIL THEN!
12-8
SCHULZ

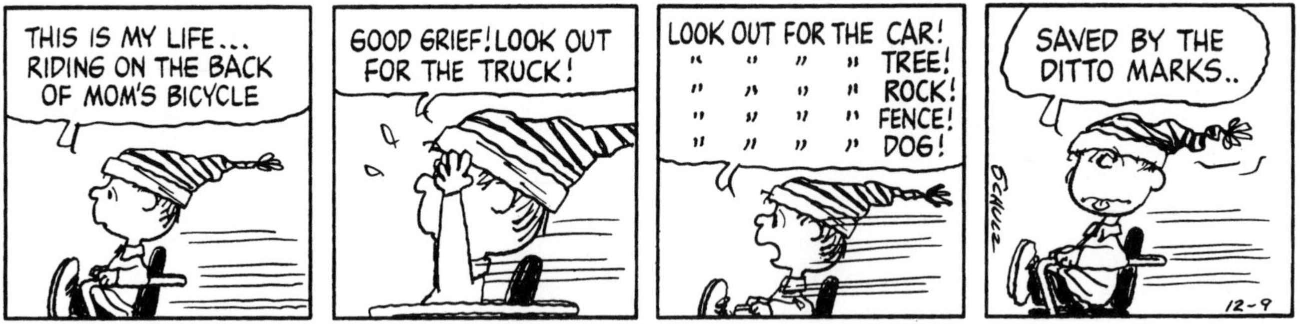
THIS IS MY LIFE... RIDING ON THE BACK OF MOM'S BICYCLE
GOOD GRIEF! LOOK OUT FOR THE TRUCK!
LOOK OUT FOR THE CAR!
" " " " TREE!
" " " " ROCK!
" " " " FENCE!
" " " " DOG!
SAVED BY THE DITTO MARKS..
SCHULZ
12-9

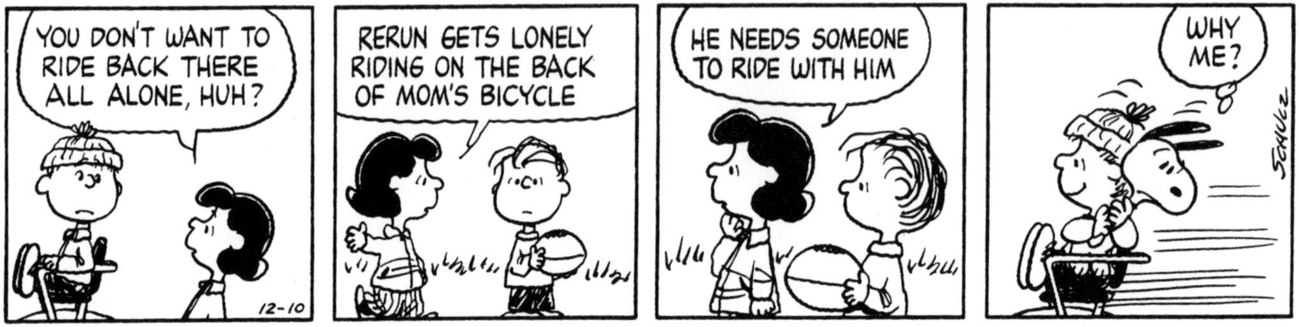
YOU DON'T WANT TO RIDE BACK THERE ALL ALONE, HUH?
12-10
RERUN GETS LONELY RIDING ON THE BACK OF MOM'S BICYCLE
HE NEEDS SOMEONE TO RIDE WITH HIM
WHY ME?
SCHULZ

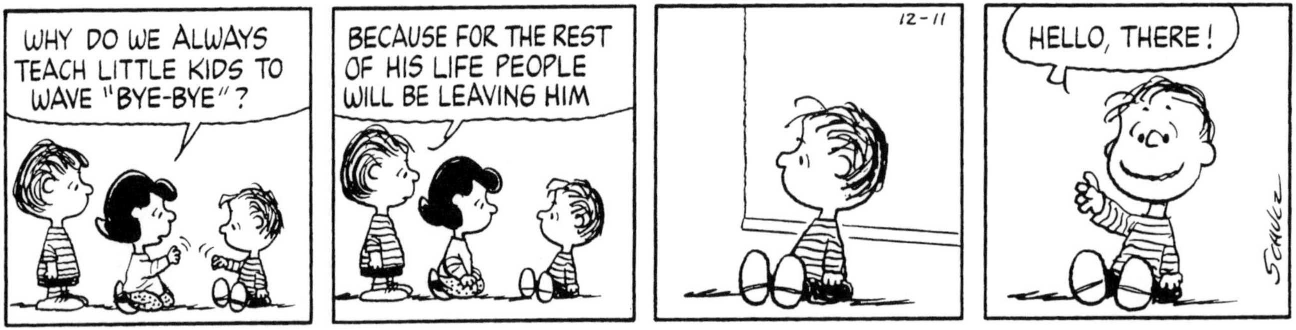
WHY DO WE ALWAYS TEACH LITTLE KIDS TO WAVE "BYE-BYE"?
BECAUSE FOR THE REST OF HIS LIFE PEOPLE WILL BE LEAVING HIM
12-11
HELLO, THERE!
SCHULZ

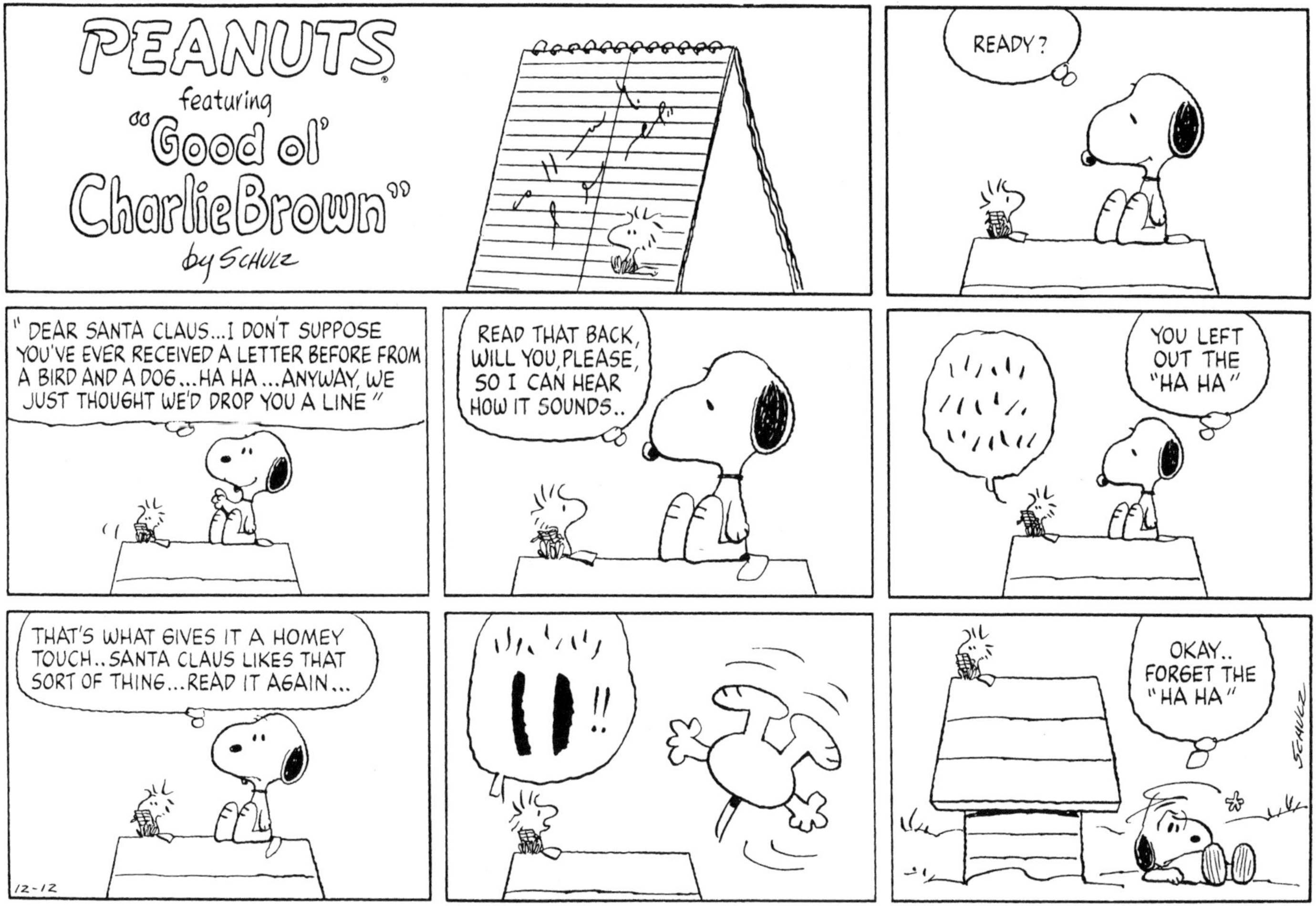
PEANUTS
featuring
"Good ol' Charlie Brown"
by SCHULZ
READY?
" DEAR SANTA CLAUS...I DON'T SUPPOSE YOU'VE EVER RECEIVED A LETTER BEFORE FROM A BIRD AND A DOG...HA HA...ANYWAY, WE JUST THOUGHT WE'D DROP YOU A LINE "
READ THAT BACK, WILL YOU, PLEASE, SO I CAN HEAR HOW IT SOUNDS..
YOU LEFT OUT THE "HA HA"
THAT'S WHAT GIVES IT A HOMEY TOUCH..SANTA CLAUS LIKES THAT SORT OF THING...READ IT AGAIN...
!!
OKAY.. FORGET THE "HA HA"
SCHULZ
12-12

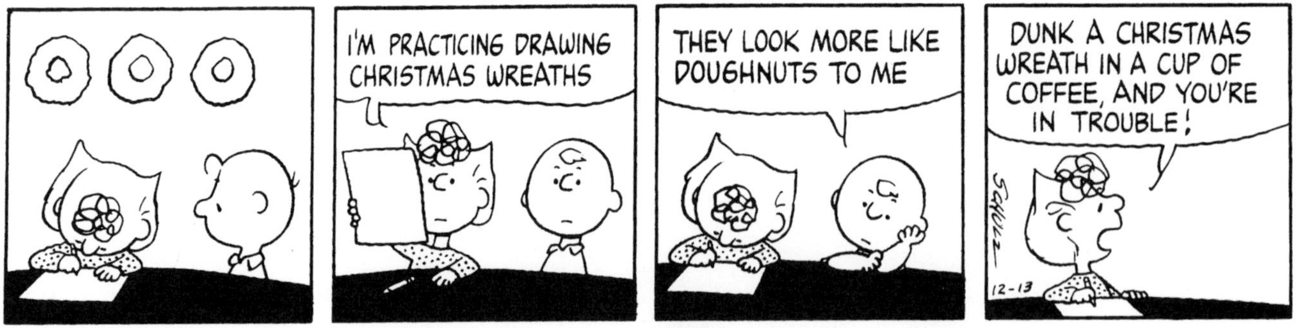
I'M PRACTICING DRAWING CHRISTMAS WREATHS
THEY LOOK MORE LIKE DOUGHNUTS TO ME
DUNK A CHRISTMAS WREATH IN A CUP OF COFFEE, AND YOU'RE IN TROUBLE!
12-13

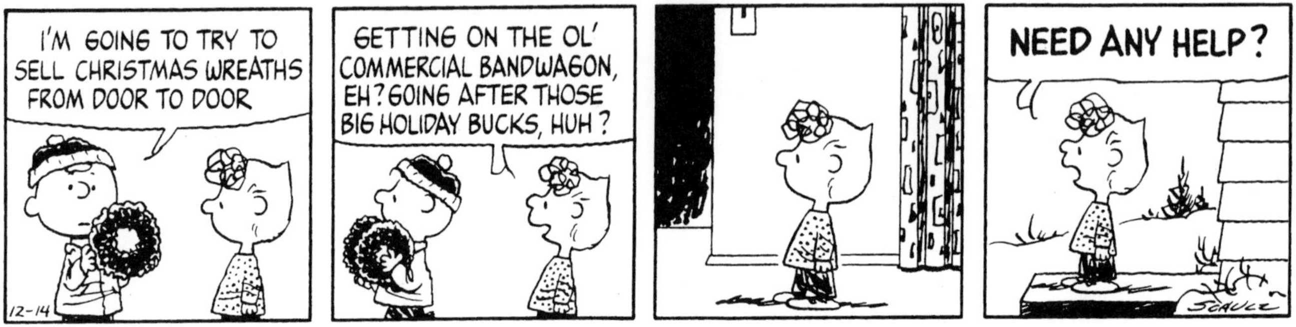
I'M GOING TO TRY TO SELL CHRISTMAS WREATHS FROM DOOR TO DOOR
12-14
GETTING ON THE OL' COMMERCIAL BANDWAGON, EH? GOING AFTER THOSE BIG HOLIDAY BUCKS, HUH?
NEED ANY HELP?

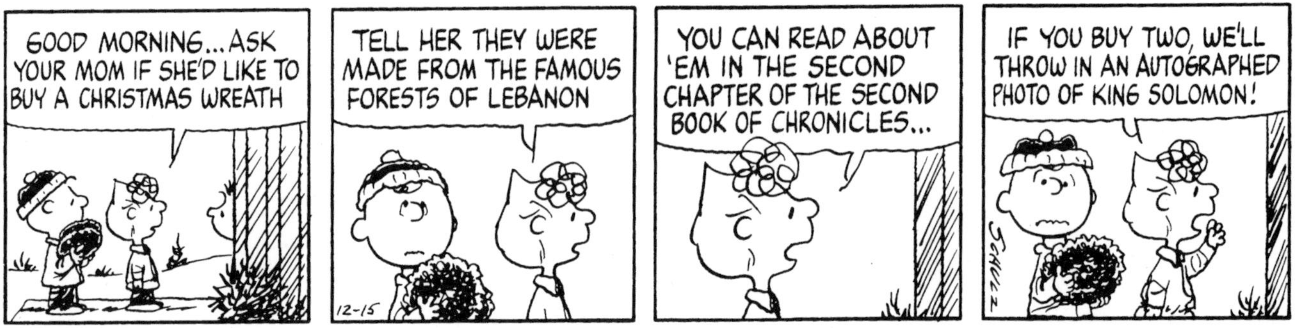
GOOD MORNING... ASK YOUR MOM IF SHE'D LIKE TO BUY A CHRISTMAS WREATH
TELL HER THEY WERE MADE FROM THE FAMOUS FORESTS OF LEBANON
12-15
YOU CAN READ ABOUT 'EM IN THE SECOND CHAPTER OF THE SECOND BOOK OF CHRONICLES...
IF YOU BUY TWO, WE'LL THROW IN AN AUTOGRAPHED PHOTO OF KING SOLOMON!

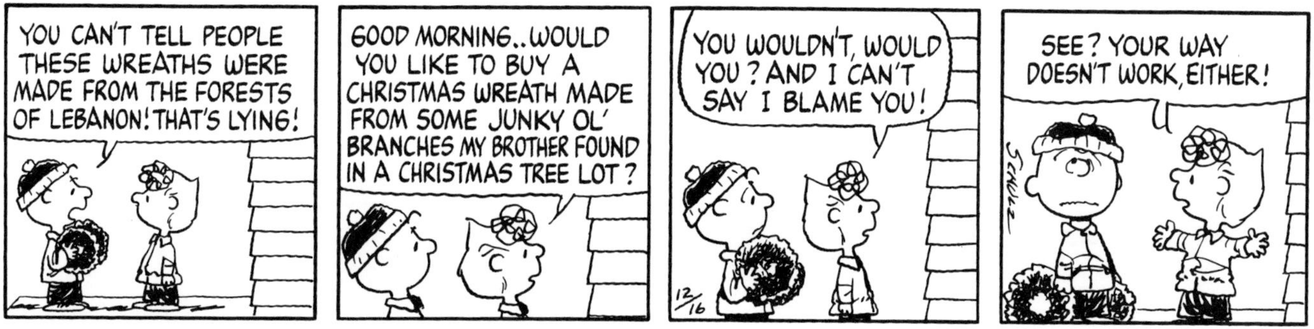
YOU CAN'T TELL PEOPLE THESE WREATHS WERE MADE FROM THE FORESTS OF LEBANON! THAT'S LYING!
GOOD MORNING..WOULD YOU LIKE TO BUY A CHRISTMAS WREATH MADE FROM SOME JUNKY OL' BRANCHES MY BROTHER FOUND IN A CHRISTMAS TREE LOT?
YOU WOULDN'T, WOULD YOU? AND I CAN'T SAY I BLAME YOU!
12/16
SEE? YOUR WAY DOESN'T WORK, EITHER!

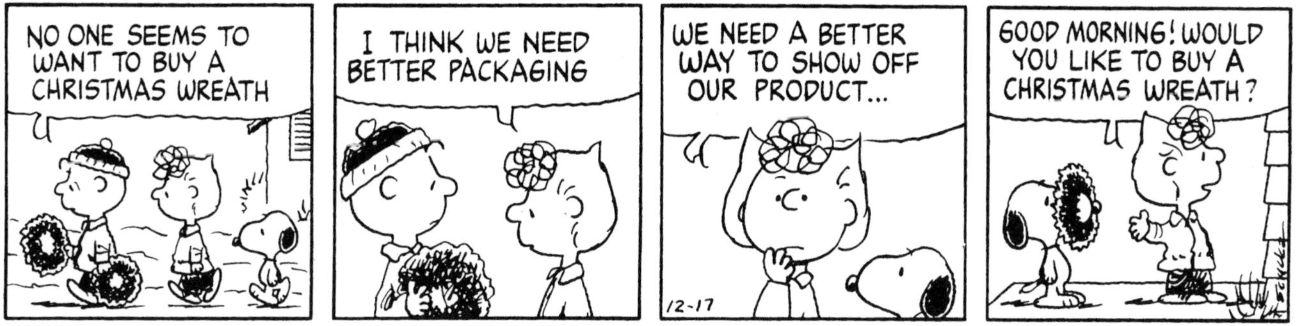
NO ONE SEEMS TO WANT TO BUY A CHRISTMAS WREATH
I THINK WE NEED BETTER PACKAGING
WE NEED A BETTER WAY TO SHOW OFF OUR PRODUCT...
12-17
GOOD MORNING! WOULD YOU LIKE TO BUY A CHRISTMAS WREATH?

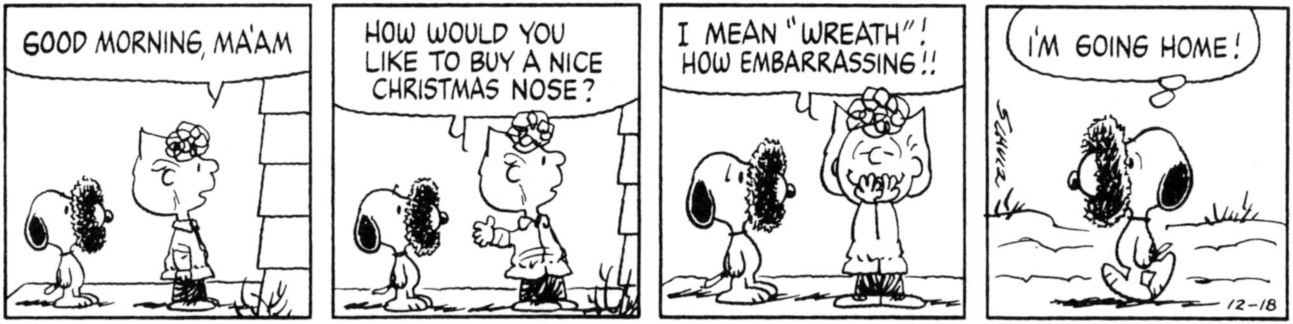
GOOD MORNING, MA'AM
HOW WOULD YOU LIKE TO BUY A NICE CHRISTMAS NOSE?
I MEAN "WREATH"! HOW EMBARRASSING!!
I'M GOING HOME!
12-18

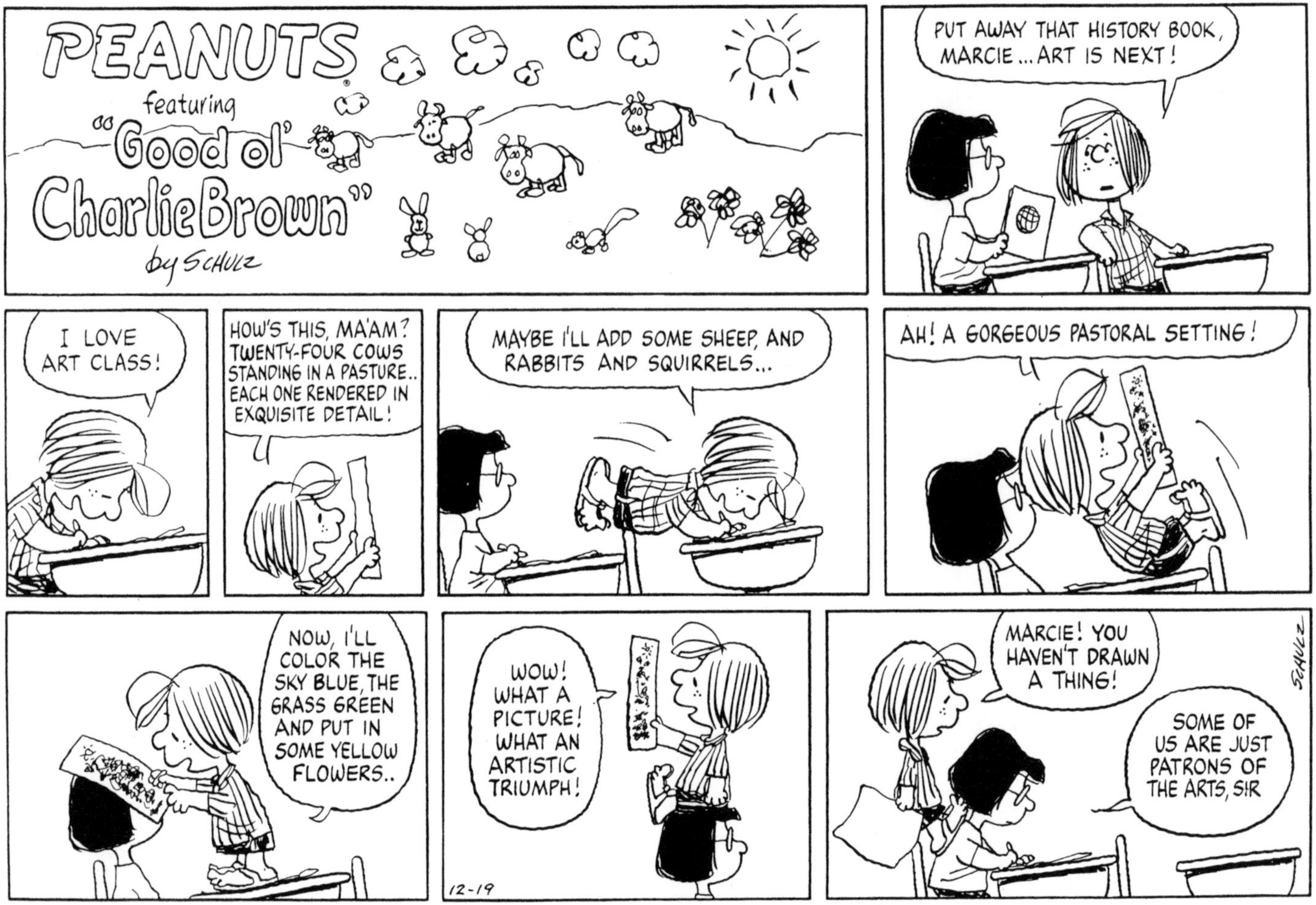
PEANUTS
featuring "Good ol' CharlieBrown"
by SCHULZ
PUT AWAY THAT HISTORY BOOK, MARCIE ... ART IS NEXT!
I LOVE ART CLASS!
HOW'S THIS, MA'AM? TWENTY-FOUR COWS STANDING IN A PASTURE.. EACH ONE RENDERED IN EXQUISITE DETAIL!
MAYBE I'LL ADD SOME SHEEP, AND RABBITS AND SQUIRRELS...
AH! A GORGEOUS PASTORAL SETTING!
NOW, I'LL COLOR THE SKY BLUE, THE GRASS GREEN AND PUT IN SOME YELLOW FLOWERS..
WOW! WHAT A PICTURE! WHAT AN ARTISTIC TRIUMPH!
12-19
MARCIE! YOU HAVEN'T DRAWN A THING!
SOME OF US ARE JUST PATRONS OF THE ARTS, SIR
SCHULZ

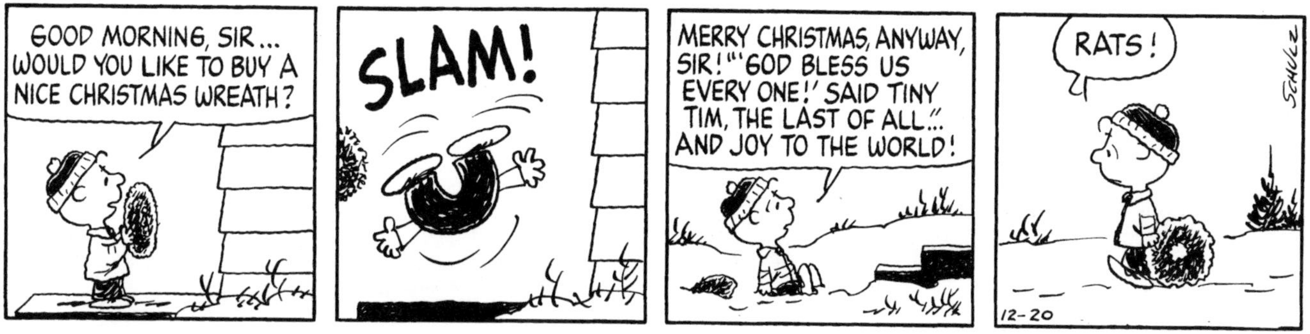
GOOD MORNING, SIR... WOULD YOU LIKE TO BUY A NICE CHRISTMAS WREATH?
SLAM!
MERRY CHRISTMAS, ANYWAY, SIR! "'GOD BLESS US EVERY ONE!' SAID TINY TIM, THE LAST OF ALL".. AND JOY TO THE WORLD!
RATS!
SCHULZ
12-20

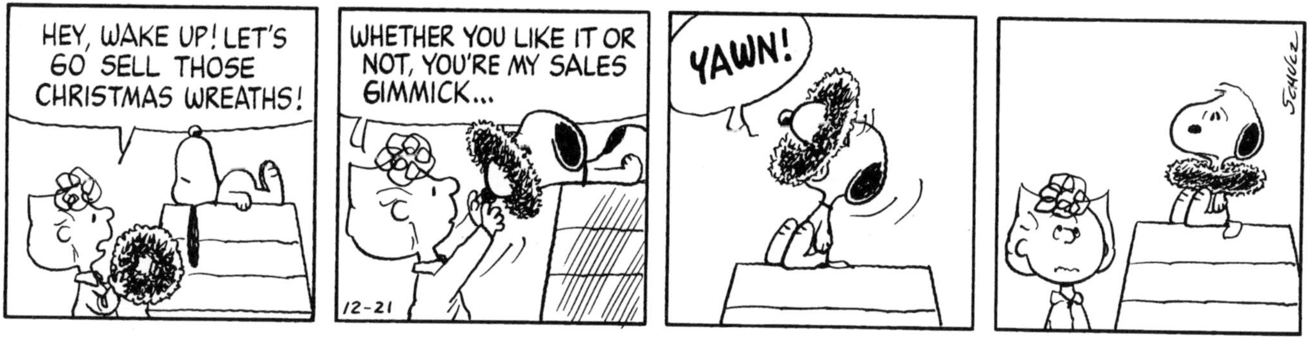
HEY, WAKE UP! LET'S GO SELL THOSE CHRISTMAS WREATHS!
WHETHER YOU LIKE IT OR NOT, YOU'RE MY SALES GIMMICK...
12-21
YAWN!
SCHULZ

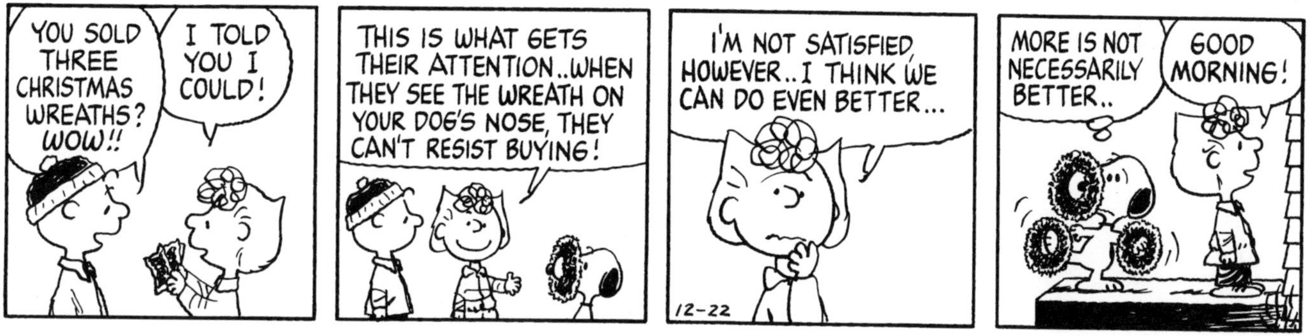
YOU SOLD THREE CHRISTMAS WREATHS? WOW!!
I TOLD YOU I COULD!
THIS IS WHAT GETS THEIR ATTENTION..WHEN THEY SEE THE WREATH ON YOUR DOG'S NOSE, THEY CAN'T RESIST BUYING!
I'M NOT SATISFIED, HOWEVER.. I THINK WE CAN DO EVEN BETTER...
12-22
MORE IS NOT NECESSARILY BETTER..
GOOD MORNING!

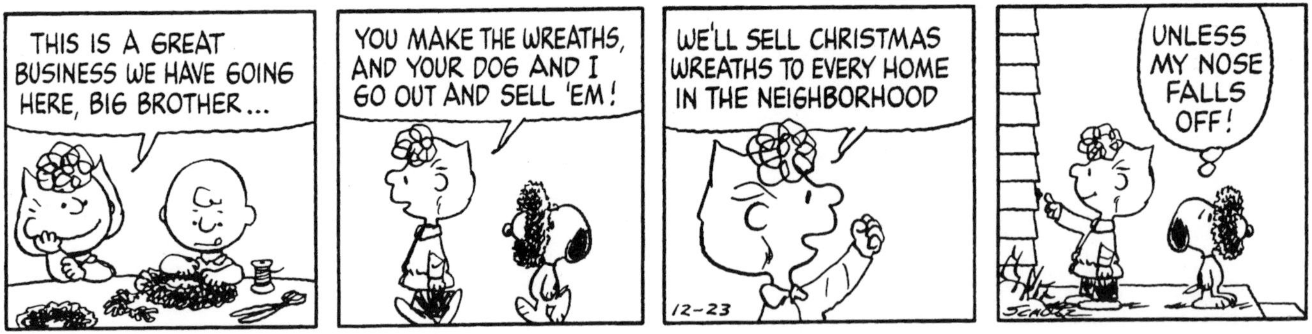
THIS IS A GREAT BUSINESS WE HAVE GOING HERE, BIG BROTHER...
YOU MAKE THE WREATHS, AND YOUR DOG AND I GO OUT AND SELL 'EM!
WE'LL SELL CHRISTMAS WREATHS TO EVERY HOME IN THE NEIGHBORHOOD
12-23
UNLESS MY NOSE FALLS OFF!
SCHULZ

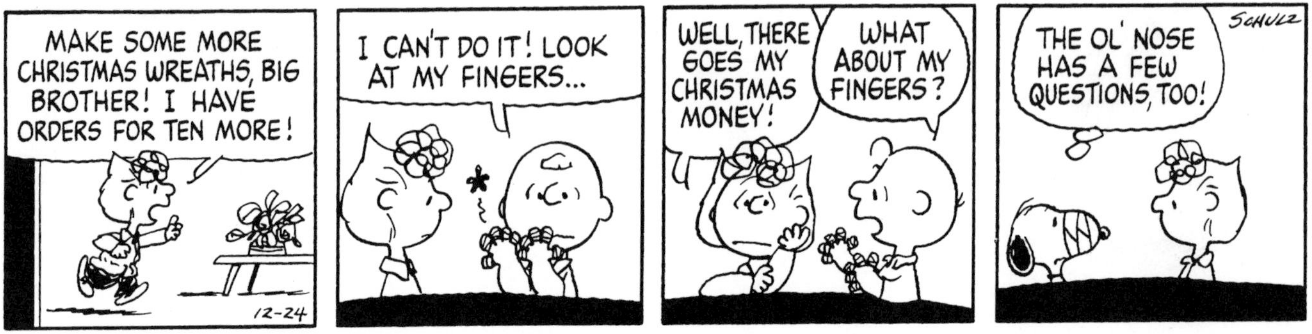
MAKE SOME MORE CHRISTMAS WREATHS, BIG BROTHER! I HAVE ORDERS FOR TEN MORE!
12-24
I CAN'T DO IT! LOOK AT MY FINGERS...
WELL, THERE GOES MY CHRISTMAS MONEY!
WHAT ABOUT MY FINGERS?
SCHULZ
THE OL' NOSE HAS A FEW QUESTIONS, TOO!

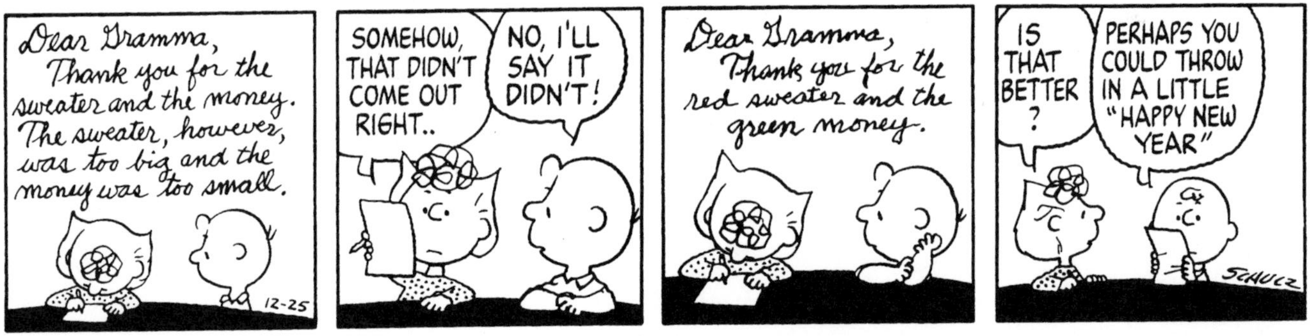
Dear Gramma, Thank you for the sweater and the money. The sweater, however, was too big and the money was too small.
12-25
SOMEHOW, THAT DIDN'T COME OUT RIGHT..
NO, I'LL SAY IT DIDN'T!
Dear Gramma, Thank you for the red sweater and the green money.
IS THAT BETTER ?
PERHAPS YOU COULD THROW IN A LITTLE "HAPPY NEW YEAR"
SCHULZ

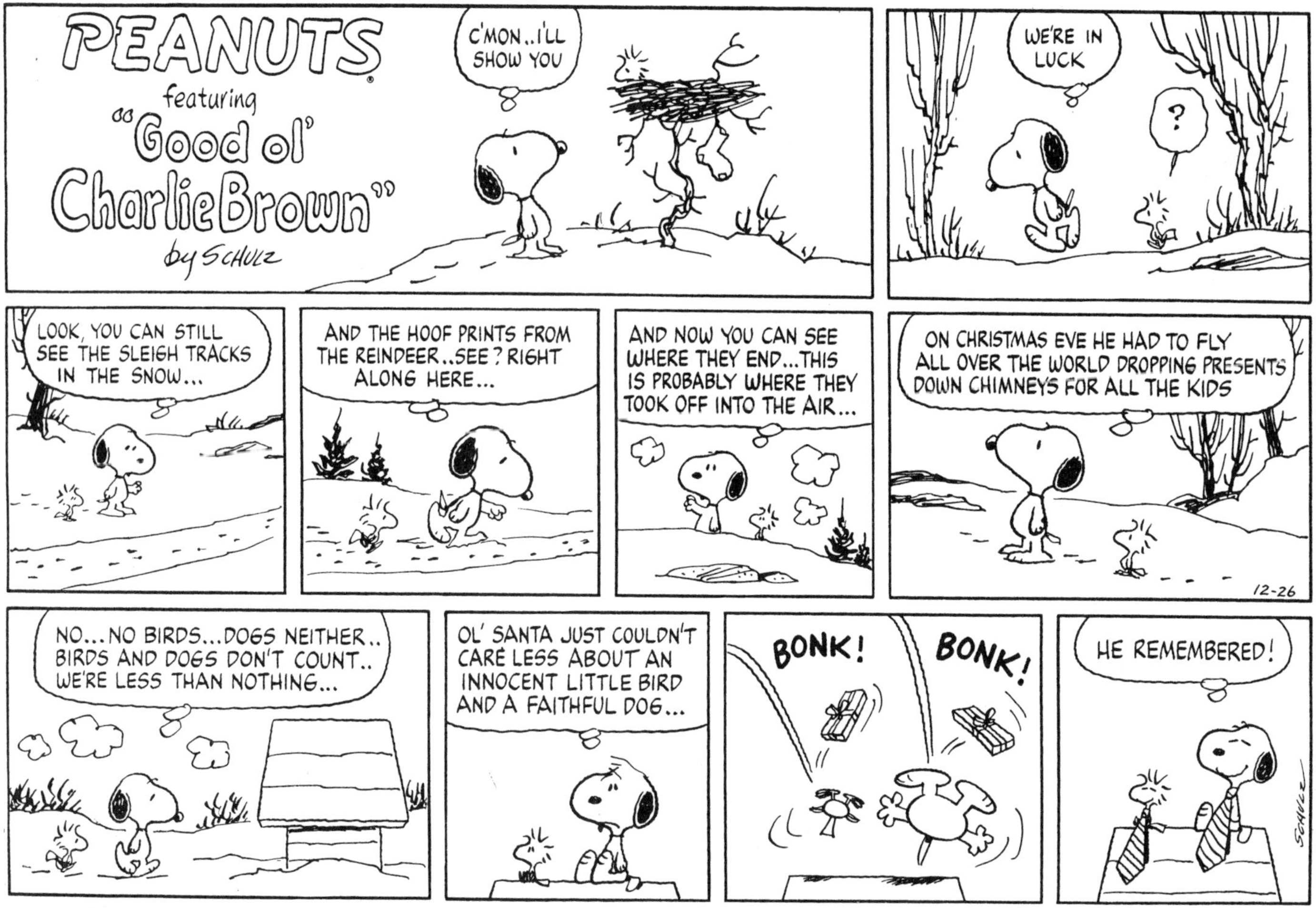
PEANUTS
featuring "Good ol' Charlie Brown"
by SCHULZ
C'MON..I'LL SHOW YOU
WE'RE IN LUCK
?
LOOK, YOU CAN STILL SEE THE SLEIGH TRACKS IN THE SNOW...
AND THE HOOF PRINTS FROM THE REINDEER..SEE? RIGHT ALONG HERE...
AND NOW YOU CAN SEE WHERE THEY END...THIS IS PROBABLY WHERE THEY TOOK OFF INTO THE AIR...
ON CHRISTMAS EVE HE HAD TO FLY ALL OVER THE WORLD DROPPING PRESENTS DOWN CHIMNEYS FOR ALL THE KIDS
12-26
NO...NO BIRDS...DOGS NEITHER.. BIRDS AND DOGS DON'T COUNT.. WE'RE LESS THAN NOTHING...
OL' SANTA JUST COULDN'T CARE LESS ABOUT AN INNOCENT LITTLE BIRD AND A FAITHFUL DOG...
BONK!
BONK!
HE REMEMBERED!
SCHULZ

AS LONG AS WE'RE JUST PRACTICING, I HAVE A SUGGESTION

MAYBE YOU SHOULD SHOOT AT THE OTHER GOAL FOR A WHILE...

12-27

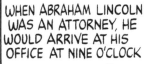

WHEN ABRAHAM LINCOLN WAS AN ATTORNEY, HE WOULD ARRIVE AT HIS OFFICE AT NINE O'CLOCK

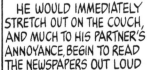

HE WOULD IMMEDIATELY STRETCH OUT ON THE COUCH, AND MUCH TO HIS PARTNER'S ANNOYANCE, BEGIN TO READ THE NEWSPAPERS OUT LOUD

I'LL HAVE TO REMEMBER THAT

THE SECRET TO BEING A GOOD ATTORNEY IS TO ANNOY YOUR PARTNER

12-28

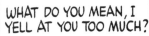

WHAT DO YOU MEAN, I YELL AT YOU TOO MUCH?

I'VE ONLY YELLED AT YOU THREE TIMES TODAY

THREE TIMES IS TOO MUCH

12-29

THAT'S ONE MORE THAN A RECOMMENDED DAILY ALLOWANCE!

IT'S VERY EASY TO NEGLECT WRITING LETTERS OF APPRECIATION

THIS IS A GOOD TIME OF YEAR TO WRITE AND TELL SOMEONE HOW MUCH THEY HAVE REALLY MEANT TO YOU...

12-30

Dear Supper Dish,

12-31

IS IT NEW YEAR'S ALREADY?

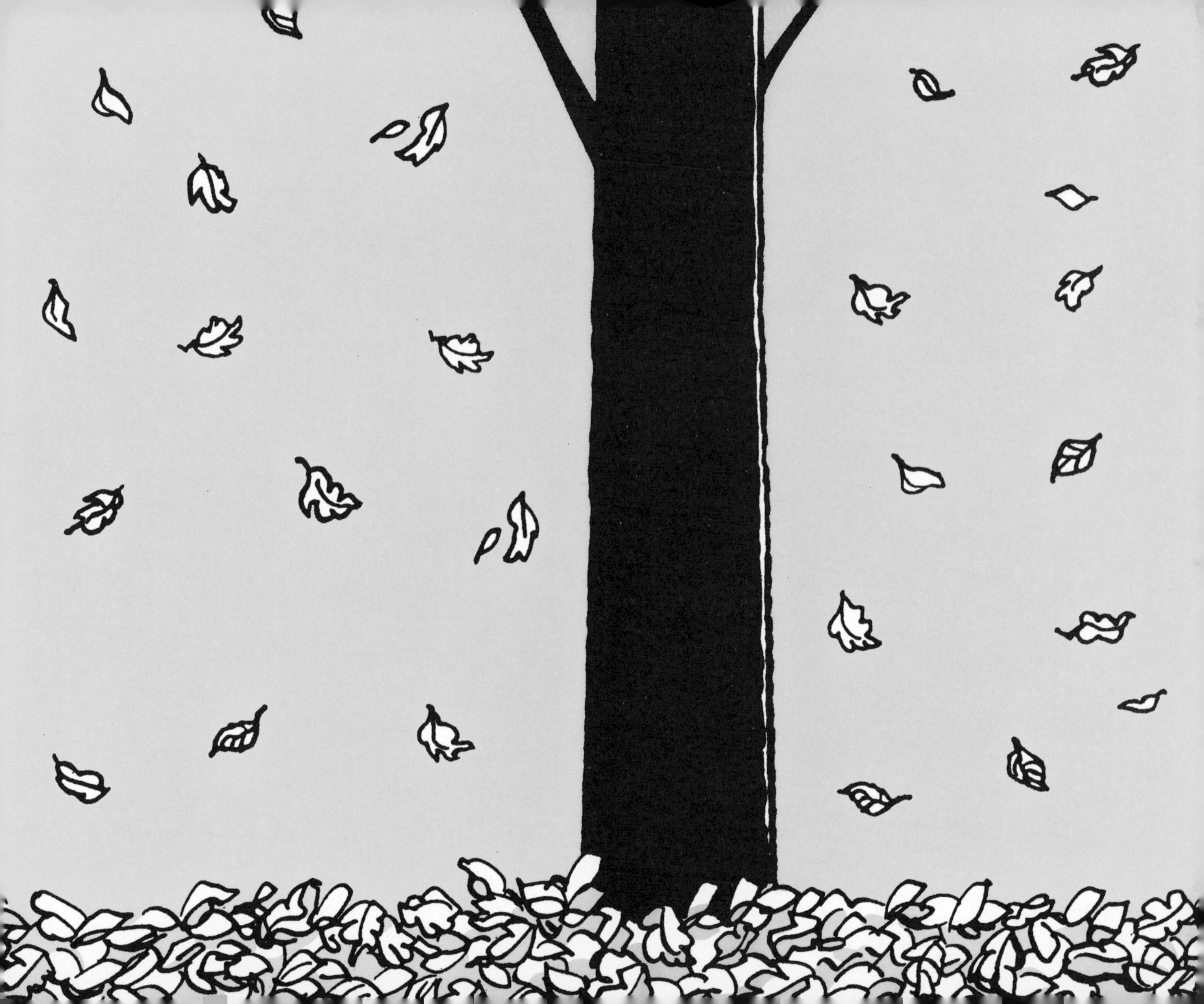

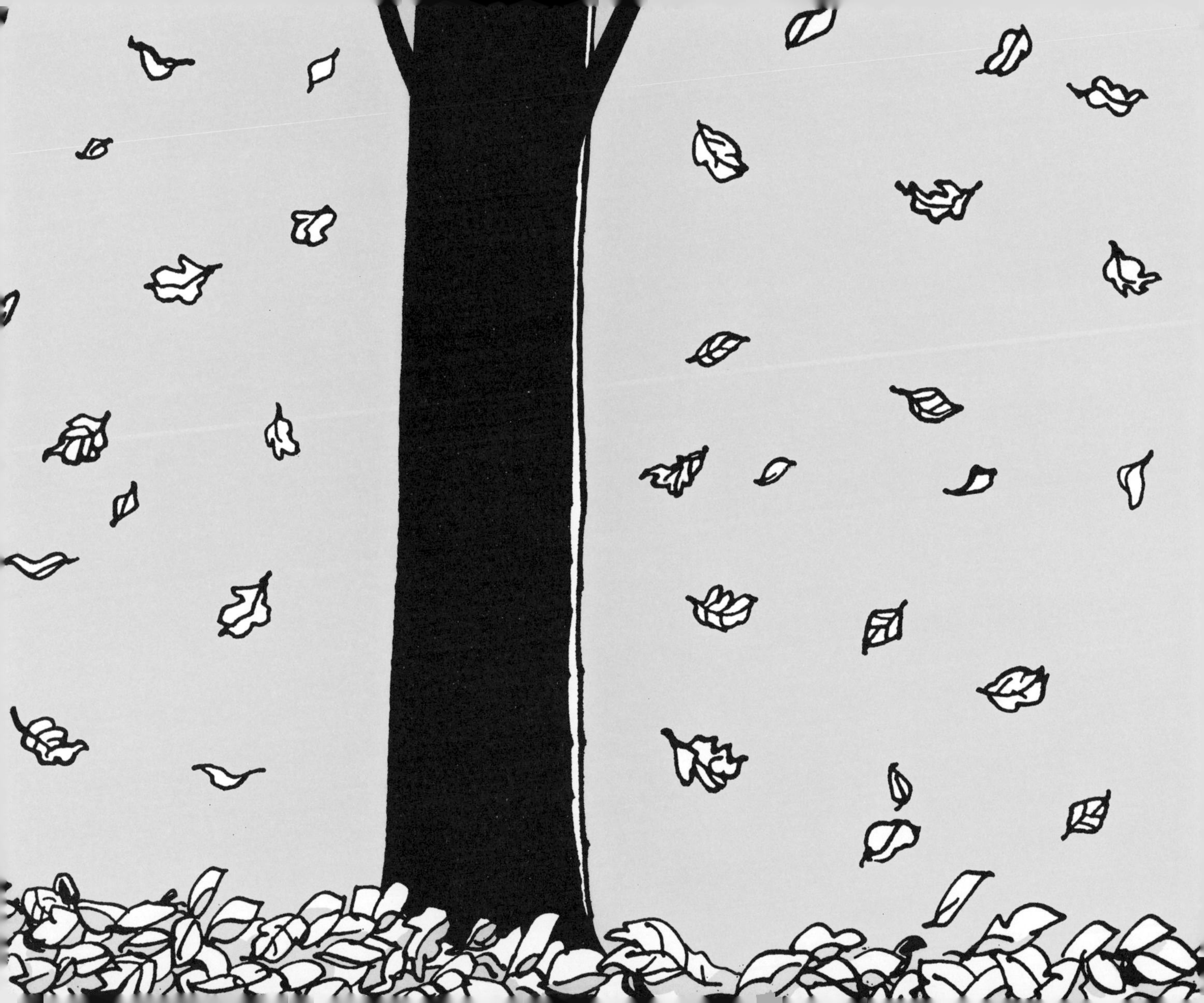

INDEX

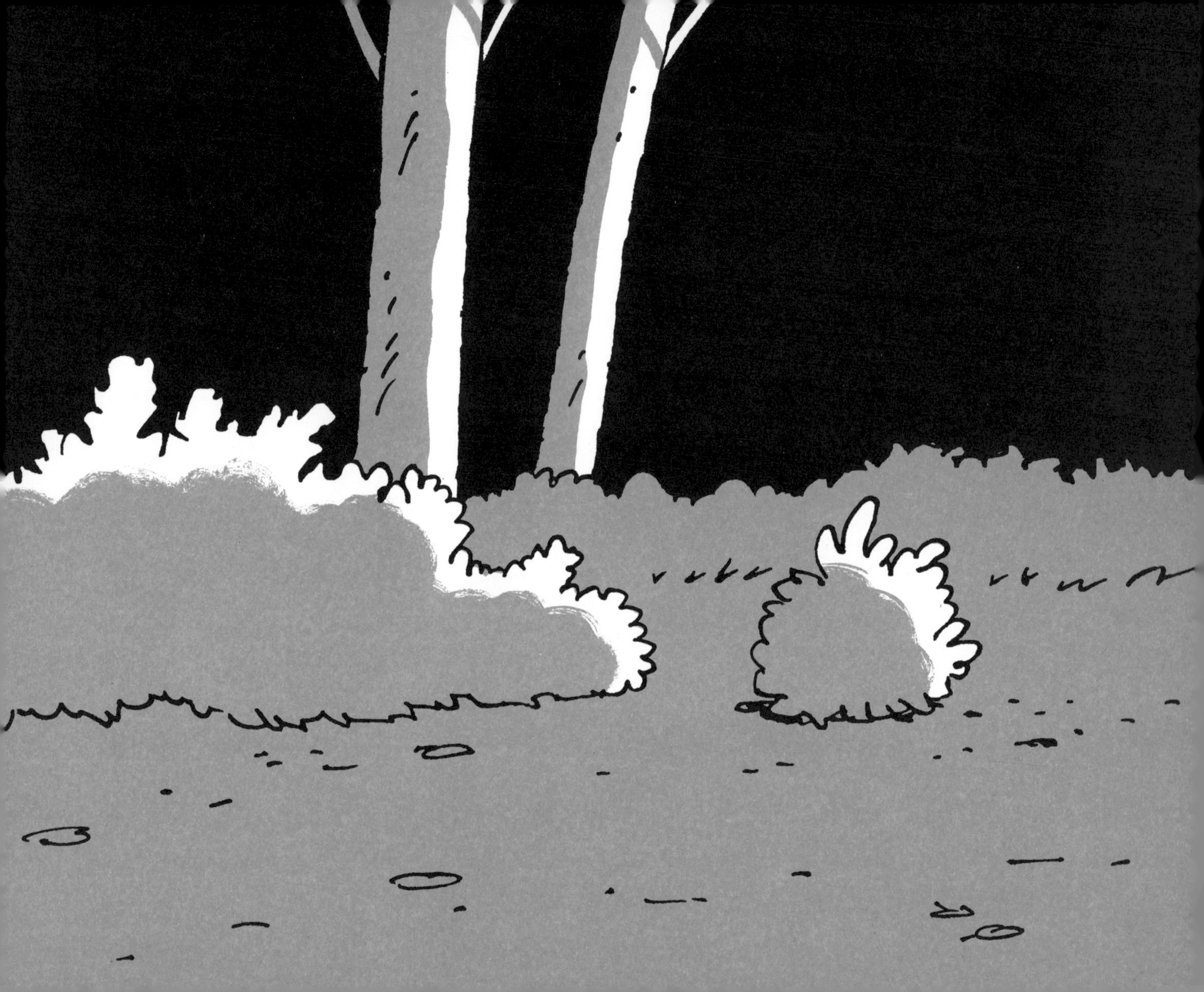

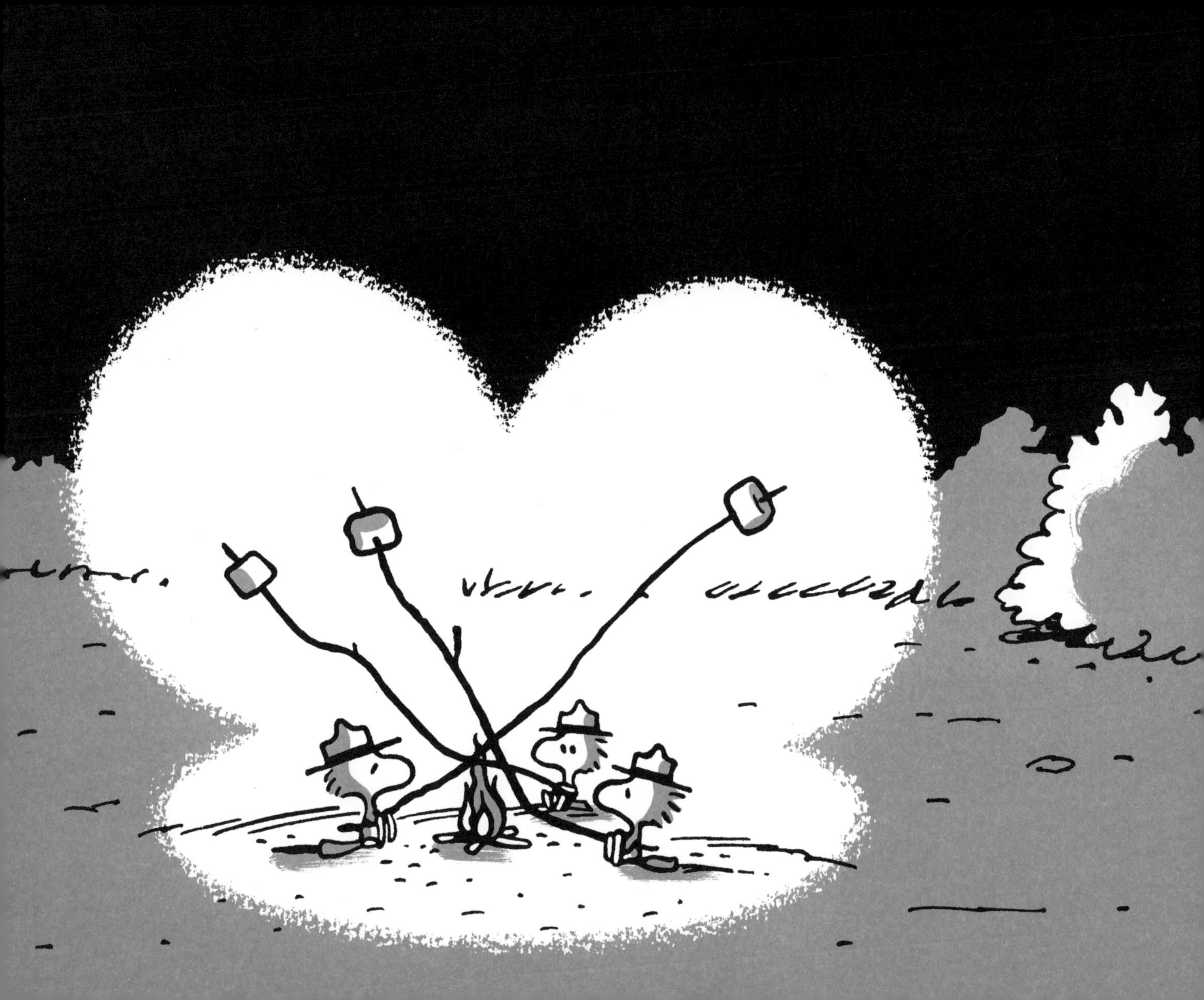

CHARLES M. SCHULZ · 1922 to 2000

Charles M. Schulz was born November 25, 1922 in Minneapolis. His destiny was foreshadowed when an uncle gave him, at the age of two days, the nickname Sparky (after the racehorse Spark Plug in the newspaper strip *Barney Google*).

Schulz grew up in St. Paul. By all accounts, he led an unremarkable, albeit sheltered, childhood. He was an only child, close to both parents, his eventual career path nurtured by his father, who bought four Sunday papers every week — just for the comics.

An outstanding student, he skipped two grades early on, but began to flounder in high school — perhaps not so coincidentally at the same time kids are going through their cruelest, most status-conscious period of socialization. The pain, bitterness, insecurity, and failures chronicled in *Peanuts* appear to have originated from this period of Schulz's life.

Although Schulz enjoyed sports, he also found refuge in solitary activities: reading, drawing, and watching movies. He bought comic books and Big Little Books, pored over the newspaper strips, and copied his favorites — *Buck Rogers*, the Walt Disney characters, *Popeye, Tim Tyler's Luck*. He quickly became a connoisseur; his heroes were Milton Caniff, Roy Crane, Hal Foster, and Alex Raymond.

In his senior year in high school, his mother noticed an ad in a local newspaper for a correspondence school, Federal Schools (later called Art

Instruction Schools). Schulz passed the talent test, completed the course and began trying, unsuccessfully, to sell gag cartoons to magazines. (His first published drawing was of his dog, Spike, and appeared in a 1937 *Ripley's Believe It Or Not!* installment.)

After World War II had ended and Schulz was discharged from the army, he started submitting gag cartoons to the various magazines of the time; his first breakthrough, however, came when an editor at *Timeless Topix* hired him to letter adventure comics. Soon after that, he was hired by his alma mater, Art Instruction, to correct student lessons returned by mail.

Between 1948 and 1950, he succeeded in selling 17 cartoons to the *Saturday Evening Post* — as well as, to the local *St. Paul Pioneer Press*, a weekly comic feature called *Li'l Folks*. It was run in the women's section and paid $10 a week. After writing and drawing the feature for two years, Schulz asked for a better location in the paper or for daily exposure, as well as a raise. When he was turned down on all three counts, he quit.

He started submitting strips to the newspaper syndicates. In the Spring of 1950, he received a letter from the United Feature Syndicate, announcing their interest in his submission, *Li'l Folks*. Schulz boarded a train in June for New York City; more interested in doing a strip than a panel, he also brought along the first installments of what would become *Peanuts* — and that was what sold. (The title, which Schulz loathed to his dying day, was imposed by the syndicate). The first *Peanuts* daily appeared October 2, 1950; the first Sunday, January 6, 1952.

Prior to *Peanuts*, the province of the comics page had been that of gags, social and political observation, domestic comedy, soap opera, and various adventure genres. Although *Peanuts* changed, or evolved, during the 50 years Schulz wrote and drew it, it remained, as it began, an anomaly on the comics page — a comic strip about the interior crises of the cartoonist himself. After a painful divorce in 1973 from which he had not yet recovered, Schulz told a reporter, "Strangely, I've drawn better cartoons in the last six months — or as good as I've ever drawn. I don't know how the human mind works." Surely, it was this kind of humility in the face of profoundly irreducible human question that makes *Peanuts* as universally moving as it is.

Diagnosed with cancer, Schulz retired from *Peanuts* at the end of 1999. He died on February 12th 2000, the day before his last strip was published (and two days before Valentine's Day) — having completed 17,897 daily and Sunday strips, each and every one fully written, drawn, and lettered entirely by his own hand — an unmatched achievement in comics.

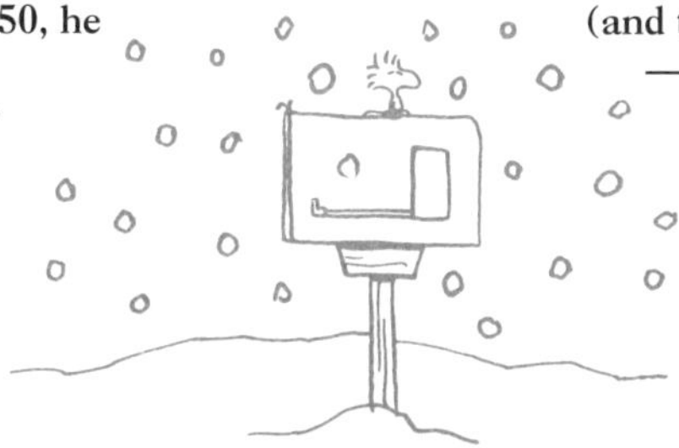

—Gary Groth

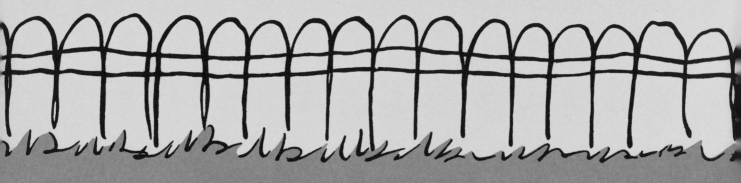

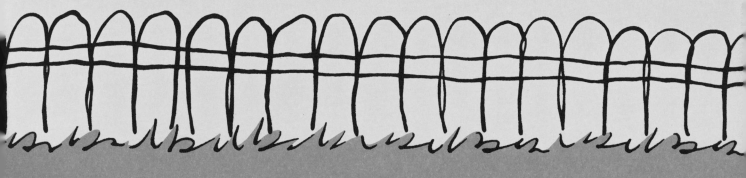

THE COMPLETE PEANUTS

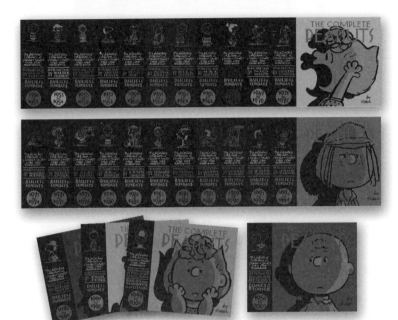

The definitive collection of
Charles M. Schulz's comic strip masterpiece

"An American treasure"
BARACK OBAMA

CANON GATE

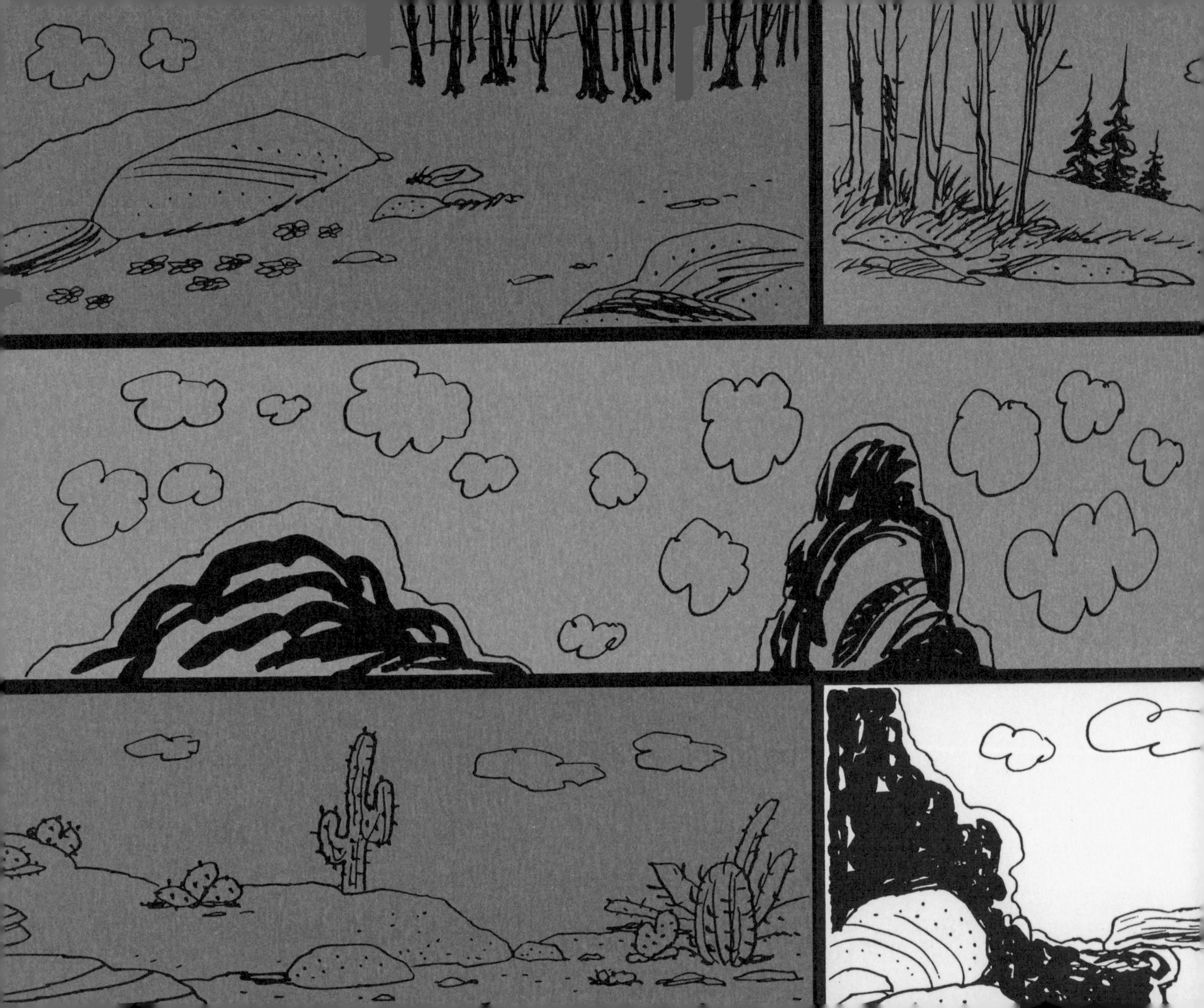